Prague

Penguin Books

PENGUIN BOOKS

Published by the Penguin Group
Penguin Books Ltd., 27 Wright's Lane, London, W8 5TZ, England
Penguin Putnam Inc., 375 Hudson Street, New York, New York 10014, USA
Penguin Books Australia Ltd., Ringwood, Victoria, Australia
Penguin Books Canada Ltd., 10 Alcorn Avenue, Toronto, Ontario, Canada M4V 3B2
Penguin Books (NZ) Ltd., Private Bag 102902, NSMC, Auckland, New Zealand

Penguin Books Ltd., Registered offices: Harmondsworth, Middlesex, England

First published 1995
Second edition 1997
Third edition 1998
10 9 8 7 6 5 4 3 2 1

Colour reprographics by Precise Litho, 34–35 Great Sutton Street, London EC1
Mono reprographics, printed and bound by William Clowes Ltd, Beccles, Suffolk NR34 9QE

Edited and designed by

Time Out Guides Limited
Universal House
251 Tottenham Court Road
London W1P 0AB
Tel: 0171 813 3000
Fax: 0171 813 6001
guides@timeout.co.uk
www.timeout.com

Editorial

Managing Editor Peter Fiennes
Editor Jonathan Cox
Deputy Editor Lesley McCave
Consultant Editor Will Tizard
Listings Editor Katka Suranska
Proofreader Tamsin Shelton
Indexer Sarah Matthews

Design

Art Director John Oakey
Art Editor Mandy Martin
Designers Benjamin de Lotz, Scott Moore,
Lucy Grant, Paul Mansfield,
Scanner Operator Chris Quinn
Picture Editor Kerri Miles
Picture Researcher Emma Tremlett

Advertising

Group Advertisement Director Lesley Gill
Sales Director Mark Phillips
Advertisment Sales (Prague) Creative Partners

Administration

Publisher Tony Elliott
Managing Director Mike Hardwick
Financial Director Kevin Ellis
Marketing Director Gillian Auld
General Manager Nichola Coulthard
Production Manager Mark Lamond
Accountant Catherine Bowen

Features in this guide were written and researched by:

Introduction Will Tizard. **Prague by Season** Carole Cadwalladr, Julia Gray, Michael Halstead, Will Tizard.
History Jonathan Cox, Paul Lewis, Will Tizard. **Prague Today** Mark Baker, Victor Gomez.
Architecture Jonathan Cox, Damon McGee. **Sightseeing** Carole Cadwalladr, Jonathan Cox, Lacey Eckl,
Dave Rimmer, Will Tizard. **Museums** Julie Ashley, Jonathan Cox. **Art Galleries** Will Tizard.
Accommodation Mark Nessmith. **Restaurants** Will Tizard. **Cafés, Pubs & Bars** Will Tizard.
Shopping & Services Emma McClune. **Children** Julia Ashley. **Film** Julia Gray. **Gay & Lesbian Prague** Julia Gray.
Literary Prague Julie Ashley. **Music: Classical & Opera** Michael Halstead, Will Tizard.
Music: Rock, Folk & Jazz Will Tizard. **Nightlife** Will Tizard. **Sport & Fitness** Julia Gray.
Theatre & Dance Julia Ashley, Laura Zam. **Trips Out of Town** Carole Cadwalladr, Jonathan Cox, Julia Gray, Dave
Rimmer, Anna Sutton, Will Tizard. **Directory** Julie Ashley, Mark Baker, Mark Nessmith, Katka Suranska, Will Tizard.
Further Reading Dave Rimmer.

The Editor would like to thank the following:

Sophie Blacksell, Selena Chalk, Tomas Fanta, Sarah Halliwell, Sara Hannant, Dave Rimmer, Katka Suranska and
last, but definitely not least, Will Tizard for inspiration, application and probably too much perspiration.
Maps by JS Graphics, Hill View Cottage, 17 Beadles Lane, Old Oxted, Surrey RH8 9JG.

Photography by Sara Hannant except for: page 19 AKG; page 26 Magnum Photos; page 169 Ed Marshall; page
192 Ed Marshall; pages 221, 238, 239, 240, 241 Jonathan Cox. Illustrations on pages 11, 12, 16 by Carl Flint.

Contents

Introduction	1

In Context

Prague by Season	5
History	10
Prague Today	29
Architecture	34

Sightseeing

Staré Mêsto	42
Nové Mêsto	53
Prague Castle & Hradčany	60
Malá Strana	74
Further Afield	81

Museums & Galleries

Museums	90
Art Galleries	96

Sleeping, Eating, Shopping

Accommodation	104
Restaurants	118
Cafés, Pubs & Bars	138
Shopping & Services	153

Arts & Entertainment

Children	176
Film	180
Gay & Lesbian Prague	185
Literary Prague	188
Music: Classical & Opera	190
Music: Rock, Folk & Jazz	197
Nightlife	201
Sport & Fitness	208
Theatre & Dance	214

Trips Out of Town

Trips Out of Town	222

Directory

Resources A-Z	245
Getting to Prague	253
Getting around Prague	254
Business	260
Media	263
Studying in Prague	266

Further Reading	269
Index	270
Advertisers' Index	276
Maps	277
Street Index	289

About the Guide

This is the third edition of the *Time Out Prague Guide*, one of our ever-expanding series of guides to the world's most exciting cities. This latest edition has been shaken out, dusted down, held up to the light and taken out for a good hot meal. We've checked Prague's credentials, reassessed its attractions and mapped the changing shape of this volatile post-revolutionary city.

Reflecting the huge improvement in culinary options, we list twice as many restaurants as the last edition. Other enhancements are improved maps (including new coverage of the Hološovice and Vinohrady/Žižkov areas) and complete map referencing throughout the book. You will now find all practical information in the Directory section in the back and sights listed by the area of the city in which they are found.

This is much more than a book for tourists and casual visitors. We try to avoid PR hype and tell you the downsides as well as the many ups to one of the world's most fascinating cities. While listing the main sights and major monuments, we've also strayed far off the beaten track to direct you to the Czech capital's coolest cafés, most happening restaurants, sharpest shopping opportunities and most uncompromisingly underground clubs.

We've also laboured tirelessly to maintain the guide's accuracy and practical usefulness: addresses, telephone numbers, opening times, admission prices and credit card details have all been updated and included wherever possible.

Checked & correct

All information in this guide was checked and correct at the time of going to press. But Prague is one place where the only thing certain is that nothing will stay the same. The commercial sector – especially bars, clubs, restaurants and shops – is in a constant state of flux. Even trams and buses are liable to sudden re-routings in the summer months when roadworks disrupt half of the city. It is wise, therefore, wherever possible, to check opening times, dates of exhibitions and other important details before setting out, or maybe just have an alternative plan up your sleeve to cope with sudden and unexpected closures.

Many prices we list should be treated as guidelines rather than gospel. Prices change constantly, and in many cases there are different rates for Czechs and foreigners.

Addresses

Prague is divided into ten districts, arranged haphazardly on the map. The central district, Prague 1, ancient heart of the city, is further subdivided into areas: **Hradčany** (the Castle), **Malá Strana** (Lesser Quarter), **Staré Město** and **Josefov** (the Old Town and Jewish Quarter) and **Nové Město** (the New Town). Many buildings have two sets of numbers: the one on the blue plaque is the street number; the one on the red plaque is the registry number within the city and, for the purposes of this guide, can be safely ignored.

We've avoided abbreviations where possible, but on maps you might find the following: **square** *náměstí (nam.)*; **embankment** *nábřeží (nábř.)*; **street** *ulice (ul.)*. Other map terms are **market** *(trh)*; **avenue** *(třída)* and **bridge** *(most)*.

Credit cards

Payment by credit card is becoming increasingly easy in Prague, although acceptance still lags considerably behind that found in the USA and Western Europe. Where we've listed them, the following abbreviations apply: **AmEx** *American Express*; **DC** *Diners Club*; **EC** *EuroCard*; **MC** *MasterCard*; **V** *Visa*. **Where we have listed none, they take none.**

Right to reply

It should be stressed that the information we give is impartial. No organisation has been included in this guide because its owner or manager has advertised in our publications. We are sure you'll enjoy the *Time Out Prague Guide*, but if you disagree with any of our assessments, or have a particularly bad experience, let us know. We also want to hear from you if you discover great establishments not featured in these pages or if you have any opinions on how the guide can be improved. Your comments will help us update the fourth edition – you'll find a reader's reply card at the end of the book.

There is an online version of this guide, as well as weekly events listings for several international cities, at
www.timeout.com

Introduction

Visitors to this city cannot help but be stunned. If the impossibly fairy-tale landscape of the Old Town doesn't leave you speechless, be assured that a shop clerk's lack of concern for your needs will. The finest beer you've ever tasted will be plonked on your table in a pub with original battlements – possibly by a surly, tipsy waiter who pads the bill. You'll wind down deserted medieval lanes in Malá Strana by night, then find them choked with reckless drivers and scarred by brown coal pollution by day. Enchanting old-world ways will catch your eye, from the shy deference of young people to the kindness shown to old folks on trams. Then you'll see the driver ejecting Gypsy boys into the street as the other passengers sit idly by.

The rhythm of reverie, then rude reality, is a constant yin and yang in Prague.

Perhaps the city has morphed so completely since 1989 that it's easy to forget how new freedom is here – and then be shocked when you discover people who still take no responsibility for creating a civil society.

So if you come here seeking a Bohemia of libertine lifestyles, hoping for a taste of lingering post-Velvet Revolution euphoria, and to glory in a new society that hasn't yet set the confining rules that chafe free spirits back home… oddly enough, you'll find it.

And when you consider that the average Czech's monthly income is just 6,578 Kč (just over £126), that their cost of living has increased 40 per cent since 1994 – and their rent has jumped 80 per cent in that time – this is wonder enough. It may just be too much to ask, then, to expect this same Czech to be unconditionally welcoming to the new rules – or for that matter to foreign partiers who espouse global awareness while taking months off work to discover themselves in Prague. Can a local even be expected to be scrupulously honest in circumstances like these? Particularly in a society where honesty has historically proven to be the one surefire way to get yourself beheaded, shot or, with luck, just demoted to garbage collector?

Mind you, the disparities are growing less significant all the time. A Praguer's monthly wage is nearly double the average above; EC membership is on the immediate agenda and incomes and investment are still on the rise despite a chaotic current administration and recognised widespread corruption. There can be no mistake:

even if completely in spite of itself, Prague is on the rise.

But even as things stand today, you cannot help but be impressed by this backdrop of Romanesque arches, Gothic spires and postmodern curves, with genteel chamber music pouring from palace windows and the perfectly proportioned river Vltava running through it all, reflecting the Prague Castle lights. It might even make as lasting an impression as the streets filled with Eva Herzigová lookalikes. Or the remarkable affordability of it all – to visitors, anyway.

So don't be dismayed by the distance Prague still has to go on the route to world-class cultural capital. It's covering the ground in record time. And the correspondents who've researched this Guide have enclosed complete directions to the fast lane.

Just take heed of a recent public service message plastered throughout the city: 'Rychle, ale bezpečně,' read the words, superimposed over images of train wrecks, plane crashes, devastation of all kinds.

Intended to remind Czech drivers of the city's astoundingly high accident rate (among the highest in Europe) the motto reads: 'Quickly, but safely.' Absurdism worthy of a Václav Havel play it may be. But let's do try not to lose our head out there.
Will Tizard

In Context

Prague By Season   **5**   Prague Today   **29**
History   **10**   Architecture   **34**

Prague by Season

Everyone's heard of the Prague Spring – but summer, autumn and winter hold their own in this amazingly cyclical land.

Few cities undergo such a severe form of seasonal schizophrenia as Prague. Winter Prague and summer Prague are two very different cities. Fur hats, boots and vistas of Charles Bridge shrouded in smog or snow give winter Prague an undeniably melancholic air, yet this is when the city seems most 'itself'. As soon as spring arrives, the gloom is thrown off and the place fills up with tourists. But although summer Prague is a much more cosmopolitan city, you're equally likely to encounter a music festival or some bizarre folk tradition at any time of year.

INFORMATION

For more information on events, try the listings section of the *Prague Post*. Many events are held at various locations throughout the city; admission price will depend on whether you buy your tickets through an agency (*see page 195*) or direct from the organisers. Unless otherwise stated, events are free.

Public holidays

Compared with other countries, the Czechs do rather poorly, with only ten national holidays: 1 January, Easter Monday, 1 May (Labour Day), 8 May (Liberation Day), 5 July (Cyril & Methodius Day), 6 July (Jan Hus Day), 28 October (Independence Day), 24-26 December.

Spring

Czech men start sporting sandals and socks and the tourist buses begin to roll into town.

Easter Monday

Date Mar/Apr. Public holiday.
Men with willow sticks rush around the countryside beating women on the backside. The women respond with gifts of painted eggs and shots of alcohol. This ancient fertility rite is rarely seen in central Prague, but painted eggs and willow sticks are on sale all over the city.

Witches' Night

Date 30 Apr.
Witches' night (pálení čarodějnic) is Hallowe'en and Bonfire Night rolled into one and marks the death of winter and the

May rituals *at the Mácha statue. See page 7.*

You can get there from here.

Calling around the world is easy. Really. Just dial the AT&T access number of the country you're calling from. An AT&T Operator or English-language voice prompt will help connect you to the States and over 80 countries quickly and easily. It's that simple. With easy billing to either your AT&T Card or U.S. Local Telephone Company calling card, or by calling collect.* So when someone tells you you can't get there from here, pick up the phone and call 'em on it.

Call with AT&T.

From Czech Republic dial
00-420-00-101

For more information about
AT&T Global Service
call collect + 44 171 505 6580

*Applies only to

birth of spring. Bonfires are lit to purge the winter spirits, an effigy of a hag is burnt (a relic of historical witch hunts), and some more daring adherents of the custom leap over the flames. Most fires are out in the country but there's occasionally a pyre or two to be found in the capital, for example on the top of Petřín Hill.

May rituals

Petřín Hill (Petřínské sady), Prague 1. Metro Malostranská/12, 22 tram. **Date** May. **Map 1 C5**
Czech lovers with the sap rising make a pilgrimage to the statue of Karel Hynek Mácha on Petřín Hill to place flowers and engage in a spot of necking. Mácha was a nineteenth-century romantic poet who spawned many myths, several bastards and an epic poem called *Máj* (May). It's actually a rather melancholy tale of unrequited love but nobody lets that spoil their fun. You might also get pulled underneath a lilac tree and energetically snogged to keep you from being 'dry' in the coming year.

Prague International Book Fair and Writer's Festival

info from PIS (544 444). **Date** May.
Czech (and occasional international) literary stars get together to read extracts and hob-nob with foreign writers specially imported for the occasion. Here's your chance to see Ivan Klíma's improbable hairdo and the quirks of other great Prague literary icons.

Labour Day

Date 1 May. Public holiday.
You are now no longer in danger of being run over by a tank when walking down Wenceslas Square, but May Day is still a good excuse to throw a demonstration. The communists, in a somewhat pitiful attempt to keep the faith alive, usually throw a small rally in Letná Park and encourage pensioners to complain about the perils of the free market, while the anarchists sometimes hold an altogether unanarchic parade.

VE Day

Date 8 May. Public holiday.
The Day of Liberation from Fascism used to be 9 May, but as good Euro-citizens, the Czech government fell into line with the rest of the Continent and moved it to 8 May, despite the fact that the Red Army didn't reach Prague until a day later. Flowers and wreaths are laid on Soviet monuments such as the place where a Soviet tank used to stand in Smíchov and the Garden of Rest at Olšany Cemetery (*see p86*).

Prague Spring Festival

info: Hellichova 18, Prague 1 (2451 0422/fax 536 040/ festival@login.cz/www.festival.cz). Metro Malostranská/ 12, 22 tram. **Admission** varies. **Date** mid-May-early June. **Map 2 D4**
The biggest and best of Prague's music festivals begins on the anniversary of Smetana's death with a performance of his tone poem *Má Vlast* (My Country). The festival is very popular, so book tickets well in advance. *See also p195.*

Prague Jazz Festival

info from PIS (see above) or AghaRTA Jazz Centrum (2221 1275). **Admission** varies. **Date** May-Oct.
Prague has a fine tradition of jazz and AghaRTA is one of the city's more dynamic clubs. The festival is small, but with excellent performances by top international acts that now tend to be spread over most of the year, both at the **Lucerna** music bar (*see p198*) and outdoors. *See also p200.*

Summer

In sticky heat, the streets throng with German and Japanese tour parties, hippies with acoustic guitars, gangs of Italian youths, and American backpackers with Lenny Kravitz goggle shades. Locals tend to clear out if they can and many institutions close down for the duration.

Balls! Balls! Balls!

Balls are big in Bohemia. The Czech ball (*ples*) tradition was at its zenith around a century ago, when balls were a bastion of Czech language and culture in the midst of the country's period of Germanisation. In the red old days, when all pubs slammed their doors in synchronicity come 10pm, balls were among the few opportunities to keep the party going until the wee hours.

The onslaught of discos and late-night clubs has changed all this, but ball season is still going strong – partly because most Czech teenagers must suffer through courses of ballroom dancing. From January to March, however, all that two-stepping pays off. Every village, every bizarre union and each district in Prague hosts its own ball. Most of them, though, are a far cry from the glass-slippers-and-taffeta affairs you might be imagining. Take the **Moravian Ball** (traditionally held in the Národní dům Smíchov), where dancers in traditional garb take centre stage with their elaborate, foot-stomping dances, and room after room of displaced southerners slug wine from bottles and sing folk songs in unison. Or the **Hunters' Ball**, held in the elegant National House of Vinohrady (Národní dům na Vinohradech), where old couples polka in the mirrored ballroom against a background of freshly killed game, which is raffled off throughout the course of the evening. Or the **Prague-Vienna Ball** in the Obecní dům, traditionally Prague's swankiest affair, where the city's élite waltz to the tune of four different orchestras. Tickets for balls run from around 150 Kč for the humbler variety, and up to 2,000 Kč for almost any event held in Žofín on Slovanský island or the Obecní dům, and can be bought at the venue, in advance or at the door. Anyone can attend, although it can be difficult to track down information. Try each district's Národní dům, the Žofín hall or **Lucerna** (for information, call 2421 2003; *see also page 198*).

*No labour for these old folk no more: dancing away **Labour Day** at Výstaviště. See page 7.*

Tanec Praha (Dance Prague)

info: Jirsíkova 4, Prague 8 (2481 7886/2481 3899/ fax 231 9576/office@tanecpha.cz/www.tanecpha.cz). Metro Florenc/8, 24 tram. **Admission** varies. **Date** June/July.

Tanec Praha, an international festival of modern dance, has proved to be one of the more successful new festivals in Prague. Participants come from all over the world to perform in the major theatres as well as giving free exhibitions in public outdoor spaces. There are workshops, a symposium on dance theory and video demonstrations. *See also p217.*

Anniversary of Kafka's death

Jewish Cemetery (Židovský hřbitov), Izraelská 1, Prague 3 (733 022). Metro Želivského/11, 16, 19, 26 tram. **Date** 3 June. **Map 8 E2**

Fans make a pilgrimage to Kafka's grave (number 21-14-33) at the Jewish Cemetery (*see p86*), and prayers are said in the Old-New Synagogue.

Commemoration of the death of Heydrich's assassins

Orthodox Cathedral of Sts Cyril and Methodius (Kostel sv. Cyrila a Metoděj), Resslova 9, Prague 2 (295 595). Metro Karlovo náměstí/4, 7, 9, 14, 16, 18, 22, 24 tram. **Open** 10am-4pm Tue-Sun. **Admission** 30 Kč adults; 10 Kč children, students. **Date** 18 June. **Map 5 H8**

The crypt of this baroque church was the site of one of the most poignant events of World War II in Prague – the last stand of the Czech assassins of Nazi Reichsprotektor Reinhard Heydrich. Every year a memorial mass is held to commemorate those who died in the reprisals following the assassination. *See also p59.*

Autumn

Catch it while you can: Prague's autumn is short and very sweet. Still an alarming number of tourists, though.

Prague Autumn

info: Přiběnická 20, Prague 3 (627 8740/fax 627 8642). **Date** mid-Sept. **Admission** varies. **Map 8 A1**

Offering the next best thing to Prague Spring, this festival attracts world-renowned talents every year to Prague's best concert venues, such as the splendid Rudolfinum.

St Vitus's Celebration

(Svatováclavské slavnosti) info: Kolejní 4, Prague 6 (2018 1710). **Admission** varies. **Date** mid-Sept.

A chance to hear spiritual music, both ancient and modern, performed at Prague Castle and in some of Prague's most splendid churches while the weather is still clement enough to make sitting for an extended period in an unheated building not an endurance test.

Burčák arrives

Date late Sept-early Oct.

Burčák, half-fermented early-season wine, hits town some time in the autumn. It's a cloudy, young Moravian vintner's speciality, served straight from the barrel. It looks like murky wheat beer, tastes like cherryade but will sneak up on you if you don't give it a healthy respect.

Festival of Best Amateur and Professional Puppet Theatre Plays

info from Union of International Marionettists (438 471). **Admission** varies. **Date** Oct.

A festival that exploits Bohemia's long tradition of puppet-making. Some of the most innovative artists in the country continue to use them, including the celebrated animator Jan Švankmajer, and there's even a faculty at the university devoted to the craft.

Anniversary of the Creation of Czechoslovakia

Date 28 Oct. Public holiday.

The nation no longer exists but the people still get a day off. Republicans spend the day in mourning and various factions hold demonstrations on Wenceslas Square.

All Souls' Day

Date 2 Nov.

Best time of year to visit any one of the city's cemeteries. Whole families turn out to light candles, lay wreaths and say prayers for the dead. The best place to go is the enormous Olšany Cemetery (*see p86*).

Anniversary of the Velvet Revolution

Národní třída & Václavské náměstí. Metro Národní třída & Muzeum. **Date** 17 Nov. **Map 3 H5 & 6 L6**

To commemorate the demonstration that began the Velvet Revolution in 1989, flowers are laid and candles are lit on the memorial on Národní třída (next to the passage by no.20) and in Wenceslas Square (near the statue).

Winter

The tourists finally leave and Prague battens down the hatches for the winter months. Smog, smog and more smog, but the city is beautiful in the snow.

St Nicholas's Eve

around Charles Bridge, Staroměstské náměstí & Karlovo náměstí. Metro Staroměstská & Karlovo náměstí.
Date 5 Dec. **Maps 2 F3, 5 H7 & 3 H3**
Grown men spend the evening wearing unlikely dresses, drinking large amounts of beer and terrorising small children. They parade through the streets in threesomes, dressed as St Nicholas, an angel and a devil, symbolising confession, reward and punishment. Instead of a red polyester cloak, St Nicholas usually looks quite fetching in a long white vestment, with a white mitre and a gold cross. The angel hands out sweets to children who have been good, while the devil is on hand to dispense rough justice to those who haven't.

The week before Christmas

The streets suddenly sport huge tubs of water filled with carp. It's the traditional Christmas dish, and while some people buy them live and store them in the bathtub (like most bottom-feeders, they taste of mud otherwise), the more squeamish have the fish of their choice killed and gutted in front of a crowd of less squeamish onlookers.

New Year's Eve

Václavské náměstí & Staroměstské náměstí. Metro Můstek, Muzeum & Staroměstská. **Date** 31 Dec.
Maps 4 K5 & 3 H3
New Year's Eve is known in these parts as St Sylvester's Day, and the streets are invariably packed with a rag-tag bunch of Euro-revellers, with much of the fun centred on Wenceslas Square and the Old Town Square. Fireworks are let off everywhere and flung around with frankly dangerous abandon, then champagne bottles are smashed.

Anniversary of Jan Palach's death

Olšanské hřbitovy & Václavské náměstí. Metro Flóra & Muzeum. **Date** 19 Jan. **Maps 8 D2 & 6 L6**
Jan Palach set fire to himself on 19 January 1969 in Wenceslas Square as a protest against the Soviet invasion. His grave sports candles and flowers all year round, but many people make the trip to Olšany Cemetery *(see p86)* or the 'memorial to the victims of communism' near the St Wenceslas statue *(see p53)* to lay a few more.

Out of town

For admission prices for the following events, it's best to check nearer the time.

Miss Czech Republic

info from Art Production Praha (292 053/2491 5735).
Date Apr.
Banned under the communists, beauty contests have now exploded across the land with incredible popularity. Cutthroat competition is assured as the lovelies vie not only for fame and fortune but also a Škoda.

Karlovy Vary Beer Olympiad

Karlovy Vary (info 017 203 569/fax 017 24667).
Date May.
Sponsored by major Czech breweries and attended by about 20,000 people – this is a chance to take part in a 1,000-person beer relay or attempt the world record for drinking a half-litre while standing on your head (the time to beat is 9.4 seconds).

Fungi frenzy

Come September and October, Czechs begin a frantic scramble for wild mushrooms. Families rise as early as 5am and head for the woods in a desperate search for these treasures of the forest. Unwilling children are roped into the fray and sent on ahead like sniffer dogs. The competition, particularly near Prague where there are more people than mushrooms, is fierce and merciless: everyone has their own 'secret place', and woe betide anyone who encroaches upon it. Disputes about ownership arise, and lifelong friends fall out. At the end of the day, exultant families cannot resist showing off their booty to friends and neighbours, as if they had just won the national lottery. Those who are not as successful are left to gnash their teeth in envy, vowing revenge.

Once collected, the fungi are dried, pickled or stewed. Every Czech housewife is well versed in the art of preserving mushrooms. Though you can buy them in markets, this is commonly regarded as being a bit infra dig: if you haven't got your mushrooms by your own efforts, it doesn't really count. As for the danger of picking the wrong kind, annual casualties average only two or three. After all, every self-respecting Czech sees himself as a mushroom expert. And if he's not sure, he can always take his haul to the Mushroom Institute in Prague for verification. Honest.

Karlovy Vary International Film Festival

info from Film Festival office (2423 5412/2423 8225/2423 8244/fax 2423 3408). **Date** July.
This genteel spa town plays host to the Czech version of Cannes. While hardly in the same league, the long-running festival does show an interesting mix of foreign and homegrown features. *See also p184 & p234.*

Anniversary of the Battle of Hradec Králové, 1866

Chlum battlefield, Hradec Králové (info 049 551 3139).
Date early July.
Czechs love to re-enact this epic battle between two of their oldest adversaries, the Austrians and the Prussians, who, for once, went for each others throats instead of the Czechs'. In the biggest fight for supremacy of the nineteenth century, half a million soldiers fought, with the Prussians coming from behind to trounce the superior Habsburg numbers. Expect drunken post-battle celebrations in town afterwards.

Buchlov Festival of Folk Music

Buchlovská svíca, near Uherské Hradiště, South Moravia (06 323 288). **Date** late July/early Aug.
Folk festivals abound in Bohemia and Moravia during the summer months, but this one has a presidential endorsement as Václav Havel usually shows up (when his health allows it).

Key Events

The Přemyslid dynasty

c400 BC Celtic Boii tribe occupies Bohemia
7th century AD Slavic tribes settle in the region
c700 The Přemyslid dynasty begins
863 Cyril and Methodius bring Christianity to Bohemia
929 Good 'King' Wenceslas is killed by his brother and becomes a martyr and the Czech patron saint
973 Prague is made a bishopric
1235 Staré Město gets a Royal Charter; Jews forced into the ghetto
1253 Otakar II becomes king and conquers half of Central Europe
1257 Malá Strana receives town status
1306 Přemyslid dynasty ends with murder of Václav III

Hussites & Habsburgs

1346 Charles IV becomes Holy Roman Emperor and King of Bohemia
1348 Charles IV founds Central Europe's first university, in Prague
1352 Swabian architect Peter Parler begins work on St Vitus's Cathedral
1357 The first stone of Charles Bridge is laid
1378 Charles's son Wenceslas IV becomes king
1389 3,000 Jews killed in pogrom
1403 Jan Hus, Rector of Prague University, begins preaching against Church corruption
1415 Hus, having been excommunicated and declared a heretic, is burned at the stake in Constance
1419 Hussite mob throws the Mayor out of the New Town Hall window; beginning of the Hussite wars
1420s-1430s Hussites repel all attacks
1434 Moderate Hussites wipe out the radicals and the Pope agrees to allow them considerable religious freedom
1458 Czech noble George of Poděbrady becomes the 'People's king' but is soon excommunicated by the Pope
1471-1526 The Jagellon dynasty rules in Bohemia
1526 Habsburg rule begins with Ferdinand I
1556 Ferdinand invites the Jesuits to Prague to counter fierce anti-Catholicism in Bohemia
1583 Habsburg Emperor Rudolf II moves the court to Prague, where it remains for the next two decades
1609 Astronomer Johannes Kepler publishes his *Laws of Planetary Motion*; Rudolf concedes religious rights to Bohemia's Protestants
1618 Protestants throw two Catholic councillors from a window in the castle, thus starting the Thirty Years' War
1619 Frederick of the Palatinate is elected King of Bohemia

Wars, revolutions & the Republic

1620 Protestants lose the Battle of White Mountain
1621 27 Protestant leaders executed in Old Town Square
1648 The Thirty Years' War ends on Charles Bridge as the citizens of Prague repel the Swedes
1740 Maria Theresa becomes empress
1743 French attack Prague
1757 Prussians attack Prague
1781 Emperor Joseph II abolishes 'useless' religious orders, including the Jesuits, and closes monasteries
1787 Mozart conducts the first performance of *Don Giovanni* in the Estates Theatre

1848 Revolutions in Europe; unsuccessful uprisings in Prague against Austrian troops
1891 Radical Young Czechs calling for independence sweep the Bohemian Diet elections
1893 The clearing of the Jewish ghetto begins
1914 Outbreak of World War I; Habsburgs refuse concessions on federalism and Czech soldiers desert to the Allies
1918 The Czechoslovak Republic is founded. Tomáš Masaryk becomes its first President

War & totalitarianism

1938 Chamberlain agrees to let Hitler take over the Sudetenland
1939 Hitler takes all Czechoslovakia
1941 Terezin ghetto established as a 'model' community for Jews, masking the reality of the Nazis' genocide programme at Auschwitz, where its survivors were taken

1942 Czech paratroopers assassinate Reichsprotektor Reinhard Heydrich. Nazis destroy villages Lidice and Ležáky in revenge
1945 Prague uprising; the Red Army enters the city
1948 The communist party assumes power under Klement Gottwald
1951 The Slánský show trials and mass purges against the regime's enemies
1968 Reformist communist Dubček becomes First Secretary and promotes 'socialism with a human face', but the Prague Spring is crushed by Warsaw Pact troops
1969 Philosophy student Jan Palach sets fire to himself in protest and 200,000 people march to his funeral
1977 The underground movement Charter 77 is established by playwright Václav Havel to monitor human rights abuses
1988 Soviet leader Gorbachev hints at support for a reformist government in Prague

The Velvet Revolution

1989 Student demonstrations turn into full-scale revolution and the communist regime falls
1990 Václav Havel is elected President of Czechoslovakia
1992 Free marketeer Václav Klaus elected Prime Minister
1993 The Slovak Republic and Czech Republic become separate, independent states
1994 New freedoms prove hazardous. Some 250,000 car accidents occur nationwide, the largest-ever cache of proliferated weapons-grade plutonium is seized (from a car), and 288 police officers are charged with crimes abuses
1996 Michael Jackson's statue briefly takes up the spot vacated by Stalin's in Letná Park, as part of his understated HIStory tour
1997 Jan Svěrák wins best Foreign Film Oscar for *Kolja*

History

They've had the best of times, they'd had the worst of times – but finally they're a nation.

The Přemyslid dynasty

In around 400 BC, a Celtic tribe called the **Boii** occupied the region where the Czech Republic now lies and gave it the name Bohemia. The Boii successfully repelled attacking armies for the best part of 1,000 years, but they were eventually driven out by the Germanic Marcomanni and Quadi tribes who in turn were wiped out by Attila the Hun in AD 451. Slavic tribes are believed to have moved into the area sometime during the seventh century. They were ruled over by the Avars whose harsh regime provoked a successful Slavic rebellion.

The Czechs had to wait until the eighth century and the founding of the **Přemyslid** dynasty for real independence. The dynasty's origins are shrouded in myth (*see below*). One relates that, in the absence of a male heir, **Čech** tribe leader Krok was succeeded by his soothsaying daughter Libuše. But the men of the tribe, indignant at being ruled over by a woman, told her to go and find a husband. Libuše went into a trance and sent her white horse over the hills. The horse, she foretold, would find a ploughman with two spotted oxen and he would become their leader. Her horse quickly located the farmer, whose name was **Přemysl**.

Prague, too, is supposed to have been founded following a similar trance-induced vision. This time Libuše declared from the hilltop at **Vyšehrad** that 'a city whose splendour will reach to the stars' would be created nearby. Everyone then went into the woods again, this time to find a craftsman making a door sill (*práh* in Czech), for, as Libuše said, 'mighty Lords bend before a low door'. When her subjects found the craftsman, the site of the city was determined.

Mything the point...?
Libuše & Přemysl

Much of the responsibility for establishing the Libuše/Přemysl origins of Prague and the Czechs is down to dean Cosmas of Prague Cathedral in his jaunty *Chronicle of the Bohemians* (1119-25). He was well aware of the importance of the Libuše (or Libussa) legend in legitimising the Přemysl dynasty. Later writers seized on and developed the story to represent everything from the historical destiny of the Czech people to the romance of the Bohemian forests.

Yet, in the 1960s, Czech scholar Vladimír Karbusický demonstrated that Cosmas's work was less a gathering of local lore (as had been assumed) than a collation and rationalisation of stories and poems from all over Europe. The humble plowman as ruler is a common tradition (in Hungary and Rome, for instance) and the theme of strong, mystical women (alternately appealing and appaling to male chroniclers) is also not unique to Cosmas's story. His Libuše is

I foresee a city of a million tour groups with a McDonalds on every street corner!

clearly influenced by a contemporary woman ruler of great power and competence – Matilda of Tuscany (1046-1115).

THE COMING OF CHRISTIANITY

In the ninth century, Charlemagne briefly occupied the area and a Slavic state was created in Moravia under Prince Mojmír. In 860 Mojmír's successor, Rostilav, appealed to the Pope for Christian apostles with a knowledge of the Slavic language to help him put an end to the worship of sun gods. The Byzantine Emperor sent two Greek monks, **Cyril** and **Methodius**, who had designed a Cyrillic script for the Slavic tongue, but Frankish and German priests objected to this initiative and, following Methodius's death in 885, Slavonic liturgy was prohibited.

Rostilav's nephew **Svatopluk** (871-94) had sided with the Germans over the liturgical issue and with their assistance ousted his uncle. Svatopluk built an empire encompassing Moravia, Bohemia and Slovakia. After Svatopluk's death the Magyars grabbed a chunk of Slovakia. They held on to it right up until the twentieth century, and their presence in the area was to disrupt all attempts to unite Slovaks and Czechs.

GOOD 'KING' WENCESLAS

Over the next four centuries, Bohemia rode a rollercoaster that alternately descended into chaos and rose to the heights of political supremacy in Central Europe. Things continued peacefully enough in the early tenth century under the humane rule of Prince **Václav** or **Wenceslas** (921-9; *see below*). Although Christmas carols still sing his praises, many Czech nobles felt that Good 'King' Wenceslas had sold out to the Germans and neglected Slavic interests. The nobles sided with Wenceslas's brother **Boleslav** (the Cruel, 935-67), who had Wenceslas murdered in 929. Boleslav then fought the Germans for the next 14 years.

Bohemia was briefly united with Moravia. Prague was made a Bishopric in 973 and the process of bringing Christianity to Bohemia was soon completed. By the end of the twelfth century, however, internal bickering over succession had become so bad that, in the words of the historian Palacký, 'in the storm of ages the Czechs were about to drown as a state and a nation'. The turning point came in 1197 when **Otakar I** confronted his brother Vladislav outside Prague in a showdown for the throne. But in this case sibling rivalry had its limits. Diplomatic negotiations on the night before the battle resulted in the two princes agreeing a deal that made Otakar I Bohemian King and Vladislav Margrave of

Mything the point...?
Good 'King' Wenceslas

Much of the St Wenceslas (Václav) legend was established by no less a personage than Charles IV, keen to establish his own noble descent. He wrote of Wenceslas's gentle nature, his great piety, his many good deeds, and of his devoted servant Podiven, who would warm himself in his master's glowing footsteps on wintry days. And if the historical Duke (not King) Wenceslas wasn't quite the paragon of virtue his hagiographers and the nineteenth-century carol made out, he was certainly an unusually otherworldly figure in the grittiest of times.

He christianised most of Bohemia, which annoyed the pagan nobility, and bolstered the economy by bringing in German merchants and craftsmen, which annoyed the native commercial classes. When his impatient brother, the aptly named Boleslav the Cruel, decided enough was enough and had him dispatched, Wenceslas was actually about to renounce his dukedom in Boleslav's favour to allow him to go to Rome to be consecrated as the first bishop of Bohemia. Wenceslas's martyrdom sped him on

Guten tag, meine freunde - have a lucrative trading monopoly

Vyser si oko!

his way into the saintly canon and into the hearts of every Czech, to whom this head-in-the-clouds, peaceable if unrealistic medieval duke transmogrified into the mighty martial saviour of the nation personified in Wenceslas Square's epic equine statue.

Moravia. By Otakar's death in 1230 a period of peace and prestige had been achieved. His son and successor **Václav I** was made one of the seven electors of the Holy Roman Empire.

With national prestige reaching new heights, **Přemysl Otakar II** (1253-78) made his territorial claims. He snatched Cheb from the Germans and won and lost Slovakia twice. For a while his empire stretched from Florence to Poland, gaining him the title 'King of Gold and Iron'. But Otakar was getting too powerful for Rudolf of Habsburg, especially when he challenged Rudolf for the throne of the Holy Roman Empire.

The title went to the Habsburg and in 1276 Rudolf invaded Bohemia. He left his rival with only a rump empire – Bohemia and Moravia. Thereafter Otakar's successor Václav II (1278-1305) was forced to look eastwards for conquests in Poland, Hungary, Croatia and Romania. His son Václav III was assassinated in 1306, allegedly by Habsburg agents. Since he left no heir, the Czech Přemyslid dynasty came to an abrupt end.

THE GERMANS ARRIVE

During this period the demographic nature of Bohemia changed significantly. The Přemysls encouraged German immigration and German women married Czech nobles. German clerics filled top positions in the Church, and German merchants gave life to the towns, introducing new laws and administration methods. Prague was reorganised into three autonomous areas: Malá Strana, Hradčany and the Old Town (Staré Město). The Jewish community of Malá Strana was forced into a ghetto in the Old Town to give the Germans more *Lebensraum*.

Successive kings drew upon the economic power of the towns to counterbalance the rural nobility. The Prague Germans demanded an ever-greater voice and by the fourteenth century Czech and German nobles began a conflict that would underlie much of subsequent Czech history.

In 1310 **John of Luxembourg**, 14-year-old son of the Holy Roman Emperor, was elected King of Bohemia. The first years of his reign were marked by tussles with the Czech nobles over the extent of royal power. He was married to the second daughter of Václav II in order to give him Přemyslid credentials, but his loyalties went no further.

His interest in Prague was ephemeral and obscure. He once attempted to recreate the Knights of the Round Table by inviting all the great knights of Europe to the city, but none of them turned up. While John was successfully wheeling and dealing in the diplomatic circles of Europe, the nobles' power grew substantially. Prague gained a town hall and became the dominant centre of Bohemia. It was raised from a Bishopric to an Archbishopric in 1344.

The rise of Hussitism

John died a noble death in a kamikaze charge against Welsh archers at the Battle of Crécy. His son **Charles IV** was elected Holy Roman Emperor in 1346 making his position as King of Bohemia unassailable. His support for the development of Prague had the full force of Empire behind it and ushered in a golden age for the city. Charles (1346-78) brought to Bohemia the stability that his father John had failed to achieve. The Czechs could not have asked for more.

THE GOLDEN AGE OF CHARLES IV

Charles had been educated at the French court and learnt to speak several languages fluently, including Czech. Although in his youth he had a reputation for wild parties and very tight pants, he became a devout Christian when the Pope rebuked him following his coronation. Through his mother he laid claim to direct lineage with the Přemyslid dynasty. Consequently, he became known as 'Father of his Country' and the 'Priest Kaiser'. Prague escaped the Black Death that ravaged Europe in 1348 and under Charles emerged as one of the most dazzling centres in Europe.

Charles brought the 23-year-old Swabian architect **Peter Parler** to Prague to build **Charles Bridge** and to work on **St Vitus's Cathedral**, a Gothic masterpiece reflecting Prague's spiralling glory in Europe.

In 1348 Charles established Central Europe's first university, declaring that Bohemians should 'no longer be obliged to beg for foreign alms but find a table prepared for them in their own kingdom'. He founded the **New Town** (Nové Město), which was constructed around wide streets, effectively relieving the Old Town of the stress created by the concentration of artisans' workshops. And he undercut the power of the nobility in 1356 by reorganising the electoral system.

Availing himself of his omnipotent position in the Holy Roman Empire, Charles declared the union of Bohemia, Moravia, Silesia and Upper Lusatia indissoluble, and grafted chunks of Germany on to Bohemia. He abandoned claims to Italian territories but refused to accept Papal dictates north of the Alps. In 1364 he and the Habsburgs declared that the succession of the Empire's territories would go to whichever royal family outlived the other. The Habsburgs benefited from the agreement.

Charles was a devout Christian. Under his rule the clergy came to own half the land in the kingdom. But at the same time he was intensely conscious of the growing corruption in the Church and often sided with the fiery preachers who condemned its excesses. These included the rabble-rousing Jan Milič of Kroměříž, who had a tendency to go a little over the top. He stunned the crowds by declaring their beloved Charles was really the Antichrist. He urged his followers to prepare for the imminent apocalypse, and since he preached in Czech rather than German, the anti-clerical hysteria he inspired became closely identified with Czech nationalism. It was an explosive mix.

NOT SO GOOD KING WENCESLAS

The seeds of religious indignation were sown during Charles's reign but the bitter fruits were not tasted until the reign of his incorrigible son **Wenceslas IV** (1378-1419). When the Archbishop of Prague ordered the burning of all of the Protestant writings of the English reformer John Wycliffe, Wenceslas, aware of the religious sensitivities of his subjects, forced the Archbishop to compensate the owners of the manuscripts. A champion of the common man, he would go out shopping dressed in commoners' clothing, but if shopkeepers cheated him he would have them executed. Despite (or perhaps because of) notorious displays of temper such as roasting the chef who had spoilt his lunch, chroniclers wrote that under his reign there was a virtual absence of crime in Prague.

Wenceslas and quiet piety never sat easily together. At his christening he was alleged to have urinated into the holy water and he was still unable to control himself at his coronation. He was perhaps closest to God the morning after a pub crawl and is said to have spent most of his last years in a drunken stupor. The nobles were not impressed and formed a 'League of Lords' to have him imprisoned, but he escaped while in the royal bathhouse, seducing the beautiful bath attendant and persuading her to row him down the Vltava to safety.

JAN HUS

Wenceslas lacked the moral and intellectual authority to steer Bohemia through the dangerous religious waters ahead. In 1403 the Rector of Prague University, **Jan Hus**, influenced by Wycliffe's reformist doctrines, took up the campaign against Church corruption. The battleground moved to the university where Czech supporters of Hus squabbled with the Germans. The King decreed in favour of the Czechs and the German academics left for Leipzig to found their own university. The Church establishment was quick to start a counter-campaign. Hus's arguments were declared heretical, although he was in fact a moderate compared to the reformers who subsequently campaigned in his name. Even so, he was persuaded by Wenceslas, under pressure from the Church, to leave Prague in 1412. The obstinate preacher continued his crusade in the countryside.

In November 1414, Hus was summoned by Wenceslas's brother Sigismund, King of Hungary, to appear before the General Council at Constance.

Hus went in good faith carrying a safe conduct pass granted by Sigismund. But on arrival he was thrown in jail. The Council ordered Hus to recant his teachings and accused him of portraying himself as a fourth addition to the Holy Trinity. He challenged the Council to prove from the Scriptures that what he preached was false, but he was told that he should recant simply because his superiors had told him to do so. He refused and on his forty-sixth birthday, 6 July 1415, Hus was burnt at the stake.

Hus embodied two vital hopes of the Czech people: reform of the established Church and independence from German dominance. It was not, therefore, surprising that he was to become a martyr. His motto 'truth will prevail' and the chalice, which represented lay participation in the Sacrament, became rallying symbols for his followers. The main tenets of Hussitism were contained in the Four Articles of Prague. These demanded unrestricted preaching of the word of God; communion in both kinds ('sub utraque specie' – his followers were known as Utraquists, although, ironically, this was never advocated by Hus himself), allowing congregations to partake in not just the bread, but also the wine of the Eucharist; removal of the large estates and possessions from monks and clergy; and strict punishment of sins committed by members of the Church.

HUSSITISM & CZECH NATIONALISM

A few weeks after Hus's death, several hundred nobles in Bohemia sent a protest to the Council of Constance, declaring their intention to defend Hus's name and promote his teachings. The groundswell of popular feeling soon engulfed Wenceslas IV. Under pressure from the Church, he suppressed the Hussites. Then, on 30 July 1419, an angry Hussite crowd stormed the Town Hall protesting at the detention of prisoners who had been arrested for creating 'religious disorder'. The mob threw the Mayor and his councillors through the window to their deaths (*see also page 73*). Prague's first defenestration finally shattered hopes for peace.

Wenceslas withdrew his decrees and died in an apoplectic fit a few days later. Hussite mobs marked the occasion by rioting and sacking the monasteries. Sigismund, who had been complicit in the burning of Hus, elbowed his way on to the Bohemian throne, and moderate Utraquist nobles, keen to find a compromise, greeted him with sycophantic deference. But radical preachers like Jan Želivský furiously denounced Sigismund and Rome, prompting the Pope to call for a holy crusade against Bohemia.

Prague was almost under siege but the Hussites were undaunted. Again the Utraquists approached Sigismund, only to report back that he swore to destroy all heresy by fire and sword. Meanwhile the radical Hussites arrived in the city in force and, as a sign of their seriousness, burnt alive nine monks in front of the Royal Garrison.

THE HUSSITE WARS

Rome's call to arms against the heretic nation was taken up all over Europe and the Czechs soon found themselves surrounded. They were united, however, behind a powerful moral cause and had a freshness and zeal that came from being independent and free. They also had in their ranks a brilliant one-eyed general called **Jan Žižka**. He not only repelled the enemies from Vitkov hill in what is now Žižkov in Prague, but, by 1432, he and his 'Warriors of God' (as the Czechs called themselves) were pillaging all the way up to the Baltic coast. Women fought and died equally alongside men.

The Hussites were united during times of greatest danger but as the battle turned in their favour, old divisions re-emerged. The majority, known as **Praguers**, were moderate and middle class and their leaders were based at the University of Prague. The more extreme group, known as **Táborites**, were based on a fortified hillside called Tábor. They banned all class divisions, shared their property and held religious services only in Czech.

Once the Pope realised that the holy war had failed, he reluctantly invited the Czechs to discuss a peace settlement. The Táborites were cynical about the Pope's overtures whereas the Praguers had never wanted to break with Rome and viewed their Hussite allies in Tábor as a little too revolutionary. In 1434, the Prague nobles marched their army down to confront the Táborites and wiped out 13,000 of them at the **Battle of Lipany**, thereby settling the issue of negotiations with Rome.

In 1436 the Pope and the Utraquists signed the Basle Compacts, which recognised the Czechs as 'faithful sons of the Church', and accepted Utraquist demands for communion in both kinds. But there was no agreement on the issue of corruption in the Church. The Táborites' lack of trust in Rome was to prove well founded. A Papal envoy was sent to Prague to cool things down. On his arrival he reproached the Praguers for conducting religious services that diverted from Roman practice. It was pointed out to the envoy that the Pope had agreed to this in the Basle Compacts. When the envoy denied any knowledge of the Compacts, he was shown the original document as proof, whereupon he and the document disappeared. He was pursued by troops across Bohemia who found it in his suitcase.

A HOME-BORN KING

Without a strong king, Prague was descending into national, religious and class anarchy. The King, Ladislav the Posthumous of Habsburg, was dependent on the Utraquist noble, **George of Poděbrady** (Jiří z Poděbrad), who allegedly advised him to drink poisoned wine. George was formally elected to the throne in 1458. From the outset he was hemmed in by hostile opponents. He eliminated the rump of the radical Táborites and suppressed a separatist pacifist Christian movement called the Unity of Czech Brethren, which was becoming immensely popular. He also fought and defeated a confederacy of plotting nobles. He kept the reactionary Catholics at bay while trying not to antagonise Rome, and resisted the demands of the German population for more power. George feared another holy crusade against his country and as a diversionary tactic he tried to form a League of Christian Kings and Princes to provide mutual assistance against the menace of the Turks. The idea was pooh-poohed by princes and bishops as an impertinence against the Pope and the Holy Roman Emperor. For his part, the Pope reneged on the Basle agreement and excommunicated George.

Since the Hussite wars the political balance in the land had altered substantially. The Church's power had been devastated and the vacuum was filled by the nobles who seized Church property and ruled mercilessly over the peasants. A hard-fought power struggle between the King and the nobles forced George to look abroad to the Polish **Jagellon** dynasty for a successor. Following his death in 1471, Vladislav II became the King of Bohemia, to be followed by Ludvík in 1516.

THE INSTABILITY CONTINUES

The two Jagellon monarchs, ruling *in absentia*, failed to keep the nobles in check. In 1500 the nobility extracted a new constitution confirming their status, reducing that of the peasants to serfdom and stripping the towns of their power. Lutheran ideas, which were close to Hussitism, seeped in from Germany and religious tensions soon flared up again. Anxious Utraquists, fearing a reproach from Rome, tried to keep the lid on these developments. They redirected all their efforts to suppressing the Unity of Czech Brethren, but the Brethren only grew in strength.

The Habsburg dynasty

When the second Jagellon King, Ludvík, was drowned in a swamp while running away from the Turks at the Battle of Mohács in 1526, the Estates of Bohemia elected the Austrian Habsburg Duke **Ferdinand I** as King of Bohemia; the dynasty was to last until 1918. Ferdinand knew how precarious his status was as a foreign Catholic monarch in a fiercely anti-Catholic country. At first he was sensitive to his new subjects, and refrained from persecuting the growing number of Lutherans. In 1546 he called upon the Estates to raise finance and an army to fight the Turks. When it transpired that he intended to use the army against Protestants in Germany, the Bohemian army refused to cross the Saxon border. The Estates, outraged at being tricked, sent a list of 57 demands to the King.

The time had come for Ferdinand to stop pussy-footing around. He sent troops into Prague and began a systematic suppression of all Protestant dissidents, in particular the Czech Brethren. He appointed Catholics to key official posts and in 1556 he invited the Jesuit Order to Bohemia. The Jesuits, who were organised on quasi-military lines, spearheaded the Counter-Reformation assault. They were put in control of higher education throughout the kingdom and became tutors to the sons of leading nobles.

Ferdinand's Habsburg successors understood the importance of Bohemia. It was one of the Electors of the Holy Roman Empire and was also extremely wealthy. Bohemia was already footing most of the bill for the disastrous war against the Turks, who had by now taken the Hungarian capital. Until 1618 the Habsburgs engaged in a game of religious brinkmanship with Bohemia's mostly Protestant population.

When **Maximilian II** became King in 1562 he hoped to divide and rule Bohemia by supporting the conciliatory Utraquist movement (which was middle class and nominally Catholic) and suppressing the resilient Unity of Czech Brethren. Instead, in a series of rearguard concessions he allowed Bohemia to unhook itself from the Roman Church and gave his approval, albeit verbally, to the adoption of the 'Confessio Bohemica', which set out the key elements of Hussite and Lutheran practices.

RUDOLFINE PRAGUE

The Estates were pleased with their gains. They duly voted through new taxes for the Turkish wars and approved Maximilian's choice of successor, **Rudolf II** (1576-1611). In 1583 Rudolf moved his court from Vienna to Prague and for the first time in 200 years, the city became the centre of an empire. The Empire badly needed a man of action, vision and direction to deal with the Turkish invaders and the demands of Bohemia's Protestants. What it got was a dour, eccentric and

---

Mything the point...?
Rabbie Löw & the golem

Born in 1520, Rabbi Judah Löw ben Bezalel was a towering figure of the Prague Renaissance, yet popular history remembers him for one thing – creating a monster out of mud, the golem. Few versions of the story agree on how the rabbi brought the clay figure (intended to protect the Jewish community) to life, but walking around the body seven times in an anti-clockwise direction, quoting the seventh chapter from the second book of Genesis, and placing a *shem* (a sacred stone tablet) in his mouth to keep him well behaved, are taken to be the three key ingredients. As man-made monsters tend to, the golem ran amok when the rabbi one day forgot to renew the power of the shem. The tormented monster stormed into the Old-New Synagogue, the *shem* was removed and all that remained was a lifeless lump of clay and a new staple of Prague folklore.

Yet the depiction of Löw as the archetypal figure of mystical, kabbalistic Prague couldn't be much farther from the truth. Author of countless sober books and commentaries, the stern, moralistic rabbi was a pedagogical reformer of the first rank, balancing new Renaissance ideas

Bugger off, I'm busy. Are you entirely shem-less?

with fundamental belief in the Jewish tradition. Stories of golems predate Löw, and it wasn't until more than 200 years after his death that the first golem story linked to him appeared in print. Prague's German and Czech *fin de siècle* decadents gave the story further publicity, and it became a favourite theme for later German writers and film-makers.

melancholic monarch who was engrossed in alchemy and astrology and tended to ignore everyone except Otakar his pet lion. While Europe headed inexorably towards the Thirty Years' War, Prague drifted into a surreal fantasy world.

While political life was frustrated by the Emperor's political inertia, Rudolfine Prague was experiencing a dazzling confluence of artistic, scientific and mystical experimentation. Rudolf played host to scores of international artists. These included the Dutch painter Spranger, whose allegorical scenes of alchemy and astrology reflected the concerns of the court. His compatriot Von Aachen painted portraits of nubile princesses from across Europe that were intended, vainly, to stimulate Rudolf's thoughts of marriage. Rudolf's fascination with planetary movements brought the astronomers Tycho Brahe and Johannes Kepler to his court. The latter published his *Laws of Planetary Motion* in 1609 with an effusive dedication to his patron.

Mystics and alchemists were welcomed with lodgings and a royal salary and, as news of the Emperor's hospitality spread, scores of geniuses, eccentrics and fraudsters rolled into town. Intellectual debates raged through the city on subjects ranging from squaring the circle to the existence of ancient giants. Anyone claiming an insight into the mysteries of the universe, from foreign astrologers to rabbis from the Jewish ghetto, had the Emperor's ear.

Rudolf had a staunch sense of Habsburg and Catholic destiny, but little stomach for a fight. He was more interested in developing a higher religious synthesis to heal the divisions in European Christendom than in adopting the proselytising approach of the Jesuits. In later years, in a state of semi-secluded insanity, he would issue violent threats against his Protestant nobles. But by then the Papacy had long since written him off as a liability to the Counter-Reformation.

But as the Turkish armies thrust northwards, the Habsburgs relied more than ever on the military and financial support of the Protestant Estates. Protestantism may have been considered undesirable, but it was clearly thought preferable to Islam. An attack on Vienna was looming, and Protestant support was by no means assured. Rudolf dealt with the crisis simply by hiding away in Prague Castle, and a flabbergasted coterie of Archdukes concluded that he had to go. His brother Matthias picked up the reins.

DEFENESTRATION

Despite their promises to Bohemia, Matthias and his successor **Ferdinand II**, both strong Counter-Reformation Catholics, turned out to be more formidable than expected. The Bohemian Estates found themselves playing a frenzied game of threats, bluff, false promises and provocation

with the new rulers. It would only be a matter of time before Bohemia (and as a result, Europe) would explode.

The fuse was lit in the towns of Broumov and Hrob, where Protestants had built chapels in accordance with the guarantees of the Letter of Majesty. When the Bishop of Prague ordered the destruction of one chapel and the Abbot of the Břevnov Monastery closed the other, fuming Protestants summoned an assembly of the Estates in Prague and issued a stinging rebuke to Vienna. The Emperor heightened the stakes by banning the Estates from further meetings.

In Prague anger was reaching fever pitch. On 23 May 1618, the whole assembly led by Count Thurn marched to the Royal Castle. They were met by the diehard Roman Catholic councillors of the Emperor, Slavata and Martinic, whom they accused of being behind the ban. The two councillors were dragged to the window and thrown out, their secretary quickly following them. Miraculously, they all survived, landing 15m (50ft) below in a pile of rubbish and excrement. (*See also page 73*.)

Prague's most famous defenestration was the first violent act of the devastating **Thirty Years' War** – and an emotive and symbolic event over which all Europe could take sides. But what actually made the crucial difference in the cold world of seventeenth-century realpolitik was the election to the Bohemian throne of **Frederick of the Palatinate**, son-in-law of James I of England and Scotland and head of the Protestant Union of German Princes. His election tipped the balance of power between Protestant and Catholic Electors within the Holy Roman Empire four-three in favour of the Protestants.

Ferdinand II was ready to fight it out but, unfortunately for Bohemia, the likeable young Frederick had little notion of what a battlefield looked like. While Ferdinand was preparing for war, Frederick was swimming nude in the Vltava and enjoying courtly life. The Czechs nevertheless believed that their new man would rally all the powerful Protestant princes of Europe to defend Bohemia.

THE BATTLE OF WHITE MOUNTAIN

By November 1620 the combined forces of the Roman Catholic League, consisting of Spain, Italy, Poland and Bavaria, were massing in support of Ferdinand. Frederick had failed to rally anyone except the Protestants of Transylvania. On 8 November 1620 the two armies faced each other at White Mountain (Bílá Hora) on the outskirts of Prague. Many expected the Czechs to fight with the same startling bravery and military skill that their forebears the Hussites had shown. But on the second Imperial charge the Protestant infantry fled with their officers in pursuit yelling at them to come back and fight.

On the first anniversary of the infamous defenestration a large crowd gathered in Prague's Old Town Square to witness the beheading of 27 leading Protestant nobles and scholars. The less privileged also had their tongues ripped out, hands chopped off and their heads skewered on the towers of Charles Bridge. While the Thirty Years' War raged on in Europe, Ferdinand settled once and for all the Habsburg's hereditary claim to Bohemia.

HABSBURG ABSOLUTISM

Ferdinand made no bones about his plan for Bohemia when he confided that it was 'better to have no population than a population of heretics'. In the ensuing years Bohemia lost three-quarters of its native nobility, along with its eminent scholars and any vestiges of national independence. The country was ravaged by the war, which reduced its population from three million to 900,000. Three-quarters of the land in Bohemia was seized and used to pay war expenses. All Protestant clergy and anyone refusing to abandon their faith were driven from the country or executed. Thirty thousand wealthy Protestant families had all their possessions confiscated and were sent into exile. While the depopulated towns and villages filled up with another influx of German immigrants, the peasants were forced to stay and work the land. The slightest opposition from them was suppressed ruthlessly and Jesuits swarmed into the countryside to 're-educate' them.

Ferdinand moved his court back to Vienna in 1624. In 1627 he formally cancelled all significant powers of the Bohemian Diet (Parliament). He ruled virtually by royal decree, maintaining Bohemia as a separate entity so that the Habsburgs could cast an extra vote in the election of the Holy Roman Emperor. The Czechs were taxed to the hilt and the money used to prettify Vienna and pay off war debts. The confiscated estates of the Protestant nobles were handed over to subservient Catholics at court, and Catholic nobles from abroad, sensing a bonanza, swooped in to pick up some cheap assets.

THE END OF THE THIRTY YEARS' WAR

During the Thirty Years' War, Prague was invaded by Saxon Protestants but then retaken by **General Wallenstein**. The Bohemian-born Wallenstein (Valdštejn in Czech) was a converted Protestant who rose from obscurity to become leader of the Imperial Catholic armies of Europe, and the greatest creditor of the Habsburg Empire. He totted up a spectacular series of victories but was hugely disliked by the Emperor's Jesuit advisors who conspired to have him dismissed. Meanwhile Wallenstein, who had been secretly negotiating with the Swedish enemy, switched sides. When he entered Bohemia in 1634, the Czech exiles suddenly pinned their hopes on a Wallenstein victory. He didn't get far. Later that year a band of Irish mercenaries burst into his Cheb residence where the general was recovering from gout. He was gagged, stabbed and dragged down the stairs to an inglorious end. The Thirty Years' War, which had begun in Prague Castle, petered out on Charles Bridge in 1648, as Swedish Protestants scuffled with newly Catholicised students and Jews from the ghetto.

By the mid-seventeenth century, German had replaced Czech as the official language of government. Czech nobles sent their sons to German schools, Charles University was renamed Charles-Ferdinand University and handed over to the Jesuits who taught in Latin. The lifeline of Czech heritage now rested with the enslaved and illiterate peasants. In 1650, at the depth of Bohemia's despair, the exiled leader of the Unity of Czech Brethren, Jan Comenius, exhorted his people to keep hope alive, with the desperate words: 'I believe that after the tempest of God's wrath shall have passed, the rule of thy country will again return unto thee, O Czech nation.'

Paradoxically, this period of oppression produced some of Prague's most stunning baroque palaces and churches. Infused with the glorification of God and Rome, the baroque served to overwhelm and seduce Prague's citizens. The Czech writer Milan Kundera has called the baroque explosion 'the flower of evil' and 'the fruit of oppression', but it did its job; before the century was out the vast majority of the population had reverted to Catholicism.

A BACKWATER

The eighteenth century was a dull time for Prague. Empress **Maria Theresa** lost Silesia to the Prussians and woke up to the fact that unless the Empire was efficiently centralised more of the same was going to happen. A new wave of Germanisation in schools and government was soon under way and the small Prague cog turned within the grand Viennese machine. Life occasionally brightened up when Mozart rolled into town to conduct a new opera, but the Czechs felt that they could do little but merely survive and wait for better times.

Maria Theresa's successor, the enlightened despot **Joseph II**, had little patience with the Church. He kicked out the Jesuits, closed monasteries, nationalised the education system, freed the Jews from the ghetto and vastly expanded the Empire's bureaucracy. In 1775 the peasants had been revolting and a spate of health and other reforms meant that they could now get married without their masters' permission. Internal tolls were abolished and the industrial revolution was getting under way. It was all good news for the Czechs except for one thing: the reforms were taking place in the German language.

Nationalism & independence

For the first 75 years of the eighteenth century, Czech virtually became the dodo of literary cultures. It was practised, rather than spoken, as the quaint hobby of eccentric intellectuals. But gradually Czechs began asserting themselves culturally with a vigour that recalled the good old Hussite days. It started with the revival of the Czech language, and ended in 1918 with political independence.

The peasants had never abandoned the Czech language, though scholars were obliged to teach and write about their history in German. By the end of the eighteenth century a number of suppressed works were published, notably Balbín's *Defence of the Czech Language* with its often-quoted rallying cry, 'Do not let us and our posterity perish'. The Bohemian Diet began to whisper in Czech; the Church, seeing rows of empty pews, started to preach in Czech; and Emperor Leopold II even established a chair in Czech Language at Prague's university. However, Napoleon's conquests made it harder for Czech leaders to claim it was all just a harmless cultural development.

Emperor **Francis I** (1792-1835) feared Napoleon and was taking no chances with liberal nationalist nonsense. In his will he had only two words of advice for his successor, **Ferdinand V** (1835-1848): 'Change nothing!' Nevertheless, the revival continued, with scholars, artists and historians setting a trailblazing pace: philologist Josef Dobrovský produced his *Detailed Textbook of the Czech Language* in 1809; Jungmann reconstructed a pure Czech literary language; historian František Palacký wrote his mammoth *History of the Czech Nation*; František Škroup composed the Czech national anthem; Prague's theatres staged patriotic dramas; and Čelakovský had the nation singing Czech verses.

THE EVENTS OF 1848

The cultural revival inevitably took a political turn. The Czechs demanded equal rights for their language in government and schools. Then in 1848, revolution once again swept through Europe. A pan-Slav Congress was held in Prague during which a conservative scholarly group led by Palacký clashed with radicals. Copycat demonstrations were multiplying throughout the Empire, finally bringing down the previously impregnable Viennese government of Prince Metternich. Shaken, Emperor Ferdinand V bought time by tossing promises in Prague's direction.

In Prague the force of reaction came in the sinister figure of Prince Windischgrätz. He fired on a peaceful gathering in Wenceslas Square intentionally provoking a riot to give himself an excuse for wholesale suppression. Thus, new Emperor **Franz Josef** (1848-1916) came to the throne on 2 December 1848 riding a tidal wave of terror. In 1849 he issued the March Constitution, which declared all the Habsburg territories to be one entity ruled from the Imperial Parliament in Vienna.

AN EMBRYO NATION

After taking a bashing from Bismarck in 1866, on his way to unifying Germany, the Habsburgs introduced a new constitution that codified some basic civil rights. But Czech claims for independence were ignored in the new dual Austro-Hungarian structure. Francis Joseph refused even to take a coronation oath as King of Bohemia.

The old-guard Czech deputies, led by Palacký, battled on for concessions in the Imperial Parliament. They threw in their lot with the conservative Polish and Austro-German deputies, and won concessions on language. But it meant accepting an electoral system in Bohemia that heavily favoured the German population. A group known as the **Young Czechs** attacked the Old Czechs for pursuing a 'policy of crumbs'. There was in fact little alternative, but national passions were running high.

The Young Czechs adopted Jan Hus as their hero and were supported by the Realist Party leader Professor **Tomáš Garrigue Masaryk**. Masaryk focused attention on the moral traditions of Czech history and pointed to the Hussite and the National Revival movements as spiritual light-

The much revered Tomáš Garrigue Masaryk.

houses for the nation. In the 1891 elections to the Diet, the Young Czechs swept the board.

The Czechs began to forge the political, social and economic infrastructure of a nation. Rapid industrialisation transformed the region with highly successful industries such as brewing, sugar production, metalworking, coal mining and textiles. An efficient rail network criss-crossed Bohemia and Moravia and linked it to the European economy as a whole. Industrialisation gave rise to working-class political movements, and Catholic parties also emerged.

Culturally, the Czech arts also flourished. The era produced the composers Smetana, Dvořák and Janáček, and painters such as Mucha. An indigenous literature blossomed in the work of Mácha, Neruda, Vrchlický and others. The Czech Academy of Sciences and Arts achieved international renown. Only the political expression of nationhood remained frustrated.

WORLD WAR I

The outbreak of World War I broke the stalemate. At first the Czechs assumed that they could win concessions on a federal constitution in return for Czech support for the war. However, the mere mention of the 'F' word provoked repressive measures from Vienna. It would prove to be a costly policy for the Empire. The Czechs soon realised that their hopes lay in the downfall of the Empire itself and, along with millions of soldiers of other minority groups, they deserted en masse to the other side. Six divisions of Czechs were soon fighting for the Allies on the Russian, Italian and French fronts while in Prague an underground society known as the Mafia ceaselessly carried out a campaign of agitation against the regime.

Meanwhile, Masaryk and **Edvard Beneš** were trying to drum up allied support for a future independent state. They found, however, that the Habsburgs were often viewed more as misguided conspirators than as evil warmongers like the Kaiser. In fact, many diplomats had no wish to see the Austro-Hungarian Empire pulled apart. Europe's crown heads and aristocrats were certainly opposed to the destruction of a powerful member of their club.

Even so, the United States took the lead, granting de jure recognition to a provisional Czechoslovak Government under Masaryk. On 18 October 1918 Masaryk declared 'the Habsburg dynasty unworthy of leading our nation' and the provisional National Committee agreed upon a republican constitution. But their power was only theoretical. The key to actual power lay in controlling the Empire's food supplies. Bohemia was the breadbasket of the Empire and the Habsburg generals, fearing a Soviet-style social revolution if food did not get through to the population, gave the nod to the Provisional Council.

On 28 October a National Committee member, Antonín Švehla, marched into the Corn Institute and announced that the Committee was taking over food production. Later that day the Habsburg Government sent to American President Woodrow Wilson a note acquiescing to Czechoslovak independence. The population of Prague spilled on to the streets in triumphant celebration of their new nation. Not a single shot was fired in opposition.

THE FIRST REPUBLIC

The new Republic of Czechoslovakia had a positive start in life. It had suffered hardly any destruction during the war; it was highly industrialised, with generous reserves of coal and iron ore; and it had an efficient communications infrastructure and a well-trained and educated bureaucracy. Its workforce was literate and politically represented. The national leadership, in particular Masaryk and Beneš, were internationally respected diplomats, and the new nation bloomed into a liberal democracy.

Ethnic rivalry was the biggest strain on the new nation. The Pittsburgh Agreement, which had promoted the concept of a new state, referred to a hyphenated Czecho-Slovakia in recognition of the two different histories. Slovaks were predominantly agricultural people and had been ruled by Magyars not Habsburgs, and, unlike the Czechs,

Memorial to the Heydrich assassins.

looked upon the Catholic Church as a symbol of freedom. The Slovaks resented what they felt was a patronising air from Prague, but until the late 1930s only a minority of voters backed the separatist Slovak People's Party under the pro-fascist leaders Hlinka and Tiso.

In Prague ethnic tensions were characterised more by rivalry than by jealousy. The Jews, who comprised only 2.5 per cent of the country's population, were mainly concentrated in Prague and formed a significant part of the intelligentsia. That most Jews spoke German also created some resentment on the part of the Czechs. But Jews were not a focus of hatred until the German population in Czechoslovakia began to look at them through Nazi eye-glasses.

The Germans, who formed 23 per cent of the population and had their own spectrum of political parties, presented the biggest obstacle to a united nation. Educated, professional and relatively wealthy, they were spread throughout the Czech lands, although Prague and the Sudeten area near the German border had the greatest concentration. The Czechs were sensitive, if also a little sanctimonious, towards minority rights and permitted the Germans to run their own schools and universities.

A SUDETEN SPANNER IN THE WORKS

Only a few years earlier, however, the German language had dominated the region and the Germans were not pleased with their sudden minority status. They had lost out in the land reforms, their businesses had suffered disproportionately from the depression of the 1930s, and Sudeten savings kept in Weimar Republic bank accounts had gone up in inflationary smoke. The economic and ethnic resentments found a political voice in young German gymnastics teacher **Konrad Henlein**, who vaulted to prominence as head of the pro-Hitler Sudeten German Fatherland Front. By 1935 the Sudeten Party was the second largest parliamentary bloc. But the sizeable Czech communist party was ordered by Stalin to back the liberal Beneš in the presidential elections in order to counter the Henlein threat, and Beneš took an easy victory.

In March 1938 Henlein told Hitler, 'We must always demand so much that we can never be satisfied.' In 1938 after intimidating their rivals, the Sudeten Nazis won 91 per cent of the German vote and demanded union with Germany. British Prime Minister Neville Chamberlain was not wholly unsympathetic to their claim. For him the Sudeten crisis was a 'quarrel in a faraway country between people of whom we know nothing'. Chamberlain went to Munich with the French premier and met Mussolini and Hitler. All parties involved in the crisis (except Czechoslovakia, which wasn't invited) agreed that Germany should take the Sudetenland. In return Hitler guaranteed that he would make no further trouble, and he even signed his name on a piece of paper saying as such, which naïve Neville waved to the world promising 'peace in our time'.

The announcement was met with demonstrations in Prague. Czechoslovakia had a well-armed, well-trained army but was in a hopeless position. With Poland and Hungary also eyeing up her borders, Czechoslovakia found herself encircled, outnumbered, abandoned by her allies and attempting to defend a region that did not want to be defended. Beneš capitulated. Six months later Hitler took the rest of the country, with Poland snatching Těšín and Hungary grabbing parts of southern Slovakia. On 14 March, 1939 a day before Hitler rode into Prague, the Slovaks declared independence and established a Nazi puppet government. Hitler dubbed the remnants of Czechoslovakia the Reich Protectorate of Bohemia and Moravia. The Czechs acquiesced peacefully, thus sparing themselves the destruction Poland suffered less than six months later.

The lights go out

Except for its Jews and gypsies, Czechoslovakia survived occupation far better than most other European countries. German was made the official language of government (Hitler wanted to reduce Czech to a patois within a generation) and a National Government of Czechs was set up to follow Reich orders. Hitler had often expressed his hatred of 'Hussite Bolshevism' but he needed Czech industrial resources and skilled manpower for the war. Almost all of Czechoslovakia's military hardware was transferred to Germany.

NAZI OCCUPATION

Many Czechs opted to avoid suicidal acts of defiance by sitting out the war and hoping for allied victory. Hitler lost no time in demonstrating the ferocity of his revenge on those who did resist. When a student demonstration was organised, nine of its leaders were executed, 1,200 students sent to concentration camps and all Czech universities were closed. **Reinhard Heydrich**, who had just chaired the Wannsee Conference on the 'Final Solution' of the 'Jewish Question', was appointed Reichsprotektor. Aiming to wipe out further resistance, he instituted rounds of calculated terror and executions against the intelligentsia while enticing workers and peasants to collaborate.

Beneš had fled to London where he had joined Jan Masaryk (son of Tomáš) to form a provisional Czechoslovak government in exile. They were joined by thousands of Czech soldiers and airmen who fought alongside the British forces. Czech intelligence agents passed approximately 20,000 messages to London, including the details of Germany's ambitious planned invasion of the Soviet Union.

THE ASSASSINATION OF HEYDRICH

Fearful that the accomplishments of the Polish resistance were overshadowing Czech resistance activities, Beneš finally approved a plan for the assassination of Reinhard Heydrich. The underground leaders in Prague doubted its effectiveness and advised heavily against it. But they were overruled, and British-trained Czech parachutists were dropped into Bohemia. On 27 May 1942, **Jan Kubiš** and **Josef Gabčik** ambushed Heydrich's open-top Mercedes, botching the assassination attempt but fatally injuring the Reichsprotektor, who died several days later.

German reprisals were swift and terrible. The assassins and their accomplices were hunted down to the crypt of the **Church of Sts Cyril and Methodius** (*see also page 59*) where they resisted all attempts to dislodge them. The last two survivors used their final rounds on each other. The Germans then went on an orgy of revenge. Anyone with any connection to the paratroopers was murdered. The villages of **Lidice** and **Ležáky** were mistakenly picked out for aiding the assassins and razed to the ground. All the adult males of the villages were murdered, the women were sent to concentration camps (in Ležáky they were shot) and the children were either 're-educated', placed with German families or killed. The transportation of Jews to concentration camps was stepped up.

Occasional acts of sabotage continued. But the main resistance took place in the Slovak puppet state where an uprising began on 30 August 1944 and lasted four months. It achieved little except, perhaps, to remove the country's stain of collaboration. The Czechs' act of defiance came in the last week of the war. On 5 May 1945 an uprising took place in Prague in which 5,000 died in four days of fighting. However, without the defection of the Russian 'Vlasov' soldiers who had fought for the Nazis, the rising might have followed the tragic course of the Warsaw rising. The reward of the Vlasov troops, who later threw themselves on the mercy of the Americans, was to be returned to Stalin for transportation and death in his camps.

LIBERATION?

The US forces that had just liberated Pilsen (Plzeň) to the west were only a few miles from Prague. But the allied leaders at Yalta had agreed other plans. Czechoslovakia was to be liberated by the Soviets, and General Eisenhower ordered his troops to pull back. General Patton was willing to ignore the order and sent a delegation to the leaders of the Prague uprising asking for an official request for American troops to liberate the capital. The communist leaders refused. Although communist power was not consolidated until 1948, the country had found itself inside the Soviet sphere of influence.

THE END OF JEWISH PRAGUE

More than 300,000 Czechoslovaks perished in the war, most of them Jews. The Jewish population of Czechoslovakia was destroyed. Most were rounded up and sent to the supposedly 'model' Theresienstadt (Terezín; *see page 227*) ghetto, 64 km (40 miles) north of Prague. Many died there, but the remainder were transported to Auschwitz and other concentration camps.

Around 90 per cent of Prague's ancient Jewish community who stayed on in the city had been murdered. It had been one of the oldest Jewish communities in Europe, arriving at least 1,000 years earlier and possibly even before the Czechs themselves. For most of this period the community had been walled into a ghetto in the Old Town and life there was characterised by pogroms, poverty, mysticism and countless Prague legends. Between the time they left the ghetto in the late eighteenth century and before the Nazi occupation, Jews had dominated much of Prague's cultural life. Now the rich literary culture that had produced Franz Kafka had been wiped out. Indeed, Kafka's family also perished in Auschwitz. The only thing that saved some of Prague's synagogues and communal Jewish buildings from the Nazis' routine destruction was the Germans' intention to use them after the war to house 'exotic exhibits of an extinct race'.

The Czech government under the Reich Protectorate actively supported the extermination of its Romany citizens and helped run dozens of concentration camps for Gypsies in Bohemia and Moravia. An estimated 90 per cent of the Czech Romany population died in Nazi concentration camps, mostly in Germany and Poland.

THE COMMUNIST NOOSE TIGHTENS

Beneš's faith in liberalism had been badly dented by the way the Western powers had ditched his country. He began to see the political future of Czechoslovakia as a bridge between capitalism and communism. His foreign minister Jan Masaryk was less idealistic, stating that 'cows like to stop on a bridge and shit on it'.

Beneš needed a big power protector and believed that if he could win Stalin's trust, he could handle the hugely popular communist party of Czechoslovakia while keeping the country independent and democratic. During the war he signed a friendship and mutual assistance treaty with the Soviet Union, and later established a coalition government comprised principally of communists and socialists friendly to the Soviet Union. In 1945 Stalin knew that a straightforward takeover of a formerly democratic state was not politically expedient. He needed Beneš as an acceptable front in order to buy time. For all his tightrope diplomacy (he often referred to diplomacy as a 'vulgar profession'), Beneš was shuffling his country into

Soviet clutches. Before he died, he wrote: 'my greatest mistake was that I refused to believe to the very last that even Stalin lied to me cynically.'

THE COMMUNISTS TAKE POWER

The Soviets and Czech communists were widely regarded as war heroes and won a handsome victory in the 1946 elections. **Klement Gottwald** became Prime Minister of a communist-led coalition. Beneš, still hoping that Stalinist communism could co-exist in a pluralistic democracy, remained President. The communists made political hay while the sun shone. They set up workers' militias in the factories, installed communist loyalists in the police force and infiltrated the army and rival socialist coalition parties.

One of the first acts of the government, approved by the allies, was to expel more than two and a half million Germans from Bohemia. It was a popular move and, as Gottwald remarked, 'an extremely sharp weapon with which we can reach to the very roots of the bourgeoisie.' Thousands were executed or given life sentences, and many more were killed in a wave of self-righteous revenge. (After 1989 President Havel acknowledged that the collective nature of the expulsions had been wrong. Today, with growing pressure from Sudeten groups, the issue is worming its way back on to the political agenda.)

In 1947 Czechoslovakia was forced to turn down the American offer of economic aid under the Marshall Plan for the rebuilding of the economy. Stalin knew that aid came with strings and he was determined to be the only puppetmaster. In February 1948, with elections looming and communist popularity declining, Gottwald sent the workers' militias on to the streets of Prague. The police occupied crucial party headquarters and offices, and the country was incapacitated by a general strike. Beneš's diplomatic skill was no match for the brutal tactics of the Moscow-trained revolutionaries. With the Czech army neutralised by communist infiltration and the Soviet army casting a long shadow over Prague, Beneš capitulated and consented to an all-communist government. Gottwald now became Czechoslovakia's first 'Working Class President'.

Shortly after the coup, **Jan Masaryk** fell to his death from his office window. The communists said it was suicide. But when his body was found, the window above was tightly fastened. The defenestration had a distinctly Czech flavour but the purges that followed had the stamp of Moscow. They were directed against resistance fighters, Spanish Civil War volunteers, Jews (often survivors of concentration camps) and anyone in the party hierarchy who might have posed a threat to Moscow. The most infamous trial was of **Rudolf Slánský**, a loyal sidekick of Gottwald who had orchestrated his fair share of purges.

After being showered with honours, he was arrested a few days later. In March 1951, Slánský and ten senior communists (mostly Jews) were found guilty of being Trotskyite, Titoist or Zionist traitors in the service of US imperialists. They 'confessed' under torture, and eight were sentenced to death. The country had descended into a mire of fear and lunacy.

Prague Spring to revolution

Gottwald dutifully followed his master, Stalin, to the grave in 1953 and the paranoia that had gripped Prague took a long time to ease. By the 1960s, communist student leaders and approved writers on the fringes of the party hierarchy began tentatively to suggest that, possibly, Gottwald and Stalin had taken the wrong route to socialism. A drizzle of criticism turned into a shower of awkward questions. On 5 January 1968 an alliance of disaffected Slovak communists and reformists in the party replaced Antonín Novotný with the reformist Slovak communist, **Alexander Dubček**.

PRAGUE SPRING

For the next eight months, the world watched developments in Prague with passionate hope as Dubček rehabilitated political prisoners and eased and then virtually abandoned press censorship. Moscow was alarmed and tried to intimidate Dubček by holding full-scale military manoeuvres in Czechoslovakia, but the reforms continued. On 27 June, 70 leading writers signed the popular, widely published *Two Thousand Word Manifesto* supporting the reformist government and declaring that they would 'stand by it with weapons if need be, if it will do what we give it a mandate to do'. Suppressed literature was published or performed on stage, Prague was infused with the fresh air of freedom. Dubček called it 'socialism with a human face'.

The Soviet leader Leonid Brezhnev, following 'full and frank' discussions, failed to influence the Czechoslovak leader. On the night of 20 August 1968, nearly half a million Warsaw Pact troops entered the country, took over the Castle and abducted Dubček and his closest supporters to Moscow. The leaders expected to be shot, but Brezhnev needed an acceptable front for a policy of repression with a human face.

Meanwhile on the streets of Prague thousands of citizens confronted the tanks, appealing to their fellow Slavs to turn back. Free radio stations using army transmitters continued to broadcast, and newspapers went underground and encouraged Czechs to refuse any information or assistance to the occupiers. Street signs and house numbers were removed, and the previously Stalinist workers' militia defended a clandestine meeting of the national party conference.

1948 – 1989

1969

16.I
19.I   25.II

Jan Palach   Jan Zajíc

OBĚTEM KOMUNISMU
...ORY OF THE VICTIMS...
...IS DER OPFER...

HUSÁK TAKES OVER

The resistance prevented nothing. Dubček stayed in power for eight more months and watched his collaborators being replaced by pro-Moscow ministers. In April 1969 Dubček, too, was removed in favour of **Gustav Husák** who was eager to push Moscow's 'normalisation'. Husák purged the party and state machinery, the army and the police, the unions, the media, every company and every other organ of the country that might have a voice in the nation's affairs. Anyone who was not for Husák was assumed to be against him. Within a very short time every aspect of Czechoslovak life was filled with Husák's mediocre yes-men. Husák was able to subdue the nation into an unquestioning apathy by permitting a small influx of consumer goods.

THE MARTYRDOM OF JAN PALACH

On 16 January 1969, a 21-year-old philosophy student called **Jan Palach** stood on the steps of the National Museum at the top of Wenceslas Square, poured a can of petrol over himself and set himself alight. He died four days later. A group of his friends had agreed to burn themselves to death one by one until the restrictions were lifted. On his deathbed he begged his friends not to go through with it, though some did.

The newsreader announcing his death was in tears. Some 200,000 people went to Wenceslas Square to place wreaths at the spot where Palach fell; and a vast procession made its way to Charles University. Crowds of mourners stretched 3km (2m). His coffin was taken to the Old Town Square where 100,000 people heard the bells of Týn Church ring out and a choir sing a Hussite chorale.

Palach's death symbolised, with malicious irony, the extinguishing of the flame of hope. As dissident playwright Václav Havel wrote: 'People withdrew into themselves and stopped taking an interest in public affairs. An era of apathy and widespread demoralisation began, an era of grey, everyday totalitarian consumerism.'

Instead of brutal mass arrests, tortures and show trials, the communists now bound up the nation in an endless tissue of lies and fabrications, and psychologically bludgeoned all critical thought in an Orwellian nightmare where people were rewarded for not asking awkward questions and punished for refusing to spy on their neighbours. Punishment could mean spells in prison and severe beatings, but for most it meant losing a good job and being forced into menial work. Prague possessed an abormally high percentage of window cleaners with PhDs, and was probably the only city where professors became street

The 'memorial to the victims of communism' – on the spot where Jan Palach and Jan Zajíc immolated themselves.

sweepers, a phenomenon well chronicled in Ivan Klima's *Love and Garbage* and Milan Kundera's *The Unbearable Lightness of Being*.

CHARTER 77

There were some, however, who refused to be bowed. A diverse alternative culture emerged in which underground (*samizdat*) literature was painstakingly copied and circulated around a small group of dissidents. In December 1976 a group led by **Václav Havel** issued a statement demanding that the Czechoslovak authorities observe human rights obligations, and specifically those contained in the Helsinki Agreement of 1975, which the government had signed. **Charter 77** became a small voice of conscience inside the country, spawning a number of smaller groups trying to defend civil liberties. In 1989 it had 1,500 signatories. But there seemed little hope for real change unless events from outside took a new turn. Then, in the mid-1980s, the unbelievable began to happen. Mikhail Gorbachev came to power in the Soviet Union and initiated his policy of perestroika.

THE VELVET REVOLUTION

The Soviet leader came to Prague in 1988. His spokesman was asked what he thought the difference was between the Prague Spring and glasnost. He replied, '20 years.' As usual it was change in the international environment that was required to alter conditions in Czechoslovakia. In the autumn of 1989 the Berlin Wall came down and the communist regimes of Eastern Europe began to falter. The Czechoslovak government, one of the most hardline communist regimes in Eastern Europe, seemed firmly entrenched until 17 November. When police violently broke up a demonstration on Národní třída commemorating the fiftieth anniversary of the closure of the universities by the Nazis, a rumour, picked up by Reuters news agency, said that a demonstrator had been killed. Another demonstration was called to protest against police brutality.

Two days later 200,000 people gathered in Prague to demand the resignation of the government. The police behaved with restraint and the demonstrations were broadcast on television. The government then announced that the man who had allegedly been killed on the 17th was alive and well. Some months after the revolution it emerged that the KGB had probably been behind the rumour as part of their plan to force out the government and replace it with something more in line with Soviet glasnost.

That there had not been a death made little difference to the growing crowds. A committee of opposition groups formed themselves into the **Civic Forum** (Občanské fórum) and was led by Václav Havel, who addressed the masses in

Dubček and Havel toast the new democratic Republic.

Wenceslas Square. The next day a quarter of a million people assembled in the Square. Two days later, Dubček, who had just spoken to crowds in Bratislava, came to Prague and, with Havel, addressed a crowd of half a million. The government had lost control of the media, and millions more watched the scenes on their television screens. On the evening of 22 November, party General Secretary Miloš Jakeš resigned. He was followed by the whole Politburo and then the government. It was not enough. Students from Prague raced out to factories, farms and mines to galvanise the workers into supporting a general strike for the 27th. Workers' militias had put the communists into power in 1948; it was crucial that they were persuaded not to stand by communism in its final hour.

On 25 November three-quarters of a million were on the streets as Havel and Dubček addressed them again. This time the acting communist Prime Minister, Adamec, also appealed to the crowds, and further purges within the communist party ranks followed. The party then declared that the 1968 Soviet invasion had been wrong, and promised free elections and a multi-party coalition. It was all too late. A new government of reformist communists was proposed, but it was rejected by Civic Forum. The negotiations continued between

the communists and Civic Forum until 27 December, when a coalition of strongly reformist communists and a majority of non-communists – mainly from Civic Forum – took power with Havel as President. Not a single person died. Havel's co-revolutionary Rita Klimová called it the Velvet Revolution. But in some ways, given the KGB's involvement in the handover of power, it might as well have been called the Velvet Putsch.

Re-awakening

Czechoslovakia entered the last decade of the twentieth century a free country. On New Year's Day Havel spoke to the reborn nation: 'For the past 40 years on this day you have heard my predecessors utter different variations on the same theme, about how our country is prospering, how many more billion tons of steel we have produced, how happy we are, how much we trust our government and what beautiful prospects lie ahead of us. I do not think that you put me into office so that I, of all people, should lie to you. Our country is not prospering. The great creative and spiritual potential of our nation is not being used to its full potential... We have become morally ill because we have become accustomed to saying one thing and thinking another... all of us have become accustomed to the totalitarian system accepting it as an unalterable fact and thereby [keeping] it running. None of us is merely a victim of it, because all of us helped to create it together.'

For months after the revolution Prague floated in a dream world. The novelty of the playwright President captured the world's imagination.

THE NATION SPLITS

But the serious issues of economic transformation and the relationship between Czechs and Slovaks loomed as formidable challenges. In the summer of 1992 the right-of-centre Civic Democratic Party (ODS), led by **Václav Klaus**, the no-nonsense free marketeer and economic disciple of Margaret Thatcher, was voted into power. But just as Klaus got down to the business of privatisation and decentralisation, calls for Slovak independence grew to a deafening roar. Nationalist sentiments had grown in Slovakia but remained a fringe issue until the electoral rise of **Vladimír Mečiar**'s Slovak separatist HZDS party. Slovaks had always resented what they had felt was a benign neglect by Prague, and Havel had never been hugely popular among them. One of his first acts as President was to abandon the arms trade. Unfortunately, his pacifist intentions took the heart out of the economy in central Slovakia where the arms industry was based. Slovaks complained that economic reforms were going too fast. Klaus, however, would not compromise, and he had an overwhelming mandate from Czech voters (though not Slovak ones) to press on. Mečiar upped his separatist threats to Prague until, with Machiavellian manoeuvring, Klaus called Mečiar's bluff and announced that he would back Slovak independence.

The two respective leaders divided up the assets of the state, and the countries peacefully parted ways on 1 January 1993 without so much as a referendum. Their currencies split and within months the Slovak currency fell by ten per cent. Havel was elected President of the new Czech Republic, but Klaus had also outmanoeuvred him, forcing Havel into a predominantly ceremonial role.

Klaus indicated that he had little time for a policy of flushing out communists from responsible positions (known as 'lustration'). Thus communists successfully dodged the spotlight amid a blizzard of accusations and counter-accusations. A significant number of Czechs seemed to have skeletons in their cupboards, and it became impossible to untangle the good from the bad. Communists remained in charge of the country's largest factories, and dissidents watched helplessly as their former tormentors sped past in new sports cars.

The first four years of the Czech Republic under Klaus's leadership produced massive economic changes, which helped make the Czechs the envy of the East and the pride of the West. Foreign investors and businesses quickly capitalised on the massive opportunities for profit and development. Unlike the Slovaks, whose reputation in the West has been severely damaged by recent political scandals, the Czechs are among the first on the list of East European countries to be granted membership in the European Union and NATO.

But economic differences between the haves and have-nots have increased drastically since 1992. Klaus's Pragocentric policies and the decision to prioritise macroeconomic issues backfired in the 1996 elections when Miloš Zeman and his Czech Social Democratic Party garnered nearly as many seats as Klaus's party. These days, issues like lustration and privatisation are taking a back seat to the more down-to-earth concerns of all the industrial workers, doctors, farm labourers, teachers – just about anyone working in the state sector, a majority of the Czech population – who haven't benefited at all from Prague's new wealth. While there is little likelihood of communists returning to the political centre, as has happened in Poland and Hungary, demands for an immediate solution to problems in health care, education and housing are something that Klaus's new government can no longer ignore.

In 1997, with the boom days of foreign investment clearly over and embarrassing headlines alleging his party had accepted secret campaign funding from interested parties, Klaus shocked the nation by stepping down. A caretaker government was formed but by the July 1998 election Klaus was already campaigning for his old office again. Social Democrat Zeman was elected Prime Minister, confirming the death of the first post-Velvet Revolution government, but Klaus, ever convinced of his indispensible vision, struck a deal with Zeman. In a pact called absurd by everyone including Havel, Zeman's leftists took charge of the cabinet, while Klaus's conservatives were given control of parliament. Among Havel's reservations was a further deal by the pair to limit the power of smaller parties.

Havel, the symbolic conscience of the nation, has been stricken not just by power politics: twice hospitalised for emergency surgery, he has forced the public to consider for the first time the possibility of life without their moral leader. As they do so, it's increasingly apparent there are no others in line who could take his place in that role. One source of comfort for the ailing widower President (aside from his recent remarriage to young Czech actress Dagmar Veškrnová) was the 1998 Winter Olympics. For the first time in nearly two decades, the Czech ice-hockey team defeated the Russians and struck gold. Old Town Square had not held such massive cheering mobs since the Velvet Revolution.

FiLm
Guide

'Without doubt, the "bible" for film buffs.'
British Film and TV Academy News

Updated annually to include over 11,500 films from around the world and fully cross-referenced with extensive indexes covering films by genre, subject, director and star, this A-to-Z directory is the ultimate guide for movie lovers.

The *Time Out* Film Guide is available at a bookshop near you.

Prague Today

After a decade of capitalism and democracy, the Czech Republic is still struggling to come to terms with its past and present.

The taste of life since the Velvet Revolution has a distinctly bitter-sweet flavour.

For the first time since the '89 revolution, Prague finally seems to be settling down and finding its feet. The euphoria unleashed by the Velvet Revolution is long over, and after ten years of adjustment, most people seem to be getting on with their lives under conditions that are both better and worse than those they knew from the former system.

The evidence of stability is all around. On the streets, the influx of new shops and restaurants that marked the first years after the revolution has abated. The early years of free-market capitalism in Prague produced thousands of economic casualties as entrepreneurs vainly tried to predict what consumers wanted, but that process is over. What was a bank or grocery store last year is more likely than not to stay a bank or grocery store this year. In the tourist-heavy centre, that means shop after shop of tacky souvenirs, T-shirts and glassware. In outlying areas, most neighbourhoods are reasonably well served by grocers, chemists, laundries and the like.

On a social level, too, many of the early disruptions seem to have abated. The widespread predictions of mass unemployment – as workers were tossed out of inefficient socialist enterprises – never really came to pass. Billions of tourist dollars flowed into the city and country, creating new jobs overnight and helping to build a national economy that is now twice as big as it was ten years ago. Prague's unemployment rate hovers around one per cent – well below what economists regard as 'full employment' (although the situation in the rest of the country is not so rosy).

The influx of money has meant that prices for housing and utilities have increased, especially in the more desirable areas of the centre and in the Vinohrady (Prague 2) and Dejvice (Prague 6). But most of that increase has been borne by foreigners newly arriving in the city. Czechs have been buffered by complex rent and housing laws. Many locals have also realised a large capital gain on their flats as property values have risen. It's not surprising then that even with rising prices, most people have found a way to keep their houses, cars and weekend homes, while coming up with a little extra to remodel the kitchen or upgrade the home video. No one knows how long rents can stay fixed at artificially low levels. The quality of the housing stock remains sharply degraded from communist times and little has changed since then.

The Republican Party – they want foreigners out, they get kicked out of parliament.

STRAPPED FOR CASH

For all the progress, though, serious problems remain. The emphasis on private consumption at the expense of public investment has left local government and institutions with almost no cash. Hospitals and schools are starved of money, and doctors, nurses and teachers are among the lowest-paid workers in the country. Many health-care workers have left the field in search of better money in the private sector. Doctors and teachers threaten to strike, it seems, at least once a month. The city's main university, venerable Charles University, has coasted on its reputation for centuries, and students and teachers complain that many of the university's programmes are woefully underfunded. It's hard to see where the money will come from, since education and health care are almost exclusively in the public domain. A stalemate in the government over which area should get priority has aggravated the problem.

Prague's City Hall is also desperately short of money. The city is divided into ten districts, but most of the resources are concentrated in Prague 1 – the Old Town, Malá Strana and the Castle. The sprawling system of roads and mass transit outside the centre is falling apart and many revitalisation projects have been put on permanent hold. The low wages among city workers have opened the door to widespread corruption. The Czech Republic routinely finishes near the top of the list of the world's most corrupt countries. Who, in a sense, can blame an official in the city's planning office for taking a £10,000 bribe to supplement his £200 a month salary. Still, the corruption under-

mines people's faith in the system and breeds a belief that somehow nothing has changed since the old regime, when it was taken for granted public officials lined their pockets whenever they could.

MARRIED TO THE MOB

The new freedoms have bred a host of problems that were almost unknown under communism, including organised crime, theft, graffiti and drug addiction. Mobsters, many from Russia, Yugoslavia and Ukraine, are as common a sight on Prague's streets as the guys flogging squawking chickens and jester's caps on Old Town Square. You'll see them everywhere – usually sporting bad haircuts and tracksuits – as they cut deals over mobile phones from the comfort of Mazdas and BMWs. Competing mobs have carved the city into little fiefdoms and control many of the restaurants, discos, souvenir shops and gambling joints that line Wenceslas Square and other prime locations. At night, the lower end of the square and adjoining streets of the Old Town are filled with prostitutes plying their trade.

On the other side of the legal line from the Mafia are the Western businessmen, advisers, managers and bankers drawn to Prague to 'promote free enterprise', 'develop the market economy' or any other euphemism that translates roughly into 'make a buck'. In Prague's loopholed landscape, these guys differ from their Eastern European counterparts chiefly by the cut of their suits. The means of control – the deal-making, the cronyism, the bribes – are the same. In their defence, it should be said the legit businessmen are less interested in prostitution and drugs (except perhaps for personal use) and are more interested in controlling the country's breweries, telecommunications, banks and consumer goods companies. They are now leading the move to clean up the stock market and rid the banks of corruption, but after ten years of making shady deals, it seems a case of too little, too late.

The police are helpless to control the rising crime level. In addition to being starved of precious funding, the force is inexplicably divided into cops who serve only the city and those who serve the country at large. The division creates a bureaucratic nightmare. The police force commands almost no respect from ordinary citizens, who still think it is staffed only by spies and former communists. It's not uncommon to see the police turn a blind eye to obvious violations of the law – especially at night on Wenceslas Square. In spite of the

increase in crime, though, the city remains relatively safe for tourists. The most serious threat a visitor is likely to face is roving bands of pickpockets on the Metro or on Wenceslas Square.

Drug addiction merits special mention. The availability of cheap heroin, home-grown speed and other drugs, combined with changes in lifestyle, fashion and weak law enforcement, have caused an explosion in the number of addicts in the past year. Some reports say the number of addicts in the country has risen sevenfold since 1994 to around 70,000 today, most of whom are concentrated in Prague. The areas around Náměsti Republiky, the Národní třída metro station and Kaprova in the Old Town are prime spots for dealers. Officials tightened drug laws in the past year, and the city's reputation for being the Amsterdam of Eastern Europe is probably over.

Friends, Romanies or countrymen?

The Romany question is a particularly difficult – and longstanding – one in the Czech Republic. Ever since the first Romanies, or Roma, migrated to the Czech lands from Asia in the fifteenth century, they have been routinely victimised by successive rulers and governments in the region. During World War II, Romanies were targeted for extermination; recent historical research has shown that it was actually Czech officials, rather than Nazi German occupiers, who organised and staffed special concentration camps for them in Bohemia and Moravia. Almost all of the inmates perished – either here or in other Nazi death camps.

After the war, many Romanies from Slovakia moved or were settled in the Czech lands to fill a need for unskilled labour. The split of Czechoslovakia at the end of 1992 led to problems for many of the descendants of these Slovak Romanies. The Czech Republic passed a citizenship law, widely criticised at the time, that made it difficult for them to obtain Czech citizenship – even if they were born in the Czech lands.

More recently, in summer 1997, the situation made international headlines when several hundred Romanies tried to obtain refugee status in Canada and Great Britain. While most of them were either turned away or returned to the Czech Republic of their own accord, two families in Canada and one in Britain were granted refugee status. In a telling reaction to this development, almost 60 per cent of respondents to one poll in the Czech Republic claimed that the government should offer help to Romanies wanting to leave the country.

These days, discrimination against Romanies in the Czech Republic ranges from employers who refuse to give jobs to Romany applicants, to violent attacks by skinheads. Even getting served in pubs and restaurants can prove impossible for them. According to a recent survey, a large number of Czechs would like to see tougher laws applied to Romanies. In one of the most alarming developments yet, the northern industrial town of Usti nad Labem is planning to erect a wall around its 8,000-strong Romany community in a chilling echo of Nazi policy towards the Jews.

While some Czechs openly admit to a racist bias against them, many argue that they are being realistic rather than racist, claiming that repeated attempts to integrate the Romanies into the broader Czech society have failed and that the two lifestyles clash. Whether or not this is true, the attitudes of many Czechs seem to a great extent to be the result of 40-odd years of isolation behind the Iron Curtain. Aside from a largely invisible Slovak minority and the Romanies, who make up only about two to five per cent of the population, the Czech Republic is almost completely homogenous. Many observers believe that travel, immigration and the integration of the Czech Republic into Europe could in time serve to reduce racism and xenophobia in the country. In the meantime, there is a glimmer of hope that the tide could at long last be turning: the ousting from parliament in the 1998 elections of the extreme-right Republican Party, led by Miroslav Sládek (a dead ringer for Mr Bean), can only be a hopeful portent.

- ♦ American Roulette
- ♦ Black Jack
- ♦ Poker
- ♦ Pontoon
- ♦ Slot machines

Add a little excitement to your stay in Prague!

Casino & Bar open daily from 1 p.m.

Free entrance

Lucky Chips available on entry

Major credit cards accepted

CASINO PALAIS SAVARIN
Na Příkopě 10, Praha 1

WHICH WAY NOW?

The inability of the city and country to come to grips with some of these problems has lent weight to the view that somehow Czech society isn't on the right road. The lack of consensus showed clearly in the 1998 parliamentary elections, which were split down the middle between right-leaning parties that support the status quo and the centre-left Social Democrats, who have called for more attention to social problems. The political right, led by Václav Klaus, has argued that the economy comes first – and that tax proceeds from growing incomes will solve the problems. That stzrategy fell apart in 1997 when the national economy ground to a halt (largely because of too much consumption at the expense of investment) and the currency was devalued by more than ten per cent. The Social Democrats don't necessarily oppose the emphasis on the economy but say a more active role is needed to solve specific problems such as crime and corruption. The party took advantage of the collective frustration following the economic slowdown to become the single most popular party in the '98 elections. It isn't clear, though, whether they have enough support to form a sustainable government.

If there was a bright spot in the elections, it was that the far-right Republican Party was voted out of parliament. The failure of the party, which was run on a relentlessly racist, anti-Romany and xenophobic platform, can only be taken as good news. Some of Prague's poorer or outlying areas can still be dangerous places for foreigners, blacks, Asians or pretty much anyone who can't pass as a Czech at first glance. In post-Velvet Prague, skinheads, anarchists, nationalists and malcontents of all stripes have found common cause in fearing their particular version of the future. Several thousand so-called anarchists went on the rampage in the spring of 1998, destroying fast-food restaurants in the centre of town, to protest at what they see as increasing 'globalisation'. Their actions were deplored by the vast majority of the population, who, after their experiences under communism, are still sceptical of any '-ism'. But it's not clear how important these groups will become, especially as Prague's foreign population grows and the city becomes more cosmopolitan.

BUT ENOUGH OF THAT

Few of these problems will impinge on visitors who largely confine their trips to the well-worn tourist paths of the Old Town and Malá Strana. Indeed, from the perspective of a short-term visit, Prague seems to have staged a dramatic recovery from the dreary normalisation period of the 1970s and '80s, when Czechoslovakia was the sternest state of the Eastern bloc.

In many instances, the improvements are real. One clear winner is cuisine. The city is undergo-

ing a true culinary revolution. It was slow to take off in the early '90s as incomes lagged behind prices and the city's relatively small middle class had better things to spend its money on than meals out, but hundreds of restaurants and cafés have opened up in the past couple of years. The quality is also on the up. Gone is the cardboard and ketchup that communists used to call pizza. Salads are bigger and fresher. Service – never a strong point – seems to be improving.

Prague's notoriously dirty air is also getting cleaner. The city still has a long way to go, but the number of winter pollution alerts has dropped markedly since the early '90s as many of its coal-fired heating plants have been replaced with gas. The gains have been offset somewhat by a huge increase in the number of cars on the roads, but more and more people are leaving their Škodas and Trabants at home and driving cleaner-burning Western models. It's not clear if the same types of improvements are happening to the city's water – which is still best avoided as a beverage – but at least it seems that the quality is now being monitored more closely.

The supply of consumer goods is improving too. Maybe only Mafia dons and their girlfriends can shop at the new Donna Karan boutique or at Versace in the Old Town; the local department stores – with real prices for real people – are approaching Western standards of quality and selection. Tesco and Kotva have excellent grocery stores in their basements. The same improvements can be seen in home furnishings, cosmetics, and household and sporting goods. The changes are obvious on the street where it's no longer possible to tell Czechs from Westerners simply by their clothes. Many of the labels are the same – and Western designers are as popular in Prague as they are just about anywhere else.

The economic future looks secure. The Czechs are front-runners for membership in NATO and the European Union, and both should serve to stabilise the economic base and encourage further investment. Prague, as the country's leading city, will garner the lion's share of these benefits.

LET'S DO THE TIME WARP

Yet, for all the changes, modern Prague remains an anachronism. In spite of the hordes of tourists choking the main streets of the Old Town, there are still plentiful quiet back lanes and alleys to take you back several centuries. Ride the Soviet-built metro out to one of the massive housing estates near Háje station, complete with a stop at the monument to cosmonaut Yuri Gagarin, and it's back to the days of Brezhnev and the Cold War. Hit an all-night techno party at Roxy with the kids in skateboard gear and suddenly it's the eve of the millennium. Ultimately, it's these startling juxtapositions that make the city so compelling.

Architecture

A millennium of marvellous buildings is Prague's greatest attraction.

'Architectural creation has two functions,' wrote Jan Kotěra, father of the Czech modern movement. 'First the creation of space, and then the decoration of that space. The creative conception of space is truth itself, and decoration is the expression of that truth.'

Prague is a decorated city – decorated in a way that not only shows architectural movements but also the fingerprints of the past and its peoples. Walking through Prague is as much about time as it is about seeing. There are 1,100 years of architecture here, and the juxtaposition of styles only reinforces the vagaries and agendas of history. And unlike many other cities in this region, its history has survived more or less intact.

BEGINNINGS

The city lies in a basin encircled by seven hills. Though inhabited for 250,000 years, it was Slav tribes who came down from the safety of the highlands in the seventh century to settle on the banks of the Vltava. At first they built wooden structures, none of which survives. Then, in the second half of the ninth century, a stone fortress was built on a rocky outcrop on the left bank, and, in the early tenth century, another castle was contructed on the right bank a little upstream. Around these structures – **Prague Castle** (*see page 60*) and Chrasten Castle (now **Vyšehrad**; *see page 84*) – the settlements began to develop that were eventually to coalesce into Prague.

Five of the best examples of buildings from each period are listed below. All are in Prague 1 unless otherwise stated.

Romanesque

From the eleventh to the thirteenth century, architecture in Prague was characterised by the simple forms, heavy, rounded arches, tunnel and cross vaults and thick columns of the Romanesque. Few

*One of Prague's few remaining Romanesque buildings – Vyšehrad's **Rotunda of St Martin**.*

complete buildings from the period remain, but the style can be most clearly observed in the three surviving rotunda, the oldest of which is the **Rotunda of St Martin** at Vyšehrad. The most extensive surviving Romanesque building in the city is **St George's Basilica** (*see page 62*) in the Castle complex, which was established in the early tenth century.

The marshy right bank, hitherto less densely populated than the area around the Castle and more liable to flood, began expanding with the creation of a market place (now **Old Town Square**) in 1100 and saw a profusion of Romanesque buildings. By 1170 the two settlements were linked by the Judith Bridge (later replaced by Charles Bridge) and the Old Town was established by decree in 1287. A later decree raised the level of the city by about ten feet to avoid flooding, leaving many Romanesque rooftops at the street level of new Gothic buildings. Romanesque structures made perfect foundations and many Romanesque basements remain (such as that in the **House of the Lords of Kunštát and Poděbrady**; *see page 52*).

Romanesque Prague

St George's Basilica
(tenth century; rebuilt in eleventh century)
Prague Castle. **Map 2 D2**

Rotunda of St Martin
(2nd half of eleventh century) *Vyšehrad, Prague 3.*
Map *see map p84*

Rotunda of St Longinus
(late eleventh century) *Na rybníčku, Prague 2.*
Map 6 K7

Rotunda of the Holy Cross
(early twelfth century) *corner of Karoliny Světlé &
Konviktská.* **Map 3 G5**

Basement of the **House of the Lords of Kunštát
and Poděbrady**
(late twelfth century) *Řetězová 3.* **Map 3 H4**

Gothic

Gothic architecture, imported from France around 1230, offered greater spatial dynamism through ribbed vaulting, pointed arches and buttressing. Now it became possible to construct taller, wider, more delicate buildings, allowing for complex tracery and stained glass.

The **Old-New Synagogue** (*see page 52*), built around 1280, is a significant example, but the oldest Gothic complex in Bohemia is **St Agnes's Convent** (*see page 51*), started 50 years earlier. From 1233, a number of fine buildings were erected, including the **Minorite Church of St Francis** (completed around 1240).

The reign of Charles IV (1346-78) saw a flourishing of Gothic architecture in Prague. The German **Peter Parler** was summoned by the enlightened Charles to oversee his master plan of creating a completely new fortified city. Planned

Benedict Ried's **Vladislav Hall** *in the Castle.*

in four geometric sections, its central axis lay on **Wenceslas Square** (*see page 53*); the construction of this New Town (begun in 1348, the same year Charles University was established) doubled the size of the city. Parler was also responsible for the seamless yet innovative additions to the French-modelled **St Vitus's Cathedral** (*see page 61*; his vault in the Chapel of St Wenceslas is a masterpiece), and for **Charles Bridge** (*see page 45*).

Many townhouses in Prague contain Gothic elements, but few retain an original Gothic façade and plan. An exception is **Dům U kamenného zvonu** ('House of the Stone Bell') on the Old Town Square, next to the Golz-Kinský Palace.

The northward-moving Renaissance was architecturally anticipated in **Benedict Ried's** audacious **Vladislav Hall** in the Castle complex (completed 1502). Its rational, stacked rectilinear windows unashamedly clash pure Renaissance with the beautiful, massively complex organic vaulting of the late Gothic roof.

Gothic Prague

St Agnes's Convent
(1233-c.1380) *Anežská 12.* **Map 3 J1**

Old-New Synagogue
(1280) *Červená ulice.* **Map 3 H2**

St Vitus's Cathedral
(1334-1929) *Prague Castle.* **Map 2 D2**

'House of the Stone Bell' (Dům U kamenného zvonu)
(c.1340) *Staroměstské náměstí 13.* **Map 3 H3**
Church of Our Lady before Týn
(1365-1511) *Staroměstské náměstí.* **Map 3 J3**

Renaissance

Bricks and mortar took on a pivotal role under the first of the Habsburgs, Ferdinand I (1526-64). Cheaper and easier than hewing raw stone and allowing more rapid construction, brick facilitated the Renaissance renovation of Malá Strana after the fire of 1541. Where new buildings were not raised, Renaissance façades were tacked on to surviving Gothic ones. The Renaissance saw a move towards more human, horizontal spaces – simpler masses and clearer forms, punctuated by columns, pillars and pilasters.

The Renaissance truly arrived with the construction of **Paolo della Stella**'s extraordinary **Belvedere** in the Royal Gardens by the Castle, completed in 1563 (*see page 69*). In the same gardens is **Bonifác Wohlmut**'s **Ball Game Court** (Míčovna; 1568), which shows off wonderfully the sixteenth-century love of decorative sgraffito work. This technique of scratching through black or brown mortar to create a pattern or picture was particularly suited to *trompe l'oeil*.

The sgraffito-ed **Schwarzenberg Palace.**

effects such as imitations of stonework, as seen in the hulking **Schwarzenberg Palace** on Hradčanské náměstí.

Perhaps the period's most striking and unusual building, however, is the **Hvězda** ('Star') **Hunting Lodge** in Prague 6, built in the form of a six-pointed star.

Renaissance Prague

'The Stone Ram' (U kamenného berana)
(fifteenth century; adapted around 1520) *Staroměstské náměstí 17.* **Map 3 H3**
The Belvedere
(1538-52 & 1557-63) *Královská zahrada.* **Map 2 E1**
Schwarzenberg Palace
(1545-67) *Hradčanské náměstí 2.* **Map 1 C3**
Hvězda Hunting Lodge
(1555-7) *Obora Hvězda, Prague 6.*
Ball Game Court
(1563-8) *Královská zahrada.* **Map 2 D1**

Baroque

The first baroque palace, designed by Giovanni Pieronni, was the titanic Wallenstein Palace (1624-30), constructed for and named after the megalomaniac commander of the Imperial Catholic armies. This building prefigured the dominance of the baroque after the Thirty Years' War, fuelled both by resurgent Catholicism and the need to rebuild much of war-damaged Prague.

After 1648, enormous city-wide baroque fortifications were built (dwarfing the Gothic ones) and paid for by the city. With Bohemia now securely within the Habsburg empire, the task of consolidating the Counter-Reformation was handed to the Jesuits, who started a new building programme. The **Church of St Saviour** (sv. Salvátor) in the Clementinum, an elegant and more austere example of early baroque (finished 1640) was the most important result. Czech baroque flitted between the plainer French and the more sensual Italian high baroque styles, intended to seduce the city back into the Catholic fold. Baroque was all about ostentation: decoration, scale, curves, complexity. The father and son team of **Christoph** and **Kilian Ignaz Dientzenhofer** built Prague baroque's *magnum opus*, the gaggingly opulent **Church of St Nicholas** (*see page 80*). It used every trick in the book: imitation marble, *trompe l'oeil, memento mori* motifs, lots of gold, layered vistas, spatial complexity, curving façades.

The War of Austrian Succession and the Seven Years' War caused more tremendous damage to the city. **Niccolo Pacassi** restored the south side of the **Castle** for Empress Maria Theresa (1740-80) and gave it the late baroque unity that we see today from Charles Bridge.

The majority of Prague's churches are baroque in design or at least incorporate baroque elements into an older structure. Similarly, a large number of the city's fine townhouses are baroque or have baroque façades (the Gothic **House of the Stone Bell** – *see above* – has had its baroque coating removed).

Baroque Prague

Wallenstein Palace
(1623-30) *Valdštejnské náměstí 4.* **Map 2 E2**

The Loreto
(1626, 1711-25 & 1746-51) *Loretánské náměstí.* **Map 1 B3**

Clementinum
(1653-1770) *Křížovnické náměstí 4.* **Map 3 G4**

Troja Château
(1679-85) *U trojského zámku 6, Prague 8.*

Church of St Nicholas
(1704-11, 1737-52 & 1755) *Malostranské náměstí.* **Map 2 D3**

Revivalism

In 1780 the newly crowned Joseph II introduced regulations to govern the height, materials and construction methods for new buildings, while also issuing an edict of religious tolerance. This marked the end of baroque and the beginning of revivalist architecture. The neo-classical **Estates Theatre** (*see page 46*) was built for Count Nostitz by **Antonín Haffenecker** a year later. New materials such as cast iron favoured neo-classical forms to express the new no-nonsense rationality of the Enlightenment.

The manufacturing middle classes now took the lead, rather than the church or nobility. Prague's first suburb, **Karlín**, was constructed within a generous, rational grid plan and included factories. Blocks of flats began to appear with common water facilities and dry toilets. The invention and spread of railways and growing engineering expertise combined in the first train station, **Masarykovo nádraží**. A massive undertaking, employing 4,000 workers, it was one of the most impressive in Europe when completed in 1845. Austrian influence, revival movements (neoclassicism and romanticism) and growing democratisation began to dominate the changing city landscape. Municipal construction responded to newly recognised social needs – schools, houses and hospitals, instead of churches and palaces. A new sense of independence was forming, which was to culminate in the Czech National Revival movement.

On 16 May 1858, 50,000 people walked in procession behind the foundation stone for the **National Theatre** (*see page 55*), designed by **Josef Zítek** (who was also responsible for the **Rudolfinum**). The project employed a whole generation of artists and designers – called, in fact, the National Theatre Generation. Shortly after opening, it burnt to the ground. Yet, within two months, money was raised by subscription

The Loreto – *over-the-top baroque.*

to rebuild it, this time according to the designs of one of Zítek's colleagues, **Josef Schulz**, who was also to build the **National Museum** (*see page 91*).

Prague's Czech population thirsted for all the usual grand municipal symbols and the National Theatre was a focal point for emerging Czech national identity. Neo-Renaissance and neobaroque were the order of the day: heavy, monumental, civic. Architectural decoration leant on Czech folklore and historical motifs – such as the newly restored painted façade of the **Wiehl House** (*see page 38*) – all of which, by the end of the century, was beginning to leave Prague looking somewhat parochial.

Revivalist Prague

Estates Theatre
(1781-3) *Železná ulice 11.* **Map 3 J4**

Masarykovo nádraží
(1844-5) *Hybernská.* **Map 4 L3**

National Theatre
(1868-83) *Národní třída.* **Map 5 G6**

Wiehl House
(1868-83) *Václavské náměstí 34.* **Map 4 K5**

National Museum
(1885-90) *Václavské náměstí.* **Map 6 L6**

Hit or myth? The folk-inspired, neo-Renaissance **Wiehl House**. *See page 37.*

Art nouveau

The rise of a business class (banking wealth and investment was switching from Viennese to Czech hands) and the desire to throw away historicism urged a new direction. The move towards decorativism, symbolism and decadence found inspiration in art nouveau (or secession, as it was known in the Austro-Hungarian Empire). The Viennese-trained architect **Friedrich Ohmann** first introduced the style to Prague. His **Café Corso** of 1898, now destroyed, was one of the city's first art nouveau buildings.

Ohmann's next project, the former **Hotel Central**, was a competent art nouveau facsimile with glass cornice and armfuls of floral motifs. Its heavy debt to the French style was more than mere serendipity. Spurred on by Rodin's exhibition and visit to Prague in 1902, Czechs responded to the notions of individualism, universality and democracy implied in Republican French culture. Municipal and residential art nouveau buildings started to spread across the city, still visible in neighbourhoods such as Vinohrady and Vršovice.

Between 1903 and 1905, one of Ohmann's collaborators, **Osvald Polívka**, built both the heavily ornamented **Prague Insurance Building** (the windows below the cornice spelling out 'Prague') and the much more restrained **Topič Building** next door. The stylistic opposition was intentional. Polívka saw the culmination and possibly the death of art nouveau in the extraordinary **Municipal House** (Obecní dům; *see page*

59). Nine years in construction under **Antonín Balšánek**'s plans (Polívka was responsible for the interior), this was another project that brought together the artistic luminaries of the day. With its excessive ornamentation (now burnished, thanks to a massive, expert renewal project), it was already something of an anachronism when it opened in 1912.

Art nouveau Prague

Hlavní nádraží (Main Station)
(1901-9) *Wilsonova.* **Map 4 M5**

Hotel Central
(1902) *Hybernská 10.* **Map 4 L3**

Grand Hotel Evropa
(1903-5) *Václavské náměstí 25.* **Map 4 K5**

Prague Insurance Building & Topič Building
(1903-5) *Národní 7 & 9.* **Map 3 H5**

Municipal House (Obecní dům)
(1905-12) *Náměstí Republiky 5.* **Map 4 K3**

From Kotěra to cubism

Jan Kotěra, a pupil of the Viennese master Otto Wagner, is considered the father of Czech modern architecture. As the decorative art nouveau excesses fell away, he concentrated on geometric functionalism – an approach that was to influence the later modernist movement. His **Urbánek Publishing House** used planes of brick to create a pared-down, singular façade. With the waning of Viennese influence and the aspirations of independence, Czech architects were beginning to leave their mark on the city.

Some architects rejected Kotěra, however, claiming his work lacked spirituality. The painter **Bohumil Kubišta** introduced cubism from Paris and artists in all fields saw in it a chance to forge a new, unified mode of expression. Cubist architecture, unique to Bohemia, was first exemplified by **Josef Gočár**'s 'House of the Black Madonna' (now home to a collection of Czech cubist paintings and furniture). Constructed over a newly developed concrete skeleton, it opened the way for more than half a dozen further cubist works. The greatest concentration can be found beneath the Vyšehrad rock, where **Josef Chochol** built a number of fine villas and tenement blocks. Sadly, the outbreak of World War I meant that cubist architecture never moved beyond its germinal stage.

Cubist Prague

'House of the Black Madonna' (**Dům U Černé matky boží**)
(1911-12) *Celetná 34.* **Map 4 K3**

Urbánek Publishing House
(1911-12) *Jungmannova 20.* **Map 3 J5**

Vyšehrad houses
(1911-13) *Neklanova 2 & 30, Libušina 3 & 49, and Rašínovo nábřeží 6-10, Prague 2.* **Map** *see p84.*

Cubist lamp-post
(1912) *in front of the Church of Our Lady of the Snows, Jungmannovo náměstí.* **Map 3 J5**

Diamant House
(1912) *Spálená 82/4.* **Map 5 H6**

Czech modernism

German surrender and the collapse of the Austro-Hungarian Empire ushered in the First Republic. In 1920, the new president, Tomáš Garrigue Masaryk, asked Slovenian **Josip Plečnik** to renovate and modernise **Prague Castle**. His sensitivity, innovation and expert craftsmanship greatly enhanced the ancient structure; the classically inspired Columned Hall, in particular, is sublime. In contrast, the clashing styles of Plečnik's **Church of the Sacred Heart** in Vinohrady, ugly and beautiful by turns, anticipate postmodernism.

The colourful, heavy and awkward style of the short-lived **rondo-cubism** (also known as National Style) can be seen at the former **Bank of the Czechoslovak Legions**, designed by Josef Gočár. Russian constructivism and the influence of **Adolf Loos** (his remarkable Müller Villa is in Střešovice at Nad hradním vodojemem 14) impacted on modernist buildings. The constructivist icon, the **Veletržní palác** in Holešovice (now the Gallery of Modern and Contemporary Art), used reinforced concrete liberally. Its huge atrium is wonderful. The shabby but elegant functionalist **Mánes Building** is of the same year (1928). Monumentalism, as in the **cenotaph** at Žižkov Hill, is modernism writ extremely large.

Perhaps the most fascinating modernist project in the city is the model colony of houses built on a

Diamant House – *cutting-edge cubism.*

hillside in Dejvice as a permanent exhibition of modern living during the early 1930s: the **Baba Villas**. More than 30 of these functionalist middle-class family homes were constructed; all were individually designed by the leading architects of the time, and all are still occupied.

Modernist Prague

Bank of the Czechoslovak Legions
(1921-3) *Na Poříčí 24.* **Map 4 L3**

Veletržní palác
(1928) *Dukelských hrdinů 47, Prague 7.* **Map 7 D2**

Mánes Building
(1928) *Masarykovo nábřeží 1.* **Map 5 G7**

Church of the Sacred Heart
(1929-32) *Náměstí Jiřího z Poděbrad, Prague 3.* **Map 8 C3**

Baba Villas
(1931-6) *Na ostrohu, Na Babě, Nad Paťankou & Průhledová, Prague 6.*

Communism

Communism was an architectural disaster. The Stalinist wedding cake-style **Holiday Inn Praha** (formerly the Hotel International) does have its own chilling, monumental grandeur, but otherwise Prague was merely ringed by gargantuan and soulless housing estates, where shoddy blocks of flats (*paneláky*) jut like rotting teeth. The laughable **Palace of Culture** (completed 1980) squats next to the brutal, vast span of the **Nusle Bridge** (Nuselský most), which helped to link many of the southerly and easterly lying housing estates to the city centre.

The buffoonery, compromise and laziness characteristic of the era is demonstrated perfectly in the lower halls of **Hlavní nádraží** (Main Station). Cowering under Josef Fanta's monumentally regal, secessionist, former station above, it is neither comfortable enough for drunks nor useful enough for passengers. Communism's last gasps produced the clean-lined, kitschy **Žižkov TV Tower** (*see page 86*), which dominates the entire city and seems set to blast off into space at any moment.

Communist Prague

Holiday Inn Praha
(1953-9) *Koulova 15, Prague 6.*

Nusle Bridge
(1965-9) *Prague 2.*

Lower halls of Hlavní nádraží (Main Station)
(completed 1979) *Wilsonova.* **Map 4 M5**

Palace of Culture
(1975-80) *Vyšehrad, Prague 2.*

Žižkov TV Tower
(1985-8) *Mahlerovy sady, Prague 3.* **Map 8 C2**

Beyond the Velvet Revolution

Since 1989, Prague and its citizens have been preoccupied with restoration and enrichment. Banks have sprouted on street corners. Enormous infrastructural investments are being made and many

complex state and private renovations are taking place, but disputes over the restitution of property are stalling much advance. Prague really does change every day, and no longer at the quotidian level. Restorations, some careful, some ghastly, are to be seen all over town. Renaissance façades have been newly splashed with wedding-cake colours and in some cases resemble hunks of Austria dropped into the heart of Prague. And the whole of Vinohrady, a neighbourhood of gentility since Mozart's time, is in a constant state of being torn up, rewired, mended and turned into luxury apartments and offices.

Though a procession of slick malls has invaded downtown Prague in the last couple of years, the most eyecatching new addition to the city skyline remains Frank Gehry's **'Fred & Ginger' building**, also known to Czechs as 'Taneční dům', or 'Dancing House', corner of Resslova and Rašínovo nábřeží. It depicts a tango-ing couple as a glass-skirted hourglass with a hairdo of twisted reinforcing steel being spun by a goofy angular concrete tower (*see picture page 56*). The office and restaurant project stands as the most significant postmodern creation since the Velvet Revolution, though it is about to lose its status as most controversial.

A nine-storey glass Graham cracker box, known turgidly as **Astra 2** (or, if you really want to get crazy, 'the Můstek Tower'), has been approved for the very bottom of Wenceslas Square. It is destined to teach a painful lesson to any critic of 'Fred & Ginger' who ever pleaded for moderation. Entirely out of character with the living museum of great architecture that is this square, this office/retail monolith will offer one principal gift to the millions who will pass before it here in the city's most visible location: a lesson in how well entrenched – and directionless – the permit bureaucracy remains nearly a decade after the official overthrow of the grey suits.

Other glass-and-steel mega-projects have been building up to this, to be sure (the **Darex** shopping and office complex at Václavské náměsti 11 and the **Myslbek** centre around the corner at Na přikopě 19/21), but it seems that not all interest in integrity has been lost to speculators. The monumentally crafted 1911 **Municipal House** (Obecní dům; *see page 59*) on Náměstí Republiky has been reopened, after more than two years of expert restoration, to its original, prime art nouveau state, providing a world-class home for the Prague Symphony Orchestra, a smart café, an exhibition hall and a French restaurant. The interiors, featuring the work of Alfons Mucha and Max Švabinský, Bohemian oak trim, cut-glass skylights and ceiling dome mosaics of old Czech myths, virtually cry out its challenge to both bureaucrats and rabid developers: just try to ignore this legacy.

Sightseeing

Staré Město   **42**   Malá Strana   **74**
Nové Město   **53**   Further Afield   **81**
Prague Castle & Hradčany   **59**

Staré Město

With its squares, churches and Prague's most famous bridge, the Old Town is, not surprisingly, the highlight of many agendas.

Map 3

It's almost impossible not to get lost in Staré Město (the 'Old Town') and much the best way to get a true measure of its charm is to do exactly that. Settled in the tenth century, it has always been where the town's business got done. While the city's rulers plotted and intrigued up on the hill, the town's merchants got on with making a quick buck, a skill that is re-emerging in post-communist times as the natives learn to wash the tablecloths, smile at the customers and quadruple the bill.

The Powder Gate to the Old Town Square

The **Powder Gate** (Prašná brána; *see below*), a Gothic gateway dating from 1475 at the eastern end of Celetná, marks the boundary between the Old and New towns and is also the start of the so-

*Looking down on the **Old Town Square**.*

called Královská Cesta, or **Royal Route,** the traditional coronation path taken by the Bohemian kings and now a popular tourist track. The first stretch runs west down **Celetná**, a pleasant pedestrianised promenade lined with freshly restored baroque and Renaissance buildings. A more recent addition is the house **'The Black Madonna'** ('U černé matky boží'), at no.34, the first cubist building in the city (built in 1913; *see also page 38*), and now, appropriately, housing an exhibition of Czech cubist art, furniture and architecture (*see page 98*). The madonna herself, a treasured artefact that adorned the outside corner, has been moved indoors for safekeeping and a copy will replace it – hopefully alleviating the need for protective bars.

On the other side of Celetná an alley leads in to **Templová**, where you'll be immersed in a part of the town where ancient façades are jumbled in with fresh new pastel paint jobs, and meticulous restoration has revitalised long-dormant lanes. Round here is the hub of expat nightlife, where backpackers, tourists and foreign residents disappear into a plethora of bars, clubs and restaurants, most of which, for some reason, have French names: **La Provence** (*see page 127*), **Chapeau Rouge** (*see page 139*), **Le Saint-Jacques** (*see page 128*) and the **Marquis de Sade** (*see page 141*) are all within a block of each other, and the **Radegast** pub (*see page 141*) and U Hynků are just around another corner. Late at night, the strip outside Chapeau Rouge (which has the longest hours of all these places) is filled with youths of all nationalities, vomiting on the street, copulating in corners, conducting minor drug deals and arguing with the Chapeau's neanderthal bouncers.

Opposite is the **Church of St James** (sv. Jakuba; *see below*) on Malá Štupartská – a typical baroque reworking of an older Gothic church (*see below*). From here you can stroll through the crisply restored, café and restaurant-lined square of **Týn**, better known by its German name of **Ungelt**, emerging behind the **Church of Our Lady before Týn** (Kostel Matky boží před Týnem; *see below*), Staré Město's parish church since the twelfth century, and eventually come out on the Old Town Square. The Týn church is a scary structure, looming ominously over the square and somehow redolent of a Monty Python animation – you almost expect the building to uproot itself and set off squelching tour groups across the city.

*Just about the best known sight in Prague – the **Astronomical Clock**. See page 52.*

The Old Town Square

For centuries the beautiful **Old Town Square** (Staroměstské náměstí), edged by an astonishing jumble of baroque and medieval structures, has been the natural place for visitors to the city to gravitate. This was the medieval town's main market place and has always been at the centre of the action: criminals were executed here; martyrs were burnt at the stake; and, in 1948, this is where huge crowds greeted the announcement of the communist takeover. Most of the houses are much older than they look, with Romanesque cellars and Gothic chambers hiding behind the pastel-coloured baroque and Renaissance façades. If the effect seems somewhat toy-town today, especially in comparison to the crumbling structures in some of the surrounding streets, it should come as no surprise to learn that it was the communists who spent an unprecedented US$10 million smartening up the square for the fortieth anniversary of the Czechoslovak Socialist Republic.

The west side is lined with stalls selling kitschy crafts and untempting souvenirs. The grassy area behind them was thoughtfully provided by the Nazis, who destroyed much of the **Old Town Hall** on 8 May 1945 when the rest of Europe was holding street parties and celebrating the end of World War II. The town lost most of its archives, though it gained a fine vista of the lovely **Church of St Nicholas** (sv. Mikuláš). Built in 1735 by Kilián Ignaz Dientzenhofer, this is an inside-out church: the exterior, with its white stucco and undulating façade, is even more ornate than the interior. An added attraction in winter is the heated seats installed to prevent your bottom freezing during organ concerts.

The **Old Town Hall** (Staroměstská radnice; *see below*) was begun in 1338, after the councillors had spent several fruitless decades trying to persuade the king to allow them to construct a suitable chamber for their affairs. John of Luxembourg finally relented, but with the bizarre proviso that all work was to be financed from the duty on wine. He obviously underestimated the high-living inhabitants of the Old Town, because within the year they had enough money to purchase the house adjoining the present tower. You can go and look at what remains of the Old Town Hall after the Nazis' handiwork, although trying to decipher the extraordinary components of the **Astronomical Clock** (orloj; *see below*) is more rewarding. It was constructed in the fifteenth century, sometime before the new-fangled notion that Prague revolves around the sun and not vice versa. Undismayed, the citizens kept their clock with its gold sunburst swinging happily around the globe. One of Prague's most famous tourist rituals is waiting for the clock to strike the hour while tacky-gift sellers buzz around. The brief appearance of figures of the apostles over the clock is remarkably short and laughably unspectacular. Far more entertaining is watching the embarrassed faces of the crowds as they exchange 'is that it?' looks with one another before shuffling away.

Perhaps the finest of the houses that make up what is left of the Old Town Hall is **The Minute House** (U minuty), the beautiful black and white sgraffitoed house on the corner, which dates from 1611. Franz Kafka lived here as a boy; opposite the Astronomical Clock is the **Café Milena**, named after Milena Jesenská, the radical journalist who is best remembered for being Kafka's girlfriend. The area teems with other Kafka sites. The writer was born in a house at U Radnice 5 (the ground floor of the building that replaced it contains one of Prague's better classical CD outlets, **Music shop Trio**; *see page 171*), lived for a while at **Oppelt's House** on the corner of Pařížská and the square (this is the house where *Metamorphosis* takes place), went to primary school on nearby Masná and later attended the strict German *Gymnasium* on the third floor of the **Golz-Kinský Palace**. This frothy stuccoed affair in the northeast corner of the square once contained Kafka's father's fancy goods shop; it's now the **Franz Kafka Bookshop** (Knihkupectví Franz Kafky). Adjoining the palace is the **House of the Stone Bell** (Dům U kamenného zvonu), the baroque cladding of which was removed in the 1980s to reveal a fourteenth-century façade beneath.

The focal point of the square is the powerful, though regrettably graffiti-festooned **Jan Hus Monument** dedicated to the reformist cleric, designed by Ladislav Saloun and unveiled in 1915 (and received as a passé artistic flop). Here tourists and school groups pause to rest their feet, chat, consult their guidebooks, sing along with buskers and occasionally get fined by the police for clambering about on the structure itself. On the orders of the Pope, Hus was burnt at the stake in 1415 for his revolutionary thinking, although the Catholic Church, some 500 years after the fact, has belatedly decided to appoint a commission to decide whether the punishment fitted the crime. (*See also page 14.*) Hus's fans are optimistic, as the quote on the side reads 'Truth will prevail', words echoed by President Gottwald in the 'Glorious February' of 1948.

The Old Town Square to Charles Bridge

The most obvious route from the Old Town Square to Charles Bridge is along **Karlova**, although twisting and curling as it does, it wouldn't be particularly obvious were it not for the inevitable crowds proceeding along it. This is the continuation of the Royal Route and becomes an unrelenting bottleneck in the summer when tourists and hawkers vie for supremacy on the narrow way.

To reach Karlova, walk past the Old Town Hall into **Malé náměstí** (Little Square). In the centre is a plague column well enclosed by an ornate Renaissance grill and overlooked by the neo-Renaissance **Rott House**, built in 1890 and entirely decorated with murals of flowers and peasants by Mikoláš Aleš. (The house now contains the excellent multi-floor food and wine store **Dům lahůdek u Rotta**; *see page 165*.) There's a branch of jeweller Mappin & Webb on the corner, evidence of the rapid upmarket trajectory of this area. (On the other side of the square, a block down

Celetná, there's a large, glowing Versace shop, and Pařížská is crowded with designer outlets of all kinds.)

The twists and turns of Karlova lead past a procession of souvenir shops, although there are a few worthwhile places along the way, such as **Bontonland Music Stop** (*see page 168*) at no.23, a decent classical CD store, and **Maximum Underground** (*see page 171*), one of Prague's few dance music shops, at nearby Jilská 22.

The third twist on Karlova winds past the massive, groaning giants that struggle to hold up the portal of the **Clam-Gallas Palace** (Clam-Gallasův palác) on Husova. Designed by Fischer von Erlach and completed in 1719, the palace now houses the city's archives.

The vast bulk of the **Clementinum** (*see below*) makes up the right-hand side of Karlova's last stretch. After the Castle, it's the largest complex of buildings in Prague. The Jesuits, storm troopers of the Counter-Reformation, set up home here on the site and carried on the tradition of book-burning and brow-beating.

Like much of the Old Town, Karlova is best viewed at night when most of the tour groups are safely back at their hotels. And if you get peckish along the way there are two all-night eateries: **U zlatého stromu** at Karlova 6, where there's a non-stop restaurant in a bizarre complex that also includes a hotel, disco and softcore strip show, and **Pizzeria Roma Due** (*see page 130*) at Liliová 18. Further up Liliová is the **James Joyce** (*see page 140*), Prague's principal Irish pub, and the **U krále Jiřího** (*see page 142*), which serves radically cheaper beer next door. The excellent **V Zátiší** (*see page 124*) restaurant is also along here at Liliová 1.

At the foot of Karlova, tourists have trouble crossing the road past the continuous stream of trams and cars that race through **Křižovnické náměstí** (Knights of the Cross Square). The eponymous Knights, an elderly bunch of neo-medieval crusaders, have come out of retirement and reclaimed the **Church of St Francis** (sv. František). Designed by Jean-Baptiste Mathey in the late seventeenth century, the church, which has a massive red dome and has been described as looking as if it has been 'gouged out of so much Dutch cheese', is unusual for Prague, not least because its altar is facing the wrong way. The gallery next door houses a job-lot of religious bric-a-brac that the Knights extricated from various museums, and a subterranean chapel decorated with stalactites made out of dust and eggshells, an eighteenth-century fad that enjoyed unwarranted popularity in Prague.

On the eastern side of the square is the **Church of St Saviour** (sv. Salvátor), which marks the border of the Clementinum. Opposite, guarding the entrance to Charles Bridge is the **Old Town**

Bridge Tower (Staroměstská mostecká věž; open *winter* 9am-6pm, *summer* 10am-7pm daily; *admission* 30 Kč adults; 20 Kč children), a Gothic gate topped with a pointed, tiled hat. Built in 1373 along the shadow line of St Vitus's Cathedral, it was badly damaged in 1648 by marauding Swedes, but the sculptural decoration on the eastern side by Peter Parler survives. Climb the tower for a perfect bird's-eye view of Prague's domes and spires, the naff **Corona Bar** (*see page 140*) and even naffer **Klub Lávka** below on the river, and the wayward line of Charles Bridge beyond.

Charles Bridge

Charles Bridge (Karlův most) is the most popular place in the city to come and get your portrait painted, take photos of the Castle, have your pocket picked or pick up a backpacker. The range of entertainment is always dodgy and diverse, from blind folk-singers to the man who plays Beethoven concertos on finger bowls.

The stone bridge was built in 1357 (replacing the earlier Judith Bridge that collapsed in a flood in 1342) and has survived over 600 years of turbulent city life, although a large and embarrassing chunk of it fell into the Vltava in 1890. The statues lining it were added during the seventeenth century, when Bohemia's leading sculptors, including Josef Brokof and Matthias Braun, were commissioned to create figures to inspire the masses as they went about their daily business. The strategy proved more effective than an earlier Catholic decoration – the severed heads of Protestant nobles. More mundane statues were added in the nineteenth century by the Max brothers.

The third statue on the right from the Old Town end is a crucifixion that has a Hebrew inscription in gold. This was added in 1696 by a Jew found guilty of blaspheming in front of the statue; his punishment was to pay for the inscription 'Holy, Holy, Holy Lord' to be added.

St John of Nepomuk – perhaps the most famous figure – is eighth on the right as you walk towards Malá Strana and recognisable by his doleful expression and the cartoon-like gold stars fluttering around his head. According to popular belief, John was flung off the bridge after refusing to reveal the secrets of the queen's confession, but he was actually just in the wrong place at the wrong time during one of Wenceslas IV's anticlerical rages. The statue – placed here in 1683 – is the bridge's earliest. It was cast in bronze and has survived better than the sandstone statues, which have been badly damaged by the elements and have mostly been replaced by copies.

Further towards Malá Strana, fourth from the end on the left, is the Cistercian nun **St Luitgard**, made by Matthias Braun in 1710, and shown in the middle of her vision of Christ. The statue is considered by many, including Prince Charles, to be the finest statue on the bridge, and he has pledged the money to save her from the elements, which are threatening to wipe the look of wonder off her face.

On the same side, second from the Malá Strana end, is the largest and most complex grouping on the bridge. It commemorates the founders of the Trinitarian Order – **Saints John of Matha** and **Felix of Valois** (accompanied by his pet stag) – plus a rogue **St Ivan**, included for no obvious

Strolling a sodden but unusually tourist-free **Charles Bridge**.

The **Old-New Synagogue** – the oldest in Prague, and still used for services. See page 52.

reason. Below them stand a lethargic figure of a Turk and his snarling dog framing three imprisoned Christian souls.

If you've fallen for the city, then you should seek out the gold cross located halfway across the bridge: touch it, make a wish and it's guaranteed that you will return. The very best time to come is at night when the Castle is floodlit in various pastel shades and appears to hover above your head.

Southern Staré Město

Canny German merchants were the first to develop the area south of the Old Town Square. They built a church dedicated to St Havel (more commonly known as St Gall) when Charles IV generously donated some spare parts of the saint from his burgeoning relic collection. The onion domes of the existing **Church of St Havel** (on Havelská) were added later in 1722 by the Shod Carmelites (the Barefooted Carmelites settled on the other side of the river). The opposite end of Havelská is lined with slightly bowed baroque houses precariously balanced on Gothic arcades. The merchants have at last returned, and the street now contains Prague's best **market** (*see page 155*). As well as handmade wooden toys, there are abundant piles of fruit and vegetables.

Between here and Celetná, in Ovocný trh, is one of Prague's finest neo-classical buildings: the **Estates Theatre** (Stavovské divadlo; *see page 217*). Known under three different official names in its time, the theatre has always suffered from something of an identity problem, and it is currently unofficially dubbed 'The Mozart Theatre'. Unlike Vienna, Prague loved Mozart and Mozart loved Prague. During the composer's lifetime, the

theatre staged a succession of his greatest operas, including the première of *Don Giovanni*, conducted by Wolfgang Amadeus himself. The building was paid for by Count Nostitz, after whom it was named when it opened in 1783 – aimed at promoting productions of works in the German language. But by the late nineteenth century most productions were being performed in Czech, and the name was changed to the Tyl Theatre, after the dramatist JK Tyl. His song *Where Is My Home?* was played here for the first time and later adopted as the Czech national anthem.

The massive oriel window overlooking the theatre belongs to the **Carolinum** (*see page 99*), the university founded by Charles IV. Charles never made a move without first consulting the stars, and ascertained that Aries was an auspicious sign for the first university in Central Europe, which was founded on 7 April 1348. It came to grief at the hands of another Aries, Adolf Hitler, when it was badly damaged in World War II.

Opposite the Estates Theatre is the former **Soviet House of Science and Culture**. Fancy boutiques have taken over most of the complex, although there's a permanent exhibition of gaudy Russian paintings and some Russian books and CDs on sale.

Just around the corner on Michalská is the ominous shape of tourist attractions to come: **St Michael's Mystery** (*see below*). Dig deep into your pockets to experience this 'cultural show' in a renovated Romanesque church; it aims to transport the visitor 'into a completely different, virtual world by means of grand-scale multimedia techniques, authentically recreated backdrops and film scenery'.

Around Betlémské náměstí

Once the poorest quarter of the Old Town and a notorious area of cut-throats and prostitutes (their present-day sisters can be seen lining Perlova and Na Perštýně a few blocks away), this was the natural breeding ground for the radical politics of the late fourteenth century. On the north side of Bethlehem Square are the swooping twin gables of the ascetically plain **Bethlehem Chapel** (Betlémská kaple; *see below*), a reconstructed version of the 1391 building where Jan Hus and other independent-minded Czech preachers passed on their vision of the true church to the Prague citizenry. Across the courtyard is the **Galerie Jaroslav Fragnera**, with the **Klub Architektů** (*see page 130*) offering passable cheap eats in the vaulted basement and, in the summer, also at tables outside. The square's other refreshment station is the **Gulu Gulu** (*see page 140*), a cool café by day and sweaty bar by night. From these two establishments, pockets of retro hippies and other youth types spill out to sprawl on benches in the middle and treat passers-by to their accomplishments on the acoustic guitar.

On the other side of the square is the **Náprstek Museum** (*see page 91*). After making his fortune by inebriating the masses, Vojta Náprstek installed a collection of ethnological knick-knacks in the family brewery. A nineteenth-century do-gooder, he didn't just spend his time hunting down shrunken heads, but also founded the first women's club in the country. The room, untouched for 100 years, can still be seen, although the peephole he drilled through from his office draws into question the purity of his motives.

One of the three Romanesque rotundas in the city, the **Church of the Holy Rood** (Rotunda sv. Kříže), is on nearby Konviktská. The tiny, charming building, dating from the early twelfth century, was built entirely in the round so that the devil had no corner to hide in. Today it's dwarfed by the surrounding tenement buildings. If you don't manage to get a look inside, try the **Hostinec U rotundy**. Covered with lovely sgraffito, it's as authentic a pub as you'll find in the Old Town, with cheap beer and a contingent of locals who'll try to stare you out when you walk in.

On Husova, to the north-east, is the **Church of St Giles** (sv. Jilji), a massive Gothic structure that looks like a fortress from the outside. It was built by the Dominicans in 1340-70, an order that has recently come back to reclaim its heritage and inhabit the monastery next door. Nearby is **U Zlatého tygra** (The Golden Tiger; *see page 142*), favourite watering hole of Bohumil Hrabal (*see page 189*), author and Nobel Prize nominee, who spent half his life inside a pub and the other half writing about what goes on inside pubs. The irascible octagenarian died in 1997. If the snarling old-timers within make you feel unwelcome, go instead to the **House of the Lords of Kunštát and Poděbrady** (Dům pánů z Kunštátu a Poděbrad; *see below*) on Řetězová. In the basement are the atmospheric remains of a Romanesque palace, and temporary exhibitions from the puppet faculty of Charles University, spookily spotlit against the crumbling vaults and pillars. In the courtyard is one of the best spots for summer drinking in the Old Town.

Parallel to Konviktská is the unnaturally quiet Bartolomějská. Czechs still avoid its environs – a legacy of the role it played in communist times. Police departments line the street and most dissidents of note did time in the StB (Secret Police) cells in the former convent. The building, now containing the **Pension Unitas** (*see page 115*), has been restored to the Sisters of Mercy and you can stay the night in the cell where President Havel was once sent to ponder the error of his ways.

The river is only a few dozen yards away and from here you have a perfect view across it to Kampa, with the Castle high up on the hill. Turning right will take you past Novotného lávka, a cluster of buildings jutting into the river centred around a nineteenth-century water tower and a small cluster of bars, and back to Charles Bridge. Turn left to reach the National Theatre and the start of the New Town.

Josefov

The main street of Josefov (Jewish Quarter) is **Pařížská**, an elegant, tree-lined avenue of designer shops and airline offices, which leads from the Old Town Square down to the Intercontinental Hotel and the river. Here you'll find swishy places like the **Jewel of India** restaurant (*see page 120*), **Barock Bar & Café** (*see page 123*) and **Bugsy's** cocktail bar (*see page 139*). This is all, however, in sharp contrast to the rest of what was once Prague's Jewish quarter.

The spiritual heart of Josefov is the **Old-New Synagogue** (Staronová synagoga; *see below*), which stands on a wedge of land between Maiselova and Pařížská. Built around 1270, this is the oldest synagogue in Europe. Legend has it that the foundation stones were flown over by angels from the Holy Temple in Jerusalem under the condition (*al tnay* in Hebrew) that they should be returned on Judgement Day, hence the name Alt-Neu in German or Old-New in English.

Next door is the former **Jewish Town Hall** (Maiselova 18), dating from the 1560s, with a rococo façade in various delicate pinks, and a Hebraic clock whose hands turn anti-clockwise. The money to build the Town Hall and neighbouring High Synagogue was provided by Mordecai Maisel, a contemporary of Rabbi Löw's (*see page 16*) and a man of inordinate wealth and

the rhythm
of the city

www.everydayprague.com

Jewish Prague

For more than a millennium, Jews have lived and worked in Prague, and for most of that time they have inhabited a tiny portion of Staré Město. Their history – at times turbulent and frequently terrifying – can be traced through the monuments that remain in the triangle of land bounded by Pařížská, Kaprova and the Vltava. The first Jewish settlers preferred the land across the river, but at the time of the first crusade, in 1096, they were rounded up and enclosed in the area that is now Josefov.

Surrounded by high ghetto walls, and subject to the vicissitudes of royal rulers, the Jews' first break came in 1245 when Přemysl Otakar II declared that they were royal property whose damage would be punishable by death. Even so, discrimination, persecution and pogroms were commonplace. At Passover in 1389, for instance, 3,000 Jews were massacred by rampaging Christians. Yet Jewish Prague was a vibrant, productive place, producing numerous entrepreneurs and scholars of the highest calibre, such as Mordecai Maisel and Rabbi Löw (*see page 16*).

It was many more centuries before conditions significantly improved. By his 1781 Edict of Tolerance, the enlightened Joseph II (after whom the quarter was named), among other liberal measures, permitted Jews to live in other parts of town and no longer forced them to wear yellow garments. After the revolution of 1848 the walls of the ghetto were finally demolished and Jews were granted the rights of citizens.

The inter-war years of the twentieth century were an especially fruitful time for Prague's Jewish community, producing a large group of writers including, most famously of all, **Franz Kafka**. He was born on the border between the Jewish Quarter and the Old Town, an opposition that prefigured the antagonism and contradictions of his life and writing. After the ghetto was cleared at the end of the nineteenth century, Kafka wrote: 'Living within us are still those dark corners, mysterious corridors, blind windows, dirty backyards and noisy inns. Our hearts know nothing about the new sanitation. The unhealthy Jewish town within us is much more real than the hygienic new town around.'

The *fin-de-siècle* tenements that replaced the ghetto tenements can seem eerie, not least because out of a pre-war population of around 50,000, only 1,500 Jews remain in the city today. Although restitution of property is bringing a little Jewish life back to the area, Josefov is still more of a sad museum to a culture that no longer exists in the city – and an overpriced tourist trap that swarms with crowds of visitors all year round. It's all distastefully like what Hitler had in mind when he collected together in Prague a vast range of Jewish paraphernalia for his intended Museum of an Extinct Race.

JEWISH MUSEUM
The **Jewish Museum** in Josefov consists of five separate buildings: the Klausen, Maisel and Pinkas synagogues, the Old Jewish Cemetery and the Ceremonial Hall. For detailed reviews of all five, *see page 94*.

Matana
Maiselova 15, Prague 1 (232 1954/www.tours.cz/ matana/matana@ms.anet.cz). Metro Staroměstská/ 17, 18 tram. **Open** 9am-6.30pm Sun-Fri.
Map 3 H3
This Jewish travel agency sells tickets for the Jewish Museum sights, the Old-New Synagogue, tours of Prague and trips to Terezin (*see p227*). The knowledgeable English-speaking staff can also book boat tours, meals in kosher restaurants and accommodation.

discriminating taste. The Town Hall has been the centre of the Jewish community ever since. The **High Synagogue** (Vysoká synagoga), which was built at the same time as the Town Hall and is attached to it, was returned to the community early in 1994 and is now, once again, a working synagogue serving the Jewish community (not open to sightseers).

Further down Maiselova you'll find the **Maisel Synagogue** (*see page 95*), also funded by the wealthy sixteenth-century money-lending mayor. Sadly, the current building is a reconstruction of the original (apparently the most splendid synagogue of them all), which burnt down in the great fire of 1689 when all 316 houses of the ghetto and 11 synagogues were destroyed. The present structure, sandwiched between tenement blocks, dates from 1892-1905, and houses a permanent exhibition of Jewish history from its origins in Bohemia to the nineteenth century.

On U starého hřbitova is the **Old Jewish Cemetery** (*see page 95*), a small, unruly patch of ground that contains the remains of thousands of bodies. Forbidden to enlarge their burial ground, the Jews had no choice but to bury bodies on top of each other in an estimated 12 layers, so that today crazy mounds of earth are jammed with lopsided stone tablets.

Typical post-ghetto architecture in Maiselova in the heart of Josefov.

To the left of the entrance is the **Klausen Synagogue** (Klausova synagoga; *see page 94*), built in 1694 by the same craftsmen responsible for many of Prague's baroque churches. Inside, the pink marble Holy Ark could almost pass for a Catholic altar were it not for the gold inscriptions in Hebrew. Here you'll find displayed various religious artefacts and prints as well as explanations of Jewish customs and traditions. Facing the synagogue is the **Ceremonial House** (*see page 94*), designed in the style of a Romanesque castle at the beginning of this century, which hosts an exhibition of funeral ceremony and ornament.

On the other side of the cemetery is the **Pinkas Synagogue** (*see page 95*), built as the private house of the powerful Horowitz family in 1607-1625. The building is now primarily given over to a memorial to the 77,297 Jewish men, women and children who died in Nazi concentration camps according to German transport lists. Since the inception of the project, other historical sources have upped the number of names to over 78,000. The names of every one have been painted on the walls since April 1997.

Josefov's final synagogue, the **Spanish Synagogue** (Španělská synagóga), was built just outside the boundaries of the ghetto in 1868, on Dušní. It was constructed for the growing number of Reform Jews, and its façade is of a rich Moorish design. Since being returned to the community it has been meticulously restored and is now a working synagogue again. It is scheduled to open to the public as well in November 1998 with a permanent exhibition on recent Jewish history in the Czech lands up to the beginning of World War II.

Northern Staré Město

The site along the banks of the Vltava wasn't incorporated into the new design of Josefov, and the grandiose buildings have their backs turned upon the old ghetto. Going down Kaprova towards the river will bring you to **Náměstí Jana Palacha**, named after Jan Palach, the student who set himself on fire on 16 January 1969 in protest at the Soviet invasion (*see page 25*). Dominating the square is the **Rudolfinum** (Dům umělců) or the 'House of Arts', built between 1876 and 1884 (and named after Rudolf II) in neo-classical style and entirely funded by the Czech Savings Bank to display its 'patriotic, provincial feelings'. You can see its corporate logo, the bee of thrift, in the paws of the two sphinxes with remarkably ample breasts who guard the riverfront entrance. In 1918 the concert hall became home to the parliament of the new Republic. When Chamberlain returned to England from meeting Hitler in 1938 disclaiming responsibility for the 'quarrel in a faraway country between people of whom we know nothing', it was here that 250,000 of these unknown people came to take an oath and pledge themselves to the defence of the Republic. The Nazis, having little use for a parliament building, turned it back into a concert hall and called it 'The German House of Arts'. Legend has it that a statue of the Jewish composer Mendelssohn was ordered to be removed for obvious reasons, but the workmen, not knowing what Mendelssohn looked like, took their lessons in racial science to heart and removed the figure with the biggest nose – which turned out to be Richard Wagner. Opposite, with its back to the Old Jewish Cemetery, is the fine **Museum of Decorative Arts** (*see page 90*).

Few visitors make it over to the streets of semi-derelict art nouveau tenement houses in northern Staré Město, but they are well worth inspection, even without the attraction of St **Agnes's Convent** (Klášter sv. Anežky české), the oldest example of Gothic architecture in the city. Its founder St Agnes died a full 700 years before the Pope deigned to make her a saint. Popular opinion held that miracles would accompany her canonisation, and sure enough within five days of the Vatican's announcement the Velvet Revolution was under way. The convent is now owned by the **National Gallery**, which displays its nineteenth-century Czech collection here (*see page 97*).

Nearby is **Dlouhá** or 'Long Street', which contained no less than 13 breweries in the fourteenth century when beer champion Charles IV forbade the export of hops. These days its main attraction is the **Roxy** at no.33 (*see page 204*). It's a semi-demolished cinema that was once the headquarters of the Communist Youth Association and is now the city's most atmospheric club. In the enjoyably quiet streets between Dlouhá and the river lie several convivial bars and cafés, including the French-style **Chez Marcel** (*see page 140*), the Irish-style **Molly Malone's** (*see page 141*), the neo-Bohemian-style **Blatouch** (*see page 139*) and that Czech all-American **Žíznivý pes** (Thirsty Dog; *see page 142*).

Sights

Bethlehem Chapel

(Betlémská kaple) Betlémské náměstí, Prague 1 (no phone). Metro Národní třída/6, 9, 18, 22 tram.
Open 9am-6pm, *winter* 9am-5pm, daily.
Admission 30 Kč adults; 20 Kč children, students.
Map 3 H4
The Bethlehem Chapel, a huge, plain, barn-like structure dating from 1391, was where the proto-Protestant Jan Hus delivered sermons in the Czech language accusing the papacy of being, among other things, an institution of Satan. Unsurprisingly, he was called to task and burnt at the stake in 1415. His last request before being thrown to the flames was for 'history to be kind to the Bethlehem Chapel'. In response, the fanatical Jesuits bought up the site and promptly turned it into a woodshed. In the eighteenth century, German merchants moved in and built two houses within the walls. Hus's wish was finally fulfilled under the communists who regarded him as a working-class revolutionary thwarted by the forces of imperialism and spared no expense in the extensive restoration of the chapel. Three of the original walls remain and still show the remnants of the scriptures that were painted on them in Czech to enable people to follow the service. A team of friendly ladies are happy to answer any queries. Upstairs is a small exhibition, captioned in spectacularly broken English, that chronologically runs through the development of Hussitism and the history of the chapel.

Church of Our Lady before Týn

(Kostel Matky boží před Týnem) Staroměstské náměstí 14, Prague 1 (232 2801). Metro Náměstí Republiky or Staroměstská/17, 18 tram. **Closed** at time of going to press, but normally open 30 minutes before services at 5.30pm Mon-Fri; 1pm Sat; 11.30am, 9pm Sun. **Map 3 J3**

The twin towers of Týn topped by what look like witches' hats are one of the landmarks of the Old Town. The church dates from the same period as St Vitus's Cathedral (the late fourteenth century), but whereas St Vitus's was constructed to show the power of King Charles IV, Týn was a church for the people. As such it became a centre of the reforming Hussites in the fifteenth century, before being commandeered by the Jesuits in the seventeenth. They commissioned the baroque interior, which blends uncomfortably with the original Gothic structure. At the end of the southern aisle is the tombstone of **Tycho Brahe**, Rudolf II's personal astronomer, famous for his false nose-piece and his fine line in gnomic utterances. If you look closely at the red marble slab, you'll see the former, while the lines above provide evidence of the latter, translating as 'Better to be than to seem to be'. Lit up at night, the Týn looks like some kind of monstrous spacecraft. If you're lucky, you may see bats swooping around the steeples at dusk, completing the fairy-tale Gothic image.

Church of St James

(Sv. Jakuba) Malá Štupartská. Metro Náměstí Republiky/ 5, 14, 26 tram. **Open** 9.30am-12.30pm, 2.30-4pm, Mon-Sat; 2-3.45pm Sun. **Map 3 J3**.
St James's boasts a grand total of 21 altars, some fine frescoes and a dessicated human forearm hanging next to the door. This belonged to a jewel thief who broke into the church in the fifteenth century and tried to make off with some gems from the statue of the Virgin. The Madonna grabbed him by the arm and kept him captive until the offending limb had to be cut off. However, its appearance – it looks like a piece of dried up salami – could be explained by the fact that the church's most prominent worshippers were members of the Butchers' Guild.

Clementinum

(Klementinum) Mariánské náměstí 4, Prague 1 (2166 6311). Metro Staroměstská/17, 18 tram. Library **Open** 9am-7pm Mon-Sat. *Chapel of Mirrors open for concerts only.* **Map 3 G3/4**
In the twelfth and thirteenth centuries this complex of buildings was the Prague headquarters of the Inquisition, and when the Jesuits moved in during the sixteenth century, kicking out the Dominicans who had set up home there in the meantime, they carried on the tradition of fear, intimidation and forcible baptising of the city's Jews. They replaced the medieval **Church of St Clement** with a much grander design of their own (rebuilt in 1711-15 and now used by the Greek Catholic Church) and gradually constructed the building of today, which is arranged around five courtyards, demolishing several streets and 30 houses on the way. Their grandest work was the **Church of St Saviour** (sv. Salvátor), whose opulent but grimy façade faces the Staré Město end of Charles Bridge and was designed to reawaken the joys of Catholicism in the largely Protestant populace. It was built between 1578 and 1653 by the Jesuits and was the most important Jesuit church in Bohemia. The Jesuits' main tool was education and their **library**, only occasionally open to the public, is a masterpiece. It was finished in 1727, and has a magnificent *trompe l'oeil* ceiling split into three parts, showing the three levels of knowledge, with the Dome of Wisdom occupying the central space. However, the ceiling started crumbling and to prevent the whole structure from collapsing the **Chapel of Mirrors** was built next door in 1725 to bolster the walls. The interior, decorated with fake pink marble and the original mirrors, is lovely. Mozart used to play here and it is still used for chamber concerts today, which is the only way you can get in to see it. At the very centre of the complex is the **Astronomical Tower**, where Kepler, who lived on nearby Karlova, came to stargaze. It was used until the 1920s for calculating high noon: when the sun crossed a line on the wall behind a small aperture at the top, the Castle would be signalled and a cannon fired.

House of the Lords of Kunštát and Poděbrady

(Dům pánů z Kunštátu a Poděbrad) Řetězová 3, Prague 1 (2421 2299 ext 22). Metro Staroměstská/17, 18 tram. **Open** *May-Sept* 10am-6pm Tue-Sun. **Admission** 20 Kč. **Map 3 H4**

This house is one of the few accessible examples of Romanesque architecture in Prague. It was begun in 1250, originally built as a walled-in farmstead, but like its neighbours in the Old Town was partially buried in the flood-protection scheme of the late thirteenth century, which reduced the vaulted ground floor to a cellar. By the mid-fifteenth century it was quite palatial, a suitably grand dwelling for George of Poděbrady, who set out from here for his election as king. The upper storeys were later greatly altered. Now it houses a modern art display and an interesting little exhibition in honour of George of Poděbrady whose well-meaning scheme for international co-operation is hailed as a forerunner of the League of Nations.

Old-New Synagogue

(Staronová synagoga) Červená 2, Prague 1 (232 1954). Metro Staroměstská/17, 18 tram. **Open** *Nov-Mar* 9am-5pm Sun-Thur; 9am-2pm Fri; *Apr-June* 9am-6pm Sun-Thur; 9am-5pm Fri. **Admission** 200 Kč adults; 140 Kč children, students; free under-6s. **Map 3 H2**

The Old-New Synagogue is a rather forlorn piece of medievalism. The oldest survivor of the ghetto and the spiritual centre of the Jewish community for over 600 years, it has now been returned to the community and is still used for services. The austere exterior walls give no clues to its peculiar Gothic interior. An extra rib was added to the usual vaulting pattern to avoid the symbolism of the cross. Instead the décor and structure revolve around the number 12, after the 12 tribes of Israel: there are 12 windows, 12 bunches of sculpted grapes, and clusters of 12 vine leaves decorate the pillar bases. The interior was left untouched for 500 years as a reminder of the blood spilled here during the pogrom of 1389, when the men, women and children who sought sanctuary in the synagogue were slaughtered by Christians. The nineteenth-century neo-Gothic crusaders, however, couldn't resist the temptation to 'restore' the original look and slapped a fresh coat of paint over the top.

Oak seats line the walls facing the *bema*, or platform, protected by a Gothic grille, from which the Torah has been read aloud every day for more than 700 years (except during the Nazi occupation). The tall seat marked by a gold star belonged to Rabbi Löw *(see p16)*, the most famous inhabitant of the ghetto. The rabbi lived to the age of 97, and a sculpture by Ladislav Saloun to the right of the New Town Hall (in Mariánské náměsti) depicts the manner of his death. Unable to approach the scholar, who was always absorbed in study of the scriptures, Death hid in a rose that was offered to Löw by his innocent granddaughter. The rabbi's grave is in the Old Jewish Cemetery, recognisable by the quantity of pebbles and wishes on scraps of paper that are placed upon the tomb to this day.

Despite its historical and religious significance, there's not much to see inside the synagogue and precious little explanation.

Old Town Hall & Astronomical Clock

(Staroměstská radnice/orloj) Staroměstské náměstí, Prague 1 (2448 2909). Metro Staroměstská. **Open** 11am-5pm Mon; 9am-6pm Tue-Sun (until 5pm in winter). **Admission** 30 Kč adults; 20 Kč children. **Map 3 H3**

The Old Town Hall, established in 1338, was cobbled together over the centuries out of several adjoining houses, but only around half of the original remains standing today. The present Gothic and Renaissance portions have been carefully restored since the Nazis blew up a large chunk of it in the last days of World War II. The Old Town coat of arms, adopted by the whole city after 1784, adorns the front of the **Old Council Hall**, and the **clock tower**, built in 1364, has a viewing platform that is definitely worth the climb. The twelfth-century dungeon in the basement became the headquarters of the Resistance during the Prague Uprising in 1944 when reinforcements and supplies were spirited away from the Nazis all over the Old Town via the connecting underground passages. Four scorched beams in the basement (not open to the public) remain as a testament to those Resistance members who fell there. On the side of the clock tower is a plaque in four languages, marked by crossed machine guns, giving thanks to the Soviet soldiers who liberated the city in 1945. There's also a pot of soil from Dukla, a pass in Slovakia where the worst battle of the Czechoslovak liberation took place, resulting in the death of 84,000 Red Army soldiers.

The **Astronomical Clock** (orloj) has been ticking, tocking and pulling in the crowds since 1490. Every hour on the hour between 8am and 8pm crowds gather to watch wooden saint statuettes emerge from behind trap doors while below a lurid lesson in medieval morality is enacted by Greed, Vanity, Death and the Turk. Much more than a mere clock, the Orloj shows the movement of the sun and moon through the 12 signs of the zodiac as well as giving the time in three different formats: Central European Time, Old Czech Time (in which the 24 hour day is reckoned around the setting of the sun) and, for some reason, Babylonian Time. A particularly resilient Prague legend concerns the fate of the clockmaker, Master Hanuš, who was blinded by the vainglorious burghers of the town to prevent him from repeating his triumph elsewhere. In retaliation Hanuš thrust his hands inside the clock and simultaneously ended his life and (for a short time at least) that of his masterpiece. Below the clock face is a calendar painted by Josef Mánes in 1865, depicting saints' days, astrological signs and the labours of the months.

Powder Gate

(Prašná brána) U prašné brány, Prague 1. Metro Náměstí Republiky/5, 14, 26 tram. **Open** 10am-6pm daily. **Closed** winter. **Admission** 20 Kč adults; 10 Kč under-6s. **Map 4 K3**

The Powder Gate, or Tower, is a piece of late fifteenth-century flotsam, a lonely relic of the fortifications that used to ring the whole town. The bridge that incongruously connects it to the art nouveau masterpiece of Obecní dům (the **Municipal House**; *see p59*) used to give access to the royal palace that stood on the same site during the tenth century. By the mid-fourteenth century Charles IV had founded the New Town, and the city's boundaries had changed. The Powder Gate remained mouldering until it at last gained a purpose, and a name, when it became a store for gunpowder in 1575. This unfortunately made it a legitimate target for invading Prussian troops and it was severely damaged during the siege of 1757. It was once again left to crumble until the neo-Gothic master Josef Mocker gave it a new roof and redecorated the sides in the 1870s. Today you can climb a precipitous staircase to the top.

St Michael's Mystery

Michalská 27-29, Prague 1 (2421 3253). Metro Staroměstská/6, 9, 18, 22 tram. **Open** 10am-8pm daily. **Admission** 355 Kč. **Credit** EC, MC, V. **Map 3 H4**

A massive cash infusion has transformed St Michael's Church from ruined baroque cathedral into the supremely kitschy St Michael's Mystery. Billed as a 'Kafka-esque' tour through Prague history, it assails visitors with 14 Disney-style scenes and audio in English, German and Czech, featuring talking file drawers, polystyrene figures from the Old Town clock tower, a souped-up theatrical elevator and old newsreel footage. If all that isn't enough to justify the staggering entry fee, visitors are also granted the privilege of a fries and coffee at quadruple the usual price in the adjoining, sensitively designed 'Snack Bar Mike's'.

Nové Město

Real life in Prague starts beyond the Old Town tourist precincts.

Maps 4, 5 & 6

Nové Město, the New Town, is far from new and no longer a township. It was founded in 1348 by Charles IV, who'd had a premonition that the Old Town would be destroyed by fire and floods. Despite frequent fires and floods, the Old Town is still standing, but the decision was a good one: his far-sighted urban planning, which led to the creation of wide boulevards and broad squares, has meant the area has adapted well to the rigours of modern life. While tourists trawl Malá Strana and the Old Town, Nové Město is where the real business of Prague daily life goes on: offices and shops, cinemas and theatres, fast-food outlets and financial institutions are all located here.

Old and New Towns meet along the line of Národní třída, Na příkopě and Revoluční. Nové Město, bounded to the east by traffic-pounded Wilsonova, wraps around the Old Town and Josefov, stretching from the river to the north down to Vyšehrad in the south.

Wenceslas Square

Wenceslas Square (Václavské náměstí), once known as the Horse Market, is the hub of city life. You'll find yourself passing through it several times a day. More of a broad boulevard than a square, it was laid out over 600 years ago under the auspices of Charles IV, and has always been a good place to check out the changing fortunes of the city. This century, Nazis, communists, anti-communists and a naked Allen Ginsberg have all paraded its length.

The May Day parades have these days been replaced by a sleazy collection of pimps, pick-pockets and crooked cab drivers. You'll be assailed by the smell of frying sausages and if you're a fat businessman, by any number of thin prostitutes. The shops, which used to have dull names like House of Fashion, House of Food or House of Shoes, have been privatised and glamourised, though they're still more interesting for their architecture than their contents.

The bottom end of the square is pedestrianised, invariably thronging with tour parties, backpackers and Euro-teens heading for the last surviving disco (there used to be a clutch of them here) whose lights pulse out over the scene. The kiosks here are the place in town to buy foreign newspapers and magazines.

A tour of the square

Almost every architectural style of the last 150 years is represented somewhere on the square. Starting at the lower end by the newsstands, the revolutionary **Baťa** building (Ludvík Kysela, 1927-9) at no.6, with its massive expanses of plate glass, was an important functionalist structure. Pioneering cubist architect Emil Králíček, together with Matěj Blecha, built the asiatic-inspired **Adam Pharmacy** at no.8, giving it a cubist interior. Jan Kotěra's first building in Prague, **Peterka House**, stands a few doors up at no.12, signalling art nouveau's first moves towards more geometric forms. Unashamedly retro, the **Wiehl House** (1896) on the corner of Vodičkova was built by Antonín Wiehl in neo-Renaissance style and decorated with elaborate sgraffito (*see page 36*). Beyond are the arcades of the **Lucerna** complex (*see page 57* **Arcades**) and Blecha's **Supich Building** (1913-16) at nos.38-40, complete with likeably bizarre Assyrian-style masks adorning its façade. The second-floor balcony of the **Melantrich Building** (no.30) became the unlikely venue for one of the most astounding events of the Velvet Revolution: on 24 November 1989, in front of a crowd of over 300,000 people, Václav Havel and Alexander Dubček stepped forward here and embraced, signifying the end of 21 years of 'normalisation'. Within weeks the entire cabinet had resigned.

Up at the top end, and crowning the whole square, is Josef Schulz's massive neo-Renaissance **National Museum** (1885-90; *see page 91*), a swaggering, monumental nineteenth-century block, cut off from the rest of the square by an expressway. Across the road is the ugly 1970s building that housed the Federal Assembly until the Czech-Slovak split in 1993. The building has now become the new base of **Radio Free Europe**, which, after playing its part in the toppling of totalitarianism, moved in to take advantage of the cheap rent.

Also at the top end of the square are two of Prague's most symbolic sites – one ancient in inspiration, one modern. The former is Josef Václav Myslbek's huge equestrian **statue of St Wenceslas** (Václav). Although a monument to the Czech patron saint has stood here since the late seventeenth century, Myslbek's serene prince wasn't unveiled until 1912. The surrounding statues of saints Agnes, Adalbert, Procopius

The **National Theatre** – *few buildings are more powerfully emotive for Czechs.*

and Ludmila, Wenceslas's mother, were added in the 1920s. The other site, a little further down the square, is where, on 16 January 1969, Jan Palach burned himself alive in protest at the Soviet invasion of the previous August. The still-flower-strewn '**memorial to the victims of communism**' commemorates his sacrifice, and that of Jan Zajic, who immolated himself on the same spot a month later.

Coming back down the north side, past the Soviet-style **Jalta Hotel**, is perhaps the square's best-known building, the glittering (on the outside at least) art nouveau **Grand Hotel Evropa** at nos.25-27, built by Alois Drýak and Bendřich Bendelmayer (1903-6). Passing the carbuncle that is the **Krone/Julius Meinl** department store, at the end of the square is Antonín Pfeiffer's **Koruna Palace** (1912-14), a fine example of the 'Babylonian'-inspired buildings that enjoyed a vogue at the time as a result of well-publicised contemporary archaeological digs in Mesopotamia.

Northern Nové Město

The pedestrianised **Na příkopě** runs from Wenceslas Square to Náměstí Republiky along the line of what was once a moat. It has been quaintly dubbed 'Prague's Wall Street' because of its concentration of banks, and the financial institutions range from the neo-Renaissance **Živnostenská banka** at no.20 to the art deco **Komerční banka** at no.28. With the opening of branches of **Planet Hollywood** and **TGI Friday's** it seems clear which way the tone of the street is going. **Čedok**, the national tourist office, is at no.18. Here you can buy tickets to major events, as well as international train and bus tickets. There is one surprisingly good restaurant and coffee bar hidden among all the tourist places – **Segafredo** (*see page 125*) at no.10.

Dominating **Náměstí Republiky** is the luscious art nouveau **Municipal House** (Obecní dům; *see below*), which stands on the border of the Old and New Towns. Built between 1905 and 1911, and recently restored, this extravagant combination of colour and curves was where Czechoslovakia was signed into existence in 1918. Incongruously attached to it is the blackened Gothic **Powder Gate** (Prašná brána; *see page 52*), which predates it by half a millennium.

Facing the Municipal House is the neo-classical former customs house, **U Hybernů** (The Hibernians), now the site for occasional exhibitions. Running east from Náměstí Republiky is Hybernská, named after the Irish monks who settled here in the sixteenth century after falling foul of Elizabeth I. Their contribution to city life was to introduce the potato, an event from which Czech cuisine has never recovered. The street itself is unremarkable save for the presence of the **American Center for Culture and Commerce** in the baroque Lidový dům at no.7, a building which ironically used to house the Lenin Museum. At no.4 once stood the Café Arco, meeting place of the self-styled 'Arconauts' who included Franz Kafka and Max Brod. Across the road in the Masaryk railway station – Prague's first, built in 1845 – is the late-night buffet, serving fried cheese until 11pm every night to the cream of the city's unsavouries.

The largely anonymous streets south of here contain Prague's newest museum, the **Mucha Museum** (*see page 90*), on Panská, and the main post office, on Jindřišská. The latter is an extraordinary place – a covered courtyard filled with newly modernised booths but still bustling with all the routine paperwork transactions of life in an extremely bureaucratic state.

Two buildings make it worth braving the streaming traffic of the Wilsonova expressway, bounding Nové Město in the east. The **State Opera** (Státní opera; *see page 194*), built by the Viennese architects Fellner and Helmer in 1888, was something of a last gasp assertion of identity by Prague's German community in the midst of the great Czech National Revival. More interesting, though, is the city's **Main Station** (Hlavní nádraží; also known as Wilsonovo nádraží). Smelly, crumbling, inhabited by lowlifes and one of Prague's main gay cruises, the station might seem an unlikely place to seek out the pleasures of Prague's bourgeois age. That it had been dedicated first to Emperor Franz Joseph and then to the American President Wilson gave the communists two very good reasons to plant a high-speed bypass outside its front door and create a modern soulless extension beneath. The upper levels, which were left to rot in obscurity until the **Fantova Kavárna** opened there recently, are an atmospheric remnant of a bygone age. The restaurant contains some of the best art nouveau murals anywhere in Prague, with languorous women serving as a backdrop to the diehard beer drinkers beneath. The cavernous lower levels are tacky, dirty, bustly and a must for fans of communist architecture.

Just north of Náměstí Republiky is the **Kotva** department store (*see page 154*). This was once one of the shopping showpieces of the Eastern Bloc, and 75,000 people a day would come from as far away as Bulgaria to snap up its fine selection of acrylic sweaters, orange plastic cruets and official portraits of Gustav Husák. It has now been overhauled and the communist idea of fashion replaced by the German one. There's another classic communist-era department store, **Bílá labuť** (*see page 154*), not far away on busy Na Poříčí; its glass-curtain wall is a classic functionalist feature. Almost opposite is a rare example of the rondo-cubist style: Pavel Janák's Banka Legii from the early 1920s. On the other side of the hideous Wilsonova flyover is the beleagured neo-Renaissance block containing the **Museum of the City of Prague** (*see page 91*).

Further north, beyond the **Postage Stamp Museum** (*see page 95*), on nábřeží Ludvíka Svobody next to the river, stands a monolithic structure, recognisable by a dome that glows orange at night. This is the Ministry of Transport, built in the 1920s and for a spell the HQ of the Central Committee of the communist party. It was here that on 21 August 1968 tanks arrived to escort Alexander Dubček to the Kremlin where he was flown for 'fraternal discussions'.

Southern Nové Město

Just south of the Old Town end of Wenceslas Square is Jungmannovo náměstí, site of the world's only **cubist lamp-post**. Tucked away in an obscure corner, Emil Králíček's bizarre and somewhat forlorn-looking creation, much derided when it was completed in 1913, has become something of a Prague cultural icon. It stands in front of the towering church of **Our Lady of the Snows** (*see below*), a wannabe St Vitus's Cathedral. A path from here leads to the unexpected oasis of the **Franciscan Gardens** (Františkánská zahrada), a haven of clipped-hedge calm in the middle of the city.

From Jungmannovo náměstí, Národní třída (National Avenue) divides the Old and New towns, meeting the river at the most Legií. Národní was the playground of generations of Czechs in the last century and the battleground of another generation this century. Standing proudly on the banks of the Vltava, topped by a crown of gold and with sculptures of bucking stallions lining the balustrade, the **National Theatre** (*see also page 218*) is a product and symbol of the fervour of nineteenth-century Czech nationalism. It took 20 years to persuade the general public to cough up the money to begin construction, and from 1868 to 1881 to build it. Then, days before the curtain was to go up on the first performance, it was gutted by fire in a single night. An emotive appeal, launched immediately by the leading lights of the city's cultural institutions, raised enough money to start all over again in just six weeks. In 1883 the building finally opened with a gala performance of *Libuše*, an opera about the mythical origins of the Czech nation written especially for the occasion by Smetana. A bronze memorial halfway down on the south side (by no.20) pays tribute to the events of 17 November 1989, where the violent police suppression of a student demonstration sparked the beginning of the Velvet Revolution.

The department store on the corner of Spálená is a barometer of the changes that have occurred since then. It used to be called Máj after the most sacred date in the communist calendar, 1 May. It then belonged to K-mart and became a source of peanut butter for the legions of Americans in town. These days it's owned by **Tesco** (*see page 154*).

By the memorial at no.20 is **Reduta** (*see page 200*), the venerable jazz club where Bill Clinton tested his saxophone skills before a global audience. Further down at no.7, through an exquisite wrought-iron entrance, is **Viola**, once a literary hangout that sports one of the three framed Václav Havel signatures to be found in various drinking holes around town. Next door, with a fine view across the river to the Castle, is the redoubtable **Slavia** (*see page 142*), once the centre of Prague's café life and, after a long closure, happily reopened and hoping to regain its past glory.

The embankment running south contains a fine if unremarkable collection of art nouveau apartment houses. At no.78 is the block containing Václav Havel's flat. In a deliberate break with tradition Havel declined to move into the swanky presidential quarters at the Castle and stayed in his own down-at-heel tenement across the river. Now the gesture has been made, admired and written about, he has bought an altogether more upmarket residence in Prague 6. Not that he can be blamed, however, since the plot next door was for some time a building site on which a controversial Frank Gehry construction now stands: the so-called **'Fred & Ginger' building**, which supposedly resembles the pair of dancing Hollywood stars. Most Czechs hate it; many visitors love it.

The climax of this art nouveau promenade is **Palackého náměstí**, which is dominated by the monumental sculpture by Stanislav Sucharda of nineteenth-century historian František Palacký, who dedicated 46 years of his life to writing a history of the Czech people. Palacký looks pretty solemn, seated on an enormous pedestal, book in hand and utterly oblivious to the bevy of beauties and demons flying around him. Behind him rise the two modern spires of the altogether more ancient **Emmaus Monastery** or Monastery of the Slavs (klášter Na Slovanech), which was founded by Charles IV, the towers added after the baroque versions were destroyed by a stray Allied bomb in World War II.

The island closest to the embankment, at the bottom of Národní třída, is **Slovanský Island**. In the days before slacking was an art form, Berlioz came here and was appalled at the 'idlers, wasters and ne'er-do-wells' who congregated on the island. With a recommendation like that it's hard to resist the outdoor café or a few lazy hours in one of the rowing boats for hire. There's also a fine statue of Božena Němcová, as seen on the back of the 500 Kč note. She was the Czech version of George Sand, a celebrated novelist whose private life scandalised polite society. At the southern tip is the art gallery **Výstavní síň Mánes** (*see page*

*The irreverent **'Fred & Ginger' building** sashays along the Vltava embankment.*

Arcades

Most of the buildings up and down Wenceslas Square are riddled with *pasáže* – passages – providing covered shopping areas and connections between neighbouring streets. The majority were built in the second decade of the twentieth century, a full hundred years after the first arcades began appearing in Paris.

In their nineteenth-century heyday, the arcades of cities like Paris, Moscow or Berlin were enclaves of small shops offering luxury goods – precursors of the department store, which largely replaced them. Those in Prague, by contrast, were built later, in the early days of cinema. Most of the Wenceslas Square arcades are constructed around movie houses, such as the **Rokoko** passage, which contains Prague's most uncomfortable cinema, the **Hvězda**. The **Blaník** at no.56, the **Jalta** at no.43 and the **Praha** at no.17 contain cinemas and very little else.

Most famous is the **Lucerna**, the ground floor of a seven-storey complex built between 1912 and 1916 by a consortium including Václav Havel's grandfather. The reinforced concrete structure with suspended ceiling was a ground-breaking piece of early modern architecture, and despite an unfortunate 1960s redecoration, still impresses with its air of faded grandeur. Lucerna and its adjoining halls run between Wenceslas Square, Štěpánská, Vodičkova and V Jámě streets, and houses a rock club (*see page 198*), a beautiful art nouveau concert hall, the **Lucerna** cinema (Prague's prettiest, which also includes a quiet café; *see page 183*) and all manner of strange, small shops.

On the other side of Vodičkova, the **Světozor** passage contains another cinema, one of Prague's best ice-cream shops and an extraordinary piece of stained glass advertising the now-struggling Czech electronics company, Tesla.

The trade in luxuries is rapidly returning to the passages of Prague. The **Černá rože** ('Black Rose') at Na příkopě 12, for example, has gone from musty to overtly trendy, with obligatory designer shops cropping up seemingly overnight. The most complete postmodern makeover, though, is certainly the **Koruna**, at the bottom end of Wenceslas Square. This art nouveau arcade was recently renovated and now houses the **Bontonland Megastore** music shop (*see page 168*). Here is the probable shape of passages to come.

102), a 1930s functionalist building incongruously attached to a medieval water tower. The left-wing intelligentsia used to gather here between the wars, as did the Union of Propertyless and Progressive Students (presumably because they had no home to go to), while in 1989 Civic Forum churned out posters and leaflets from here. The island is also home to the newly restored cultural centre Žofín – a large yellow building dating from the 1880s that has long been associated with the Czech cultural psyche, and hosted tea dances and concerts until just before World War II.

Around Karlovo náměstí

There are some fine backstreets to explore between Národní třída and Karlovo náměstí, as well as some major thoroughfares. Jungmannova contains the **Bontonland (Supraphon)** and **Popron** music shops (*see pages 168 & 171*). The best-known fixture in this area is **U Fleků** (*see page 145*), at Křemencova 11, the world's oldest still-operating brew pub and the place to go if you want to unload some cash and meet a lot of Germans bellowing drinking songs (if you can put up with that, the beer tastes wonderful). Its entrance is marked by a picturesque old clock, hung like a tavern sign. At Spálená 82 is the **Diamant House**, designed by Emil Králíček in 1912, which takes its name from the broken-up prisms that constitute the façade. The ground floor has now become a Škoda showroom and the neon strip lights that adorn it are a dubious aesthetic addition. A nice touch is the cubist arch which shelters a piece of baroque statuary and bridges the gap, literally and historically, between this building and the eighteenth-century Church of the Holy Trinity next door.

Karlovo náměstí is an enormous expanse that used to be a cattle market and the site of Charles IV's relic fair. Once a year he would wheel out his collection of saints' skulls, toenails and underwear, the townsfolk dutifully gawped, cripples would throw down their crutches and the blind would miraculously regain their sight. These days you're most likely to come across the square in a night tram, minor miracles in their own right. Its other attractions include the fourteenth-century **New Town Hall** (Novoměstská radnice). It was from here that several Catholic councillors were ejected from an upstairs window in 1419 – and the word 'defenestration' entered the language (*see also page 73* **Window dropping**).

On the eastern side of the square is the splendidly restored Jesuit **Church of St Ignatius** (sv. Ignác), an early baroque affair in cream, pink and orange stucco, with gold trimmings. No.24 was once a restaurant used for training waiters employed by the secret police. The James Bonds of the catering world learnt how to plant bugs in

dissidents' soup and dish up the sauce to their eager employers. In the south-west corner is the **Faust House** (Faustův dům), an ornate seventeenth-century building that has more than a few legends attached to it. Edward Kelley, the earless English alchemist, lived here, as apparently did the Prince of Darkness, who carried off a penniless student and secured the house a place in Prague's mythic heritage.

Halfway across the square on Resslova is baroque **Cathedral of Sts Cyril & Methodius** (*see below*), scene of one of the most dramatic and poignant events of World War II – the last stand of the assassins of Reichsprotektor Reinhard Heydrich. Going in the opposite direction up the hill is Ječná, where Dvořák died at no.14; but rather than staring at the plaque on the wall, go to the **Dvořák Museum** (*see page 92*) on nearby Ke Karlovu, where you can catch a chamber recital. It's housed in a gorgeous Dientzenhofer-designed summer house – the Villa Amerika – surrounded nowadays by incongruous modern bits of concrete.

At the far end of the street is a museum of a very different sort – the **Police Museum** (*see page 94*). Brek, the stuffed wonder dog responsible for thwarting the defection of hundreds of dissidents, has been given a decent burial, but there's still plenty of gruesome exhibits to delight the morbid.

If it all gets too much, you can seek sanctuary in the unusual church next door, which is dedicated to Charlemagne, Charles IV's hero and role model. The octagonal nave of **Na Karlově** was only completed in the sixteenth century, although the superstitious townspeople refused to enter it for years, convinced that it would collapse. The ornate, gilt frescoed walls inside were restored after the building was partially destroyed in the Prussian siege of 1757, but bullets can still be seen embedded in them. From the garden there are extensive views across the Nusle Valley to Vyšehrad on the other side. Close by on Vyšehradská is the **Church of St John on the Rock** (sv. Jan na skalce), a fine Dientzenhofer structure built in the 1730s, perched at the top of an impressive double stairway; a little further to the south are the delightful but little-visited Botanical Gardens, where the hothouses have recently been rebuilt and the tranquil terraces retain a strong attraction for pram-wielding mothers and old folk.

Sights

Church of Our Lady of the Snows

*(Kostel Panny Marie Sněžné) Jungamannovo náměstí, Prague 1 (265 742). Metro Můstek. **Open** 6am-7.30pm daily. **Map 3 J5***

Charles IV founded the church to mark his coronation in 1347, intending it to stretch more than 100m (330ft), but, after the 33-m (110-ft) high chancel was completed in 1397, funds dried up. What remains is a voluptuous, vertiginous affair that sweeps the eyes upwards, scaling the towering

The sun shines on **Our Lady of the Snows.**

and typically over-the-top black and gold baroque altarpiece. Despite this oppressive presence, the church is a wonderfully light, tranquil space, with an interesting marbling effect on the walls. The church was erected 1,000 years after the Virgin Mary appeared to fourth-century Pope Liberius in a dream, telling him to build a church where the snow fell in August. He knocked up Santa Maria Maggiore in Rome.

Municipal House

(Obecní dům) Náměstí Republiky 5, Prague 1 (232 0839). Metro Náměstí Republiky/5, 14, 26 tram. **Map 4 K3**
All the leading artists of the day were involved in the creation of the Obecní dům (1905-11), a masterpiece of stained glass, coloured mosaics, tiled murals and gold trimmings. Built during the death throes of the Austro-Hungarian Empire, the building became a symbol of the aspirations of the new republic, representing a stylistic and structural break with the *ancien régime*. It was here that the newly independent state of Czechoslovakia was officially created in 1918, and a plaque on the side pays a now rather sad tribute to a country that no longer exists.

Following a major renovation, it is once again possible to attend concerts in the spectacular Smetana Hall, and see the other magnificent civic rooms including, most splendid of all, the Lord Mayor's Salon, which is covered with murals by Alfons Mucha depicting heroes of Czech history. The façade is by Osvald Polívka who also designed the exquisitely ornamented café *(see p144)* and restaurant; the monumental mosaic called 'Homage to Prague' above the main entrance, featuring languid ladies in an altogether unurban setting, is by Karel Špillar. It is offset by Ladislav Šaloun's sculptural composition entitled 'The Humiliation and Resurrection of the Nation'. The café and restaurant, basement bars and gallery are all open to the public, though a guided tour provides access to the other splendid corners.

Orthodox Cathedral of Sts Cyril & Methodius (National Monument of the Heydrich Terror – Place of Reconciliation)

(Kostel sv. Cyrila a Metoděje) Resslova 9, Prague 2 (295 595). Metro Karlovo náměstí/4, 7, 9, 12, 14, 16, 18, 22, 24 tram. **Open** 10am-4pm Tue-Sun. **Admission** 30 Kč adults; 10 Kč children, students. **Map 5 H8**
This baroque church, built in the 1730s, was restored and taken over by the Czech Orthodox Church in the 1930s. A plaque and memorial outside, together with numerous bullet holes, still attract tributes and flowers today, and are clues to what happened inside during World War II. In 1942, two Czech paratroopers trained in England were flown into Bohemia, together with five colleagues, to carry out the assassination of Reinhard Heydrich, Reichsprotektor of Bohemia and Moravia and the man who chaired the infamous Wannsee Conference to organise 'The Final Solution'. Josef Gabčík, Jan Kubiš and their co-conspirators were given sanctuary in the crypt of this church after the event, until they were betrayed to the Germans. In the early hours of 18 June, 350 members of the SS and Gestapo surrounded the church and spent the night bombarding it with bullets, grenades, water cannon and smoke. The men who survived until dawn used their final bullets to shoot themselves.

The incident did not end there, however. Recriminations were swift, brutal and arbitrary. Hundreds of people, many of them Jews, were rounded up in Prague and shot immediately, while five entire villages and most of their inhabitants were liquidated, the most famous being Lidice. The events brought about a turning point. Britain repudiated the Munich Agreement and Anthony Eden declared that Lidice had 'stirred the conscience of the civilised world'. The story of the assassination and its aftermath is movingly told (in English) in the crypt of the church (entrance on Na Zderaze) where the Czech soldiers made their last stand.

Prague Castle & Hradčany

Home to a thousand years of Czech history – and a million tourists.

Maps 1 & 2

For more than 1,000 years the silhouette of **Prague Castle** (Pražský hrad) has formed the most distinctive feature of the city's skyline – a symbol of the power of Prague's rulers, the political and spiritual centre of the country, and still the presidential seat today. To Czechs it therefore evokes ambivalent feelings, encapsulating both national pride and foreign oppression.

The surrounding streets, stretching north and west from the Castle across the hilltop, form the district of **Hradčany**, a quiet, beautiful and less heavily touristed area than the Castle itself and its immediate environs. Aside from the Castle grounds, there's not much in the way of commerce up here, and to find somewhere to stop for rest and refreshments, it's probably best to head back down the hill into Malá Strana. The recently opened gastro complex **Bazaar Mediterranée** (*see page 126*) is a good choice and has a wonderful terrace.

Prague Castle

Founded in the ninth century by the Přemysl princes, the impressive, if somewhat sombre, collection of buildings that makes up the Castle – including a palace, three churches and a monastery – has been added to, destroyed and rebuilt over the centuries. The final touches were not added until the early twentieth century and, thus, the Castle resembles a vast museum of architectural styles stretching back to the Romanesque.

The grandiose façade enclosing the complex is the result of the Empress Maria Theresa's desire in the mid-eighteenth century to bring some coherence to the clumsy collection of awkward parts that the Castle had become. But the result of **Nicolo Pacassi**'s monotonous design is uninspiring – 'an imposing mass of building in the factory style of architecture', as one nineteenth-century commentator put it. After Maria Theresa's son, Joseph II, attempted to turn the Castle into a barracks, it was largely deserted by the Habsburgs. Václav Havel has chosen not to live here, although he has an office in the Castle. He has done his best to enliven the palace, throwing open

doors that were kept tightly closed during the years of communist paranoia and hiring the costume designer from the film *Amadeus* to remodel the guards' uniforms.

You really can't get away without spending at least half a day up here. Unfortunately, that's what every visitor to Prague thinks. The result is a notable lack of any real city life, and an awful lot of chattering tour groups and whirring video cameras. To avoid the worst of the crush, come as early or as late as you can.

ENTRANCE

(information in English and Czech 2437 3368). Metro Malostranská/12, 22 tram. **Open** *May-Oct* 9am-5pm daily; *Nov-Mar* 9am-4pm daily. **Admission** 100 Kč adults; 50 Kč children, students, OAPs; 150 Kč families. Tickets are valid for three days. **No credit cards.** **Map 1 C2**

There's no charge to enter the precincts of the Castle, but you'll need a ticket to see the main attractions. An audio guide (available in English) costs extra and is available from the information centre in the third courtyard. One ticket covers entrance to the **Old Royal Palace**, the **Basilica of St George**, the **Powder Tower** and the choir, crypt and tower of **St Vitus's Cathedral**. Entrance to the art collection of **St George's Convent** (*see p97*) and the **Toy Museum** (*see p95*) costs extra.

It's a stiff walk up to the Castle from Malá Strana and Malostranská metro station. The least strenuous approach is to take the 22 tram, which snakes around the back of the hill, and get off at the Pražský hrad stop. There are several cafés within the Castle, providing reasonable food and liquid refreshment.

The first & second courtyards

The most obvious way to enter the Castle is the same way that visiting heads of state do: through the first courtyard from the broad open space of Hradčanské náměstí. The gateway has been dominated by Ignatz Platzer's monumental sculptures of battling Titans since 1768. They create an impressive, if not exactly welcoming, entrance. The changing of the guard takes place in this courtyard, a Havel-inspired attempt to add some ceremonial pizazz to life in the Castle. Though the change is carried out hourly every day between 5am and 10pm, the big crowd-pulling ceremony takes place at noon. The two tapering flagpoles are the work of the Slovenian architect **Josip Plečnik**, who was brought in by President Masaryk during the 1920s to tidy up the Castle's loose ends.

To reach the second courtyard go through the **Matthias Gate** (Matyášova brána), a baroque portal dating from 1614, topped by a German Imperial Eagle that pleased Hitler when he came to stay in 1939. The monumental stairway on the left leads up to the magnificent gold and white **Spanish Hall** (Španělský sál; open to the public only during occasional concerts), built in the seventeenth century for court ceremonies. The décor was overhauled in the nineteenth century when the *trompe l'oeil* murals were covered with white stucco, and huge mirrors and gilded chandeliers brought in to transform the space into a suitable venue for the coronation of Emperor Franz Joseph I. Franz Joseph, however, failed to show up and it was not until the 1950s that the hall was given a new use – it was here the Politburo came to discuss the success of their latest five-year plan (protected from assassins by a reinforced steel door).

Behind the austere grey walls of the second courtyard lies a warren of opulent state rooms whose heyday dates from the time of Rudolf II. The state rooms of the second courtyard, which are rarely open to the public, housed Rudolf's magnificent art collection and such curiosities as a unicorn's horn and three nails from Noah's ark. The bulk of the collection was carried off in 1648 by Swedish soldiers, although the remnants are housed in the **Prague Castle Picture Gallery** (*see page 98*) on the north side of the courtyard by the **Powder Bridge** (U Prašného mostu) entrance. In the middle of the courtyard is a seventeenth-century baroque fountain, and the **Chapel of the Holy Rood**, which was rebuilt in neo-baroque style in the late nineteenth century.

St Vitus's Cathedral

The third courtyard – the oldest and most important site in the Castle – is entirely dominated by the looming towers, pinnacles and buttresses of **St Vitus's Cathedral** (Katedrála sv. Víta). Although it was only completed in 1929, exactly 1,000 years after St Wenceslas had been laid to rest on the site, the cathedral is undoubtedly the spiritual centre of Bohemia. This has always been a holy place: in pagan times Svatovít, the Slavic god of fertility, was worshipped on this site, a clue perhaps to why his near namesake St Vitus (or *svatý Vít* in Czech) – a Sicilian peasant who became a Roman legionary before being thrown to the lions – had the cathedral dedicated to him. Right up until the eighteenth century young women and anxious farmers would bring offerings of wine, cakes and cocks.

The cathedral's Gothic structure owes its creation to Charles IV's lifelong love affair with Prague. In 1344 he managed to secure an archbishopric for the city, and work began on the construction of a cathedral under the instructions of French architect Matthew of Arras. Inconveniently, Matthew dropped dead eight years into the project, so the Swabian Peter Parler was called in to take up the challenge. He was responsible for the 'Sondergotik' or German Late Gothic design. But it remained unfinished until it was adopted and completed by nineteenth-century nationalists, according to Parler's original plans. The skill with which the later work was carried out means it is difficult to tell where the Gothic ends and the neo-Gothic begins.

Outside, the most dominant feature is the **Great Tower**, a Gothic and Renaissance structure topped with a baroque dome. It houses **Sigismund**, the largest bell in Bohemia, weighing in at 15,120kg (33,333lbs). Getting Sigismund into the tower was no mean feat: according to legend it took a rope woven from the hair of the city's noblest virgins to haul it into position. Below the tower is the Gothic **Golden Portal** (Zlatá brána), decorated with a mosaic of multicoloured Venetian glass depicting the Last Judgement. On either side of the arch are sculptures of Charles IV and his wife Elizabeth of Pomerania, whose talents apparently included being able to bend a sword with her bare hands.

Inside, the enormous nave is flooded with multicoloured light from the gallery of stained glass windows created at the beginning of this century. All 21 of them were sponsored by financial institutions including (third on the right) an insurance company whose motto – 'those who sow in sorrow shall reap in joy' – is incorporated into the biblical allegory. The most famous is the third window on the left, in the Archbishop's Chapel, which was created by Alfons Mucha and depicts the Christian Slavonic tribes; it was paid for, appropriately enough, by Banka Slavia.

On the right is the **Chapel of St Wenceslas** (Svatováclavská kaple), which stands on the site of the original tenth-century rotunda where Prince Wenceslas (*see page 12*) was buried. Built in 1345, the chapel has 1,345 polished amethysts, agates and jaspers incorporated into its design, and contains paraphernalia from the saint's life, including his armour, chain shirt and helmet. Unfortunately, it is closed to the public now – too many sweaty bodies were causing the gilded plaster to disintegrate – but its glinting treasure-trove glory can be glimpsed over the railings. Occasionally, on significant state anniversaries, the skull of the saint is put on display, covered with a cobweb-fine veil.

A door in the corner leads to the chamber that contains the **crown jewels**. A papal bull of 1346 officially protects the jewels, while popular legend unofficially prescribes death to anyone who uses them improperly. Reichsprotektor Reinhard Heydrich was the last person to test the legend, and was assassinated within a year of placing a crown upon his head (*see page 21*). The door of the chamber is locked with seven keys held by seven different people, after the seven seals of Revelations.

The most extraordinary baroque addition to the cathedral was the **silver tombstone of St John of Nepomuk**, the priest who was flung from Charles Bridge in 1393 as a result of King Wenceslas IV's fit of anti-clerical pique. The tomb, designed by Fischer von Erlach the Younger in 1733-6, is a flamboyant affair. Two tons of silver were used to create the pedestal, statue of the saint and fluttering cherubs holding up a red velvet canopy. The phrase 'baroque excess' scarcely does it justice.

Close by is the entrance to the **Crypt**. Down below lie the remains of a choice selection of Czech kings and queens, including George of Poděbrady and Rudolf II. The most eyecatching tomb is Charles IV's startlingly modern-looking, streamlined metal affair by Kamil Roškot (1934-5).

The third courtyard

After the cathedral, the second most noticeable monument in the third courtyard is the somewhat incongruous 17-m (50-ft) high granite obelisk, a memorial to the dead of World War I erected by Plečnik in 1928.

Close to the Golden Portal is the entrance to the **Old Royal Palace** (Starý královský palác), which contains three levels of royal apartments. Six centuries of kings called the palace home and systematically built new parts over the old. In what is now the basement you can see the dingy twelfth-century Romanesque remains of Prince Soběslav's residence. The top floor contains the highlight of the palace, the **Vladislav Hall**. Designed by Benedict Ried at the turn of the sixteenth century, its exquisitely vaulted ceiling signalled the last flowering of the Gothic, while the large, square windows are the first expressions of the Renaissance in Bohemia. It is here that the National Assembly elects its new president. The specially designed **Rider's Steps** allowed knights to enter the hall without dismounting. Higher up again (in the Louis Wing) is the **Bohemian Chancellery** and the window through which the victims of the defenestration of 1618 (*see page 73* **Window dropping**) were ejected.

At the eastern end of the cathedral is Jiřské náměstí, named after **St George's Basilica** (Bazilika sv. Jiří). Stand far enough back from the basilica's crumbling red and cream baroque façade to get a good look at the two Romanesque towers jutting out behind. The Italian craftsmen who constructed them in 1142 built a fatter male tower (Adam, on the left) standing guard over a more slender female one (Eve, on the right). The basilica, founded by Prince Vratislav in 921, has burned down and been rebuilt over the centuries. Its first major remodelling took place 50 years after it was first erected when a Benedictine convent was founded next door. A major renovation in the early twentieth century swept out most of the baroque elements and led to the uncovering of the original arcades, remnants of thirteenth-century frescoes and the bodies of a saint (Ludmila, who was strangled by assassins hired by Prince Wenceslas's mother Drahomíra) and a saint-maker (the notorious Boleslav the Cruel, who turned his brother Prince Wenceslas into a martyr by having him stabbed to death). The basilica's refound simplicity and clean lines seem far closer to godliness than the mammon-fuelled baroque pomposity of most of Prague's other churches.

On the left of the main entrance is an opening built to give access for the Benedictine nuns from the **St George's Convent** next door (which now houses part of the **National Gallery's** wonderful collection of Gothic, Renaissance and baroque art; *see page 97*) and to keep to a minimum their contact with the outside world.

The lane Vikářská, on the north side of the cathedral, is where Picasso and Eluard came to drink in the Vikářská tavern, and gives access to the fifteenth-century **Mihulka** or **Powder Tower** (Prašná věž). It was here that wacky Rudolf II stationed his many alchemists, who were engaged in attempts at distilling the Elixir of Life and transforming base metals into gold. The tower now houses a museum of alchemy, bell- and cannon-forging, and Renaissance life in the Castle.

Elsewhere in the Castle

Going down the hill from St George's, signposts direct you to the most visited street in Prague, **Golden Lane** (Zlatá ulička). The tiny multicoloured cottages that cling to the castle's northern walls were thrown up by the poor in the sixteenth century out of whatever waste materials they could find. The name is allegedly a reference to the alchemists of King Rudolf's time who were rumoured to live here. Another theory is that soldiers billeted in a nearby tower used it as a public urinal. In fact, the name probably dates from the seventeenth century when the city's goldsmiths worked here. Houses used to line both sides of the street, leaving barely enough space to pass in between, but in the eighteenth century hygiene-conscious Joseph II ordered a spot of demolition. Although the houses look separate, a corridor actually runs the length of their attics and used to be occupied by the sharp-shooters of the Castle Guard. The house at no.22 was owned by Kafka's sister Otla, and he stayed here for a while in 1917, reputedly drawing the inspiration for his later

Stop for a moment to enjoy the views of Malá Strana from the **Castle**.

novel, *The Castle*. If he were to rewrite it today, he'd call it *The Souvenir Shop*. Atmospheric at night, by day the lane is one long traffic jam of shuffling tourists.

At the eastern end some steps take you under the last house and out to the **Dalibor Tower** (Daliborka), named after its most famous inmate, Dalibor, who spent time here on death row and amused himself by playing the violin. According to legend (and Smetana's opera *Dalibor*), he attracted crowds of onlookers who turned up at his execution to weep en masse.

Continuing down the hill takes you past another **Lobkowicz palace** (Lobkovický palác), one of several in the town. This one, finished in 1658, houses the unexciting **Historical Museum** (*see page 91*). Opposite is Burgrave House, now the **Toy Museum** (*see page 95*). The statue of a naked boy in the courtyard fell victim to Marxist-Leninist ideology when President Novotný decided that his genitals were not an edifying sight for the masses and ordered them to be removed. Happily the boy and his equipment have since been reunited. The lane passes under the **Black Tower** (Černá věž) and ends at the **Old Castle Steps** (Staré zámecké schody), which lead to Malá Strana. Before descending, pause at the top for a view over the red tiled roofs, spires and domes of the 'Little Quarter'.

An even better view can be had from the **Paradise Gardens** (Rajská zahrada; open Apr-Oct 9am-5pm; *see page 79*) on the ramparts below the Castle walls (enter from the Bull Staircase –

Art attack outside the **Castle**.

Keep off the glass inside the magnificent **St Vitus's Cathedral***. See page 61.*

see below – or from outside the Castle, to the right of the first courtyard). This is where the victims of the second and most famous defenestration fell to earth (*see also page 73* **Window dropping**) and for centuries was little more than a spot for the emptying of medieval chamber pots. Although they were laid out in 1562, the gardens were redesigned in the 1920s by Josip Plečnik. The spiralling **Bull Staircase** leading up to the Castle's third courtyard, and the huge granite bowl, are his work. When their restoration is at long last complete, it will be possible to make the descent to Malá Strana by the terraced slopes of the beautiful Renaissance **Ledebour Gardens** (*see page 79*).

The Royal Garden & the Belvedere

Crossing over the **Powder Bridge** (U Prašného most) back by the Castle's second courtyard, you reach the **Royal Garden** (Královská zahrada), which lies on the outer side of the **Stag Moat** (Jelení příkop). It was laid out in the Italian style for Emperor Ferdinand I in the 1530s and originally included a maze and a private zoo, but the area was devastated by Swedish soldiers during the seventeenth century.

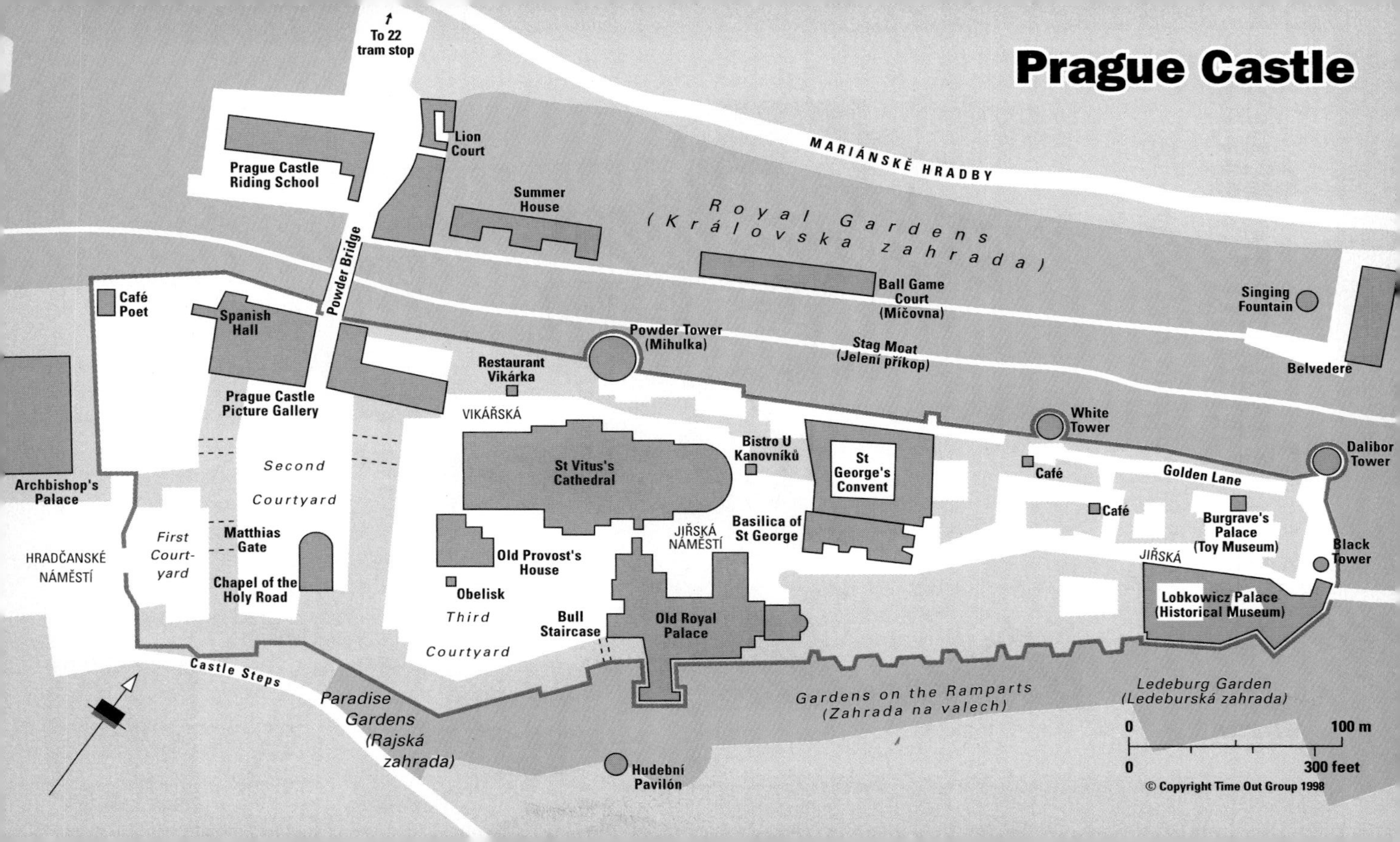

Prague Castle

MARIÁNSKÉ HRADBY

Royal Gardens
(Královská zahrada)

Singing Fountain

Belvedere

Ball Game Court (Míčovna)

Stag Moat (Jelení příkop)

Summer House

Lion Court

To 22 tram stop

Prague Castle Riding School

Spanish Hall

Café Poet

Prague Castle Picture Gallery

Powder Bridge

Second Courtyard

Matthias Gate

Chapel of the Holy Road

First Court-yard

Archbishop's Palace

HRADČANSKÉ NÁMĚSTÍ

Castle Steps

Paradise Gardens (Rajská zahrada)

Powder Tower (Mihulka)

Restaurant Vikárka

VIKÁŘSKÁ

St Vitus's Cathedral

Old Provost's House

Obelisk

Third Courtyard

Bull Staircase

Hudební Pavilón

Bistro U Kanovníků

St George's Convent

Basilica of St George

JIŘSKÁ NÁMĚSTÍ

Old Royal Palace

Gardens on the Ramparts (Zahrada na valech)

White Tower

Café

Café

Golden Lane

Burgrave's Palace (Toy Museum)

JIŘSKÁ

Lobkowicz Palace (Historical Museum)

Dalibor Tower

Black Tower

Ledeburg Garden (Ledeburská zahrada)

0   100 m
0   300 feet

© Copyright Time Out Group 1998

Refreshment in **Hradčany**. See page 71.

At the eastern end of the gardens is the **Belvedere** (open *summer* 10am-6pm; *winter* 10am-5pm; *closed* Dec-Feb), which was itself the target of French fire during the eighteenth century, but was saved for posterity by the payment of 30 pineapples by the canny head gardener. A stunning Renaissance structure built by Paola della Stella between 1538 and 1564 (though construction work was interrupted by a fire at the Castle in 1541), its strangely shaped green copper roof is supported by delicate arcades and Ionic columns. The Belvedere was the first royal structure in Prague to be dedicated to pleasure-seeking rather than power-mongering – it was commissioned by Ferdinand I as a gift for his wife Anne – a loveshack one remove away from the skulduggery of life in the Castle. But the long-suffering Anne never got to see 'the most beautiful piece of Renaissance architecture north of the Alps' (as it is invariably dubbed in the city's tourist brochures) – she drew her last breath after producing the fifteenth heir to the throne. The royal couple are immortalised in the reliefs adorning the façade. The Belvedere went on to become the site of all sorts of goings-on: mad King Rudolf installed his astronomers here and the communists bricked up the windows of the upper level to prevent armed assassins getting too close to the president. People come here today to see occasional art shows (*see page 99*). In front of the palace is the so-called **Singing Fountain**, cast in bronze by Bohemian craftsmen in the 1560s, which used to hum as water splashed into its basin before it was reconstructed, hence the name.

On the southern side of the garden overlooking the Stag Moat is another lovely Renaissance structure, which is covered with elaborate black and white sgraffito and was completed by Bonifác Wohlmut in 1563 to house the king's **Ball Game Court** (Míčovna). The sgraffito has to be renewed every 20 years, although the last time this was done some decidedly anachronistic elements were added to the allegorical frieze depicting Science, the Virtues and the Elements. For example, look carefully at the lovely ladies on the top of the building and you'll see that the woman seated next to Justice (tenth along from the right) is holding a hammer and sickle.

On the same side of the garden, closer to the entrance, is the mustard-coloured Dientzenhofer **Summer House** (Zahradní dům), which acted as the presidential residence between 1948 and 1989. During this period, large sections of the Castle were closed to the public and huge underground shelters were built to connect the president's residence with the rest of the complex. No sooner were the shelters completed than it was decided that the underground passages might help to conceal counter-revolutionary enemies, and the exit shafts were blocked off with huge concrete slabs.

Hradčany

Hradčany owes its grand scale and pristine condition to the devastating fire of 1541, which destroyed the medieval district, and the frenzied period of Counter-Reformation building following the Protestant defeat at the Battle of White Mountain in 1620 (*see page 17*). Little has changed here in the last two centuries.

The area's focal point is **Hradčanské náměstí**, one of the grandest squares in the city, lined with imposing palaces built by the Catholic aristocracy, anxious to be close to the Habsburg court. It was nonetheless cut off from the Castle and its neurotic inhabitants by a complicated system of moats and fortifications, which remained until Empress Maria Theresa had a grand spring clean in the mid-eighteenth century. Along with the moat went the tiny Church of the Virgin Mary of Einsedel, which used to stand next to the castle ramp. Lovely as this was said to have been, it's hard to believe that it was lovelier than the superb panorama of Malá Strana, the Strahov Gardens and Petřín Hill that the demolition opened up.

On the north side of the square, next to the Castle, is the domineering sixteenth-century **Archbishop's Palace** (Arcibiskupský palác), tarted up with a frothy rococo façade in 1763-4. Next door, slotted in between the palace and a row of former canons' houses, stands the **Sternberg Palace** (Šternberský palác), which houses the **National Gallery**'s fourteenth- to eighteenth-century collection of European art (*see page 97*). Opposite is the heavily restored **Schwarzenberg Palace** (Schwarzenberský palác), one of the most imposing Renaissance buildings in Prague. It was built between 1545 and 1563, the outside exquisitely decorated with 'envelope' sgraffito. It now contains the **Military Museum** (*see page 92*), which brims with as comprehensive a collection of killing instruments as you would expect from a country that gave the world the words 'pistol' and 'Semtex'.

Further along Loretánská is the pub **U Černého vola** (The Black Ox; *see page 151*), a simple Renaissance building with a crumbling mural on the façade. As a result of some direct action in 1991, it's one of the few places left in Hradčany where the locals can afford to drink. The regulars foiled several attempts at privatisation by forming a co-operative to run it themselves in conjunction with the Beer Party, now downgraded from a political party to a civic association. You don't have to feel guilty about the amount you drink here – all profits go to a nearby school for the blind.

The pub looks out on to **Loretánské náměstí**, a split-level square built on the site of a heathen cemetery, half of which is occupied by a car park for the Ministry of Foreign Affairs based in the monolithic **Černín Palace** (Černínský palác).

This is an enormous and unprepossessing structure, its long grey façade articulated by an unbroken line of 30 pillars. Commissioned in 1669 by Humprecht Johann Černín, the Imperial ambassador to Venice, its construction financially ruined his family and the first people to move in were hundreds of seventeenth-century squatters. In 1948, Foreign Minister Jan Masaryk took a dive from an upstairs window and was found dead on the pavement below a few days after the communist takeover (*see page 73* **Window dropping**).

Dwarfed by the Černín Palace is the **Loreto** (*see below*), a baroque masterpiece and a monument to the power of the Catholic miracle culture that swept the Czech lands after the Thirty Years' War. The façade (1721) is a swirling mass of stuccoed cherubs, topped with a bell-tower. The 27 bells ring out every hour with a cacophonous melody called 'We Greet You a Thousand Times'.

The streets behind the Loreto are some of the prettiest and quietest in Hradčany. The quarter was built in the sixteenth century for the Castle staff; now its tiny cottages are the most prized pieces of real estate in the city. Going down Kapucínská, you pass the **Domeček** or 'Little House' at no.10, once home to the notorious Fifth Department – the counter-intelligence unit of the Defence Ministry. At no.5 on nearby Černínská is **Gambra** (*see page 102*), a quirky gallery that specialises in surrealist art from the 1930s to the present day. Its owner, the world-renowned animator Jan Švankmajer, lives in the house next door. At the foot of the hill is **Nový Svět** ('New World'), a street of brightly coloured cottages restored in the eighteenth and nineteenth centuries that is all that remains of Hradčany's medieval slums. Most of the rest were destroyed in the Great Fire of 1541. Tycho Brahe, the Danish alchemist notorious for his lack of a nose (which he lost in a duel) and spectacular death (of an exploding bladder), lived at no.1, called 'The Golden Griffin'. Up from Loretánské náměstí is Hradčany's last major square: **Pohořelec**. The passage at no.8 leads to the peaceful surroundings of the **Strahov Monastery** (Strahovský klášter; *see below*). The monastery's magnificent libraries and fine collection of religious art are well worth a visit.

Sights

The Loreto

(Loreta) Loretánské náměstí 7, Prague 1 (2451 0789).
Tram 22. **Open** 9am-12.15pm, 1-4.30pm, Tue-Sun.
Admission 40 Kč adults; 25 Kč children, students.
Map 1 B3
The Loreto is probably the most outlandish piece of baroque fantasy in Prague. Its attractions include a painting of a bearded lady, the skeletons of two female saints, an ecclesiastical extravagance, and the highest concentration of cherubs to be found anywhere in the city. It was built as part of a calculated plan to reconvert the masses to Catholicism after the Thirty Years' War.

Pražské panoptikum

Come with us to an exciting trip through past and present. Walk on a 19th century lane and also meet Kafka.
Shake hands with Mozart and talk to Václav Havel.
You can meet them all at Pražské panoptikum.
See also our holographic projection.

◊

Open daily 10am - 8pm.
Groups are always welcome.
For group rates, please call us.

Pražské panoptikum, Praha 1, Národní třída 25
inside the passage of Palác Metro

(200m from the National Theatre).tel.+420-2-21085318,fax+420-2-21085229
www.waxmuseum.cz, panoptikum@highland.cz

At its heart is a small chapel, the **Santa Casa**, whose history is so improbable that it quickly gained cult status. The story goes that the original Santa Casa was the home of Mary in Nazareth until it was miraculously flown over to Loreto in Italy by angels, spawning a copycat cult all over Europe (there are 50 in Bohemia alone). This one, from 1626-31, boasts two beams and a brick from the 'original', as well as a crevice left on the wall by a divine thunderbolt that struck an unfortunate blasphemer. The red colour scheme makes it look more like a place to hold a black mass than a virgin's boudoir.

The shrine was a particular hit with wealthy ladies who donated the money for baroque *maestri* Christoph and Kilian Ignaz Dientzenhofer to construct the outer courtyards and the **Church of the Nativity** (1716-23) at the back. They also sponsored the painting of St Wilgefortis, the patron saint of unhappily married women, who grew a beard as an extreme tactic to get out of marrying a heathen (in the corner chapel to the right of the main entrance), and that of St Agatha the Unfortunate, who can be seen carrying her severed breasts on a meat platter (in the Church of the Nativity). The famous **diamond monstrance**, designed in 1699 by Fischer von Erlach and sporting some 6,222 stones, is in the treasury.

Strahov Monastery

(Strahovský klášter) Strahovské nádvoří 1, Prague 1 (2051 7451). Tram 8, 22/143, 149, 217 bus. **Open** 9am-12.30pm, 1-5pm, Tue-Sun. **Admission** 40 Kč adults; 20 Kč children. **No credit cards. Map 1 A4**
The Premonstratensian monks set up home here in 1140, and embarked upon their austere programme of celibacy and silent contemplation. The complex still has a quiet air of seclusion, a fragrant orchard stretching down the hill to Malá Strana and, since 1990, several cowled monks who've returned to reclaim the buildings that were nationalised by the communists in 1948. Their services are once again held in the **Church of Our Lady**, which retains its twelfth-century basilica ground plan, although it was remodelled in the early seventeenth century.

The highlight of the complex is without a doubt the superb libraries. Within the gilded, frescoed **Theological** and **Philosophical Halls** are 130,000 volumes (there are a further 700,000 in storage) forming the most important collection in Bohemia. Visitors cannot, alas, stroll around the libraries, but have to be content with gawping from their doors. The comprehensive acquisition of books didn't begin until the late sixteenth century; when Joseph II effected a massive clampdown on religious institutions in 1782, the Premonstratensians outwitted him by masquerading as an educational foundation, and their collection was swelled by the contents of the libraries from less canny monasteries. Indeed, the monks' taste ranged far beyond the standard ecclesiastical tracts, including such highlights as the oldest extant copy of *The Calendar of Minutae* or *Selected Times for Bloodletting*. Nor did they merely confine themselves to books: the 200-year-old curiosity cabinets house a collection of deep-sea monsters that any landlocked country would be proud to own.

In another part of the complex, the **Strahov Gallery** (*see p99*) contains a fine exhibition of a small part of the monastery's considerable collection of religious art.

Window dropping

Prague is home to perhaps the most perverse form of political assassination ever invented: defenestration. At critical times in the country's turbulent history, somebody or other goes out through a window. Here we consider the scenes of the crimes.

Bohemian Chancellery

Map 2 D2
Relations between the Bohemian Protestants and their Catholic Habsburg rulers were never easy during the sixteenth century. Events finally came to a head on 23 May 1618. A band of noblemen plotted the death of two Catholic governors appointed by Ferdinand II, marched up the steps to the Castle and after a fierce struggle succeeded in throwing them and their secretary out of the window. Their fall was broken, however, by a dung heap that had collected beneath that very window, and the event sparked the bitter Thirty Years' War, which was to devastate half of Europe (*see p17*). The Chancellery (Česká kancelář), within the **Old Royal Palace** (*see p62*), is open to the public and you can admire the same view over the roofs of Malá Strana that the three unfortunates took in moments before their fall.

Černín Palace

Map 1 A3
The Černín Palace (Černínský palác) in Lorentánské náměstí (closed to the public; *see also p71*) is famous for being the largest palace in Prague, but it certainly isn't the prettiest. Started in 1669, it reflects the gargantuan ambitions – and lack of vision – of its original owner Humprecht Johann Černín, the Imperial Ambassador to Venice. By 1851 it had become a barracks, and in World War II it was the Nazi's Prague headquarters, but after hostilities ceased the Ministry for Foreign Affairs moved back into the building. On 10 March 1948, just days after the communist coup d'état had been announced, the Foreign Minister Jan Masaryk was found dead on the cobblestones outside the palace, having apparently fallen from a bathroom window. Whether he fell or was pushed has never been satisfactorily resolved. The son of Tomáš Masaryk, founding father of the Czechoslovak Republic, he was the only liberal voice left in the cabinet and had raised strong objections to the communist takeover. The comrades insisted it was suicide, but their claim would have been rather more convincing had they released the details of the autopsy. Recent research suggests that Masaryk actually plumeted from a ledge rather than a window, which, strictly speaking, would disqualify him as a genuine defenestration. Only purists are likely to quibble on the point though.

New Town Hall

Map 5 J7
The New Town Hall (Novoměstská radnice) on Karlovo náměstí, the largest square in the city, was the site of Prague's first, trendsetting defenestration. The present building is a fourteenth-century remnant of the original New Town Hall. It was here that in 1419 an irate mob, egged on by Jan Želivský, Hussite preacher and rabble rouser extraordinaire, gathered, demanding the release of several prisoners incarcerated within the walls. Several Catholic councillors were hurled from an upstairs window and a fashion was started. It's now a popular place to get married, but Želivský is not forgotten. The revisionist historians of the 1960s recast him as a precursor of communism and a statue of him was erected in front of the building. There's also a metro station named after him.

Malá Strana

Great bars, ancient streets and a wealth of little-known gardens.

Map 2

The name Malá Strana means the 'Little Quarter' or 'Lesser Town' – a typically Bohemian understatement for an area that contains hulking palaces and ornate, formal gardens, as well as baroque churches and tiny, crumbling cottages.

It was founded by the Přemyslid Otakar II in 1287, when he invited merchants from Germany to set up shop on the land beneath the castle walls. Very little remains of this Gothic town – the present-day appearance of the quarter dates from the seventeenth century. The area was transformed into a sparkling baroque town by the wealthy Catholic aristocracy, who won huge parcels of land in the property redistribution that followed the Thirty Years' War. When the fashionable followed the court to Vienna in the seventeenth century, the poor took over the area. It has been the spiritual and actual home of poets, drunks and mystics ever since, living cheek-by-jowl with the ambassadors and diplomats who also inhabit what is one of Prague's two diplomatic quarters – the British, American, Irish, German, Italian and French embassies, among others, are all in Malá Strana.

Today, the character of the quarter is changing rapidly, as accountancy firms, bankers and frou-frou wine bars set up here. It's still remarkable, though, just how few businesses there are in what is one of the most central Prague districts. Malostranské náměstí now throbs with life deep into the night, but this is mostly down to the tourist trade, and its many bars, restaurants and music venues. Apart from stores selling souvenirs and cut glass, there is very little shopping in the area.

Malostranské náměstí & around

The main drag between Charles Bridge and Malostranské náměstí is **Mostecká**. It's a continuation of the Royal Route – the path taken by the Bohemian kings to their coronation – and is lined with elegant baroque dwellings. At no.15 is the **Kaunitz Palace** (Kaunicův palác), built in 1773 for Jan Adam Kaunitz, an advisor to Empress Maria Theresa, who sycophantically had the exterior painted her favourite colours – yellow and white. It's now the embassy of the former Yugoslavia. Just off Mostecká are the **Blue Light** jazz pub (*see page 148*) and **U Patrona** restaurant (*see page 125*), both pricey establishments but oases of quality in a stretch otherwise characterised by naff souvenir shop after naff souvenir shop.

At the heart of the quarter is **Malostranské náměstí**, a lively square edged by large baroque palaces and Renaissance gabled townhouses perched on top of Gothic arcades. Here you'll find the 100-year-old **Malostranská kavárna** (*see page 150*), which, when it reopened a few years ago, added a much-needed boost to Prague's once-vibrant café culture. Bang in the middle, dividing the square in two, is the **Church of St Nicholas** (*see below*), a monumental late baroque affair, whose dome and adjoining belltower dominate the skyline of Prague's left bank. Built between 1703 and 1755, it's the largest and most ornate of the city's Jesuit-founded churches. During its construction, the Society of Jesus waged a battle against the local residents who were understandably loath to let go of the two streets, two churches and various other inconveniences that had to be demolished to make room for it.

The grim block next door at no.25 is yet another Jesuit construction, built as a college for their priests and now housing harassed-looking maths students. More appealing is the **Lichtenstein Palace** (Lichtenštejnský palác) opposite, finished in 1791. The Lichtensteins used to be major landowners in Bohemia and the alpine principality has been waging a battle to regain the palace, which was confiscated in 1918. They have been unsuccessful so far, and the palace is currently used as a venue for classical concerts. Also in the square, located in the former town hall at no.21, is the club **Malostranská beseda** (*see page 198*), where music of a more jazz/blues/pop bent is played. Opposite the south side of St Nicholas is a whole parade of pubs and restaurants. The American backpacker hangout **Jo's Bar**, the late-opening theatre-café **Studio A Rubín**, the stereotypical Irish pub **Scarlett O'Hara's** (*for all three, see page 150*) and the **Avalon** and **Circle Line** (*see pages 124 & 119*) restaurant complex are all on this stretch. The tables outside Avalon, in the south-west corner of the square, are a grand spot for summer dining.

Nerudova heads up from the north-west corner of the square towards the Castle, and is a fine place for deciphering the ornate signs that decorate many Prague houses: there's the Three Fiddles at no.12, for example, or the Devil at no.4. This practice of distinguishing houses continued up until 1770, when that relentless modernist Joseph II spoiled the fun by introducing new-fangled numbers.

An urban idyll – the Malá Strana end of Charles Bridge

The street, which is crowded with cafés, restaurants and shops aimed at the ceaseless flow of tourists to and from the Castle, is named after its famous son, the nineteenth-century novelist **Jan Neruda**. He lived at no.47, the Two Suns (U dvou slunců). The house was turned into a pub and during the communist period was a favourite hangout of the Plastic People of the Universe, the underground rock band who were later instrumental in the founding of Charter 77. The place is now a joyless tourist trap. Also to be ignored is the turquoise drinking establishment at no.13 where Václav Havel, in an uncharacteristic lapse of taste, took Yeltsin for a mug of beer. 'As for heads of state,' Havel is quoted as saying, 'I haven't met anyone whose eyes didn't shine when I suggested that after the official reception we should go and get a beer somewhere...' A better bet is U **Kocoura** at no.2. It's owned by the Friends of Beer, formerly a political party, now a civic association. Although their manifesto is a bit vague, their ability to pull a good, cheap pint is beyond question. The newcomer **Bazaar Mediterranée** (*see page 126*) at no.40 is a fine spot for lunch.

The alley next door leads up to the British Embassy, at Thunovská 14, which a former ambassadorial wag christened 'Czechers'. Leading up from here are the **New Castle Steps** (Nové zámecké schody), one of the most peaceful (and least strenuous) routes up to the Castle, and a star location in the film *Amadeus*.

There are more embassies back on Nerudova, the Italians occupying the **Thun-Hohenstein Palace** (Thun-Hohenštejnský palác) at no.20, built by Giovanni Santini-Aichel in 1726 and distinguished by the contorted eagles holding up the portal, the heraldic emblem of the Kolowrats for whom the palace was built. The Italians have been trumped by the Romanians, however, who inhabit the even more glorious **Morzin Palace** (Morzinský palác) opposite at no.5. Also the work of Santini-Aichel (1714), it sports two very hefty Moors, a pun on the family's name, who hold up the window ledge. Their toes have been rubbed shiny by passers-by who believe this will bring them luck.

Following the tram tracks from Malostranské náměstí in the direction of the river brings you to the **Church of St Thomas** (sv. Tomáš; *see below*), whose rich baroque façade is easy to miss, tucked into the narrow side street of Tomášská. Based on a Gothic ground plan, the church was rebuilt in the baroque style by Kilián Ignaz Dientzenhofer for the Augustinian monks. The symbol of the order – a flaming heart – can be seen all over the church and adjoining cloisters (now an old people's home) and even in the hand of St Boniface, a fully dressed skeleton who occupies a glass case in the nave.

On the other side of the street is Josefská, a street that takes its name from the **Church of St Joseph** (sv. Josef), a tiny baroque gem set back from the road and designed by Jean-Baptiste Mathey. Since 1989 it has been returned to the much-diminished Order of English Virgins, who were also one-time owners of the nearby **Soldiers' Gardens** (Vojanovy sady; *see page 79*), one of the most tranquil spots in the city.

Running parallel to U lužického semináře is **Cihelná**, a street named after the now-derelict brick factory, which provides an opening on to the river and an almost perfect view of the Vltava. Back on Letenská, towards Malostranská metro station, is a door in a wall leading into the best-kept formal gardens in the city. The early seventeenth-century **Wallenstein Gardens** (Valdštejnská zahrada; *see page 79*) belonged, along with the adjoining **Wallenstein Palace**, to General Albrecht von Wallenstein (Valdštejn), successful commander of the Catholic armies in the Thirty Years' War and a formidable property speculator. The palace (now the Ministry of Culture) is enormous. Designed by the Milanese architect Andrea Spezza between 1624 and 1630, it once had a permanent staff of 700 servants, and 1,000 horses.

This whole area of Malá Strana, between Malostranská metro station and the square, is largely devoid of commerce or other signs of modernity. Walking deserted Letenská at night, in the ancient glow cast by old-fashioned street lamps, only the occasional tram disturbs the feeling that you've stepped right back into the seventeenth century.

Kampa Island

Crossing over Charles Bridge from the Staré Město side, you'll see one of the best photo opportunities in the city: the twin towers of the bridge, framing an almost perfect view of the Church of St Nicholas and the Castle behind. Before continuing, however, take the flight of steps on the left, leading down to Na Kampě, the principal square of **Kampa Island**. Until 1770, it was known simply as Ostrov or 'island', which understandably led to confusion with the other islands of the Vltava.

The narrow **Čertovka**, or Devil's Stream, which slices Kampa from the mainland, went by the altogether unromantic name of the Ditch until it was cleaned up and rechristened in the nineteenth century. The communists proposed filling the Čertovka to create a major road but were luckily thwarted by the forces of sanity, and this singular place, with its medieval water wheels, has survived.

Kampa is an oasis of calm on even the most crowded August day. One of the loveliest parks in the city is located at its southern end. This was created in the nineteenth century when an egalitarian decision was made to join the gardens of three private palaces and throw them open to the public. While washerwomen once rinsed shirts on the banks (note the Chapel to St John of the Laundry near the southern end), today it's taken up by snoozing office workers and bongo-beating Eurohippies. The river and bridge views are as romantic as they come, while the chestnut trees make shady spots for reading and recharging. In spring the park is filled with pink blossom. **Kampa Park** the restaurant (*see page 123*), one of Prague's classier and pricier eateries, is actually at the other end of the island, where the Čertovka runs back into the river.

Beatle's about – John lives on.

Between Kampa & Petřín Hill

Across the tiny bridge on Hroznová that leads to tranquil Velkopřevorské náměstí is the elegant **Buquoy Palace** (Buquoyský palác), a frothy, pink stucco creation dating from 1719, which now houses the French Embassy. Opposite is the **John Lennon Wall**, which, during the 1980s, became a place of pilgrimage for the city's hippies, who dedicated it to their idol and scrawled their messages of love, peace and rock 'n' roll across it. The secret police, spotting a dangerous subversive plot to undermine the state, lost no time in painting over the graffiti, only to have John's smiling face reappear a few days later. This continued until 1989 when the wall was returned to the Knights of Malta as part of a huge property package under restitution. The Knights proved even more po-faced than the secret police and were poised ready to whitewash the graffitti when an unlikely Beatles fan, in the form of the French Ambassador, came to the rescue. Claiming to enjoy the strains of *Give Peace a Chance* wafting through his office window, he sparked a diplomatic incident but saved the wall. In the summer of 1998, the Knights had a change of heart, the graffiti and crumbling remains of Lennon's face were removed, the wall was replastered and the scouser's portrait repainted by artist František Flasar. The John Lennon Peace Club is encouraging modest graffiti – preferably in the form of a little flower. Ahhh.

Just around the corner is the lovely **Maltézské náměstí**. The Knights of Malta have lived here since Vladislav II offered them a refuge in Prague. Their eight-pointed cross can be seen all over the square, since the order (which was dissolved by the communists) regained great swathes of property under the restitution laws. Round the corner on Prokopská, **U Maltézských rytířů** restaurant (*see page 125*) occupies a candlelit Gothic cellar that was formerly a hospice operated by the Knights. The baroque building on the corner of the square was once the Museum of Musical Instruments. It has suffered more than its fair share of blows: its priceless Flemish tapestries were given to Von Ribbentrop, Hitler's foreign affairs adviser, its Stradivarius violins were stolen in 1990, and now the museum is closed for good.

Although the museum is gone, the sound of students practising at the nearby conservatory provides a soundtrack to your sightseeing. The highlight of the square is the **Church of Our Lady Beneath the Chain** (Panny Marie pod řetězem). This strange building was originally built by a military-religious order to guard the original Romanesque Judith Bridge that formerly spanned the Vltava close to where Charles Bridge stands today. Two solid towers still protect the

What an eiffel! The **Petřín Tower.** *See p80.*

entrance – they now contain the most unusual flats in Prague. The Hussite wars interrupted the construction of the church and it was never finished. In place of a nave is an ivy-covered courtyard that leads up to a baroque addition (dating from 1640-50) built in the apse of the original structure. Inside, by the altar, are the chains from the original bridge that give the church its name.

At the foot of the Petřín Hill runs **Újezd**, which becomes **Karmelitská** as it runs north before leading into Malostranské náměstí. On the way, there are a couple of peculiar diversions. The first is the **Michna Palace** (Michnův palác), a fine baroque mansion built in 1640-50. It was intended to rival the Wallenstein Palace (*see above*), which was itself built to compete with the Castle. Considering these gargantuan ambitions, it's no surprise that Francesco Caratti took Versailles as his model when it came to designing the garden wing of Michna. Today the gardens contain tennis courts, a clue to the site's present incarnation as the **Tyrš Sport and Physical Training Museum** (closed for an indefinite period at the time of going to press), the headquarters of the Sokol sporting organisation and a youth hostel (*see page 116*).

Further along Karmelitská, at no.9, is the **Church of Our Lady Victorious** (Panny Marie Vítězné; *see below*), the first baroque church in Prague (built 1611-13). It belongs to the Barefooted Carmelites, an order that returned to the city in 1993 and has taken charge of the church's most celebrated exhibit: the doll-like, miracle-working **Bambino di Praga**. Heading left up the hill from Karmelitská is Tržiště, on the corner of which stands **U Malého Glena** (also known as Little Glen's; *see page 151*), a convivial sort of Czech-Irish pub owned by a short American named Glen. A little further up is the hip **St Nicholas Café** cellar bar (*see page 150*). The seventeenth-century **Schönborn Palace** (Schönbornský palác), now the American Embassy, is at Tržiště 15. It was built by Giovanni Santini-Aichel, who, despite his name, was a third generation Praguer, and one of the descendants of Italian craftsmen who formed an expat community on Vlašská just up the hill.

From here, Tržiště becomes a tiny lane that winds up the hill, giving access to some of the loveliest hidden alleys in Malá Strana. Washing hangs out above the streets, old ladies stare out of windows, and at no.22 is **Baráčnická rychta**, one of the most traditional – and certainly the most insalubrious – drinking establishments in the Little Quarter.

Vlašská runs on up the hill from Tržiště and contains the German Embassy, housed in the **Lobkowicz Palace** (Lobkovický palác) at no.19. This is one of four Lobkowicz Palaces in Prague and its design (1703-69) is based on Bernini's unrealised plans for the Louvre. You can get a glimpse of the gorgeous gardens through the gate, though access to the original aviary and bear pit is forbidden. In 1989 thousands of East Germans ignored the Verboten signs and scaled the high walls, setting up camp in the garden until they were granted asylum. The Lobkowicz family were major landowners in Bohemia until the nationalisation of property in 1948, and although they haven't reclaimed the palace, they have succeeded in regaining five castles, and the *vinárna* next door serves a good selection of wines from their estate in Mělník (*see page 225*).

Across from the palace and a few yards up Šporkova you'll find the **Faros** restaurant (*see page 126*), an acceptable Greek place that is one of the area's better spots for lunch. Nearby is the excellent **Hotel Sax** (*see page 111*) on Janský vršek. Vlašská ambles on upwards, fading out as it passes a hospital and chapel founded in the seventeenth century by the area's Italian community, and eventually leads back on to Petřín Hill.

Petřín Hill

Rising up in the west of Malá Strana is **Petřín Hill** (Petřínské sady), the highest, greenest and most peaceful of Prague's seven hills. This is the largest expanse of greenery in central Prague – a favourite spot for sledging children in winter and kissing couples in summer. 'Petřín' comes from the Latin word for rock, a reference to the fact that the hill was the source for much of the city's building material. The southern edge of the hill is traversed by the so-called **Hunger Wall** (Hladová zed), an eight-metre (23-ft) high fortification commissioned by Charles IV in 1362 to provide some work for the poor of the city.

The lazy (and fun) way up to the top of the hill is to catch the funicular from Újezd (running roughly every ten minutes, and stopping halfway up by the pricey restaurant **Nebozízek**). At the top is a fine collection of architectural absurdities. Climb the 299 steps of the **Petřín Tower** (*see below*) – a fifth-scale copy of the Eiffel Tower – for spectacular views over the city. This was erected in 1891 for the Jubilee Exhibition, as was the neighbouring mock Gothic castle that now houses the **Mirror Maze** (*see below*), a fairground-style hall of wacky mirrors and, somewhat incongruously, a tableau with wax figures representing the defence of Charles Bridge against the Swedes in 1648. There's a café at the base of the tower, and another basic refreshment hut nearby.

The third and least-frequented of the Petřín trio of attractions is **Štefánik Observatory** (*see below*), near to the top of the funicular. It's well worth a peek, though. On clear days you can look at sunspots and possibly a planet or two; on good nights there are views of the stars and craters on the moon.

The secret gardens

Don't be led astray by the long, blank walls that hide them – Malá Strana is home to some of Prague's finest gardens. Their nature may be more vest-pocket than the rambling woods of nearby Stromovka, but they retain a character of grace and elegance that belies their roots as pleasure respites for one-time nobles. Peacocks wander from statue to hedgerow and high walls banish even the memory of the tourist throngs passing by, unawares, just beyond them.

The French and Italian Renaissance and baroque layouts, ornamented by vases, balustrades, stairs, ponds and colonnades, provided soothing havens for a select few long before public parks were established in Prague. To this day, the intimacy remains for the few people who duck through a small unadorned entrance.

For Malá Strana's other green spaces, see **Kampa Island** and **Petřin Hill** in this chapter.

Ledeburg Gardens

(Ledeburská zahrada) Valdštejnské náměstí 3. Metro Malostranská/12, 22 tram. **Opening** pending. **Map 2 E2**
Though still undergoing restoration work at the time of going to press, the magnificently terraced criss-crossing paths of the Ledeburg Gardens look to be nearly ready to reopen to the public and so are worth trying; they are unparalleled for location. The terraces lead directly up to Prague Castle's southern flank, offering a stunning view of the pantiled roofs that are a distinct Malá Strana charm.

Paradise Gardens/ Gardens on the Ramparts

(Rajská zahrada/Zahrada na valech) Prague Castle, third courtyard (2437 3368). Metro Malostranská/12, 22 tram. **Open** *Apr-Oct* 9am-5pm daily. **Map 2 D2**
Once you do make it to the Castle, you can actually improve on the Ledeburg Gardens' vista, but you'll have to find the Bull Staircase (just south of St Vitus's Cathedral). Descend into Prague Castle's 'other' garden while most visitors are uniformly lured off to the Royal Gardens on Hradčany's north slope. As you mingle with a handful of Prague natives and take in the best non-Castle vista in the city, don't miss the twin obelisks that solemnly mark the holy spots where the defenestrated Catholic councillors were saved by dung heaps (*see p17*). They fit in well with the First Republic makeover worked by Josip Plečnik (*see p38*), who also created that remarkable Bull Staircase and the grandiose neo-classical vases.

Soldiers' Gardens

(Vojanovy sady) U lužického semináře. Metro Malostranská/12, 18, 22 tram. **Open** *May-Sept* 9am-7pm daily. **Map 2 E/F3**
This island of tranquillity, only accessible by a small door in the street-side wall, is invariably overlooked by visitors, yet it has quietly bloomed in spring for longer than any other green spot in the city – since the Carmelites established it in 1248. Peacocks have the run of the place, not soldiers, except possibly during summer brass concerts. Aside from the winding paths, a tiny chapel looking as if it were made from candle drippings serves as a temple to Elijah.

Wallenstein Gardens

(Valdštejnská zahrada) Valdštejnské náměstí 4. Metro Malostranská/12, 18, 22 tram. **Open** *May-Sept* 9am-7pm daily. **Map 2 E2**
Once the private puttering ground of megalomaniac Catholic warlord Albrecht von Wallenstein (*see p18*), these rambling paths and blossoming trees were reclaimed by the public long ago – a small compensation for the homes Wallenstein's palace gobbled up in the first place. At least he did it in style, contracting Milanese architect Andrea Spezza in 1624 to turn out this splendid spot (and the vast halls of the noble residence attached) and sculptor Adrian de Vries to adorn it. The statues remaining today are copies, the originals having so impressed the marauding Swedes during the Thirty Years' War that they spirited them off. Catch a summer concert here. *See picture below.*

While kids get the most out of the hilltop attractions, Petřin's labyrinthine paths are the attraction for grown-ups. It's possible to wind through the apple, pear and rowan trees for hours, never quite working out when you will come across the statue of Karel Hynek Mácha, unofficial patron saint of all lovers. The unlit bowers are a favourite of his disciples, who begin to gravitate here as soon as the first buds appear and linger until the last leaf has fallen.

If you don't want to descend the hill, take a gentle downhill stroll to the **Strahov Monastery** (*see page 73*) and the 22 tram stop.

Sights

Church of Our Lady Victorious

(Kostel Panny Marie Vitězné) Karmelitská 9, Prague 1 (530 752). Tram 12, 22. **Open** 9am-7pm Mon-Sat; 10am-8pm Sun. **Map 2 D4**

The early baroque church is entirely eclipsed by its diminutive but revered occupant: **Il Bambino di Praga** (Pražské Jezulátko). This 400-year-old wax effigy of the baby Jesus draws pilgrims, letters and cash from grateful and/or desperate believers the world over. The list of miracles that the Infant of Prague is supposed to have performed is impressive and over 100 stone plaques of thanks attest to his powers. The effigy was brought from Spain to Prague in the seventeenth century, placed under the care of the Carmelite nuns just in time to protect them from the plague, and was later granted official miracle status by the Catholic Church. A wardrobe of over 60 outfits befits this dazzling reputation: the baby Jesus is always magnificently turned out, and his clothes have been changed by the Order of English Virgins at sunrise on selected days for 200 years. While he is said to be anatomically correct, the nuns' blushes are spared by a specially designed wax undershirt. At the back of the church is a shamelessly commerical bambino gift shop where tour parties grapple for miraculous souvenirs.

Church of St Nicholas

(Chrám sv. Mikuláše) Malostranské náměstí, Prague 1 (536 983). Metro Malostranská/12, 22 tram. **Open** *May-Sept* 9am-4.30pm daily; *Oct-Apr* 9am-4pm daily. **Admission** 30 Kč adults; 15 Kč children, students. **Map 2 D3**

The immense dome and bell-tower of St Nicholas, which dominate Malá Strana, are monuments to the money and effort that the Catholic Church sank into the Counter-Reformation. The rich façade by Christoph Dientzenhofer, completed around 1710, conceals an interior and dome by his son Kilián Ignaz dedicated to high baroque at its most flamboyantly camp – bathroom-suite pinks and greens, swooping golden cherubs, swirling gowns and dramatic gestures; there's even a figure coyly proffering a pair of handcuffs.

Commissioned by the Jesuits, it took three generations of architects, several financial crises and the demolition of much of the neighbourhood between presentation of the first plans in 1653 to final completion in 1755. Inside, a *trompe l'oeil* extravaganza created by the Austrian Johann Lukas Kracker covers the ceiling, seamlessly blending with the actual structure of the church below. Frescoes portray the life and times of St Nicholas, best known as the Bishop of Myra and the bearer of gifts to small children, but also the patron saint of municipal administration. Maybe this is why St Nicholas's was restored by the communists in the 1950s when the rest of Prague's baroque churches were left to crumble.

Church of St Thomas

(Kostel sv. Tomáše) Josefská 8, Prague 1 (530 218/5731 3142). Metro Malostranská/12, 22 tram. **Open** 10.45-1pm, 2.30-6pm, daily. **Admission free. Map 2 E3**

It's worth craning your neck to get a good look at the curvy pink façade of St Thomas's. The lopsided structure is the legacy of an earlier Gothic church built for the Order of Augustinian hermits. After the structure was damaged by fire in 1723, Kilián Ignaz Dientzenhofer was employed to give it the baroque touch. The newly rich burghers of Malá Strana provided enough cash for the frescoes to be completed at breakneck speed (in only two years) and for Rubens to paint the altarpiece *The Martyrdom of St Thomas*. They even bought the bodies of two saints. The original altarpiece is now part of the National Gallery's collection on show in the **Sternberg Palace** (*see p97*) and has been replaced by a copy, but the skeletons of the saints dressed in period costume are still on display. Next door are the seventeenth-century cloisters, where the monks dabbled in alchemy before realising that transforming hops into beer was easier and more lucrative than making gold out of base metals. A door on Letenská leads to their former brewery, now the tourist-infested restaurant **U sv. Tomáše**.

Mirror Maze

(Zrcadlové bludiště) Petřin Hill, Prague 1 (531 362). Tram 12 or 22, then funicular railway. **Open** *Apr-Oct* 10am-7pm daily; *Nov-Mar* 10am-5pm Sat, Sun. Closed in bad weather. **Admission** 30 Kč adults; 20 Kč children. **Map 1 C5**

Housed in a cast-iron mock Gothic castle complete with drawbridge and crenellations is a hall of distorting mirrors that, rather touchingly in this age of computer entertainment, still causes remarkable hilarity among kids and their parents. Alongside is a diorama of one of the proudest historical moments for the citizens of Prague: the defence of Charles Bridge against the Swedes in 1648.

Petřin Tower

(Rozhledna) Petřin Hill, Prague 1 (531 786). Tram 12 or 22, then funicular railway. **Open** *Apr-Oct* 9.30am-7pm daily; *Nov-Mar* 9.30am-5pm Sat, Sun. Closed in bad weather. **Admission** 25 Kč adults; 10 Kč students; 5 Kč children. **Map 1 B5**

At the time that the Parisians were still debating the aesthetic value of the newly erected Eiffel Tower, the Czechs decided they liked it so much they constructed their own version out of recycled railway tracks in just 31 days for the 1891 Jubilee Exhibition. Its fiercest opponent was Adolf Hitler, who looked out of his guest room in the Castle and made an immediate order for 'that metal contraption' to be removed. Somehow it survived, although these days it's pretty tatty, but the stiff climb to the top is made worthwhile by phenomenal views over the city. This is about the only vantage point that gives a view of St Vitus's Cathedral as a complete building, and not merely a set of spires poking over the top of the rest of the Castle. Just try not to think about the alarming way the tower sways in the wind.

Štefánik Observatory

(Hvězdárna) Petřin Hill, Prague 1 (5732 0540). Tram 12, 22, then funicular railway. **Open** *Apr-Aug* 2-7pm, 9-11pm, Tue-Fri; 10am-noon, 2-7pm, 9-11pm, Sat, Sun. Shorter opening hours during rest of year. **Admission** 15 Kč adults; 5 Kč children, students; free under-6s. **Map 1 C5**

Prague is justly proud of its historical astronomical connections. Both the haughty Dane Tycho Brahe and his protégé Johannes Kepler were one-time residents, and the duo feature in the observatory's displays (which contain enough English labelling to be helpful), along with stellar information and a CD-Rom about famous space missions. Telescopes offer glimpses of sun spots and planets during the day and panoramas of the stars and the moon on fine nights.

Further Afield

When you tire of the standard tourist trail and long to be far from the maddening crowds, head out of the centre and discover the Prague few visitors see.

Holešovice, Letná & Troja

Map 7

At first glance, **Holešovice** is an unremarkable turn-of-the-century suburb filled with tenement buildings overlaid with a thick layer of grime from neighbouring factories, and containing one of Prague's two international train stations. However, this district to the north of the Old Town over the Vltava also contains two of the finest green spaces in the city and is rapidly throwing off its post-war torpor. New shops and bars have appeared, and, with the opening of the new Gallery of Modern & Contemporary Art, it looks set to become one of the liveliest areas in town and a good spot to pass a leisurely day.

Down towards the river on Kostelní is the **National Technical Museum** (*see page 93*), a constructivist building dating from 1938-41. Its dull name belies a fascinating collection that includes an atrium packed with steam trains, aeroplanes, a hot-air balloon, innumerable cars and a flying sledge, and a coal mine in the basement.

Five minutes' walk east of here is Holešovice's main drag, Dukelských hrdinů. Here stands another constructivist building, the enormous **Veletržní palác** (Trade Fair Palace), built in the mid-1920s to house the trade fairs when they had outgrown Výstaviště (*see below*). When Le Corbusier first visited the palace he described it as 'breathtaking', although he later dismissed it as 'a very important building which after all is not refined enough to be called architecture'. It was gutted by fire in 1974 but has been splendidly restored; the stunning white-painted atrium rises up seven storeys lined with sweeping guard rails, giving it the feel of a massive ocean liner. Pop in to peak at the atrium even if you don't want to look around the National Gallery's **Gallery of Modern & Contemporary Art** (*see page 96*) within. This is a stunning exhibition space in which to view the impressive collection of twentieth-century Czech art.

If museum fatigue is setting in, head for parallel Janovského, one of the centres of Prague's extensive twentysomething slacker scene. Here you'll find **The Globe** (*see also pages 151 & 158*), an American-run bookshop/café and a great spot for brunch.

Bring me the head of Joseph Stalin

It wasn't until 1 May 1955, two years after the dictator's demise, that Prague's Stalin Monument was unveiled to cheering crowds. It was the largest figure of Stalin ever erected – a 14,000-ton, 30-m (98-ft) high granite monster that had taken 600 workers 500 days to create. One of its designers, Otokar Švec, had committed suicide shortly before, leaving all his money to a school for blind children, for they at least would not have to view his creation. Everyone else in Prague could see it, though, as the towering tyrant high on Letná Park led a procession of monumental workers in a tableau popularly dubbed *tlačenice* – the crush – for its resemblance to a communist-era bread queue.

The following year, Stalin was denounced by Nikita Khrushchev, tripping off a mild thaw throughout the Eastern Bloc. Always sluggish to catch on to liberalising trends, it took Czechoslovakia six years to remove the embarrassing monument, which was finally reduced to rubble in 1962. Legends linger about the fate of Stalin's massive head. Some claim that the night before the statue was swept on to the rubbish heap of history, an ardent fan removed it and hid it somewhere in Prague. Others claim that it rolled into the Vltava where it remains to the present day.

The statue was replaced by a giant, ponderously slow metronome. Once in a while, this thing actually works. Set the contraption to 160 beats per minute, and the Stalin Monument site would be a fabulous location for an outdoor techno rave.

A couple of minutes' walk to the north is **Výstaviště** ('exhibition ground'; entrance 10 Kč; *see below*), an unusual wrought-iron pavilion built to house the Jubilee Exhibition of 1891 and considered the first expression of art nouveau in the city. Here, in the **Lapidarium** (*see page 98*), you'll find an intriguing collection of reject monuments that once stood around the city. Come on a summer evening to see the floodlit Křižík fountain swoop and soar in time to music, or – if you're brave – have a go on the old rollercoaster in the adjacent funfair, **Lunapark** (*see page 178*). From the top of the ferris wheel there are fine views over the woody environs of **Stromovka**, a vast park laid out by Rudolf II in the sixteenth century, as a place where he could commune with nature. Rudolf's interests ranged from the eclectic to the perverse and his favoured companion at Stromovka was the English alchemist and mathematician John Dee, who got the job when he claimed to understand both the language of the birds and the one in which Adam conversed with Eve in Paradise. Today, the leafy park makes a wonderful spot for a stroll, a bike ride or a picnic. Towards the centre is one of Prague's earliest neo-Gothic buildings, the **Místodržitelský letohrádek** (built 1805).

If you still have the energy, take the half-hour walk back to the Old Town via the sedate embassy-land of Bubeneč, past the **Sparta Stadium** and through **Letná Park** (Letenské sady). This is where the biggest demonstration of 1989 took place, attended by nearly a million people. On the edge of the park, with a fine view overlooking the town, is the plinth where the statue of Stalin used to stand (*see page 81*). The area around here is a favourite spot for Prague's enthusiastic but generally incompetent skateboarders.

Alternatively, a 20-minute walk north of Stromovka (or you can take the 112 bus from Nádraží Holešovice metro station) brings you to **Troja Château** (Trojský zámek; *see below*). Commissioned by Count Šternberg in the 1700s and built by a French architect and Italian craftsmen, it contains some stunning *trompe l'oeil* frescoes, fakes within fakes that completely steal the limelight from the nineteenth-century paintings exhibited here. Count Šternberg's horses were particularly fortunate, inhabiting a sumptuous stable block with marble floors and decorated with frescoes of their noble forebears. The inmates of Prague's **zoo** (*see page 176*) across the road can only curse their historical mis-timing, for, despite having found a new patron in Coca-Cola, their living conditions are altogether less salubrious.

Troja Château

(Trojský zámek) U trojského zámku 1, Prague 7 (689 0761/855 1726). Metro Nádraží Holešovice/112 bus. **Open** 10am-5pm Tue-Sun. **Admission** 100 Kč adults; 50 Kč children, students.

After winning huge tracts of land in the property lottery that followed the Thirty Years' War, Count Šternberg embarked upon creating a house worthy of his ego. As a native Czech nobleman he was anxious to prove his loyalty to the Habsburg emperor and literally moved mountains to do so. The hillside had to be dug out to align the villa with the royal hunting park of Stromovka and the distant spires of the cathedral; the Burgundian architect, Jean-Baptiste Mathey, had to be defended against the Italian building mafia; sculptors had to be imported from Dresden and painters from Flanders. The result is a paean to the Habsburg dynasty, modelled on a classical Italian villa and surrounded by formal gardens in the French style, interspersed with fountains and sculptures. On the massive external staircase (by Johann Georg Heerman and his nephew Paul), gods hurl the rebellious giants into a dank grotto. In the Grand Hall (by Abraham and Isaac Godyn) the virtuous Habsburgs enjoy a well-earned victory over the infidel Turks. This, a fascinating though slightly ludicrous example of illusory painting, is the main attraction of Troja. To see it you have to don huge red slippers to protect the marble floors, which have the effect of making visitors look like Smurfs. An insensitive restoration programme has destroyed the atmosphere of the villa, and the installation of a small collection of nineteenth-century Czech painting does little to redeem it.

Výstaviště

Prague 7 (2010 3111/2010 3204). Metro Nádraží Holešovice/5, 12, 17 tram. **Open** 2-10pm Tue-Fri; 10am-10pm Sat, Sun. **Admission** weekends 10 Kč. **Map 7 D1**
Built out of curvaceous expanses of wrought iron to house the Great Exhibition of 1891, Výstaviště signalled the birth of the new architectural form in Prague. During the 1940s it became the site of various communist congresses, but today it is principally used to house car and computer expos. It's worth dodging past the salesmen to see the interior. The industrial feeling created by the wrought-iron structure is offset by vivid stained glass and exquisite floral decorations. The best view of the exterior is from the back, where a monumental modern fountain gushes at night in time to popular classics, accompanied by a light show. The grounds are filled with architectural oddities (the **Lapidarium**; *see p98*), an open-air cinema and a delightfully delapidated funfair (**Lunapark**; *see p178*), which nevertheless pulls in crowds of Czech families at the weekends.

Dejvice & further west

Some of the most exclusive residences in the city are located in Prague 6, the suburbs that lie beyond the Castle. You'd never guess this, though, from the rather desolate hub of the area, Vítězné náměstí, where a statue of Lenin used to stand. Nearby is the **U Cedru** restaurant (*see page 129*), serving up the some of the best Middle Eastern food in Prague.

Leading north from the square is the wide Jugoslávských partyzánů (Avenue of Yugoslav Partisans) at the end of which you'll find the **Holiday Inn Prague**. This monumental piece of wedding-cake socialist realism built in the 1950s is one of the last remaining bastions of Marxist-Leninist interior decoration in the city. The bars, which used to be populated by morose party officials after a hard day spent inventing production figures, have now been taken over by morose mafioso types.

Vyšehrad Cemetery – home to all the Czech arts greats, and to some great funeral art.

On the hill above the hotel are the **Baba Villas**, a colony of constructivist houses built after, and inspired by the huge success of, the 1927 Exhibition of Modern Living in Stuttgart. Under the guidance of Pavel Janák, all 33 of the houses were individually commissioned to provide simple but radically designed living spaces for ordinary families. However, they were quickly snapped up by leading figures of the Czech avant-garde, and many of them are still decorated with original fixtures and fittings. None, alas, is open to the public, but they are still a must-see for any fan of modern architecture. Take bus 131 to U Matěje and walk up Matějská to reach the estate.

On the western fringe of the city, just off Patočkova (bus 108, 174, 180, 217), is the **Břevnov Monastery**, inhabited by Benedictine monks since AD993 and modelled on 'God's perfect workshop'. The monks celebrated their millennium with an enormous spring clean, sweeping out traces of the Ministry of the Interior, which for the last 40 years had used the **Basilica of St Margaret** (sv. Markéta) as a warehouse for its files on suspicious-looking foreigners. This Romanesque church was remodelled by the Dientzenhofer father-and-son act in the early eighteenth century, and is one of their most successful commissions, with a single high nave and unfussy interior.

Close by, near the terminus of tram 22, a small stone pyramid marks the site of **Bílá Hora**, or White Mountain, where the decisive first battle of the Thirty Years' War took place in 1620 (*see page 17*). Within the park is the **Hvězda Hunting Lodge** (Letohrádek Hvězda), an extraordinary product of the Renaissance mind, its angular walls and roof arranged in the pattern of a six-pointed star (*hvězda* in Czech). It was built in the 1550s for Archduke Ferdinand of Tyrol who, when he wasn't feuding with Rudolf II over possession of the Habsburg narwhal horn, was obsessed with numerology, and the whole is conceived as an intellectual conundrum. Today it houses the rather dull **Jirásek and Aleš Museum** (closed at time of going to press; *see page 94*).

North of here, off Evropská, is the extensive and wonderfully wild **Divoká Šárka** (*see also pages 210 & 212*), a fine place to stroll, swim or cycle, away from the city crowds and fumes. The summer nude sunbathing area also makes an impression.

Smíchov & Barrandov

Smíchov has undergone quite a few changes since the days when Mozart stayed here. Rapid industrialisation rather spoilt the ambience of the aristocracy's summer houses and the area has since been taken over by factories (including the Bass-owned Staropramen Brewery) and factory workers. Proletarian glories are still commemorated in the massive socialist realist murals in Anděl metro station. You can get an idea of what Smíchov was once like at **Bertramka**, the house with lilac-scented gardens that belonged to František and Josefina Dušek and is now a museum devoted to their most famous house guest, Wolfgang Amadeus Mozart (**Mozart Museum;** *see page 92*).

South of Smíchov is **Barrandov**, the Czech version of Hollywood (*see also page 180*). On the cliffs below there are even white Hollywood-style letters that spell out B-a-r-r-a-n-d-e, although this is actually in homage to the nineteenth-century geologist after whom the quarter takes its name. Enormous studios were built here in the 1930s and the site has been the centre of the Czech film industry ever since. On the hills below the studios are some interesting modern villas, among them a former terrace restaurant built by an uncle of Václav Havel in the constructivist style. There are plans to revamp it, although at present it's a down-at-heel reminder of the glory days of the First Republic.

Vyšehrad

Vyšehrad, the rocky outcrop south of Nové Město, is where all the best Prague myths were born. **Libuše**, the mother of Prague, fell into a trance and sent her horse out into the countryside to find her a suitable spouse. The horse returned with a strapping young ploughman called Přemysl, after whom the early Bohemian kings take their name (*see also page 10*). Alas, no evidence has been uncovered to back up the legend, but it has emerged that a castle was founded here in the first half of the tenth century, enjoying a period of importance when King Vratislav II (1061-92) built

a royal palace on the rock. Within 50 years, though, the Přemyslid rulers had moved back to Prague Castle and Vyšehrad's short period of policital pre-eminence was over. The historical myths were revived by the nineteenth-century romantics who rebuilt the Church of Sts Peter and Paul, created a public park and established a national cemetery for the biggest names in Czech arts.

The easiest way to reach Vyšehrad is to take the metro to the Vyšehrad stop, under the enormous road bridge spanning the Nusle valley. When it was built in the 1970s, the bridge was hailed as a monument to socialism, an epithet hastily dropped when large chunks of concrete began falling on passing pedestrians, and it became the most popular spot for suicides in the city. Walk away from the towering **Corinthia Hotel Forum** (whose fitness centre and pool boast one of the best views in the city; *see page 104*) and past the entirely unappealing, monolithic concrete **Palace of Culture** (Palác kultury), completed in 1980 and the supreme architectural expression of the years that were referred to as 'normalisation', then through the baroque gateway into the park. The information centre to the right can provide maps of the area.

One of the first sights you will pass is the over-restored **Rotunda of St Martin**. Dating from the second half of the eleventh century, it is the oldest complete Romanesque building in Prague.

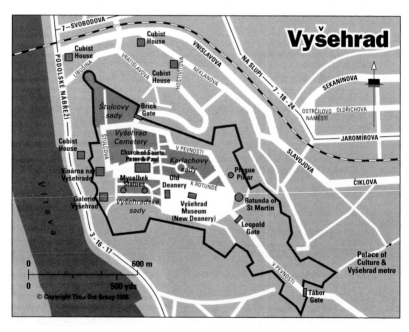

There's been a church on the same site at Vyšehrad since the fourteenth century, but it was apparently irrevocably damaged when Lucifer, angered by an insubordinate cleric, threw three large rocks through the roof. The granite slabs (known as the **Devil Pillars**) can be found close to the **Old Deanery**, but the holes are gone and Joseph Mocker's neo-Gothic **Church of Sts Peter and Paul** (sv. Petr a Pavel) dates from the beginning of the twentieth century. Restoration has brought out the best of the splendid polychrome interior, decked out with art nouveau-style saints and decorative motifs.

Next door is the **Vyšehrad Cemetery**, conceived by the nineteenth-century National Revival movement and last resting place of the cream of the country's arts worthies, including the composers Dvořák and Smetana, writers Karel Čapek and Jan Neruda and painter Mikoláš Aleš. The **slavín** (pantheon), designed by Antonín Wiehl, jointly commemorates further big cheeses such as painter Alfons Mucha and sculptor Josef Václav Myslbek. Surrounded by Italianate arcades, the cemetery contains a wealth of fine memorials, many displaying art nouveau influences.

On the south side of the church are four monumental sculptural groups by Myslbek depicting mythological heroes from Czech history; the thrusting couple nearest to the church are the legendary founders of Prague – Přemysl and Libuše (*see page 10*).

The park extends to the cliff edge overlooking the Vltava, from where there are fine views across the water to the Castle. A walk along the ramparts, an al fresco bite and a drink at the basic **Vinárna na Vyšehradě** by the church and a leisurely mooch around the Vyšehrad sights is a fine and (usually) not too crowded way to pass an afternoon.

If you continue down the hill from Vyšehrad along Přemyslova, you'll find one of the most outstanding pieces of cubist architecture in the city, a corner apartment block designed by **Josef Chochol** at Neklanova 30 (1911-13). He also designed the house on Libušina 3, further to the west near the river. Peep over the fence on the embankment to see the overgrown remains of some cubist landscaping. Some way south is a railway bridge popularly known as 'The Bridge of Intelligence', because it was built by the intellectual élite who worked as labourers after losing their jobs during the purges of the 1950s.

Vinohrady & Žižkov

Map 8

Vinohrady came into existence in what the communist guidebooks called the period of Bourgeois Capitalism, and it's an area of magnificent, if crumbling, *fin de siècle* tenements. The heart of the neighbourhood is Náměstí Míru, with the twin spires of the neo-Gothic **Church of St Ludmila** (sv. Ludmila) and the opulent **Vinohrady Theatre** (Divadlo na Vinohradech). The **Radost/FX** café, gallery and nightclub complex (*see pages 129, 152 & 203*), past its prime but still one of Prague's premier clubs, is nearby on Bělehradská. The **Medúza** café (*see page 152*) on quiet Belgická is one of the city's nicest daytime spots.

The main artery of Vinohrady, however, is Vinohradská, a little further north. Formerly called Stalinova třída, it was here that the fiercest street battles of 1968, against the Warsaw Pact troops, took place. On the parallel Mánesova is **U Knihomola** (*see page 158*), an English-language bookshop and pricey café. Vinohradská heads east past the **Pavilon** designer mall and up to the fine Náměstí Jiřího z Poděbrad. Art nouveau apartment blocks line the sides, looking out on to the **Church of the Sacred Heart** (Nejsvětější Srdce Páně), one of the most inspiring pieces of modern architecture in the city, dominated by its huge glass clock. It was built in 1928-32 by **Josip Plečnik** (*see page 39*), the pioneering Slovenian architect.

Fans of ecclesiastical modernism might also like to look at Pavel Janák's 1930s **Hussite Church** (Husův sbor) on the corner of U vodárny and Dykova, and Josef Gočar's uncompromising functionalist **Church of St Wenceslas** (sv. Václav) on náměstí Svatopluka Čecha.

A few streets north of Plečnik's church is the **Akropolis** (*see pages 152 & 198*), a hip bar, a restaurant and music venue. Looming above it is the infamous, space-age **Žižkov TV Tower** (Žižkovský Televizní vysílač; *see below*), which was completed in 1989 and still suffers from excessive unpopularity, at least among native Praguers.

Tumbling down the hill to the north and east is **Žižkov**, a district notorious for its insalubrious pubs and whorehouses and for its large Romany population. One of the only pubs welcoming to outsiders is **U vystřeleného oka** (the Shot-Out Eye; *see page 152*) on U božích bojovníků. Žižkov has always been a working-class district, so it's not surprising that the post-war presidents chose to be interred here, in the massive **National Memorial** (Národní památník; *see below*) on top of Vitkov Hill. Outside this mausoleum stands the largest equestrian statue in the world, a 16.5-ton effigy of Hussite hero Jan Žižka who, for a time, vanquished the combined Catholic armies and gave his name to the suburb (*see also page 15*). The corpses were ejected from the mausoleum in 1990, but it's still an eerie, neglected place, though there are plans to turn the hill into a huge leisure complex. It has already hosted a massive rave party.

Further east on Vinohradská are two fine cemeteries. The first, **Olšany Cemetery** (Olšanské hřbitovy; *see below*), is the largest in Prague – an enormous city of the dead. Since 1989 the cemetery has begun to suffer from the usual urban blights (graffiti) as well as some more unusual ones (grave-robbing). The cemetery extends from the Flora metro station to Jana Želivského, and includes a Garden of Rest, where the Red Army soldiers who died liberating Prague are buried. Their graves are marked by sculptures of crossed machine guns, and wreaths are still left by those who haven't forgotten them.

Next door is the **Jewish Cemetery** (Židovské hřbitovy), where fans of Franz Kafka come to leave stones and pay their respects at his simple grave (follow the sign at the entrance by Želivského metro station; it's about 200m (660ft) down the row by the southern cemetery wall). The cemetery is in stark contrast to the cramped quarters of the Old Jewish Cemetery in Josefov. It was founded in 1890 and only a fraction of the graveyard has been used since the decimation of the population in World War II.

National Memorial

(Národní památník) U památníku, Praha 3 (627 8452). Metro Florenc/133, 168, 207 bus. **Map 8 C1**
The National Memorial is one of the city's best-known and least liked landmarks. Looming above the eastern working-class suburb of Žižkov, the massive, constructivist, rectangular block and equally enormous equestrian statue high up on Vitkov Hill can be seen from many points around the city. It was built in 1925 by Jan Zázvorka as a dignified setting for the remains of the legionnaires who fought against the Austro-Hungarian Empire in World War I. In 1953 it was refitted out by the communist regime and turned into a mausoleum for the Heroes of the Working Class. The mummified remains of Klement Gottwald, first communist president, were kept here, tended by a team of scientists who (unsuccessfully) tried to preserve his body for display, Lenin-style, before the project was abandoned and the body fobbed off on Gottwald's family in 1990.

No one is quite sure what to do with the memorial or the mausoleum. Opening times are unpredictable, but it doesn't really matter as most of what you might want to see can be seen from the outside. In front stands the massive equestrian statue of one-eyed General Žižka, scourge of fourteenth-century Catholics and the darling of the communists who adopted him in an effort to establish genuine Bohemian credentials. It's more impressive for its entry in the *Guinness Book of Records* than for any artistic merit. One developer has further plans to turn the entire complex into a park that'll eventually stand as the pride of Žižkov.

Olšany Cemetery

(Olšanské hřbitovy) Vinohradská/Jana Želivského, Praha 3. Metro Flora or Želivského. **Open** dawn-dusk daily. **Map 8 D2**
The overgrown yet beautiful Olšany Cemetery is the last resting place of two unlikely bed fellows: the first communist president, Klement Gottwald, who died after catching a cold at Stalin's funeral, and the most famous anti-communist martyr, Jan Palach, the student who set fire to himself in Wenceslas Square in 1969. In death their fates have been strangely linked, as neither of their mortal remains have been allowed to rest in peace. Palach was originally buried here in 1969, when 800,000 people attended his funeral, but his grave became such a focus of dissent that the authorities disinterred his body and reburied it deep in the Bohemian countryside. In 1990 he was dug up and brought back to Olšany. You can find his grave just to the right of the main entrance. Gottwald is harder to locate,

hidden away in Section 5 and sharing a mass grave with various other discredited party members. In 1990 his mummified remains were ejected unceremoniously from the National Mausoleum (*see above*) and returned to the family. An unusual index of popular opinion is to check which grave is sporting the most floral tributes and candles.

Žižkov TV Tower

(Televizní vysílač) Mahlerovy sady, Praha 3 (6700 5784). Metro Jiřího z Poděbrad/5, 9, 26 tram. **Open** *tower* 10am-11pm daily; *café* 11am-11pm daily. **Admission** 30 Kč; under-10s free. **Map 8 C2**
The huge, thrusting, three-pillared television tower in Žižkov has been dubbed the *Pražský pták* or 'Prague Prick'. Seemingly modelled on a Soyuz rocket ready for blast-off, or maybe something out of *Thunderbirds*, it has been more of a hit with space-crazy visitors than with the locals. It was planned under the communists (who tore up part of the adjacent Jewish Cemetery to make room for it), completed early in 1989, and no sooner started operating in 1990 than it came under attack from nearby residents who claimed it was guilty of, among other things, jamming foreign radio waves and giving their children cancer. Although cleared on both counts, it is easy to understand the Big Brother analogies. You can take a lift up to the eighth-floor viewing platform, or have a drink in the fifth-floor café, but in many ways standing at the base and looking up the 216m (709ft) of grey polished steel is even more scary. Views from the platform and the café are splendid, except at night, when they're obscured by reflections off the glass. More than 20 TV channels broadcast from behind the white plastic shielding that defends against the elements. Lower transmitters deal with radio stations and emergency services.

Jižní Město & Háje

To the south and east lies the wilderness of Prague 4. Though parts are very old and beautiful, the post-code has come to mean only one thing for Praguers: *paneláky*. *Panelák* is the Czech word for a tower block made out of pre-fabricated concrete panels. These blocks mushroomed throughout the 1960s and 1970s as a cheap solution to the ever-present housing crisis. Jižní Město, or Southern Town, in Prague 4 has the greatest concentration of them and houses 100,000 people. Possibly the worst aspect of the *panelák* is that they all look identical both outside and in, although residents claim that even worse is the knowledge that they can't even be blown up and would have to be demolished the way they went up, panel by dreary panel.

Similar housing developments now ring the whole city, but Háje, the last metro stop on the red Line C, is as good a place as any to go to see the best of the worst. Before the big name change of 1989, Háje used to be known as Kosmonautů, a nod in the direction of the sister state's space programme and there's still a rather humorous sculpture of two cuddly cosmonauts outside the metro. **Galaxie**, Central Europe's first multiplex cinema, is nearby (*see page 182*), as is the popular swimming spot of **Hostivař Reservoir** (*see page 212*).

The much-maligned but nonetheless magnificent **Žižkov TV Tower** *prepares for take-off.*

Museums & Galleries

Museums 90
Art Galleries 96

Museums

Jewish history, famous composers and... er... wax figures dominate Prague's collections.

*Browsing at the **Mucha Museum**, Prague's newest high-profile museum.*

Prague's collection of museums is rich and varied. As with its galleries, revolution and restitution have taken their toll, and some collections either remain homeless (for example, the splendid collection of the Museum of Musical Instruments) or have disappeared altogether (the Museum of National Security and Interior Ministry, for obvious reasons). However, many museums, freed from state control and pressed into action by the need to be commercial, are trying to make their collections more accessible to the public.

For national collections of paintings and sculpture and a note on opening hours and listings, *see* chapter **Art Galleries**.

Decorative arts

Mucha Museum

(Muchovo muzeum) Kaunický palác, Panská 7, Prague 1 (628 4162/museum@mucha.cz/www.mucha.cz). Metro Můstek/3, 9, 14, 24 tram. **Open** 10am-6pm daily. **Admission** 120 Kč; 60 Kč students. **Map 4 K4**
Prague's newest museum (opened 1998) celebrates the artistic range and mastery of Alfons Mucha (1860-1934), perhaps the most famous of Czech visual artists. Best known for commercial work including mass-produced decorative panels and advertising posters for Sarah Bernhardt's theatre performances, Mucha also influenced his contemporaries by publishing the *Encyclopedia For Craftsmen* (1902), a kind of catalogue of art nouveau decorative elements, forms and designs. Though he lived most of his early years abroad, Mucha returned to his Czech roots later in life, creating a stained-glass window for St Vitus's Cathedral (*see p61*) and his Slavonic Epic, a series of gigantic narrative oil paintings (now housed at the castle at Moravský Krumlov, south-west of Brno). As well as posters, panels and paintings, the spacious museum displays drawings, sketches, notebooks, a re-creation of the artist's Paris studio and a video of his life. There's also a café with a summer terrace.

Museum of Decorative Arts

(Uměleckoprůmyslové muzeum) ulice 17. listopadu 2, Prague 1 (2481 1241). Metro Staroměstská/17, 18 tram. **Open** 10am-6pm Tue-Sun. **Admission** 40 Kč; 20 Kč 10-15-year-olds, students, OAPs; free under-10s. **Map 3 G2**
Built between 1897 and 1900 in neo-Renaissance style, this museum is a work of art in itself, with richly decorated halls, stained-glass and etched-glass windows, and intricately painted plaster mouldings. The lower floor hosts temporary exhibitions of Czech and international decorative art. Only a fraction of the museum's 190,000 items are permanently displayed in a single floor of galleries upstairs. Arranged chronologically, they document the impressive craftsmanship, decorative styles and, occasionally, the hideous taste of previous centuries. The lavishly crafted pieces here include exquisite furniture, tapestries, pottery, clocks, books, monstrances, a small but beautifully preserved collection of clothing, and fine displays of ceramics and glass. Bohemian glassmakers were highly inventive and managed to perfect techniques such as engraving, facet-cutting and ruby-glass manufacture that their competitors found hard to rival. The tradition continues today, and the museum's extensive holdings of twentieth-century glass art, as well as other items not included in the permanent exhibition, are occasionally shown at other galleries around the city.

History

Historical museum at the Lobkowicz Palace

Lobkovický palác, Jiřská 3, Prague 1 (537 3641/537 218). Metro Malostranská/22 tram. **Open** 9am-5pm Tue-Sun. **Admission** 40 Kč; 20 Kč children, students, OAPs. **Map 2 E2**

Part of the sgraffitoed façade of the original Renaissance building on this site in the Castle complex can be seen from the café in this museum's courtyard. However, the palace itself was rebuilt in the late seventeenth century by the Lobkowicz family and today houses a large two-floor permanent exhibition called 'Treasures From the Nation's Past'. Although the English-language texts can be difficult to follow, archaeology and history buffs will nonetheless be fascinated by the museum's collections of sculptures, coins, documents, instruments of torture, armour, musical instruments, jewellery, furniture and scores of other items including copies of the Czech coronation jewels. The exhibits trace the region's history from Celtic culture in the second century AD, through medieval kingdoms, the Hussite wars and on to the National Revival and industrial revolution. An imposing, gorgeously frescoed banquet hall is used for concerts, recitals and the occasional temporary exhibition.

Komenský Pedagogical Museum

(Pedagogické muzeum JA Komenského) Valdštejnská 20, Prague 1 (2421 0802 ext 104/134). Metro Malostranská/ 12, 22 tram. **Open** 10am-noon, 1-5pm, Tue-Sun. **Admission** 10 Kč; 5 Kč children, students, OAPs. **Map 2 E2**

You may never have even heard of Jan Amos Komenský (Comenius), Czech philosopher and Protestant pedagogue, but he remains a great source of Czech national pride. The museum traces his tragic life (1592-1670) during the turbulent times of the Bohemian Counter-Reformation, as well as his extensive European travels and mind-bogglingly large body of work. Best-known for his contributions to modern education theory, Komensky published 132 works while alive; a further 62 were published posthumously. Though the exhibits are in Czech, the friendly museum attendants will provide visitors with an English-language information sheet, and perhaps even an enthusiastic tour.

Museum of the City of Prague

(Muzeum hlavního města Prahy) Na Poříčí 52, Prague 1 (2481 6772). Metro Florenc/3, 8, 24 tram. **Open** 9am-6pm Tue-Sun. **Admission** 30 Kč; 15 Kč children, students, OAPs. **Map 4 N2**

Antonin Langweil spent 11 years during the early nineteenth century building an incredibly precise paper model of Prague, which is now the museum's prize exhibit. If you've ever wondered what the city looked like before the Jewish ghetto was ripped down, here's your chance to find out. The lower floor's displays begin with artefacts, re-creations and explanations of Prague's pre-history, and follow the city's development and changes through to the seventeenth century. English translations are provided in only a few of the rooms. The upstairs galleries host temporary exhibitions related to Prague's past.

Vyšehrad Museum

Soběslavova 1, Prague 2 (296 651/296 652). Metro Vyšehrad/17 tram. **Open** 9.30am-5.30pm daily. **Admission** 10 Kč; 6 Kč children; 30 Kč day pass to all exhibitions. **Map** *see p85*

The rocky outcrop of Vyšehrad, rising above the east bank of the Vltava, has played an important role in the history of Prague since the first ancient Slav fortifications were built here in the tenth century. Today, it's a vast archaeological monument where layers of history, from Romanesque to baroque, have been uncovered. The monuments of the ancient citadel are co-ordinated by a tiny museum (near the

Romanesque Rotunda of St Martin). A quick glance at the models of Vyšehrad's Gothic and baroque fortress provides a useful background to the citadel's history, layout and architecture. Another small exhibition of the Prague and Vyšehrad fortifications is housed in the Cihelná braná (Brick Gate) at the north entrance to the citadel, where books and information pamphlets can also be purchased. *See also p84.*

Natural history & ethnography

Náprstek Museum

(Náprstkovo muzeum) Betlémské náměstí 1, Prague 1 (2421 4537/2421 4538). Metro Můstek or Národní třída/6, 9, 17, 18, 22 tram. **Open** 9am-noon, 12.45-5.30pm, Tue-Sun. **Admission** 30 Kč; 10 Kč children, students, OAPs; free under-6s. **Map 3 G4/5**

Nineteenth-century nationalist Vojta Náprstek had two passions: modern technology and primitive cultures. While the gadgets he collected are now in the **National Technical Museum** *(see p93)*, the ethnographic bits and bobs he acquired from Czech travellers are housed in an extension to his own house, an ungainly building that smells strongly of disinfectant. Displays concentrating on the native peoples of the Americas, Australasia and the Pacific Islands are interesting and excellently arranged. English-speakers may become frustrated trying to match the items displayed with the confusing explanations in the English-language information binders. Still, fans of archaeology and primitive art shouldn't miss this impressive collection.

National Museum

(Národní muzeum) Václavské náměstí 68, Prague 1 (2423 0485/2449 7111). Metro Muzeum. **Open** *May-Sept* 10am-6pm daily; *Oct-Apr* 9am-5pm daily. **Closed** first Tue of month. **Admission** 60 Kč; 30 Kč 6-15-year-olds, students, OAPs; free under-6s; 50 Kč family ticket; free first Mon of month. **Map 6 L6/7**

The city's grandest museum is also its biggest disappointment. The vast building dominates the top of Wenceslas Square, its neo-Renaissance flamboyance promising an interior bursting with delights. Instead it is filled with roomfuls of dusty fossils and minerals, and more cabinets of stuffed animals than you can shake a stick at. Apart from an introductory sheet in English for each of the 'Prehistory', 'Palaeontology', 'Mineralogy/Petrology' and 'Zoology' sections, all the exhibit labelling is in Czech only. If rocks are your thing, the 10,000-plus specimens on display (one of the largest collections in Europe) might impress – gem fans note the unique green Brazilian beryls – but otherwise it's the big woolly mammoth head and skeleton of a fin whale that are most memorable. It's worth strolling around the pantheon, a collection of sculptures of the big cheeses of Czech history, science and the arts.

The museum's most appealing feature, however, is its architecture. Designed by Josef Schulz (who collaborated on the National Theatre) and finished in 1890, it was a proud symbol of the Czech nationalist revival. Figures representing Bohemia, flanked by Vltava, Elbe, Moravia and Silesia, decorate the façade; the interior contains murals by František Ženíšek and Václav Brožík depicting key events in Czech history, including Libuše summoning Přemysl to rule over the Czechs and Charles IV founding Prague University in 1348.

Military

Aeronautical & Cosmonautical Exhibition

(Letecké muzeum) Mladoboleslavská, Prague 9 (2020 4933/2020 4926/824 709). Metro Českomoravská, then 185 or 259 bus to Kbely. **Open** *May-Oct* 10am-6pm Tue-Thur, Sat, Sun. **Admission** 40 Kč; 25 Kč children, students, OAPs.

The **National Museum**: grand in design, bland in content. See page 91.

It's a long haul out to Kbely airport, but if you are interested in glimpsing the other side of the Cold War, a visit here is essential. Three hangars house a huge collection of military and civil aircraft, ranging from World War I biplanes to a McDonnell Douglas Phantom and a veritable squadron of MiGs. A small cosmonautical section, displaying space suits and segments of rockets, is popular with children, but it's the threatening collection of Russian tanks and military vehicles – including mobile tactical missiles from the 1970s – that's the show-stopper.

Army Museum

(Armádní muzeum) U památníku 2, Prague 3 (no phone). Metro Florenc/107, 133 bus. **Open** May-Oct 10am-6pm Tue-Thur, Sat, Sun. **Closed** Nov-Apr. **Admission** 20 Kč; 10 Kč children, students, OAPs; free Tue. **Map 8 B1**

This museum covers the modern military history of Czechoslovakia, with an emphasis on World Wars I and II, including a fascinating section on the free Czech troops parachuted into the country during the Nazi occupation. Despite more modest forays into recent military activities, such as the anti-chemical unit sent by Czechoslovakia to the Gulf War in 1991, the collection seems unfinished. The well-illustrated displays are directed more towards Czech speakers than foreigners, who will find the dearth of English-language text frustrating.

Military Museum

(Vojenské muzeum) Schwarzenberský palác, Hradčanské náměstí 2, Prague 1 (2020 2020). Metro Malostranská/ 22 tram. **Open** 10am-6pm Tue-Sun. **Admission** 40 Kč; 25 Kč 6-15-year-olds, students, OAPs; free Tue. **Map 1 C3**

Located just a few metres from the main Castle gate, where sculpted giants mercilessly batter invaders, the magnificently sgraffitoed Schwarzenberg Palace seems an apt place for a museum devoted to historical weaponry. Exhibits bristling with bloodthirsty weapons chart bygone Czech military campaigns, from thirteenth-century battles against marauding Mongols and Tartars, up to the end of World War I. The collection of scale models should please anyone who ever owned a set of toy soldiers.

Music & musicians

Dvořák Museum

(Muzeum Antonína Dvořáka) Villa Amerika, Ke Karlovu 20, Prague 2 (298 214). Metro I.P. Pavlova. **Open** 10am-5pm Tue-Sun. **Admission** 30 Kč; 15 Kč children, students, OAPs. **Map 6 K8**

This dinky red and ochre villa, built by Kilian Ignaz Dientzenhofer in 1720 for Count Jan Václav Michna (it was originally known as the Michna Pavilion), was used as a cattle market during the last century. Happily, it has since been restored and put to more appropriate use as the home of the Dvořák Society's well-organised tribute to the best-known of Czech composers. The ground floor displays cover the composer's life, with memorabilia, photographs and the gown he wore to receive an honorary doctorate from Cambridge University. Upstairs is a recital hall (used for concerts during the summer), decorated with frescoes by Jan Ferdinand Schor, plus further exhibits and information on all of Dvořák's considerable musical output. An English-language translation of the exhibit labelling and CDs are available.

Mozart Museum

Bertramka, Mozartova 169, Prague 5 (543 893). Metro Anděl/4, 7, 9, 14 tram. **Open** Apr-Oct 9.30am-6pm, Nov-Mar 9.30am-5pm, daily. **Admission** 50 Kč; 30 Kč children, students, OAPs; 10 Kč under-6s.

Mozart stayed at Bertramka several times, as a guest of the villa's owners, composer František Dusek and his wife Josefina. He was here in 1787 while working on *Don Giovanni*, composing the overture at Bertramka the night before its première in what is now the Estates Theatre. The house and grounds have been restored to their eighteenth-century glory (the building was badly damaged by fire in 1871) and, since much of the memorabilia displayed has only tenuous connections to the composer, the museum works better as a homage to Mozart's era than as a monument to the man himself. Nonetheless, some interesting artefacts are on display. Tranquillity is the villa's greatest asset – in mid-morning or late afternoon, you can linger over cappuccino in the courtyard café relatively undisturbed by tour groups. Evening recitals held on the terrace cash in further on the Mozart connection, sometimes incorporate period costumes.

Smetana Museum

(Muzeum Bedřicha Smetany) Novotného lávka 1, Prague 1 (2422 9075). Metro Staroměstská/17, 18 tram. **Open** 10am-5pm Wed-Mon. **Admission** 40 Kč; 20 Kč students, OAPs; 5 Kč 6-15-year-olds. **Map 3 G4**

The imaginatively revamped Smetana Museum displays an extensive collection of documents, photos, playbills, musical scores and other memorabilia connected with the life and works of Bedřich Smetana (1824-84). Only serious fans will care enough to match the thick binder's worth of English language text (only one copy is available at the door) with all the items exhibited. Others can browse a few moments, then make a beeline for the rear of the museum, where a clever interactive display lets the visitor stand at an orchestra conductor's podium and point a baton at one of a dozen music stands – each devoted to a separate Smetana composition. Aim well and press a little button on the wand to hear a snippet of the work in question. Be sure to check the beautiful view of the river and Castle from the museum's windows.

Science & technology

City Transport Museum

(Muzeum MHD Střešovice) Patočkova 4, Prague 6 (325 776/325 777). Tram 1, 8, 18. **Open** Apr-Oct 9am-5pm Sat, Sun, public holidays. **Admission** 20 Kč; 8 Kč 6-15-year-olds.

Filled with a mesmerising collection of big shiny engines, and very popular with children and their fathers, the City Transport Museum contains nearly every model of tram and trolley bus that ever ran the streets of Prague, polished and oiled to perfection. In summer you can also take a trip on a historical tram that runs from here to the city centre and back, taking in assorted sights along the way. A far cry from today's plastic-seated, advertising-plastered vehicles, the early twentieth-century trams' wooden seats, dinging bells and spiffy red and tan paint jobs can make you feel like you've stepped back into history. Note that the museum is only open at weekends and public holidays.

National Technical Museum

(Národní technické muzeum) Kostelní 42, Prague 7 (373 651/383 825). Metro Hradčanská or Vltavská/1, 8, 25, 26 tram. **Open** 9am-5pm Tue-Sun. **Admission** 30 Kč; 10 Kč children, students, OAPs. **Map 7 C3**

Don't let the mundane name put you off: this is a fascinating collection, enjoyable for kids and adults. One of the few museums in Prague to use interactive displays, it traces the development of technology and science within the Czech Republic, which, until the communist era, was one of the most innovative and industrially advanced of Western European nations. The Transport Hall, filled with steam trains, vintage motorcycles, racing cars and the obligatory set of bi-planes, forms a sharp contrast to the claustrophobic mine in the basement, where all manner of sinister coal-cutting implements are displayed in tunnels. Guided tours of the mine leave from the ticket office and are available in English. There's also an extensive photography and cinematography section, and a collection of rare and fascinating astronomical instruments.

Wax museums

Two wax museums have opened in Prague in the last few years. Surprisingly, both have some cultural merit, representing the best-known characters from Prague's eventful history and legends, as well as twentieth-century political leaders. For visitors with some knowledge of the region's history, the museums provide a uniquely visual journey through Bohemia past and present. Those less familiar with the history might want to take along a guidebook with a good index as a reference, as neither museum provides much information other than simple name placards next to the figures. Both museums also offer different versions of '3-D' films based on Prague's culture, architecture and lore.

Prague Wax Museum

(Pražské panoptikum) Národní třída 25, Prague 1 (2108 5217). Metro Národní třída/6, 9, 18, 22 tram. **Open** 10am-8pm daily. **Admission** 119 Kč; 59 Kč students; 49 Kč 6-15-year-olds, OAPs; free under-6s. **Credit** EC, MC, V. **Map 3 H5**

The elder of Prague's wax museums has fewer dummies but far better sets than its competitor. In a dusty medieval library, alchemist Edward Kelley mixes a concoction while Rudolf II watches and a cauldron bubbles, Tycho Brahe and Johannes Kepler gaze out of a window at a starry sky, and an appropriately haunted Franz Kafka merits a mirrored corner in an eerily beautiful turn-of-the-century Prague street scene. Only Miloš Forman, Václav Klaus and Václav Havel

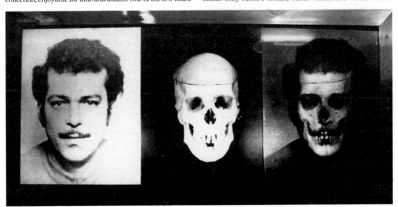

Don't fancy yours much. Be Sherlock for a day at the **Police Museum**. *See page 94.*

represent the post-socialist era. The movie offerings, labelled 'pseudoholography', feature tiny 3-D projections dancing through a tiny set – entertaining for five minutes, tops.

Wax Museum Prague
(Muzeum voskových figurín) 28 října 13, Prague 1 (2419 5203). Metro *Můstek.* **Open** 9am-8pm daily. **Admission** 120 Kč; 60 Kč children, students, OAPs; 250 Kč family ticket. **Map 3 J5**
This museum's Kafka looks disconcertingly happy, but its perfect, rosy soldier Švejk quaffs a frosty stein, and astronomer Tycho Brahe is properly outfitted with the metal proboscis he wore after losing his nose in a duel. Unlike its competitor, this museum has a long hall of international luminaries, including Rasputin, Einstein, Picasso, the Pope and an unconvincing Arnold Schwarzenegger. Princess Di and Hitler each rate a separate chamber, while major communist leaders (Czech and international) share a conference table. The clever film set-up projects MTV-influenced videos of Prague artefacts and architecture onto a screen surrounded by a short hall of mirrored panels, to kaleidoscopic effect.

Jirásek & Aleš Museum
Letohrádek Hvězda, Obora Hvězda, Prague 6 (367 938/362 600). Metro *Hradčanská, then 8, 18, 22 tram.*
This museum, jointly dedicated to writer Alois Jirásek (1851-1930) and artist Mikoláš Aleš (1852-1913), is closed for reconstruction until at least autumn 1998. However, its home, the stunning sixteenth-century star-shaped **Hvězda Hunting Lodge** (*see p83*), is well worth a look.

Police Museum
(Muzeum policie ČR) Ke Karlovu 1, Prague 2 (298 940/2413 5708). Metro *I.P. Pavlova/6, 11 tram.* **Open** 10am-5pm Tue-Sun. **Admission** 10 Kč; 5 Kč children, students, OAPs. **Map 6 K10**
A former convent attached to the Karlov Church is the incongruous home of Prague's surprisingly interesting yet rarely visited Police Museum. Once you've got beyond the cases of uniforms, there are displays on policing and crime detection techniques. Visitors can take their own finger-

The Jewish Museum

The museum was founded in 1906 to preserve the historical monuments of the former Jewish ghetto, at the time when the surrounding area was under reconstruction. However, by the most gruesome of ironies, it was Hitler who was responsible for today's comprehensive collections. He ordered the quarter to be preserved as a Museum of an Extinct Race, and the property belonging to the 153 Jewish communities of Bohemia and Moravia was sent to Prague for cataloguing and storage. It remained here after the war because there was nobody to return it to. *See also page 49* **Jewish Prague**.

Today, the collection is housed in five different buildings in Josefov, and makes up one of Prague's most popular tourist draws. To visit the following sites you can buy an **all-in-one ticket**, costing 450 Kč for adults and 330 Kč for students and 6-15-year-olds (for a guided tour, it's an additional 200 Kč per person) – good value if you want to see them all. It's also possible to buy a ticket for just the **Old Jewish Cemetery** (*see below*) and also for the **Old-New Synagogue** (*see page 52*), which is not officially part of the Jewish Museum.

Tickets can be bought at a number of locations in the area, including the Maisel and Pinkas synagogues, by the Former Ceremonial Hall on U starého hřbitova and at **Matana** travel agency at Maiselova 15 (232 1954). English-language tours are conducted from Sunday to Friday, usually at 10am, from the Maisel Synagogue (call the Jewish Museum beforehand to check on 2481 0099). Groups and private guides in several languages are also available from Matana for higher rates.

All sites are open from 9am to 6pm (until 4.30pm from November to March) Monday to Friday and Sunday (and are closed Saturday and Jewish holidays). The nearest metro station is Staroměstská or you could take the 17 or 18 tram.

Former Ceremonial Hall
(U starého hřbitova) Prague 1 (231 7191/231 0302). **Map 3 H2**
Turreted and arched, the Romanesque details of this building located at the exit of the Old Jewish Cemetery make it appear as old as the gravestones. In fact, it was built relatively recently in 1906 for the Prague Burial Society, which only got to use the building for 20 years. It currently houses an exhibition consisting primarily of Jewish funereal items.

Klausen Synagogue
(Klauzová synagóga) U starého hřbitova 3a, Prague 1 (231 0302). **Map 3 H2**
The original Klausen Synagogue, along with 318 houses and ten other synagogues, was destroyed in the great ghetto fire of 1689. The present-day building, which was hastily constructed on the same site in 1694, has much in common with Prague's baroque churches, some of which were built by the same craftsmen. Lack of space meant that the synagogue was built on the extreme edge of the ghetto, on a street that had been frequented by ladies of ill repute since the Middle Ages. Inside, a permanent exhibition of Hebrew manuscripts, prints and artefacts details the place of religion in the daily lives of the ghetto's former inhabitants. The religious artefacts displayed were used in many rituals, ranging from birth and circumcision through to death and the preparation of the body for burial. Accompanying texts explain their meaning, use and relevance to Jewish life.

The best view of the synagogue is from inside the Old Jewish Cemetery, where the simple façade rises behind the ancient gravestones, topped by two tablets of the decalogue engraved with a golden inscription. The exact shape of the tablets is echoed in the two semicircular vaulted windows at the top, two larger ones lower down, and in the decorative details on the balustrade.

prints and try to work out what's happened in a creepy scene-of-the-crime mock-up. The extensive criminology section also contains accounts of murder mysteries illustrated with photographs, weapons and photo-fits. Kids love it, though you should be warned that some of the photographs are pretty graphic. The final room contains an arsenal of home-made weaponry that James Bond would be proud of: sword sticks, home-made pistols, pen guns, and even a converted lighter. The only downside to this fascinating place is that labelling is almost entirely in Czech.

Postage Stamp Museum

(Poštovní muzeum) Nové mlýny 2, Prague 1 (231 2006/ 231 2160). Metro Náměstí Republiky. **Open** 9am-5pm Tue-Sun. **Admission** 15 Kč; 5 Kč children, students, OAPs. **Map 4 L1**

Unless you're a big philately fan, 15 minutes will suffice for browsing through this riverside museum's ground floor, which contains 300 pull-out displays of Czechoslovak and European stamps, as well as a few other post-related artefacts, such as postal weights, printing plates for stamps,

a map of old postal routes, and a nineteenth-century postman's costume (complete with trumpet). The real charms of the museum reside on the upper floor of the villa, where a postal library is combined with temporary art exhibitions. These beautifully maintained rooms boast ornate old furnaces and clever *trompe l'oeil* frescoes by the nineteenth-century artist Josef Navratil.

Toy Museum

(Muzeum hraček) Jiřská 4, Prague 1 (2437 2294/2437 1111). Metro Malostranská/22 tram. **Open** 9.30am-5.30pm daily. **Admission** 40 Kč; 20 Kč students, OAPs; under-15s free; 50 Kč family ticket. **Map 2 E1**

Part of Czech émigré Ivan Steiger's large collection is displayed on the two floors of this museum. Brief, bland explanatory texts accompany cases of toys, which range from the adorable to the ingenious, from wooden folk toys to an incredibly elaborate train set made of pure tin. Kitsch fans will love the case of toy robots and the enormous collection of Barbie and friends clad in vintage costumes throughout the decades. Good for a rainy day, but don't get too excited.

Maisel Synagogue

(Maiselova synagóga) Maiselova 10, Prague 1 (2481 0099/0232 1814). **Map 3 H3**

Rabbi Mordecai Maisel (1528-1601), mayor of Prague's Jewish ghetto during the reign of Rudolf II, was one of the richest men in sixteenth-century Europe. Legend traces his wealth to the lucky intervention of goblins, but more realistic historians suggest that Rudolf II granted Maisel a lucrative trading monopoly. Funded by Rabbi Maisel, the original building on this site was apparently the most splendid of all the quarter's synagogues, but it burned down along with almost all the others in 1689's ghetto fire. The present structure, sandwiched between tenement blocks, dates from 1892 to 1905. It contains an exhibition detailing the Jewish history of Bohemia and Moravia and also displays the museum's silver collection, including some exquisite eighteenth- and nineteenth-century spice holders, as well as religious ornaments used for dressing the Torah scrolls. The rows of Torah pointers and ceremonial crowns on display here are only a fraction of the treasures owned by the museum, but there's no space to display them all.

Old Jewish Cemetery

(Starý židovský hřbitov) U starého hřbitova 3, Prague 1. **Admission** 250 Kč adults, 130 Kč 6-15-year-olds, students; 200 Kč extra per person for a guided tour; *see also above for inclusive ticket.* **Map 3 H2**

The Old Jewish Cemetery, where all of Prague's Jews were buried until the New Jewish Cemetery was founded in 1787, is one of the eeriest remnants of the city's once thriving Jewish community. The 12,000 tombstones crammed into this tiny, tree-shaded patch of ground graphically demonstrate the terrible lack of space accorded to Prague's Jewish ghetto, which remained walled until the late eighteenth century. Forbidden to enlarge their burial ground, the Jews had no choice but to bury bodies on top of each other. An estimated 100,000 bodies were piled in, in some cases as many as 12 layers deep, so that today crazy mounds of earth are jammed with lopsided stone tablets.

Burials began here in the early fifteenth century, although earlier gravestones were brought in from a cemetery nearby, including that of Avigdor Kara, who died in 1439. His is the oldest tombstone in the cemetery (the original has now been replaced by a copy). Kara was just a boy when he witnessed the pogrom that took place during the Passover of 1389 when 3,000 people were massacred by Christians rampaging through the quarter. One of the few survivors, he wrote an elegy of remem-

brance that to this day is recited on Yom Kippur every year in the Old-New Synagogue. The most prominent tombs, easily identified by their coverings of pebbles and messages, belong to Rabbi Maisel (*see above*) and Rabbi Löw ben Bezalel (1512-1609; *see p16*).

Decorative reliefs on the headstones symbolise the deceased's name or their occupation: a pair of scissors, for example, indicates a tailor. The black headstones are the oldest, carved from fifteenth-century sandstone; the white ones, of marble, date from the sixteenth and seventeenth centuries. Nowadays the graveyard is as busy with chattering tourists as with teetering headstones. For a more contemplative perspective, visit the first floor of the Museum of Decorative Arts (*see p90*), from which you can gaze down on the cemetery in peace and quiet.

Pinkas Synagogue

(Pinkasova synagóga) Široká 3, Prague 1. **Map 3 H2/3**

Rabbi Pinkas – according to a contemporary chronicler a member of the clan of 'recalcitrant, sharp tongued Pinkases' – founded this synagogue in 1479 after falling out with the elders at the Old-New. The building was enlarged in 1535, and a Renaissance façade added in 1625. In the 1950s, the names of 77,297 men, women and children of Bohemia and Moravia who died in the Holocaust were inscribed on the synagogue's walls as a memorial. (Recent scholarship suggests that 78,000 is a more accurate figure.) Taken from duplicates of the transport files that the Jewish clerks secretly compiled, the names cover every available wall space. In 1967, after the Six Day War, the Czechoslovak government expelled the Israeli ambassador and closed the synagogue for 'restoration'. During the ensuing 22 years, the communist authorities let the names decay into indecipherability. Only in 1989 was the museum able to start the long task of restoring the monument.

Today, the Pinkas Synagogue also houses a powerful exhibition of drawings by children interned in Terezin (*see p227*), the last stop of the Jewish population before being sent to the death camps in the east. The images the children drew are both shocking and poignant: the mass dormitories and stormy skies of the camp stand next to idyllic recollections of fields and flowers. In the synagogue's courtyard, a fifteenth-century ritual bath, or *mikveh*, has been uncovered. The Jewish community is in the process of building a new ritual bath here, since for more than 40 years the city has been without this essential part of Orthodox life.

Art Galleries

There's Mucha more to Czech art than Alfons.

If Prague is the world's greatest living museum, then it should follow that its labyrinth of galleries offers a proper assault on the senses. You would expect no less from a city with connections to the twentieth-century's major art movements. Still, a kind of identity crisis has predictably arisen since the death of state control over the arts and the legacy is still colouring what you see. In the castle and state galleries, a top-heavy administration has survived all attempts at modernisation, but recent coups such as the city-wide **Rudolphine Renaissance** summer festival in 1997 have shown that there is a gradual return to co-ordinated, intelligent curating. The state's reputation has not been helped, however, by ongoing intrigues at what should be the city's most exciting new cultural venture – the massive Veletržní palác modern art space in Holešovice.

Meanwhile, Prague's artists and curators are still reeling from trying to cram into eight years the four decades of worldwide artistic development that they missed. Lapses into tired surrealist exercises, which may have once been forbidden but are not necessarily relevant nowadays for that, are common fare at the major venues. And high street private galleries still tend toward pedestrian daubings aimed unashamedly at tourists. Yes, there are fresh ideas – both Czech and foreign – out there; it's just a question of tracking them down at the handful of breakaway galleries listed below. Sometimes they might even be relegated to bars and bookstores (*see chapter* **Cafés, Pubs & Bars**).

Still, how could a mere 40 years of insularity pose any real threat to the birthplace of visionary medieval court painters, fourteenth-century fruit portraiture, erotic allegory, bewitching romantic landscapes of Bohemia, the art nouveau splendour of Alfons Mucha and cubism?

Even under communism, all was not merely socialist realism. The conceptualist Milan Knížák, the print-maker Jiří Anderle and documentary photographer Josef Koudelka, for example, were able to produce original and thought-provoking work from the 1960s onwards. Additionally, the city is scattered with small, intriguing spaces such as František Bílek's villa, which is designed after a wheatfield.

Prague's place on the contemporary international circuit also makes it a great city in which to catch travelling exhibitions by noteworthy foreign artists.

INFORMATION

For up-to-date information on cultural events in Prague, including exhibitions in galleries and museums, consult the listings pages of the *Prague Post*, *Culture in Prague* (*Kultura v Praze*) – a white listings booklet available from newstands, available in English at some central locations and online (www.culture.cz) – or *Atelier*, a Czech fortnightly broadsheet with an English summary and listings of all exhibitions in the country.

This chapter covers the city's major public collections, as well as principal exhibition spaces and the more interesting commercial galleries. Most galleries and museums are closed on Mondays and in August, but it's always best to check that the one you want to visit hasn't 'temporarily' closed before setting out. Unless stated otherwise, credit cards are not accepted.

National Gallery

The National Gallery is actually a conglomerate of three relatively small permanent collections, a towering, controversial modern art centre and a handful of exhibition spaces across the city (*see page 101* **Prague Castle Riding School** and **Wallenstein Riding School**). Its permanent collections span a millennium and contain a surprising degree of genuine artistic riches considering how often Prague's treasures have been raided by foreign powers. This, combined with increasing borrowings of works from abroad, has led to recent successes like the summer-long Veletržní palác exhibition of avant-garde avatar František Kupka. Another hurdle to be overcome is the legacy of communist-purloined art works, many of which have now been returned to their legal owners. But the latter hasn't diminished the overall quality of the National's holdings as much as might be expected; the ownership of masterworks is high-maintenance stuff and many of the art heirs have thus allowed the state to continue housing their works.

The National Gallery information line is 2051 4599 and its website (www.ng-ssu.cz) is regularly updated with all the major current exhibitions.

Gallery of Modern & Contemporary Art

(Galerie moderního umění Veletržní palác, Dukelských hrdinů 47, Prague 7 (2430 1111). Metro Vltavská/ 5, 12, 17 tram. **Open** 10am-6pm Tue, Wed, Fri-Sun; 10am-9pm Thur. **Admission** 80 Kč; 40 Kč students, OAPs; free under-15s, art students; 120 Kč family ticket. **Map 7 D2**

Despite funding scandals and a succession of fired directors, the public reception of the city's brightest modern art treasure has been overwhelmingly positive. One look around the soaring white space of this open plan high-rise will explain why. The cubist sculpture of Otto Gutfreund, the moody Czech take on impressionism typified by Jan Preisler and Antonín Slavíček, the perceptual explorations of Emil Filla and Bohumil Kubišta and even the inevitable assorted surrealists fit in here so well you would think the place was made to be the first comprehensive centre for Czech twentieth-century art. But the translation of Veletržni palác is 'Trade Fair Building' and it was as such that Oldřich Tyl and Josef Fuchs designed it in 1924. And, incredibly, despite the gallery's standing, the decision to use it for art in 1978 remains a continuing source of doubt to the National Gallery administration.

St Agnes's Convent

(Klášter sv. Anežky české) U milosrdných 17, Prague 1 (2481 0628). Metro Náměstí Republiky/5, 14, 26 tram. **Open** 10am-6pm Tue-Sun. **Admission** 70 Kč; 40 Kč children, students, OAPs; free under-10s. **Map 3 J1**

Taking up where St George's Convent leaves off (*see below*), the gallery of St Agnes displays nineteenth-century Czech art. It starts with the founders of nationalist painting: Antonín Machek, who specialised in portraits of Czech intellectuals, and Antonín Mánes, known for his romanticised views of the Czech landscape. His son, Josef Mánes, was one of the dominant figures of mid-nineteenth-century painting, experimenting in styles and subject matter but most admired for his depictions of Czech legends and country life. Historical painting, which popularised heroic events in newly discovered Czech history, became a dominant theme. It was carried out most convincingly by Jaroslav Čermák and Mikoláš Aleš and most laughably by František Ženíšek. (The last two were both members of the so-called National Theatre Generation of the 1870s.) Despite a significant cross-fertilisation between Paris and Prague, impressionism was virtually ignored in the Czech lands. A new vision is hinted at, however, in the deeply atmospheric night views of Prague by Jakub Schikaneder, normally in the St Agnes collection, but on loan at the time of going to press to the **Wallenstein Riding School Gallery** (*see below*).

St George's Convent

(Klášter sv. Jiří) Jiřské náměsti 33, Prague 1 (5732 0536/ 535 240). Tram 22. **Open** 10am-6pm Tue-Sun. **Admission** 70 Kč; 40 Kč children, students, OAPs; free under-10s. **Map 2 D2**

This gallery houses Bohemian painting and sculpture from the early Middle Ages to around 1800. Its glory is the early section, filled with the lyricism and humanity of Czech medieval art. During the reign of Charles IV (1348-78), Prague was in the forefront of European artistic development and this is still in evidence in the convent. The bronze statue of St George and the Dragon, for example, is so advanced, so Renaissance in spirit, that scholars are still arguing over its date. One innovation was portraiture, an example of which can be seen in the Votive Panel of Jan Očko of Vlašim, where the emperor and archbishop Očko are painted with compelling realism. The panels by Master Theodoric – just a few of the many hundred executed for the Chapel of the Holy Rood at Karlštejn – show a similar interest in realism.

The outstanding artist of the end of the fourteenth century was the Master of Třeboň. His many-panelled altarpiece that includes the *Resurrection of Christ* shows a change in mood – realism has been replaced by an atmosphere of mystery and miracle. Another of his paintings, the *Madonna of Roudnice*, is an example of the so-called 'Beautiful Style' that prevailed until the outbreak of the Hussite wars. The following rooms show how the Gothic style remained popular in Bohemia right up to the sixteenth

century. These end with an extraordinary wood carving by the monogrammist IP – in it, the skeletal, half-decomposed figure of Death is brushed aside by the Risen Christ.

The galleries upstairs begin with a handful of paintings that survive from the collections of Rudolf II (1575-1608). They include masterpieces by the Antwerp painter Bartholomaeus Spranger, whose sophisticated colours, elegant eroticism and obscure themes are typically mannerist; and landscapes by Roelandt Savery that show the growing interest in the natural world.

The next rooms are devoted to baroque art, starting with Karel Škréta, the founder of baroque painting in Bohemia. He spent his youth as a Protestant exile in Rome but returned to Prague in 1638, a convert ready to serve the Counter-Reformation. He was a down-to-earth painter, in contrast to Michael Leopold Willmann and Jan Kryštof Liška, whose work was feverishly religious. A distinct characteristic of baroque art was the way in which painting and sculpture borrowed from each other. This can be seen in the following rooms, where the paintings of Petr Brandl, the most acclaimed artist of the early eighteenth century, are displayed beside the sculpture of Mathias Bernard Braun, the finest sculptor. The other great sculptor of the period was Ferdinand Maximilián Brokof, the creator of the swaggering Moors who once guarded the château of Count Morzini.

At the end of the eighteenth century, Bohemian arts went into decline. The work of Norbert Grund is interesting not for its style, which is an uninspired version of French rococo, but for its subject matter. His small studies of artists' studios give a rare glimpse of the craftsman's daily grind.

Sternberg Palace

(Šternberský palác) Hradčanské náměsti 15, Prague 1 (2051 4599/2051 4634-7). Tram 22. **Open** 10am-6pm Tue-Sun. **Admission** 70 Kč; 40 Kč children, students, OAPs; free under-10s. **Map 1 C2**

The Sternberg Gallery was founded in the 1790s by the Society of Patriotic Friends of the Arts in Bohemia, a group of enlightened aristocrats determined to rouse Prague from its provincial stupor. Now it houses the National Gallery's European Old Masters. It's not a large or well-balanced collection but it does include some outstanding paintings, including the *Haymaking* landscape by Pieter Brueghel, a brilliant portrait by Frans Hals, and Dürer's *Feast of the Rosary*.

The collection's earlier paintings were acquired through random gifts and purchases, but the twentieth-century galleries benefited from the systematic approach of Vincenc Kramář, the Gallery's director during the First Republic. He was an extraordinarily perceptive critic and one of the first people to recognise the importance of Picasso. His Parisian spending sprees in 1925, 1934 and 1935 gave the Czech public a superb collection of French contemporary art. The corner devoted to Picasso and Braque – small, select and instructive – is a perfect introduction to cubism.

Other collections

Bílek Villa

(Bílkova vila) Mickiewiczowa 1, Prague 6 (2432 2021/341 439). Metro Hradčanská/18, 22 tram. **Open** 15 May-15 Oct 10am-6pm Tue-Sun; 16 Oct-14 May 10am-5pm Sat, Sun. **Admission** 80 Kč; 40 Kč children, students, OAPs. **Map 7 A3**

This must be the only museum in the world designed in the form of a wheatfield. It was built in 1911-12 by the mystic sculptor František Bílek as his studio and home, and still contains much of his work. Bílek went to Paris in his youth to study as a painter but finding he was half colour-blind turned to sculpture and illustration instead. Repelled by the decadence of modern life, he embarked on a spiritual quest to uncover a universal cosmic truth that would unite the vis-

A far cry from its beginnings as a trade fair hall, the stunning Veletržní palác, makes a

ible and invisible world. The wheatfield, representing spiritual fertility and the harvest of creative work, was only one of the many symbols on which he dwelt. Light was an emanation of creative energy, trees were associated with Man and the continual cycle of birth and decay. This is strong stuff, and the work it inspired ranges from the sublime to the sickening.

House of the Black Madonna

(Dům U Černé matky boží) Celetná 34, Prague 1 (2421 1732). Metro Náměsti Republiky/5, 14, 26 tram.
Open 10am-6pm Tue-Sun. **Admission** 35 Kč; 15 Kč children, students. **Map 4 K3**
Worth a visit for the building alone, perhaps the finest example of Prague cubist architecture. Having been renovated by the Czech Museum of Fine Arts, the gallery now houses a permanent exhibition of Czech cubism, featuring furniture design and architecture along with painting. The lower floors host temporary exhibitions, frequently of Western European artists from the modernist era.

House of the Gold Ring

(Dům U Zlatého prstenu) Týnská 6, Prague 1 (2482 7022). Metro Náměsti Republiky/5, 14, 26 tram.
Open 10am-6pm Tue-Sun. **Admission** 100 Kč; 50 Kč children, students; free under-6s. **Map 3 J3**
The city of Prague's latest showpiece proves that the National Gallery isn't the only body willing to invest in the revival of Czech modern art. This Gothic gem contains a broad spectrum of well-organised late twentieth-century works and a fine basement exhibition space for rising artists as well.

Lapidárium

Výstaviště, Prague 5 (373 198). Metro Nádraži Holešovice/5, 12, 17, 25 tram. **Open** noon-6pm Tue-Fri; 10am-6pm Sat, Sun. **Admission** 20 Kč; 10 Kč children, students, OAPs. **Map 7 D1**

Officially the Lapidárium is the last resting place of sculptures that have been rescued from demolished buildings or taken in from the weather. Unofficially, it's also a testimony to the city's recent swings in fortune. The collection includes the Marian column from the Old Town Square, which was erected in 1648 in gratitude for the defence of Prague from the Protestant Swedes; a fine equestrian statue of Emperor Francis II, one of the least attractive Habsburgs (and that's saying something) who was responsible for the country's atrophy in the first half of the nineteenth century; and a magnificent bronze group of the Austrian marshal Josef Radecký, which formerly stood in Malostranské náměsti. All these were torn down in 1918 as symbols of Habsburg rule: communist monuments are still not yet on view. This handsome, well-modernised gallery also includes the original baroque masterpieces from Charles Bridge and copies of Peter Parler's famous heads. Tantalisingly out of view in St Vitus's Cathedral, these date from the late fourteenth century and are among the first European portraits. Parler was rightly proud of his achievements and included himself in the exalted company of kings, queens, bishops and clergy.

Prague Castle Picture Gallery

(Obrazárna Pražského hradu) Prague Castle (second courtyard), Prague 1 (2437 3539). Tram 22.
Open 10am-6pm daily. **Admission** 100 Kč; 50 Kč children, students, OAPs; free under-6s; 150 Kč family ticket. **Map 1 C2**
Home of the infamous *Vertumnus*, the mannerist work by Giuseppe Arcimboldo, who cast Emperor Rudolf II as a Roman harvest god using only fruit and grains. Also worth a look are the other highly unorthodox erotic depictions of scenes from antiquity, all bankrolled by the Habsburg family's wildest member and the only one to reside in Prague Castle.

perfect home for the **Gallery of Modern & Contemporary Art**. *See page 96.*

Strahov Gallery
(Strahovský klášter) Strahovské nádvoří 1/132, Prague 1 (2051 7451). Tram 22. **Open** 9am-noon, 12.30-5pm, Tue-Sun. **Admission** 40 Kč; 20 Kč children, students, OAPs. **Map 1 A4**

The Strahov paintings, sculpture and metalwork form one of the most important monastic collections in Central Europe. It was seized by the state – like all other church property – in the early 1950s but has now been restored to its rightful owner. Strahov's gain has been the National Gallery's loss, for the collection includes paintings such as the fourteenth-century Strahov *Madonna* and Spranger's *Resurrection of Christ* that not so long ago took pride of place down at the Castle. Unfortunately, space restrictions mean that only a small proportion of the collection can be displayed.

Exhibition spaces

Temporary exhibition spaces come and go in Prague, but the main organising bodies are the National Gallery, the Office of the President of the Republic (the Castle) and the Gallery of the City of Prague. Shows organised by them tend to be increasingly large-scale, though sometimes curated without much vision or cohesiveness.

Private curators form the leading edge in revitalising both the global awareness and the sense of adventure so vital to art, two areas still recovering from the pre-'89 era. State-curated exhibitions are more generally devoted to the reappraisal of Czech artistic heritage. To give you an idea, previous ones have covered the national fixation with surrealism, the early photographic expressionism of František Drtikol, the avant-garde inter-war years and Stalinist socialist realism.

The Belvedere
(Belvedér) Letohrádek královny Anny, Prague 1 (2437 2327). Metro Hradčanská/22 tram. **Open** *summer* 10am-6pm Tue-Sun; *winter* 10am-5pm Tue-Sun. **Closed** Dec-Feb and in bad weather. **Admission** 80 Kč; 40 Kč children; 120 Kč family ticket. **Map 2 E1**

Stunning Renaissance-style space for occasional large touring shows. *See also p69.*

Carolinum
(Výstavní síň Karolinum) Železná 9, Prague 1 (2449 1111/2449 1653). Metro Můstek. **Open** 10am-5pm Tue-Sun. **Admission** 20 Kč; 10 Kč children, students, OAPs. **Map 3 J4**

The vaulted ground floor of the Carolinum makes an excellent gallery space for both international travelling exhibitions and shows by Czech artists. A labyrinth of subterranean rooms has just been added. One of the galleries is run by the **Czech Museum of Fine Arts** (*see below*) and is definitely worth checking out.

Czech Museum of Fine Arts
(České muzeum výtvarných umění) Husova 19-21, Prague 1 (2422 2068). Metro Národní třída or Staroměstská/9, 17, 18, 22 tram. **Open** 10am-noon, 1-6pm, Tue-Sun. **Admission** 20 Kč; 10 Kč children, students, OAPs; free under-6s. **Map 3 H4**

This organisation, based in an elegant baroque townhouse close to Charles Bridge, mostly exhibits twentieth-century Czech art, but also organises international exhibitions and retrospectives of foreign artists. *See also above* **Carolinum**.

Galerie Hollar

Smetanovo nábřeži 6, Prague 1 (2423 5243). Metro
Národní třída/6, 9, 17, 18, 22 tram. **Open** 10am-1pm, 2-
6pm, Tue-Sun. **Admission** 5 Kč; 3 Kč children, students,
OAPs. **Map 3 G5**

The gallery of the Union of Czech Graphic Artists is on
the ground floor of the University's Faculty of Sociology.
The building faces the river but, sadly, is rather swamped
by traffic noise from the busy embankment. Apart from
monthly exhibitions – normally of Czech or Slovak artists
– there are also large racks of prints to browse through
and/or buy.

Galerie Jaroslava Fragnera

Betlemské náměstí 51, Prague 1 (2422 8304). Metro
Národní třída/6, 9, 17, 18, 22 tram. **Open** 10am-6pm
Tue-Sun. **Admission** free. **Map 4 H4**

Having been extensively renovated, the location of this
beautiful Gothic space beneath the Bethlehem Chapel is
its best feature. The large, low-ceilinged hall is interrupted
by the remains of the church's ancient foundations.
Entry is down a spiral staircase leading off from the chapel's
east courtyard.

Galerie Rudolfinum

Alšovo nábřeži 12, Prague 1 (2489 3205/2489 3252).
Metro Staroměstská. **Open** 10am-6pm Tue-
Sun. **Admission** 40 Kč; 20 Kč children, students, OAPs;
free under-15s, art students. **Map 3 G2**

A series of grand rooms in this newly refurbished nineteenth-century concert building, which is used as an exhibition space under the auspices of the Ministry of Culture.
Top touring shows often stop here, and the curators also
favour more established contemporary Czech work.

Golz-Kinský Palace

(Palác Kinských) Staroměstské náměstí 12, Prague 1
(2481 0758). Metro Staroměstská. **Open** 10am-6pm Tue-
Sun. **Admission** 30 Kč; 10 Kč children, students, OAPs.
Map 3 J3

The exhibition rooms are nondescript but they hold interesting shows drawn from the National Gallery's collection
of prints and drawings. At the time of going to press, the
palace was closed for refurbishment.

House of the Stone Bell

(Dům U kamenného zvonu) Staroměstské náměstí 13,
Prague 1 (2481 0036/232 7851). Metro Staroměstská.
Open 10am-6pm Tue-Sun. **Admission** 30 Kč; 15 Kč
children, students, OAPs. **Map 3 J3**

A Gothic sandstone building on the east side of the Old
Town Square that was opened to the public after extensive
renovation in 1986. Inside, a gorgeous baroque courtyard
is surrounded by three floors of exhibition rooms, some
of which are still with their original vaulting. Concerts are
also held here.

Imperial Stables

(Cisařské koníma) Prague Castle (second courtyard),
Prague 1 (2437 3531). Tram 22. **Open** 10am-6pm Tue-
Sun. **Admission** 60 Kč; 30 Kč children, students, OAPs;
90 Kč family ticket. **Map 1 C2**

Rudolf II would probably be pleased to find that his stables
are now an art gallery. The exhibitions are always well
curated and beautifully displayed.

Municipal House Exhibition Hall

(Obecni dům výstavni sál) Náměsti Republiky 5, Prague 1
(2200 2674). Metro Náměsti Republiky/5, 14, 26 tram/

Czech modern artists: a sampler

In the tradition of Josef Čapek, Emil Filla and
František Kupka, Czech modern artists are continuing the irreverent, often spiritual pursuit of
an artistic mode that transcends the accepted limits of canvas or plaster. Two generations of contemporary artists have taken up this tradition of
late and now enjoy exposure not imaginable since
the times of their pre-war mentors: those formerly banned and those who've grown up unfettered
but facing the arts vacuum that followed 1989.

Hence, a sampler of a few prominent members
of the former group, all experimenters who share
a thread of anarchy and more than a few surrealist influences – one relatively safe area of expression practised under the days of state oversight:

Václav Stratil – representing the 'Hu haba'
school of Brno, named after a nonsensical out-
burst once overheard from a street drunk, his
sculpture and paintings are suitably abstract
and chaotic.

František Skála – A sculptor more inclined
toward cybernetic metals and melting effects,
who also knows the feeling of exhibiting in
secret – his designs were slipped into the Palác
Akropolis pub and concert hall.

Martin Mainer – Icons that play at pagan rituals and Buddhist temple rites, among other
topics, generally using incongruous materials
like beer coasters and coloured clay.

Among the newer talents seeking newer ground
are:

Jiří Příhoda – A recent star whose installations, including a sensational collaboration with
Brian Eno, focus on structural elements,
exposed building materials and strange lighting from within to evoke a re-examination of
physical form.

Petr Kvícala – Vibrant colour abstracts that
employ geometric patterns to create tension,
woven strands being a favourite device.

Adriena Šimutová – Also interested in form,
playing with the ideas of how ordinary objects
are perceived, such as dining room chairs done
up to look more like wounded soldiers hastily
bandaged.

Veronika Bromová – Exploits hi-tech image
manipulation to achieve hyper-realistic portraits
emphasising the body as an almost elastic form.

Galerie Jiří Švestka *showcases the best of Czech and international contemporary art.*

505, 509 bus. **Open** 10am-6pm daily. **Admission** 60 Kč.
Credit AmEx, MC, V. **Map 4 K3**
Within the stunning art nouveau Obecni dům (Municipal
House) lies this new exhibition gallery for extended shows
on broad themes like the relationship between crafts and
their surroundings. Thoroughly enjoyable indulgence in
another world, thanks to the gleaming marble, oak and brass.

Municipal Library
*(Městská knihovna) Mariánské náměstí 1 (entrance on
Valentýnská), Prague 1 (231 0489/231 3357). Metro
Staroměstská.* **Open** 10am-6pm Tue-Sun. **Admission** 40
Kč; 20 Kč children, students, OAPs. **Map 3 H3**
A proud Czech modern art exhibition space since 1945, this
combination of modern and classical details and large,
well-lit rooms easily rivals the National Gallery's spaces.
Usually shows Czech art.

Prague Castle Riding School
*(Jízdárna Pražského hradu) U Prašného mostu 55,
Prague 1 (2437 3232). Tram 22.* **Open** 10am-6pm Tue-
Sun. **Admission** 60 Kč; 30 Kč children, students, OAPs;
90 Kč family ticket. **Map 1 C1**
This and the **Wallenstein Riding School** (*see below*) are
the National Gallery's principal venues for major exhibitions. The Castle Riding School was built in 1694 to designs
by Jean-Baptiste Mathey and restored by Pavel Janák after
World War II. Its book stall is a good source of current and
remaindered catalogues on Czech art.

Wallenstein Riding School
*(Valdštejnská jizdárna) Valdštejnské náměstí 3, Prague 1
(536 814). Metro Malostranská/12, 18, 22 tram.*
Open 10am-6pm Tue-Sun. **Admission** 80 Kč; 40 Kč
children, students, OAPs. **Map 2 D2**
See above **Prague Castle Riding School**. Forming part
of the Wallenstein Palace, completed by the overambitious
general in 1630, the Wallenstein Riding School has recently established itself as host to the most experimental and
thought-provoking exhibitions in the city. Explorations of
technology and social questions trade off here with baroque
sculpture and romantic landscape shows.

Commercial galleries

Prague could hardly be described as the centre
of the international art market, but the commercial
scene is alive and kicking and can be viewed at
a host of small galleries. Artists to watch out for
include Václav Stratil, Viktor Pivovarov, Jiří
David, František Skála and Petr Nikl.

Exhibitions vary widely in quality but a number of spaces show consistently good work.
Outstanding galleries such as **Jiří Švestka** and
Nová síň provide tantalising incentives for the
hunt. Contemporary Czech art can be found
dependably at galleries **Behémót** and **MXM**.

Galerie Behémót
*Elišky Krásnohorské 6, Prague 1 (231 7829). Metro
Staroměstská/17, 18 tram.* **Open** 1-7pm Tue-Sun.
Map 3 H2
Owner Karel Babiček considers display conditions to be just
as important as the original creative act and thus favours
installations, resulting in some of the most interesting and
dynamic shows in Prague. The artists are mostly young,
Czech and Slovak, and their more portable work upstairs
can be viewed upon request.

Galerie Jednorožec s harfou
*Bartolomějská 13/Průchodní 4, Prague 1 (2423 0801).
Metro Národní třída/6, 9, 18, 21, 22 tram.*
Open 11am-11pm Mon-Fri; 1-10pm Sat, Sun.
Map 3 H5
The 'Unicorn With a Harp' gallery shows the work of men-
tally and physically handicapped artists. It's a quiet space
and has a tiny café that is a peaceful respite from the bustle
of nearby Národní třída.

Galerie Jiří Švestka
*Jungmannova 30, Prague 1 (9000 2185). Metro Národní
třída/3, 9, 14, 24 tram.* **Open** noon-7pm Tue-Fri; 11am-
6pm Sat. **Map 5 J6**

Well-known as a curator, Jiří Švestka operates a shop in the former Mozarteum specialising in bold, internationally recognised modern art. Top-quality solo and group installations of both Czech and foreign work from the likes of Dan Graham and Bořek Šípek.

Galerie MXM

Nosticova 6, Prague 1 (531 564). Metro Malostranská/ 12, 18, 22 tram. **Open** noon-6pm Tue-Sun. **Map 2 E4**
Conceived in 1990 as a private gallery that would represent Czech artists, this small vaulted space, hidden in the heart of Malá Strana, is, believe it or not, the oldest private gallery in Prague. It also used to be one of the most influential. Only Czech artists are shown here and the gallery has built up a stable of 18 of them from all generations. Exhibitions are consistently good and recent ones have included works by Petr Nikl, Jiří David, Karel Malich and Tomáš Cisařovský. Ring bell for entry.

Galerie Na Jánském Vršku

Jánský vršek 15, Prague 1 (533 9271/538 257). Tram 12, 22. **Open** 10.30am-5.30pm Tue-Sun. **Map 2 D3**
Focusing on Czech artists who translate the traditional Bohemian medium of glass from craft well into modern art, this tiny respected gallery consistently exhibits fresh perspectives. Among the bold innovators to look out for are Dana Zámečníková, Václav Cigler, František Vizner and Vladimír Kopecký.

Galerie Peithner-Lichtenfels

Michalská 12, Prague 1 (2422 7680). Metro Můstek. **Open** 10am-7pm daily. **Closed** Sat, Sun in July, Aug. **Map 3 H4**
A small gallery in the Old Town with a permanent collection of nineteenth- and twentieth-century Czech art, including artists such as Beneš, Kolář and Kokoschka, shown in conjunction with five or six temporary exhibitions a year. Poor lighting makes the space seem cluttered.

Galerie Vltavín

Masarykovo nábřeží 36, Prague 1 (2491 4540). Metro Národní třída/6, 9, 17, 18, 22 tram. **Open** 10am-noon, 1-6pm, daily. **Map 5 G6**
Overlooking the Vltava and close to the National Theatre, the pocket-sized Vltavin has become a popular venue for Czech artists. Focusing mainly on contemporary work by the older generation, exhibitions are usually low-key. **Branch**: Ostrovni 6, Prague 1 (298 141).

Gambra

Černinská 5, Prague 1 (2051 4785). Metro Hradčanská/ 1, 8, 18, 25, 26 tram. **Open** *Mar-Oct* noon-6pm Wed-Sun; *Nov-Feb* noon-6pm Sat, Sun. **Map 1 A2**
Tucked away in a beautiful Hradčany street is a gallery whose unprepossessing exterior hides one of the city's most interesting exhibitions. It's the gallery of the Czech surrealist movement and is part-owned by the cult hero of animated filmmaking, Jan Švankmajer. Švankmajer has always said that his films are only a small part of his work as a surrealist: it's possible to see the other side here, where some of his lithographs and ceramics are on show. The gallery's emphasis is on group work, however, and equal importance is given to the other members of the movement, both classic and contemporary, such as Medek, Karel Baron and Švankmajer's wife, Eva.

Gandy Galerie

Školská 12, Prague 1 (2421 0774). Metro Národní třída/3, 9, 14, 24 tram. **Open** *Mar-Aug* 2-6.30pm Mon-Fri; 11am-4pm Sat; *Sept-Feb* 1-6pm Tue-Fri. **Map 5 J6**
Tiny new space dealing in known Western artists, especially French ones (it's owned by a Frenchwoman). Also minor exhibitions by not-so-minor names such as Lydia Lunch and Nan Golden.

Czech Union of Fine Arts

Exhibitions organised by the Czech Union of Fine Arts are always by contemporary Czech artists; the quality of the work on show varies enormously, but entry tends to be cheap (and is sometimes even free) and the galleries are usually worth a visit. Works can be purchased direct from the artists: this can usually be arranged through the individual galleries.

Galerie Václava Špály

Národní třída 30, Prague 1 (2421 3000). Metro Národní třída/6, 9, 18, 22 tram. **Open** 10am-1pm, 2-6pm, Tue-Sun. **Admission** 10 Kč; 5 Kč students. **Map 3 H5**
Larger than it seems from the street, this well-established gallery has been going for 40 years in its present incarnation, and is made up of three floors of exhibition space. Recent shows have included artists from the avant-garde Brno school and their Prague counterparts.

Nová síň

Voršilská 3, Prague 1 (292 046). Metro Národní třída/ 6, 9, 18, 22 tram. **Open** 11am-6pm Tue-Sun. **Admission** 10 Kč; 5 Kč students. **Map 5 H6**
A single bright, clean room tucked away in a building close to Národní. The excellent lighting makes it a great place to view work by contemporary Czech artists. Samplers of their stuff and the latest issues of art magazines *Umělec* and *Divus* crowd the rack at the entrance.

Výstavní síň Mánes

Masarykovo nábřeží 250, Prague 1 (295 577). Metro Karlovo náměstí/3, 4, 7, 14, 16, 17 tram/ 176 bus. **Open** 10am-6pm Tue-Sun. **Admission** 25 Kč; 15 Kč students, OAPs; children free. **Map 5 G7**
Both the largest and most important of the Czech Union of Fine Art's galleries, and a beautiful piece of functionalist architecture (built by Otakar Novotný in 1930; *see also p57*). The riverside Mánes usually hosts two exhibitions at the same time, ranging from international travelling shows to those of classic and contemporary Czech artists. The home of the Mánes Graphic Artists Society, the gallery's steadily reviving into something like the vibrant centre it used to be. The cubist ceiling frescoes on the lower ground floor should not be missed.

Photography galleries

Fotogalerie U Řečických

Vodičkova 10, Prague 1 (2421 3618). Metro Můstek/9 tram. **Open** 11am-6pm daily. **Admission** 20 Kč; 10 Kč students. **Map 5 J6**
Well-planned exhibits in two creaking, timbered rooms from another age with consistently compelling work by such diverse lights as Manhattan newshound Bedřich Grünzweig, Czech parodists of American billboards and early Russian silver plate pioneers.

Josef Sudek Gallery

Úvoz 24, Prague 1 (533 851). Tram 22. **Open** 10am-noon, 1-6pm, Tue-Sun. **Admission** 10 Kč; 5 Kč students. **Map 2 E5**
The father of Czech photography and an inspiration to the art around the world almost seems to be hanging about the corners in his former studio, now an exhibition space for his still lifes, defracted light studies and classic Prague vignettes.

Sleeping, Eating, Shopping

Accommodation   **104**   Cafés, Pubs & Bars   **138**
Restaurants   **118**   Shopping & Services   **153**

Accommodation

No longer a standing joke, Prague's hotels are stepping out in style. Aside from a few comedy-sketch gems, that is.

As is the case with most things in Prague, it's becoming increasingly more difficult to find stark relics from those pre-'89 days when the customer was never right, but the comrade always was. For the most part, that's a welcome development for travellers. But for others, finding a still-pulsing bit of the past can be part of the fun.

Stare struktura (literally, 'old structure') is one of those quirky descriptions, used to describe a pub, restaurant or, in this case, hotel, with bland, greasy food, surly and incompetent service, rank toilets and cheap beer. Ask any Prague-based expat, though, and they'll tell you about another type of *stare struktura* joint. These cosy places are inevitably distinguished by an increasingly elusive charm, bumbling but good-natured service, a slightly gaudy décor that only an *apparatchik* could love, and still cheaper beer. Okay, so there might be bright orange curtains, clunky, red plastic rotary phones and a Soviet bloc TV set in each room. But a *stare struktura* hotel will at least be clean, with an adequate array of travellers' services, a taste of the not-so-distant past and, perhaps best of all, a budget price. After all, sometimes bad is good, right?

INFORMATION & BOOKING

The surviving *stare struktura* hotels complement the sky-rocketing number of quality, Western-styled lodging options available. For the less adventurous tourist (or those less nostalgic for the days before the playwright president, the pink tank and the inevitable velvet hangover), there is now an amazing number of renovated or brand-new hotels to choose from, including modern, family-run inns and giant, corporate-owned multi-star hotels. And though accommodation in Prague is generally still pricey compared with other European cities, there are ways to beat the system: many hotels give discounts to groups and for longer stays (normally around ten days or more). And, generally, rooms are 20-25 per cent cheaper in the off-season, roughly November to March.

But, be warned: while the number of hotel rooms in Prague increases each year, so, it seems, does the demand. If you come to the city in peak months without reservations, expect to have to pound the pavement for hours looking before you find a clean, well-lit place. Even off-peak, it's still wise to book.

Most of the more expensive hotels will have English-speaking staff; those at cheaper establishments may struggle, though you can usually make yourself understood. Many hotels can arrange airport pick-ups for a fixed price, which will save you time, money and hassle.

PRICES & CLASSIFICATION

Hotels are classified below according to their cheapest double room; prices include breakfast, unless stated otherwise. Note that these prices may not be available in the peak season, and also be aware that some of the more upmarket hotels fix their room rates in German marks or US dollars. For ease of use we have converted all prices into crowns but be warned that fluctuations in the value of the crown will affect these rates. Note that hotels with no credit card details in the listings information don't accept any plastic.

All rooms in the 'Luxury' and 'Expensive' categories will have an en-suite bath and/or shower and toilet. This also applies to the 'Moderate' category, unless otherwise stated. Facilities in other categories vary; it's always best to check exactly what you'll be getting when you book. For longer-term accommodation, *see page 247*. For hotels that are particularly welcoming to gay people, *see page 187*.

Luxury (7,000 Kč upwards)

Every hotel in this category offers (unless otherwise stated) currency exchange, fax, laundry, a lift, multilingual staff, at least one restaurant, a bar, babysitting, air-conditioning, business and conference facilities, a limousine service and parking facilities; all rooms are equipped with a hairdryer, minibar, room service, satellite TV, safe and telephone. The services listed below each review are in addition to the above.

Corinthia Hotel Forum

Kongresová 1, Prague 4 (6119 1238/fax 6121 1673/forum-reservations@ts-hotels.cz). Metro Vyšehrad/7, 18, 24 tram. **Rooms** 531. **Rates** *single* 7,920 Kč; *double* 8,270 Kč; *triple* 9,770 Kč; *junior suite* 11,620-13,200 Kč. **Credit** DC, EC, MC, V.

The Forum spent much of spring 1998 making headlines in the Czech press. Not because of its wide array of facilities, but because it became an unwitting pawn in international politics when the US government dubbed it off limits to Americans because of its new owners' alleged ties to Libya. Whatever the case, US citizens should consult the embassy in Prague before considering the Forum. One thing the new owners have done is crank the service up a notch, and the hotel continues to have a loyal following of business travellers. Although slightly out

of the centre, it's right next to the metro, a major motorway and the city's biggest conference centre.
Hotel services *Beauty salon. Bowling. Casino. Disabled: access, rooms adapted. Fitness facilities. Hairdresser. Interpreting services. No-smoking rooms. Pool. Sauna. Solarium. Squash court.* **Room services** *Fax (some rooms). Radio.*

Grand Hotel Bohemia

Králodvorská 4, Prague 1 (2480 4111/fax 232 9545). Metro Náměstí Republiky/5, 14, 26 tram. **Rooms** 78. **Rates** *single* 6,100 Kč; *double* 8,450 Kč; *extra bed* 2,200 Kč (1,100 Kč for 7-12s; free for under-6s). **Credit** AmEx, DC, EC, MC, TC, V. **Map 4 K3**
Grand indeed, this gorgeous hotel – under Austrian management – is situated between the art nouveau gem Obecni dům (Municipal House) and Old Town Square. Even standard rooms are chock full of amenities, including a fax machine and trouser press. If you're booking a suite, be sure to ask for one with a view of the Castle. The Boccaccio Room doubles as a grand ballroom or an extravagant conference room for up to 140 suits.
Hotel services *Disabled: room adapted. No-smoking floor.* **Room services** *Radio. VCR.*

Hotel Palace Praha

Panská 12, Prague 1 (2409 3111/fax 2422 1240/palhoprg@mbox.vol.cz/www.hotel-palace.cz). Metro Můstek/3, 9, 14, 24 tram. **Rooms** 124. **Rates** *single* 7,400 Kč; *double* 8,800 Kč; *triple* 11,000 Kč. **Credit** AmEx, DC, EC, MC, V. **Map 4 K4**
Quite possibly the best service in Prague. An enthusiastic staff that insists the hotel should really have six stars, simple but comfortable rooms, two restaurants and a piano bar, and a location just close enough – but thankfully not too close – to Wenceslas Square. Some of the more expensive rooms have a fax machine.
Hotel services *Disabled: access, rooms adapted. Interpreting services. No-smoking floors.*
Room services *Radio.*

Hotel Paříž Praha

U Obecního domu 1, Prague 1 (2422 2151/fax 2422 5475/prgpariz@mbox.vol.cz). Metro Náměstí Republiky/5, 14, 26 tram. **Rooms** 95. **Rates** *single* 7,510 Kč; *double* 8,140 Kč. **Credit** AmEx, DC, EC, MC, TC, V. **Map 4 K3**
This gorgeous art nouveau classic is a perfect architectural complement to nearby Obecni dům (Municipal House) and has been family-run since the days when it was immortalised in Bohumil Hrabal's *I Served the King of England*. That said, however, it's in dire need of an injection of new life; renovating the interior would be a solid start, as would lessons in charm for the staff. Don't count it out, though – this is a Prague fixture for a reason and it won't stay down for long.
Hotel services *Café.* **Room services** *Radio.*

Hotel Savoy

Keplerova 6, Prague 1 (2430 2430/fax 2430 2128/savoyhoprg@mbox.vol.cz). Tram 22. **Rooms** 61. **Rates** *single or double* 7,400 Kč; *extra bed* 1,850 Kč; free under-12s. **Credit** AmEx, DC, EC, MC, TC, V. **Map 1 A2**
Stepping into the Savoy's dignified lobby, complete with reading room and fireplace, it may seem hard to imagine this as a haven for rock stars and celebs such as Tina Turner and Cher. But the divas aren't the only ones who know this as a peaceful bastion of first-class service and tasteful, modern rooms. For a terrace overlooking the city, reserve room 304. No air-conditioning in rooms at the time of going to press.
Hotel services *Beauty salon. Disabled: access, rooms adapted. Fitness facilities. Hairdresser. Interpreting services. Jacuzzi. No-smoking rooms. Sauna.*
Room services *Fax. Radio. Refrigerator. VCR.*

Prague Hilton Atrium

Pobřežní 1, Prague 8 (2484 1111/fax 2484 2378/sales_prague@hilton.com). Metro Florenc/8, 24 tram. **Rooms** 788. **Rates** *single* 7,920 Kč; *double* 8,280 Kč, *extra bed free; junior suite* 9,720 Kč; *executive suite* 11,160 Kč; *family apartment* 24,660 Kč. **Credit** AmEx, DC, EC, MC, $TC, V.
Not surprisingly, this massive, mirrored cube frames the largest atrium in the Czech Republic. Huge leather armchairs, lots of greenery and gently bubbling fountains all spell relaxation and recreation, as do the pool, sauna, salon and indoor tennis courts. Not the place for those raring to grab a map and tramp through the city sights, which might explain the hotel's list of former Presidential Suite occupiers: Richard Nixon, Nelson Mandela and the Clintons. There is an equal abundance of services for both business guests and tourists.
Hotel services *Beauty salon. Casino. Disabled: access, rooms adapted. Fitness facilities. Hairdresser. Interpreting services. No-smoking rooms. Pool. Sauna. Solarium.* **Room services** *Refrigerator. Voice mail.*

Renaissance Prague Hotel

V celnici 7, Prague 1 (2182 2100/fax 2182 2200/www.renaissancehotels.com). Metro Náměstí Republiky/3, 5, 14, 24, 26 tram. **Rooms** 315. **Rates** *single* 8,000 Kč; *double* 8,600 Kč; *suite* 9,500 Kč-14,000 Kč. **Credit** AmEx, DC, EC, MC, TC, V. **Map 4 L3**
The most centrally located of Prague's giant luxury hotels, the Renaissance offers stellar service for tourists and business folk. While the prices may be a bit steep, you do get what you pay for. The Renaissance's two gourmet restaurants attract a good number of discerning local diners too; Sunday jazz brunches are a highlight. The nearby Masarykovo train station may attract a strange lot, but the denizens are, on the whole, harmless, and in any case, just about everything you'll want to walk to is in the other direction.
Hotel services *Fitness facilities. No-smoking rooms. Pool. Sauna. Solarium.* **Room services** *Radio. Refrigerator. VCR (extra charge).*

Expensive (4,000-7,000 Kč)

Every hotel in this category offers (unless otherwise stated) a bar, restaurant, fax and laundry; all rooms are equipped with a hairdryer, minibar and telephone. The services listed below each review are in addition to these.

Best Western City Hotel Moráň

Na Moráni 15, Prague 2 (2491 5208/fax 297 533). Metro Karlovo náměstí/3, 4, 14, 16 tram. **Rooms** 57. **Rates** *single* 3,510-5,120 Kč; *double* 4,520-6,110 Kč; *extra bed* 840-1,000 Kč. **Credit** AmEx, DC, EC, MC, V. **Map 5 G9**
Clean and bright rooms in a comfortable hotel with a good location near the river. Not great value, but the staff are friendly and capable. At the time of going to press, the management was planning to expand the hotel.
Hotel services *Air-conditioning. Babysitting. Car park. Currency exchange. Lift. Limousine service. Multilingual staff. Safe.* **Room services** *Radio. Room service. Satellite TV.*

Diplomat Hotel Praha

Evropska 15, Prague 6 (2439 4111/fax 2439 4215/diphoprg@mbox.vol.cz/www.diplomat-hotel.cz). Metro Dejvická/2, 20, 26 tram. **Rooms** 382. **Rates** *single* 4,750-5,500 Kč; *double* 5,280-6,500 Kč; *extra bed* 1,460 Kč; *suite* 10,560-15,100 Kč; free under-12s. **Credit** AmEx, DC, EC, MC, TC, V.
Located a short drive from the airport and right at a metro stop, the Diplomat has a lot to offer for guests interested in

both business and pleasure. From fully kitted-out suites to a go-kart racing course in the basement, there's no shortage of things to do here – and no shortage of things to pay top-dollar for.

Hotel services *Air-conditioning. Beauty salon. Business services. Car park. Conference facilities. Currency exchange. Disabled: access, rooms adapted. Fitness facilities. Hairdresser. Interpreting services. Lift. Limousine service. Multilingual staff. No-smoking rooms. Safe.* **Room services** *Radio. Room service. Satellite TV.*

Don Giovanni

Vinohradská 157a, Prague 3 (6703 1111/fax 6703 6704). Metro Želivského/10, 11, 16, 26 tram. **Rooms** 400. **Rates** *single* 5,280 Kč; *double* 6,250 Kč; *junior suite* 7,000 Kč. **Credit** AmEx, DC, EC, MC, TC, V. **Map 8 E2**

This relative newcomer may just be the best value in this class; especially for business travellers. The lobby contains an impressive array of original art and sculpture and more philistine guests will appreciate the stellar business services. Don't be put off by the location out of the centre; the hotel is right by the Želivského metro stop, so downtown is less than ten minutes away. And no hotel is closer to Franz Kafka's final resting place. Rock-solid value.

Hotel services *Air-conditioning. Business services. Car park. Conference facilities. Currency exchange. Disabled: access, rooms adapted. Fitness facilities. Lift. Multilingual staff. No-smoking rooms.* **Room services** *Radio. Refrigerator. Room service. Safe. Satellite TV.*

Holiday Inn Prague

Koulova 15, Prague 6 (2439 3111/fax 2431 0616). Tram 20, 25. **Rooms** 243. **Rates** *single* 3,750 Kč; *double* 4,700 Kč. **Credit** AmEx, DC, EC, MC, TC, V.

Modelled on Stalin's colossal Seven Sisters in Moscow and adorned with heroic socialist realist friezes, the 14-storey Holiday Inn is perfect if you want a communist nostalgia trip. Reconstruction in 1996-7, however, has left the interior pleasant, modern and not at all like one of Uncle Joe's *gulags*. For those here to make money, there are fax/modem connections in all rooms; for those here to lose it, there's a casino. As the hotel is located off the beaten path, Holiday Inn guests either learn to get around on the tram or rely on taxis.

Hotel services *Air-conditioning. Babysitting. Beauty salon. Business services. Car park. Conference facilities. Currency exchange. Disabled: access, rooms adapted. Fitness facilities. Garden. Hairdresser. Interpreting services. Lift. Limousine service. Multilingual staff. No-smoking. Sauna. Solarium.* **Room services** *Fax. Radio. Room service. Satellite TV.*

Hotel Hoffmeister

Pod Bruskou 7, Prague 1 (5731 0942/fax 530 959/ hotel@hoffmeister.cz/www.hoffmeister.cz). Metro Malostranská/12, 18, 22 tram. **Rooms** 42. **Rates** *single* 5,480 Kč (*deluxe* 5,915 Kč); *double* 6,250 Kč (*deluxe* 6,855 Kč); *extra bed* 1,160 Kč. **Credit** AmEx, DC, EC, MC, TC, V. **Map 2 F1**

A good option for those more interested in exploring romantic Prague than in networking and closing the deal. It's located right on a busy junction on the edge of Malá Strana, but all windows have been soundproofed and tranquillity has the upper hand over traffic. The lobby is filled with original works by artist Adolf Hoffmeister and downstairs you'll find a superb wine bar that boasts a cosy, 1920s speakeasy feel and offers a well-thought-out selection of rare Moravian and international vintages. Breakfast costs extra. No restaurant.

Hotel services *Air-conditioning. Babysitting. Business services. Car park. Currency exchanged. Garden. Lift. Limousine service. Multilingual staff. Safe.* **Room services** *Radio. Refrigerator. Room service. Satellite TV.*

Superb **Hotel Palace Praha.** *See page 105.*

LISTEN TO OUR
PRAGUE TRIO

*F*irst violin is masterfully played by the Hotel Savoy.

Nestled in the historic district near Prague Castle, 61 luxuriously appointed rooms and suites, including a grand Presidential Suite, await the discerning guest. Personal VCR, satellite TV, advanced telecommunications technology and complimentary soft mini-bar are just some of the standard features of all guest rooms. For substance and style, look to the Hotel Savoy!

*T*he Hotel Palace Praha delights with a virtuoso performance every time!

This intimate Art Nouveau hotel situated in the very heart of Prague offers 124 stylish, deluxe rooms and suites. Enjoy the exciting and innovative cuisine of the „Club Restaurant" - one of Prague's premier gourmet restaurants. However, it is the gracious, personal service and attention to detail that distinguishes the Hotel Palace Praha. Our warm hospitality will be music to your ears!

*T*he dynamic violoncello best describes the Diplomat Hotel.

Strategically located, this modern business hotel features excellent meeting room and conference facilities. Whether you are holding a private company celebration or a multimedia presentation, our experienced staff will ensure the success of your event. Your partners and clients alike will notice the *tempo allegro* and subtle nuance of service. The Diplomat Hotel - a masterpiece of function and flair!

Hotel Savoy*****

Keplerova 6
CZ ~ 118 00 ~ Praha 1
Phone: ++420(2)2430 2430
Fax: ++420(2)2430 2128
E-mail: savhoprg@mbox.vol.cz
http://www.hotel-savoy.cz

Hotel Palace Praha*****

Panská 12
CZ ~ 111 21 ~ Praha 1
Phone: ++420(2)2409 3111
Fax: ++420(2)2422 1240
E-mail: palhoprg@mbox.vol.cz
http://www.hotel-palace.cz

Hotel Diplomat****

Evropská 15,
CZ ~ 16041 ~ Praha 6,
Phone: ++420(2)2439 4111,
Fax: ++420(2)2439 4215,
E-mail: diphoprg@mbox.vol.cz,
http://www.diplomat-hotel.cz

managed by
VIENNA INTERNATIONAL
Hotels & Resorts

*Paris comes to Prague in the form of the art nouveau **Hotel Paříž Praha**. See page 105.*

Hotel Pod Věží

(Under the Tower) Mostecká 2, Prague 1 (533 710/531 895/fax 531 859). Metro Malostranská/12, 22 tram.
Rooms 12. **Rates** *single* 3,900-4,500 Kč; *double* 5,300-7,200 Kč; *suite* 6,000-8,400 Kč. **Credit** AmEx, DC, EC, MC, TC, V. **Map 2 E3**
To tout this as 'a place of retreat for the visitor, service for the guest who – as we know – is the messenger of joy' might be overdoing it just a bit. Nevertheless, this *is* a good option for tourists who want to be in the thick of Malá Strana. The hotel is located just a few cobblestones further from Charles Bridge than **U Tří pštrosů** (*see below*) and offers slightly lower prices.
Hotel services *Babysitting. Car park (400 Kč per day). Conference facilities (10 people). Currency exchange. Garden (summer). Hairdresser. Lift.* **Room services** *Room service. Safe. Satellite TV. VCR.*

Hotel Praha

Sušická 20, Prague 6 (2434 1111/fax 2431 1218). Metro Dejvická. **Rooms** 124. **Rates** *single* 4,690-5,790 Kč; *double* 5,490-6,790 Kč; *apartment* 6,950-8,690 Kč; *suite* 9,590-18,990 Kč. **Credit** AmEx, DC, MC, V.
This showcase of 1970s flamboyance – with its big bulbous lights, extravagant leather upholstery – used to be reserved exclusively for high-ranking communist party officials and visiting dignitaries. Now mere mortals – albeit mortals with expense accounts – can relax in rooms that have hosted dignitaries from the dictatin' likes of Colonel Gadaffi to the hip-shakin' likes of BB King. Having access to a car (or lots of taxis) is a virtual necessity if you want to see the city sights. Children under 12 stay free.
Hotel services *Air-conditioning. Beauty salon. Billiards. Bowling. Business services. Car park. Conference facilities. Currency exchange. Disabled: rooms adapted. Fitness facilities. Garden. Hairdresser. Interpreting services. Lift. Limousine service. Multilingual staff. Pools. Safe. Sauna. Solarium. Tennis.* **Room services** *Room service. Safe (some rooms). Satellite TV.*

Hotel U páva

(The Peacock) U Lužického semináře 32, Prague 1 (5732 0743/5831 5867/fax 533 379/hotelupava@tnet.cz).
Metro Malostranská/12, 18, 22 tram. **Rooms** 11.
Rates *single* 3,800-4,900 Kč; *double* 4,000-5,300 Kč; *extra bed* 600-800 Kč; *suite* 5,900-6,400 Kč. **Credit** AmEx, EC, MC, V. **Map 2 F3**
The combination of U páva's dark oak ceilings and crystal chandeliers doesn't synthesise as well as the seamless elegance of **U krále Karla** (also owned by Karel Klubal; *see below*). Still, an ideal location in a serene corner of Malá Strana makes one quite forgiving (as does the attentive service). Suites 201, 301, 401 and 402 have views of the Castle.
Hotel services *Car park. Multilingual staff.*
Room services *Room service. Satellite TV.*

Romantik Hotel U raka

Černínská 10, Prague 1 (2051 1100/fax 2051 0511/uraka@login.cz/www.romantikhotels.com). Tram 22.
Rooms 6. **Rates** *single* 5,600 Kč; *double* 5,900 Kč; *triple* 7,200 Kč. **Credit** AmEx, EC, MC, TC, V. **Map 1 A2**
Dating back to 1739, this small, rustic pension is a good choice for couples not in a hurry. It's located a short stroll from the Castle and within earshot of the bells of the Loreto. There are six rooms here (two in the main house and four adjacent cottages) plus a beautiful breakfast room/inn/café/reading room with brick hearth. No children under 12. No bar.
Hotel services *Air-conditioning. Car park. Currency exchange. Limousine service. Multilingual staff. Safe.*
Room services *Radio. Room service. TV.*

U krále Karla

(King Charles) Úvoz 4, Prague 1 (538 805/533 618/fax 538 811). Metro Malostranská/22 tram. **Rooms** 19.
Rates *single* 3,750-5,300 Kč; *double* 4,100-5,800 Kč; *suite* 5,400-6,400 Kč; *extra bed* 600-900 Kč. **Credit** AmEx, EC, MC, V. **Map 1 B3**
The solid oak furnishings, painted vaulted ceilings, stained-glass windows and various baroque treasures lend this hotel

Book the **Holiday Inn Prague**. See page 107.

– once owned by the Benedictine order – the feel of an aristocratic country house. If the daily hike up the hill from the tram seems daunting, try **U krále Karla's** cousin, **U Pava** (*see above*), opposite the Vojanovy Gardens.
Hotel services *Babysitting. Car park. Lift. Multilingual staff.* **Room services** *Radio. Safe. Satellite TV.*

U Tří pštrosů

(The Three Ostriches) Dražického náměstí 12, Prague 1 (5732 0565/fax 5732 0611). Metro Malostranská/12, 22 tram. **Rooms** 18. **Rates** *single* 4,000-5,050 Kč; *double* 5,400-6,900 Kč; *suite* 6,800-9,900 Kč. **Credit** AmEx, DC, EC, MC, TC, V. **Map 2 E3**
The location (at the base of Charles Bridge) may scare away some who fear the non-stop din of tourists shrieking 'This is just like Disney World!' in 34 different languages. Still, once inside, the noise factor is surprisingly minimal and the helpful staff go out of their way to make your stay peaceful. The 18 rooms feature gorgeous wooden floors and original ceiling beams; the result is a rustic feel without 'olde-world' overload. The stairs are steep, so this is not a good choice for less agile people. If you want a view of the bridge, ask for it. No restaurant or hairdryer in rooms.
Hotel services *Babysitting. Car park. Currency exchange. Multilingual staff. Limousine service.*
Room services *Radio. Refrigerator. Room service. Safe. Satellite TV.*

Moderate (2,500-4,000 Kč)

All rooms in this category have a telephone and satellite TV, in addition to the services listed below each review.

Betlém Club

Betlémské náměstí 9, Prague 1 (2421 6872/fax 2421 8054). Metro Národní třída/6, 9, 18, 22 tram.
Rooms 22. **Rates** *single* 2,400-2,600 Kč; *double* 3,200-3,400 Kč. **Map 3 H4**
A homely hotel on an agreeable square, only a twist and a turn away from Charles Bridge or, in the other direction, Wenceslas Square. Fairly spacious rooms are punctuated by a little too much brass, but are nevertheless clean, attractive and well stocked with necessities. With the money you save here, treat yourself to dinner at nearby **V Zátiší** (*see p124*).
Hotel services *Laundry. Lift.* **Room services** *Minibar.*

Cloister Inn

Bartoloměsjká 9, Prague 1 (232 7700/fax 232 7709/ cloister@cloister-inn.cz/www.cloister-inn.cz). Metro

Národní třída/6, 9, 18, 22 tram. **Rooms** 25. **Rates** *single* 2,700 Kč; *double* 3,400 Kč. **Credit** AmEx, EC, MC, £$TC, V. **Map 3 H5**
Resting above the cheaper **Pension Unitas** (and run by the same people; *see below*), this three-star hotel has a lot going for it. Bright rooms, attentive staff, great location, good prices and a nearby house full of nuns in case you commit a little mortal sin and need redemption. There are plans to extend the hotel to 80 rooms in 1999.
Hotel services *Babysitting. Business services. Car park. Currency exchange. Fax. Interpreting service. Laundry. Lift. Multilingual staff.* **Room services** *Hairdryer. Safe.*

Hotel Axa

Na Poříčí 40, Prague 1 (2481 2580/fax 2421 4489/ axapraha@mbox.vol.cz). Metro Florenc or Náměstí Republiky/3, 5, 9, 14, 24, 26 tram. **Rooms** 131. **Rates** *single* 1,760-2,350 Kč; *double* 2,750-3,250 Kč. **Credit** AmEx, DC, MC, V. **Map 4 M2**
For a step back to the not-so-distant past, try this old-timer. The rooms are in dire need of renovation and the carpets in need of a torch (steam cleaning wouldn't be enough). Still, the location – just about halfway between two downtown metro stations – is good and the prices quite fair. Consider this a solid choice if the hotel you originally wanted is fully booked. If you're a light sleeper, ask for a room at the back of the hotel away from the tram tracks. There is a good-size workout centre in the building, though it is not run by the hotel and therefore costs extra.
Hotel services *Bar. Beauty salon. Business services. Car park. Currency exchange. Disabled access. Fax. Fitness facilities. Hairdresser. Laundry. Lift. Multilingual staff. Restaurant. Safe. Sauna. Sports facilities (gym & pool).*

Hotel Sax

Jánský vršek 328/3, Prague 1 (538 422/fax 538 498) Metro Malostranská/12, 22 tram. **Rates** *single* 3,300-3,650 Kč; *double* 3,950 Kč; *suite* 4,700 Kč, *extra bed* 1,000 Kč. **Credit** AmEx, DC, EC, MC, V. **Map 1 C3**
As crisp and comfortable as the lobby and rooms in this hotel are, the real Sax appeal is its location, up the hill from Malostranské náměstí, and perfect for tourists who want to be in the heart of the Castle district. And service? The staff at the Sax won't blow it.
Hotel services *Bar. Car park. Currency exchange. Fax. Laundry. Lift. Limousine service. Multilingual staff. Restaurant.* **Room services** *Hairdryer. Minibar. Radio. Room service.*

Hotel 16 U sv. Kateřiny

Kateřinská 16, Prague 2 (295 329/fax 293 956). Metro I.P. Pavlova/7, 18, 24 tram. **Rates** *single* 2,100 Kč; *double* 2,800 Kč; *suite* 2,600-3,800 Kč. **Credit** EC, MC, V. **Map 6 K8**
St Catherine's is a family-run inn on a quiet, sloping street near the Botanical Gardens that is everything a small hotel should be: tranquil, intimate and well run by its friendly owners, who will cater to individual needs. Not exactly centrally located, but well worth the money.
Hotel services *Bar. Currency exchange. Fax. Multilingual staff.* **Room services** *Hairdryer. Minibar. Safe.*

Julián

Elišky Peškové 11, Prague 5 (5731 1150/542 312/ fax 5731 1149/547 525/casjul@vol.cz). Tram 6, 9, 12. **Rooms** 31. **Rates** *single* 1,980-2,780 Kč; *double* 2,680-3,880 Kč; *extra bed* 600-900 Kč. **Credit** AmEx, DC, V. **Map 3 H1**
On the edge of Smichov, the Julián is slightly off the beaten path, yet just ten minutes' walk (or a quick tram ride) from Malá Strana. Just off the reception area is the Julián's jewel: its cosy reading room with fireplace, with translated Czech works for sale. The fourth floor is air-conditioned and all

PRAGUE'S FORMER
Famous Alcron Hotel
OPENS AGAIN

Despite the abundance of Art Nouveau in the city, it is extremely rare to find examples of true Czech Art Deco. The former Alcron Hotel, long since closed, was one such example. After nearly a decade of planning, this Prague landmark is now being re-opened as the glorious, five star, Radisson SAS Hotel Praha. Centrally located in the heart of the city, the Radisson SAS Hotel Praha provides the ideal venue to host your meetings and conferences.

Constructed in 1930, the Alcron enjoyed the enviable reputation of being Jazz-age Prague's "in" hotel, offering cocktails at the bar, relaxed dining and the opportunity to see powerful, glamorous people in a striking, luxurious environment. This charmed existence came to an abrupt end in 1939 with the onset of the Second World War. It is only now that under the management of the Radisson SAS can this exceptional hotel again command center stage.

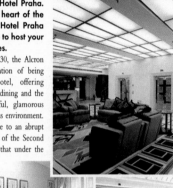

In restoring the Alcron to its former glory the Radisson team, headed by General Manager Philippe Pellaud and Sales and Marketing Director Stefan Buchs, made sure that the clean lines of the original layout were faithfully followed. Much of the interior is historically significant and had to be preserved appropriately. Many unique items have been renovated, from the weighty chandeliers and rich Italian marble to the creamy "milk glass" throughout the hotel.

The Radisson SAS offers outstanding meeting facilities. The Crystal Ballroom, with its soaring rib-like frame of steel with glass roof, is the focal point. This impressive ballroom can accommodate meetings from 10 to up to 150 persons. Five comfortable private salons provide the ideal meeting space for hosting conferences, presentations, board meetings and seminars. The hotel prides itself on having 100% guest satisfaction combined with the best available service.

The hotel contains 211 luxurious, airy rooms and suites with high ceilings and classic period furnishings. A state of the art, on-line in-room entertainment system has been added, providing Internet access and video games for every guest. The first of its kind in Central Europe, it is ideal for the business traveller. Every room contains three phones, a mini-bar, a trouser press, fax and PC connections, in-room movies, a warm, stylish ambiance and, of course, marble and chrome fittings. In addition, the latest security features have been installed throughout the hotel.

The hotel includes the 130-seat La Rotonde restaurant, a professionally equipped fitness center with sauna and solarium, central parking, boutiques, a travel agency and 24-hour limousine service plus the Radisson's Worldwide Hospitality Programme for corporate guests. One of the hotel's most exciting features is its Art Deco BeBop bar where waiters glide past in crisp, long aprons, with live jazz by local musicians.

The former Alcron's return to the Prague scene is truly more than welcome. With everything from an internationally trained staff to the tradition of 5 star service, guests can look forward to experiencing a unique environment.

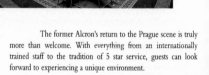

ŠTĚPÁNSKÁ 40, 110 00 PRAHA 1 CZECH REPUBLIC
Tel.: ++ 4202 2282 0111, Fax: ++ 4202 2282 0120
Toll Free: 0800 374 411, E-mail: sb@traveller.cz

apartments have kitchenettes. The only drawback here is the lurid pink sheets on every bed. Services on offer will be boosted by a planned fitness centre and sauna. Pets are accepted by arrangement if you can't bear to leave Henry at home. **Hotel services** *Bar. Car park (200 Kč per day).* *Disabled: access, rooms adapted. Fax. Internet. Laundry.* *Lift. Multilingual staff.* **Room services** *Hairdryer. Safe.*

Kampa Stará Zbrojnice

Všehrdova 16, Prague 1 (5732 0508/fax 5732 0262). *Metro Malostranská/22 tram.* **Rooms** 84. **Rates** *single* 2,000-2,200 Kč; *double* 3,150-3,550 Kč. **Credit** AmEx, DC, EC, MC, V. **Map 2 E5**
Despite the baroque setting, this place has a distinct *staré struktura* (old structure) feel; a throwback to pre-1989. Still, it's good value considering the prime location on a quiet backstreet on Malá Strana. The service may be a bit lethargic but at least it's inoffensive.
Hotel services *Car park. Currency exchange. Fax.* *Garden. Laundry. Lift. Multilingual staff. Restaurant.* *Safe.* **Room services** *Minibar. Radio.*

U krále Jiřího

(King George) Liliová 10, Prague 1 (2422 2013/tel/fax 2422 1983). Metro Staroměstská or Národní třída/17, 18 tram. **Rooms** 9 (all en suite). **Rates** *single* 1,500-1,900 Kč; *double* 2,600 Kč; *triple* 3,500 Kč; *2-person apartment* 3,000 Kč. **Credit** AmEx, MC, V. **Map 3 G4**
Tucked down a picturesque lane, this pension has attic rooms with sloping ceilings and ancient beams that are so snug you may never want to get out of bed. But if you manage to, you'll find a trendy Irish pub downstairs (the James Joyce; *see p140*) and Charles Bridge and Old Town Square just cobblestones away.
Hotel services *Currency exchange. Fax. Garden. Safe.* *Wine bar.* **Room services** *Radio.*

U Zlaté studny

(The Golden Well) Karlova 3, Prague 1 (tel/fax 2421 0539). Metro Staroměstská/17, 18 tram. **Rooms** 6. **Rates** *double* 3,500-3,900 Kč; *suite* 3,990-4,600 Kč; *extra person* 500 Kč; free under-15s. **Credit** AmEx, MC, V. **Map 3 H4**
Four roomy suites (and two doubles) decorated in Louis XIV style in a classy Renaissance structure, a location less than five minutes from Old Town Square or Charles Bridge, and super staff make this one of the best-value hotels in this category. A perfect choice for those hoping to explore most of the historic areas of Prague on foot.
Hotel services *Bar. Currency exchange. Fax. Laundry.* *Lift. Multilingual staff. No-smoking rooms. Restaurant.* **Room services** *Hairdryer. Minibar. Radio. Safe.*

Budget (under 2,500 Kč)

See also **Libra-Q**, *page 116*.

Dům U Velke Boty

(House of the Big Shoe) Vlašska 333/30 Prague 1 (5731 1107). Metro Malostranská/12, 22 tram. **Rooms** 12. **Rates** *single* 1,350 Kč; *double* 2,100 Kč; *triple* 2,860 Kč. **Map 1 B4**
Set in a building that dates back to the 1470s, the House at the Big Shoe has the pleasant feel of a rustic cottage or inn. The eccentric owners, Charlotta and Jan Rippl, refuse to hang 'some garish sign' on their hotel, so just look for the door buzzer marked 'Rippl'. Attentive (without being overattentive) service and loads of gorgeous period furniture make this the perfect nest from which to explore romantic Prague. Frequented by many European writers, artists, actors and the like. Breakfast is an extra 150 Kč.
Hotel services *Fax. Laundry. Fitness facilities.* *Multilingual staff.* **Room services** *Hairdryer. Telephone.*

Grand Hotel Evropa

Václavské náměstí 25, Prague 1 (2422 8117/fax 2422 4544). Metro Můstek/3, 9, 14, 24 tram. **Rooms** 93 (53 en suite). **Rates** *single* 1,280-2,450 Kč; *double* 2,160-3,400 Kč; *triple* 2,790-4,350 Kč; *quad with bath* 5,200 Kč; *apartment* 4,700-5,000 Kč. **Credit** AmEx, EC, MC, V. **Map 4 K5**
This nostalgic feast offers a unique opportunity to savour the dying breaths of two bygone eras (Graham Greene would revel in both). The building is a stunning art nouveau landmark inside and out. Still, the First Republic is long gone and now, if you listen closely, you can actually hear the elegance fading. The other, less-fondly remembered era kept alive at the Evropa is the bad old communist days. The indifferent (sometimes flat-out incompetent) service is a distinct throwback to this time, as are the clunky rotary phones and hallways with the lights turned out their entire length. Perhaps they're still using the excuse that they need to conserve the workers' energy. The restaurant's dinners are criminally overpriced. To get a bit more value for money, request a room with a renovated bathroom.
Hotel services *Bar. Currency exchange. Fax. Laundry.* *Lift. Multilingual staff. Restaurant. Safe.* **Room services** *Telephone.*

Hotel Anna

Budečská 17, Prague 2 (2251 3111/2251 5158). Metro Náměstí Míru/4, 16, 22, 34 tram. **Rooms** 23. **Rates** *single* 1,500-1,800 Kč; *double* 2,340-2,880 Kč; *triple* 2,880-3,960 Kč. **Credit** AmEx, EC, MC, V. **Map 8 B3**
This part of leafy Vinohrady is just off the beaten tourist path, a bonus when summer crowds overwhelm. The hotel's stained-glass windows, wrought-iron staircase, tall French doors and abundant greenery make this an exceptionally tasteful option in this price category. Anna is just a short walk from the metro and a number of good, medium-priced

U Zlaté studny – *great location, great price.*

restaurants. The hotel was planning a renovation at the time
of going to press, so be sure to check before you book.
Hotel services *Air-conditioning. Bar. Car park.
Currency exchange. Fax. Laundry. Lift. Multilingual staff.
Restaurant. Terrace.* **Room services** *Satellite TV.
Telephone.*

Hotel Legie
*Sokolská 33, Prague 2 (2492 0254/fax 2491 4441). Metro
I.P. Pavlova/4, 6, 16, 22 tram.* **Rooms** 41 (all en suite).
Rates *double* 2,200-2,600 Kč; *triple* 3,100-3,500 Kč; *quad
with bathroom* 2,200 Kč; *without* 1,700 Kč. **Map 6 L8**
With recently renovated rooms, Legie might just be Prague's
best bet in this category. The socialist-flavoured exterior of
this beast is almost as hideous as its location is good – just
a ten-minute walk from Wenceslas Square. But don't let the
ugly concrete exterior of this former military recreation centre put you off, comrade. The rooms are clean and almost
modern – just not fancy. Best of all, they're cheap. If you're
a light sleeper, bring your earplugs: the traffic can get loud.
Hotel services *Bar. Car park. Currency exchange. Fax.
Lift. Multilingual staff. Restaurant.* **Room services**
Satellite TV. Telephone.

Pension City
*Belgická 10, Prague 2 (691 1334/fax 691 0977). Metro
Náměstí Miru/4, 6, 11, 16, 22, 34 tram.* **Rooms** 19 (7 en
suite). **Rates** *single* 1,100-1,700 Kč; *double* 1,500-2,300 Kč;
triple 1,750-2,600 Kč; *quad* 1,900-2,800 Kč. **Credit** AmEx,
DC, EC, MC, TC (AmEx), V. **Map 6 M9**
Depending on how you look at it, this is either a two-star hotel
or a three-star pension. The difference has to do with the facil-
ities in the different rooms (12 of which are family rooms).
But the common denominator is good value for the no-frills
traveller who wants an affordable, quiet, central location.
Hotel services *Café. Currency exchange. Fax. Hairdryer
on request. Lift. Multilingual staff. Safe.* **Room services**
Radio on request. Satellite TV (70 Kč per day). Telephone.

Koruna
*Opatovická 16, Prague 1 (2491 5174/fax 292 492).
Metro Národní třída/6, 9, 18, 22 tram.* **Rooms** 23.
Rates *single* 1,200-1,650 Kč; *double* 2,200-2,850 Kč;
triple 3,200-3,600 Kč; *suite* 4,500-5,000 Kč. **Credit** MC, V.
Map 5 H6
The Koruna's elegant, nineteenth-century exterior is let down
by its dingy dingy rooms, seemingly unchanged since the
1950s. But the location near the National Theatre and a number of choice cafés and inexpensive restaurants is a major
plus. If this place were more accessible by car, it would likely go upmarket in no time. For now, though, it's a haven for
budget travellers.
Hotel services *Fax. Lift. Safe.* **Room services** *Radio.
Satellite TV. Telephone.*

Penzion Dientzenhofer
*Nosticova 2, Prague 1 (531 672/538 896/fax 5732 0888).
Metro Malostranská/12, 22 tram.* **Rooms** 7. **Rates** *single*
1,500-1,900 Kč; *double* 2,000-2,800 Kč; *1-person suite* 2,300
Kč; *4-person suite* 4,700 Kč. **Credit** AmEx, DC, EC, MC,
TC (AmEx), V. **Map 2 E4**
Outrageously good value (but note that rates are set to rise
slightly in 1999). Run by genuinely nice people, the Dientzen-
hofer is in a quiet neighbourhood, yet is still in the heart of
Malá Strana. The management has taken care to provide for
the needs of guests in wheelchairs. Room 2 has a nice view
of the garden. Dogs and cats are welcome, though they have
to fork out 100 Kč per night. Suites have a minibar and safe.
Hotel services *Babysitting. Bar. Business services.
Car park. Disabled: access, rooms adapted. Fax.
Garden. Hairdresser. Laundry. Lift. Limousine service.
Multilingual staff. No-smoking rooms. Restaurant.*
Room services *Hairdryer. Minibar. Radio. Room
service (24 hours). Safe. Satellite TV. Telephone.*

Pension Unitas
*Bartolomějská 9, Prague 1 (232 7700/fax 232 7709/
unitas@cloister-inn.cz/www.cloister-inn.cz/unitas/
unitas.htm). Metro Národní třída/6, 9, 18, 22 tram.*
Rooms 35. **Rates** *single* 1,020 Kč (*with en-suite bath*
2,700 Kč); *double* 1,200 Kč (*with en-suite bath* 3,400 Kč).
Map 3 H5
This hostel is housed in the same building as the **Cloister
Inn** (*see above*). One floor has standard, comfortable hostel
rooms; in the basement you'll find communist-era prison cells
that have been converted into rooms. Big Brother locked
playwright/dissident Václav Havel in room P6. This floor
can feel eerie, but the rooms are fine and clean. A bargain.
Hotel services *Babysitting. Business services.
Car park. Currency exchange. Fax. Hairdryer on request.
Interpreting services. Laundry. Lift. Multilingual staff.
No-smoking rooms.*

Pension Větrník
*U Větrníku 40, Prague 6 (2061 2404/fax 361 406/
milos.opatrny@telecom.cz). Metro Hradčanská, then
1, 18, 26 tram.* **Rooms** 6 (all en suite). **Rates** *double*
2,000 Kč; *apartment* 3,000 Kč, *extra bed* 500 Kč.
Credit EC, MC.
A fair way from the centre but a prime spot for those who
favour comfort over location. The six rooms in this restored
eighteenth-century windmill overlook a large secluded garden whose high walls block out the ugly cluster of buildings
nearby. Charming owners (including Arnost, the docile St
Bernard) and private tennis court are further enticements.
Hotel services *Car park. Garden. Laundry.
Multilingual staff. Restaurant. Safe.* **Room services**
Hairdryer. Radio. Satellite TV. Telephone.

Pension Vyšehrad
*Krokova 6, Prague 2 (424 813). Metro Vyšehrad/8, 24
tram.* **Rooms** 4 (none en suite). **Rates** *single* 900 Kč;
double 1,300 Kč; *triple* 1,750 Kč.
Want to get the feel of staying in a Czech family's home, yet
still be just minutes from downtown? Well, this is the place.
Run by Mila Kovarikova and her English-speaking daughter Eva, this tiny pension allows travellers to get away
from tourist overkill and step right into peace, quiet and hospitality. There's no sign, so just ring the bell marked
'Kovarikova'. Even if Eva is not there, just say 'pension?' and
you're set. The family cat has the run of the house, so aller-
gy sufferers beware. Use of washing machine.
Hotel services *Car park. Garden. Telephone.*
Room services *Radio.*

U medvídků
*Na Perštýně 7, Praha 1 (2421 1916/fax 2422 0930).
Metro Národní třída.* **Rooms** 18 (10 en suite). **Rates**
double 1,500-3,000 Kč. **Credit** AmEx, MC, V. **Map 3 H5**
The Little Bears offers comfortable rooms and good service
above one of a dying breed of Prague pubs (the kind that still
attracts locals in search of great beer and food at good prices).
This pub's only nods to the tourist trade upstairs are bad
translations on the menu and some poor sap walking around
squeezing an accordion. *See also p142.*
Hotel services *Bar. Currency exchange. Fax. Garden.
Multilingual staff. Restaurant. Safe.* **Room services**
Minibar. Refrigerator. Telephone. TV.

Hostels

Most hostels have shared bathrooms.

Charles University dorms
*Central office: Terronská 28, Prague 6 (2431 1105/2491
3692/fax 2431 1107). Metro Dejvická/20, 25 tram.*
Reception open 9am-7pm daily. **Rates** (per person)
double, triple or *quad* 200-400 Kč.

*Too much clowning and you might get barred from the **Clown & Bard Hostel**.*

One central office takes care of booking some 1,000 dorm rooms scattered throughout the city. Only available from late June to late September, however.

The Clown & Bard

Bořivojova 102, Prague 3 (272 436). Metro Jiřího z Poděbrad/5, 9, 11, 26 tram. **Beds** 85. **Reception open** 24 hours. **Rates** *hostel bed* 200 Kč; *double room* 350 Kč; *apartment* 300 Kč. **Map 8 B2**

A cheap hotel that doubles as a hostel. The staff here encourage a laid-back, friendly (and trusting) environment; guests are logged in by first name only. Rooms are sparse but clean, and include appealingly shabby antiques. The ground-floor pub features live music several nights a week and attracts an eclectic mixture of hotel guests, expats and young, hip Czechs from the neighbourhood (*see also p152*). There's no shut out, but there are a few things to bear in mind: no breakfast, no phone reservations, and you should try to arrive by 7pm. **Hostel services** *Bar. Fax. Garden. Laundry. Safe.*

Club Habitat

Na Zbořenci 10, Prague 2 (290 315/293 101/fax 290 315/293 101). Metro Karlovo náměstí/3, 6, 9, 18, 24 tram. **Beds** 55. **Reception open** 24 hours. **Rates** (per person) 350 Kč. **Map 5 H7**

Set back from the main drag in a fourteenth-century courtyard and just five minutes' walk from the city centre, this hostel is one of the friendlier places for budget tourists to bed down for the night. Club Habitat has four- to ten-person rooms, including one with a kitchenette (at no extra charge). Luggage can be stored here if you can't face lugging your stuff around. All hostel proceeds go to support Czech children's charities. Breakfast is an extra 60 Kč. **Hostel services** *Car park. Fax. Multilingual staff.*

Hostel Sokol

Újezd 40/450, Prague 1 (5700 7397/5700 7340). Metro Malostranská/12, 22 tram. **Beds** 90. **Reception open** 24 hours. **Rates** (per person) 220 Kč. **Map 2 E5**

In a nutshell, ultra-cheap lodging in an ultra-great location. Follow a labyrinth of halls through the Sokol sports centre to get to reception. Signs allegedly lead the way, but it's easy to get lost. Once you manage to find the reception desk, however, you're in budget travellers' paradise. Sip beer on the desolate terrace while watching the moon over Petřín hill. Or walk to Charles Bridge. The staff struggle with English. **Hostel services** *Kitchenette. Multilingual staff.*

Libra-Q

Senovážné náměstí 21, Prague 1 (2423 1754/2210 5536/fax 2422 1579). Metro Hlavní nádraží, Můstek or Náměstí Republiky/3, 9, 14, 24 tram. **Rooms** 28 (14 en suite). **Reception open** 24 hours. **Rates hostel**: *single* 750 Kč; *double* 890 Kč; *triple* 1,320 Kč; *quad* 330 Kč *per person; 8-person room* 310 Kč *per person*; **hotel**: *single* 980 Kč; *double*, 1,380 Kč; *triple* 1,630 Kč. **Map 4 L4**

The Libra has two type of lodgings. Its hostel rooms are, well, hostel rooms. The clean, bare-bones 'hotel' rooms have shower and WC but no TV, phone or other usual hotel amenities. A good, practical (if unromantic) location between the main train station and Wenceslas Square. Luggage can be stored for 10 Kč per day, and breakfast costs 50 Kč. **Hostel services** *Bar. Fax. Restaurant. Safe.*

Travellers' Hostels

Booking office: Dlouhá 33, Prague 1 (231 1318/231 1234/fax 231 6161/hostel@terminal.cz). Metro Náměstí Republiky/5, 14, 26 tram. **Reception open** 24 hours (all branches). **Rates** (per person) *double* 490 Kč; *triple* 430 Kč; *quad* 400 Kč; *10-person dorm* 350 Kč. **Map 3 J3**

This hostel and booking office connects travellers to any of a network of hostels. The two constants are good value and a glut of English-speaking backpackers. **Hostel services** *Bar. Fax. Laundry.* **Branches** Růžová 5, Prague 1 (2422 8566); Střelecký ostrov 336, Prague 1 (2491 0188); U Lanové dráhy 3, Prague 1 (533 160); Křižovnická 7, Prague 1 (232 0987); Husova 3, Prague 1 (2421 5326).

Accommodation agencies

Unless otherwise noted, each of the following agencies organises private accommodation in flats and also books hostel beds, pensions and hotels at no extra service charge. Getting a flat outside the centre can cut the cost by around 35 per cent.

AVE

Hlavní nádraží, Wilsonova 8, Prague 2 (2422 3521/2422 3218/fax 2422 3463/avetours@avetours.anet.cz). Metro Hlavní nádraží. **Open** 6am-11pm daily. **Credit** AmEx, DC, EC, MC, V. **Map 4 M5**

Pick of the bunch: Best…

… haven for the overwhelmed

Staff at the **RHIA Tours** office (*see page 117*) do a damn fine job of finding bargain beds that fit travellers' particular needs. Let's say you want a hotel not too far out of the centre that will accept your pit bull, has safe parking for your rented Harley-Davidson and a sauna. This would be a good place to start.

… to reminisce about communism and still live to tell (and laugh) about it

From the bell-hop to the management, the folks working here at the **Grand Hotel Evropa** (*see page 113*) seem a bit puzzled by all that's happened during the last ten years or so. They know they're sitting on a gem of a building in a jewel of a city. But they'd probably be happier if all those damn foreigners would stop coming by and insisting on giving money in order to sleep here.

… to park your time machine

At **Dům U Velke Boty** (*see page 113*), you can kick your shoes off and soak up the atmosphere of a hotel filled not just with old stuff, but with relics that have been purposefully chosen by owners Charlotta and Jan Rippl to complement the ambience. If you have an hour or so, get a cup of coffee and a cigarette and ask Charlotta to fill you in on the history of the place.

… to meet, eat and drink with the weird

From neighbourhood teens rolling up joints, to drunken Aussies quaffing absinthe, to expat bands howling blues, rock or bluegrass, the pub of the **Clown & Bard Hostel** (*see page 116*) has a smoky atmosphere reminiscent of early '90s Prague. That was when young, idealistic foreigners flocked to Czechoslovakia carrying backpacks, smoking cheap hash and wearing Doc Martens – instead of these days' more commonly observed briefcases, Cohibas and Bruno Maglis.

… to bring Spot or Tiddles

The **Pension Dientzenhofer** (*see page 115*) not only accepts dogs but is located just seconds away from prime walking territory, Kampa Park. Here your pooch can mingle with the locals who often bring their masters for a stroll on the island.

Located in the main train station, this is probably the most convenient option for those who arrive at a late hour with no place to go. Service seems to have improved of late, but can still be erratic.
Branches: Na příkopě 16, Prague 1 (261 013); Pohořelec 9 & 18, Prague 1 (531 020); Ruzyně Airport, Prague 6 (316 4266); Nádraži Holešovice, Prague 7 (6671 0514); Staroměstska Mostecká věž, Prague 1 (summer only; 536 010); Staroměstské náměstí 2, Prague 1 (2448 2018).

City of Prague Accommodation Service

Haštalská 7, Prague 1 (231 0202/fax 2481 0603). Metro Náměsti Republiky/5, 14, 26 tram. **Open** 9am-7pm daily. **Map 3 J2**
A reputable firm that offers good service.

Mary's Accommodation Service

Anny Letenské 17, Prague 2 (2225 4007/2225 3510). Metro Náměsti Míru/11 tram. **Credit** AmEx, MC, V. **Map 6 M7**
A friendly, English-speaking low- to mid-priced agency that places visitors in pensions, hotels and private apartments throughout the city. The minimum rate is for two people, and reservations must be guaranteed with a credit card (for which a surcharge is added). Generally, breakfast is not included in the prices.

RHIA Tours

Školská 1, Prague 2 (2491 4514/291 765/fax 294 843). Metro I.P. Pavlova, Můstek or Národní třida/3, 9, 14, 24 tram. **Open** 10am-8pm daily. **Map 5 J7**
A full-service travel agency offering great alternatives to hostels for just a bit more dosh. Staff can arrange accommodation with safe parking, and you can also change currency here.

Stop City

Vinohradská 24, Prague 2 (2423 1233/tel/fax 2422 2497). Metro Muzeum or Náměsti Míru/11 tram. **Open** *Apr-Oct* 10am-9pm daily; *Nov-Mar* 11am-8pm daily. **Credit** AmEx, EC, MC, V. **Map 6 M6**
Stop City's helpful staff are ready to book you into a pension, hotel, private room or apartment. They don't handle hostel bookings, however.

Tom's Travel

Ostrovni 7, Prague 1 (293 972/290 696/299 349/fax 291 866/toms@travel.cz). Metro Národní třida/6, 9, 18, 22 tram. **Open** *June-Aug* 8am-10pm daily; *Sept-May* 8am-8pm daily. **Credit** EC, MC. **Map 5 G6**
Tom's can book two- to five-star hotels, pensions and apartments – and it offers free airport transfer with advance bookings. Also a handy option for booking rooms in other Czech cities.

Campsite

Autocamp Trojská

Trojská 375/157, Prague 7 (tel/fax 854 2945). Metro Nádraži Holešovice, then bus 112. **Open** all year round. **Rates** *tent* 90-150kč; *person* 90 Kč; *car* 90 Kč; *caravan* 150-190 Kč; *bungalow* 250 Kč per person; *room in house* 350-500 Kč; 70 Kč *6-15s*; 30 Kč *under 6s*; *electricity* 70 Kč.
A pretty suburban garden with the added possibility of staying in a bungalow or a room in the house if the charms of al fresco living pale. Management is friendly and easygoing. There's also a garden restaurant, snack bar, use of a washing machine and common kitchen with fridge. There's a small camp tax per person per day.
Facilities *Fax. Telephone.*

Restaurants

You've never had it so good. Honest.

When asked what a visitor to Prague should eat, Marlène Salomon, owner of the city's finest French bistro, answers without hesitation: 'Czech food.' Then she adds immediately, '*I* tried it once – I won't do it again.'

Gallic pride aside, her advice encapsulates the essential dilemma of dining in Prague. Going native usually involves leaving your tastebuds at the door, but to dine on Western or world cuisine here is to miss out on the very heart of Czech life. Slavic cuisine, like that in much of Eastern Europe, involves high-starch foods that keep well in winter, will fuel a ploughman all day, and are preferably pickled, boiled into mush, salted, fried, slathered with gravy, set in aspic or smothered in mayonnaise. Put it this way: steak dripping in butter is considered the height of refinement.

Yet, believe it or not, there are few things closer to the Slavic heart than food. Listen in on any conversation between Czech women over 40 and the word *brambory* (potatoes) will invariably be heard, followed by the latest market price. Ask any of the younger generation their most cherished experience and they will probably tell you of their grandmother's *cibulačka* (onion soup) or *česnekova* (garlic soup), soaked up in the heavy brown rye bread that Czechs pine for in vain outside this country. So how do you get in on the act while sticking strictly to the palatable? Simple. Use the solution to all intractable geopolitical paradoxes: compromise.

Czech wonder meals, brought off with inspiration at a handful of establishments, are game platters (*see page 135* **Fair game**), *guláš* (okay, so it's borrowed from Hungary) and fresh river fish, which is generally available in autumn. But if you're prepared to look beyond what you see on your plate, you'll come away with a few unforgettable experiences (in the good sense). How about dinner for two in a candlelit Gothic cellar; at the edge of the glistening Vltava; or at a street table on an ancient, cobbled square? And all for the price of a couple of cheeseburgers at the Hard Rock Café back home.

And while Prague has yet to score its first Michelin star, the number of restaurants in the capital is on the increase (nearly 1,200, up 20 per cent from just two years ago). Pakistani, Thai, Japanese, Tex-Mex, Indian, French, North African, fresh seafood and organic vegetarian now join the growing list of better-than-ever Italian, Chinese and Middle Eastern.

NO MORE VEGGIE HELL

For vegetarians as well, survival prospects have improved, with an increasing number of places offering salads that resemble works of art, and a few actually going so far as to wow you with reasonably fresh dishes and appetising ethnic creations. Even in pubs, a meat-free (*bez masá*) dinner is possible, though it may be nothing more than fried cheese (*smažené sýr*), fried cauliflower (*smažené květák*) or fried mushrooms (*smažené žampiony*). Other possible last resorts include an omelette with cheese, mushrooms or peas (*omeleta s sýrem, žampiony* or *hráškem*), dumplings with egg or spinach (*knedlíky s vejci* or *špenát špenát*) or the inevitably bland cheese plate (*sýrový talíř*).

Establishments with a unique understanding of veghead ways are **Lotos**, **U Govindy Vegetarian Club**, **Sports Café Cornucopia**, **Bar Bar**, **Adonis**, **Safir Grill**, **Country Life** and **Le Gourmand**. Or follow the expat trail to Western-oriented cafés with imaginative vegetarian alternatives, such as **FX Café**, **Jo's Bar** (*see page 150*), **The Globe Bookstore & Coffeehouse** (*see page 151*) and **Érra** (*see page 140*). Upmarket veggie-friendly restaurants include **V Zátiši**, **Le Bistrot de Marlène**, **Bellevue**, **U Patrona**, **Le Café Colonial** and **Avalon**. All these places are listed below, unless otherwise stated.

THE MENU

Traditional Czech menus list two types of main course: *minutky*: cooked to order, and *hotová jidla*: ready-to-serve fare like slow-cooked meats in sauces (such as *guláš* and *svíčková*), accompanied by dumplings (*knedlíky*). Lunch dishes (*obědy*) are usually available until about 4pm; after this time more expensive dinner dishes (*večeře*) are served. Usual sides are rice, potatoes or fried béchamel dough (*krokety*), ordered separately. The closest thing to fresh vegetables in these places is usually *obloha*, a garnish of pickles or a tomato on a single leaf of lettuce or cabbage. Surprisingly tasty appetisers are Prague ham with horseradish or rich soups, while dessert faves include *palačinky*, pancakes filled with either fruit, chocolate or ice-cream (and sometimes all three).

DRINKS

Beer is a national treasure in the Czech Republic; Czech beer (*see page 147*) is a treasure throughout the world. A half-litre mug from the tap is often cheaper than a Coke or cup of coffee. Wines, mostly from southern Moravia (*see page 144* **Not just here for the beer?**), aren't as grand, and are sometimes even poured half-and-half into glasses of the most popular mineral waters, the carbonated Mattoni and Dobrá Voda ('Good Water', which is also available still). Espresso, generally from bitter, low-grade Central European grounds, is the most popular coffee, while anything called Turkish coffee (*turek*) is strictly for masochists and those who don't mind parting with a few teeth. *See also chapter* **Cafés, Pubs & Bars** for more on drinking in Prague.

THE BILL

Highly suspect maths skills remain pervasive at some places – or worse, two sets of menus, one reasonable, in Czech, and a much higher-priced one in English or German. A well-loved scam comes in the form of a preposterously high charge for the unbidden salted almonds put out when you sit down. Don't touch them unless you're prepared to pay up. Also look out for an illegal additional 23 per cent VAT on restaurant bills: this charge is already incorporated into menu prices.

A more usual and benign custom in traditional Czech establishments is the little slip of paper a waiter places on your table with his chicken-scratch record of your order on it, which translates at leaving time into a bill. In such places you pay the guy with the big black folding wallet in his waistband, not your waiter (ask him 'Za platim, prosim?'– 'May I pay, please?'). A small cover charge and extra charges for everything from milk in your coffee to a single slice of bread taken from the proffered basket is usual, as is minimal tipping (except, perhaps, at top-of-the-range places where adding ten per cent is usual), usually by asking them to round the figure up to the nearest ten crowns (rather than leaving the tip on the table).

GENERAL ADVICE

These days you'll encounter fewer of the communist-era problems for which Prague restaurants were once infamous, but you'll probably be irritated often enough. Comically surly and/or glacial service is still no surprise, nor is a kitchen that closes at 9pm when the posted closing hour is midnight. Much less frustrating is sharing a table with other patrons who, like you, should ask 'Je tu volno?' ('Is it free?') and may also wish each other 'dobrou chu' before chowing down. The national toast is 'na zdravi'. Prague dines with an extremely relaxed dress code and reservations are necessary at only the fanciest spots in town.

Also, little details such as phone numbers and opening hours – or being open at all – are still changing fast in this topsy-turvy culinary adventure. So, as with many other aspects of Prague life, be sure to bring a sense of humour and a back-up plan with you.

Note that although you should have little trouble making a reservation in English by phone in swankier establishments, it may be easier to book in person whenever possible.

RESTAURANT CATEGORIES

The following restaurants are listed by price range, based on **an appetiser and a main course with accompanying side dish for one person, but no dessert or drinks**. They are divided into five categories: Bank-breakers (900 Kč upwards); Pricey (750-900 Kč); Moderate (450-750 Kč); Inexpensive (300-450 Kč); and Cheap (under 300 Kč). Note that establishments only take credit cards where specified.

Dinner can be had at a *restaurace*, a *vinárna* or wine bar (varying widely in quality), a *pivnice* or beer hall (which generally has an extremely basic menu, though we've listed notable exceptions); you can also grab a bite at a fast-food counter (which in Prague provides either the healthiest or the only food available, depending on the hour). *See chapter* **Cafés, Pubs & Bars** for more wine bars and beer halls.

Bank-breakers (900 Kč upwards)

Bellevue
Smetanovo nábřeži 18, Prague 1 (2422 7614). Metro Národni třida/17, 18 tram. **Open** noon-3pm, 7-11.30pm, Mon-Sat; 11am-3.30pm (jazz brunch), 5.30-11pm, Sun. **Average** 1,300 Kč. **Credit** AmEx, EC, MC, V. **Map 3 G5**
Parnas was almost universally lauded as Prague's finest restaurant prior to moving up the street and changing its name to Bellevue. Now, during any heavenly Sunday jazz brunch, with a bottomless mimosa before you, along with pan-fried quail in Drambuie sauce or veal tenderloin topped with fresh truffles, it's clear that nothing was left behind during the move. Service is generally head and shoulders above the competition, but bear in mind this is Prague: there's no such thing as guaranteed pleasant dining. Still, this star of Sanjit Suri's group, which includes **V Zátiší**, **U Patrona** and **Avalon** (for all, *see below*), is still the guiding light with service and castle views that set the standard in the city.
Air-conditioning. Booking essential. Tables outdoors (24, terrace).

Circle Line
Malostranské náměsti 12, Prague 1 (5753 0023/ fax 530 276). Tram 12, 22. **Open** 6-11pm Mon-Sat. **Average** 1,000 Kč. **Credit** AmEx, EC, MC, V. **Map 2 D3**
Fresh seafood, which arrives on Wednesdays and Fridays, is served in an elegant, high-ceilinged cellar downstairs from the cheaper **Avalon** (*see below*). The live piano music can be a bit cloying, but otherwise this place is hard to fault. The restaurant has recently been revamped, and the cruise ship theme décor has now been softened with curtains and big vases of dried reeds. The service is impeccable; the seasonal salads are a work of art; the fish, lamb and chicken dishes are imaginatively prepared and presented according to French and Italian ideas, and there's always a vegetarian option on the menu. The wine list is good but will punish your wallet – you can sample the same vintages upstairs at Avalon for around half the price.
Tables outdoors (20, pavement).

When Good 'King' Wenceslas last looked out, he probably wasn't chilling out with his mates

David

Tržiště 21, Prague 1 (539 325). Tram 12, 22. **Open**
11.30am-11pm daily. **Average** 1,100 Kč. **Credit** AmEx,
EC, MC, V. **Map 2 D3**
Top of the list of every touring rock star is this family-run,
discreet little dining room, where they know how to pam-
per, old club-style. Nestled between the American, German
and Italian embassies, David features waiters who seem
more like butlers as they whisk roast boar and port to your
table. A small vegetarian menu satisfies moody bass players, while the rest make do with definitive Bohemian classics such as roasted duck with red and white cabbage, and
rabbit fillet with spinach leaves and herb sauce.
Booking essential. Tables outdoors (10).

Jewel of India

*Pařížská 20, Prague 1 (2481 1010). Metro
Staroměstská/17, 18 tram.* **Open** 11.30am-3pm, 5.30-
11.30pm, daily. **Average** 1,000 Kč. **Credit** AmEx, MC,
V. **Map 3 H2**
The surroundings are sumptuous, with a ground-floor
bar and a spacious cellar dining room. Tandoori special-
ties lead a menu that could do with being a little more
adventurous, though it's mostly well prepared and at least
not under-spiced. (Avoid anything with mushrooms,
though, unless tinned ones are your thing.) Service is typically Indian – a sort of teeming caste system of waiters –
while British diners, at least, could probably do without
their detailed explanation of every last item. ('This is nan

bread…'). The *nawabi* and *begumi khazanas*, respectively
meat and vegetarian at 700 and 600 Kč, offer the chance to
try a little bit of everything.

Opera Grill

*Karoliny Světlé 35, Prague 1 (265 508/0602 203 962).
Metro Staroměstská/6, 9, 17, 18, 22 tram.*
Dinner served 7pm-2am daily. **Average** 1,200 Kč.
Credit AmEx, EC, MC, V. **Map 3 G5**
A speakeasy fantasy. First locate the tarnished, unlit brass
sign, walk into the nondescript apartment building, rap on
a knocker, then you're whisked into a gorgeous little dining room that's as lush and sugary as the sweetest dessert.
Guests sit in large, overstuffed armchairs, surrounded by
voluminous draperies and statuettes, while a pianist plays
in one corner. The international, nouvelle cuisine menu (on
hand-lettered and handmade paper) is short but nevertheless manages to cover all the basics, from beef and game
(in season) to pasta and seafood. The wine list includes a
number of well-chosen Moravian vintages that will pleasantly surprise oenophiles.
Booking essential.

Ostroff

*Střelecký ostrov 336, Prague 1 (2491 9235). Tram 6,
9, 17, 18, 22.* **Open** *restaurant* noon-2pm, 7pm-
midnight, daily; *bar* 11am-3am daily; *terrace* 11am-
midnight daily. **Average** 1,200 Kč. **Credit** AmEx,
EC, MC, V. **Map 2 F5**

and enjoying the views from the terrace at **Fromin**. *See page 123.*

A perfect idyll, a classy bar perch and a thoroughly decadent splurge, all rolled into one. This marvel, on an island
on the Vltava, sets a new Prague standard with a great terrace on which to enjoy decent salads and desserts, the
longest, best-run water's-edge bar in town and a vaulted cellar restaurant serving a range of delicate Sicilian and
Tuscan delights – as well as the most definitive Italian wine
list in the Republic. Recommended dishes include the guinea
fowl salad, the home-made linguini with scorpion fish sauce,
and, for dessert, the marbled strawberry cheesecake. The
restaurant is just a short walk across Most Legii (Legion-
naire's Bridge) to Střelecký ostrov (Shooter's Island).
Tables outdoors (75, terrace).

Parnas
*Smetanovo nábřeží 2, Prague 1 (2421 1901). Tram 6,
9, 17, 18, 22.* **Meals served** 11.30am-3pm, 6-11pm,
daily. **Average** 1,200 Kč. **Credit** AmEx, EC, MC, V.
Map 3 G5
Now under new ownership, the former shining light of the
Prague dining scene has retained its classic art deco interior and fabled location above the Vltava and **Slavia** (*see
p142*). While certainly no shirk at white linen service, this
Parnas is visibly a step or two less inspired than its previous manifestation, which is now doing business up the
street as **Bellevue** (*see above*). That said, the roast duck,
among other dishes, remains a delicate delight, and the
views will always manage to pull in the punters.
Booking advisable.

La Perle de Prague
*corner of Rašínovo nábřeží & Resslova, Prague 2 (2198
4160). Metro Karlovo náměstí/17 tram.* **Open** noon-4pm,
7pm-midnight, Mon-Sat. **Average** 1,800 Kč. **Credit**
AmEx, DC, EC, MC, V. **Map 5 G8**
This bold stab at king of the hill generally succeeds with
its formula of rotating international chefs flown in for the
month and heavenly haute cuisine at celestial prices. Views,
which should be stunning from this crow's nest locale atop
Frank M Gehry's 'Fred and Ginger' building, are, ironically, the only disappointment – somehow cutting-edge design
called for smallish recessed windows. *See also p40.*
Air-conditioning. Booking essential.Tables outdoors.

U malířů
*(The Painter's) Maltézské náměstí 11, Prague 1 (5732
0317/0601 202 816). Tram 12, 22.* **Dinner served**
7-10pm daily. **Average** 1,500 Kč. **Credit** AmEx, MC, V.
Map 2 E4
Prague's most expensive restaurant by far is located within a quaint sixteenth-century house with original painted
ceilings. Though the authentic French food is good, it's
hard to escape the feeling that people mostly dine here to
impress. The menu changes seasonally: for example, in
summer, snails or pâté served with a glass of Sauternes
lead on to main courses such as sea bass, lobster, lamb and
pigeon. The cheese board is excellent, there are three fixed-
price menus as well as the carte, and the wine list includes
vintages from every wine-growing region of France –

although the price of one of these bottles will double the cost of your already ruinously expensive meal. Service is formal but not oppressive.
Air-conditioning. Booking advisable. No smoking.

Pricey (750-900 Kč)

Barock Bar & Café
Pařížská 24, Prague 1 (232 9221). Metro Staroměstská/ 17, 18 tram. **Open** 8.30am-1am Mon-Wed; 8.30am-2am Thur, Fri; 10am-2am Sat, Sun. **Average** 800 Kč. **Credit** AmEx, EC, MC, V. **Map 3 H2**
Glam dining was never more overt than at this shrine to beautiful people, complete with steel bar, floor-to-ceiling windows and free drinks if you're a model (well, Eva Herzigová at least, so be sure to wear your Wonderbra). For all that, it must be said that Barock serves up one of the finest sushi platters in town, and certainly the most stylish, with impeccable *nigiri*. Everything but prawns, practically impossible to get in this landlocked Republic, comes off expertly. A reasonably priced breakfast menu of croissants, sandwiches and powerhouse latte attracts a quiet morning crowd. *Booking advisable. Tables outdoors (40).*

Le Bistrot de Marlène
Plavecká 4, Prague 2 (tel/fax 291 077). Metro Karlovo náměstí/3, 7, 16, 17 tram. **Open** noon-3pm, 7-11.30pm, daily. **Average** 800 Kč. **Credit** AmEx, EC, MC, V. **Map 5 G10**
The chalkboard menus out front in French and Czech offer the first hint of what's to come: namely, enchanting, market-fresh meals of fine traditional Franche-Comté rural cuisine in a small, wooden-shuttered room with terracotta floor tiles and rustic hues. The seasonal pheasant, venison and boar are the only things not imported and the expertly done mushroom flan in parsley sauce, *filets mignons* and *salades niçoises* are a *cause célèbre* among Prague patrons. Service is attentive and deals courteously with awkward veggie requests. An excellent spot for a quiet business confab, a romantic tête-à-tête, or simply a damn good meal. *Tables outdoors (20, pavement).*

Brasserie Le Molière
Americká 20, Prague 2 (9000 3344). Metro Náměstí Miru/4, 22, 34 tram. **Open** 8am-1pm, 7-11pm, Mon-Fri; 7-11pm Sat. **Average** 800 Kč. **Credit** AmEx, EC, MC, V. **Map 6 M8**
Don't be put off by the ridiculous mannequins in full baroque *commedia dell'arte* costume – the *filets*, sauces and *terrine campagnarde* are fine examples of what the city's new gustatory French Wave can offer. Caution: you need more than mere willpower to resist the *millefeuille de fraises*. *Booking advisable.*

La Brise
Hládkov 6, Prague 6 (2051 6667). Tram 8, 22. **Meals served** noon-3pm, 6-9pm Mon-Sat. **Average** 800 Kč. **Credit** AmEx, EC, MC, V. **Map 1 A3**
Provençal cuisine has made major inroads in the last two years, but nowhere is your soufflé more at home than in the surroundings of this new but cosy neighbourhood bistro. *Booking advisable.*

Casablanca
Na příkopě 10, Prague 1 (2421 0519). Metro Můstek. **Open** 6-9.30pm daily. **Average** 800 Kč. **Credit** AmEx, DC, EC, MC, V. **Map 3 J4**
French-Moroccan tagines, harissa soups and home-made sweetmeats exude sincerity, but this is decidedly a place of high production values. And it's priced like one. For an evening of all-out indulgence amid satin pillows, houkahs and the odd belly dancer, however, it's hard to outdo.

Fakhreldine
Klimentská 48, Prague 1 (232 7970/tel/fax 231 1659). Metro Florenc/5, 14, 26 tram. **Open** noon-midnight daily. **Average** 750 Kč. **Credit** AmEx, DC, EC, MC, V. **Map 4 M2**
An upscale Lebanese restaurant in a hard-to-find street. The elegant, chandeliered dining room is mercifully free of tourist posters and folk crafts. Starters outnumber main courses and the most interesting way to dine here is to assemble your own meze selection, although some of the small dishes are almost as expensive as the mains. Lebanese cream cheese, grilled aubergine and courgette, houmous and *sojok* (spicy Armenian sausages) are served with home-made pitta bread. Char-grilled lamb and other meats form the bulk of the main courses, while a handful of international fish, veal and steak dishes round out the menu. Baklava from the sweet trolley and Lebanese coffee with cardamom is the perfect end to a meal. Attentive service, relaxing atmosphere. At the time of writing, Fakhreldine was planning to move to Štěpáňská 42, Prague 1, so phone before you go. *Air-conditioning.*

Francouská Restaurace
Náměstí Republiky 5, Prague 1 (2200 2777). Metro Náměstí Republiky/5, 14, 26 tram. **Open** noon-3pm, 6-11pm, daily. **Average** 800 Kč. **Credit** AmEx, EC, MC, V. **Map 4 K3**
The aesthetics don't get any better than this – the city's preeminent shrine to art nouveau (and one of its top concert halls) has been painstakingly renovated, with this continental cuisine dining room and the adjoining café cast as jewels in the crown. The potato soup's a treat– and a steal at the price – but otherwise it's an upmarket night out for rabbit and French cheese plate. *Air-conditioning.*

Fromin
Václavské náměsti 21, Prague 1 (2423 5793). Metro Můstek/3, 9, 14, 24 tram. **Open** 9.30am-2am Mon-Wed; 9.30am-4pm Thur, Fri; 11am-4pm Sat; 11am-midnight Sun. **Average** 800 Kč. **Credit** AmEx, EC, MC, V. **Map 4 K5**
If you can get over the terminally blasé attitude of your waiter, who is more concerned with being discovered and made into a star, the steaks and pastas are quite credibly done. On top of that, you get one of the best views over Wenceslas Square, thanks to a steely open-plan renovation that has transformed this formerly cheesy disco into a new lightning rod for the young and beautiful (not to mention rich). *Air-conditioning. Tables outdoors (terrace).*

Kampa Park
Na Kampě 8b, Prague 1 (5731 3493/5731 3494). Metro Malostranská/12, 22 tram. **Open** noon-midnight daily. **Average** 850 Kč. **Credit** AmEx, DC, EC, MC.
Map 2 F4
Kampa Park's location is arguably the finest in Prague – beneath Charles Bridge with a beautiful riverside terrace where the Čertovka, having carved Kampa Island from the Malá Strana mainland, rejoins the Vltava. It has much to offer, namely a slick bar room scene favoured by the business crowd, tasteful indoor dining rooms and a Thursday night Scandinavian buffet. The real joy, however, is an outdoor feast of oysters, swordfish and salad in summer featuring the rich, pungent sauces that are the specialities of owners Tommy Sjoo and Nils Jebens. If artfully presented fresh Bohemian river trout or eel sounds appealing, October is your chance, otherwise you'll have to make do with imports. Service, as at the company's **Barock** (*see above*) and **Segafredo** (*see below*) restaurants, is generally by would-be *Esquire* cover boys and girls for whom your dinner may not be a priority in life. *Tables outdoors (100).*

Prague's best cellar: the romantic **U Maltézských rytířů**.

Praha Tamura/Japanese Bufet Dai

Havelská 6, Prague 1 (2423 2056). Metro Můstek. **Open**
11am-11pm daily. **Average** 800 Kč. **Credit** AmEx, DC,
EC, MC, V. **Map 3 J4**
Arguably Prague's first and top-dog sushi establishment,
Tamura is a full-on formal Japanese experience, while the
recently added buffet (till 7pm daily) is a nod towards backpackers and Czech income levels. Just off the city's oldest
continuous open market, it has tables laden with *maki* and
curries – adding a measurable improvement to the city's
reasonable lunch options.

Rasputin

Kodaňská 47, Prague 10 (733 585). Tram 4, 7, 22, 24.
Open noon-2am daily. **Average** 800 Kč. **Credit** V.
Possibly the finest borscht in town – which is saying a lot
– with a hip demeanour, splotchy sunset-coloured décor
and live combo in the corner. What they do with fresh herbs
is astounding: try the signature Russian dill sauces over fil-
lets of pork and chicken. There's also an impressive Black
Sea fish and shellfish menu.

Sakura

*Štefánikova 7-9, Prague 5 (542 348). Metro Anděl/4, 6,
7, 9, 12, 14, 34 tram.* **Open** noon-3pm, 6-11pm, daily.
Average 800 Kč. **Credit** AmEx, EC, MC, V.
Quite possibly Prague's strangest dining environment – no
small feat in this city's wonderland of Gothic cellars and
fab, state-designed, '70s-era spaces. Sakura achieves it,
though, with late-night sushi bar, strippers, undisclosed
upstairs activities and a regular clientele that really
shouldn't be trifled with. It was once raided spectacularly
by the police, who haven't had the nerve to return since.

U Matouše

*(Matthew) Preslova 17, Prague 5 (546 284). Metro
Anděl/6, 9, 12 tram.* **Open** 11am-11pm daily.
Average 800 Kč.
A local favourite for lovers of traditional Czech food, with
the inevitable tender duck with cabbage and dumplings

and a definitively Old World, wood-heavy atmosphere. If
you're in the mood for game bird, make sure you call a day
in advance to order it.

V Zátiší

*(In Seclusion) Liliová 1, Betlémské náměstí, Prague 1
(2422 8977/2423 1187/267 848). Metro Národní třída/
6, 9, 18, 22 tram.* **Meals served** noon-3pm, 5.30-11pm,
daily. **Average** 750 Kč. **Credit** AmEx, EC, MC, V.
Map 3 G4
Situated on a narrow cobbled lane and owned by the management of **Bellevue** (*see above*) and U **Patrona** (*see
below*), this is one of the city's most elegant and pampered
dining rooms. The menu changes regularly and features
enticements along the lines of home-made pasta, fresh sea
bass, with preparation that somehow transforms relatively ordinary fare into stuffed garlic mushrooms and melon
of the gods. A daily special puts a deluxe spin on traditional
Czech cooking with such daring dishes as 'kid roll'. V Zátiši
also offers Prague's poshest lunch.
Air-conditioning. Booking advisable.

Moderate (450-750 Kč)

Avalon

*Malostranské náměstí 12, Prague 1 (530 263/fax 530
276). Tram 12, 22.* **Open** 11am-1am daily. **Average** 550
Kč. **Credit** AmEx, EC, MC, V. **Map 2 D3**
A restaurant (upstairs from the **Circle Line**; *see above*) in
the style of a California family eatery offering a reasonably
well-prepared range of grills, pastas, ribs, salads, sandwiches, seafood, Tex-Mex items and a couple of vegetarian
choices. The cramped bar mixes an exceptional Martini to
the accompaniment of jazz men playing in chrome cages.
The location, at the quiet, lovely end of Malostranské
náměstí behind the baroque Church of St Nicholas, is a definite plus. Inside, though, it's pretty bland, with humdrum
Americana on the walls. Service is erratic but well meaning.
Tables outdoors (summer only).

Le Café Colonial

Široká 6, Prague 1 (2481 8322). Metro Staroměstská.
Open 7.30am-1am Mon-Sat; 8.30am-5pm (*brunch*
11.30am-3pm) Sun. **Average** 700 Kč. **Credit** AmEx, EC,
MC, V. **Map 3 G3**
The café section of this place is replete with mini-quiches,
duck, salads, big windows and a newspaper rack featuring
Le Monde. More formal dining is on one side. The attached
pâtisserie – Prague's best source of crusty French baguettes
and *confits* – is a perfect complement for the designer veranda furniture in Matisse tones. Gloriously French.
Air-conditioning. Tables outdoors.

Don Giovanni

Karolíny Světlé 34, Prague 1 (tel/fax 265 406).
Metro Staroměstská. **Open** 11am-midnight daily.
Average 700 Kč. **Credit** AmEx, MC, V. **Map 3 G5**
In grand but understated surroundings, not far from the Old
Town end of Charles Bridge, this is the finest Italian dining
you'll find in Prague. Owner Avelino Sorgato is a member
of the Circolo Italiano di Praga, a gastronomic clique who
used to cluster around the Italian embassy and went public
with Don Giovanni in early 1995. And so far so good: the
fettucine is home-made, the Parma ham is the real stuff, the
tiramisu is excellent, and there's a range of more than 30
different grappas. Nevertheless, the menu is unadventurous, the Italian wines overpriced, and the bruschetta a major
disappointment, as are most of the colour-photo-on-a-card
desserts. Dependable but not spectacular.

Estia

*Kubelíkova 9, Prague 3 (273 892). Metro Jiřího z
Poděbrad.* **Open** noon-midnight daily (bar service
only 2.30-6pm). **Average** 500 Kč. **Credit** EC, MC, V.
Map 8 B2
Greek food arrives in the pub mecca of Žižkov, providing
a welcome splash of olive oil, aubergine, lamb with rosemary and retsina. Already on the business community dinner circuit, Estia is elegant without being fawning – a mix
that's still unusual in Prague.
Tables outdoors (80, garden).

Massada

*Michalská 16, Prague 1 (2421 3418). Metro
Staroměstská.* **Open** 11am-11pm Mon-Thur, Sun; by
reservation Fri, Sat. **Average** 700 Kč. **Credit** AmEx, EC,
MC, V. **Map 3 H4**
The city's first serious venture into kosher food since 1939
is an elegant, dark-wood-accented, strictly professional
establishment that's been a hit since it opened in 1997. With
a street-level dairy section and an upstairs meat menu, and
mashgiachs (food inspectors) approved by the Republic's
chief rabbi, Massada dishes up herring, moussaka, veggie
burekas and goulash with equal aplomb.
Booking advisable (essential Fri, Sat).

Reykavík

Karlova 20, Prague 1 (2422 9251). Metro Staroměstská.
Open 11am-midnight daily. **Average** 500 Kč.
Credit AmEx, DC, EC, MC, V. **Map 3 G4**
Smack-bang on the main tourist route to Charles Bridge,
this comfortably elegant restaurant nevertheless boasts
fresh seafood in abundance at extremely reasonable prices.
The Icelandic owners, who fly in the fish and lobster from
their homeland, suck in the crowds – and there are plenty
of those on this street. Soups, starters, burgers and chicken are not as strong as the seafood. The upstairs loft seating offers the quietest repose.
Tables outdoors (60, pavement).

Rybí trh

Týn 5, Prague 1 (2489 5447). Metro Staroměstská.
Open 11am-midnight daily. **Average** 700 Kč.
Credit AmEx, EC, MC, V. **Map 3 J3**

A posh new seafood emporium in a sleek, cavernous space
in the newly opened Ungelt (Týn) square, a block from Old
Town Square, where they'll boil or grill a pike-perch, carp
or eel, then present it with turmeric rice. Avoid the shellfish, as is usually the rule in Prague.
Tables outdoors (80, garden).

Segafredo

Na příkope 10, Prague 1 (2421 0716). Metro Můstek.
Open *restaurant* 11.30am-11pm daily; *café* 8.30am-1am
Mon-Sat; 10am-midnight Sun. **Average** 450 Kč.
Credit AmEx, DC, MC, V. **Map 3 J4**
Given its coffee company franchise and prominent location
on one of the New Town's main tourist drags (the tables
outside are always full of trippers), this Italian place is surprisingly good. While the busy café in the front serves a
variety of coffees, croissants and drinks, dining takes place
in a calm, pastel-shaded back room. There are a few daily
specials as well as a standard small menu of soups, salads,
pasta, steak and fish, though vegetarians will be disappointed with the slim choice of meatless dishes. If you stay
away from the salmon or peppered steak, it's possible to
eat much more cheaply than the average quoted above.
Probably better for lunch than dinner.
Summer garden. Tables outdoors (150, pavement).

U Maltézských rytířů

*(The Knights of Malta) Prokopská 10, Prague 1 (536
357). Tram 12, 18, 22.* **Open** 11am-11pm daily.
Average 450 Kč. **Credit** AmEx, MC. **Map 2 E4**
This candlelit, Gothic cellar restaurant, once an inn for the
marauding Knights of Malta, is a top vote-getter for Czech
game, and justly proud of its venison châteaubriand. Mrs
Černíková, whose husband and two children help run the
place, is guaranteed to appear at least once an evening,
bang a small chime, theatrically narrate the history of the
house and harass you to eat the strudel. The stone-walled
cellar, which is daubed with oil paintings, is also host to an
unmissable Halloween party every year.
Booking essential.

U modré kachničky

*(The Blue Duckling) Nebovidská 6, Prague 1
(5732 0308/0602 353 559). Tram 12, 18, 22.*
Meals served noon-4pm, 6.30-11pm, daily.
Average 600 Kč. **Map 2 E4**
On an obscure side street within strolling distance of
Charles Bridge, this fine establishment is known to parliamentarians and visiting actors for its wonderfully wrought
Czech game dishes. A sublime roast duck competes on the
menu with pheasant, wild boar or roebuck haunch in rosehip wine sauce, of course with dumplings or sauerkraut.
Service is excellent, while the restaurant's three rooms are
charming – hand-painted walls, antique furniture and plenty of wooden duck decoys as decoration. Without a doubt
one of the best restaurants in Prague.

U Patrona

*(The Patron's) Dražického náměstí 4, Prague 1 (531
497). Metro Malostranská.* **Open** 11.30am-2.30pm, 5.30-
11pm, daily. **Average** 600 Kč. **Credit** AmEx, EC, MC, V.
Map 2 E3
Under the same ownership as **Bellevue** and **V Zátiší** (for
both, *see above*), U Patrona has no difficulty meeting their
high standards. Traditional local specialities such as river
trout and game birds are rendered into light, delectable cuisine, tempered with delicious fresh vegetables that are collected each morning from the local market. If you still
suspect a stray tinned mushroom, just direct your attention
to the glass wall in the main dining room: the kitchen staff
work in full view of diners. For those who trust them
already, the tiny balcony (with a cute little table, perfect for
an intimate *à deux*) and street terrace come equipped with
enviable views of Charles Bridge.

Inexpensive (300-450 Kč)

Ambiente
Celetná 11, Prague 1 (2423 0244). Metro Náměstí Republiky. **Open** 11am-11.30pm daily. **Average** 400 Kč. **Map 3 J3**
Certainly the most overrated restaurant in Prague – and with its subtitle 'The Living Restaurant', trying hard to be the most pretentious, too – Ambiente has nevertheless been such a hit that this is the third branch in the city (and there are two more elsewhere in the country). Run by Czechs who've lived in the USA and dined once too often at TGI Friday's, it has yawnworthy Coca-Cola ads on the wall and a wacky American-style menu offering 'ribs' and 'wings', 'sirloin butt-steak' and drinks 'mixed for non-alcoholics'. The baked potatoes are good value, but the pasta is very poor and most of the rest of the stuff is pretty run-of-the-mill. At the Americká branch go for the jambalaya or the gnocchi. Star of the show is the chocolate fondue at 60 Kč, which is served in dark, light and white versions with pineapple or banana pieces to scoop it up.
Booking essential at all branches.
Branches: Americká 18, Prague 2 (691 1882); Mánesova 59, Prague 2 (627 5913).

Barracuda
Krymská 2, Prague 10 (746 881). Metro Náměstí Míru. **Open** noon-5pm Mon-Thur; 5-11.30pm Fri-Sun. **Average** 300 Kč.
Based on the regular rush at the dinner hour, Prague seems to have voted this little cellar in desert hues its best Mexican restaurant. A Californian will notice the lack of complementary tortilla chips (nationwide lack, that is), but the sizzling fajitas, unmatched anywhere else in the Republic, go a long way to compensate, as do the overstuffed tacos.
Booking advisable.

Bazaar Mediterranée
Nerudova 40, Prague 1 (9005 4510). Tram 12, 22. **Open** noon-10pm daily (*jazz brunch* 11am-3pm Sun). **Average** 350 Kč. **Credit** AmEx, EC, MC, V. **Map 2 D3**
The hands-down winner when it comes to the finest terrace views and cuisine combination in the city. Since this labyrinth of wine cellars, patios, garden restaurant and cavernous, candlelit bars opened, it has been buzzing with explorers. You could return for weeks, following the aroma of garlic and rosemary until your map is complete – and annotated with descriptions of complementary warm focaccia baskets, papillotes de saumon, aubergine cannelloni with goat's cheese and tiramisu. Follow the signs to the spiral stairs leading up to the open-air eatery – the reward is a stunning pantiled roof panorama.
Air-conditioning. Terrace seating (100).

Bella Napoli
V Jámě 8, Prague 1 (2422 7315). Metro Můstek or Muzeum. **Open** 11.30am-11.30pm Mon-Sat; 6-11.30pm Sun. **Average** 350 Kč. **Map 5 J6**
An easily overlooked pasta place worth a second glance, this relaxed if commonplace spot can too easily be overshadowed by the adjoining sleaze bar. The 75 Kč antipasti bar is well stocked with garlic spinach, marinated aubergine and peppers. But make sure you save room for the generous pastas: sauces are tasty, if lacking in flair, but the farfalle al salmone is one dish that stands out from the crowd. Hefty salads plus a couple of pastas are all that's on offer for vegetarians, but they might just be tempted by the rich wine sauces in the meat section, anyway. The wines – both Czech and Italian – are mediocre, but as an intimate (and fairly cheap) setting, this place is hard to beat. Try to time your hunger pangs to coincide with the restaurant's 20 per cent discount on meals (from 2.30-5.30pm).

Buffalo Bill's
Vodičkova 9, Prague 1 (2494 8624/fax 9623 8083). Metro Můstek/3, 9, 14, 24 tram. **Meals served** noon-11.30pm daily. **Average** 400 Kč. **Credit** AmEx, MC, V. **Map 5 J6**
Passable Tex-Mex fare and good service, but long since surpassed by **Barracuda** (*see above*). The influence of bad westerns is apparent, with an eager young crew in American jeans and red cowboy kerchiefs slinging tacos beneath the watchful gaze of Duke Wayne. Drinks come in big, Texas-sized glasses instead of the usual juice glasses.

La Cambusa
Klicperova 2, Prague 5 (0602 374 189/541 678). Tram 4, 7, 9, 34. **Open** 7pm-midnight Mon-Sat. **Average** 300 Kč. **Credit** AmEx, EC, MC, V.
From an unlikely side street in the blue-collar Smíchov district, this French-Czech seafood specialist has built a name as a dependable source of the freshest tastes around. Décor is essentially a nautical afterthought, though at least they bothered to install fish tanks.

Cantina
Újezd 38, Prague 1 (5731 7173). Tram 12, 22. **Open** noon-midnight daily. **Average** 300 Kč. **Map 2 E5**
The cactus and unpainted Arizona-style furniture generally outpace the passable Mexican food at Cantina (the straight-from-a-bag nachos are beyond excuse). Nevertheless, it's a reasonably priced and convenient trip out west, close to the Left Bank clubs and cafés. Window seats provide for better-than-average people-watching, but be warned: you might strain your neck trying to read the old *Prague Post* editions that are glued to the ceiling.

Cicala
Žitná 43, Prague 2 (2221 0375). Metro I.P. Pavlova. **Open** 11.30am-10.30pm Mon-Sat. **Average** 400 Kč. **Map 5 J7**
Get the tip on which fresh Italian wonder the proprietor has driven in this week: it might be calamari or it might be figs; either way, it will be proudly presented to you like a work of art. This subterranean two-room eatery on an otherwise unappealing street is well worth seeking out as a bastion of home cooking and a mainstay of Prague's Italian ghetto.

La Colline Oubliée
Elišky Krásnohorské 11, Prague 1 (232 9522). Metro Staroměstská. **Open** noon-midnight Mon-Sat; 6pm-midnight Sun. **Average** 400 Kč. **Credit** V. **Map 3 H1**
Small, colourful, efficient and assured, this North African island of full-flavoured couscous, brik (vegetables and meat wrapped in filo then fried) and mustard vinaigrette salads has all the ingredients to make it a real neighbourhood fave.

Dolly Bell
Neklanova 20, Prague 2 (298 815). Tram 3, 7, 16, 17. **Open** 2-11pm daily. **Average** 300 Kč. **Credit** AmEx, DC, V.
An insider's favourite, with kooky upside-down furnishings, warm service, last year's prices, along with an impressive range of Yugoslavian starters, lamb dishes and wines.

Faros
Šporkova 5, Prague 1 (5731 6945/0603 216 678). Tram 12, 22. **Open** noon-11pm daily. **Average** 300 Kč. **Credit** AmEx, MC, V. **Map 1 C3**
Authentic Greek food in a quiet backstreet near the German embassy, where the bazouki music contrasts oddly with vaulted Central European ceilings. It's a peaceful, reliable place offering well-prepared Greek standards, including spitted and grilled meats, moussaka and a large range of starters that will perk up any vegheads. Service is also pretty good. An excellent spot for lunch while exploring Malá Strana.
Tables outdoors (20, garden).

La Golosina

Na výtoni 12, Prague 2 (292 653). Tram 3, 7, 16, 17.
Open 11am-10pm daily. **Average** 350 Kč.
Credit AmEx, EC, MC, V. **Map 5 G10**
Under the banner of 'South American food', this venture of
the **Palffy Palác** (*see below*) and **Érra** café folks (*see p140*)
is curiously burrito-heavy, but with all the attention to presentation and space creation for which its predecessors are
already known. The steak and generous bowl of spicy
Mexican soup come off particularly well, while the lethal-
ly large dessert burrito is good for dividing between four.

Lotos

*(Lotus) Platnéřská 13, Prague 1 (232 2390). Metro
Staroměstská.* **Open** 11am-10pm daily. **Average** 300 Kč.
Credit EC, MC, V. **Map 3 G3**
Run by a former ministry spokeswoman who dreamed of
a place for colourful, exotic and healthy food in Prague,
Lotos is now the undisputed leader in the city's vegetarian
reformation. Though a few of the tofu-based creations have
met with lukewarm responses, the banana ragout is a consistent winner. Be sure not to miss the grocery out front,
which sells a limited range of organic fare.
No smoking.

Mailsi

Lipanská 1, Prague 3 (0603 466626). Tram 5, 9, 26.
Open noon-3pm, 5-11pm, daily. **Average** 300 Kč.
Map 8 C1
No atmosphere to speak of, just dirt-cheap Pakistani food,
which goes down well in Žižkov, one of Prague's few ethnically mixed districts. Kebabs, murgh, dahl and other traditional dishes are expertly spiced and served up with
friendly gusto. All in about half the time it would take to
get a beer in many neighbouring pubs.

Na rybárně

*Gorazdova 17, Prague 2 (299 795). Metro Karlovo
náměstí.* **Open** noon-midnight Mon-Sat; 5pm-midnight
Sun. **Average** 400 Kč. **Credit** AmEx, DC, EC, MC, V.
Map 5 G8
A carefully kept neighbourhood secret was blown when
Havel became president and let slip which place had been
his favourite nosh joint. Notoriety hasn't set it back at all,
however. It's still a good, unpretentious option for well-
grilled local freshwater fish. Just remember: October is trout
season; eel, carp and pike-perch are the other main options,
but mind the bones.

Palffy Palác

*Valdštejnská 14, Prague 1 (5731 2243/reservations
5732 0570/www.czechreality.cz/palffy). Metro
Malostranská/12, 18, 22 tram.* **Meals served** 10.30am-
10pm Mon-Fri; 10am-10pm Sat, Sun. **Average** 400 Kč.
Credit AmEx, MC, V. **Map 2 E2**
A beautiful interior, fine service, a promising brunch menu
and a fantastic terrace above a garden, but with unpredictable food. The aubergine lasagne is lovely but gone
after a few bites, lemon custard is microwave-defrosted, but
crêpes and salads are generous and delicate affairs. With
these surroundings, it's certainly worth taking a chance,
though, and excellent value for money.
*Booking advisable (one day in advance). Tables outdoors
(terrace).*

La Palma

Na hrázi 32, Prague 8 (683 2764). Metro Palmovka.
Open 11.30am-11.30pm daily. **Average** 350 Kč.
A longstanding pioneer in pasta and sauces, where the
rigatoni with olives and fresh Parmesan is still enough of
an attraction to merit a trip out to the Palmovka district
and brave the generic décor and generally less than remarkable service.
Tables outdoors (20, terrace).

Pizzeria Grosseto

*Francouská 2, Prague 2 (2425 2778). Metro Náměstí
Míru/4, 22, 34 tram.* **Open** 11.30am-11pm daily.
Average 300 Kč. **Map 8 A3**
Having added this downtown location to its booming
Dejvice location, Grosseto does big-volume, quick turnover
business with its flame-cooked pizzas; the four-cheese version is an absolute must – beware imitations elsewhere
using anything called eidam or hermelin (generic Czech
cheeses). Though you could say that shortcuts have been
taken on the minestrone, the carpaccio in tomato sauce is
a winner and the bread basket (which comes complete with
herb butter) is fresh, excellent and, above all, free. If you
fancy a bit of scene-making, with time left over for a movie,
you'd be hard-pressed to do better.
Branch: Jugoslávský partyzánů 8, Prague 6 (312 2694).

La Provence

*Štupartská 9, Prague 1 (232 4801/2481 6695/
reservations 9005 4510). Metro Náměstí Republiky/
5, 14, 26 tram.* **Meals served** noon-midnight daily.
Bar open 11am-1am daily. **Average** 400 Kč.
Credit AmEx, EC, MC, V.
Map 3 J3
Billed as a 'restaurant, bistro and tapas bar' and sharing
its premises with the **Banana Café** (*see p139*), this
establishment suffers from just a wee identity crisis. The
restaurant, with its lantern lighting and wall-to-wall
gingham pillows and rustic farm implements, offers good
service, some fine wines and decent scampi, cassoulet
and coq au vin. However, its upstairs alter ego – the neon
and throbbing-bass Banana Café – tries to cover all the
bases with alternating oldies and transvestite go-go
shows. In order to reach the calmer waters below, you'll
have to elbow your way through a dense beefcake and hair-
product mob.
Air-conditioning. Booking advisable.

Restaurant Delfy

Podolské nábřeží 1, Prague 4 (4446 3772). Tram 3, 17.
Open 11am-midnight daily. **Average** 400 Kč.
Credit EC, V.
The commotion from the packs of cars out front is for a
reason. Inside, someone is whipping up a mean moussaka.
This merits exploration, at least according to half the pop-
ulation of the Braník district, who are fortunate enough to
have this Greek wonder in their backyards.
Tables outdoors (200, terrace).

Restaurant Fondue

Slezská 20, Prague 2 (2425 0459). Tram 11, 16.
Open 11.30pm-1am daily. **Average** 300 Kč.
Credit AmEx, DC, EC, MC, V.
Map 8 C3
An easily overlooked velour bar secretly leads downstairs
to a perfect slice of '70s California culture: hanging weav-
ings, bubbling fondue pots and Sterno-heated rocks for
cooking your own meat and veg at the table. All kitsch, all
fun, all the time.

Il Ritrovo

*Lublaňská 11, Prague 2 (296 529). Metro I.P. Pavlova/6,
11 tram.* **Meals served** noon-3pm, 6-11.30pm, Mon-Sat.
Average 400 Kč. **Map 6 L8**
Over 30 varieties of pasta, four of them home-made, attract
a loyal crowd of Italian speakers, who are no doubt friends
of Florentine owner Antonio Salvatore. Having moved his
family here from Tuscany, he secretly whips up sauces that
are known only by three, offered only when you ask. Following
the menu is by no means limiting, though, not with the gar-
lic-marinated antipasti bar, four-cheese linguine and ravi-
oli in cream, sage and, if you fancy it, brandy. Keep an ear
peeled for Antonio's infamous gramophone collection of
sentimental Italian songs.

Le Saint-Jacques

Jakubská 4, Prague 1 (232 2685). Metro Náměstí Republiky/5, 14, 26 tram. **Meals served** noon-3pm, 6pm-midnight, Mon-Sat. **Average 4 Kč.** **Credit** AmEx, EC, MC, V. **Map 4 K3**

Just around the corner from **La Provence** (*see above*), this excellent restaurant is far too often overshadowed by its pricier, slicker neighbour. But Le Saint-Jacques has nothing to apologise for: the French proprietor personally lays out excellent fresh scallops (*coquilles Saint-Jacques*), beef fondues and a French onion soup to weep over. True, the décor resembles a Holiday Inn lobby, but by the time the tarte tatin arrives, you'll no longer care.

Shalimar

Balbínova 26, Prague 2 (2225 3872/2225 1550). Metro Muzeum/11 tram. **Open** noon-midnight Fri, Sat; 5pm-midnight Sun-Thur. **Average** 300 Kč. **Credit** AmEx, EC, MC, V. **Map 6 M7**

Tandoori delights, marking a significant step forward in the new wave of world-wiser Prague dining. The curries are flawless, as is the utterly unpretentious service. Order 'mild' spice if you eat jalapeños for fun, otherwise 'plain' (there's nothing plain about it). Best all-around value is the chicken kerahi sampler, with dahl, pilau rice and warm chapati. Extra mineral water is essential but not included in the price.

Taj Mahal

Škrétova 10, Prague 2 (2422 5566). Metro Muzeum/11 tram. **Open** noon-3pm, 6-11.30pm, daily. **Average** 300 Kč. **Credit** AmEx, EC, MC, V. **Map 6 L7**

Like any old UK high street Indian: same menu (onion bhaji, chicken tikka masala, vegetable biriani, tarka dahl and

other familiar standards) and pretty much the same prices – which makes it overpriced by Prague standards. **Shalimar** (*see above*) offers far better value and is just blocks away, but if a curry near the State Opera or the Lucerna is what you need, this is a dependable option. *Air-conditioning.*

Thajský Restaurant

V Holešovičkách 22a, Prague 8 (688 8740). Metro Holešovice, then 102, 156, 175 bus. **Open** 11am-3pm, 6-10.30pm Mon-Sat. **Average** 300 Kč.

Another major leap into world cuisine. Somehow the city's first credible Thai effort (with some Burmese and Indian dishes thrown in) was eight years in the making; so awaited was it that people gladly bussed out here – and still do – for the papadums alone. At these prices, and with pad Thai so thoroughly correct and a tom yam soup that is a reasonable approximation, it's clear why. Be sure not to hop on one of the other buses that run this route but pass Thajský by, and get off at the third bus stop, at Nad Rokoskou.

Thanh Long

Ostrovní 23, Prague 1 (2491 2318). Metro Národní třída/6, 9, 18, 22 tram. **Meals served** 11.30am-3pm, 5-11pm, daily. **Average** 300 Kč. **Credit** AmEx, V. **Map 5 H6**

Distinguished only by its central location and the fact that it has those big revolving tables that are so much fun. The service is bumbling and the food so bland that you forget what you've eaten almost as soon as you've swallowed it. The only saving grace (if that is what it is) is a huge moving-light painting in the back that can induce an LSD-type trip without recourse to chemicals. Unless you get off on monosodium glutamate, that is.

If you can't stand the meat...

A master chef's lot is not a happy one in the Czech Republic. Get one talking for five minutes and the war stories inevitably start pouring out. They tell you about how their staff trained at the country's best cooking school, where the difference between rare and well-done was never taught; they complain that local health inspectors haughtily forbid the use of top-grade sauces imported from Western Europe because the ingredients are not listed in Czech; that a chef's best creations are upstaged by inept waiters, then knocked in the local press by critics who don't know a béchamel from a tartar sauce; and that, occasionally, the Ukrainian mob decides to set up shop in the dining room.

'We're where Sweden was ten years ago,' mopes one acclaimed Czech chef. 'Everyone is taught to overcook meat,' he sighs. And as for flavourful spices – well, many newly hired cooks here are simply too embarrassed to ask what they're for. One North African chef, taking the kitchen helm at a world-famous hotel in the city, recalls with a shudder the sight of his cooks chain-smoking over their sauce pans.

And supplies? One impassioned French restaurateur encapsulates it nicely: 'Le poulet! C'est catastrophe!' And then there's the question of fresh seafood, which tends to be problematic in any landlocked country. In Prague, deliveries are limited to just two days a week, with major import companies coming and going like salmon flopping upstream.

While it's true to say that culinary standards in Prague *have* been raised several notches over the last couple of years, veterans of respected kitchens in Paris, Brussels and even Stockholm can still be seen shaking their heads in dismay when they hit town. Why, you have to ask, would any one of their number choose to set up shop here? An uncomfortable silence follows such a question. Could it be that the boiled vegetable mindset is just too formidable to be overcome here? Whatever the case, the true gourmet chef considers this for only the merest moment before lifting his gaze, arising and marching right back to the kitchen. 'I must be insane,' one of them admits. 'But if I can do it here, I can do it anywhere.'

U Cedru

*(The Cedar) Na hutich 13, Prague 6 (312 2974). Metro
Dejvická.* **Open** 11am-11pm daily. **Average** 400 Kč.
Credit AmEx, DC, MC, V.
The best Middle Eastern food in town is to be had at this
small, unprepossessing Lebanese restaurant out at the end
of the green metro line. There's a good choice of familiar
starters including houmous and stuffed vine leaves; dishes
based around every kind of grilled meat; and a small assortment of odd-sounding 'international' dishes such as 'Fish
with Tahina Sauce' and 'Sirloin à la Peking Art'. The mezes
are the best value, offering five, seven or ten different starters
at 315 Kč, 435 Kč and 615 Kč respectively. It also does delivery until 11pm, for a charge, and takeaway till midnight.
Branch: Na Kocince 3, Prague 6 (2431 1682).

U Čížků

*Karlovo náměstí 34, Prague 2 (298 891).
Metro Karlovo náměstí/3, 6, 14, 18, 22, 24 tram.* **Meals
served** noon-3.30pm, 5-10pm, daily. **Average** 400 Kč.
Credit AmEx, EC, MC, V. **Map 5 H8**
Eating is a communal experience in this timbered beer cellar, from the giant ceramic soup pots to the large tables
packed with German tourists. The food is fine traditional
fare – smoked pork, beef in creamy sauces and other hearty
meat dishes served with sauerkraut and dumplings – but
pricey considering that this is the same stuff to be found in
just about any Czech kitchen. Enormous portions, though.

U Kristiána

*Smetanovo nábřeží hollar, Prague 1 (9000 0601/9000
0639). Tram 17, 18.* **Open** 11am-11pm daily.
Average 300 Kč. **Map 3 G4**
Floating dining rooms generally trade dinner quality for
view, but U Kristiána, by remaining firmly docked all night,
strikes a much better compromise. The fare is standard-
issue Czech schnitzels and chicken steaks (though they're
by no means the worst in town) and the outlook on to
Prague Castle and the Vltava river traffic is a genuine pearl.
Tables outdoors.

U pastýřky

*(The Shepherdess) Bělehradská 15, Prague 4 (691
3555/691 3562). Tram 6, 11.* **Open** 6pm-1am daily.
Average 300 Kč. **Credit** AmEx, EC, MC, V. **Map 6 L8**
Highly romanticised Slovak village life, presented as an open
flame grill for any meat you can name, plus a nice, basic beer
garden outside. Traditional, dulcimer-like cimbalom music,
played live every night, completes the folk credentials.
Tables outdoors (100, garden).

U Ševce Matouše

*(Matthew the Cobbler) Loretánské náměstí 4, Prague 1
(2051 4536). Tram 22.* **Meals served** 11am-4pm, 6-11pm,
daily. **Average** 300 Kč. **Credit** EC, MC, V. **Map 1 A3**
Generous helpings of steak (in a dozen or so guises), fish and
chips are served up in what was a cobbler's workshop (until
recently, it was still possible to get your shoes repaired while
eating lunch). Prices are reasonable given the prime location.

U Supa

*(The Vulture) Celetná 22, Prague 1 (2427 2004). Metro
Náměstí Republiky or Staroměstská.* **Meals served**
11.30am-10.30pm daily. **Average** 250 Kč. **Credit** AmEx,
DC, EC, MC. **Map 3 J3**
Pork reaches its apotheosis in this traditional Czech pub-like
interior in the form of a whole roast pig, basted in beer and
lard and carved up at the table for a mere 3,000 Kč (this has
to be ordered a day in advance). 'Lighter' fare along the lines
of duck or beef, served with the ubiquitous dumplings and
cabbage, is also available. Whatever you choose, one thing's
for sure: a meal at the Vulture is not for the faint-hearted.
The location, in the Old Town's main nightlife area, is great.
No smoking. Tables outdoors (30, pavement).

Cheap (under 300 Kč)

Akropolis

*Kubelíkova 27, Prague 3 (272 184). Metro Jiřího z
Poděbrad.* **Open** 4pm-2am Mon-Sat; 4pm-midnight Sun.
Average 170 Kč. **Map 8 B2**
A hangout for a young, hip, hard-rocking, hard-smoking
set. A bar and restaurant plus adjoining basement pubs
and concert hall, with décor that looks like de Chirico gone
Tahitian – check out the coconut light fixtures, soft carved-
wood shapes and aquariums full of mechanical still lifes.
Alas, the Czech food, typically fried cheese or roast chick-
en and rice, can no longer be washed down with the city's
best draught Velkopovické Kozel: a marketing blitz has
landed Akropolis with Lobkowicz ashtrays, bar towels and,
sadly, its vastly inferior beer. *See also p198 & p204.*

Bar Bar

*(Barbarian) Všehrdova 17, Prague 1 (532 941). Tram
12, 22.* **Meals served** 11am-11pm Mon-Fri; noon-11pm
Sat, Sun. **Average** 180 Kč. **Credit** EC, MC, V. **Map 1 E5**
A pleasant, unpretentious but crowded local fave bar
and restaurant in a picturesque Malá Strana backstreet.
Though it also serves open sandwiches, salads and grill
dishes, the selection of savoury crêpes (from 39-139 Kč) is
the real highlight here. You can also get an English-style
dessert pancake with lemon and sugar for 25 Kč. Staff are
cool and the kitchen is reasonably flexible if you don't spot
quite the crêpe you want on the menu.

Černý pivovar

*(The Black Brewery) Karlovo náměstí 15, Prague 2
(244 451). Metro Karlovo náměstí/3, 6, 14, 18, 22, 24
tram.* **Meals served** 11am-10.30pm daily. **Average** 150
Kč. **Map 5 H8**
Come here for a taste of the good old, bad old days. The
giant floor-to-ceiling white glass mosaic depicting socialist
realist stereotypes of heroic workers and small farmers is
wonderful. The service does not seem to have improved one
iota since the days when such murals were *de rigueur*, while
the standard Czech food is, well, standard Czech food.
Air-conditioning.

Čínské Zátiší

*(Chinese Seclusion) Batelovská 120, Prague 4 (6121
8088). Metro Budějovická.* **Open** 11.30am-10.30pm
daily. **Average** 160 Kč.
Improbably lodged on the ground floor of a communist-era
block of flats, this is one of the few good Chinese restaurants in Prague, a fact attested to by the difficulty in getting a table. Here the chef is not afraid of heat. The hot and
sour soup is enough to make your eyes water, and the pork
balls are seriously spicy. Sadly, the quality is relative: this
place would be just one among thousands anywhere else.
Still, be grateful. At least it's not a front for an illegal immigration ring or money-laundering operation (well, not that
we know of, anyway).

FX Café/Radost

*Bělehradská 120, Prague 2 (2425 4776). Metro I.P.
Pavlova/4, 6, 16, 22, 34 tram.* **Open** 11.30am-4am daily.
Average 250 Kč. **Map 6 L8**
Vegetarian food is served both in the slightly sterile café
at the front of the Radost complex, and in the cosier bar section next to the gallery at the back. Although it's a relief for
the herbivore to find such a large selection of meatless fare
on offer – pasta, salads, falafel, spinach burgers, burritos,
sandwiches – and the place is open admirably late, the food
does tend to lack that extra something special. Still, it's
healthy and – for Prague – exotic eating. Sunday brunch
(which is served until 3pm) is popular with the English-
speaking crowd, but expect to wait 45 minutes for your
scrambled eggs or French toast. *See also p152, p203 & p206.*
No smoking area.

Hogo Fogo

Salvátorská 4, Prague 1 (231 7023). Metro
Staroměstská. **Open** noon-midnight Mon-Thur, Sun;
noon-2am Fri, Sat. **Average** 120 Kč. **Credit** AmEx, EC,
MC, V. **Map 3 H3**
Changing art exhibitions, a small women's clothes shop out
the back, a tiny bar at the front, odd lighting and booming
acoustics. As for the food, it's indifferent Czech-Italian fare
that includes a good few vegetarian options, and there's
Gambrinus on tap at 18 Kč. Despite its extremely handy
location, just near Old Town Square, Hogo Fogo remains
largely undiscovered by tourists.

Indická restaurace

(Indian) Štěpánská 61, Prague 1 (9623 6051).
Metro Muzeum or Můstek. **Meals served** noon-
10.30pm daily. **Average** 170 Kč. **Credit** AmEx, EC,
MC, V. **Map 6 K6**
For many years this was the only place in the entire country where you could get tandoori chicken. Things have
changed, but this shabby though centrally located excuse
for an Indian restaurant has yet to realise the fact. Your
average UK street-corner takeaway is better than this
(but, then again, this is Prague, not the UK). The adjoining
snack bar has a smaller, cheaper menu, however, and you
could do worse than grab some chicken and a couple of
naans for lunch.
Air-conditioning.

Klub Architektů

Betlémské náměstí 169, Prague 1 (2440 1214 ext 214).
Metro Národní třída/6, 9, 17, 18, 22 tram.
Meals served 11.30am-11pm daily. **Average** 150 Kč.
Credit AmEx, DC, EC, MC, V. **Map 3 G5**
This restaurant is located in the dim cellar of the Josef
Frágner Gallery, which specialises in architectural exhibits
(and, despite the name of the restaurant, you won't find too
many architects in here), with summer tables outside in the
courtyard of Bethlehem Chapel. Low prices, an excellent location and a selection of decent vegetarian dishes keep this
place packed to the gills. Meat dishes are hearty and typical,
though lighter than is usual for Prague. Outside, there's a
more limited menu, including a commendable pasta salad.
Pilsner Urquell is available at 20 Kč.
Air-conditioning. Tables outdoors.

Kmotra Pizzeria

(The Godmother) V jirchářích 12, Prague 1 (2491 5809).
Metro Národní třída/6, 9, 17, 18, 22 tram. **Meals served**
11am-12.15am daily. **Average** 120 Kč. **Map 5 H6**
Inexplicably one of Prague's favourite pizza joints.
Customers queue down the stairwell to get one of the cov-
eted bench seats in the cellar near the open, wood-burning
pizza oven. If you can't face the wait, it's possible to order
downstairs and then eat at one of the tables in the street-
level bar area. The pizzas are tasty enough, with fresh
ingredients but soggy centres. Still, odd-sounding combinations featuring cucumber, leeks or mayonnaise work,
more or less.
Booking advisable (two days in advance, max 6 people).

Kogo Pizzeria & Caffeteria

Havelská 27, Prague 1 (2421 4543). Metro Můstek.
Open *restaurant* 11am-11pm daily; *café* 8am-11pm daily.
Average 120 Kč. **Map 3 J4**
For such an overt hangout for the slick, this Old Town café
and adjoining restaurant offer remarkably low prices on
passable salads, pastas, pizzas plus a few exceptional desserts such as chocolate mousse. The café, with its designer wicker chairs and Kandinsky exhibition posters, is just
the right spot for a quick cappuccino and a bite of baklava, especially if you're dressed to kill. The restaurant is a
more formal, slower-paced fantasy of ochre-stained walls,
with an above-average wine list.

Modrá Zahrada

(The Blue Garden) Pařížská 14, Prague 1 (232 7171).
Metro Staroměstská. **Open** 11am-midnight daily.
Average 120 Kč. **Map 3 H2**
Upstairs, a picture-window bar redolent of Howard Hawks;
down below, a generous cellar with big wooden tables. Go
for the big, acceptable pizzas rather than the fairly dodgy
salads, all of which contain some kind of meat. It's a relaxing place, and cheap given the location. Service can be
somewhat dizzy, though.
Air-conditioning. Tables outdoors (16).

Pizza Coloseum

Vodičkova 32, Prague 1 (tel/fax 2421 4914). Metro
Můstek/3, 9, 14, 24 tram. **Open** noon-11.30pm daily.
Average 250 Kč. **Credit** AmEx, MC, V. **Map 5 J6**
A popular cellar joint just off Wenceslas Square that's a cut
above the usual Prague pizzeria. Excellent bruschetta, better-than-average flame-baked pizza, flavourful pastas
served in unfeasibly large portions, an oil-heavy antipasti
bar and a familiar range of dependable steak and fish dishes. On the down side, the Moravian house wine is poor, but
at least it's cheap; Italian vintages come at around ten times
the price. Like every other pizzeria in town, the tables groan
under an inexplicable range of ketchups.
Booking advisable.

Pizzeria Roma Due

Liliová 18, Prague 1 (270 624). Metro Staroměstská/17,
18 tram. **Open** 24 hours daily. **Average** 200 Kč.
Map 3 G4
Pizza that merits mention only because it's cheap, warm
and available around the clock. It's also within stumbling
distance of the **Roxy** (*see p204*) and **Chapeau Rouge** (*see*
p205) clubs, from which you'll be booted out well before
the first morning tram home.
Branch: Jagellonská 19, Prague 3 (0602 304 467).

Pizzeria Rugantino

Dušní 4, Prague 1 (231 8172). Metro Staroměstská/
17 tram. **Open** 11am-11pm Mon-Sat; 6-11pm Sun.
Average 100 Kč. **Map 3 H2**
Reasonably priced pizzas of above-average character are
served in this pleasant-enough white-walled dining room
just around the block from the northern edge of Old Town
Square. Spacious and good for large groups, but be warned:
if the pizza isn't listed on the menu as having cheese, then,
sure enough, it won't have cheese.
Booking advisable. No smoking area.

Pravěk

(Primeval Age) Budečská 6, Prague 2 (2425 2287).
Tram 4, 22. **Meals served** 11am-10.30pm daily.
Average 250 Kč. **Credit** AmEx, EC, MC, V. **Map 8 B3**
Leave your arteries at the door: you've just entered grilled
meat central. The pterodactyl motif and scarab fossils on
the walls are no joke: Pravěk will spit-roast anything that
moves, be it rabbit, duck, turkey, chicken, pork or beef, and
then serve it up with your choice of six sauces. Primitive,
but definitely unique.
Air-conditioning. Tables outdoors (12).

Restaurace Jáma

(The Hollow) V jámě 7, Prague 1 (2422 1783/2422
2383). Metro Národní třída or Můstek/3, 9, 14, 24 tram.
Open 11am-1am daily. **Average** 150 Kč. **Credit** AmEx,
EC, MC, V. **Map 6 K6**
American-owned Jáma has a loud, college vibe, is packed
with Czech scenesters by day and young business types by
night. The former come for reduced-price lunches under
Rolling Stones posters, the latter for drink specials (still a
rarity in Prague). With an odd hybrid menu of California-
style avocado and tuna, potato skins, Mexican food and
lasagne, the tastes vary as much as the clientele.

*Drinkers deep in discussion at **Kampa Park**, overlooking the Vltava. See page 123.*

Taverna

Revoluční 16, Prague 1 (231 7762). Metro Náměstí Republiky/5, 14, 26 tram. **Open** *10am-midnight daily.* **Average** 250 Kč. **Map 4 K2**

Affordable, authentic Greek delights in a cheery, Mediterranean tavern that somehow drifted far off course to Prague's Old Town and landed a block from the Roxy club at the former site of a horrendous pizza joint. Stuffed vine leaves in tzatziki, spinach pie and fried kaseri cheese make zesty, light intros to souvlaki, kebabs and pittas. Naturally, ouzo, retsina and cold frappé coffee are on hand to wash it down.

U Govindy Vegetarian Club

Soukenicka 27, Prague 1 (2481 6016). Metro Náměstí Republiky/5, 14, 26 tram. **Open** *11am-5pm Mon-Sat.* **Average** 50 Kč. **Map 4 L2**

Cheap although not so cheerful, Govinda offers a basic self-service vegetarian Indian meal – rice, lentils, vegetable curry, bread – for a mere 50 Kč, embellished with extras, such as pakora vegetables on a skewer, for another 25 Kč or so. Most of the ingredients are grown on the Krishnas' organic farm outside Prague. The atmosphere is a little lacking and the food fairly basic, but at these prices, who's complaining? The *cukrárna* downstairs serves teas and Indian sweets for around 10-12 Kč.

U Radnice

(The Town Hall) U radnice 2, Prague 1 (2422 8136). Metro Staroměstská. **Meals served** *11am-10.30pm daily.* **Average** 125 Kč. **Credit** AmEx, DC, EC, MC, V. **Map 3 H3**

U Radnice is one of the last places in the Old Town Square where traditional food is served at prices meant for the locals. For lunch, tasty Czech specialities including goulash and beef in a cream sauce are available for under 50 Kč. In the evening, dishes such as steak covered with cheese and topped with an egg are to the fore – vegetarians are probably better off avoiding this place altogether. Dark wood panelling and large tables (which are meant to be shared) create a comfortable pub atmosphere.

Zlatá ulička

(Golden Lane) Masná 9, Prague 1 (232 0884). Metro Staroměstská or Náměstí Republiky/5, 14, 26 tram. **Open** *10am-midnight daily.* **Average** 150 Kč. **Map 3 J2**

A tiny restaurant run by one of Prague's many Yugo-slavian entrepreneurs. The menu is made up of excellent beef and veal-based dishes that defy the usual Czech bland-is-better attitude. The veal stew with mashed potatoes is a knockout, as is the *palačinka* (sweet pancake), a sinful affair big enough for two. There are upbeat comments from former diners on the wall, mournful Yugoslavian poetry on the floor, and a kitsch decoration scheme based on the Golden Lane at Prague Castle. Ask for the pie of the day, which won't be on the menu.

Air-conditioning. Tables outdoors (20).

Branch: Pizzeria Zlatá uliăka, Petrská 21, Prague 1 (231 7015).

Pub dining

It's probably inevitable that you'll taste some standard local cooking while downing a beer – most Prague pubs offer at least a limited menu of traditional Czech food. Some are better than others, though: the following is a selection of *hospodas* where the food is as cheap and as good as the beer.

Our maître d'hotel, Mr. Miroslav Hudek, looks forward to welcoming you personally when you join us for dinner at our authentic English style "Club Restaurant". Devoted to mastering that elusive combination of first-class service and gourmet dining, our "Club Restaurant" has long been regarded as one of Prague's leading restaurants.

THE GOURMET CLUB RESTAURANT
HOTEL PALACE PRAHA
Panská 12, CZ - 111 21 Prague 1, tel.: +420/2/2409 3111, fax: +420/2/2422 1240
email: palhoprg@mbox.vol.cz
Open daily 18.00 - 24.00

RESTAURANT HRADČANY

First-class pampering in a unique atmosphere

The "Restaurant Hradčany" at the Hotel Savoy has distinguished itself among Prague's gourmets as a leader in innovative and exciting cuisine. Only the freshest ingredients, often imported from around the world, are used in creating both international dishes and hearty, traditional Czech meals. The ambience of the Restaurant Hradčany is grand and imperial. The service is friendly, attentive and personal.

RESTAURANT HRADČANY
HOTEL SAVOY
Keplerova 6, CZ - 118 00 Prague 1, tel.: +420/2/24 30 24 30, fax: +420/2/24 30 21 28
email: savhoprg@mbox.vol.cz
Open daily 15.00 - 23.00

managed by
VIENNA INTERNATIONAL
Hotels & Resorts

Eating out

Meals (jídla)

snídaně breakfast; **oběd** lunch; **večeře** dinner.

Basics (základní)

chléb brown bread; **cukr** sugar; **drůbež** poultry; **karbanátek** patty of unspecified content; **máslo** butter; **maso** meat; **ocet** vinegar; **olej** oil; **omáčka** sauce; **ovoce** fruit; **pepř** pepper; **rohlík** roll; **ryby** fish; **smetana** cream; **sůl** salt; **sýr** cheese; **vejce** eggs; **zelenina** vegetables.

Appetisers (předkrmy)

boršč Russian beetroot soup (borscht); **chlebíček** open sandwich; **hovězí vývar** beef broth; **jazyk** tongue; **kaviár** caviar; **paštika** pâté; **polévka** soup; **uzený losos** smoked salmon.

Meat (maso)

biftek beefsteak; **hovězí** beef; **játra** liver; **jehně** lamb; **jelení** venison; **kanec** boar; **klobása** sausage; **králík** rabbit; **ledvinky** kidneys; **párek** sausage/ frankfurter; **slanina** bacon; **srnčí** roebuck; **šunka** ham; **telecí** veal; **vepřové** pork; **zvěřina** game.

Poultry & fish (drůbež a ryby)

bažant pheasant; **husa** goose; **kachna** duck; **kapr** carp; **křepelka** quail; **krocan** turkey; **kuře** chicken; **losos** salmon; **pstruh** trout; **úhoř** eel.

Main meals (hlavní jídla)

guláš goulash; **sekaná** meat loaf; **šízek** schnitzel; **smažený sýr** fried cheese; **svíčková** beef in cream sauce; **vepřová játra na cibulce** pig's liver stewed with onion; **vepřový řízek** fried breaded pork.

Side dishes (přílohy)

brambor potato; **bramborák** potato pancake; **bramborová kaše** mashed potatoes; **hranolky** chips; **kaše** mashed potatoes; **knedlíky** dumplings; **krokety** potato or béchamel dough croquettes; **obloha** small lettuce and tomato salad; **rýže** rice; **salát** salad; **šopský salát** cucumber, tomato and curd salad; **tatarská omáčka** tartar sauce; **zelí** cabbage or sauerkraut.

Cheese (sýr)

balkán a saltier feta; **eidam** hard white cheese; **hermelín** soft, similar to bland brie; **madeland** Swiss cheese; **niva** blue cheese; **pivný sýr** beer-flavoured semi-soft cheese; **primátor** Swiss cheese; **tavený sýr** packaged cheese spread; **tvaroh** soft curd cheese.

Vegetables (zelenina)

česnek garlic; **chřest** asparagus; **cibule** onion(s); **čočka** lentils; **fazole** beans; **feferonky** chilli peppers; **hrášek** peas; **kukuřice** corn; **květák** cauliflower; **mrkve** carrots; **okurka** cucumber; **petržel** parsley; **rajčata** tomatoes; **salát** lettuce; **špenát** spinach; **žampiony** mushrooms; **zelí** cabbage.

Fruit (ovoce)

ananas pineapple; **banány** banana; **borůvky** blueberries; **broskev** peach; **hrozny** grapes; **hruška** pear; **jablko** apple; **jahody** strawberries; **jeřabina** rowanberries; **mandle** almonds; **meruňka** apricot; **ořechy** nuts; **pomeranč** orange; **rozinky** raisins; **švestky** plums; **třešně** cherries.

Desserts (moučník)

buchty traditional curd-filled cakes; **čokoláda** chocolate; **dort** layered cake; **koláč** cake with various fillings; **ovocné knedlíky** fruit dumplings; **palačinka/palačinky** crêpe/crêpes; **pohár** ice-cream sundae; **šlehačka** whipped cream; **zákusek** cake; **závin** strudel; **žemlovka** bread pudding with apples and cinnamon; **zmrzlina** ice-cream.

Terms & expressions

bez masá or **bez masá jídla** without meat; **čerstvé** fresh; **domácí** home-made; **grilované** grilled; **míchaný** mixed; **na roštu** roasted; **pečené** baked; **plněné** stuffed; **smažené** fried; **špíz** grilled on a skewer; **vařené** boiled.

Do you have...? *Máte...?*
I am a vegetarian *Jsem vegetarián/vegetariánka (m/f)*
Can I have it without...? *Mohu mít bez...?*
The bill, please *Účet, prosím*
May I see the menu? *Mohu vidět jídelní lístek?*
I can't eat this and I won't pay for it (use with extreme caution) *Nedá se to jíst. Nezaplatím to*

Drinking

Drinks (nápoje)

čaj tea; **káva** coffee; **mléko** milk; **pivo** beer; **pomerančový džus** orange juice; **sodovka** soda; **víno** wine; **voda** water.

Terms & expressions

čistý straight; **denní bar** bar open during the daytime; **hospoda** pub; **led** ice; **pivnice** beer hall; **sladký** sweet; **suché** or **sekt** dry; **sušený** barrelled; **vinárna** wine bar.

A beer, please *Pivo, prosím*
Two beers, please *Dvě piva, prosím*
Same again, please *Ještě jednou to samé, prosím*
What'll you have? *Co si dáte?*
Not for me, thanks *Pro mě ne, děkuji*
No ice, thanks *Bez ledu, děkuji*
He's absolutely smashed *Je totálně namazaný*

Hospodka U Kašpárka

Dubečská 4, Prague 10 (628 0647). Metro Strašnická/ 22, 24, 26 tram. **Meals served** noon-11pm Mon-Fri; 1-11pm Sat, Sun.

This place does possibly the best fried cheese and potato pancakes in Prague, not to mention good fish and beef stir-fry dishes. The staff are hip and friendly, the patio is an oasis, especially in summer, and prices are remarkably low. All this, plus you can get Guinness on tap at 40 Kč. It's almost worth a special trip out this way (it's the penultimate stop on the green metro line).
Tables outdoors (50, garden).

Keltská Retaurace

Srbínská 4, Prague 10 (782 1295). Metro Strašnická/ 22, 24, 26 tram. **Meals served** 11am-midnight daily.

Just look for the big sign that says Biker Bar 666 to find this pub with Tahitian-style thatch hut tables, Elvis playing on the stereo and such enticing-sounding delights as 'Lobster meat in potatoe doughes' on the menu for around 45 Kč. Radegast on tap costs just 10 Kč, so it's easy to see where the appeal of the place lies. The biker bar, if you're that interested, is downstairs.
Tables outdoors (100).

Fair game

One menu that has remained above reproach in the Czech lands, even during the dark days of state-controlled recipes, is that of the hunt lodge. Rabbit with bacon dumplings, crisply browned duck in red and white cabbage, and boar in wine sauce all constitute something of a sacred cow in these parts, dating back to the royal blood sport established here a full millennium ago.

Head-to-toe green woollen hunting suits, ancestors' rifles with hand-engraved filigree by Czech craftsmen such as Jan Becher, and arcane codes of etiquette all must take their turn even today before your waiter can bring you a game platter. (For those who would mock the full huntsman kit, be advised that the traditional penalty for touching the little brush in someone's forester cap band is a sharp flick on the nose.)

Despite some wildly excessive hunting by overfed monarchs like the Archduke Ferdinand, this brazenly bourgeois tradition was secretly admired and adopted even by the Poliburo's highest mugwumps, who carried on shooting parties through the 41-year communist regime. The proletariat's most-honoured bureaucrats donned full greens just as their gentrified predecessors did, and motored out to game preserves established by royal Hapsburg families. There they'd load up and open fire, sometimes with the help of more experienced huntsmen, whose job it was to secretly lure a buck out of hiding with a pile of corn cobs, or even down the poor beast while insisting it was the Comrade Minister's shot that did it.

Officially, of course, game hunting could be seen as counter-revolutionary when the party deemed it useful. Thus Alexander Dubček, the Czechoslovak President whose liberal reforms prompted the Warsaw Pact invasion of 1968, was the only person ever to be formally investigated at the highest party level for shooting a bear. As it happened, the Slovak-born Dubček was a crack marksman and had ambushed a critter that was terrorising villagers in the Tatra mountains.

It's not so surprising that a tradition as deeply ingrained as game hunting could survive polar political wind shifts; even the doddering Archduke, who recorded 300,000 kills at his castle in Konopiště (before finally catching a fatal dose of black powder himself in Sarajevo at the onset of World War I), couldn't give it too bad a name. Just catch a whiff of the game at one of the city's best providers (among them **Opera Grill**, **U Matouše**, **U Maltézských rytířů**, **U modré kachničky** and **U Patrona**), and you'll begin to understand why.

Na Kampě 15

Na Kampě 15, Prague 1 (539 710). Metro Malostranská/ 12, 22 tram. **Open** noon-midnight daily. **Credit** AmEx, DC, EC, MC, V. **Map 2 F4**
If you can't afford the pricey restaurant, just swing around the corner to the pub of the same name. It features goulash and dumplings for 90 Kč, fried mushrooms for 55 Kč and Purkmistr on tap for 25 Kč. Outdoor tables on the edge of Kampa Park are among the perks, and waiters don't mind if you roam with drinks down to the bank of the Vltava a few metres away.

Novoměstský Pivovar

Vodičkova 20, Prague 1 (2423 3533/2423 7552). Metro Můstek/3, 9, 14, 26 tram. **Open** 11.30am-11.30pm Mon-Sat; noon-10pm Sun. **Credit** AmEx, EC, MC, V. **Map 5 J6**
One of the few brew pubs in Prague (nearly all buy in from local breweries), this once-charming spot has fallen a few notches recently. With a vast underground labyrinth of rooms, it's still a fascinating experience and you'll still get a fine glass of suds, but the waiter's addition skills will prove ever more remarkable – your schnitzel may well cost you twice what it says on the menu, so check your bill. *Booking advisable.*

Pivnice U Pivrnice

Maiselova 3, Prague 1 (232 9404). Metro Náměstí Republiky/5, 14, 26 tram. **Open** 11am-11.30pm daily. **Map 3 H3**
Traditional Czech cooking done with above-average presentation right in the heart of the Jewish Quarter. Lots of pork and tasteless cartoons on the wall from some of the country's best lampoonists. Try the Bohemian skewer with a well-tapped cheap Radegast.

Restaurace Pivovarský dům

corner of Lipová & Ječná, Prague 2 (9621 6666). Tram 4, 16, 22, 34. **Open** 11am-11.30pm daily. **Credit** EC, MC, V. **Map 5 J8**
A brewer and chemist have joined forces to launch the city's newest and most fashionable brew pub, which offers a distinctive Pilsner of its own creation, in addition to such imaginative varieties as coffee beer and champagne beer. The wheat beer, generally a 'safer' bet, is a true rarity in Prague, as is the surprisingly edible pub grub of *utopenci* (literally, 'drowned man' – sausages immersed in vinegar) and pork with dumplings. *Air-conditioning.*

Fast food

Fast food the world over has lost its original meaning. Drive-thrus serve everything from baked potatoes to sushi, while some upmarket restaurants, often part of a chain, bring your your bill before you've even sat down. Not so Prague. If a movie or a concert is on the agenda tonight, you'd better scrap plans to go to a restaurant first. The best of them will keep you for at least two hours; even

some cafés, serving lighter fare, can take almost as long. Thus are Prague's corner falafel stands and salad bars oases of quick service – and hours no restaurant can match.

Adonis

Jungmannova 21, Prague 1 (268 908). Metro Národní třída/6, 9, 18, 22 tram. **Open** 11am-7pm daily. **Map 5 J6**
The most pleasant option when it comes to cheap falafel or tzatziki. Booth seating and cheerful service elevate this Middle Eastern cafeteria to the top of its genre. Though it closes early, it's handy if you fancy a quick bite before getting fleeced at one of the nearby theatres on Národní třída, and offers better side salads and veggies than its nearest competition, **Safir Grill** (*see below*).

Country Life

Melantrichova 15, Prague 1 (2421 3366). Metro Můstek. **Open** 9am-3pm, 6-9.30pm, Mon-Thur; 9am-7pm Fri; 11am-6pm Sun. **Map 3 H4**
Though it has expanded from a shop with salad bar into a full-blown cafeteria with seating and lovely Old Town street views, Country Life has managed to remain a low-key, dirt-cheap source of organically grown vegetarian fare. Massive DIY salads, fresh carrot juice, delectable lentil soups, wholegrain breads, along with slightly disquieting mashed potato casseroles. Note that it's salads and sandwiches only until 11am Monday-Friday and during the staff's midday break. *No smoking.*
Branch: Jungmannova 1, Prague 1 (2454 4419).

Le Gourmand

Vaclávské náměstí 18, Prague 1 (0602 242 227). Metro Můstek/3, 9, 14 tram. **Open** 8am-2am daily. **Map 4 K5**
Unbeatable hours have given rise to something long believed impossible in this city: a fast, credible, any-time salad on Wenceslas Square, and all this for mere pocket change. The name, by the way, is hopelessly exaggerated.

Grill Bono/Občerstvení

Spálená 43, Prague 1 (290 232). Metro Národní třída. **Open** 8.30am-1am daily. **Map 5 H6**
Actually two places, side by side, separated by a building entryway. Grill Bono only offers roast chicken and doesn't stay open late, while Občerstvení serves up falafel, kebabs and mini-pizzas (and stays open till the kebabs run out). Not much more than a hole in the wall for fast, cheap falafel and pizza, but its late hours make it a club habitué's lifeline on many a winter night.

Gyros Falafel Arik

Vodičkova 15, Prague 1 (0603 201 231). Metro Můstek/3, 9, 14, 24 tram. **Open** 10am-2am daily. **Map 5 J6**
The best falafel around, spiced with seasoned carrot and more dependably available than at any other such stand, plus basic salad greens and saffron veggies.

Safir Grill

Havelská 12, Prague 1 (260 095). Metro Můstek. **Open** 10am-8pm Mon-Sat. **Map 3 J4**
Formerly Queenz Grill, this handy falafel, houmous and tahini counter has been opened out into a pleasant, blond-wood sitting space for a quick bite. Perfect for refuelling after perusing the market stalls out front or a nibble on the run when heading for a Wenceslas Square movie or concert. *No smoking.* Tables outdoors.

Sports Café Cornucopia

Jungmannova 10, Prague 1 (2422 0950). Metro Můstek/3, 6, 9, 14, 22, 24 tram. **Open** 8am-10pm Mon-Fri; 10am-8pm Sat, Sun. **Map 5 J6**
Satellite coverage of all the best matches is half the appeal of this unpretentious and convenient little hole in the wall.

DIY picnics

A classic taunt of one Prague expat to another has always been, 'Say, wouldn't you like to know where I got these lovely fresh chickpeas? You can't imagine the houmous I can make with these!' After which the subject is normally changed to the unusually mild spring weather this year, perfect for picnics, and the answer is somehow never given.

Food emporia with international scope, Lebanese grocers, flower shops with live rosemary plants (such as the one in the Muzeum metro passage), extended hours at Country Life (home of the first takeaway salads and veggie burgers in the Republic) and even a dependable seven-days-a-week supply of tofu, frozen oysters and tortilla chips at Tesco have killed the evil joy of this game somewhat in the last year or two. There are other consolations, however, in cruising the fresh parsley and radish piles of the odd open market – for the money you'll spend, you can very likely assemble the best-tasting and healthiest repast you'll have in this city. Once properly outfitted, grab some friends and trot your bounty over to Střeleký Island, Kampa Park or Malá Strana's immaculately manicured Valdštejnská zahrada for a sublime brunch under the trees.

Essential sources for the DIY al fresco repast include **Havelská Market** (*see page 155*), **Dům lahůdek u Rotta**, **Fruits de France** (*for both, see page 165*) and **Potraviny U Cedru** (*see page 166*). For other specialist food shops, *see page 165*. For takeaway and delivery options, *see page 166*.

The other half is in the fast, custom-built submarine sandwiches, Mexican food menu, home-baked brownies, and decent fry for Sunday brunch.

U Bakaláře

Celetná 13, Prague 1 (2481 1870). Metro Náměstí Republiky/5, 14, 26 tram. **Open** *summer* 9am-9pm Mon-Fri; 10am-9pm Sat, Sun. **Map 3 J3**
This convenient Old Town lunch buffet is a good standby for toasted sandwiches, pancakes and soup. Communal seating, friendly-ish service and, of course, way too much salt.

U Rozvařilů

Na Poříčí 26, Prague 1 (2481 1736). Metro Náměstí Republiky/5, 14, 26 tram. **Open** 7.30am-7.30pm Mon-Fri; 7.30am-7pm Sat; 10am-5pm Sun. **Map 4 L3**
A chrome-covered, mirrored remake of that pre-revolutionary classic, the worker cafeteria. The cast of characters, from servers in dirty white aprons to harassed-looking customers in white socks and sandals, all remain, thankfully, as do the incredibly cheap soups, *guláš*, dumplings and *chlebíčky* (open-faced mayonnaise and meat sandwiches).

Cafés, Pubs & Bars

The trad Czech boozer is legendary, but don't miss out on a reviving café culture and the inexorable rise of the teahouse.

Wise Czech forefathers pass on to their children one guiding principle for living in this society: 'Don't spit under the table; your friends could be down there.'

That pubs in Prague are not easy to walk out of is evident to anyone who has ever tasted the undisputed finest beer in the world – and paid about the price of breath mints for the privilege. But there is also a culture that surrounds the night-long build-up of a good, sloppy beer drunkard that has remained essentially unaltered for the last half a millennium. And a better way to cut to the heart of the Bohemian spirit is scarcely imaginable. The ritual of the automatic refill; the long, communal benches and heavy, stained tables; the air choked with smoke by winter, or mild and clear under stars by summer; the utter mystery of the cuneiform tab handed to you by the sweaty, over-worked and inevitably irritable waiter; the occasional fossil of an accordion player in the corner; the slow slippage floorward of your friends…

The authentic, full pub experience is growing noticeably harder to find these days as establishments 'westernise' (not necessarily synonymous with 'improve'). Treasured exceptions are **U Zlatého tygra**, **U Kotvy**, **Baráčnická rychta**, **U Černého Vola** and the back room of **U medvídků**; student-favoured versions of same are **Studio A Rubín**, **U krále Jiřího** and **Radegast Pub**; and a prime surviving specimen of a terrace pub is **Na zvonařce**.

Café society, once the lifeblood of brilliant depressives like Franz Kafka, Karel Čapek, Jan Neruda, Jaroslav Seifert, Max Brod, Jiří Kolář and Václav Havel, once emulated Vienna's coffeehouse flavour but was dealt a decisive one-two blow by communist neglect then capitalist property values. It now appears to be reviving little by little. Nicotine-fuelled creative discourse has already taken root at **Malostranská Kavárna**, **Galerie Baraka Café**, **Galerie Café Chiméra**, **Jazz Café č. 14**, **Literární kavárna GPlusG**, **Blatouch** and **St Nicholas Café**. For a pure caffeine rush that might have doubled Kafka's output (or left him bewildered at the aroma of Sumatran

Arabica coffee beans) try **Káva káva káva** or **Vzpomínky na Afriku**, while modern foodie cafés like **Bohemia Bagel**, **Érra Café** and **Pták Loskuták** offer noticeably savoury menus and sometimes décor to match. The symbolic bur-nished leaders of the vanguard are the reopened worker heroes of **Kavárna Obecní dům** and the **Slavia**, the latter being home to nearly all of the aforementioned illuminati. Neither is now even imaginable as its former grotty self.

TEA TIME

In the void between pub floor and the heights of café palaver, one new and wholly unique phenomenon has hit Prague with no signs of abating. The Prague conception of tearoom combines the soundtrack, lighting, carpets, steeping methods and, yes, countless leaf varieties of traditional tea-houses from Tunis to Shanghai via Kathmandu. Recommended escapes from all worldly cares include **Dobrá čajovna**'s two legal locations and its hidden room at the **Roxy** (*see page 204*), **U Zlatého kohouta**, newly opened tearooms in a number of more beer-based locales including **U Vystřelenýho oka**, and, though it does involve conventional chairs and tables, **U zeleného čaje**. *See page 149* Ceylonging for a cuppa.

Another growing institution of gentility, at least among expats, is the Sunday hangover brunch, available in fine form at **Radost** (*see page 129 & page 203*), **The Globe** and **Jáma**. The splashy full-scale version is served at **Palffy Palác** (*see page 127*), **Bellevue** (*see page 119*) and **V Zátiší** (*see page 124*).

All usher in a smooth return to conscious life. No, to expectorate in a shrine is bad karma indeed.

Staré Město

Andy's Café

V kolkovně 3, Prague 1 (no phone). Metro Staroměstská/ 17, 18 tram. **Open** 10am-6am Mon-Thur; 10am-8am Fri; noon-6am Sat; noon-6am Sun. **Map 3 J2**

The 'No drug dealers' sign on the window isn't just there for show: this is the genuine article. Open all night, it attracts all the folks hungry enough to brave these dreadful fries and salads and willing to eat under enormous sculptures of

Homer Simpson. Which basically means club kids from the **Roxy** (*see p204*) and junkies. As virtually the only option for any-hour feeding besides **Pizzeria Roma Due** (*see p130*), it's at least jumping with colourful clientele.

Banana Café

Štupartská 9, Prague 1 (232 4801). Metro Náměstí Republiky/5, 14, 26 tram. **Open** 8pm-1am daily. **Map 3 J3**

Upstairs from **La Provence** (*see p127*), this daft Euro-trash hangout features dated disco music, go-go dancers, a sardine-can dancefloor and bizarre entertainments, such as a woman in an improbable wig sitting knitting on the bar. Worth one drink and a giggle on your way to somewhere else.

Belle Epoque

Křížovnická 8, Prague 1 (232 1926). Metro Staroměstská/17, 18 tram. **Open** noon-2am daily. **Map 3 G3**

Ushering in the still-groundbreaking advent of a grill bar, this place appeals to a mixed crowd of Czech Moderns bent on having a thoroughly Western cocktail experience and willing to pay double the usual rate for it. Mobile phone bearers can be seen gathered around Long Island ice teas amid the rough-hewn brick walls and candles. The drinks list is civilised enough, but the staff need a bit more practice. Still, at least they're willing to slap anything you can name onto the barbecue.

Blatnička

Michalská 6, Prague 1 (263 812). Metro Můstek/6, 9, 18, 22 tram. **Open** 11am-11pm daily. **Map 3 H4**

Hidden just off Karlova and away from the tourist hordes, this wine cellar masquerades as a tiny, smoke-filled bar that appears most unwelcoming. Walk to the back and down the stairs, though, and you find yourself in a snug little restaurant that serves unimaginative Czech food to soak up their drinkable Moravian wines, on tap in half- and one-litre jugs. The tiny glasses make you think you haven't drunk a thing, which can cause confusion when you find yourself at eye-level with the waiter's shoes when you try to stand up.

Blatouch

Vězeňská 4, Prague 1 (232 8643). Metro Staroměstská/17, 18 tram. **Open** 11am-midnight Mon-Fri; 2pm-1am Sat; 2pm-midnight Sun. **Map 3 J2**

Two sisters run this gentle and reasonably priced café, a favourite of clean-cut Czech students and intellectuals. Jazz and soul music wafts through the narrow, high-ceilinged room and up the metal stairwell to the floor above, carpeted and filled with armchairs. The wooden floors and bookcase add to the civilised atmosphere. Salads and melted cheese amalgams are available but can't be recommended.

Internet cafés

Get online at one of the following:
Cybeteria, *see page 143.*
Dobrá čajovna, *see page 149.*
Internet Café, *see page 140.*
Kavárna Obecní dům, *see page 144.*
Najada, *see page 151.*
Pl@neta, *see page 152.*
Studio A Rubín, *see page 150.*
Terminal Bar, *see page 144.*
U zeleného čaje, *see page 149.*

Bugsy's

Pařížská 10 (entrance on Kostečná), Prague 1 (232 9943). Metro Staroměstská/17, 18 tram. **Open** 7pm-2am daily. **Map 3 H3**

An establishment as swish as the street outside, offering a book-size drinks menu including 200-plus cocktails and bar staff good enough to mix them properly. Prices prohibit all but Czech *nouveaux riches*, foreign businesspeople, and a complement of babes waiting for some nice wealthy fellow to buy them a drink. The bar is fun to perch at; the tables less inviting. Packed in mid-evenings.

Café bar Na zábradlí

Anenské náměstí, Prague 1 (2422 1933). Metro Staroměstská/17, 18 tram. **Open** 11am-1am daily; closed in summer. **Map 3 G4**

Temperamental opening hours, and officially it's just for theatre patrons after 6pm, but when luck is with you, the boisterous local theatre crowd in this café adjoining Václav Havel's old stage make for a rollicking night out. It provides (much overlooked) relief from the higher tourist prices charged all around it, with a few basic mini-salads and a cobbled courtyard out back thrown in for good measure.

Café Louvre

Národní třída 20, Prague 1 (297 665). Metro Národní třída/6, 9, 18, 22 tram. **Open** 8am-11pm daily. **Map 3 H5**

A long, lofty café that somehow manages to get away with a garish cream and turquoise colour combination, perhaps because it leads to a fine back-room pool hall. Prices are above average, but then so is the food (there's also a restaurant in the next-door room, past the fancy fountain). Good for solid weekend breakfasts.

Café Milena

Staroměstské náměstí 22, Prague 1 (260 843). Metro Staroměstská or Můstek. **Open** 10am-9pm daily. **Map 3 J3**

Milena Jesenská was one of Kafka's lovers. The quiet, carpeted rooms, overseen by waiters in grey waistcoats, are trying to recreate a bygone atmosphere, but come off a little too clean-cut. Depending on your mood, you can sit in the grey room or sunny yellow room. (There's also a red one reserved for members of the Franz Kafka Society.) An assortment of cakes, pancakes and ice-cream can be eaten while looking out of the window at the astrological clock.

Café Rincon

Melantrichova 12, Prague 1 (2421 4593). Metro Můstek. **Open** 9am-2am daily. **Map 3 H4**

Ever the scene for a fashionable Czech clientele, this hollow of orange-splotchy walls and worn wood trim lies just past the bottom of Wenceslas Square, and stocks some rare, lesser-known brews, plus crude attempts at sangria. Conversation is shouted, but it's a comfortable sort of chaos. Come for one of the wacky theme nights (anyone for karaoke?) or for breakfast (till noon every day).

La Casa Blů

Kozí 15, Prague 1 (302 3774). Metro Staroměstská. **Open** 2-11pm daily. **Map 3 J2**

Sarapes draped over hard-back chairs, Mexican street signs and tequila specials still pass for Latin culture in Prague. It does make for a break from beer hall row, and is generally packed, but the film, music and art promised on the programme rarely come through. Try the buzzer even if the door is locked – people routinely wheedle their way in and carry on well past closing hour.

Chapeau Rouge

Jakubská 2, Prague 1 (no phone). Metro Náměstí Republiky/5, 14, 26 tram. **Open** *winter* 4pm-4am, *summer* 4pm-5am, daily. **Map 4 K3**

Multinational college crowds cram nightly into this loud and smoky epicentre of young Prague nightlife. It's open longer than anywhere else. Good place to find drugs or pick up a one-night stand. Otherwise, there's little to recommend it. *See also p205.*

Chez Marcel

Haštalská 12, Prague 1 (231 5676). Tram 5, 14, 26. **Open** 8am-1am Mon-Fri; 9am-1am Sat, Sun. **Map 3 J2**
Classy, elegant but unpretentious – a favourite watering hole for Prague sophisticates. Reasonably priced French wines complement a good, basic bistro menu of quiches, massive salads and top-drawer fries. It also makes a perfect site to wind down an evening with its mellow glow, gentle arches and dark-wood-panelled interior. Set on one of the Old Town's last great quiet, cobbled squares.

Corona Bar

Novotného lávka 9, Prague 1 (2108 2208). Metro Staroměstská/17, 18 tram. **Open** 6pm-1am Mon-Wed; 6pm-3am Thur-Sat; 6pm-midnight Sun (terrace from noon-midnight in summer). **Map 3 G4**
No fewer than four slick, upmarket bars, a tapas menu and a tiny terrace out back looking on to the Charles Bridge. Guitarists stand under the expensive décor – meant to suggest a humble Mexican village – and strum odd versions of *Guantánamera* as fairly accurate mixed drinks are whisked about them. Some may actually buy the bottled Mexican beer at three times the price of supreme Czech pilsner.

Cheesy snacks

When it comes to Czech pubbing, it's easy to tell the men from the boys – and not by the filterless cigarettes. No, not even by the way they chow down grease-soaked, garlic-packed, cold potato pancakes, smoked meat slices or hours-old schnitzels with curling corners. You have to look more closely at their plates.

The true connoisseurs of beer-hall culture prove themselves only through their grasp of *utopenci*, *zavináči* and *pivní sýr*. You could order *utopenec* – 'drowned man' – a sausage left floating in a jar of vinegar, much as a hardboiled egg would in a Depression-era diner. Or how about *zavináč*: an 'ampersand' of rolled fish, scales and all, served cold?

But these are nothing compared with *pivní sýr*, the true hallmark of pub couture (not to mention will-power). This little culinary delight consists of a plate of mild curd cheese served with a dollop of hot mustard and raw onion chunks or sardines and, if you're lucky, a sprinkling of paprika. The technique is deceptively simple. Mash it all up with your fork then pour a bit of your beer over it. So far, so good. Now you just have to eat it.

Congratulations: you've been elevated to the rank of seasoned brewhouse veteran. Just don't expect to pull tonight.

Érra Café

Konviktská 11, Prague 1 (2423 3427). Metro Národní třída/6, 9, 17, 18, 22 tram. **Open** 10am-midnight Mon-Fri; 11am-midnight Sat, Sun.
Map 3 G5
Looking much like a copy of Czech *Elle* exploded in an Old Town cellar, with mylar-coated settees and a psychedelic colour scheme that manages giddiness without slipping into pretence. The menu parties as well, with salads of duck and artfully arranged spinach leaves, garlic-sesame chicken baguettes and rich banana milkshakes. Whimsical gay-friendly scene by night that's brought off by the cooks at **Palffy Palace** (*see p127*).

Gulu Gulu

Betlémské náměstí 8, Prague 1 (900 121 581). Metro Národní třída/6, 9, 17, 18, 22 tram. **Open** 10am-midnight daily. **Map 3 H4**
With large floor-level windows looking out over Betlémské náměstí and a Miró-esque décor that engages the senses without overpowering them, Gulu ranks high among central meeting places. A good coffee selection and a fresh copy of *The Times* make it attractive at 10am, but suspiciously cheap chef's specials are a major gamble. Low-price Radegast and eight kinds of vodka draw young, hip crowds from around 10pm.

Internet Café

Národní třída 25, Prague 1 (2108 5284). Metro Národní třída/6, 9, 18, 22 tram. **Open** 9am-10pm Mon-Fri; 2-10pm Sat, Sun. **Map 3 H5**
Nothing much to recommend it except cheap and convenient Internet access. The bar is a packaged juice and bottled beverage counter and the staff are more or less cheerful and more or less oblivious if you don't know your way around the World Wide Web.

James Joyce

Liliová 10, Prague 1 (2424 8793). Metro Staroměstská/17, 18 tram. **Open** 11am-1am daily. **Map 3 G4**
The Hooray Henry hangout of the expat crowd. Few Czechs can afford the prices here, and Joyce himself would probably have blanched at the hiked Guinness and Kilkenny rates, along with those on the menu. That is partly the purpose of this expat 'oasis', but such arrogance aside, you have to admit that the swaying hearties who come here know how to have a piss-up. A newly improved offer of Irish stews and fry-ups is also well done amid this interior imported from a nineteenth-century Belfast church.

Káva Káva Káva

Národní třída 37, Prague 1 (268 409). Metro Národní třída/6, 9, 18, 22 tram. **Open** 7am-9pm Mon-Fri; 9am-9pm Sat, Sun. **Map 3 H5**
Prague's first full-blown coffee (*káva*) emporium is a far kinder, gentler kind of Starbucks, with a quiet courtyard sipping experience and a dozen beans on offer. Through a sweetheart deal with Bohemia Bagel, it also offers credible snacks. Carrot cake and a latte go well with the parade of characters before the shady outside tables during the summer heat.

Kavárna Rudolfinum

Alšovo nábřeží 12, Prague 1 (2489 3317). Metro Staroměstská/17, 18 tram. **Open** 10am-6pm Tue-Sat. **Map 3 G3**
Just about the best spot in town for an hour or two of refinement, quiet and contemplation with a glass of indifferent wine. Soaring ceilings, blond wood, diffused natural light and sometimes great art are the décor in this often overlooked café within the grand neo-classical Rudolfinum's art gallery (enter from the riverfront side, around the corner from the concert hall).

Konírna

(The Stable) Anenská 11, Prague 1 (no phone). Metro Staroměstská/17, 18 tram. **Open** noon-midnight Mon-Fri; 6pm-midnight Sat, Sun. **Map 3 G4**
A narrow, civilised stable bar tucked into a cobbled side street within staggering distance of Charles Bridge, which serves cheap drinks and a smattering of basic salads. Service is quick and friendly. Quiet scribblers hang out during the day, while at night the bar is usually packed with laid-back Czechs.

Kozička

Kozí 4, Prague 1 (2481 8308). Metro Staroměstská. **Open** noon-4am Mon-Fri; 4pm-4am Sat, Sun. **Map 3 J2**
Secret insider's tip: The iron-clad success formula for packing a bar every night of the week in the Czech Republic is to grill a LOT of bargain-priced meat. Try 500g (1lb) rump steaks charred to juicy perfection in this brick and wood-trimmed underground maze of Krušovice taps. That is, if you can work your way to the bar (and get your order in before the kitchen closes at 1am). Afterwards, the nutrition comes purely in liquid form, but proves every bit as popular.

Marquis de Sade

Templová 8, Prague 1 (no phone). Metro Náměstí Republiky/5, 14, 26 tram. **Open** 11am-2am (food until 11pm) daily. **Map 4 K3**
The Old Town's crossover bar, featuring a little bit of everyone who's out and, despite nightly live jazz, enough peace and quiet for them to talk to each other. The splendid, large, picture-windowed room was the centrepiece of a lavish First Republic whorehouse, and there are vague plans afoot for expansion into its deeper recesses. Good bar for perching, excellent location, mediocre but cheap salads and sandwiches, plus inexcusably poor Lobkowicz beer. *See also p205.*

Metamorphosis

Malá Štupartská 5, Prague 1 (2482 7058). Metro Náměstí Republiky/5, 14, 26 tram. **Open** 9am-1am daily. **Map 3 J3**
Shaded outside tables in a hushed stone courtyard, sunny service and décor, plush turquoise seating in amoebic shapes and a cellar restaurant complement the live jazz here. Sedate and capable, this family-run pasta café on the newly refurbished Ungelt (Týn) Square has just one disadvantage: the square's location directly on the route from Metro to Old Town Square.

Molly Malone's

U Obecního dvora 4, Prague 1 (534 793). Metro Náměstí Republiky/5, 14, 26 tram. **Open** noon-12.45am Sun-Thur; noon-1.45am Fri, Sat. **Map 3 J2**
The Platonic archetype of Irish pubs everywhere. Roaring log fire, mismatched chairs and tables constructed out of beds and sewing machines, the Pogues playing incessantly, 'traditional Irish food' and lots of rowdy English businessmen. But, much as you want to hate it, the place does have a certain charm. The bar is great for propping up, the Guinness is better than any you'll taste in London, the food is actually good, and in winter there's a warm and welcoming atmosphere. In summer, you risk an irate neighbour from this quiet corner of the Old Town throwing a plant pot at you if you stand outside after 9pm, but that's all part of the fun.

O'Ché's

Liliová 14, Prague 1 (9005 1079). Metro Staroměstská/17, 18 tram. **Open** 10am-1am daily. **Map 3 G4**
Everything **Jo's Bar** *(see p150)* should be and isn't. Appealing, roomy, with a wacky theme, a mix of folksy young foreigners, taps that pour Guinness and appetising (if overpriced) burgers and pastas. Presiding over all are Cuban flags and images of that mad motorcycle diarist Che Guevara, brought back to life in the form of an Irish publican. In such poor taste that it's got to be charming.

Radegast Pub

Templová 2, Prague 1 (232 8069). Metro Náměstí Republiky/5, 14, 26 tram. **Open** 11am-midnight daily. **Map 4 K3**
One of the last typical Czech pubs to hang on in the Bermuda Triangle of expat drinking; its main draws are the excellent beer and pub food (you could pay an extra 200 Kč in a swank restaurant and have a far better goulash). The clientele are a mixture of Czechs, expats and backpackers who can't believe they've found such a cheap place to eat and drink right in the centre of Prague. Semi-enclosed snugs give an air of privacy, but the service is iffy – orders tend to get lost in the smoke haze.

Reno

Museum of Decorative Arts (Uměleckoprůmyslové muzeum) ulice 17. listopadu 2, Prague 1 (2481 1307). Metro Staroměstská/17, 18 tram. **Open** 10am-6pm Mon-Fri; 11am-6pm Sat, Sun. **Map 3 G2**
A modern bar in the Museum of Decorative Arts *(see p90)* with friendly service, pleasant pictures and sculptures neatly arranged on the walls, as well as pretty mugs and teapots for sale from a glass display case.

Dreaming of things past in the reborn **Slavia**. *See page 142.*

Slavia

Smetanovo nábřeží 2, Prague 1 (2422 0957). Metro Národni třída/6, 9, 17, 18, 22 tram. **Open** 8am-midnight Mon-Fri; 9am-midnight Sat, Sun. **Map 3 G5**
The mother of all Prague cafés, where all the great literati once tippled and puffed, with the best strudel in town. Purists say that the art deco fixtures and the crisp service aren't true to the spirit of Jaroslav Seifert's poem 'Café Slavia' or that of fellow rabble rousers and/or National Theatre miscreants Karel Tiege, Jiří Kolář, a struggling Václav Havel and, at one point, Tolstoy. But the mix of business people, backpackers, reminiscing pensioners and the inevitable in-tellectual scribblers is unique, as are the splendid views of Prague Castle and Národni streetlife.

Tequila Sunrise

Štupartská 6, Prague 1 (2481 9383). Metro Náměstí Republiky/5, 14, 26 tram. **Open** 11am-2am daily. **Map 3 J3**
This place opens and closes regularly (and has also been known to rename itself): this year's model offers a reasonable attempt at Mexican food until 10pm, Czech waiters in mariachi kit, plus a fair range of wines. It has jettisoned the next-door pub once filled with the sound of rollicking blues.

U červeného páva

(The Red Peacock) Kamzíkova 6, Prague 1 (2423 3168). Metro Můstek. **Open** 11am-11.30pm Mon-Fri; 4-11pm Sat, Sun. **Map 3 J4**
Recently an overt gay 'rainbow' club, the Red Peacock is now a bit more subtle, placing its emphasis on wagon wheels and gallows décor, camp piano singalongs by night and amazingly cheap lunch specials for the Old Town. Well intentioned, highly random service; what you get is bound to be decent and affordable but it's anyone's guess whose table your schnitzel and Gambrinus will go to, or when.

U medvídků – *a classic Czech boozer.*

U krále Jiřího

(King George) Liliová 10, Prague 1 (no phone). Metro Staroměstská/17, 18 tram. **Open** 11am-midnight Mon-Fri; noon-midnight Sat, Sun. **Map 3 G4**
Just falling-down distance from the upscale **James Joyce** (*see p140*), this narrow cellar pub is an insider's trump card with its cheap Gambrinus 10-degree on tap and its location in the heart of Old Town. Frequented by old-time locals, itinerant buskers and long-term expats, it's a funky, bare-bones hide-out for loud debates about the meaning of Velvet Underground lyrics.

U medvídků

(The Little Bears) Na Perštýně 7, Prague 1 (2422 0930). Metro Národni třída/6, 9, 18, 22 tram. **Open** 11am-11pm Mon-Sat; 11am-10pm Sun. **Map 3 H5**
Five centuries of classic beer hall drills and still going strong, this place brushed off communism as a passing fashion. The only regime that counts here is the ritual of fine, aggressively served Budvar for a song – half-litre mugs keep coming until you tell the waiter to stop. Don't be sidetracked by the modern bar to the left of the entrance; the real goods are on the right. Where else in Prague can you try a platter of pork and *knedliky* while seated in a hay wagon?

U Zlatého tygra

(The Golden Tiger) Husova 17, Prague 1 (2422 9020). Metro Staroměstská/17, 18 tram. **Open** 3-11pm daily. **Map 3 H4**
Once the headquarters of Prague's favourite native son writer, the crotchety Bohumil Hrabal (*see p189*), this place has lost virtually all its appeal since his mysterious death by hospital window fall. The tourists who have always besieged it still do, the Pilsner Urquell is no bargain and the remaining regulars are none too happy about this state of affairs and are likely to blow unfiltered cigarette smoke your way.

Vzpomínky na Afriku

corner of Rybná & Jakubská, Prague 1 (0603 441 434). Metro Náměstí Republiky/5, 14, 26 tram. **Open** 10am-7pm daily. **Map 4 K3**
King of the coffee bean hill, with dozens of fresh-roasted Arabica and Robusta beans, ground up for your mug on the spot or bagged for home defibrillation. An expert, English-speaking staff is surprisingly non-jumpy and willing to steer you from Colombian Medellin roast to bitter Indonesian options. Opportunities to sit 'n' sit here are not great, however, unless you manage to grab the single table available.

Žíznivý pes/Thirsty Dog

Elišky Krásnohorské 5, Prague 1 (231 0039). Metro Staroměstská/17, 18 tram. **Open** 11am-1am Sun-Thur; 11am-2am Fri, Sat. **Map 3 H2**
A shrine to the golden days of expat slacking whose long-closed original location at Obecní dům was once immortalised by Nick Cave, who apparently felt very sorry there. Nowadays it's burgers, Murphy's Stout and Lobkowicz, jubilant disporting by Yanks and a handful of Czechs, and summer breezes in the little patio out back.

Nové Město

Café Archa

Na Poříčí 26, Prague 1 (232 4149). Metro Náměstí Republiky or Florenc/3, 24 tram. **Open** 9am-10.30pm Mon-Fri; 10am-8pm Sat; 1-10pm Sun. **Map 4 M2**
This glass fish tank café, with long dangling lamps as bait, seems to have hooked a young laid-back clientele with cheap drinks, pristine surfaces and posters and photos from the theatre and rock worlds. You can stare out at the passers-by as you drink, though they're more likely to be staring in at you.

Cybeteria

Štěpánská 18, Prague 1 (2423 3024). Metro Muzeum/3, 9, 14, 24 tram. **Open** 10am-8pm Mon-Fri; noon-6pm Sat. **Map 6 K6**

Prague's first Internet café is still dead last in the rankings, with lamely 'spacey' atmosphere, insolent service and poor drink selection. Hourly prices for computer use are higher than all competitors', and if you can't figure out their software don't bother asking for help – the staff don't know how to use it either.

Dunkin' Donuts

Václavské náměstí 1, Prague 1 (2422 6526). Metro Můstek. **Open** 7am-10pm Mon-Fri; 8am-10pm Sat, Sun. **Map 3 J5**

Part of the advancing corporate takeover of Wenceslas Square without question, but its early-morning supply of the classic American junk food breakfast with filtered coffee packs in Czechs at any hour of the day. Sole supplier of outsize blueberry muffins to the republic as well, with prime picture window views out on to the Old Town end of Wenceslas Square.

Evropa Café

Grand Hotel Evropa, Václavské náměstí 25, Prague 1 (2422 8117). Metro Můstek or Muzeum/3, 9, 14, 24 tram. **Open** 10am-11pm daily. **Map 4 K5**

This decaying art nouveau hotel café still retains a certain dusty charm, with its ageing prostitutes and bearded jazz trios who tinkle, scrape and puff their way through old favourites. Nowadays, most tables are filled with businessmen and backpackers, and a nominal cover charge is levied when the band cranks up. Service is so appalling it will either make you laugh or cry, the food is expensive and limited, and the coffee's not that great either, but it's worth looking in at least once.

French Institute Café

Štěpánská 35, Prague 1 (2421 6630). Metro Můstek/ 3, 9, 14, 24 tram. **Open** 9am-6pm Mon-Fri. **Map 6 K6**

A critical source of croissants and good, strong espresso before the opening of Chez Marcel and **Le Café Colonial** (*see p125*), the French Institute carries on as a Gallic nerve centre with unapologetically Francophile art gallery downstairs, and free cinema adjoining. Elegant, prime posing with an open courtyard and a fair chance of starting an intellectual romance.

Galerie Módy

Štěpánská 61, Prague 1 (2421 1514). Metro Můstek/ 3, 9, 14, 24 tram. **Open** 10am-8pm Mon-Sat. **Map 6 K6**

Prague's top fashion designers, led off by Helena Fejková, have joined forces to open this glassed-in perch overlooking the wonderfully yellowed Lucerna Passage, a former shopping arcade glory of the First Republic (*see p57*). In this last great time capsule of Wenceslas Square, a designer tea among the black satin dress racks (and the models pawing them) is a supreme way to prepare for a movie or concert in the vast halls below the floor.

Jáma

(The Hollow) V jámě 7, Prague 1 (264 127). Metro Můstek/3, 9, 14, 24 tram. **Open** 11am-1am daily. **Map 6 K6**

Loud and collegiate year-round, this long bar with Mexican food is the choice of the real local business crowd, as opposed to the execs and lawyers that hit the overpriced **James Joyce** (*see p140*). The Arizonans who run it sponsor the literary quarterly *The Prague Revue*, but you'd never guess it from their extensive cocktails (often on special), faux cacti and Mexican food lunch discounts. Décor is early Elvis Costello poster and service above average for Prague.

Hot shots

To go with Prague's beer, you can also take your pick of numerous home-grown chasers. Here are the ones you are most likely to find.

Topping the list is **Becherovka**, a sweetish yellow herb liqueur made to a secret recipe (of course) in Karlovy Vary; known as **Beton** ('concrete') when cut with tonic. **Fernet** – like a cross between Italian Fernet Branca and Branca Menta – is more bitter, though its taste can be lightened by irrigating it with tonic water to make what is called, for some strange reason, **Bavorský pivo** – 'Bavarian beer' or **Bávorak**. The result is similar to Pimms, and quite refreshing. Both drinks are often recommended as a hair of the dog (they're both also supposed to be good for the stomach), but many people just use them as the dog itself.

The cheapest way to get out of your head is to go for **Tuzemský Rum**, favourite tipple of indigenous winos. Drunk neat it resembles rocket fuel, but with sugar, hot water and a slice of lemon it makes a good warming grog to see you through Prague's protracted winter.

Borovička is a juniper-based spirit, more Slovak than Czech and not unlike Dutch Jenever, while **Slivovice** (plum brandy), if not home-made, is smooth and goes down a treat. **Myslivecká** – so-called because of the hunter on the label – is deceptively mild, tasting a bit like weak bourbon, but should be treated with respect. **Griotte** is a cherry brandy, and best for sloshing over ice-cream. And then, of course, there's **Absinthe**…

Jazz Café č. 14

Opatovická 14, Prague 1 (no phone). Metro Národní třída/6, 9, 18, 22 tram. **Open** 11am-11pm daily. **Map 5 H6**

A crowd of local writers and arty types clearly considers this a fine, if smoky, hideaway for the winter, with an easy, mismatched furniture feel, congenial service and a constant jazz soundtrack (which, absurdly, is never live). The cold-pressed olive oils, groovy loose teas and honey on display in the old hives are all for sale and make nice, cheap mementos.

John Bull Pub

Senovážná 8, Prague 1 (2422 6005). Metro Náměstí Republiky/3, 5, 9, 14, 24, 26 tram. **Open** 8am-2am Mon-Fri; 11am-2am Sat; 11am-midnight Sun.* **Map 4 K4**

Part of an international conspiracy of theme pubs whose sole purpose seems to be to unload on to Eastern Europe all the bitter too awful even for the English. The Czechs, rampant anglophiles as they are, lap it up and come back for more. Near Prague's financial district, at lunchtime you could be in any City of London pub – braying besuited wideboys, tatty red velvet chairs, *Punch* prints, wobbly stools and all.

Not just here for the beer?

If you read the reports, you'd be forgiven for thinking that your only decent wine options in Prague are Bulgarian reds or sweet Hungarian Tokay. But make no mistake, a fine Moravian vintage is one of the great, overlooked joys of the beer capital of the world. True, you won't happen upon it easily in Prague. The sterling produce of small, family-owned vineyards seldom makes it to the big city. The surest option, therefore, is to jump on a train for the sunny south-eastern border towns such as Mikulov, Znojmo, Šobes or Valtice, then just wander from village to village. There you will inevitably be accosted by locals intent on proving to you that their personal cellars and grapes are the region's *raison d'être*.

But city-bound Bohemians can do almost as well by taking one of two approaches: The first is a discriminating eye for wine-savvy restaurants and shops, of which there are, regrettably, still but a handful. The **Hotel Hoffmeister** (*see page 107*), a magnet for genteel film and stage stars during the inter-war days of the First Republic, has revived some of its glory days with juried wine tastings. The results are published in the Czech business press, pushing the industry's standards of excellence, and the Hoffmeister stocks what it deems best. **Opera Grill** (*see page 120*) and **U modré kachničky** (*see page 125*) are also both excellent at hunting down the best work of local vintners.

Be warned, though: most of the city's otherwise top restaurants stock the same mass-produced Vinium and Znovin wines that are peddled at the local grocery, except they're marked up by about fourfold. A better bet is to take the initiative and pick up a bottle yourself at any of the new-generation wine shops such as **Cellarius**, **Dům lahůdek** or **Vinotéka Galerie**. Then head over to a friend's house if it's cold out or, if the weather's mild, take your score to Stromovka park and let your chums find their way to you.

The second approach is to bring an empty plastic water bottle into any corner tavern marked *sudové víno* (utterly unspecified 'barrelled wine', available in simply red or white) and have them fill 'er up, usually for around 50-75 Kč per litre. It's peasant wine you could cut with a knife, but it's very likely the same stuff you'll be served in a swank Old Town dining room.

Don't be fooled by the phrase 'Archivní' on a bottle – winemaking standards are improving measurably every year so something from the '93 or '92 archives is a poor bet. And Bohemian wine can stand up against Moravian, at least in the case of **Château Mělník**, and increasingly, the table wine **Ludmila**, both produced in the region north of Prague. **Bohemia Sekt**, a champagne-wannabe normally sweet to excess, is quite palatable when available under the award-winning label **Château Roudnice**.

Kavárna Obecní dům

Náměstí Republiky 5, Prague 1 (2200 2763). Metro Náměstí Republiky/5, 14, 26 tram. **Open** 7.30am-11pm daily. **Map 4 K3**
The magnificently restored Municipal House (1905-11) is rightly one of Prague's most celebrated buildings. It features a stunning art nouveau concert space, galleries and a decent French restaurant but its café takes the cake. Replete with impossibly elaborate *jugendstil* brass chandeliers, balconies, a pianist and, somewhat incongruously, a few Internet terminals, a cup of espresso here is not likely to be forgotten. *See also p59.*

Master's Bar 23

Křemencova 23, Prague 1 (292 086). Metro Národní třída/6, 9, 18, 22 tram. **Open** 6pm-1am daily. **Map 5 H7**
The small space resembles an indoor patio garden with a slight touch of New York art deco. Patronised by a cast of regulars and the occasional lost sheep tourist, it's a nice, calm place to pause for an espresso or whisky.

Posezení Na řece

Slovanský ostrov, Prague 1 (294 868). Tram 6, 9, 17, 18, 22. **Open** 11am-11pm daily (summer). **Map 5 G7**
Barge pubbing on one of the Vltava's most idyllic islands has to be the reason God gave us summer nights. This one's lack of amenities is therefore no dissuasion. With a glass in hand, watching the rowboats slip by, you won't even notice the plastic garden chairs.

Praha-Roma

V jámě 5, Prague 1 (2416 2475). Metro Národní třída or Můstek/3, 9, 14, 24 tram. **Open** 9am-11pm daily. **Map 6 K6**
Decorated with pink 1920s lampshades and pink tablecloths, this café sells a good selection of forward-thinking cakes.

Terminal Bar

Soukenická 6, Prague 1 (2187 1223/2187 1224/technical support 2187 1666/www.terminal.cz). Metro Náměstí Republiky/5, 14, 26 tram. **Open** 10am-2am daily. **Map 4 L2**
The only genuinely helpful and friendly international Internet café in Prague doubles as a repository for expat counter culture, outlandish interior decorating concepts and a mean cappuccino. Other inducements are multilingual technical advice during work hours, fast connections and a relaxed cybertrash vibe throughout (free screenings of B-movie classics in the downstairs videotheque, and English-language cult video rental for members).

Wines worth seeking out

WHITES

Müller Thurgau – Like most Central European whites, it's more of a sweet dessert wine than a dry complement to seafood, but with a dependable, colourful body.

Neuburské – Not as fruity and more to the point, but still widely consumed.

Pálava – Complex, award-winning hybrid of riesling and veltlinské.

Rulandské bílé – Actually a pinot, though no match for the sun-kissed French competition.

Rulandské šedé – A lauded, strong pinot gris with a lovely bouquet.

Ryzlink rýnský – A more effervescent riesling, made capably by Znovín's premium line, Vinařská oblast Znojmo, from Šobes grapes.

Ryzlink vlašský – Also bottled well by the above and sweet as love.

Sauvignon – Best from Hodonice, with a richer, more aromatic quality.

Tramín – Right up there with vlašský – almost cloying.

Veltlínské zelené – Aromatic with a hint of bite, also done well in Znovín's top line.

REDS

Frankovka – Ruby-hued, sweet and fruity, the Vino Mikulov is recommended.

Portugal modrý – A rarely seen medium red with nothing whatsoever to do with Portugal.

Rulandské červené – Pinot noir that favours the Moravian soil of Hnízdo.

Svatovavřinecké – The heartiest of the bunch and a good match for game.

Respectable wine sources

Cellarius
Štěpanská 61 (in the Lucerna Passage), Prague 1 (2421 0979). Metro Můstek/3, 9, 14, 24 tram. **Open** 9.30am-9pm Mon-Sat. **Map 6 K6**

Dům lahůdek u Rotta
Malé náměstí 3, Prague 1 (269 537/267 094). Metro Staroměstská. **Open** 9.30am-7pm Mon-Sat; noon-7pm Sun. **Map 3 H4**

Hotel Hoffmeister
Pod Bruskou 9, Prague 1 (5731 0942). Metro Malostranská/12, 18, 22 tram. **Open** *restaurant* noon-11pm daily. **Map 2 F1**

Národní banka vín
Platnéřská 4, Prague 1 (2110 8244/2110 8245). Metro Staroměstská/17, 18 tram. **Open** 10am-7pm Mon-Fri; 11am-3pm Sat. **Map 3 H3**

Vinotéka Galerie
Míšeňská 8, Prague 1 (no phone). Metro Malostranská/12, 22 tram. **Open** 11am-1pm, 2-9pm, daily. **Map 2 E3**

Cheap and efficacious sources

Blatnička
Michalská 6, Prague 1 (226 169). Metro Můstek/ 6, 9, 18, 22 tram. **Open** 3pm-3am daily. **Map 3 H4**

U sudových vín
Bořivojova 61, Prague 3 (2423 6751/9003 1048). Metro Jiřího z Poděbrad/5, 9, 26 tram. **Open** 10am-6pm Mon-Fri. **Map 8 B2**

U Fleků
Křemencova 11, Prague 1 (2491 5118). Metro Národní třída/3, 6, 14, 18, 24 tram. **Open** 9am-11pm daily. **Map 5 H7**
Without doubt the most famous pub in Prague, U Fleků has brewed fine 13-degree dark beer on the premises for centuries. You are automatically assumed to be here for the beer and may be treated like cattle – or a nice, fleecy lamb when it comes to billing time. The courtyard is shaded by overhanging trees and surrounded by a picturesque sgraffitoed wall; coachloads of hearty Germans sing and swing glasses to oompah-pah music within. Hair-raising atmosphere, but fun if you're in the mood – and the beer is incomparable.

U Kotvy
(The Anchor) Spalená 11, Prague 1 (291 161). Metro Národní třída/6, 9, 18, 22 tram. **Open** 24 hours daily. **Map 5 H6**
In winter, this smoky little hole-in-the-wall wouldn't rate a second glance, at least until after midnight, when it comes into its own as an all-night drinking den inhabited by assorted intriguing mutants. In summer, the large garden hidden out the back offers a leafy haven for getting gently plastered over an afternoon. Slow service, passable food, and beware the toilets.

U Rozvařilů
Na Poříčí 26, Prague 1 (2481 1736). Metro Náměstí Republiky/3, 24 tram. **Open** 7.30am-7.30pm Mon-Fri; 7.30am-7pm Sat; 10am-5pm Sun. **Map 4 L3**
One of last great *bufets*, a singular Prague dining experience of the pre-revolutionary days wherein grumpy old women in dirty aprons slopped *guláš* and tepid, salt-choked potato soup on to your tray. Mercifully, this is a modernised version with reasonably cheerful, Czech-only service, not-so-bad food and a bizarre interior of chrome and mirrors on every possible surface.

U Sudu
(The Barrel) Vodičkova 10, Prague 1 (2421 3499). Metro Karlovo náměstí/3, 9, 14, 24 tram. **Open** 11am-midnight Mon-Fri; 2pm-midnight Sat, Sun. **Map 5 J6**
Originally a small, dark wine bar on the ground floor, U Sudu has expanded down into two Gothic cellars and what seems to be somebody's spare room next door. The cellars have been claimed by students, while upstairs sees everyone from artists to business types to little old ladies. The service is wonderful, the wine nothing to shout about, although it is worth visiting when the *burčák* (a half-fermented, traditional Czech wine punch) arrives in September.

Beer makes beautiful bodies

Czechs love their beer and you will too. The average citizen drinks something like 280 pints (160 litres) a year, making the Czechs the world's biggest beer drinkers by a wide margin. Old ladies are said to drink it for the vitamins; construction workers think it helps steady their hands; girls say it helps expand their bra size; and men use it to fashion their big bellies – still a source of pride in some neighbourhoods. It's an excellent complement to the national dish – roast pork, dumplings and sauerkraut – though some Czechs seem to drink it at every meal, even breakfast. Don't feel constrained if you feel like doing the same.

It's no mystery really why the beer is so popular. Czech hops (the main ingredient in beer) are considered to be the best in the world and beer has been brewed on the territory of the Czech Republic for a thousand years. Beer was kept good and relatively cheap during the communist times as a way of keeping the masses docile. It is celebrated widely in literature, song and film – a popular movie from the '60s was even called *The Hop Pickers*.

Types of beer

Czech beer comes in many strengths and shades, but the most popular is the light, hoppy variety we commonly call lager, or 'pils', developed during the last century in the southern Bohemian town of Plzeň (Pilsen in German). Darker beers are becoming more popular, but you'll still have to look around to find a good one. **U Fleků** (*see page 145*) is a good if touristy place to sample the dark, slightly sweetish Prague-style brew that used to be common – a couple of centuries ago – throughout the city.

You can buy beer just about anywhere, but the best place to drink it is in a pub (*pivnice*), which will usually know how to store and tap the beer properly. To order, just tell the waiter 'pivo prosim'. Most pubs offer only one or two kinds of beer, so you usually won't have to specify which brand you want. You might be offered a choice between 10-degree and 12-degree beer, the former being a little lighter and with less alcohol. In more traditional pubs, once you've ordered, the waiter will continue to bring rounds until you tell him to stop. Signal that you've drunk enough by placing a beermat on top of your glass. The waiter will mark down rounds as he brings them on a small slip of paper. At the end of the evening, he'll tot up the damage.

Draught beer is best, and drinking out of bottles is not nearly as tasty or economical. Canned beer is reserved strictly for tourists. The alcohol level varies from brand to brand but ranges from about 3.5 per cent to a little more than 5 per cent. The dark beers tend to be sweeter than the lights, which have a full-bodied flavour but can be bitter. If you don't care for the hoppiness of the lights and the dark beer is too sweet, then ask for a *rezane*, which is a mix (it literally means 'cut') of the two.

The price of beer depends on where you drink it, not on the brand or type. A half litre in a decent pub shouldn't cost more than 20 Kč. Prices in the most heavily touristed parts of Prague rise accordingly. It's worth seeking out smaller – and often grimier – neighbourhood pubs where your money can often go three or four times as far.

Brands on the run

Thanks to worldwide distribution, the biggest Czech beers are increasingly well known abroad. **Pilsner Urquell** is probably the leading beer and the one that Czechs commonly cite as their favourite – although **Gambrinus** is the biggest seller. Another international favourite, **Budvar** (or Budweiser), bears no resemblance to its American namesake. It's a top seller among Czechs too for its faintly sweet and smooth taste. Bass nowadays is making a big international push for its **Staropramen** label. All three are great beers, but there are lots of smaller regional breweries worth seeking out that are virtually unknown outside the country (we've listed some in our taste test below). A few names to look for include **Regent**, **Bernard** and **Herold**. Bernard has a particularly loyal following because it's one of the few breweries that still uses wooden vats throughout the brewing process. One beer, **Velvet**, deserves special mention – if only because it's become so popular so quickly. It's the newest entrant on to the pub scene, unwelcomingly similar to the mock Irish beers found in Britain, such as Caffrey's and Kilkenny, and is the first brew to be openly marketed as a gimmick. Some dismiss out of hand the hip retro tap and the chemical concoction that passes for lager. Others say 'Pour me another, please'. You decide.

The Czechs enjoy seeing people sampling their national treasure, even to excess. However, you do stand a fair chance of being picked up by the police if you come across drunkenly loud or belligerent; so act harmless, tip well, drink up and tread softly.

Best of the brews

(The *Time Out* Taste Test)

The head of the Prague brewers' association says it's pointless to ask which Czech beer is best. It's like asking whether gentlemen prefer blondes, brunettes or redheads. Basically, it's down to individual preference – and they're all good anyway. To help you sort out the major brands, we offer the following unbiased rec-ommendations (all taste-tested by *Time Out* writers and editors). The beers are divided into lighter beers (around 4% alcohol content) and stronger beers (more than 5% alcohol). We list our top five from each category. The degree, by the way, refers to the original gravity, which indicates the density of malt and sugars.

Light beers (10 degree)

Gambrinus

The surprising favourite among the *Time Out* staff. Lively, with a clean finish. Leaves a hint of an aftertaste, which is avoidable if you carry on drinking. From the makers of Pilsner Urquell.

Bernard

Earthy, flavourful and unique. From a small brewery that eschews modern methods. Tough to find on tap, but worth looking for.

Branik

Creamy and light, with a slight bitterness to the finish. The quality on tap can vary as the brew-ery is little-changed from communist times.

Velkopopovický Kozel

Tongue-numbingly strong in both its light and heavier varieties. The beer for people who love the taste of beer. Relatively easy to find in pubs. *Kozel* means 'goat' (there's one on the label).

Radegast

A light beer that can hold its own with stronger brews. Amber coloured and slightly sour. Goes well with pretzels.

Heavier beers (12 degree)

Samson Premium

An all-round great beer. Difficult to find on tap, but widely available in bottles. Hoppy and light – what you'd expect from a classic pilsner.

Staropramen

Owned by the folks who churn out Bass, but still a good beer. Surprisingly fragrant and fruity– even possibly overpowering. Made by Prague's biggest brewery and found in pubs all over town.

Bernard

Most people prefer the light beer, but still a great choice. Light, smooth and a little cloudy.

Gambrinus

This beer outsells all others in the Czech Republic. A solid choice, with a strong bite and a weak finish.

Radegast

A perennial blue-ribbon at best beer contests, this Moravian label is still a little hard to find in Prague. Crisp with a strong bite. Best drunk very cold.

U Svatého Vojtěcha

(Saint Vojtěch) Vojtěšská 14, Prague 1 (2491 0594).
Metro Národní třída/6, 9, 17, 18, 22 tram.
Open 8am-10pm Mon-Fri; 10am-10pm Sat, Sun
(July, Aug open from 10am daily).
Map 5 G7
Just behind the National Theatre and largely unmolested
by non-Czechs, this quiet, unassuming café is frequented
by actors and intellectual types who sit by the large win-
dow, have a leisurely smoke and leaf through the morning
papers. No food.

Velryba

(The Whale) Opatovická 24, Prague 1 (2491 2391).
Metro Národní třída/6, 9, 18, 22 tram.
Open 11am-2am daily (kitchen closes at 11pm).
Map 5 H6
Granddaddy of the young Czech hipster hangouts, the
Whale comes equipped with clamorous front-room dining
on pastas and chicken steaks, back-room chess sets and
Beton (Becherovka cut with tonic) and cellar gallery spe-
cialising in what looks suspiciously like art therapy.
Curiously, the bar only serves bottled Gambrinus. The lack
of air once actually prompted a brave/foolish no-smoking
policy that lasted about a week before the nicotine-crazed
clientele won the day. Avoid the healthy-sounding tofu
karbanátky – it isn't anything of the sort.

Vltava

Rašínovo nábřeží 1 (near Palackého náměstí), Prague 1
(294 964). Metro Karlovo náměstí/3, 4, 16, 17, 24 tram.
Open 11am-10pm daily. **Map 5 G9**
Smetana may have made a lot of it, but Praguers seem
strangely indifferent to their river. Consequently, waterside
life is curiously and disappointingly absent, although this
embankment pub tries to make up for that with generally
atrocious food and a definite *On the Waterfront* vibe. Soak
up the afternoon sun and the seedy diner feel, then watch
deck hands lug beer kegs on to awaiting Vltava cruise
boats, or idly count the swans gliding by.

Malá Strana/Hradčany

Baráčnická rychta

(Patriots' Hall) Tržiště 22, Prague 1 (530 679). Metro
Malostranská/12, 22 tram. **Open** 11am-11pm daily.
Map 2 D3
Czech pubgoers moan that the tourist trade has all but killed
the pub culture – immortalised in Jan Neruda's *Prague Tales*
– that has thrived in Malá Strana since the nineteenth century. But there are still a few authentic places and this is one
of them. Just off Nerudova, Baráčnická rychta eludes the mob
behind a series of archways. Beyond, it's split into two – a
small beer hall frequented by hardcore pivo drinkers, both
students and middle-aged, and an infrequently opening
downstairs that looks like a converted gym. Obvious tourists
may catch a scowl, but in general it's a friendly place.

Blue Light

Josefská 1, Prague 1 (531 675). Metro Malostranská/
12, 22 tram. **Open** 6pm-3am daily. **Map 2 E3**
Cosy Czech-owned bar featuring occasional live jazz music,
or jazzy sounds on the stereo, and jazz posters all over the
distressed walls. It's a convivial spot to sit with a friend,
especially when there's room at the bar. Overpriced house
brews such as Staropramen, Bass and Corona somehow fail
to drive away the locals. Good selection of whiskies.

Bohemia Bagel

Újezd 16, Prague 1 (530 921). Tram 12, 22. **Open** 7am-
2am Mon-Fri; 9am-2am Sat; 9am-midnight Sun. **Map 2 E5**
Another offshoot of the Red, Hot & Blues/U Malého
Glena *(see p151)* empire, this latest addition constitutes
the sole source of bagels, bagel sandwiches and decent coffees during late hours. The boiled, baked Yiddish wonder
food comes cheap, flavoured with cinnamon, onion or egg
dough and filled with egg, salsa or mozzarella and tomato.
All but the lox and cream cheese version (the latter ingredient makes up 90 per cent of it) are up to par and downed
pleasantly enough in the blond-wood booths.

Al fresco summer fun at **U Kotvy**. *See page 145.*

Ceylonging for a cuppa?

Mysticism has been brewing in the Czech lands since nomads settled in what is now Letná Park some 250,000 years ago. During the late Renaissance, Emperor Rudolf II's court attracted every nut with a Hermetic theory in Europe. Until the advent of Prague's tearoom boom, however, it was all just a practice run.

Anyone in doubt should try slipping down a dark, stony mews by the name of Boršov, locating the address of Lubos Rychvalsky at number 2, and pulling on the weird, misshapen bell handle hanging outside it. After a tense moment, a dark-robed figure greets you, bows and admits you to the inner sanctum. All around the semi-darkness, people converse in hushed tones over shipping crates, sipping miniature earthen cups of Nepalese Yogi tea, Chinese red (no, there aren't just green and black varieties) or South American macha. This last group tends to curse quietly and wear lip blisters until they get the hang of drinking from a gourd using a white-hot metal straw.

All appear to have committed to memory the appropriate chá rituals enumerated in the Chinese Book of Tea. Never sip during heavy rain, but rather during a fine drizzle, preferably in a bamboo grove. Sip in the company of 'agreeable friends and slim concubines', never with garrulous people. Sip while seated 'under unusual rocks', not while opening mail…

What looks like a modern-day opium den is in fact **Dobrá čajovna**, the head office of a thriving local business chain with three locations in Prague, 14 nationwide and contracts to supply half as many tearooms again owned by competitors. All of which is to the chagrin of Mr Rychvalsky, who merely wanted to be the first Czech *čajovník* (tea master). The former seminary student of Jewish history and Hussitism had no idea he was planting the seeds of an imbibing revolution when he agreed in 1989 to help cater a New Year's party for the new president and borrowed Persian rugs and samovars from the Barrandov film studios. Now, having made himself an expert on the art of tea service and steeping according to half a dozen cultures worldwide, he is responsible for Prague's mellowest retreats, perfect opposite compass points from the beer halls all around. Listed below are Prague's best teahouses; *see also* **Najada**, *page 151*, and **U Vystřeleného oka**, *page 152*.

Raise then a lumpen demi to the spirit guide responsible for improvisation.

Dobrá čajovna

(The Good Teahouse) Václavské náměstí 14, Prague 1 (2423 1480). Metro Můstek/3, 9, 14, 24 tram. **Open** 10am-9pm Mon-Sat; 3-9pm Sun. **Map 3 J5**

The first beachhead in the conversion of Praguers from beer guzzlers to tea aficionados, this teahouse set up shop shortly after the Velvet Revolution with a calming, softly lit, idealised Asian fantasy setting and hasn't looked back since. Choose from dozens of Darjeelings, Assams, Algerian mint leaves and unpronounceable Chinese varieties, each prepared more-or-less faithfully to its culture, then ring the brass bell that comes with your menu to summon a serene, sandalled waiter. At the Boršov branch, pull the door ringer to get in. Dobrá čajovna also has a room at the **Roxy** (*see p204*).
Branch: Boršov 2, Prague 1 (269 9794).

Malý Buddha   •

Úvoz 44, Prague 1 (265 9916). Tram 22. **Open** 11am-10pm Tue-Sun. **Map 1 B3**

Another milestone in the evolution of Prague's now unstoppable tea culture, this refuge of incense and spring rolls has upped the ante with an actual Buddhist altar in the back. Good for a ceramic Peking dog as well, should you need one, but undeniably it's primarily a soothing, vaulted, sipping space. And one located, improbably, just up the street from Prague Castle.

U zeleného čaje

(The Green Tea) Nerudova 19, Prague 1 (5753 0027). Metro Malostranská/12, 22 tram. **Open** 11am-9.30pm daily. **Map 2 D3**

Fragrant pot pourris of dried lilac and incense, tea and biscuits and Czech children's books for sale, making for a tearoom several shades lighter than the shadow houkah-and-gong variety elsewhere around town. Well-placed on the main route up to Prague Castle, it provides a gentle break from the hawkers and scams all around.

U Zlatého kohouta

(The Golden Rooster) Michalská 3, Prague 1 (2421 3455). Metro Můstek/6, 9, 28, 22 tram. **Open** 10am-9.30pm Mon-Fri; 2-9.30pm Sat, Sun. **Map 3 H4**

Muted and shadowy by day or night, this early arrival in the Prague teahouse movement makes a point of its tolerance for herbs of all sorts, whether steeped or smoked. The friendly staff brews and sells the usual arsenal of loose teas from this homey space in a courtyard off a street leading to the otherwise madding Old Town masses.

Absinthe

Whether Prague in the 1990s bears any resemblance to Paris in the 1920s has been the subject of much debate. But those scouring for similarities are likely to find their best proof – all 170 of it – in a translucent green beverage that pours freely in Prague's cafés.

Absinthe, made from fermented wormwood and tasting like alcoholic shampoo, is illegal in most of the world. But not in the Czech Republic, where the beverage's tendency to cause unsavoury side effects like hallucination, addiction and brain disease has done nothing to thwart its popularity. In 1917, Czech distillery Hills Liqueurs began making the stuff, and by World War II it was considered such a staple that every adult got a monthly half-litre ration.

In communist times the drink was banned for being bourgeois, but in 1991 Hills Liqueurs reopened the old distillery. Hills says there is one crucial difference between its absinthe and that which pickled the great minds of Paris. Hills' is 75 per cent alcohol, while the old absinthe was 80 per cent, and that five per cent is the crucial threshold in which the concentration of wormwood becomes harmful. The jury is still out on that one.

It is a grave *faux pas* to imbibe absinthe without observing the proper ritual. Take a spoonful of sugar and dunk it in the liqueur. Light the wet sugar. A little alcohol fire will burn in the spoon, caramelising the sugar. When the sugar turns to liquid, the fire will go out. Dump the contents into the drink and stir.

Then close your eyes, take a big sip and try not to think about tomorrow.

Galerie Baraka Café

Míšeňská 2, Prague 1 (532 283). Metro Malostranská/ 12, 22 tram. **Open** 11am-midnight.
Map 2 E3
It's more likely that a promising young artist's work will show up here than at any of the lauded, but clubby, art galleries in Prague. What's more, it can be soaked up with the aid of cheap wine or draught.

Galerie Café Chiméra

Lázeňská 6, Prague 1 (no phone). Metro Malostranská/ 12, 22 tram. **Open** 11am-11pm daily.
Map 2 E3
Remarkably mellow for somewhere so near the Malá Strana tourist throng. This quiet room of plank floors, overstuffed living-room chairs and canvases by atavistic artists is best for red wine, conversation and, if you're starving, one or two of their toasted cheese sandwiches and a strudel.

La Habana

Míšeňská 12, Prague 1 (5731 5104). Metro Malostranská/12, 22 tram. **Open** 10am-1am daily.
Map 2 E3
What was once a funky but sleepy Malá Strana cellar eatery has somehow morphed into the hub of Prague's latest craze: Latin dance. Fuel up with steaks, tortillas and Havana Club rum, then get briefed on mambo and salsa by a patient instructor when the doors first open in early evening. Later, when you see the impossible moves of the competition on the dancefloor, you'll be glad you took advantage of the crash course.

Jo's Bar

Malostranské náměstí 7, Prague 1 (531 251). Metro Malostranská/12, 22 tram. **Open** 11am-2am daily.
Map 2 E3.
This narrow bar gets so crammed with backpackers that some nights there's a copy of *Let's Go Europe* on every table. You can play chess, listen to loud rock, eat passable Mexican food, take coffee refills and get liquored quick on occasional drink specials. On a bad night it's like a mawkish American college reunion, but the cramped Gothic cellar dance space (where exactly are the fire exits?), when blasting Iggy Pop tunes, can be a kick with partiers stripping off and dancing on the bar top until 4am. *See also p203.*

Malostranská Kavárna

Malostranské náměstí 5, Prague 1 (533 092). Metro Malostranská/12, 22 tram. **Open** 9am-11pm daily.
Map 2 E3
The reopening of the Malostranská, which was founded in 1874, has gone a long way to restoring Prague's all-but-dead traditional café culture. Its returning former clientele – a cross-generational mix of pensioners, shoppers and students from the neighbouring maths and physics university faculty – evidently approve of what the new owners have done to this place. An ideal rest stop for a very Central European fix of coffee and cream cake.

Scarlett O'Hara's

Mostecká 21, Prague 1 (534 793). Metro Malostranská/ 12, 22 tram. **Open** noon-2am daily.
Map 2 E3
An Irish pub brought to you by the creators of **Molly Malone's** (*see p141*). So what's the difference? Well, this one's bigger, it's got TV, it's a lot less atmospheric than its sibling, and it must be the only joint in Prague to serve draught cider. A fine place to watch sport on the box, should that be your thing.

St Nicholas Café

Tržiště 10, Prague 1 (0603 460 570). Metro Malostranská/12, 22 tram. **Open** noon-1am Mon-Fri; 4pm-1am Sat, Sun. **Map 2 D3**
An atmospheric vaulted cellar decked out with steamer trunk tables, arches embroidered in red tempera and decent Pilsner Urquell on tap, where a mellow but lively crowd gathers in the nooks for late evening conversation about nothing in particular. This is a good spot for giving the brew a rest and taking up a glass of Havana Club rum, priced for a song.

Studio A Rubín

Malostranské náměstí 9, Prague 1 (535 015). Metro Malostranská/12, 22 tram. **Open** noon-midnight daily.
Map 2 E3
Having joined the seemingly inexhaustible teahouse rage with the obligatory basement throw-pillow shrine, this former underground performance space for dissident thespians has revived the tiny stage in the next-door bar as well. Troops such as Ensemble Grotesque now put on comic guerilla performances, well keyed in to the wacky, young show-tune-loving crowd of drama students.

*'You've got how many REM albums?' Backpacker heaven at **Jo's Bar**.*

U Černého Vola

*(The Black Ox) Loretánské náměstí 1, Prague 1
(2051 3481). Tram 22.* **Open** 10am-10pm daily.
Map 1 B3
One of the best pubs in Prague. The murals make it look
like it's been here forever, but in fact the Black Ox was
built after World War II. Its superb location, right above
the Castle, made it a prime target for redevelopment in the
post-1989 building frenzy, but the rugged regulars, in
co-operation with the former Beer Party, bought it up to
ensure that all the local bearded artisans would have at least
one place they could afford to drink. The Velkopopovický
Kozel beer is pure perfection and, although the snacks are
pretty basic, they do their job of lining the stomach for a
good long session.

U Malého Glena

*(Little Glen's) Karmelitská 23, Prague 1 (535 8115).
Metro Malostranská/12, 22 tram.* **Open** 10am-2am daily.
Map 2 E4
Two-level pub that has captured a good percentage of the
Malá Strana market by appealing to both tourists and
Czech thirtysomethings, thirsty for a taste of imported
brews and live music in a casual, upscale pub atmosphere.
Upstairs is intimate without being suffocating, sporting
long wooden benches, Margaritas and light sandwich fare.
Downstairs you'll find a tiny bar that hosts jazz and reg-
gae shows (*see p200*).

U Závěsnýho kafe

*(The Hanging Mug) Radnické schody 7, Prague 1 (no
phone). Metro Malostranská/12, 22 tram.* **Open** 11am-
midnight daily. **Map 2 D3**
Considering it's on the steps leading from Nerudova to the
Castle, it's a wonder this place manages to keep prices low
and tourists at bay. Within lurk long-haired adolescents
studying for their *maturitas* and university students
downing cheap Měšťan beer. Excellent jukebox with Karel
Gott and other naff 1960s Czech pop stars, though it's often
out of order.

ZanziBar

*Lázeňská 6, Prague 1 (no phone). Metro Malostranská/
12, 22 tram.* **Open** noon-3am Mon-Sat; 5pm-3am Sun.
Map 2 E3
If you can handle the thoroughly obnoxious service (waiters easily out-pose their university-age customers), then
you can choose from ZanziBar's phenomenally well-stocked
bar and voluminous list of mixed drinks. In season, it's
shoulder-to-shoulder after 9pm or so, but it does offer fair
prospects as a pink neon pick-up joint. *See also p205.*

Further afield
Holešovice

The Globe Bookstore & Coffeehouse

*Janovského 14, Prague 7 (6671 2610/globe@login.cz/
www.ini.cz/globe). Metro Vltavská/1, 5, 8, 12, 14, 17, 25,
26 tram.* **Open** 10am-midnight daily. **Map 7 D2**
The city's original bookstore-café has been pegged from the
outset as the literary heart of post-revolutionary Prague, sad-
dled with cultivating all the budding Hemingways. The
Globe carries its burden graciously, offering up a cosy reading den and comfortable café environs to scribblers of both
novellas and postcards to Wisconsin. Home-made scones and
pasta salads, regular readings by local and foreign authors
and poets, rocket-propellant café au lait, excellent brownies
and great Sunday brunch are all part of the attraction.

Karlín

Najada

*Křižíkova 115, Prague 8 (231 4647). Metro Křižíkova/8,
24 tram.* **Open** 2-11pm Mon-Sat.
The only cyber tearoom in town with cheap Internet hook-
ups and a mostly Czech-speaking staff. They make the
most of this rather nondescript and somewhat inconveniently located place.

Vinohrady

Literární kavárna GPlusG
Čerchovská 4, Prague 2 (627 3332). Metro Jiřího z Poděbrad/11 tram. **Open** 10am-10pm daily. **Map 8 B2**
A clean, well-lit place to catch a jazz trio or the opening of a Slovak dadaist exhibition. It's all par for the course at this small press publisher-cum-coffeehouse, which stocks a wide array of Czech-language indie books and culture 'zines, plus wonderfully illustrated children's books. It's all in Czech, but with a very welcoming vibe.

Medúza
Belgická 17, Prague 2 (258 534). Metro Náměstí Míru/4, 22, 34 tram. **Open** 11am-1am Mon-Fri; noon-1am Sat, Sun. **Map 8 A3/6 M9**
A relaxed and friendly women-run café with good coffee, a limited menu of snacks and sandwiches, portraits and old photos on the walls, and classical music or old Czech cabaret songs playing in the background. Good place to chill out.

Na zvonařce
(The Bellmaker's) Šafaříkova 1, Prague 2 (2425 1990). Tram 11, 34. **Open** 11am-10pm daily. **Map 6 M10**
Known to locals as 'the pub at the end of the world', this terrace is one beery idyll in mild weather, with Bohemian duck served more or less cheerfully under the chestnut trees and plastic tables looking over the Nusle Valley. Incongruously, the indoor bar goes topless from 6-9pm on Thursdays.

Pl@neta
Vinohradská 102, Prague 3 (6731 1182). Metro Jiřího z Poděbrad/11 tram. **Open** 8am-10pm daily. **Map 8 B3**
Friendly English-speaking staff, low-priced surfing, and a minimum of coffee and libations. Like all Prague Internet cafés (except the off-the-wall **Terminal Bar**; *see p144*), it's more office than bar, but still the most relaxed around.

První Prag Country Saloon Amerika
Korunní 101, Prague 1 (2425 6131). Metro Náměstí Míru/16 tram. **Open** 11am-1am Mon-Sat. **Map 8 B3**
Somehow picked up whole from Praha, Texas and blown by dust storm into fashionable Vinohrady, this is a Czech cowboy's hoedown dream. Live country and western bands fiddle nightly while would-be Hosses and their gals crowd into hard wood seating, tuck into steaks and admire the inexplicable animal skins on the walls. Just remember that the locals take this very seriously and some risked jail for years while collecting stetsons and six-shooters. *See also p200.*

Pták Loskuták
Slezská 23, Prague 3 (2425 2481). Metro Jiřího z Poděbrad/11 tram. **Open** 2pm-2am Mon-Sat; 2pm-midnight Sun. **Map 8 C3**
Further evidence of a sad Prague social shift – the disappearance of decrepit student drinking holes. This was once a classic example, but the smudged purple and green walls have been done over in clean, bright yellows and the snarling barman have been replaced by cheery waitresses. They've decorated each table as a gewgaw collage under glass, put in pool tables and, worse still, the menu now features chicken steaks drizzled in lemon and onion soup. Where can this end?

Radost/FX Café
Bělehradská 120, Prague 2 (2425 4776). Metro I.P. Pavlova/4, 6, 11, 16, 22, 34 tram. **Open** 11.30am-6am daily. **Map 6 L8**
Back-room gallery, Sunday poetry readings, downstairs disco with free video nights on Mondays, and a street-front vegetarian café with one of the city's mainstay Sunday brunches. Radost tries to be all things to all people – and succeeds pretty well. The bulletin board is a critical link in the Prague housing and job food chain. Foreign residents may moan but can't stay away. *See also p129, p203 & p206.*

Rhythmeen
Londýnská 71, Prague 2 (251 124). Metro I.P. Pavlova/4, 6, 11, 16, 22, 34 tram. **Open** 4pm-4am daily. **Map 6 L8**
Perhaps it's sheer coincidence that the antithesis of glammy Radost is located a street away, consituting a sort of yin-yang of bars. This small, smoke-filled dive, formerly called Ješěrka, is full of teens with unnatural hair colours and improbable shoes, skipping school to down an ultra-cheap beer and joints galore. Friendly, phlegmatic and a good place to witness the decline of post-communist youth.

U Knihomola
Mánesova 79, Prague 2 (627 7768). Metro Jiřího z Poděbrad/11 tram. **Open** 10am-11pm Mon-Thur; 10am-midnight Fri, Sat; 11am-8pm Sun. **Map 8 B3**
Below the bookshop of the same name, this café serves excellent (if pricey) coffees, cakes, quiches and salads, but is just a little dodgy in the atmosphere department – too much Gypsy Kings in the background, with pretentious expat chatter over the top. Good place to sip a latte and leaf through the *Guardian* you bought upstairs. Hosts readings and art shows.

Žižkov

The Clown & Bard
Bořivojova 102, Prague 3 (279 9655). Metro Jiřího z Poděbrad/5, 9, 26 tram. **Open** 8am-1am daily. **Map 8 B2**
About as entertaining as hostel bars get, and it can be quite entertaining if you manage to come on a night when one of the undiscovered bands that regularly play here is good. Otherwise, it's strictly backpacking, backgammon, cheap brews and comparing notes on the sights. Handy if you drink yourself into needing a bed. *See also p116.*

Akropolis
Kubelíkova 27, Prague 3 (697 5491/akropol@terminal.cz/www.spinet.cz/akropolis). Metro Jiřího z Poděbrad/5, 9, 26 tram. **Open** 10am-1am Mon-Fri; 4pm-1am Sat, Sun. **Map 8 B2**
The current Prague hub of world music and its most happening concert space is also a growing labyrinth of bars. With four of them and a photo gallery at last count, the themes range from proto-*Alien* (street level and equipped with fryer-favouring kitchen) to hayseed country and western (innermost cellar). They can't build them fast enough to satisfy the demand by hip Žižkov patrons, however, who carouse late every night.

Propast
Lipanská 3, Prague 3 (9000 3371). Tram 5, 9, 26. **Open** 6pm-midnight Mon-Fri; 6pm-3am Sat, Sun. **Map 8 C1**
A particularly grotty bar when not a punk venue, featuring dirt-cheap Kozel beer, anarchist posters, ska fanzines and a crowd of international punky types. Don't be put off by the metal-barred door – inside it's a pretty friendly place. You'll probably have to pay a small cover charge.

U Vystřelenýho oka
(The Shot-Out Eye) U božích bojovníků 3, Prague 3 (627 8714). Metro Florenc, then 135 or 207 bus. **Open** 3.30pm-1am Mon-Sat. **Map 8 C1**
Beneath the ominous giant statue of General Jan Žižka (the renowned warrior whose battle injury inspired the gory name), this pub embodies the inebriated spirit of the neighbourhood. Žižkov has more pubs than any other area of Prague, but this is undoubtedly the best of the lot, and the only one that's genuinely welcoming to foreigners. A three-level outdoor beer garden serves up bargain-basement Měšťan, while indoor taps flow non-stop to a Psí Vojáci soundtrack. Upstairs is a quiet, Indian-style tearoom somewhat out of place amid the chaos, but inviting nonetheless.

Shopping & Services

Let's face it – no-one comes here to shop. But things are on the up.

By all means, try shopping in Prague. Just don't be surprised if, after hours of trudging around town, you end up tearful and desperate in Marks & Spencer, Benetton or – even worse – McDonald's. It's not that there's nothing to buy in Prague, it's just that all the best stuff is imported – most of the home-grown stuff is plain old tourist tat. The best shopping plan is to have a plan in the first place – know what you want to buy, then go buy it. It sounds ludicrously easy, but the streets are full of red-faced, over-heated tourists desperately trying to find Little Johnny a giftie from Prague in their last couple of hours before boarding the bus for the airport.

Locally produced CDs – classical in particular *(see page 192)* – are incredibly cheap and, for the most part, just as good as their Western counterparts. Czech glass, especially the plainer, modern stuff, can be a good buy. The old-fashioned, cut-glass crystal is pretty chunky and ugly, unless you're into that sort of thing. Locally produced, plain wooden toys for children are still staple gifts, as are bottles of Czech-produced spirits. When it comes to fashion, the situation is a lot better than it used to be. Prague underwent a retail boom a few years back and the floodgates opened for the Western retail giants. The trouble is, the success of outlets such as Diesel and Stefanel took all the wind out of the local competition's sails – the standard of Czech fashion shops is a bit ho-hum at best. But don't fall for the old 'We're in Central Europe, it's got to be cheaper' fallacy – the word on the street is that some of these Western fashion chains use this market to offload a lot of last season's fashion. Also, you'll see no price advantage in buying from Western outlets based here. Some stores even keep the British price tags on the clothes, and just convert from pounds into crowns at the cash till.

*Gloves-off bargaining, native-style, at **Havelská Market**. See page 155.*

Most shop assistants, at least in the centre of town, speak good English. But if you're looking to spend a lot of money on something extra special you'd be wise to bring a dictionary along with you. Anyone who speaks even a few words of Czech will find *Zlaté stránky* (Yellow Pages) invaluable. There is an English-language index in the back of the book. Otherwise turn to *The Prague Phone Book*, a limited English-language phone book on sale at bookshops in the centre.

On the services side, the desire to earn money is slowly winning out over the communist legacy of surly attitudes, sloppy work and unreasonable delays – these days the customer is at least not always wrong. And services in Prague can often be extraordinarily cheap and of high quality, as long as you're not looking for something that requires imported Western materials or technology such as computer repairs.

Unless otherwise stated, the following places do not take credit cards.

Department stores

Bílá labuť
Na Poříčí 23, Prague 1 (2481 1364/2421 1473). Metro Náměstí Republiky/3, 5, 14, 24, 26 tram. **Open** 8am-7pm Mon-Fri; 8am-6pm Sat. **Credit** AmEx, MC, V.
Map 4 M2
When it opened in 1937, Bílá labuť was the height of modernity. Today it all seems a bit of a jumble, with a pretty grotty supermarket in the basement. The new branch on Václavské náměstí is no better – nothing but ugly '80s clothes and cheap jewellery.
Branch: Václavské náměstí 59, Prague 1.

Kotva
Náměstí Republiky 8, Prague 1 (2480 1111). Metro Náměstí Republiky/5, 14, 26 tram. **Open** *department store* 9am-8pm Mon-Fri; 9am-6pm Sat; 10am-6pm Sun; *potraviny* 8am-8pm Mon-Fri; 8am-6pm Sat; 9am-6pm Sun. **Credit** AmEx, EC, MC, V. **Map 4 K3**
Ugly but well stocked. Work your way up past glossy cosmetics stalls, stationery, bed linen, fashion, sports gear, car accessories and end up with the fairly naff furniture and lighting. There's a travel agency, bureau de change and shoe repairs in the basement, next to a glossy, modern split-level supermarket. Good for gourmet chocolates and French wines – less so for fruit and vegetables and pre-packed meat. Kids will love the ramp escalator that takes the shopping carts from level to level, though.

Krone/Julius Meinl
Václavské náměstí 21, Prague 1 (2423 0477). Metro Můstek/3, 9, 14, 24 tram. **Open** *main shop* 9am-8pm Mon-Fri; 9am-7pm Sat; 10am-6pm Sun; *bread and cake shop* 8am-8pm Mon-Fri; 8am-7pm Sat; 9am-6pm Sun; *potraviny* 8am-9pm Mon-Fri; 8am-8pm Sat; 10am-6pm Sun. **Credit** MC, V. **Map 4 K5**
The best thing here is the basement grocery. You can stagger right into the metro with your purchases.

Tesco
Národní třída 26, Prague 1 (2422 7971-9). Metro Můstek or Národní třída/6, 9, 18, 22 tram. **Open** *department store* 8am-8pm Mon-Fri; 9am-6pm Sat; 10am-6pm Sun; *potraviny* 7am-8pm Mon-Fri; 8am-6pm Sat; 9am-6pm Sun. **Credit** EC, MC, V. **Map 3 H5**

This department store has weathered a few changes in recent years. Originally known as Máj, it was the pride of communist Czechoslovakia's retail industry. Soon after the revolution it was sold to the American chain K-mart, which spent a lot of money revamping the store, only to sell it on to Tesco in 1996. Currently it has a good mix of Czech and Western products and a popular supermarket that stocks American peanut butter, decent baked beans and British biscuits.

Malls

A couple of years back, Prague underwent a mammoth retail boom that spawned a string of shiny, new malls. The economy then went into tail-spin, imported goods became more expensive and the retail industry took a hit. Today, many of these new developments are still half empty and eerily quiet.

Černá růže (The Black Rose)
Na příkopě 12, Prague 1 (no phone). Metro Můstek/3, 9, 14, 24 tram. **Open** 10am-6pm Mon-Fri.
Map 4 K4
A teensy-weeny passage without much inside it yet except gleaming new interiors, a lonely security guard, an Italian designer clothes boutique and entrances to the adjoining **Moser** crystal shop (*see p157*) and good old TGI Friday's.

Darex
Václavské náměstí 11, Prague 1 (2162 9567). Metro Můstek/3, 9, 14, 24 tram. **Open** 10am-8pm Mon-Fri; 10am-6pm Sat; noon-6pm Sun. **Credit** AmEx, EC, MC, V.
Map 3 J5
A horribly crowded and claustrophobic mall with not much in the way of big name stores – it's all just Nike, sunglasses, perfume and bad fashion. There's quite a good lingerie shop on the top floor.

Koruna Palace
Václavské náměstí 1, Prague 1 (2421 9526). Metro Můstek/3, 9, 14, 24 tram. **Open** 9am-8pm Mon-Sat. **Credit** AmEx, EC, MC, V. **Map 3 J4**
Glitzy but not exactly inspiring. Dunkin' Donuts, overpriced shoes and a massive music shop in the basement – **Bontonland Megastore** (*see p168*) with the best selection of Czech recordings, both classic and pop, in Prague. Avoid the overpriced coffeeshop in the mall foyer: there are far better (and cheaper) places for a quick pitstop in the centre.

Myslbek Center
Na příkopě 19/21, Prague 1 (2423 9550). Metro Můstek/3, 9, 14, 24 tram. **Open** 8.30am-8.30pm daily.
Map 4 K4
You could be forgiven for thinking you're back in Britain. Marks & Spencer, Next, Tie Rack, Clinique, Mothercare, Kookaï and Vision Express fill the swankiest and certainly most crowded mall of all. For an interesting lesson in sensitive modern architecture, check out the back face of the mall in comparison with the surrounding Ovocný trh square outside.

Pavilon
Vinohradská 50, Prague 2 (2423 3125). Metro Náměstí Míru/11 tram. **Open** 9.30am-9pm Mon-Sat; noon-6pm Sun. **Credit** AmEx, EC, MC, V. **Map 8 A3**
Prague's first yuppie mall is a bit off the beaten track. There's a good supermarket in the basement, plus the usual big name shops upstairs: Levi's, Christian Dior, Benetton, Ray-Ban, Nina Ricci, etc.

Tesco – the biggest department store chain in the Czech Republic. No joke.

Markets

If you're looking for one of those fabled flea markets jam-packed with '50s-era biker jackets and old vinyl, try Berlin. Or better yet, try some of the *bazars* listed below under **Antiques**. Prague outdoor markets are invariably disappointing fruit 'n' veg affairs. Some special Christmas and Easter markets spring up along the main tourist routes seasonally. If you're lucky enough to catch one of the Christmas markets in Old Town Square, Václavské náměstí or Náměstí Republiky, warm yourself with a glass of steaming mulled wine – *svařené víno* or *svařák* – while you browse.

Havelská Market

Havelská, Prague 1 (no phone). Metro Můstek or Národní třída/6, 9, 18, 22 tram. **Open** 7.30am-6pm Mon-Fri; 8.30am-6pm Sat, Sun. **Map 3 J4**
Officially known as Staré Město Market, but universally referred to by its location, this is probably the best market in town for both greens and a taste of daily Bohemian life. Fresh fruit and vegetables are crammed alongside wooden toys, puppets, tourist trinkets and bad art. Good for gifts, but watch your purse. Havelská has recently become a prime pickpocket hunting ground. Not a bad place to stop for a quick bite – check out the cheap falafel and Japanese food places on the same street. Flowers are a tremendous bargain as well but just be sure to hit it in the morning, before the trinket hawkers take over three-quarters of the stalls.

Karlovo náměstí Market

Karlovo náměstí (no phone). Metro Karlovo náměstí/3, 4, 6, 14, 16, 18, 22, 24, 34 tram. **Open** 8am-6pm Mon-Fri. **Map 5 H8**
Cheap fruit and vegetables, overpriced second-hand clothes and nasty perfume. Don't bother unless you're passing.

Market at the Fountain

Národní třída (no phone). Metro Národní třída/6, 9, 18, 22 tram. **Open** 7.30am-7pm daily. **Map 3 H5**
Excellent fruit and vegetable market just outside Tesco – usually cheaper, too.

Prague Market

(Pražská tržnice) Bubenské nábřeži 306, Prague 7 (800 592). Metro Vltavská/1, 3, 14 tram. **Open** 8am-6pm Mon-Fri; 8am-2pm Sat. **Map 7 E3**
Nothing much here but bruised fruits, bad quality clothes, cheap cigarettes and microwave ovens. Avoid the morning granny-rush at all costs.

Antiques

There may be few true antique shops in Prague, but there are myriad junk shops, selling everything from old irons and typewriters to prints by Alfons Mucha. If an antiques shop is on a main tourist route, then you can be fairly sure that the prices are aimed at foreigners. For cheaper and more unusual items, seek out *bazar* stores, which are like a better class of junk shop. There are a few listed here, but many more can be found in the *Zlaté stránky* (Yellow Pages). Prague also has some wonderful antiquarian bookshops (*see page 158*).

Alma

Valentinská 7, Prague 1 (232 5865). Metro Staroměstská/17, 18 tram. **Open** 10am-6pm daily. **Credit** EC, MC, V. **Map 3 H3**
Classy antiques shop with plenty of unchipped porcelain and clean lace. A few interesting pieces of vintage clothing, including several full-dress traditional Czech costumes – if your budget can stretch that far.

Antique

*Kaprova 12, Prague 1 (232 9003). Metro Staroměstská/
17, 18 tram.* **Open** 10am-1pm, 2-6pm, Mon-Sat; 10am-
3pm Sun. **Credit** DC, EC, MC, V. **Map 3 G3**
Expensive but rewarding. Check out the antique art deco
watches – they're pretty stylish and affordable.

Antique Anderle

*Václavské náměstí 17, Prague 1 (2400 9166). Metro
Můstek/3, 9, 14, 24 tram.* **Open** 10am-7pm Mon-Sat;
10am-4pm Sun. **Credit** AmEx, DC, EC, MC, V. **Map 3 J5**
Super-expensive antique store with the best selection of
above-par art and Russian icons (with export certificates)
in town. For serious collectors only.

Art Deco

*Michalská 21, Prague 1 (261 367). Metro
Staroměstská/6, 9, 18, 22 tram.* **Open** 2-7pm Mon-Fri.
Credit AmEx, EC, MC, V. **Map 3 H4**
A tribute to a golden era when Prague was the fashion center of the East. Vintage 1920-40s clothes, beaded hats and
costume jewellery at fair prices. Check out the women's magazines for an interesting take on pre-war fashion. Nothing
here is dirt cheap, but still reasonable by Western standards.

Bazar nábytku

*Libeňský ostrov, Prague 8 (684 3070). Metro
Palmovka/1, 3, 12, 14 tram.* **Open** *summer* 9am-5pm
Mon-Thur; 9am-3pm Fri; *winter* 8am-5pm Mon; Wed
8am-6pm Thur; 8am-3pm Fri; 9am-1pm Sat.
There's little here of real value, but good for the odd
wardrobe or sofa for first-time home-makers. Not much
you'd want to lug back home with you, though.
Branches: Bělehradská 20, Prague 4; Moskevská 1,
Prague 10.

Jan Huněk Starožitnosti

*Pařížská 1, Prague 1 (232 3604). Metro
Staroměstská/17, 18 tram.* **Open** 10am-6pm daily.
Credit AmEx, DC, EC, MC, V. **Map 3 H3**
Exquisite and expensive Czech glass from the eighteenth
century to the 1930s. For true collectors only.
Branch: Husitská 31, Prague 1.

Rudolf Špičák Vetešnictví

*Ostrovní 26, Prague 1 (297 919). Metro Národní třída/
6, 9, 18, 22 tram.* **Open** 10am-5pm Mon-Fri.
Map 5 H6
A great junk shop in a damp basement. Among the old telephones, bashed-in violins and faded furniture you can find
real communist-era magazines and postcards, as well as
the odd Stalin badge.

Vinohradský bazárek

*Mánesova 64, Prague 2 (2224 3759). Metro Jiřího z
Poděbrad/11 tram.* **Open** 10am-noon, 1-6pm, Mon-Fri.
Map 8 B3
A good selection of high-class knick-knacks such as moth-
er-of-pearl opera glasses and gentlemen's vanity cases.
Reasonable prices.

Bookshops & newsagents

English-language books in Prague are reasonably
priced by Western standards, outrageous by local
standards. If you're on a budget and none too
picky, try one of the *antikvariáty* listed below.
Although most of the bookshops listed can order
new books specially, be prepared for a three- to
five-week wait – hardly practicable if you're only
here for a week.

Academia

*Václavské náměstí 34, Prague 1 (2422 3511/2422
3512). Metro Můstek.* **Open** 9am-8pm Mon-Fri; 10am-
8pm Sat, Sun. **Map 4 K5**
Newly opened in the fabulously restored Wiehl building,
this friendly two-storey bookstore will (hopefully) define
the future of Prague retail. Though predominantly Czech,
Academia also stocks a wealth of English-language history, art and language texts, plus coffee-table books and a
wide array of culture magazines and journals with some
English content. Clean, well-lit place for a quiet espresso in
the Literární café upstairs.

Crystal balls?

Glassmaking in Bohemia dates back to the thirteenth century when craftsmen started blowing
glass in monastery workshops. By 1936 the
country's craftsmen were producing ten per
cent of the world's glass. Success was due to
plentiful supplies of quartz and the vast beech
forests of North Bohemia, which supplied the
potash for the mix, and heat for the kilns.

This tradition was brought to a standstill
after World War II, when the Sudeten Germans,
who possessed much of the technical and commercial know-how, were expelled and the industry was nationalised. Now factories are being
privatised and modernised, while designers are
slowly revamping the products. Most of the
stuff aimed at the tourist market is still pretty
unimaginative, though. For a potted history of
Czech glassmaking and a list of shops, muse-

ums and producers, buy *A Guide to Czech and
Slovak Glass* by Diane E Foulds from **Moser** or
a large bookshop.

Erpet

*Staroměstské náměstí 26, Prague 1 (2422 9755/2421
5257). Metro Staroměstská.* **Open** 10am-8pm daily.
Credit AmEx, DC, EC, MC, V. **Map 3 J3**
Not a whole lot of bargains here but an extremely wide
and varied selection.

Moser

*Na příkopě 12, Prague 1 (2421 1293-4). Metro
Můstek/3, 9, 14, 24 tram.* **Open** 9am-7pm Mon-Fri;
9am-4pm Sat. **Credit** AmEx, DC, EC, MC, V. **Map 4 K4**
Moser glass, made in Karlovy Vary since 1857, claims to
be the 'King of Glass' and the 'Glass of Kings'. The lead-
free formula produces a crystal of great brilliance and
durability. Being the only Czech crystal that's truly worth
seeking out, naturally it is very expensive indeed. You
could content yourself with a tiny ashtray for over 500 Kč.

Anagram Bookshop

Týn 4, Prague 1 (2489 5737/fax 2489 5738/anagram@ terminal.cz). Metro Náměstí Republiky/5, 14, 26 tram. **Open** 9.30am-7.30pm Mon-Sat; 10am-6pm Sun. **Credit** DC, EC, MC, V. **Map 3 J3**
This new, American-owned bookshop has a great second-hand English-language rack, with an emphasis on health, fitness, philosophy, self-help and alternative medicine.

Big Ben Bookshop

Malá Štupartská 5, Prague 1 (231 8021/books@ bigbenbookshop.com). Metro Náměstí Republiky/5, 14, 26 tram. **Open** 9am-7pm Mon-Fri; 10am-6pm Sat, Sun. **Credit** AmEx, DC, EC, MC, V. **Map 3 J3**
This extremely friendly bookshop has the standard books on Prague, several shelves of bestsellers and a fair selection of English-language newspapers and magazines.
Branch: British Council, Národní 10, Prague 1.

The Globe Bookstore

Janovského 14, Prague 7 (6671 2610/www.ini.cz/glo/ globe@login.cz). Metro Vltavská/1, 5, 8, 12, 17, 25, 26 tram. **Open** 10am-midnight daily. **Credit** V. **Map 7 D2**
The Globe is something of an institution in certain expat circles, and is always teeming with travellers, journalists, budding poets and English-language teachers perusing the large selection of fiction, periodicals and second-hand paperbacks. Popular café attached (*see p151*).

Knihkupectví Jan Kanzelsberger

Václavské náměstí 42, Prague 1 (2421 7335). Metro Můstek/3, 9, 14, 24 tram. **Open** 8am-7pm Mon-Sat; 9am-7pm Sun. **Credit** AmEx, EC, MC, V. **Map 4 K5**
Very central, with more coffee-table books of Prague, a reasonably good selection of Czech fiction in translation and an odd assortment of guidebooks.

Bibliophile heaven: **The Globe Bookstore.**

Knihkupectví Na Můstku

Na příkopě 3, Prague 1 (2421 6383). Metro Můstek/3, 9, 14, 24 tram. **Open** 8.30am-7pm Mon-Fri; 9.30am-6pm Sat, Sun. **Credit** DC, MC, V. **Map 3 J4**
Apart from the usual Prague travel guides, calendars and Czech-English dictionaries, there is a respectable number of English-language novels and translated Czech literature here. Very centrally located, right at the bottom of Wenceslas Square.

Knihkupectví U Černé Matky Boží

Celetná 34, Prague 1 (2421 1155). Metro Náměstí Republiky/5, 14, 26 tram. **Open** 9am-8pm Mon-Sat; 10am-8pm Sun. **Credit** AmEx, EC, MC, V.
Map 4 K3
It's worth tracking down this arty bookshop just to gaze up at the building's wonderful cubist exterior (House of the Black Madonna; *see p39*). The bookshop itself is good for gift-hunting, with hundreds of art prints, T-shirts, translated Czech authors and coffee-table books and calendars.

Mega Books

Rostovská 4, Prague 10 (7174 0026/megabook@ bohem-net.cz). Tram 4, 6, 7, 22, 24, 34. **Open** 8am-5pm Mon-Thur; 8am-3pm Fri. **Credit** EC, MC.
Mega Books is a mecca for English-language teachers seeking inspiration from perhaps the best selection of teaching resource and language exercise books on offer anywhere. You'll never find it without a map of the city.

Trafika Můstek

Václavské náměstí, Prague 1 (no phone). Metro Můstek/3, 9, 14, 24 tram. **Open** 9am-8pm daily.
Map 3 J5
These two green magazine stands at the bottom of Wenceslas Square stock everything from *Forbes* to *Film Threat*. When it comes to Western periodicals, if you can't find it here, then you can't find it in Prague.

U Knihomola

Mánesova 79, Prague 2 (627 7770). Metro Jiřího z Poděbrad/11 tram. **Open** 10am-11pm Mon-Thur; 10am-midnight Fri, Sat; 11am-8pm Sun. **Credit** AmEx, EC, MC, V. **Map 8 B3**
An impressive selection of Czech and European literature in English translation, an outstanding art book section, some history and new age, a comprehensive range of guidebooks, newspapers, magazines, and a desultory few shelves of 'light reading'. The basement Unamuno Café exhibits works of art and serves gourmet chocolate cakes and good French wines, complete with soft acoustic guitar serenades. *See also p152.*

Old books & prints

Prague's second-hand bookshops, which also sell prints, maps and graphics, are known as *antikvariáty*. If you're looking for a one-of-a-kind Prague souvenir, you couldn't do better than a 1970s-era Prague coffee-table book or a dirt-cheap print by a unknown Czech artist. *Antikvariáty* are also the best places to find bargain-priced second-hand novels in English.

Ad Plus

Dlážděná 7, Prague 1 (262 980). Metro Náměstí Republiky/3, 5, 9, 14, 24, 26 tram. **Open** 9am-6pm Mon-Fri; 10am-3pm Sat. **Map 4 L4**
More a used bookstore than a collectors' shop, this out-of-the-way *antikvariát* offers little for those seeking true rarities, but has old postcards, songbooks, and prints from the 1920s and 1930s. A few old English-language books, too.

After an old map or book? Try an antikvariát.

This second-hand bookshop specialises in technical literature (only in Czech, of course), but it also has quite a good selection of prints and, if you're interested, copious quantities of English-language books on business and management matters.

Makovský & Gregor

Kaprova 9, Prague 1 (232 8335). Metro Staroměstská/ 17, 18 tram. **Open** 9am-7pm Mon-Fri; 10am-6pm Sat. **Credit** AmEx, DC, EC, MC, V. **Map 3 H3**

Dusty, crowded and dimly lit – this store is everything a good *antikvariát* should be. Makovský & Gregor is jam-packed with old books, prints, engravings and coffee-table picture books dating back to the 1950s. There's also a reasonable range of second-hand novels in English from as little as 30 Kč.

Computers

Apple Macintosh was slow to enter the Czech market, and the choice of computers on offer today still isn't the best. You'll be able to find PC outlets on every street corner, and the list of suppliers in the *Zláté stránky* (Yellow Pages) is endless. Pray that your computer doesn't malfunction in Prague. But if it does, we list below a few places to get it fixed.

Global Ameritech

Pod Kavalírkou 18, Prague 5 (2421 1544). Tram 4, 7, 9. **Open** 8am-4pm Mon-Fri.

An authorised repairer for IBM and Compaq computers, and the only repair centre in the country that can cope with hand-held Intermec computers. Repairs usually take less than a week.

Branch: Rytířská 10, Prague 1 (2421 2167/2421 0493).

MacSource

Krkonošská 2, Prague 2 (627 2224). Metro Jiřího z Poděbrad/11 tram. **Open** 9am-5pm Mon-Fri. **Credit** AmEx, MC, V. **Map 8 B2**

Probably the largest and best Mac outlet. If you need your Macintosh fixed in Prague, then, unfortunately, you have to come here. MacSource has improved its service admirably over the last couple of years, but few consultants speak English. Shipping in special replacement components can take up to one month. Simple repairs can take half a day. For an extra fee, MacSource consultants will come to your home.

Maximac

Jindřišská 7, Prague 1 (263 684). Metro Můstek/ 3, 9, 14, 24 tram. **Open** 9.30am-6pm Mon-Fri. **Map 4 K5**

Central Mac repair outfit, with a fair number of English-speaking consultants.

Signet

Hanusova 9, Prague 4 (6121 8690-2). Metro Pankrác. **Open** 8.30am-5pm Mon-Fri.

Repairs Macs and all kinds of PCs in anything from a few minutes to a few months.

Spilka & Group

Naskové 1, Prague 5 (5731 3183/5731 3184). Metro Anděl, then bus 123. **Open** 8.30am-6pm Mon-Fri.

Licensed sales and repairs of Brother and Hewlett Packard computers as well as Toshiba notebooks, UPS boxes, Eizo monitors and a whole range of printers and fax machines. Once again, importing special spare parts can take up to a month, but this centre tries hard to fix your computer so you can use it while waiting for the component.

Antikvariát Galerie Můstek

28. října 13, Prague 1 (268 058). Metro Můstek/6, 9, 18, 22 tram. **Open** 10am-1pm, 2-6pm, Mon-Fri; 10am-1pm Sat. **Credit** AmEx, DC, EC, MC, V. **Map 5 H6**

A discriminating *antikvariát* with fine antiquarian books (nineteenth-century natural history especially) and a steady stream of key works on Czech art.

Antikvariát Kant

Opatovická 26, Prague 1 (2491 6376). Metro Národní třída/6, 9, 18, 22 tram. **Open** 10am-6pm Mon-Fri; 10am-3pm Sat. **Map 3 J3**

An eclectic mix of shoddy and superb prints and dust-encrusted books. There's an impressive selection of second-hand titles in English covering everything from *Jaws* to Germaine Greer.

Antikvariát Karel Křenek

Celetná 31, Prague 1 (232 2919). Náměstí Republiky/5, 14, 26 tram. **Open** 10am-6pm Mon-Fri; 10am-2pm Sat. **Credit** AmEx, DC, MC, V. **Map 3 J3**

The nineteenth- and twentieth-century graphic work is excellent, but prices have spiralled of late. If you're skint, go for the book plates; if adventurous, ask for the erotica.

Antikvariát Pařížská

Pařížská 8, Prague 1 (232 1442). Metro Staroměstská/ 17, 18 tram. **Open** 10am-6pm daily. **Credit** AmEx, MC, V. **Map 3 H3**

Gorgeous prints and maps exclusively from the sixteenth to nineteenth centuries.

Eva Kozáková

Myslíkova 10, Prague 1 (294 402). Metro Karlovo Náměstí/17 tram. **Open** 9am-6pm Mon-Fri; 10am-2pm Sat. **Credit** AmEx, MC, V. **Map 5 H7**

*Too long in **Laundry Kings** can have a serious effect on your mental health.*

Cosmetics & perfumes

In addition to the places listed below, most of the department stores above have big-name cosmetic booths on their ground floors.

Body Basics
Pavilon, Vinohradská 50, Prague 2 (2423 3125 ext 105). Metro Náměstí Miru/11 tram. **Open** 9.30am-9pm Mon-Sat; noon-6pm Sun. **Credit** AmEx, EC, MC, V. **Map 8 A3**
This shameless rip-off of the Body Shop has affordable, pleasant-smelling cosmetics that are guaranteed to be not tested on animals.
Branches: Bílá labuť, Na Poříčí 23, Prague 1; Koruna Palace, Václavské náměstí 1, Prague 1; Ovocný trh, Prague 1; Myslbek Center, Na příkopě 19/21, Prague 1.

Botanicus
Týn 1049, Prague 1 (2489 5446). Metro Náměstí Republiky/5, 14, 26 tram. **Open** 10am-8pm daily. **Credit** AmEx, EC, MC, V.
Map 3 J3
An all-Czech hippy version of the Body Shop. Tons of soaps, shampoos, body lotions and creams infused with herbs and other natural ingredients, all lovingly wrapped in brown paper.

Christian Dior
Pařížská 7, Prague 1 (232 6229/232 7382). Metro Staroměstská/17, 18 tram. **Open** 10am-6pm Mon-Fri; 10am-3pm Sat. **Credit** AmEx, DC, MC, V.
Map 3 H3
Branch: Národní třída 17, Prague 1.

Clinique
Myslbek Center, Na příkopě 19/21, Prague 1 (2423 3562). Metro Můstek/3, 9, 14, 24 tram. **Open** 9.30am-8pm; 9.30am-7pm Sat; noon-6pm Sun. **Credit** AmEx, EC, MC, V. **Map 4 K4**

Elizabeth Arden
Rybná 2, Prague 1 (232 5471). Metro Náměstí Republiky/5, 14, 26 tram. **Open** 9.30am-6.30pm Mon-Fri; 10am-2pm Sat. **Credit** AmEx, DC, MC, V. **Map 4 K2**

Nina Ricci
Pařížská 4, Prague 1 (2481 0905). Metro Staroměstská/17, 18 tram. **Open** 10am-6pm Mon-Fri. **Credit** AmEx, V. **Map 3 H3**

Parfumerie Lancôme
Jungmannovo náměstí 20, Prague 1 (2421 7189). Metro Můstek/6, 9, 18, 22 tram. **Open** 9am-7pm Mon-Fri; 10am-2pm Sat. **Credit** AmEx, EC, MC, V. **Map 3 J5**

Yves Rocher
Václavské náměstí 47, Prague 1 (2162 5570-72). Metro Můstek/3, 9, 14, 24 tram. **Open** 8.30am-7pm Mon-Fri; 9am-6pm Sun. **Credit** AmEx, DC, EC, MC, V. **Map 4 K5**
Branch: Vodičkova 15, Prague 1.

Dry cleaners & launderettes

All three launderettes in Prague charge roughly the same for a wash and a dry, so your choice depends more on location than anything else.

9

Service washes are quite good value and usually take two days. Dry cleaners in Prague rarely offer guarantees, so it's probably best to wait until you get home to dry clean your grandmother's silk cocktail dress.

Dája
V celnici, Prague 1 (2421 2787). Metro Náměstí Republiky/5, 14, 26 tram. **Open** 7am-7pm Mon-Fri; 8am-1pm Sat. **Map 4 L3**
Alterations and dry cleaning.

Golden Clean
Dlouhá 27, Prague 1 (no phone). Metro Náměstí Republiky/5, 14, 26 tram. **Open** 8am-8pm daily. **Map 3 J2**
Claims to use the most modern technology to dry clean everything from furs and leathers to upholstery.

Laundry Kings
Dejvická 16, Prague 6 (312 3743). Metro Hradčanská/2, 20, 25, 26 tram. **Open** 6am-10pm Mon-Fri; 8am-10pm Sat, Sun.
Self and service washes as well as dry cleaning. CNN satellite news will keep to informed while you wait. Scouring the public notice board is a great way to hook up with a travelling partner or a future flatmate, or to sell a bike or find a guitar teacher.

Laundryland
Londýnská 71, Prague 2 (251 124). Metro I.P. Pavlova. **Open** 8am-10pm daily. **Map 6 M9**
Self and full service laundromat and dry cleaning. There's also a pretty handy alteration service. Friendly atmosphere. **Branch:** Pavilon, Vinohradská 50, Prague 2.

Prague Laundromat
Korunní 14, Prague 2 (255 541). Metro Náměstí Míru/16 tram. **Open** 8am-8pm daily. **Map 8 A3**
Self and service washes and dry cleaning.

Fashion
General

Adelaide
Kaprova 8, Prague 1 (232 0972). Metro Staroměstská/17, 18 tram. **Open** 10am-7pm daily. **Credit** AmEx, MC, V. **Map 3 H3**
Hand-painted clothes in rainbow hues. Everything here is a mite hippy, bordering on twee, but unusual, nevertheless. The prices are more than fair, and anyway, you might just dig that pink, suede mini-skirt with a hand-painted pussycat on the front.

Black Market
Petrské náměstí 1, Prague 1 (231 7033). Metro Náměstí Republiky/3, 5, 14, 24, 26 tram. **Open** noon-7pm Mon-Fri; 10am-5pm Sat. **Map 4 L2**
Itsy-bitsy cotton tops and lycra dresses, catering to skinny-girl club queens. The prices are higher than they might be elsewhere in town, but it is the only place in Prague to get silver lamé hot pants. There's usually a bargain rack of cords, jeans and thrift store-style woollies at the back of the shop.

The Gap/Banana Republic
V Kolkovně 6, Prague 1 (231 7817). Metro Staroměstská. **Open** 10.30am-7pm Mon-Fri; 11am-6pm Sat. **Credit** AmEx, DC, EC, MC, V. **Map 3 J2**
A two-in-one store in the backstreets of the Old Town. Everything you expect, including English-speaking staff.

Gianni Versace
Celetná 7, Prague 1 (231 8851). Metro Staroměstská/5, 14, 26 tram. **Open** 10.30am-7pm Mon-Sat. **Credit** AmEx, DC, MC, V. **Map 3 J3**
It's here if you can afford it. **Branch:** U Prašné brány 3, Prague 1.

Kooka¨i
Myslbek Center, Ovocný trh 8, Prague 1 (2423 5734). Metro Můstek/3, 9, 14, 24 tram. **Open** 10am-7pm Mon-Sat; noon-6pm Sun. **Map 4 K4**
Most Czech girls go to Kooka¨i to have a hearty laugh at the prices.

Nostalgie
Jakubská 8, Prague 1 (232 8030). Metro Náměstí Republiky/5, 14, 26 tram. **Open** 10.30am-6.30pm Mon-Sat. **Credit** AmEx, EC, MC, V. **Map 4 K4**
Flowing linen clothes in neutral shades designed by Marie Fleischmannová. Everything in the store can be altered to fit for a nominal fee. **Branch:** Husova 8, Prague 1.

Original Móda
Jilská 18 (entrance also at Michalská 19) (2421 4626). Metro Můstek. **Open** 11am-6pm Mon-Fri. **Credit** AmEx, EC, MC, V. **Map 3 H4**
Handmade, elegant, classic garments, ceramics and gifts by a collective of a dozen Czech artists and designers. For genuine and stylish Prague crafts, you'll not find better than the painted silk dresses, hand-stained soufflé dishes and button-eyed children's toys.

Piano Boutiques
Národní třída 37, Prague 1 (2421 3282). Metro Národní třída/6, 9, 18, 22 tram. **Open** 10am-7pm Mon-Fri, 11am-3pm Sat. **Credit** AmEx, DC, MC, V. **Map 3 H5**
Czech-designed business wear. Reasonable prices but a bit hit-or-miss on quality. **Branch:** Vinohradská 47, Prague 2.

Red or Dead
Myslíkova 31, Prague 1 (2491 9219). Metro Karlovo náměstí/3, 6, 14, 17, 18, 22, 24 tram. **Open** 10am-7pm Mon-Fri; 10am-2pm Sat. **Credit** AmEx, EC, MC, V. **Map 5 H7**
Super-trendy British fashion wear. There's no price advantage whatsoever in buying designer clubwear in Prague.

Sanu Babu
Michalská 22, Prague 1 (216 32401). Metro Můstek/6, 9, 18, 22 tram. **Open** 11am-7.30pm Mon-Sat; noon-7pm Sun. **Credit** AmEx, MC, V. **Map 3 H4**
The waft of incense and mystical wailings betrays that you've entered ethnically inspired clothes and accessories. It's not all new agey stuff, though – the linen shirts are eminently desirable and (by Western standards) attractively priced. **Branches:** Karlova 22, Prague 1; V kolkovně 3, Prague 1.

Senior Bazar
Senovážné náměstí 18, Prague 1 (2423 5068). Metro Náměstí Republiky/3, 5, 9, 14, 24, 26 tram. **Open** 8.30am-4pm Mon-Thur; 8.30am-2pm Fri. **Map 4 L4**
A veritable Prague institution, and the only second-hand clothes shop worth visiting. There are hundreds of second-hand shops in Prague, but most only sell ugly 1980s clothes bought in bulk from Germany. Senior Bazar gets its stock straight from Prague's most stylish citizens – the octogenarians. Pick up a handmade 1950s summer dress or leather coat for peanuts. But get there in the morning. All the *Elle* and *Cosmopolitan* girls who work nearby do a clean sweep on their lunchbreaks. **Branch:** Karolíny Světlé 18, Prague 1.

Children

Creation Stummer
Jungmannova 18, Prague 1 (2422 8668). Metro Národní třída/3, 9, 14, 24 tram. **Open** 9am-6pm Mon-Fri; 9am-noon Sat. **Map 3 J5**
An Austrian 'baby boutique' with its own brand. Most of the stock is for babies and toddlers up to five years.

Lego Kids Wear & Toys
Malá Štupartská 3, Prague 1 (2482 8054). Metro Náměstí Republiky/5, 14, 26 tram. **Open** 11am-7pm Mon-Fri; 10am-4pm Sat. **Credit** AmEx, DC, EC, MC, V. **Map 3 J3**
Brightly coloured Lego trademarked clothes for kids. The idea, presumably, is that mum ends up buying baby a Lego set, too. We'll see if this marketing idea pans out.

Mothercare
Myslbek Center, Na příkopě 19/21, Prague 1 (2423 9550). Metro Můstek/3, 9, 14, 24 tram. **Open** 9.30am-7pm Mon-Fri; 9am-6pm Sat; 11am-6pm Sun. **Credit** AmEx, EC, MC, V. **Map 4 K4**
The Empire strikes back with British babywear and toys on the top floor of the Myslbek shopping mall. For all ages from infants to early adolescents.

Pinito
Křemencova 17, Prague 1 (0602 376 133). Metro Národní třída/6, 9, 18, 22 tram. **Open** 10am-6pm Mon-Fri; 9am-3pm Sat. **Map 5 H6**
'All-grown-up' kiddywear from Spain – suits and dicky bows abound.

Zerodocci of Benetton
Na příkopě 16, Prague 1 (2421 1146). Metro Můstek/3, 9, 14, 24 tram. **Open** 9.30am-7pm Mon-Fri; Sat 9.30am-6pm. **Credit** AmEx, EC, MC, V. **Map 3 J4**
Benetton for children and babies.

Jewellery & accessories

Granát
Dlouhá 30, Prague 1 (231 5612). Metro Náměstí Republiky/5, 14, 26 tram. **Open** 10am-6pm Mon-Fri; 10am-1pm Sat. **Credit** AmEx, DC, EC, MC, V. **Map 3 J2**
Czech garnets, found in the Vltava basin south of Prague, are considered the finest in the world. They've been used since the Middle Ages, but took off as an industry in the nineteenth century. Since then, garnet jewellery has been a perennial favourite with traditionally minded Czechs. Under communism, its production was confined to the Granát co-operative in Turnov, whose wares are displayed here.

Helena Fejková
Lucerna passage, Štěpánská 61, Prague 1 (2421 1514). Metro Můstek/3, 9, 14, 24 tram. **Open** 10am-8pm Mon-Sat. **Credit** AmEx, DC, EC, MC, V. **Map 6 K6**
Look past the racks of so-so Czech-designed clothes and you'll find the great designer jewellery section at the back of the store. Getting up to the shop is tricky, though. Once you're in Lucerna Passage, look up, spot the shop, and then make for the cinema staircase. Turn right on the landing, and you're in. There's also a nice, quiet coffee shop from which you can gaze down at the shoppers below.

Mappin & Webb
Karlova 27 (entrance on Malé náměstí), Prague 1 (2423 7075). Metro Staroměstská/17, 18 tram. **Open** 10am-6.30pm Mon-Sat; 10am-5pm Sun. **Credit** AmEx, DC, EC, MC, V. **Map 3 H4**
It seems a little odd to buy British crystal in the Czech Republic, but the jewellery and watches are both fabulous and fabulously expensive.

Lingerie

Chez Parisienne
Pařížská 8, Prague 1 (231 9689). Metro Staroměstská/17, 18 tram. **Open** 10am-7pm Mon-Fri; 10am-6pm Sat. **Credit** AmEx, DC, EC, MC, V. **Map 3 H3**
High quality boxers, lingerie, T-shirts and pajamas at sky-high prices. Also, inexplicably, sells vintage Triumph motorcycles.

Jane
Darex, Václavské náměstí 11, Prague 1 (no phone). Metro Můstek/3, 9, 14, 24 tram. **Open** 9am-8pm Mon-Fri; 10am-6pm Sat, Sun. **Map 3 J5**
Small and sensible. You can really sweep up on the big name bras at one of the regular sales.

Judita
Jakubská 8, Prague 1 (9000 4847). Metro Náměstí Republiky/5, 14, 26 tram. **Open** 10am-6.30pm Mon-Fri; 11am-4pm Sat. **Map 4 K3**
All the major brands of bras, undies and tights. The nice, motherly ladies with tape measures are glad to help out, but they don't speak English. One changing room available.

Marks & Spencer
Myslbek Center, Na příkopě 19/21 (2423 5735). Metro Můstek/3, 9, 14, 24 tram. **Open** 9am-8pm Mon-Fri; 9am-7pm Sat; 11am-6pm Sun. **Credit** DC, EC, MC, V. **Map 4 K4**
Can M&S become as indispensable a feature of Czech women's undies drawers as they are to the Brits? Probably.

Palmers
Královodvorská 7, Prague 1 (231 6915). Metro Náměstí Republiky/5, 14, 26 tram. **Open** 9am-6pm Mon-Fri; 10am-3pm Sat. **Credit** AmEx, MC, V. **Map 4 K3**
An Austrian company selling its own brand plus swimwear. **Branch:** Billa, Vysočanská 20, Prague 9.

Shoes & leather goods

Adidas
Na Poříčí 42, Prague 1 (232 5168). Metro Florenc/3, 24 tram. **Open** 9am-7pm Mon-Fri; 9am-3pm Sat. **Credit** AmEx, MC, V. **Map 4 M2**
The days when Czechs would line up outside the door simply to get a glimpse of brand-name sportswear are long gone. However, Adidas is still doing brisk business with its street-smart tennis shoes and sportswear. **Branch:** Na příkopě 8, Prague 1.

Allinari
Rybná 2, Prague 1 (232 8249). Metro Náměstí Republiky/5, 14, 26 tram. **Open** 10am-7pm Mon-Fri; 10am-1pm Sat. **Credit** AmEx, EC, MC, V. **Map 4 K2**
Posh Italian shoes for men and women.

ART
Štěpánská 33, Prague 1 (2423 0257). Metro Muzeum/3, 9, 14, 24 tram. **Open** 9.30am-7pm Mon-Fri; 9am-4pm Sat. **Credit** AmEx, MC, V. **Map 6 K6**
Doc Martens and other big, clunky shoes.

Bama
Na příkopě 25, Prague 1 (262 894). Metro Můstek/3, 9, 14, 24 tram. **Open** 9.30am-7pm Mon-Fri; 10am-4pm Sat. **Credit** AmEx, EC, MC, V. **Map 4 K4**
Bama, a German label, has sensible shoes at sensible prices. They boast of a special sole designed to protect your feet from Old Town cobblestones, but dedicated followers of fashion might well be turned off by the round-toed, flat-heeled designs.

Baťa

Václavské náměstí 6, Prague 1 (2421 8133). Metro Můstek/3, 9, 14, 24 tram. **Open** 9am-8pm Mon-Fri; 10am-6pm Sat, Sun. **Credit** AmEx, DC, EC, MC, V.
Map 3 J5

The Baťa family, whose shoe-making operation was one of the world's first multinationals, saw trouble coming in 1938, fled the country and re-established their headquarters in Batawa in Canada. The rump of the parent company was nationalised by the communists ten years later. Now the Baťa family is firmly back in the driving seat and has refurbished the original 1928 modernist flagship store on Wenceslas Square.
Branches: Jindřišská 20, Prague 1; Moskevská 27, Prague 10.

Belt

Pařížská 10, Prague 1 (231 5182). Metro Staroměstská/17, 18 tram. **Open** 10am-7pm Mon-Fri; 10am-3pm Sat, Sun. **Credit** AmEx, DC, MC, V.
Map 3 H3

Beautiful leatherware for big spenders. The labels include Joop!, Adpel, Picard and Giorgio Armani.

Humanic

Národní třída 34, Prague 1 (2494 6695). Metro Můstek or Národní třída/6, 9, 18, 22 tram. **Open** 9am-7pm Mon-Fri; 9am-4pm Sat. **Credit** EC, MC, V. **Map 3 H5**

Cheap and cheerful fashion shoes. Popular among trendy teenagers on a tight budget.

Sedlářské práce

Ambrožova 14, Prague 3 (893 179). Tram 1, 9, 16. **Open** 8am-8pm Mon-Fri.

Handbags, bags and belts hand-crafted to customer specifications – you can even go along to the workshop and have your own design or ornamental detail made for you. The prices knock the spots off anything else available in the shops, but you have to call ahead for an appointment. Little English spoken.

Shoe repairs

There are shoe repair shops in **Baťa** (*see above*), and **Tesco** and **Kotva** supermarkets (*see page 154*); or you can try either of the places listed below. Failing that, look in *Zlaté stránky* under 'obuv-opravy'.

Austria Miniservis

Spálená 37, Prague 1 (2491 0822). Metro Národní třída/6, 9, 18, 22 tram. **Open** 9am-5pm Mon-Fri.
Map 5 H6

Jan Ondráček

Navrátilova 12, Prague 1 (296 653). Metro Národní třída/3, 9, 14, 24 tram. **Open** 8am-6pm Mon-Fri.
Map 5 J7

Costume & formal dress hire

Every school and workplace holds its own *ples*, or ball, sometime between November and April – there are even annual balls for hunters, miners and Moravians held in Prague (*see also page 7*). If you are invited to a ball, and left your tux, evening gown or Napoleon outfit at home, try the places below. It is best to make arrangements several days in advance, and take your passport as proof of identity.

Barrandov Studio, Fundus

Křiženeckého náměstí 322, Prague 5 (6707 1111). Metro Smíchovské nádraží, then bus 246, 247, 248. **Open** 8am-3.30pm Mon-Fri.

Prague's main film studio rents everything from bear costumes to military uniforms from its extensive wardrobe of over 240,000 costumes and accessories, including 9,000 wigs. None of this comes cheap, however. Deposits start at around 4,000-8,000 Kč for an antique ballgown, including an 800 Kč fee for a one- to seven-day hire period.

Hudební divadlo Karlín

Křižíkova 13, Prague 8 (231 2051). Metro Křižíkova/8, 24 tram. **Open** 9am-5pm Mon-Thur; 9am-4pm Fri.

Colourful but slightly shoddy operetta-style ball gowns and theatre costumes. Put down 150 Kč deposit for each item per day (a weekend counts as a day), then pay between 200-400 Kč per dress or costume per day.

Ladana

Opatovická 20, Prague 1 (291 890/269 7134). Metro Národní třída/6, 9, 18, 22 tram. **Open** 9am-6pm Mon, Wed, Thur; noon-4.30pm Tue, Fri; *July & Aug* 9am-6pm Wed, Thur only. **Map 5 H6**

Small costume shop with some amusing dresses, period costumes and masks as well as wedding and bridesmaid dresses, Czech national costumes and dinner jackets. Very cheap, very friendly. Pay just 500 Kč for a Wizard costume for a one- to three-day hire. No deposit, although the staff may ask to take down your passport number.

Florists

There's no shortage of flower shops in Prague, but most are more or less the same. Your local corner *květinařství* is likely to be as good as the centrally located places listed below. When sending flowers out of the country, be sure to plan well in advance as most florists require four or five days' notice.

Ateliér Kavka

Elišky Krásnohorské 3, Prague 1 (232 0847). Metro Staroměstská/17, 18 tram. **Open** 9am-6pm daily. **Credit** AmEx, V. **Map 3 H2**

Unlike most flower shops, the arrangements here are graceful and modern. Good dried flowers are also available, from as little as 150 Kč for a small bunch to 3,500 Kč for an imposing urn-full.

Bohemian Flowers

Lucemburská 3, Prague 3 (697 5522/272 002). Metro Jiřího z Poděbrad/ 1, 8, 25, 26 tram. **Open** 8.30am-5pm Mon-Fri. **Credit** AmEx, MC, V. **Map 7 B2**

A tiny, old-fashioned shop that can hand-deliver everything from name-day sprigs to wedding bouquets anywhere in Prague.

Clivia

Václavské náměstí 55, Prague 1 (265 078). Metro Muzeum/3, 9, 14, 24 tram. **Open** 10am-8pm daily. **Credit** AmEx, EC, MC, V. **Map 6 K6**

An Interflora outlet with standard rates for international deliveries.
Branch: Štefánikova 61, Prague 5.

Floraservis

Bubenské nábřeží 9, Prague 7 (805 635). Metro Vltavská/1, 3, 14 tram. **Map 7 E3**

Everything here from single red roses at around 50 Kč to full-blown bouquets, wedding sprigs and buttonholes.

Celetná Crystal

The tradition of Bohemian glassmaking dates back to the thirteenth century.
Today, beautiful Czech glass from the most famous regions of Bohemia and Moravia
are available in this luxurious, air-conditioned three-floor emporium in the
heart of Prague. Celetná Crystal offers a wide variety of classic cut glass, paneled,
engraved, enamel and contemporary glass. In addition to the crystal, shoppers
will find Czech garnets, amber, jewelry, crystal beads, folk arts and crafts,
porcelain, ceramics and crystal chandeliers.

Free hotel delivery service and worldwide shipping.
All major credit cards accepted, Eurocheques and currencies.

All languages spoken

Celetná 15, Prague 1, Tel.: 2481 1376
Open every day except Dec. 25
Nov.-March Open 10:00 -19:00, April-Oct. 10:00 -20:00

Food & drink

Food shopping in Prague has improved beyond all recognition in recent years. Under the communists, oranges and bananas were special treats only imported at Christmas time. Now even the local grocer might sell exotica such as star fruit and sun-dried tomatoes. Western-style supermarkets are still a rarity outside of the city centre, but most everyday shopping can be done in the local *potraviny* (grocery store) and *ovoce-zelenina* (greengrocer). Don't dare enter a supermarket without a trolley; this will result in sharp words from the woman at the check-out. If you want a plastic bag you will have to pay at least 2 Kč for it, so ask for a *tašku* before the cashier totals your bill. If you're eating on the trot, and not too fussy, try one of the hundreds of stand-up snack bars (*občerstvení*) scattered throughout the city. Just don't expect to find anything that does more than fill your stomach.

Specialist

Čaj lepších časů

Národní třída 20, Prague 1 (2491 2230). Metro Národní třída/6, 9, 18, 22 tram. **Open** 10am-6.30pm Mon-Fri; 11am-4pm Sat. **Map 3 H5**
Join in the great Prague tea craze (*see also p149*). Fresh uncut teas from Sri Lanka as well as its own brand of bagged tea.

Chléb, pečivo

Kaprova 13, Prague 1 (232 5225). Metro Staroměstská/17, 18 tram. **Open** 7am-7pm Mon-Fri; 8am-1pm Sun. **Map 3 H3**
This great little Czech bakery is so centrally located, it's a wonder it has survived the invasion of KFCs, McDonald's and Pizza Huts. For just a few crowns you can pick up a *syrový uzel* (cheese-topped roll), a traditional dough-tartlet, called *koláč*, or a couple of plum or poppy seed *buchty*. There's also a reasonable selection of sandwiches and filled rolls. Be ready to point out your order – no one here speaks English.

Country Life

Melantrichova 15, Prague 1 (2421 3366). Metro Můstek. **Open** 8am-7pm Mon-Thur; 8am-6pm Fri (*winter* 8am-3pm); 11am-6pm Sun. **Map 3 H4**
Not long ago this was a rare life-saver for vegetarians in Prague who were happy to queue up for odd sesame burgers and millet salads. Now it's a fully stocked health food shop with cold-pressed oils, amaranth baked goods, corn meal and tofu. There's a full hot buffet next door that features the complete range of salad components you'd expect anywhere, as well as wondrous, dirt-cheap lentil soups, fresh carrot juice and carob dessert cakes. The one hold-over from before is the major lunchtime crush. *See also p137*.
Branch: Jungmannova 1, Prague 1.

Le Delice Belges

Pavilon, Vinohradská 50, Prague 2 (786 8063). Metro Náměstí Míru/11 tram. **Open** 9.30am-9pm Mon-Sat; noon-6pm Sun. **Map 8 A3**
Handmade chocolates shipped in each week from Belgium. The Becherovka chocolates, made specially for the Czech market, make good gifts at 20 Kč each. Gift boxes and delivery possible.

Dobra čajovna

Václavské náměstí 14, Prague 1 (2423 1480). Metro Můstek/3, 9, 14, 24 tram. **Open** 10am-10pm daily. **Map 3 J5**
More of a shrine than a teashop, this place sells a daunting array of oriental teas that can be sampled in the warm, womb-like café. It also stocks all you need for a tea ceremony: tiny ceramic teapots and cups, joss sticks and Japanese tea strainers.

Dům lahůdek u Rotta

Malé náměstí 3, Prague 1 (2423 4457). Metro Můstek/17, 18 tram. **Open** 9.30am-7pm Mon-Sat; noon-7pm Sun. **Credit** AmEx, EC, MC, V. **Map 3 H4**
From the sgraffitoed exterior, you would never guess this is a multi-level food and wine emporium trafficked by internationally minded nouvelle Czechs, let alone the former Rott hardware store for generations before that. Nevertheless, it is the place to ferret out Black Sea caviar, French duck pâté (at a mere 60 Kč a tin), Hungarian sausage and even a mild local version of goat's cheese. If you don't get your favourite deli-delight here, you won't find it anywhere in Prague. Start at the snack bar in the hall, which sells handsome spinach focaccia, open-topped sandwiches (*chlebíček*) and potato pancakes (*bramborák*), then work your way up. There's also a café in the foyer and an upmarket wine shop, **Vinotéka**, in the basement (*see p145*).

Fruits de France

Jindřišská 9, Prague 1 (2422 0304). Metro Můstek/3, 9, 14, 24 tram. **Open** 9.30am-6.30pm Mon-Wed, Fri; 11.30am-6.30pm Thur; 9.30am-1pm Sat. **Map 4 K5**
Opened by an astute Frenchwoman in 1991 when Prague was a gastronomic desert, Fruits de France is still an oasis of mouthwatering fruit, vegetables, olives, cheese, chocolate, oil and wine. Deliveries from France arrive on Thursdays, but storage is good and everything remains in excellent condition. Such luxury does not come cheap: a block of mozzarella could set you back 300 Kč. There are a couple of stand-up-and-eat tables at the back of the shop for quick deli snacks with wine.

Leonidas

Karlovo náměstí 32, Prague 2 (292 812). Metro Karlovo náměstí/3, 6, 14, 18, 22, 24 tram. **Open** 10am-5pm Mon-Fri. **Map 5 H7**
World-famous and utterly delicious Belgian chocolates at stratospheric prices.

Ocean

Zborovská 49, Prague 5 (9000 1517). Tram 6, 9, 12, 22. **Open** 10am-8pm Mon-Sat.
Every Wednesday a shipment of more than 35 types of fresh fish and seafood arrives from Belgium, and the store can special order over 60 more. Also fresh herbs and other imported produce.

Paris-Praha

Jindřišská 7, Prague 1 (2422 2855). Metro Můstek/3, 9, 14, 24 tram. **Open** 8.30am-7pm Mon-Fri; 8.30am-1pm Sat. **Credit** AmEx, EC, MC, V. **Map 4 K5**
As well as having top quality French champagnes, cognacs and bordeaux, this snack bar also sells delicious pastries. Get there early before they are snapped up by French shoppers on their way to Fruits de France.

Pekařství Odkolek

Vodičkova 30 (Lucerna passage), Prague 1 (2416 2048). Metro Národní třída or Můstek/3, 9, 14, 24 tram. **Open** 7am-8pm Mon-Fri; 8am-8pm Sat; 10am-8pm Sun. **Map 6 K6**
A café with an excellent range of patisserie. Open fruit tarts or cakes blanketed in chocolate can be taken home whole for a mere 200 Kč or so.

Potraviny U Cedru
Československé armády 18, Prague 6 (312 2119).
Metro Dejvická. **Open** 7am-11pm daily.
Any grocery with these hours is a godsend in Prague, but
one with basmati rice, houmous, vine leaves and other
Lebanese delights? Worth the trek to Dejvice, clearly. If you
don't fancy cooking, go to the restaurant, **U Cedru**, the
best Middle Eastern eatery in town (*see p129*).

Prodejna U Salvatora
Náprstkova 2, Prague 1 (9005 2325). Metro Národni
třída/17, 18 tram. **Open** 10am-6pm Mon-Fri. **Map 3 G4**
This sweet little store in the Old Town has more than 120
kinds of spices in paper packets or in little glass jars. Ask the
assistant for the catalogue which lists each item in English.

Vzpomínky na Afriku
Rybná/Jakubská (0603 441 434). Metro Náměstí
Republiky/5, 14, 26 tram. **Open** 10am-7pm daily.
Map 4 K3
The smell of dark, roasted African coffee beans hits you as
soon as you step through the doors. If you can't make up
your mind between the 30 or so coffee beans from different
African countries on offer, you can always sit at the one
and only table available and try a cup. Beans can be ground
before packaging on request.

Supermarkets

In addition to the places below, there are centrally located supermarkets in **Kotva** and **Tesco**
(*see page 154*).

Delvita
Sokolovská 14, Prague 8 (232 7015). Metro Florenc/
8, 24 tram. **Open** 7am-8pm Mon-Fri; 7am-7pm Sat;
9am-7pm Sun.
This well-stocked Belgian chain has good vegetables, meat
and wine, but poor bread and very little in the way of fish.
There are ten branches: check the Yellow Pages (*Zlaté*
stránky) for your nearest.

Pronto
Rytířská 10, Prague 1 (2421 2300). Metro Můstek/6, 9,
18, 22 tram. **Open** 7am-8pm Mon-Fri; 7am-2pm Sat.
Map 3 J4
This formerly state-owned supermarket has done an excellent job of transforming itself into a shiny Western-style
grocery store. The prices here tend to be a little higher than
in a corner *potraviny*, but it's open late and is situated in
the centre of town.
Branch: Pavilon, Vinohradská 50, Prague 2.

Food delivery
See also above **U Cedru**.

Chicago's Famous Pizza
José Martího 376, Prague 6 (316 4242/316 6135).
Tram 20, 26. **Open** 9.30am-9.30pm daily.
Average pizza delivered to your door for a pretty penny –
pizzas start at a whopping 280 Kč for a small cheese pizza
plus taxi charges – reckon on about 15 Kč a kilometre. If
you're based further afield, it might be worth your while
ordering from the Prague 4 branch listed below.
Branch: Na Pankráci 24, Prague 4.

Pizza Go Home
Argentinská 1, Prague 7 (870 026/870 277/870 869).
Metro Vltavská/1, 3, 14 tram. **Open** 24 hours daily.
Map 7 E2
Pizza vaguely reminiscent of cardboard, delivered round the

clock. Cheap, though. Only 85 Kč for a small cheese pizza
delivered by taxi at an additional 15 Kč per kilometre.

Pizza Taxi
Karlovo náměstí 28, Prague 2 (295 762/290 706). Metro
Karlovo náměstí/3, 6, 14, 18, 22, 24 tram. **Open** 11am-
10pm daily. **Map 5 H7**
There are approximately 100 items on Pizza Taxi's deliv-
ery list, but none of them except the tiramisu is any good.
Delivery charge 60 Kč.

Pizza West
Náměstí bratří Synků 5, Prague 4 (692 4341). Tram 6,
7, 11, 18, 24. **Open** 10.30am-2am Mon-Fri; 4.30pm-2am
Sat, Sun.
Cheap and edible pizza delivered until late in the evening.
Some of the receptionists speak a little English. Delivery
charge, anything from 50-150 Kč depending on your Prague
district area.

Sports Café Cornucopia
Jungmannova 10, Prague 1 (2422 0950). Metro Můstek/
3, 9, 14, 24 tram. **Open** 9am-4pm Mon-Fri. **Map 3 J5**
Sandwiches, cookies, brownies, french fries, burritos, soft
drinks, newspapers and even cigarettes delivered within
Prague 1 and 2 and parts of 3 only. Delivery charge is 45 Kč;
100 Kč minimum order. Free delivery for orders over 650 Kč.

Wine

See also **Dům lahůdek u Rotta,** *page 165.*

Blatnička
Michalská 6, Prague 1 (no phone). Metro Národni
třída/6, 9, 18, 22 tram. **Open** 10am-6pm Mon-Fri.
Map 3 H4
One of dozens of places around town to pick up cheap
Moravian table wine (look for 'sudová vína' signs marking
places where they will refill your plastic water bottle with
the stuff for next to nothing) or sample any of a dozen on
the spot. The crowd in here loves drink, certainly, though
they don't know a bouquet from Bo Diddley.

Cellarius
Štěpánská 61 (Lucerna passage), Prague 1 (2421 0979).
Metro Můstek/3, 9, 14, 24 tram. **Open** 9.30am-9pm
Mon-Sat; 3-8pm Sun. **Credit** EC, MC, V. **Map 6 K6**
One of the first Prague shops to thoroughly organise and
collect Moravian wines and an excellent place to pick up
some interesting ones that are rarely available in Prague.
International wines are less of a sure thing here, however.

Dionýsos
Vinařického 6, Prague 2 (295 342). Tram 7, 18, 24.
Open 10am-6pm Mon-Fri. **Credit** EC, MC, V.
Map 5 H10
A classy wine merchant patronised by the Prague élite.
Dionýsos has a respectable range of foreign wines but spe-
cialises in top quality local production, including older vin-
tages. The staff, who know and love their wines, will guide
you through the shelves.

General services

Affordable Luxuries
Štěpánská 15, Prague 2 (2166 1266/2166 1319). Metro
Muzeum or I.P. Pavlova/3, 9, 14, 24 tram. **Open** 8am-
5pm Mon-Fri. **Credit** AmEx, MC, V. **Map 6 K6**
This expat-run company can take care of your laundry, do
your shopping, get your clothes altered, arrange for a
housecleaner, find a babysitter, cater for a party, call a
plumber and basically do just about anything else a busy
businessperson might not have time to do.

One of Prague's ten billion souvenir shops.

Gifts

Most expats have a nervous breakdown looking for gifts around Christmas time, so don't worry if you have more than a spot of difficulty locating that special something. The trick is to avoid the tourist-tat, and go for the less obvious choices – it's just a question of knowing where to look. Czech CDs, both pop and classical, are always a good buy at approximately half the price of CDs back home, and most of the bookshops listed above stock beautiful photography calendars and Czech authors translated into English. For booze lovers, a bottle of Becherovka, that sweet, herby spirit famed throughout the nation as a 'medicine', has a certain novelty value, as do the round, chocolate wafers called Fidorkas. Don't, whatever you do, get bullied into buying one of those chicken-toys that get touted around Old Town Square. They're nothing more than half a loo roll on a string, and usually fall apart in the first ten minutes. Here's a few more suggestions to be getting on with.

See also page 173 **Toys**.

Association Club Sparta Praha

Na Perštýně 17, Prague 1 (2422 0763). Metro Národní třída/6, 9, 18, 22 tram. **Open** 10am-5pm Mon-Thur; 10am-4pm Fri. **Map 3 H5**
Football paraphernalia, including lighters, beer mugs, beach balls, keychains, T-shirts, and hats emblazoned with the name or red-star logo of Prague's biggest soccer team,

Sparta Praha. Just try to remember that Poborský, though Czech, didn't actually come from this club but the rival club from the other end of town. The shop assistants (all ardent Sparta fans) don't take too kindly to this frequent mistake.

Česká lidová řemesla

Jilská 22, Prague 1 (2423 2745). Metro Můstek. **Open** 10am-7pm Fri, Sat; 10am-6.30pm Sun-Thur. **Credit** AmEx, EC, MC, V. **Map 3 H4**
A chain of shops selling touristy but attractive folk art, including straw nativities (around 1,000 Kč), a vast range of painted Easter eggs and willow twigs for whacking girls at Easter (*see p5*). The various branches have different specialities – for example, Jilská sells textiles and wooden toys.
Branches: Melantrichova 17, Prague 1; Mostecká 17, Prague 1; Nerudova 23 & 31, Prague 1; Zlatá ulička 16, Prague 1.

Charita Florentinum

Ječná 2, Prague 2 (295 029). Metro Karlovo náměstí/4, 6, 16, 22, 34 tram. **Open** 8am-6pm Mon-Thur; 9am-5pm Fri, Sat. **Map 5 J8**
The place where Czech priests come for their robes, incense burners and other paraphernalia. Incredibly cheap candles.

Keramika

Jakubská 8, Prague 1 (no phone). Metro Náměstí Republiky/5, 14, 26 tram. **Open** 11am-6pm Mon-Fri; 11am-4pm Sat. **Map 4 K3**
Home-made ceramics took off in a big way a few years ago, giving rise to hundreds of little ceramic shops selling brightly coloured pots, mugs and teacups. This is one of the best.

Modrá Galerie

Jakubská 8, Prague 1 (232 6796). Metro Náměstí Republiky/5, 14, 26 tram. **Open** 10.30am-6.30pm Mon-Fri; 10.30am-4pm Sat. **Map 4 K3**
An arty crafts shop, packed with colourful ceramics, puppets for children, plain wooden toys and naïve-art paintings and drawings. There's virtually nothing distinctly 'Czech' here, but everything's pretty enough.

Hair & beauty

Those after the simplest of cuts should be able to get a decent trim in any *kadeřnictví* (hairdressers) or *holičství* (barbershop) for around 100 Kč. Anyone looking for something more dramatic should enquire at one of the posh hotels, or consult the following. But remember, fashions come late to the Czech Republic, so if you're looking for something ultra-new, you may like to wait until you get home.

Dream Hair

Týn 2, Prague 1 (2489 5776). Metro Náměstí Republiky/5, 14, 26 tram. **Open** 9am-8pm Mon-Fri; 9am-3pm Sat. **Map 3 J3**
A highly recommended salon, staffed mainly by English-speaking hairdressers. A ladies' cut will set you back around 450 Kč – at least twice the price of a cut by the average Czech hairdresser – but there's less risk involved.

Šarm

Jungmannova 1, Prague 1 (2422 4814). Metro Můstek/6, 9, 18, 22 tram. **Open** 7am-9pm Fri-Mon; 9am-3pm Sat (*winter only*). **Map 3 J5**
Slightly more upscale than your average *kadeřnictví*, Šarm is still incredibly reasonable. More than 17 locations, a few listed below.
Branches: Dlouhá 1, Prague 1; Králodvorská 12, Prague 1; Revoluční 25, Prague 1.

Velia

Vinohradská 53, Prague 2 (2225 2547/2225 0028).
Metro Jiřího z Poděbrad/11 tram. **Open** 8am-8pm Mon-Fri; 9am-2pm Sat. **Credit** EC, MC, V. **Map 8 B3**
Haircuts for men and women, manicures, pedicures and massages available at this Western-style salon. Most of the staff speak English.
Branches: Hotel Diplomat, Evropská 15, Prague 6; Bělehradská 118, Prague 2.

Household

Baumax

Hall 22, Pražská tržnice, Bubenské nábřeží, Prague 7 (6671 0512). Metro Vltavská/1, 3, 14 tram.
Open 8.30am-7pm Mon-Fri; 8am-4pm Sat.
Map 7 E3
Everything for the dedicated DIYer: tools, wood, paint, hardware, camping gear, gardening stuff, outdoor furniture, wading pools and garden gnomes.
Branches: Türkova, Prague 4; Jeremiášova, Prague 5.

Galerie bydlení

Truhlářská 20, Prague 1 (231 2383). Metro Náměstí Republiky/5, 14, 26 tram. **Open** 9am-7pm Mon-Fri; 9am-5pm Sat, Sun (summer only). **Credit** EC, MC, V.
Map 4 L2
Wacky, surrealistic, fun furniture design. Well on the way to kitsch.

IKEA

Skandinávská 1, Prague 5 (651 0261/5718 6111).
Metro Zličín. **Open** 10am-8pm daily. **Credit** EC, MC, V.
When the Swedish furniture giant IKEA opened its megastore in 1996, around 100,000 people – eight per cent of the population of Prague – visited it in the first four days of business. IKEA in Prague is a byword for style, and a couple of years on it has yet to meet with a serious competitor for quality and value for money. Riding the metro on a Saturday and watching the hoards of excited shoppers on their way home with their IKEA bags is entertainment in itself.

KDS

Národní třída 43, Prague 1 (265 303). Metro Můstek or Národní třída/6, 9, 18, 22 tram. **Open** 9am-6pm Mon-Fri; 9am-1pm Sat. **Map 3 J5**
Stainless steel Czech knives in every size and shape. A modest outlay buys interesting presents for foodie friends.

Modrobílá linie

Lucerna passage, Štěpanská 61, Prague 1 (2421 3710).
Metro Můstek/3, 9, 14, 24 tram. **Open** 10am-7pm Mon-Fri; 10am-2pm Sat. **Map 6 K6**
The Czech and imported pottery, candlesticks and tablecloths are far more sophisticated here than in your average *keramika* store. Most of the items seem to be in some shade of blue or white – hence the name, which means 'The Blue and White Line'.

Obi

Výtvarná 3/1033, Prague 6 (302 5228). Bus 108, 225.
Open 8am-8pm Mon-Fri; 8am-6pm Sat. **Credit** EC, MC, V.
The biggest hardware store in the country now has three locations, none of them anywhere near the centre.
Branches: Ústřední 326, Prague 4; Lhotecká 446, Prague 4.

Le Patio

Národní třída 22, Prague 1 (2491 8136). Metro Národní třída. **Open** 10am-7pm Mon-Sat; 11am-7pm Sun.
Credit AmEx, DC, MC, V. **Map 6 K6**

The Belgian owner has craftily married local iron-working skills with her own intriguingly romantic designs. Wrought-iron constructions from candleholders to birdcages are set off by the odd bunch of paper flowers or sculptural wooden bowl.
Branch: Pařížská 20, Prague 1.

Potten & Pannen

Vodičkova 2, Prague 1 (2491 2173). Metro Národní třída/3, 9, 14, 24 tram. **Open** 9am-6pm Tue, Wed, Fri; 9am-7pm Thur; 9am-4pm Sat. **Credit** AmEx, DC, V.
Map 5 J6
The last word in cookware – grinders, choppers, graters and squeezers as well as shining pots and pans. P&P also sells Calphalm aluminium saucepans from the USA and Emile Henry oven-to-tableware.

Key cutting & locksmiths

The best places to cut keys is at one of the major supermarkets in town – they're more likely to speak English and less likely to rip you off. Try either at **Bílá labuť, Tesco** or at the bottom of the escalators at the entrance to the **Kotva** supermarket (*see page 154*). For a 24-hour locksmith, try one of the following.

Bon Express zámečnictví pohotovost

Tupolevova 515, Prague 9 (858 6348).

KEY Non=Stop

Vazovova 3, Prague 4 (401 6616/401 7921).

Music

Bazar CD

Jungmannova 13, Prague 1 (2494 8565). Metro Můstek/3, 9, 14, 24 tram. **Open** 9am-6pm Mon-Fri. **Map 3 J5**
This diminutive shop stocks hundreds of second-hand CDs starting at around 120 Kč – mostly mainstream rock and pop, though.

Bontonland Megastore

Palace Koruna, Václavské náměsti 1 (2422 6236).
Metro Můstek/3, 9, 14, 24 tram. **Open** 9am-8pm Mon-Sat; 10am-7pm Sun **Credit** AmEx, EC, MC, V.
Map 3 J4
The first Western-style music megastore in Eastern Europe opened in 1996, with stereo equipment, videos, CD-Roms, books, some vinyl, posters, T-shirts, instore DJ, listening posts and a café – as well as CDs and cassettes of every genre. There's rock and pop aplenty, but stock in some non-mainstream areas such as world music and techno are a bit limited. The jazz section's good, though.

Bontonland Music Stop

Karlova 23, Prague 1 (2421 0891). Metro Staroměstská/17, 18 tram. **Open** 10am-7pm Mon-Sat; 11am-6pm Sun. **Credit** DC, EC. **Map 3 H4**
Reasonably good section of homegrown and imported classical CDs plus a sprinkling from other genres. Unmissably located on Prague's main tourist drag.

Bontonland (Supraphon)

Jungmannova 20, Prague 1 (2494 8718). Metro Národní třída or Můstek/3, 9, 14, 24 tram. **Open** 9am-7pm Mon-Fri; 9am-noon Sat. **Credit** AmEx, DC, EC, MC, V.
Map 5 J6
The former state recording company – now privatised – has its own shop. To find out what's on offer, flick through the files on the counter. Service is basic.

Souvenir Czech list

ITALIAN FASHION

- Les Copains - Borsalino - Casadei - Ruffo - Allegri -

V Kolkovně 5, Prague 1, Tel.: 232 98 23

Maximum Underground

Jilská 22, Prague 1 (628 4009). Metro Můstek, Národní třída or Staroměstská/3, 9, 18, 22 tram. **Open** 10am-7pm Mon-Sat; 2-7pm Sun. **Map 3 H4**

Within a sort of alternative culture shopping mall that includes clothes stores, tattooing and piercing parlours is this friendly shop, stocking mostly CDs and some cassettes. There's a good selection of techno, ambient and hardcore, and the staff seem to know their stuff.

Music shop – antikvariát

Národní třída 25 (Lucerna passage), Prague 1 (2108 5241). Metro Národní třída/6, 9, 18, 22 tram. **Open** 10.30am-7pm Mon-Sat. **Map 3 H5**

A collectors' paradise, with hundreds of used CDs and LPs from the 1920s onwards. It includes jazz, blues, country, folk, Czech pop/rock, classical, a pricey stack of rarities and bootlegs, and long-deleted recordings not only from this country but also from the former East Germany.
Branch: Mostecká 4, Prague 1.

Music shop Trio

U Radnice 5, Prague 1 (232 2583). Metro Staroměstská/17, 18 tram. **Open** 10am-7pm Mon-Fri; 10am-6pm Sat. **Credit** AmEx, DC, EC, MC, V. **Map 3 H3**

At the address where Franz Kafka was born, this shop specialises in Czech music, though also stocks assorted staples from the standard classical repertoire. Given the tourist location, its prices are slightly higher, but the service is attentive and knowledgeable.

Pohodlí

Benediktská 7, Prague 1 (2481 6627). Metro Náměstí Republiky/5, 14, 26 tram. **Open** 11am-6pm Mon-Fri; 10am-4pm Sat. **Map 4 K2**

This tiny, family-run ethnic music store stocks everything from Zimbabwean marimba music to Nusrat Fateh Ali Khan, plus a fair selection of Moravian folk music and Czech alternative music. The Polish owner is more than happy to let you listen to your chosen CD before purchasing and, if you're lucky, you might even get offered a cup a tea.

Popron

Jungmannova 30, Prague 1 (2494 8682). Metro Národní třída/3, 9, 14, 24 tram. **Open** 9am-7.30pm Mon-Fri; 9am-7pm Sat; 10am-6pm Sun. **Credit** MC, V. **Map 5 J6**

After Bontonland Megastore, the slickest music store in town offering a complete collection of mainstream rock. Little else of interest, though. Listen to top-selling albums on headphones while browsing the racks.

234

Bělehradská 120, Prague 2 (2425 2741). Metro I.P. Pavlova/6, 11 tram. **Open** *summer* 10am-7pm Mon-Fri; 10am-3pm Sat; *winter* 9.30am-7.30pm Mon-Fri; 10am-4pm Sat; 1-5pm Sun. **Credit** AmEx, DC, MC, V. **Map 6 L8**

In the same building as Radost nightclub, this small CD-only shop specialises in techno, house and hip-hop. Owned by a member of the 1970s Czech band Garáž, it's also an excellent place to find Czech dissident rock, such as the Plastic People of the Universe CD box set. English-speaking staff.

Musical instruments

Hudební nástroje – Jakub Lis

Náprstkova 10, Prague 1 (265 230/2423 0797). Metro Mustek or Staroměstská/17, 18 tram. **Open** 10am-7pm Mon-Fri; 10am-4pm Sat. **Map 3 G4**

Small and cheery music shop with a fair selection of second-hand electric and acoustic guitars, violins, cellos, accordians and Indian and African drums and instruments. All this, plus all the usual musicians' paraphernalia – strings, rosin and reeds.

Praha Music Center

Soukenická 20, Prague 1 (2481 0970). Metro Náměstí Republiky/5, 14, 26 tram. **Open** 9.30am-5.30pm Mon-Fri. **Map 4 L2**

Caters admirably for plugged-in musicians. There's all the usual equipment, and it's especially good for pick-ups, pedals and second-hand amps.

Opticians

Both frames and lenses can be incredibly cheap in Prague, making it possible to get a basic pair of glasses for around 1,500 Kč. Be aware, however, that the vast majority of opticians do not use shatterproof glass. The stores listed below are more upmarket than the average optician and stock high quality lenses.

AM Optik Studio

Jungmannova 19, Prague 1 (2494 8451). Metro Národní třída/3, 9, 14, 24 tram. **Open** 8am-6pm Mon-Fri. **Credit** AmEx, MC, V. **Map 5 J6**

A reasonably fashionable choice, though without much help for non Czech-speakers.

Eiffel Optic

Ječná 6, Prague 2 (295 977). Metro Karlovo náměstí/4, 6, 16, 22, 34 tram. **Open** 8am-7pm Mon-Fri; 9am-1pm Sat. **Credit** AmEx, DC, EC, MC, V. **Map 5 J8**

This place has a reputation for reliable, speedy service with a smile, as well as a small but better-than-average range of frames.

Lumia Optic

Na slupi 15, Prague 2 (297 055). Metro Karlovo náměstí, then 18, 24 tram. **Open** *summer* 8am-5pm Mon-Fri; *winter* 8am-6.30pm Mon-Fri. **Credit** AmEx, EC, MC, V. **Map 5 H10**

A wide selection of fashionable frames and sunglasses. It also does repairs.
Branch: Skořepka 1, Prague 1.

Vision Express

Myslbek Center, Na příkopě 19/21 (2423 5729). Metro Můstek/3, 9, 14, 24 tram. **Open** 9am-6pm Mon-Fri. **Map 4 K4**

Super-fast eye-tests, repairs and lens-cutting from the British optician chain. Only a few people here speak English, but they all seem to know what they're doing.

Photocopying

Akant

Myslbek Center, Na příkopě 19/21 (2224 0031). Metro Můstek/3, 9, 14, 24 tram. **Open** 9am-6pm Mon-Fri. **Map 4 K4**

Smaller than most, but centrally located. English spoken.

BossCan Reprostudio

Školská 34, Prague 1 (266 798). Metro Můstek/3, 9, 14, 24 tram. **Open** *summer* 8am-7pm Mon-Fri; 10am-5pm Sat; *winter* 8am-8pm Mon-Fri; 10am-12.30pm, 1-5pm, Sat, Sun. **Map 5 J6**

A standard photocopy shop with standard rates. Some English spoken.

*Snappers' paradise: the snappily named **Jan Pazdera obchod a opravna**.*

C-Copy Centrum

*Opletalova 5, Prague 1 (2209 8221). Metro Můstek/
3, 9, 14, 24 tram.* **Open** 8am-6pm daily.
Map 6 K6
The usual range of photocopying services, as well as harder-to-find colour double-sided copying, T-shirt printing and binding. C-Copy Centrum will also pick-up and deliver. English spoken.

Copy General

*Senovážné náměstí 26, Prague 1 (2423 0020).
Metro Náměstí Republiky/3, 5, 9, 14, 24, 26 tram.*
Open 24 hours daily; other branches 7am-10pm daily.
Map 4 L4
If you're struck by the need to get a colour copy done at four in the morning, this is the place to come. A variety of copying and binding services performed round the clock: black-and-white digital printing, full-colour digital printing, pick-up and delivery services and print-outs from ZIP, CD and JAZ discs. Some assistants speak reasonable English.
Branches: Vinohradská 13, Prague 2; Milady Horákové 4, Prague 7; Na Bělidle 40, Prague 5.

Photography
Camera shops & repairs

AZ Foto

*Senovážná 8, Prague 1 (2421 3443).
Metro Náměstí Republiky/3, 5, 9, 14, 24, 26 tram.*
Open 8.30am-6pm Mon-Fri; 9am-7pm Sat.
Map 4 K4
New and second-hand cameras and multifarious accessories. AZ Foto is particularly strong on cheap, second-hand lenses.

Fotografie Dobra

*Pařížská 12, Prague 1 (2481 6498). Metro Staroměstská/
17, 18 tram.* **Open** 2-6pm Mon-Fri. **Credit** AmEx, EC,
MC, V. **Map 3 H3**
A shop and a gallery, Fotografie Dobra is the place to track down collectable cameras as well as desirable vintage prints by renowned Czech photographers such as Sudek and Drtikol.

Fototechnika a video

*Vodičkova 36, Prague 1 (2423 2246). Metro Můstek/3,
9, 14, 24 tram.* **Open** 9am-7pm Mon-Fri; 9am-2pm Sat.
Credit AmEx, DC, EC, MC, V. **Map 5 J6**
One-stop shopping for the professional photographer: a wider range of film than any other store in the city, plus tripods, lights, enlargers, second-hand and new cameras. Prices here tend to be a little bit higher than at smaller shops, but you pay for convenience. If you're interested in old cameras, check out the second-hand section at the back of the shop and pick up an old Soviet or East German camera for around 500 Kč, or an entire black-and-white developer for under 4,000 Kč. This section is always crowded with the snapper cognoscenti, so you'll need to assert yourself if you want to get served.
Branch: Husova 23, Prague 1.

Jan Pazdera obchod a opravna

*Lucerna passage, Vodičkova 30, Prague 1 (260 683).
Metro Můstek/3, 9, 14, 24 tram.* **Open** 9am-6pm Mon-
Fri. **Map 4 K5**
Used cameras, movie cameras, enlargers, filters, microscopes, telescopes, tripods and just about every other photographic accessory you can imagine. This excellent store has plenty of second-hand cameras from the former communist bloc, which are currently quite fashionable among photographers in the West. Also does simple camera repairs.

Photo developing

Photo shops have mushroomed all over the tourist areas, so finding a decent place to get your pictures developed should not be any problem whatsoever.

Benecel
Celetná 36, Prague 1 (264 536). Metro Náměstí Republiky. **Open** 10am-6pm Mon-Fri. **Map 3 J3**
One-hour developing.

Česká tisková kancelář (ČTK)
Opletalova 5-7, Prague 1 (2209 8353/2209 8237). Metro Muzeum/3, 9, 14, 24 tram. **Open** 8am-7pm Mon-Fri; 9am-1pm Sat. **Map 6 K6**
One of the only places to get black-and-white photos developed 'quickly' – meaning a week, or three days if you pay a 50 per cent 'rush' fee. This is a professional developing place in the same building as the country's leading news agency. Not really a place to take your holiday snaps.

Fotolab
Opletalova 32, Prague 1 (2421 1393). Metro Muzeum/3, 9, 14, 24 tram. **Open** 8am-6pm Mon-Fri; 9am-1pm Sat. **Credit** AmEx, EC, MC, V. **Map 4 L5**
Fast developing services. If you ask nicely, they'll even be able to put those nice, white borders around your photos. **Branches:** Na příkopě 24, Prague 1; Rytířská 22, Prague 1.

Fotoplus
Na příkopě 17, Prague 1 (2421 3121). Metro Náměstí Republiky/5, 14, 26 tram. **Open** 9am-7.30pm Mon-Fri; 9am-7pm Sat; 10am-7pm Sun. **Credit** AmEx, EC, MC, V. **Map 4 K4**
One-hour developing. A little English spoken.

Stationery & art materials

The ubiquitous *papírnictví* shops sell everything from envelopes to toilet paper. If you can't find what you want in one, try **Kotva** (*see p154*) or one of those listed below.

Altamira
Jilská 2, Prague 1 (2421 9950). Metro Můstek, Národní třída or Staroměstská/6, 9, 18, 22 tram. **Open** 9am-7pm Mon-Fri; 10am-5pm Sat; noon-5pm Sun. **Map 3 H4**
A truly specialist art shop, crammed with stretchers, easels, canvasses, paints, chalks and brushes.
Branch: Skořepka 2, Prague 1.

Loco Plus
Palackého 10, Prague 1 (2494 7732). Metro Národní třída or Můstek/3, 9, 14, 24 tram. **Open** 8.30am-6.30pm Mon-Thur; 8.30am-6pm Fri; 9am-noon Sat. **Map 5 J6**
Masses and masses of good, cheap, local stationery and no overpriced imports.

McPaper & Co
Dukelských hrdinů 39, Prague 7 (373 803). Metro Vltavská/1, 3, 5, 8, 12, 14, 17, 25, 26 tram. **Open** 9.30am-4.30pm Mon-Fri. **Map 7 D2**
Glossy German Berlitz products, including sketch pads, wrapping paper, jiffy bags and tableware.
Branch: Vršovická 70, Prague 10.

Ráj výtvarníků
Michalská 15, Prague 1 (2423 1199). Metro Národní třída/6, 9, 18, 22 tram. **Open** 10am-6pm Mon-Fri. **Map 3 H4**
A well-stocked art shop bang in the centre, especially good for oil paints.

Toys

An invasion of Barbie dolls and Polly Pockets has hit Prague, but traditional Czech toys are holding their own – at least among visitors. There is no shortage of places to buy all the old favourites – puppets, puzzles and pull-alongs – while the department stores have large enough toy sections to please all but the pickiest kid.

Ivre
Jakubská 3, Prague 1 (232 6644). Metro Náměstí Republiky/5, 14, 26 tram. **Open** 10am-6pm Mon-Sat; 10am-5pm Sun. **Credit** AmEx, DC, EC, MC, V. **Map 4 K3**
Soft toys hand-sewn in the shape of moons, suns, puppets and pillows by Renáta Löfelmannová.
Branch: Husova 12, Prague 1.

Mc Toy
Jakubská 8, Prague 1 (232 2136). Metro Náměstí Republiky/5, 14, 26 tram. **Open** 10am-6pm Mon-Sat. **Credit** AmEx, EC, MC, V. **Map 4 K3**
This usually rather overcrowded toy shop specialises in toy animals.

Obchod loutkami
Nerudova 47, Prague 1 (530 065). Metro Malostranská/12, 22 tram. **Open** *Jan-Mar* 9.30am-6pm; *Apr-May, Oct-Dec* 9.30am-7pm; *June-Sept* 9.30am-8pm, daily. **Credit** AmEx, MC, V. **Map 2 D3**
Huge, grotesque trolls and witches leer over a pantheon of fairy-story characters in stick, string and finger form. The big puppets are expensive; the smaller are also pricey but well made.

Video rental

Terminal Video
Soukenická 6, Prague 1 (2187 1999/2187 1111/ online@terminal.cz/www.terminal.cz). Metro Náměstí Republiky. **Open** 9am-2am Mon-Fri; 9am-1am Sat; 10am-1am Sun. **Map 4 L2**
Run by **Terminal Bar** (*see p144*), this video rental store is accordingly devoted to cult weirdness, cultural exchange and all-round fun. Videos, for 50-120 Kč a night, include a wealth of Czech films with English subtitles, '60s sexploitation and obscure sci-fi. No membership fee but a refundable 1,000 Kč deposit required. Some videos are NTSC only.

Video to Go
Vítězné náměstí 10, Prague 6 (312 4096). Metro Dejvická/2, 20, 25, 26 tram. **Open** 9am-10pm Mon-Sat; 11am-8pm Sun. **Membership** 500 Kč per year. **Credit** AmEx, MC, V.
More than 2,500 English-language videos are available to rent in their original versions, in both European and American formats. Two-day hire costs 180 Kč. You can also rent a TV/VCR unit for 250 Kč a day, or a VCR for 150 Kč a night.

Video World
V Rybníčkách 13, Prague 10 (781 9064). Metro Skalka. **Open** 2-7pm Mon-Fri; 3-7pm Sun.
Video World offers the cheapest rentals in town, at just 30 Kč a day for a new release and 20-25 Kč for an older video. However, all the shop's 2,000 videos are dubbed into Czech – good for learning the local language, but not exactly making for relaxing viewing. No membership is required, but foreigners will need to leave their passport number.

Arts & Entertainment

Children	**176**	Music: Rock, Folk & Jazz	**197**
Film	**180**	Nightlife	**201**
Gay & Lesbian Prague	**185**	Sport & Fitness	**208**
Literary Prague	**188**	Theatre & Dance	**214**
Music: Classical & Opera	**190**		

Children

Wobbly mirrors, tram rides and puppets – Prague's kid-friendly attractions are decidedly old-school.

Prague is often described as a fairy-tale city, but that doesn't necessarily mean it is a great place for children. In appearance at least it is undeniably Grimm. Its enchantments are mostly dark and its historical details are grotesque enough to spook any child not weaned on video nasties. There is an old-fashioned quality to life, which will perhaps appeal more to parents brought up on Disney than their Nintendo kids. But, for the most part, everything is cheap (if you're a foreigner), the city centre is small, public transport is safe and frequent, and, with good timing and a little effort, Prague yields enough attractions to keep families occupied.

For toy shops, *see page 173*; for shops selling children's clothes, *see page 162*.

Sightseeing & activities

Some common tourist attractions, such as the astro-logical clock, and climbable towers – the Petřín's mini-Eiffel, the Old Town tower on Charles Bridge, and the Powder Gate – are as suited to children as they are to adults.

Historic tram
(info 312 3349/9612 4900). **Times** *Apr-Oct* hourly.
Fare 15 Kč; 7 Kč children.
A great sightseeing refuge for tired feet, this quaint, wood-framed tram travels a loop from Výstaviště, down the banks of Malá Strana, across to the National Theatre, through Václavské náměstí and back to Výstaviště by way of Náměstí Republiky. It can be joined at any stop on the route.

National Technical Museum
(for listings details, see p93)
Full of old vehicles, aircraft and gadgets, this museum is a sure hit with kids. A popular coal-mine tour tunnels through the building's basement. Special family rates are available and English-speaking tours can be arranged in advance.

Toy Museum
(for listings details, see p95).
An interesting collection of antique and collectable toys from ancient Greece to the present day. The Toy Museum's glass-enclosed exhibits were clearly created with children's viewing in mind, but there isn't much to play with except, in one room, kid-level push-buttons that activate elaborate displays of moving teddy bears.

Wax Museums
(for listings details, see p93)
Central Prague's two wax museums display life-size figures of internationally celebs, along with characters from Czech history and well-known twentieth-century polit-ical leaders. Both museums feature short films, described as '3-D' or 'kaleidoscopic'.

Puppets for your poppets at Charles Bridge.

Zoologická zahrada v Praze
U Trojského zámku 3, Prague 7 (688 0480). Metro Nádraží Holešovice, then 112 bus, or walk through Stromovka park and across Císařský ostrov.
Open *summer* 9am-7pm daily; *winter* 9am-4pm daily.
Admission 40 Kč; 20 Kč children, students; free under-3s.
Built in 1931, Prague's well-sited zoo had become dilapidat-ed and depressingly out-of-date by the 1989 revolution. Thankfully, recent renovation has created more humane and 'natural' spaces for many of the animals, though some still inhabit cramped, barred cages. The zoo's lovely, sloping grounds are a fine place to stroll, and its 'ski lift' provides a stunning view of the city. An excursion to the zoo can be eas-ily combined with a walk through **Stromovka** park (*see p178*) or a boat ride upriver (*see* **Boating** *below*).

Boating

A convenient and entertaining way to see central Prague, rowing boats offer prime Vltava idylls while paddleboats require at least two adult-strength pedal pushers. They can be rented for 80-120 Kč per hour

Give the tram a miss – go boating at Slovanský island.

at Novotného lávka (just to the south of the Staré Město end of Charles Bridge), at Slovanský island (located in the river near the National Theatre), and on the Malá Strana side of the river between Charles Bridge and Mánes Bridge.

PPS-EVD
(info 293 803/298 309). Central Wharf, south of Jirásek Bridge (near Palackého náměstí in Nové Město) – **Map 5 G8***; Kampa Wharf, just south of Charles Bridge (Malá Strana side) –* **Map 2 F4**.
This company's boats cruise north to Prague's zoo from the Central Wharf twice a day. In addition, 75-minute tours sail south from the same pier past Vyšehrad before turning back, offering drink service along the way; more expensive trips include meals. PPS also operates a 50-minute sightseeing tour (although half of this time is spent standing in a lock), leaving once an hour between 11am and 8pm from its Kampa Wharf.

Entertainment & sport

For children's shows and films, check out the listings magazines *Kultura v Praze* and *Přehled*, as well as the *Prague Post*, which also features a regular kids' page.

Although there's a fair bit of children's programming on Czech television, including live-action fairytales and brief animated shorts every evening, the language barrier may prevent foreign kids from enjoying it. Going to the cinema poses a similar problem: though foreign children's films are shown regularly in Prague, they are invariably dubbed into Czech. Satellite television, of course, will provide further options, including the ever-popular Cartoon Network.

In the autumn, one circus or another is usually performing in Prague. A far cry from high-tech three-ring circuses popular in the West, the circuses that come to Prague tend to be rinky-dink one-ring affairs; nonetheless, many kids adore them.

There are plenty of opportunities to go swimming, skiing and skating (*see chapter* **Sport & Fitness**). The skating rinks sometimes have special hours for children.

Puppet Theatre
Puppet theatre has a rich history in Bohemia, and two kid-oriented puppet theatres, **Theatre Minor** and **Spejbl and Hurvínek Theatre** (*see p219*), exist in Prague. Both, unfortunately, usually feature some Czech-language text. You'll also see puppeteers in tourist areas such as Charles Bridge. Quality puppet productions also tour the Czech Republic.

Children's Story Hour
The Globe Bookstore & Coffeehouse, Janovského 14, Prague 7 (6671 2610). Metro Vltavská/1, 3, 8, 12, 14, 17 tram. **Time** 10.30am Sat. **Map 7 D2**
Stories ranging from Czech legends and well-known fairy tales to traditional tales from other cultures are entertainingly told in English during The Globe's weekly story hour.

Hucul Club
Zmrzlík 3, Prague 5 (528 313). Metro Nové Butovice, then 230, 249, 256, 352 bus. **Children's lessons** Sat, Sun. **Fees** 150 Kč per hour. **Membership** 450 Kč per year (lessons free).
Czech horses tend to be very large and pretty wild. This is one of the few stables that has mounts suitable for children.

Koupaliště Divoká Šárka
Šárka, Prague 6 (368 022). Tram 26, then short walk through a rocky valley. **Open** 9am-7pm daily.
Admission 20 Kč; 10 Kč children.
A lovely outdoor swimming area, quiet and shaded, with two pools fed by spring water. The smaller one is for paddling, the larger one shallow enough for young kids to stand in.

Eating out

The bulk of Prague's restaurants and bars are a parent's nightmare – smoke-choked and loud, with sluggish kitchens and slow, surly waiting staff whose attitude snarls, 'What possessed you to bring your rug-rats here?' This intolerance of kids helps explain the popularity of **McDonald's**

Larks in the park

The sun is beaming, the trees are in bloom and you don't feel like hauling your children through the tourist masses clogging central Prague's streets. How to escape the gritty city and keep the children entertained? Look no further.

STROMOVKA

The sprawling expanse of **Stromovka** (trams 5, 12, 17 to Výstaviště or Metro C to Nádraží Holešovice) used to serve as Rudolf II's hunting grounds. Today, its scads of trees tower over a maze of paths, including a ring road perfect for biking or rollerskating. A wander through this huge park reveals flower gardens, bad communist sculpture, a man-made lake with ducks, a ruined château, picnicking families, young couples in clinches and elderly women walking their dogs. Star-gazing youngsters might enjoy shows at the city **planetarium**, just to the left of the main road some 50m from the park's entrance. Modest cafés and drink stands sprinkle the park, providing ice-cream for kids and cold beer for you. *See also page 82.*

If your kids prefer rollercoasters to trees, follow the blaring techno music and the curving ring road back to **Výstaviště**, the exhibition grounds and funfair built for the 1891 Prague Exhibition. With metal-and-glass architecture straight from Dr Seuss, the grounds include a **sculpture museum** (the **Lapidarium**; *see page 98*), an outdoor cinema (**Letní Kino**, operating only on summer evenings – Mon-Sat), a ho-hum **diorama** of the Hussite defeat at the Battle of Lipany, and the **Križik fountains**, which combine synchronised spraying with coloured lights and music. Towards the rear of Výstaviště's enclosure, **Lunapark** offers rides, including a ferris wheel, bumper cars, a pitiful excuse for a haunted house and a rickety but fun rollercoaster. **Dětský svět** (Kids' World) is an indoor play area. *See also page 82.*

PETŘÍN HILL

A centrally located haven of green, **Petřín Hill** is above all a great place for a stroll. On your way up, catch the funicular (9.15am-8.45pm daily) just uphill from the Újezd tram stop. Exit at the second and Šinal stop, turn left, and you'll find yourself in a rose garden, overlooked by the **Štefánik Observatory** (Hvězdárna). Here kids can peer through telescopes, scan an exhibition of cosmic photographs, and watch child-oriented films and slide shows (10.30am and 2.30pm Sat, Sun). Some of the pleasant staff speak English.

*Meet your wobbly twin in the **Mirror Maze**.*

Take a right from the funicular station and follow the path through an arch in the stone wall to Prague's miniature Eiffel Tower (*Rozhledna*). Trudge up the **tower**'s spiral staircase for a stunning view of the city. If you're feeling less ambitious, settle for an ice-cream in the café at the tower's base. With the mini-Eiffel behind you, you'll see several further buildings to the left. The Disneyesque pseudo-Gothic one, known as the **Mirror Maze** (*Bludiště*), houses a none-too-disorienting labyrinth of mirrors, a boring diorama of the Thirty Years' War, and, finally, a fabulous room of distorting trick mirrors that will make even the grumpiest children (and adults) giggle madly. *See also page 80.*

The best thing to do on Petřín, though, is ramble. Various zig-zag paths down the steep hillside lead to orchards, nearby Strahov Monastery, playgrounds, statues and a restaurant called Nebozizek. *See also pages 77-9.*

Other parks

Prague's other major parks include: **Divoká Šárka**, Vokovice, Prague 6 (Tram 26); **Obora Hvězda**, Liboc, Prague 6 (Metro Malostranská, then 1, 2, 18, 22 tram); **Vyšehrad**, Prague 2 (Metro Vyšehrad).

among Czech families. Say what you like about the plasticky food and mass-produced atmosphere, but, with in-restaurant playgrounds, kids' meals and free (self-advertising) balloons, McDonald's at least makes families feel welcome. If you prefer overpriced Tex-Mex fare, **Buffalo Bill's** (*see page 126*) will also cater to your tykes, providing high chairs, crayons and scribble-ready placemats. Parents with plenty of cash could try the weekend brunch buffet at **V Zátiší** (*see page 124*), which offers a wealth of food choices, child-friendly staff and high chairs. If, parental love aside, you just want the little ones out of your hair for an hour, go for the expensive brunch buffet at the Hotel Savoy's **Restaurant Hradčany** (*Keplerova 6-8; 2430 2122*). Stow your offspring in a toy-filled room where a babysitter will keep them entertained. When your kids cry for pizza, the centrally located **Pizzeria Rugantino** (*see page 130*) is a good bet. Despite a dearth of high chairs, this bright, friendly pizzeria has a non-smoking room, good grub and staff who won't give your kids the evil eye.

All over Prague, wise parents should avoid peak dining hours, when waiters may be too harassed to treat children with kid gloves and kitchens may be too busy to deliver food as promptly as your kids' stomachs (and your sanity) demand.

Practicalities

Baby requirements

Disposable nappies and baby food are widely available, both at centrally located department stores such as **Kotva** and **Tesco** (*see p154*) and at specialised stores, including the following:

Chicco *Ondříčkova 20, Prague 3 (627 6338). Metro Jiřího z Poděbrad/5, 9, 11, 26 tram.* **Open** 12.30-6pm Mon-Fri; 8am-noon Sat. **Map 8 C2**

Cinderella *Rumunská 25, Prague 2 (2425 4816). Metro I.P. Pavlova or Náměstí Míru/4, 6, 11, 22, 34 tram.* **Open** 9am-6pm Mon-Fri. **Map 6 L8**

Dětský svět *Budějovická 64, Prague 4 (no phone). Metro Budějovická/118, 121, 134, 190, 504, 505 bus.* **Open** 9am-7pm Mon-Fri; 9am-3pm Sat.

Mevis Bambino *Ječná 14, Prague 2 (2491 1239). Tram 4, 6, 16, 22, 34.* **Open** 9am-6pm Mon-Fri. **Map 5 J8**

Childminding & home help

The large hotels usually have a babysitting service. Otherwise try one of the places below.

Agentura Martina

PO Box 12, Prague 9 (684 2319/887 418/0601 205 534). With a little advance notice, Agentura Martina can arrange English-speaking babysitters.

Little Prince Fun and Learning Center

Severnychodni 4, 25, Prague 4 (7176 1701/0602 390 909). Metro Budějovická, then 121 bus. **Open** 8am-6pm Mon-Fri. **Fees** 350 Kč half-day; 500 Kč full day. Friendly English-speaking staff care for children of many nationalities at this small, private day-care centre, which also welcomes single-day or short-term visitors.

Health

Prague's **water**, though not especially tasty, supposedly conforms to international standards of cleanliness and safety. Its nitrate level, however, is not safe for the developing respiratory systems of children and infants. Bottled water is cheap and available everywhere; red caps usually indicate carbonated varieties.

Atmospheric pollution is also a problem. On some winter days the radio warns parents to keep children indoors. If you are planning to live in Prague, look for accommodation on the outskirts or on the hills of Prague 5 and Prague 6.

If you intend to travel widely around the Czech countryside, it's advisable to be vaccinated against **tick-born encephalitis**, which is endemic throughout Eastern Europe, before you enter the country. **Na Homolce Hospital** (*see below*) and **American Medical Center** (*see below*) can provide the three-injection course of the vaccine in Prague but this is only of use for expats and residents. When found, the ticks must be removed intact. One approach is to smother them in soap or Vaseline and then use tweezers to twist them off anticlockwise. Another is to place a drop of superglue on the tick. After a bath, it usually separates from the skin and the tick can be pulled away whole. Then disinfect the area thoroughly. Occasionally the bite causes a red mark around the spot, leading to infection and fever, which should be treated immediately with antibiotics. If in doubt, see a doctor.

For more information on obtaining medical treatment, *see also page 245.*

American Medical Center

(Americké Kulturní středisko) Janovského 48, Prague 7 (807 756). Metro Vltavská/1, 8, 17 tram. **Fees** nonmembers pay $215 per consultation. A yearly family membership costs $375 and includes a 30% discount on consultation, free complete annual examination and 24-hour house calls. **Map 7 D2**

The English-speaking general practitioners are from the US, Canada and the Czech Republic; the English-speaking dentist is French. All work with children. A paediatrician visits every two weeks to care for newborns and infants.

Na Homolce Hospital

(Nemocnice Na Homolce) Roentgenova 2, Prague 5 (5292 1111). Tram 4, 7, 9/167 bus. **Open** 24 hours daily.

This hospital has a paediatric department (5292 2025) with English-speaking doctors (open from 8am-4pm daily). There is also a 24-hour emergency service (5292 2043) that will make home visits if necessary.

Transport

Children up to six years old travel free on public transport. Those aged ten to 15 go half price, as do adults accompanying children up to three years old. When taking a pram on to a public bus or tram, signal the driver as the vehicle pulls up (so hopefully he'll wait long enough for you to lift the pram inside) and enter and exit through the rear door.

Film

The celluloid lining to the cloud of censorship.

Never let it be said that centuries of oppression didn't do a bit of good for the Czech Republic. If anything positive came from the country's history as a hot potato between Euro superpowers, it's an archive of remarkably brilliant films. Czech cinema has had more than its fair share of setbacks, mirroring the various stages of occupation and liberation in the country's short history. But we can thank the critical eye of the censors for inadvertently encouraging the subtle subversion and charred humour that is the trademark of decades' worth of Czech film – especially the deft, accomplished movies of the Czech new wave.

Indeed, pessimists gripe that the complex, understated films of the Czech new wave set a standard that contemporary filmmakers just can't reach. At first glance, this may seem all too true – witness the in-your-face sentimentality of Oscar-winning *Kolja*, designed to jerk tears from the eyes of people who hadn't even heard of Czechoslovakia. And even many of the less mainstream films produced today are sadly, blatantly derivative copies of the innovative films of the '60s. It can only be hoped that the next generation of Czech directors will be able to make a name for itself on its own terms.

THE EARLY YEARS

Czech film first gained international attention with the Devětsil group, pioneers of a moody surrealism that relished the possibilities of film as a then-new artistic and communicative medium. But Czech filmmaking began in earnest when the Barrandov studios – financed by Václav Havel's grandfather, an architect who was also behind the construction of the swanky Lucerna pasáž – first opened its doors in 1933. Filmmakers throughout Europe flocked to use the Barrandov facilities, and Czech cameramen were soon in considerable demand across the Continent. In its pre-war days, the studios produced around 30 films a year.

Nazi occupation left more emotional scars than physical ones upon the studio complex. In fact, the Barrandov studios remained intact – and even enjoyed significant expansion. But this simply gave Hitler more means to churn out heavily pro-Reich films; during World War II, over 100 cloyingly nationalistic films were made at Barrandov. Still, when the Nazis fell, their backhanded generosity towards the studio remained, and Prague boasted the largest undamaged film studios in all of Europe.

But it wasn't long before a new and more onerous form of propaganda began filling the reels. The communist takeover in 1948 spawned a dubious breed of social realism, producing painfully cheery flicks involving lots of heavy machinery and gleeful workers. Though these films are generally held to represent the dark age of Czech filmmaking, they're worth a glance for their sheer audacity – especially the musicals. As proven in the recent documentary *East Side Story*, it can't but raise a smile to see fields of happy workers spontaneously bursting into song.

Meanwhile, the Academy of Film (FAMU), founded in October 1945 and still going strong today, began schooling what would become a talented group of film directors, and also gave rise to a lot of ne'er-do-well arty types who began to frequent the café **Slavia** next door (*see page 142*). Staffed by seminal talents like Jan Kádár and Elmar Klos, who directed *The Shop on Main Street* (1964) about the puppet state of Slovakia, and Karel Kachyňa, the film school yielded a harvest of directors that would set the standard for Czech film.

CZECH NEW WAVE

A brief period of negligence by party officials, who had bigger problems on their hands than kids with cameras, allowed a batch of remarkable films to emerge. Beginning in 1963 and cut off in 1968, many of these young directors slipped past the censors' eyes, perhaps because they were fresh out of film school and assumed to be free of any troublesome ideological leanings.

Hardly. If anything, the directors and cameramen of the Czech new wave were familiar enough with the system to know best how to subvert it. Their thinly veiled critiques of the state were often manifested as dark, deeply psychological films that relied as much on innovative camerawork and careful lighting as plot.

Many of the most subversive films to slip by the censors were animations. Other classics of the time weren't so lucky and were immediately banned – the latter include Miloš Forman's uproarious *The Fireman's Ball* (1967); Věra Chytilová's *Something Different* (1963), an examination of the fairer sex; Jaromil Jireš's adaptation of Milan Kundera's novel *The Joke* (1969); and a whole slew of other films that gave irreverent, critical renderings of the regime.

No, you haven't stepped back in time. It's just another pesky bunch of film extras.

PRAGUE SPRING TO 1989

The 1968 Warsaw Pact invasion clamped down on the Czech new wave as much as any other form of expression. Socialist realism bared its blindly grinning head once more, and most of the promising directors skipped town rather than subject themselves to the obligatory sessions of self-criticism in front of the powers that be. The reels at Barrandov all but stopped rolling.

A few brave post-new wave films, such as Juraj Herz's *The Cremator of Corpses* (1970) and Václav Matejka's *Nakedness* (1970), were instantly banned, setting the mood for 20 years of largely uninspired and uninspiring films. During this time, the Czech film tradition was continued, somewhat vicariously, through exiled directors struggling to make a name for themselves abroad – a rough battle for most, save Miloš Forman, who imparted more than a little totalitarian chill into his award-winning *One Flew Over the Cuckoo's Nest* (1975).

THE NEXT WAVE

When the wall came tumbling down in 1989, it cleared the way for an outpouring of all the film ideas that had been stoppered up throughout those long years of oppression. And the results haven't exactly been pretty. Though many of the newer films are not particularly bad, they're simply unfocused, caught between the legacy of their predecessors and the whirlwind of influences from the West.

Furthermore, the moviegoing public's demands are changing shape as well. Czechs have traditionally been avid moviegoers, but cinema attendance took a nose-dive in the early '90s with the advent of prime-time TV programming. Though Czechs have always prided themselves on their discerning taste in cinema, smutty and super-popular TV Nova has shown that few can withstand the powerful draw of lazing on the couch watching *Baywatch* reruns.

Thus, the terrain of moviegoing in Prague has shifted to accommodate the increasingly stratified audiences. As more of the formerly state-owned neighbourhood cinemas – many of which plumbed new depths of discomfort – close their doors for good, just a handful have undergone renovations and emerged as viable art house cinemas. Conversely, film distributors who are frustrated with the still-low (though ever-rising) ticket costs, have begun to open multiplexes that have a better chance of making a profit. Multiplex plans are now in the works for Slovanský dům, a one-time rock club complex off Wenceslas Square, and even for the grounds of Výstaviště.

HOLLYWOOD COMES TO TOWN

Another odd footnote in the Czech film archives is the country's popularity as a locale for contemporary Western blockbusters. Lured by the relatively cheap production costs and the beauty of the surroundings, directors and crews have braved the bureaucracy and shot such crowd-pleasers as *Les*

Classic Czech films

Ecstasy (Extáze)
Gustav Machatý (1933)
Known primarily for the first-ever scene of nudity, courtesy of a young Slovak actress who would later be known as Hedy Lamarr, this imagistic film depicts a girl frustrated with her relationship with an older man, and the strange triangle of desire that emerges from their involvement.

The Long Journey (Daleká cesta)
Alfréd Radok (1949)
Banned by the Communists for 20 years, this film uses innovative lighting and camera techniques to depict the deportation of Jews to concentration camps.

The Great Solitude (Velká samota)
Ladislav Helge (1959)
One of the few pre-new wave movies that goes deeper than farm-tool worship, this film focuses on how tough it is to be a rural party official.

The Shop on Main Street (Obchod na korze)
Jan Kádár & Elmar Klos (1964)
Set during World War II in the Nazi puppet state of Slovakia, it's about an honest carpenter who must act as the 'Aryanizator' in a small button shop run by an old Jewish Woman. Winner of the 1966 Oscar for Best Foreign Film.

Intimate Lighting (Intimní osvětlení)
Ivan Passer (1965)
Possibly the most delightful film of the Czech new wave, it tells about the reunion of two old friends after many years of living very different lives, only to discover the musical ensemble they used to play in is as tuneless as it ever was.

Closely Observed Trains (Ostře sledované vlaky)
Jiří Menzel (1966)
Based on a novel by Bohumil Hrabal, this Oscar-winning film about wartime occupation and resistance as seen by a small-town train station signalman epitomises the darkly irreverent humour inherent in the most serious of stories.

Daisies (Sedmikrásky)
Věra Chytilová (1966)
Shot by the director's late husband Jan Kučera, Chytilová's enigmatic film offers a riotous image of youth flouting rules. Two young girls gorge themselves shamelessly at a special banquet for bureaucrats, who luckily never arrive.

Report on the Party and its Guests (O slavnosti a hostech)
Jan Němec (1966)
Along with Švankmajer, Němec continues a Czech surrealist tradition. A strong flavour of Buñuel suffuses his exploration of the increasingly uncomfortable behaviour of guests invited to a party they cannot leave.

The Firemen's Ball (Hoří má panenko)
Miloš Forman (1967)
Concentrating on small-town bureaucracy, Forman expresses with great humour the incompetence that prevents even the simplest of tasks from being carried out smoothly.

The Joke (Žert)
Jaromil Jireš (1969)
Based on a novel by Milan Kundera, Jireš's fine film unravels the absurd and terrifying ramifications of making even the mildest of jokes at the Party's expense.

Larks on a String (Skřivánci na niti)
Jiří Menzel (1969)
Set in a steel mill in the industrial town of Kladno, politics crops up but love – and plain libido – somehow always triumph. Banned soon after its release, the film was not shown again until 1989 when it won the Berlin Film Festival's Golden Bear.

The Ear (Ucho)
Karel Kachyňa (written by Jan Procházka) (1970)
The full force of surveillance terror and paranoia is

Misérables, Immortal Beloved and Mission: Impossible here. This also means that there's a brisk business in employing extras. So if your late-night bartender looks a bit familiar, who knows? You might have seen him decked out in frills and a Renaissance wig in the period movie *du jour*.

TICKET PRICES
Screening flicks at 25 Kč a head, once standard practice in Prague, barely covers the cost of renting the print, so distributors jump at any chance they can get to jack up ticket prices, which usually means that it'll cost you more to see a potentially popular film. *Evita*, at 100 Kč a ticket, was the first to break the three-digit barrier, and it's only going to go up from there – though most cinemas still adjust ticket prices to the movie in question. Certain cinemas that boast better-quality sight and

sound, such as **Cinema Broadway** and **Galaxie Multiplex**, get away with slapping the same high price on all their features. Art cinemas and out-of-the-way venues are often around half the price.

SCREENING INFORMATION
Big-time comedy flicks or movies that might be geared for children are generally dubbed, but most are kept in the original language, with Czech subtitles. Wenceslas Square is a bit of an open-air multiplex, but you'll usually find the same six action blockbusters at all the downtown cinemas. Furthermore, many of the downtown venues reach new standards in discomfort, with creaky, rickety seats and screens set neck-achingly high. Go for the balconies when you can. But spare yourself the wrath of your fellow film goers by sticking to the seat that's assigned to

exposed in this chilling film whose origins go further back than the communists to Kafka. Banned instantly, of course.

Elementary School (Obecná škola)
Jan Svěrák (1988)
Also up for an Oscar in its time, Svěrák's earlier film is far subtler and more mischievous than *Kolja* (*see below*), depicting a group of rambunctious schoolchildren who warm up to a militaristically strict teacher.

The Faust Lesson (Lekce Faust)
Jan Švankmajer (1994)
Blending puppets, claymation, object animation and live action, Švankmajer's grotesquely absorbing version of Faust draws on both Goethe and Bohemian puppet traditions.

Kolja
Jan Svěrák (1996)
The father/son film making team of Jan and Zdeněk Svěrák hilariously play out Czech-Russian antagonisms in miniature, in a late 1980s story of a Czech musician who unwittingly becomes the guardian of a young Russian boy.

Buttoners (Knoflíkáři)
Petr Zelenka (1997)
Sardonic, schizophrenic flick that shuffles the lives of several disparate characters, all vaguely connected through the bombing of Hiroshima. Sassy and clean-paced enough to have nabbed a few international awards.

you. Screening times, especially at **Galaxie Multiplex**, can be wildly erratic; nonetheless, you can get a basic idea of showings from the *Prague Post*, *DoMěsta*, or from any of the events posters plastered on kiosks around town.

Best of the cinemas

Cinema Broadway
Na příkopě 31, Prague 1 (2161 3278). Metro Můstek or Náměstí Republiky/5, 14, 26 tram. **Map 4 K4**
Huge screen, cushy seats deep enough to swallow any voyeur, and ear-ringing sound quality – this is the best place to see spectacle films. The Broadway's programming is seldom short on eye-candy.

Galaxie Multiplex
Arkalycká 874, Prague 4 (6791 0616/24-hour info line 9614 1414, only in Czech). Metro Háje.

Soon to be dwarfed by Bonton's multiplex in Slovanský dům, and not a moment too soon. The ham-flavoured popcorn, trashy pastel-patterned upholstery and claustrophobic mini-cinemas were outdated long before the plans got off the drawing board.

Kino Illusion
Vinohradská 48, Prague 2 (250 260). Metro Náměstí Míru/11 tram. **Map 8 A3**
All dressed up in faded pink, this cinema relentlessly screens new Czech films, for better or worse; *Knoflíkáři* played here for a solid five months.

Kinokavárna Jalta
Václavské náměstí 43, Prague 1 (2422 8814). Metro Muzeum/3, 9, 14, 24 tram. **Map 6 K6**
The cinema coffeehouse is a dying tradition – at one time *kinokavárnas* were relaxed, homey places where you could have a drink and a smoke while you watched the movie. This is the only one still operating, and it's little more than an informal seating plan around a small screen. Sort of like filmgoing in someone's basement. The cool thing, of course, is that this someone lives right on Wenceslas Square.

Lucerna
Vodičkova 36, Prague 1 (2421 6972-3). Metro Můstek/3, 9, 14, 24 tram. **Map 6 K6**
A true movie palace, with shabby chandeliers, ornate balconies and an adjacent bar complete with piano player.

64 U Hradeb
Mostecká 21, Prague 1 (535 006). Metro Malostranská/12, 22 tram. **Map 2 E3**
With a bluish, newish décor, a huge screen and good sound quality – plus reliably experimental programming and rare late-night screenings – this is probably Prague's best cinema.

Arthouse cinemas

Some of the venues below are film clubs, but you usually don't have to be a member to see a film; just buy a 20 Kč pass along with your ticket. In addition to the below, **Terminal Bar** (*see page 144*) has a vast archive of films to rent for 50 Kč a time; cram as many people as you can into the gold-spangled screening room.

Aero
Biskupcová 31, Prague 3 (893 601). Tram 1, 9, 16.
A battered gem in the bleaker streets of Žižkov: green-velvet wallpaper and lamps shaped like wilted lilies only help reassure you that you're enriching your soul.

Dlabačov
Bělohorská 24, Prague 6 (311 5328). Tram 8, 22.
Don't be scared off by this film club's mothership, the horrifying Hotel Pyramid. Ensconced in the basement and boasting a mammoth screen and decent sound quality, this cinema shows local and imported indies of reliable quality.

Evald
Národní třída 28, Prague 1 (2110 5225). Metro Národní třída/6, 9, 18, 22 tram. **Map 3 H5**
Property of CinemArt, the country's art-film distributor, this 30-person venue usually shows the more select of the first-run films.

Institut Français
Štěpánská 35, Prague 1 (2421 4032). Metro Můstek/3, 9, 14, 24, tram. **Map 6 K6**
Regularly offers free screenings of Czech-subtitled French films, in refined surroundings. Comfy seats and a big screen.

How to crash a film festival

It may not attract gargantuan stars; the system of ticket sales was probably designed by a bunch of drunk, blind hyenas; you'll most likely end up sleeping in a remote student dorm temporarily dubbed 'Hotel Festival'; the film you've been dying to see may be screened in its original Finnish only; and there may not be a thing to eat in the whole damned town. But the **Karlovy Vary Film Festival** is definitely worth your time.

For one thing, it's lovely to see the postcard-perfect spa town saturated with a different kind of tourism than that of the standard spa-wafer munchers. Ever eager to please, the town puts on a new face to suit the festival-going public as well, with movie posters even hovering above the central stream that flows through the main boulevard. Occasional outdoor mini-concerts and leggy attendants add to the highly charged environment that takes over the town each year.

Of course, it's highly possible that the festival, until recently a bi-annual event, would have dwindled into shabby obscurity had it not been for the spawning of the short-lived **Prague Film Festival** (otherwise known as the **Zlatý Golem Festival**). Though the Prague festival lasted for only two years, the pressure was enough for Karlovy Vary to start behaving in earnest like a grown-up gala. Jiří Bartoška, a much-respected Czech actor, was appointed president of the festival and immediately switched it from a bi-annual to an annual event. Hosted, as always, by the Hotel Thermal, itself an uninspiring concrete affair but at least small enough to prevent festival-goers from getting lost, the event has benefitted from a team of image-makers, conscripted to provide a theme for each year and make over the hotel and the surrounding town. And though the goings-on still lack the glam of many big-time film festivals, Karlovy Vary still manages to attract a clutch of interesting stars, such as Christopher Walken, Alan Alda, Julia Ormond and Steve Buscemi.

Sponsors' parties are best avoided, unless of course you think it good taste to imbue the Grandhotel Pupp's elegant dining room with the atmosphere of a high-school prom by plonking a loud band in its centre. Though the accreditation policy is tightening up, a bit of smooth talking might weasel you a pass, which will give you a better shot of avoiding the queues and crashing the incessant parties by the Hotel Thermal pool. And then the overbooked screenings, films that blacken out mid-reel, and the constantly crashing computer systems may not seem to matter any more.

For more on **Karlovy Vary**, *see page 234.*

MAT Studio

Karlovo náměstí 19, Prague 1 (2491 5765). Metro Karlovo náměstí/3, 4, 6, 14, 16, 18, 22, 24 tram. **Map 5 H8**
With a capacity of only 24 people and a consistently impressive run of Czech films with English subtitles at the unheard-of hour of 10pm, you'd better buy tickets in advance. If you're turned away, you can always repair to the bar in the basement or on the ground floor, and sip your scotch amid loose threads of film and pastel upholstery.

Ponrepo/Bio Konvikt

(Český filmový archiv/Ponrepo) Bartolomějská 13, Prague 1 (no phone). Metro Národní třída/6, 9, 18, 22 tram. **Annual membership** 120 Kč adults; 60 Kč students. **Map 3 H5**
Membership must be bought during business hours for each person in your party; then you can delve into the Republic's film heritage.

Festivals & special events

The events listed below are pretty permanent; keep your eyes open, though, for the occasional fly-by-night job like **Indies Festival** (which last happened in late 1997). The **Archa** theatre (*see page 215*) occasionally has interesting mini-festivals and multimedia screenings.

Look out also for the summer outdoor cinemas (Letní kino) in Výstaviště (2010 2104) and on Střelecký island (0602 710 696).

Days of European Film

(2423 4875). **Date** late Apr.
This (roughly) week-and-a-half-long festival takes over two of the city's top cinemas – **Lucerna** and **64 U Hradeb** (*see above*; information is available at these cinemas) – and shows co-productions and award-winning European films that have never before been screened in Prague, in their original language (usually with English subtitles). When it's over, the whole festival is screened in Brno. The festival is organised by a number of European cultural centres; the number above is for the main organiser, the Austrian Cultural Institute.

FAMU Student Film Festival

FAMU Smetanovo nábřeží 2, Prague 1 (2422 9468). Tram 9, 17, 18, 22. **Date** Apr (varies).
Discover the juvenilia of tomorrow's big Czech directors at this weekend festival, usually screened at Divadlo Archa.

Karlovy Vary Film Festival

info: Marek Brodsky, Pánská 1, Prague 1 (2423 5412). **Date** nine days in mid-July.
Centred at the Hotel Thermal, but occupying practically every available space in this small spa resort. *See above* **How to crash a film festival**. *See also p234.*

Gay & Lesbian Prague

Small and imperfectly formed the scene may be, but the action's out there if you know where to look.

For a town of its size, Prague has a decently happening gay scene, especially for men – but politically and culturally, gay life in Prague is still edging out of the closet. Not that you should necessarily expect harassment or gay-bashing if you're out and proud, but do bear in mind that mainstream queer culture is still in its infancy in this country. Most likely, any public displays of identity will win you baffled stares and whispered comments – though people will generally leave you alone.

But who wants to be left alone? Take a deeper look, and it won't take much to expose all the latent homophobia that's rampant in the Czech Republic. Media representations of homosexuality tend to be dumbfoundingly reactionary, such as David Ondříček's popular rave flick *Whisper* ('Šeptej', 1996) in which a girl converts a femmy boy to hetero living, while his suicidal prostitute lover ends up in an asylum. And the recent lobbying for a bill that would legally recognise same-sex partnerships was met with overwhelming disdain in parliament. 'Why not grant legal registration to sock fetishists as well? Fetishists are, after all, very fond of their socks,' sniffed one ODS (Social Democrat) member, while an ODA (Democratic Alliance) member was less witty, advising gays to 'go to hell… The world has bigger problems.' Ultimately the bill was rejected largely on the grounds that businessmen might feign a gay relationship just to get tax breaks.

While there are no sodomy laws, the so-called 'family law', in existence since the outset of the communist regime, sanctified the mum-dad-two-kids unit as the most effective mechanism for well-functioning proletarian families –though it could be argued that the system, by forging such strong bonds in the male workforce and creating self-sufficient, capable women – did more towards cracking that unit than building it.

But even among the more enlightened segments of the community, you'll probably find resistance towards claiming any common identity. For the would-be cruiser, this definitely takes its toll on local nightlife, as many establishments seem to

Blissed out: **Radost**'s *Hot House. See p203.*

host just the owners and their six friends. Gay men have a fair chance at a good time, with several established haunts consistently drawing in the crowds – even if you'll soon begin to notice the same faces over and over again.

But tough luck, gals – lesbian life in Prague is maddeningly domesticated. Though there seem to be a fair number of girls who like girls in this town, most seem to have already chosen partners and settled down in thinly veiled partnerships. A newer generation of baby dykes has yet to claim a niche.

Let it be said, though, that gay life in Prague is increasingly more out, more aware and more proud. AIDS awareness is on the rise, and there's an ever-widening distinction between pick-up bars and places where you can just go for a good time. And queer chic is rampant in this town. You'll find the most out organisations are those that don't trumpet their orientation: the tasteful **Medúza** (*see page 152*), run by a group of lesbians but frequented by plenty of well-heeled types; and anything by restaurateur Roman Reznicek, whose heavily stylised **Palffy Palac** (*see page 127*), **Érra Café** (*see page 140*) and **Mecca** (due to open in late 1998 or early 1999) rank among the most tasteful and cosmopolitan establishments in Prague. And **Radost** (*see page 203*) now hosts gay nights every Thursday – at press time, these were not especially well attended, but are at least a sign that queer culture is making a name for itself in the mainstream.

Bars, pubs & clubs

Many of these bars claim to be 'members only' – but are not about to turn away clientele. So just look in the know, and you'll be let in.

A-club

Miličova 25, Prague 3 (9004 4303). Tram 5, 9, 26, 55, 58. **Open** 5pm-6am Mon-Sat; 3pm-midnight Sun. **Map 8 C1**
'A' for effort. A welcome breath of good intention in Žižkov's shady gay scene, this rose-hued lesbian bar, with a microscopic dancefloor, hosts women-only nights on Fridays and occasional poetry readings, performances and a lot of girl-power art on the walls.

Drake's

Petřínská 5, Prague 5 (534 909). Tram 9, 12, 57, 58. **Open** 24 hours daily.
Everything you could possibly request in a gay bar: boys in tight T-shirts, bad disco lighting, a video-screening room and adjacent video rental store – even private dark rooms if you can't make it back to your own apartment.

Kafírna U českého pána

Kozi 13, Prague 1 (232 8283). Metro Staroměstská or Náměstí Republiky. **Open** 11am-10pm Mon-Fri; 2-10pm Sat, Sun. **Map 3 J2**
Cheery, if slightly sterile, lesbian-owned two-room bar, attracting a middle-aged crowd of lonely hearts and their lonelier friends.

Knast/Arco bar

Opatovická 12, Prague 1 (no phone). Metro Národní třída/6, 9, 18, 22, 51, 54, 57, 58 tram. **Open** *Arco Bar* 9am-8pm Mon-Fri; 11am-8pm Sat, Sun; *Knast* 9pm-5am daily. **Map 5 H6**
A little something for everyone (as long as you're male, that is; ladies won't be welcome unless they bring their girlfriends): a low-lit pub (Arco bar) with greasy-spoon Czech meals on the ground floor and, in the basement (Knast), pool tables, a video-screening room and closets for furtive groping.

L club

Lublaňská 48, Prague 2 (296 287). Metro I.P. Pavlova/6, 11, 56 tram. **Open** *club* 10pm-4am daily; *restaurant* 8-10pm daily. **Map 6 L8**
More GM than L – and suspiciously young GMs at that, who can usually be taken home for a price. Don't panic; the age of consent in this country is 15. There's a restaurant here too, plus transvestite shows on Wednesdays, and stripteases on Fridays and Saturdays.

Piano bar

Milešovská 10, Prague 3 (627 5467). Metro Jiřiho z Poděbrad/11 tram. **Open** 5pm-2am daily. **Map 8 C2**
Campy and cute, and attracts a whole spectrum from lithe young boys striking poses over the pool table to beefy old

queens hunched over the tables discussing the family dog with their partner. The piano in the back room often gets as much action as the patrons themselves.

Sam's club

Čajkovského 34, Prague 3 (no phone). Metro Jiřiho z Poděbrad/5, 9, 26, 55, 58 tram. **Open** 9pm-4am Tue-Sun. **Map 8 C2**
Billed as a leather bar for men, but the garb is none too exotic. In fact, the club has been known to forgo the leather altogether in favour of evenings in the buff.

Stella

Lužická 10, Prague 2 (2425 7869). Metro Náměstí Míru/16, 22, 34, 51, 57 tram. **Open** 8pm-5am daily. **Map 8 B3**
Consistently a blast, with an amicable amount of scamming at any given time. Increasingly popular among younger gays and lesbians who aren't interested in pulling a profit out of the evening.

Tom's bar

Pernerova 4, Prague 8 (2481 3802). Metro Florenc/8, 24, 52 tram. **Open** 9pm-2am Tue-Thu; 9pm-4am Fri, Sat.
Popular men-only bar and disco. Upstairs looks like any other Czech restaurant and serves reasonable food. The cellar houses a dancefloor, a video room and a cavernous zone.

Tunel sex club

Plzeňská 41, Prague 5 (no phone). Metro Anděl/4, 7, 9, 14, 34, 58 tram. **Open** 9pm-very late.
Not for sensitive souls, this sleek, newish club is as hardcore as Prague gets. Discover fetishes you didn't even know you had. Strictly men only.

U dubu

Záhřebská 14, Prague 2 (no phone). Metro Náměstí Míru/6, 11, 56 tram. **Open** 10am-3pm, 6pm-midnight, daily. **Map 6 M9**
What's a pretty boy like you doing in a run-down *pivnice* like this? The girls invariably turned away at the door might clue you in.

U Petra Voka

Na Bělidle 40, Prague 5 (no phone). Metro Anděl/4, 6, 7, 9, 12, 14, 34, 52, 58 tram. **Open** 8pm-late daily.
This friendly bar has all the raunchiness and friendliness – and a bit of the smell – of a local roadside truck-stop. As good-natured as the gay scene gets in Prague.

It's a travesti

Don't expect the attitude or finesse of any of the big-city shows. Prague's transvestite scene is mostly commandeered by a group called **The Screamers**, who stumble along at lip-syncs and don wigs with a sprayed-in bad hair day. Might be fun, but the crowds these places tend to attract are straight in every sense of the word, and you're lucky if you make it out having had a reasonably un-depressing time. Check for more polished solo acts at some of the places above – like the lovely **Ivana Trampová**. Or try your luck at the **Aqua club 2000** (*see below*) or...

U střelce

Karoliny Světlé 12, Prague 1 (2423 8278). Metro Národní třída/17, 18, 51, 54 tram. **Open** 9.30pm-late Wed, Fri, Sat.
A gay pub with thrice-weekly transvestite shows. Booking is essential.

Restaurants

U kapra
Žatecká 7, Prague 1 (2481 3635). Metro Staroměstská/ 17, 18, 51, 54 tram. **Open** 11am-1am daily.
Map 3 H3
Because of its location, in the dead centre of the Old Town, you may often find groups of tourists blissfully gnawing on their carp, oblivious to the stares of the regulars. Nice to find the dichotomy reversed once in a while.

U starého songu
Štitného 27, Prague 3 (2278 2047). Tram 5, 9, 26, 55, 58. **Open** 6pm-midnight Mon-Thur; 6pm-2am Fri, Sat.
Map 8 C1
Reminiscent of a queer 'Cheers', with lots of red brick and a waiter who acts like he knows your name. Subdued and homey. Though the management has recently changed hands, the food is still the sketchiest thing about the place.

Saunas

Babylona
Martinská 6, Prague 1 (2423 2304). Metro Národní třída/6, 9, 18, 22, 51, 54, 57, 58 tram. **Open** 2pm-3am daily. **Map 3 H5**
Newish, cleanish mecca of pools, steam rooms and massages.

Chaos
Dušní 13b, Prague 1 (2423 8510). Metro Staroměstská/ 17, 51, 54 tram. **Open** 5pm-3am daily. **Map 3 H2**
A little bit grungy, but the steam rooms, saunas and screening rooms keep the crowds (ahem) coming.

David
Sokolovská 77, Prague 8 (232 8789). Metro Křižíkova/8, 24 tram. **Open** 2pm-2am daily.
Prague's oldest sauna had its share of crazy times, but now has fallen out of favour with the young and steamy.

All of the above

Aqua club 2000/Connections
Husitská 7, Prague 3 (627 8971). Bus 133, 135, 207, 504. **Open** 9pm-4am daily.
Disco! Drag queens! Sauna! Swimming pool! Take your pick in this multi-tiered complex. The dancefloor – the newly renovated Connections disco next door, with an influx of new blood to boot – is the most reliable of the bunch.

Accommodation

Gay penzion David
Holubova 5, Prague 5 (9001 1293/fax 549 820). Metro Anděl, then 14 tram. **Rates** *single* 1,360 Kč; *double* 2,040 Kč; *extra bed* 510 Kč. **Credit** AmEx, EC, MC, V.
Gay visitors (male and female) will find this suburban villa, 15 minutes from the centre, a decent base for unwinding. Good value with well-equipped, clean and colourful rooms and breakfast included. Advanced booking essential. Sauna and delightful terrace restaurant open to non-residents.

Villa Andy
U šípků 10, Prague 5 (581 6681). Bus 126, 246, 247, 248. **Rates** *single* 1,500 Kč; *double* 1,800 Kč.
Credit EC, MC.
Named after everyone's favourite Slovak-born pop art supremo. Not too conveniently located, but with a sauna, city tours and all-too-willing staff, who's complaining?

Publications

Amigo
PO Box 60, Prague 8 (684 6548/amigo@czn.cz).
Bi-monthly. Calendars, horoscopes, personals and listings, plus a few nudie pics to boot. Available for 30 Kč at most of the above-listed establishments.

ProFem
V Olšinách 50, Prague 10 (no phone).
Lesbian monthly mag of creative writing, essays and photography – and 'Dykes to Watch Out For' on the back page.

SOHO Revue
Husitská 7, Prague 3 (627 8348/www.infima.cz/soho).
Somewhat texty, this monthly magazine's broad-stroke articles are aimed at gay and lesbian life in the Czech Republic. The design and the subjects are getting progressively flashy.

Information & helplines

ČSAP (HIV+ helpline)
PO Box 34, Prague 8 (2421 0956/2481 0345).
Open 10am-6pm Mon, Wed, Thur; 10am-10pm Tue.
Hours vary, but staff are usually around in the afternoon. Organises trips and activities as well as providing information and support.

Lambda
Krakovská 2, Prague 1 (739 276). Metro Muzeum.
Open 2-5.30pm, 6.30-8pm, daily. **Map 6 K7**
Moonlights as a sex shop, but also provides information about the region's festivals and parties.

LOGOS Gay Helpline
Jungmannova 9, Prague 1 (254 650). **Open** 9am-7pm Wed.
A hotline for basic counselling and support for gays and lesbians run by **Lambda** (*see above*). No English spoken.

National AIDS hotline
(08001 44444). **Open** 10am-6pm Mon, Wed; noon-10pm Tue; 10am-7pm Thur.
Can advise on prevention.

Festivals

ApriLes
*Contact **Amigo** – see above – for details.* **Date** April.
A much more self-conscious event than the Gay Man Pageant, hosting workshops, discussion groups, art exhibits and readings. Worth checking out, if only to show support and to catch the talent acts in the evenings.

Parník
*Contact **A-club** – see above – for details.* **Date** May.
Held each May, a riotous, all-day cruise down the the Vltava, with drag queens and other derelict types drinking, posing, and having a ball. If you're in town, don't miss it. Information can be procured at any one of the clubs listed above.

Rainbow Festival in Karlovy Vary
*Contact **Amigo** – see above – for details.* **Date** May.
This unlikely event features exhibits, workshops, theatre, film and music events that culminate with a bash in, of all places, the staid Grandhotel Pupp. Designed to heighten awareness of gays' contributions towards the arts.

Gay Man Pageant
(05 4721 6233). **Date** June.
Host cities vary for this fabulous, fun opportunity for queers from the provinces to show their faces.

Literary Prague

There's far more to Czech writing than Kundera and Kafka.

Modern Czech literature first took significant shape towards the end of the nineteenth century, when rising Czech nationalism encouraged a linguistic revival. In previous centuries, educated Czechs had spoken, and written, almost exclusively in German, leaving the native Slavic tongue to the peasants. Though some important Czech writers, including Kafka, continued to write in German up until World War II, the late 1800s produced the first examples of what has become, in little more than a century, an impressive body of world-class Czech-language literature.

BEGINNINGS

One of the fathers of that literature, **Jaroslav Hašek**, created in his World War I novel *The Good Soldier Švejk* an enduring and uniquely Czech anti-hero. Uncannily similar to his alcoholic creator, Švejk enjoys a series of wartime misadventures, eventually triumphing over the forces of evil (elitism) through sheer cheerfulness. Hašek himself wasn't so lucky: he drank himself to death in 1923.

A more 'respectable' writer, who emerged during the interwar period, was **Karel Čapek**. A talented journalist, novelist and playwright, and close friend of First Republic President TG Masaryk, Čapek wrote books and plays for both adults and children. Internationally, he is best known for popularising the Czech word 'robot' in his widely performed 1921 play *R.U.R.* ('Rossum's Universal Robots').

KAFKA & JEWISH-GERMAN WRITERS

While Hašek boozed his way around Europe and Čapek wrote political speeches, **Franz Kafka** lived a more anonymous life in the Bohemian capital. A member of Prague's large and vibrant German-speaking community, Kafka found Prague considerably less charming than most visitors do nowadays. One of Kafka's recurring themes – that of the individual inexplicably caught up in a nightmarish situation beyond his control

– took on new significance during the Stalinist years, when his works were banned. Today, Kafka's face broods on countless T-shirts and coffee mugs for sale in the centre of town and the adjectival form of his name has become so ubiquitous in Prague that a new tourist-attraction-cum-funhouse bills itself as 'a Kafkaesque experience'.

Kafka died in 1924, and the Final Solution effectively destroyed the rest of Prague's Jewish community. Among the survivors were **Arnošt Lustig** and **Jiří Weil**, who have written about their experiences during the Occupation.

SAMIZDAT & EMIGRES

When communism came to Czechoslovakia in 1948, those Czechs writers who refused to toe the party line, either aesthetically or politically, were banished to rotten day jobs or exile, and their writings published only in *samizdat* (typewritten manuscripts illegally circulated among intellectuals and sympathetic cultural circles). Among them was **Ivan Klíma**, president of the Czech Writers' Union during the Prague Spring, whose banned works appeared *samizdat* until 1989's revolution hauled them into the mainstream. Klima's primary themes are morality and that favourite Czech pastime, the love affair. His most recent novel, *The Ultimate Intimacy* (1997), combines his characters' painful transition from the confinements of communism to the terrifying 'freedoms' of capitalism with a framing story of a devastating clash between love and moral rectitude.

The most internationally famous of the Czech writers who came of age during the communist period is **Milan Kundera**. While his early novels like *The Joke* and *The Book of Laughter and Forgetting* depict the absurdity and bureaucracy of Stalinism, Kundera's best-known work, *The Unbearable Lightness of Being*, concentrates on his other obsession: the perils and cruelties of sexuality. Foreigners will find Kundera surprisingly unpopular in the Czech Republic, where his post-Prague Spring emigration (and recent literary abandonment of the Czech language) are sometimes considered betrayals of his native land.

Like Kundera, novelist **Josef Škvorecký** chose emigration over persecution. Along with writing *The Swell Season, Talking Moscow Blues,* and *The Miracle Game,* Škvorecký also established Sixty-Eight Publishers in his adopted Canada. Škvorecký and his wife not only published the works of many banned Czech writers, but they also managed to smuggle some works back into their native country.

Other famous members of the dissident generation include scientist-poet-essayist **Miroslav Holub** (*The Vanishing Lung Syndrome* and *The Dimension of the Present Moment*) and the feuilleton-writer **Ludvík Vaculík** (*A Cup of Coffee With My Interrogator*), whose polemical *2,000 Words Manifesto*, published in July 1968, helped spur the ensuing communist invasion.

Václav Havel, the playwright president, writes little except his own speeches these days, but his absurdist plays (among them *The Garden Party*, *Audience* and *Memorandum*) still make engaging reading. For an insight into Havel the man, try reading *Disturbing the Peace* (1990), in which he talks about his privileged childhood as well as events leading up to the 1968 invasion, or *Letters to Olga* (1988), written to his wife while he was in prison in the late 1970s. For an overview of Havel's main political concerns, read *The Art of the Impossible* (1997), a lucidly written and impressive (if somewhat repetitive) collection of speeches.

Bohumil Hrabal's gorgeously written and idiosyncratic masterpieces, including *Closely Observed Trains* and *I Served the King of England*, made him perhaps the best loved of post-war Czech writers. Literarily unproductive for most of the '80s and '90s, Hrabal was a famous fixture at the Old Town pub U Zlatého tygra (The Golden Tiger; *see page 142*), where literary acolytes seeking their idol rarely rated more than a snarl. Though official reports of the elderly Hrabal's death in 1997 claimed the writer 'fell' from the fifth-floor window of his hospital room while feeding birds, his works include many references to suicide.

POST-REVOLUTIONARY WRITING

Nowadays, Czech writers have lost the inflated status – as artists, thinkers and moral authorities – that they both suffered and enjoyed in more repressive times. Accordingly, most older writers have moved beyond reminiscing about socialist oppression and the Velvet Revolution. Younger writers often explicitly reject the traditional Czech role of writer as the moral and political conscience of his/her nation.

Jáchym Topol and **Michal Viewegh**, the best-known literary darlings of the up-and-coming crop of writers, both portray the moral muddle of individuals coping with post-communist life. Topol's lengthy and sometimes difficult novels appeal to critics and hip, avowedly intellectual readers; his short story *A Trip to the Train Station* has been published in a joint English/Czech version. Viewegh's humorous semi-autobiographical novels, wildly popular with readers of all ages and backgrounds, are increasingly derided by critics. His second and third novels, *The Wonderful Years*

That Sucked and *Bringing Up Girls in Bohemia*, have been made into popular films; the latter has also been published in English translation.

When he died in 1995 amid eyebrow-raising circumstances (his body was found at the foot of a cliff), **Lukáš Tomin** left behind three unique experimental prose volumes – *The Doll*, *Ashtrays* and *Kye* – each depicting a surreally disjointed and thorny world. Tomin's publisher, Prague's Twisted Spoon Press, has also printed *The Diary of Mr Pinke*, a dreamily poetic work by **Ewald Murrer**. Other interesting young authors include **Michal Ajvaz**, **Jiří Kratochvíl** and **Martin Šimecka**.

Only recently have female Czech writers begun to get the recognition they deserve. Though **Věra Linhartová** (who emigrated in 1961) has long been lauded for her experimental writing, her international reputation lags unfairly behind that of her male contemporaries. The much younger **Iva Pekárková**'s unevenly written and highly sexed novel *Truck Stop Rainbows* made a big splash in 1994, when its author still worked as a cabbie in New York City; she has published two more novels since. Few full-length books by Czech women have yet been published in English. Thus, the best place to read works by outstanding writers like **Daniela Fischerová**, **Alexandra Berková**, **Zuzana Brabcová** and **Eva Hauserová** is *Allskin and Other Tales* (Women in Translation, 1998), an anthology of contemporary Czech women writers. Female Czech writers, both established and relatively unknown, also appear in *one eye open*, a bilingual feminist journal.

For gender-neutral samplers of contemporary and recent Czech literature, pick up *This Side of Reality* (Serpent's Tail, 1996) or *Daylight in Nightclub Inferno* (Catbird Press, 1997), which include works by many of the above-mentioned authors. Previously untranslated work by contemporary Czech writers occasionally appears in the quality local English-language journals *Trafika* and *The Prague Revue*.

In the wake of an annoying 1992-4 media blitz – which repeatedly tried to button-hole Prague's expatriate writing community as budding Steins, Hemingways and Fitzgeralds boozing it up in the so-called 'Left Bank of the 1990s' – the city's many English-language writers now spend more time writing than socialising or fronting for cameras. **Beefstew**, a weekly open-mike 'poetry reading' held in the basement of **Radost/FX Café** (*see page 152*) since 1993, usually features fiction, live music, play excerpts and stand-up comedy as well as a smattering of verse. Depending on the night, the quality can range from impressive to depressing. Nonetheless, the good-humoured and amazingly tolerant audience can be counted on to applaud dutifully and Beefstew remains the best place in town to meet friendly, literary-minded English-speaking expatriates.

Music: Classical & Opera

Get ready to baroque, Bohemian style.

In keeping with its reputation as a great musical centre in the nineteenth and early twentieth centuries, Prague is anxious to re-establish itself on the contemporary international musical scene. And by and large it is succeeding. Czech conductors such as **Jiří Bělohlávek** and **Libor Pešek** are well known to British concert-goers, while singers **Eva Urbanová**, **Dagmar Pecková** and **Magdalena Koˇzená** are prominent on the international circuit. The **Prague Spring Festival**, the highlight of the musical calendar, now plays host to orchestras of the calibre of the Berlin Philharmonic and the London Symphony Orchestra as well as highly sought-after soloists such as Kathleen Battle.

Like anywhere else, however, state funding is rapidly diminishing and there is an increasing reliance upon corporate sponsorship, often to the detriment of standards of programming, although things have not yet reached the crisis level of some other European capitals. True, the Czech Philharmonic has been going through a somewhat traumatic period over the past few years, and lack of cooperation between the two opera companies, the National Theatre and the State Opera, has led to unnecessary duplication of what was already a limited repertoire. In addition, the National Theatre appears happy to forfeit the prime potential revenue season of summer by shutting down and allowing foreign companies to take over its halls.

Nevertheless, brilliant music somehow survives from year to year in Prague. There are more than 20 ticket agencies, all vying for the tourist trade. Although this sounds attractive, what it means in practice is that there are too many concerts (particularly in the churches) offering a stale repertoire of Mozart, Vivaldi and Dvořák executed by bored musicians doing it for the umpteenth time – and too often at a price well over what one would pay for a major concert by any of the principal orchestras.

That said, there is more than enough high quality musicianship to satisfy the most indefatigable music lover. The Czechs are very proud of their musical tradition – and rightly so. Although the Big Four – **Smetana**, **Dvořák**, **Janáček** and **Martinů** – are firmly established throughout the

*Opening night of the **Prague Spring Festival**.*

world, there are many composers, particularly from the baroque and classical periods, who have remained largely unknown outside the Czech Republic. Prague has always been one of the musical capitals of Europe, and it now boasts three theatres where opera is regularly performed, four major orchestras and countless smaller ensemble groups, ranging from early music to contemporary. Whatever your tastes, you are sure to find something that appeals.

Long before the première of *Don Giovanni* in Prague in 1787 (the one landmark in Czech musical history that everyone seems to know), the city and Bohemia as a whole had produced many composers whose influence extended far beyond its boundaries. Chamber concerts held in churches and palaces throughout the city provide a good introduction to the works of **Zelenka, Mysliveček, Benda, Černohorský** and **Brixi** – to name only a handful. Furthermore, as a result of recent research largely forbidden under communism, a good deal of new material has been unearthed from archives and is being given an airing for the first time in more than 100 years.

Although Mozart-mania doesn't quite reach the level of kitsch found in Salzburg, it's all but impossible to visit Prague without encountering countless Mozart references. Prague, unlike Vienna, gave *The Marriage of Figaro* a rapturous reception, and commissioned not only *Don Giovanni* (dedicated to 'the good people of Prague'), but also *La Clemenza di Tito*, written for the coronation of Emperor Leopold II as King of Bohemia. And then there is, of course, the 'Prague Symphony'. Practically every second chamber concert will include a work by the great Wolfgang Amadeus, who has seemingly been accorded the status of an honorary Czech.

The other great musical heroes are **Smetana** and **Dvořák**. The growth of nationalism in the latter half of the nineteenth century produced an emphasis on Bohemian musical folk traditions (though Smetana and Dvořák actually used folk music very rarely in their melodies). Smetana was the guiding force behind the establishment of the National Theatre, which opened in 1881 with the première of *Libuše*, his 'solemn festival tableau' dealing with the mythical foundation of the Czech nation. Regarded as 'the father of Bohemian music' (a little unfair on his baroque and classical predecessors), Smetana's status as the pre-eminent Czech composer remains undisputed. He is followed a close second by Dvořák.

The inherent conservatism of the average Czech music lover means that the two giants of Czech twentieth-century music, **Janáček** and **Martinů**, aren't so well represented (although Janáček's operas are given an increasing number of airings). Unlike in Britain and America, they are both still regarded as 'difficult' composers, though this may well be a legacy of the communist era. It took a long time for Janáček's reputation to be established in Prague; he was far more widely accepted in Brno, capital of his native Moravia. As for Martinů, his many years of self-imposed exile meant that only recently has he been granted a genuine place in the Czech musical pantheon.

There are other Czech composers worth discovering: **Josef Suk**, Dvořák's son-in-law – a late romantic who is only really recognised in the West for the *Asrael* symphony; **Zdeněk Fibich**, a contemporary of Smetana and Dvořák; and quite a few contemporary composers, with **Petr Eben** at their head, who are only now finding their own voice after years of censorship and socialist realism. Concerts of contemporary music are not nearly as ubiquitous

as the more staple repertoire, but there is a growing interest in present-day music, largely promoted by the Czech Music Information Fund. The Prague Spring Festival, for example, has a whole section devoted to works by living composers.

Principal orchestras

There are now four main orchestras based in Prague. The oldest and most venerable is the world-renowned **Czech Philharmonic**, which performs regularly in the **Rudolfinum** (*see below*). The celebration of its centenary in 1996 was marred by controversy surrounding German conductor Gerd Albrecht, the orchestra's first non-Czech musical director, who resigned amid accusations of arrogance, financial misconduct and dwindling standards of musicianship in the orchestra. For nearly two years the orchestra remained without a musical director (though Sir Charles Mackerras was appointed chief guest conductor) until **Vladimir Ashkenazy** took up the post at the beginning of 1998. The celebrated Russian pianist and conductor, whose three and a half year contract requires him to devote eight weeks a year to his duties, will no doubt go a long way to awaken what he has described as 'the last sleeping giant of Europe'.

The **Prague Symphony Orchestra**, meanwhile, has gone from strength to strength under the baton of Italian conductor **Gaetano Delogu**, who took up the post in 1995. It is now back in its main venue, the **Smetana Hall** in the newly renovated Municipal House (Obecní dům), and can turn out performances that are more than a match for the Czech Philharmonic. Rather than seeing itself as a rival to its older sibling, it intends to be an equal alternative, with a wide-ranging repertoire embracing twentieth-century and non-European music, as well as a strong commitment to works of the Russian symphonic repertoire. (Maxim Shostakovich, the composer's son, is a regular guest conductor.) Although Delogu will give up his post at the end of the 1997/8 season, he will stay on as conductor laureate, with reduced duties.

The **Radio Prague Symphony Orchestra** lacks the kudos of the other two but frequently produces more than creditable performances under director **Vladimír Válek**, which compare well with those of its more famous rivals.

A relative newcomer on the Prague musical scene is the **Prague Chamber Philharmonic Orchestra**, founded by the former director of the Prague Symphony, **Jiří Bělohlávek**. Composed chiefly of younger musicians, it has made an impressive debut both in the concert hall and on disc.

Lastly, there is the **Czech National Symphony Orchestra**, which makes the occasional appearance, chiefly under the baton of American conductor **Paul Freeman**.

Municipal House

(Obecni dům) Náměstí Republiky 5, Prague 1 (2200 2336). Metro Náměstí Republiky/5, 14, 26 tram. **Map 4 K3**
A stunning example of Czech art nouveau, this cream, verdigris and brass jewel of the Municipal House is built around the **Smetana Hall**, where the Prague Symphony Orchestra performs – and kicks off the Prague Spring Festival every year as it has for over half a century. Hearing Smetana variations on folk tunes while gazing at the ceiling mosaics of old Czech myths is an experience not to be missed. *See also p59.*

Rudolfinum

Alšovo nábřeží 12, Prague 1 (2489 3311). Metro Staroměstská/17 tram. **Map 3 G2**
One of the most beautiful concert venues in Europe. Built in neo-classical style at the end of the nineteenth century, the Rudolfinum has two halls: the **Dvořák Hall** for orchestral works and major recitals, and the **Suk Hall** for chamber, instrumental and solo vocal music. Opinions are divided about the acoustics of the Dvořák Hall, but the grandeur of the building's interior – plus the high standard of musicianship at the concerts – make an evening here eminently worthwhile.

Venues for chamber music and instrumental recitals are legion. Practically every church and palace offers concerts. Programming is mainly from the baroque and classical repertoire, with the emphasis on Czech music. The quality of performance varies but is usually good. Some of the best venues are listed below.

Basilica of St James

(Bazilika sv. Jakuba) Malá Štupartská, Prague 1 (no phone). Metro Náměstí Republiky/5, 14, 26 tram. **Map 3 J3**
Another prime example of Czech baroque architecture, and with excellent acoustics. In addition to large-scale sacred choral works, music accompanying the celebration of mass (usually at 10am) is a regular feature on Sunday mornings.

Bertramka

Mozartova 169, Prague 5 (540 012). Metro Anděl/4, 7, 9 tram.
The house where Mozart stayed when he came to Prague is now a museum devoted to him, and has regular concerts. Nearly all of them, inevitably, include at least one work by the great Austrian composer. *See also p92.*

Homegrown classics

Below we select eight excellent domestic recordings. All feature music by Czech composers that has not been better recorded or performed by foreign companies.

Antonín Dvořák: *The Spectre's Bride*

Eva Urbanová, Ludovít Ludha, Ivan Kusnjer. Prague Philharmonic Choir and Prague Symphony Orchestra, conducted by Jiří Bělohlávek.
(Supraphon SU 3091-2 231)
An accomplished live recording of Dvořák's dramatic cantata, originally commissioned for the 1989 Birmingham Festival. It is an interesting exercise to compare Dvořák's handling of the text with Martinů's.

Zdeněk Fibich: *Moods, Impressions and Reminiscences*

Marián Lapšanský (piano).
(Supraphon SU 0188-2 131 · SU 0191-2 131/SU 3248-2 131 · SU 3255-2 131) (12 individual CDs)
This massive cycle of piano miniatures by the Czech romantic composer Zdeněk Fibich is a revelation. Essentially it is a romantic journal, an expression of his deep love for his young pupil Anežka Schulzová. Much of the writing is intensely beautiful and lyrical, excellently performed with great sensitivity by Marián Lapšanský. This is the first ever recording of the work in its entirety and, as such, a highly important addition to the catalogue. If you don't want to invest in all 12 CDs, try either volume 1 (Moods) as a sampler or volumes 5 and 6, which

consist of the section titled 'Novella', which describes a holiday the lovers took at Karlovy Vary, and is thus more or less self-containedd.

Leos Janáček: *Kaťa Kabanová*

Gabriela Beňačková, Peter Straka, Eva Randová, Dagmar Pecková, Ludyěk Vele and others. Chorus of the Prague National Theatre, Czech Philharmonic Orchestra, conducted by Sir Charles Mackerras.
(Supraphon SU 3291-2 632) (2 CDs)
Mackerras's second recording of this opera does not quite have the searing intensity of his earlier reading, made 20 years previously. Nevertheless, it is an impressive achievement, with a cast that represents the best of contemporary Czech vocal talent. Of all the home-grown records of Janáček's most passionate opera, this is the one to have.

Chapel of Mirrors
(Zrcadlová kaple) Klementinum, Mariánské náměstí, Prague 1 (2166 3111 ext 331). Metro Staroměstská/17, 18 tram. **Map 3 G4**
A pink marble chapel within the vast Clementinum complex where you can catch all manner of romantic, baroque and original chamber recitals.

Church of St Nicholas
(Chrám sv. Mikuláše) Malostranské náměstí, Prague 1 (536 983). Metro Malostranská/12, 22 tram. **Map 2 D3**
One of Prague's most celebrated churches, with a stunning baroque interior. There are regular choral concerts and organ recitals. *See also p79.*

Church of St Nicholas
(Kostel sv. Mikuláše) Staroměstské náměstí, Prague 1 (no phone). Metro Staroměstská. **Map 3 H3**
Regular organ, instrumental and vocal recitals are held here, with the emphasis on baroque music.

Church of St Simon & St Jude
(Kostel sv. Šimona a Judy) Dušní, Prague 1 (232 1352/232 1068). Metro Staroměstská/17 tram. **Map 3 H2**
Recently renovated, this has become one of the city's major venues for chamber music. The Prague Symphony Orchestra, which also promotes selected ensembles, is responsible for the programming.

House of the Stone Bell
(Dům U kamenného zvonu) Staroměstské náměstí 13, Prague 1 (2481 0036). **Map 3 J3**
One of the oldest buildings in Prague, where concerts are of contemporary music as well as more staple fare.

Lobkowicz Palace
(Lobkovický palác) Jiřská 3, Prague 1 (537 364). Metro Malostranská/22 tram. **Map 3 E2**
Concerts are held in the imposing banqueting hall, with frescoes by Fabián Harovník.

Lichtenstein Palace
(Lichtenštejnský palác) Malostranské náměstí 13, Prague 1 (2451 0131). Metro Malostranská/12, 22 tram. **Map 2 E3**
Home of the Czech Academy of Music. Regular concerts are given in the Gallery and in the Martinů Hall.

Nostic Palace
(Nostický palác) Maltézské náměstí 1, Prague 1 (5731 1590). Metro Malostranská/12, 22 tram. **Map 2 E4**
The palace of the man who paid for the Estates Theatre. Concerts are of a high standard and go very well with a glass of wine, ever on sale in this fine Malá Strana venue.

Bohuslav Martinů: *The Spectre's Bride, Nipponari, Magic Nights*
Kühn Mixed Chorus, Prague Symphony Orchestra, conducted by Jiří Bělohlávek.
(Supraphon SU 11 1090-2 231)
Three hitherto neglected works by one of the giants of Czech twentieth-century music, persuasively performed under the baton of Jiří Bělohlávek. *Magic Nights*, a setting of three Chinese poems from the same anthology that Mahler used for *Das Lied von der Erde*, is a gem.

Arnold Schoenberg: *Verklärte Nacht/* Pavel Haas: *Study for String Orchestra, Overture for Radio, Psalm 29*
New Czech Chamber Orchestra, Prague Chamber Philharmonic Orchestra, Bambini di Praga, conducted by Jiří Bělohlávek.
(Supraphon SU 0010-2931)
Debut recording of the Prague Chamber Philharmonic under founder Jiří Bělohlávek. An impressive performance of *Verklärte Nacht* is coupled with three pieces by Pavel Haas (1899-1944), a student of Janáček. Haas was one of the composers rounded up by the Nazis and transported to the 'model camp' at Terezín. There the *Study for String Orchestra* was composed and first performed – before an imaginary audience – filmed by the Nazis to demonstrate the happy conditions of the inmates. Three days later Haas, the orchestra and 2,500 other inhabitants of the ghetto were hauled off to Auschwitz – most, including Haas, to their deaths.

Bedřich Smetana: *Dalibor*
Leo Marian Vodička, Eva Urbanová, Ivan Kusnjer and others. Prague National Theatre Orchestra and Chorus, conducted by Zdeněk Košler.
(Supraphon SU 0077-2 632) (2 CDs)
Smetana's most successful serious opera given a passionate and dedicated reading by the late Zdeněk Košler, whose last recording this was before his death in 1995.

Josef Suk: *Works by Suk*
Prague Radio Symphony Orchestra, conducted by Petr Vronský. Prague Symphony Orchestra, conducted by Vladimír Válek.
(Panton 81 1212-2)
Best known for his *Asrael* Symphony, Suk was a late romantic composer whose other works deserve to be more widely heard. The three pieces here are relatively early compositions, dating from the first years of the twentieth century. The orchestral suite *Pohádka* ('A Fairy Tale') is particularly beautiful.

Various: *Musica Temporis Rudolphi II*
Duodena Cantitans, Capella Rudolphina, Michael Consort, conducted by Petr Daněk.
(Supraphon SU 11 2176-2 231)
This fine selection of music from the time of Emperor Rudolf II (late sixteenth and early seventeenth centuries), some of it never recorded before, is performed on original instruments (still a rarity in Prague). There is a combination of instrumental, vocal and choral works, both sacred and secular.

*The Stamic Quartet let rip in the Clementinum's **Chapel of Mirrors**.*

St Agnes's Convent

(Klášter sv. Anežky české) U milosrdných 17, Prague 1 (2481 0828/tickets 2481 0835/2481 0628). Metro Staroměstská or Náměstí Republiky/5, 14, 26 tram. **Map 3 J1**

The acoustics in St Agnes's Convent are not without their critics, but the high standard of chamber music – usually from the classical, romantic and twentieth-century repertoire, with an emphasis on Smetana, Dvořák and Janáček – makes this venue worth a visit.

Opera

There are three venues for opera in Prague: the National Theatre, the Estates Theatre (which operates under the aegis of the National Theatre) and the State Opera. Increasing rivalry between the National Theatre and the State Opera means that it has been known for two different productions of the same opera to be given on the same night – an unnecessary and irritating extravagance in a city where state funding has decreased dramatically. Even so, standards of production and musicianship have increased impressively over the last few years, but don't expect anything approaching the level found in Berlin, Munich or Vienna.

Estates Theatre

(Stavovské divadlo) Ovocný trh 1, Prague 1 (info 2422 8503/box office 2421 5001). Metro Můstek. **Open** *box office* 10am-6pm Mon-Fri; 10am-12.30pm, 3-6pm, Sat, Sun. **Map 3 J4**

A shrine for Mozart lovers, this is where *Don Giovanni* and *La Clemenza di Tito* were first performed. The theatre was built by Count Nostic in 1784 and its beautiful dark blue and gold auditorium was almost over-renovated after the Velvet Revolution. It began life as the Prague home of Italian opera, but in 1807 became the German opera with Carl Maria von Weber as its musical director (1813-17). Today most of the programming is given over to theatre but there are regular performances of Mozart – including, of course, *Don Giovanni. See also p217.*

National Theatre

(Národní divadlo) Národní 2, Prague 1 (2491 3437/ 2490 1520). Metro Národní třída/6, 9, 17, 18, 22 tram. **Open** *box office* 10am-6pm Mon-Fri; 10am-12.30pm, 3-6pm, Sat, Sun. **Map 5 G6**

Smetana was a guiding light behind the establishment of the National Theatre, a symbol of Czech nationalism that finally opened in 1883 with a performance of his opera *Libuše.* In keeping with tradition, the theatre today tends to concentrate on Czech opera, the core of the repertoire being works by Smetana and Dvořák (including lesser known works such as Dvořák's *The Devil and Kate* and Smetana's *The Kiss*), together with some Janáček. Operas by non-Czech composers and some impressive ballets are also performed – increasingly so. *See also p55 & p218.*

State Opera

(Státní Opera) Wilsonova 4, Prague 2 (2422 7693/ box office 265 353). Metro Muzeum. **Open** *box office* 10am-5.30pm Mon-Fri; 10am-noon, 1-5.30pm, Sat, Sun. **Map 6 L6**

The State Opera (then called the German Theatre) opened in 1887. Music directors and regular conductors included Seidl, Mahler, Zemlinský, Klemperer and Szell, and up until World War II the theatre was regarded as one of the finest German opera houses outside Germany. After the war it changed its name to the Smetana Theatre and became the second house of the National Theatre. Today it's a separate organisation and presents operas from the standard Italian repertoire, with an occasional excursion into German, French and Russian opera. The appointment of the new directors Daniel Dvořák and Jiří Nekvasil, partners who were responsible for **Opera Mozart** *(see below)*, an organisation chiefly geared to the tourist trade, signals a change in the direction of business savvy. Their plans include an increasing emphasis on contemporary opera.

Festivals

The major event in the calendar is the **Prague Spring Festival**, which runs from May to June. Since the Velvet Revolution it has a much stronger international flavour and ranks with the Edinburgh Festival or the Proms in its ability to attract first-class performers from all over the

world. Traditionally, the festival opens with
Smetana's patriotic cycle of symphonic poems,
Má Vlast ('My Country'), and concludes with
Beethoven's Ninth. Many of the major events sell
out quickly and it's best to obtain tickets from the
Prague Spring Festival Office (*see below*),
rather than from agencies, which add a hefty
mark-up. Note, though, that the office only opens
a month before the festival and that there are two
price ranges, one for Czechs and one for foreigners, so if possible, get a Czech friend to go along
with you to do the talking.

There are numerous festivals out of town, usually during the summer months, in other tourist
centres such as Karlovy Vary, Mariánské Lázně
and Český Krumlov (*see chapter* **Trips Out of
Town**). There are also festivals devoted to
Smetana and Janáček in Litomyšl and Hukvaldy,
their respective places of birth.

Buying tickets

The best way of obtaining tickets is via the relevant box office. Although there are many ticket
agencies, they tend to raise prices for foreigners.
Avoid touts unless desperate. Prices for concerts
vary and some (in the smaller churches) are free,
but the cost is usually between 250 Kč and 500 Kč.

Information about forthcoming events tends to
be haphazard, but one agency with a calendar
made out months in advance – and willing to take
your phone order and credit card payment from
abroad – is **Bohemia Ticket International** (*see
below*). If already in Prague, it's worth trying to get
a ticket at the relevant venue an hour before the
beginning of any performance, even if you have
been told it is sold out. This is truer of concerts
than of opera. Like most cities in Central Europe,
Prague has a tradition of subscription evenings
and so you may find certain glittering occasions
rather difficult to get into.

Ticket agencies

Bohemia Ticket International (BTI)

*Na příkopě 16, Prague 1 (2421 5031/btünter@login.cz/
www.csad.cz/bti). Metro Můstek or Náměstí Republiky.*
Open 9am-6pm Mon-Fri; 9am-4pm Sat; 10am-3pm Sun.
Credit AmEx, EC, MC, V. **Map 4 K4**
This agency is the sole non-travel agency means for buying tickets in advance from abroad with a credit card for
opera and concerts at the National Theatre, Estates Theatre
and State Opera, in addition to numerous other orchestral
and chamber concerts. There's a significant mark-up.
Branches: Václavské náměstí 27, Prague 1 (2419 7535);
Salvátorská 6, Prague 1 (2422 7832).

Čedok

*Na příkopě 18, Prague 1 (2419 7411/2419 7203/fax
2419 7535). Metro Můstek or Náměstí Republiky.*
Open 9am-5pm Mon-Fri; 9am-1pm Sat. **Map 4 K4**
Tickets for assorted events as well as some concerts.
Branches: Pařížská 6, Prague 1 (231 6978); Rytířská 16,
Prague 1 (263 697).

Interkoncerts

*Rytířská 31, Prague 1 (2421 1180). Metro Můstek/6, 9,
18, 22 tram.* **Open** 10am-10pm daily. **Credit** AmEx,
MC, V. **Map 3 J4**
Though this box office specialises in bad black-light theatre and death metal rock, Interkoncerts does list chamber
music events as well.

Melantrich

*Pasáž Rokoko, Václavské náměstí 38, Prague 1 (2421
5018). Metro Muzeum or Můstek/3, 9, 14, 24 tram.*
Open 9am-7pm Mon-Fri. **Map 4 K5**
At one time the prime booking office for all shows in
Prague, this Lucerna passage office remains active for
now and still offers cash-only ticket sales for most major
performances.

Opera Mozart

*Žatecká 1, Praha 1 (232 2536/232 3429/fax 232
4189/festival@mozart.cz/www.mozart.cz). Metro
Staroměstská/17, 18 tram.* **Open** 10am-8.30pm
Thur-Tue; 10am-6pm Wed. **Credit** EC, MC, V.
Map 3 H3
The best-promoted classical and theatre endeavour in
Prague predictably targets tourists with four separate con-
cepts: **Mozart Open** cannily takes over the Estates
Theatre during the summer hiatus of its usual occupant,
the National Theatre, with a big-budget Mozart opera performed by foreigners (with tickets at a withering 590-1,900
Kč); **The Best of Mozart** brings costumed arias, duets
and snippets year-round to a small baroque-style space
next to a disco at Lávka (Novotného lávka 1, Praha 1); the
National Marionette Theatre hosts year-round puppet
productions of *Don Giovanni* and *Yellow Submarine* (*see
p219*) and the **Magic Theatre of the Baroque World**
runs a puppet theatre **Orfeo ed Euridice** for foreign kids
who prefer a taste of antiquity (Theatre on the Balustrade,
Anenské náměstí 6, Praha 1; *see p218*).

Pragokoncert

*Celetná 17, Prague 1 (231 5656/fax 232 0353). Metro
Náměstí Republiky/5, 14, 26 tram.* **Open** 10am-10pm
daily. **Map 2 E4**
Concert promoters, based in the Nostic Palace, who organise a range of chamber music concerts as well as major
gala events.
Branch: Nostic Palace, Maltézské náměstí 1, Prague 1
(5731 1590).

Prague Spring Festival Office

*Hellichova 18, Prague 1 (2451 0422/530 293/533 474/
fax 536 040/festival@login.cz/www.festival.cz). Metro
Malostranská/12, 22 tram.* **Map 2 D4**
Buy your tickets here in person and save a fortune from
agents' mark-ups, but remember that the office is only open
in the month before the festival.

Ticketpro

*Salvátorská 10, Prague 1 (2481 4020/fax 2481
4021/orders@ticketpro.cz/www.ticketpro.cz). Metro
Staroměstská.* **Open** 8am-8pm Mon-Fri; 9am-8pm Sat;
noon-8pm Sun. **Credit** AmEx, EC, MC, V.
Map 3 H/J3
Advance booking for major concerts and numerous smaller events. Consult *Zlaté stránky* (*Yellow Pages*) for other
branches too numerous to list here.

Wolff Travel Agency

*Na příkopě 24, Prague 1 (2421 1964/2421 3718/
fax 2422 8849). Metro Můstek or Náměstí Republiky.*
Open 9.30am-7pm Mon-Fri; 10.30am-4pm Sat;
summer only 10am-4pm Sun. **Credit** AmEx, EC, MC, V.
Map 4 K4
Tickets for the opera and chamber concerts.

Music: Rock, Folk & Jazz

From mainstream to pure mad, there'll be a venue for it in Prague.

'Who is Czech is a musician', according to an old Bohemian aphorism. Based on what's listened to and enjoyed day and night in Prague, it's got to be true – no one but an utter devotee could appreciate all the sounds you'll hear here. Thumping Top 40 derivatives at otherwise fine restaurants; buskers who can't hit a straight note to save their lives; blues in high street clubs that in any other country would be relegated to lift interiors; industrial noise utterly without notes that packs a dancefloor all night, every night.

Czechs must surely be the most musically democratic people in the world. With only a handful of round-the-clock clubs to choose from, a typical night out might offer the choice of Bud Powell-inspired straight-ahead jazz, Siberian throat-singing monks (Huun-Huur-Tu; *see picture page 198*), jungle/drum 'n' bass night with D Smack U Promotion, local trip-hoppers Significant Other, horrifying Euro-pop DJs at **Music Park** (*see page 203*), the Czech mod retro Pisnička at **Lucerna music bar**, an all-Czech country and western band at **První Prag Country Saloon Amerika** or medieval rounds done in full costume at a local community house.

Then there's the recent 'ethno' mania. Praguers have emerged from what some called the communist cultural refrigerator starved of the sounds of the rest of the world and will now settle for no less than its remotest reaches. Los Panchos, Dun an Doras, Bourama Badgi and Shamen are all regular names in the local listings while clubs like Roxy are organising world music nights with names like 'Cous-couseria', all of them a good bet for an evening's disporting. Even veteran Prague bands are making themselves over with hide drums, burlap tunics and brass bells on sticks, from the once-underground Jablkoň to the erstwhile tuxedoed big band leader Pavel Klikar.

The techno scene, a particular mainstay of semi-legal clubs like the **Roxy** (*see also page 204*) and wholly illegal summer raves at **Cibulka** (*see page 201*), is currently populated by more innovative home-grown stars than any other genre. Liquid Harmony, DJs Chris Sadler, Agent, Tráva and OO Bidlo the main players, often on the programmes of Radost, the Roxy and Punto Azul, all of which sometimes play host to guest DJs from the UK or Germany (*see also chapter* **Nightlife**). These gigs are generally well covered on Radio 1 (91.9 FM), which, despite a recent buy-out, has not much compromised its anarchic reputation. Broadcasts carry on with an up-to-date mix of experimental, hardcore, ambient, techno and rock.

And if it's dark and close enough to the fringe, more mainstream foreign rock can also be a treat in Prague. Where else can you spend 13 quid and get within feet of John Cale or David Byrne than at the Archa theatre or catch big-time rock in the Lucerna arcade's massive, balconied, subterranean, faux-marble theatre?

Such a spread was probably inevitable in a city whose musical heritage includes both a hearty inter-war jazz scene and 1960s psychedelia that regularly made the *NME*. And while Czech rock is far from exportable as yet (it's depressing enough, certainly, but vocalist garbling in the West has to degrade significantly before Czech lyrics can actually get by on New York or London airwaves), a few select Prague acts have been eyed for 'international exploitation'. PolyGram and Sony have respectively tapped a member of the local hip-hop skate punk sensation Chaozz and the Ecstasy of St Theresa.

Looks like Prague has come a long way from the Plastic People of the Universe, the former dissident band whose persecution sowed the seeds of the Velvet Revolution. A long, colourful and very open-minded way.

Tickets & information

It's easy to find out what's going on. There are flyposters on vacant hoardings all over Prague, and flyers can be picked up at clubs and record shops. Look also for listings in English in *Think, Do města* or the *Prague Post*. Tickets can be obtained in advance at the following agencies – this is an especially good idea since a surprising number of concerts sell out. Shows by local groups should cost around 100-200 Kč, while major concerts tend to go for between 500 Kč and 1,000 Kč.

Interkoncerts

Rytířská 31, Prague 1 (2161 0162-4). Metro Můstek.
Open 10am-10pm daily. **Credit** AmEx, MC, V. **Map 3 J4**
Concert organisers of most of the arena, teen rock, heavy
metal and Top 40 shows in Prague. Tickets, along with
advance programmes, are available at this office.

Pragokoncert

*Celetná 17, Prague 1 (5731 1591). Metro Náměstí
Republiky/5, 14, 26 tram.* **Open** 9am-4pm Mon-Fri.
Map 4 K3
Former state concert agency, now in charge of launching
Czech career revivals for the likes of Art Garfunkel, who
usually play the massive former communist convention hall
(Congress Centre).

Ticketpro

*Salvátorská 10, Prague 1 (2481 4020/vstupenky@
ticketpro.cz/www.ticketpro.cz). Metro Staroměstská/17, 18
tram.* **Open** 8am-6pm Mon-Fri; 9am-8pm Sat; noon-8am
Sun. **Credit** AmEx, EC, MC, V. **Map 3 H3**
Major ticket outlet for most larger concerts. Consult *Zlaté
stránky* (Yellow Pages) for other branches too numerous to
list here. Located by the side of the Church of St Salvator,
just off Dušní.

Venues

Enormous gigs

The largest venue in Prague is **Strahov Stadion**,
which has been graced in the past by President
Havel's mates, the Rolling Stones, as well as Pink
Floyd and Billy Idol. Far more regular are shows
at **Výstaviště** (good enough for Tina Turner) and
Palác kultury (big enough for Björk).

*Huun-Huur-Tu get busy at the **Akropolis**.*

Palác kultury

*(Kongresové Centrum Prahy) 5. května 65, Prague 4
(6117 2263/6117 2791). Metro Vyšehrad.*

Strahov Stadion

*Diskařská 100, Prague 6 (539 951-9). Tram 22 to Újezd,
then cable car, or 132, 143, 149, 176 bus.* **Map 1 A5**
Prague's largest stadium can take a staggering 200,000 people. The stadium runs special bus services for big gigs.

Výstaviště

*(Sportovní hala) U Výstaviště, Prague 7 (2010 3111).
Metro Nádraží Holešovice/5, 12, 17 tram.* **Map 7 D1**

Small to middling gigs

Akropolis

*Kubelíkova 27, Prague 3 (697 5491/697 6411/
akropol@terminal.cz/www.spinet.cz/akropolis). Metro
Jiřího z Poděbrad/5, 9, 11, 26, 55, 58 tram.* **Open** concerts start at 7.30pm. **Admission** 100-250 Kč. **Map 8 B2**
The former basement cinema here is not just one of the best
lit and miked concert spaces in Prague, it's also host to the
city's most progressive line-up of world music. In the first
months of 1998 alone, Akropolis offered up New York's
Klezmatics, a Bulgarian women's choir, Asian monks with
startling vocal noises and Spanish gypsy guitar group Los
Reyes. The downstairs pubs keep tunnelling in deeper, offering, at last count, four distinct happening drinking holes,
including a greasy spoon at street level. *See also p152.*

Lucerna music bar

*Vodičkova 36, Prague 1 (2427 7108). Metro Můstek/3,
9, 14, 24, 52, 53, 55, 56 tram.* **Open** concerts start at
9pm. **Admission** (concerts) 60-300 Kč. **Map 4 K5**
Downstairs from the untouched '20s-era Lucerna shopping
arcade just off Wenceslas Square, this bar and concert
space provide a truly trippy environment in which to catch
touring jazz performers like Maceo Parker or local '80s
nights. Crowds for the former sit around white tablecloths
while the latter revel in the threadbare cheesiness and
cheap beer of this remarkable wood-panelled, two-storey
basement, complete with hydraulic stage lift.

Malostranská beseda

*Malostranské náměstí 21, Prague 1 (539 024). Metro
Malostranská/12, 22, 57 tram.* **Open** 1pm-1am daily; bar
from 5pm; concerts start at 8pm. **Admission** 50-80 Kč.
Map 2 E3
In a pricey tourist area, this large, upstairs space right on
Malostranské náměstí offers reasonable (bottled) beer,
scuffed, old-fashioned wood floors for dancing and a cover
charge low enough to attract the locals. It's a good place to
catch popular Czech bands like ska crew Sto Zvířat and
rock-a-billy sounds from Lemon Nashville.

Rock Café

*Národní třída 20, Prague 1 (2491 4416/
www.radio.cz/rock-cafe). Metro Národní třída/6, 9, 18,
22, 51, 54, 57, 58 tram.* **Open** 10pm-3am Mon-Fri; 8pm-
3am Sat, Sun. **Admission** 60-300 Kč. **Map 3 H5**
With a history as a post-revolution rock pioneer, the glory
days are a bit in the past. These days it's more of a teen
hangout, and home to endless Czech 'revival' bands, who
resurrect everyone from Abba to Velvet Underground. No
atmosphere to speak of.

Roxy

*Dlouhá 33, Prague 1 (2481 0951). Metro Náměstí
Republiky or Staroměstská/5, 14, 17, 18, 26, 51, 53, 54
tram.* **Open** from 8pm daily; *tearoom* noon-midnight
daily. Occasionally closed Mondays. **Admission** (live
performances) 120-250 Kč; (DJs) 40-100 Kč. **Map 3 J3**

*Step back in time with Ondřej Havelka & the Melody Makers at the **Lucerna music bar**.*

Shows at this gracefully crumbling theatre are nearly always interesting and most usually feature house and techno shows of considerable talent, often from London or Berlin. Regular fringe film screenings, over-the-top transvestite cabarets and Latin nights are also a kick. The sound system is much improved and the back hall tearoom and art installations provide mellow correctives to the pounding of rapid BPMs. *See also p204.*

Jazz

Prague's rich jazz history stretches back to the 1930s, when Jaroslav Ježek led an adored, diffident big band while colleague RA Dvorský established a tough standard of excellence that would survive both Nazi and communist oppression. Karel Velebný, member of the renowned Studio 5 group, continued that tradition post-war, while writer Josef Škvorecký chronicled the eternal struggle of Czech sax men in countless novels.

These days, the jazz scene occupies a lower echelon of the club world, but a corps of talented musicians plays the few jazz clubs, and, despite unfulfilled dreams of the New York big-time, their appreciative fans here support and keep them energised. Thus Prague jazz, if traditional, does continually develop.

AghaRTA
Krakovská 5, Prague 1 (2221 1275). Metro Muzeum or I.P. Pavlova/4, 6, 16, 22, 34 tram. **Open** *July, Aug* 7pm-1am, *Sept-June* 5pm-midnight, daily; shows start at 9pm. **Admission** around 80 Kč. **Map 6 K6**
Just off Wenceslas Square and named after Miles Davis' most controversial LP, this is one of Prague's best spots for modern jazz and blues. A fairly even mix of Czechs and

foreigners mingle in the relatively small, but comfortable, space – perfect for sitting back and enjoying solo performances from artists such as flautist Jiří Stivín. Like many Prague jazz clubs, there's a CD store inside selling outstanding local recordings from 150-400 Kč. Look for the club's own ARTA label.

Jazz & Blues Café
Na příkopě 23, Prague 1 (2422 8788 ext 362). Metro Můstek. **Open** 6pm-midnight daily; shows start at 9pm. **Admission** 150 Kč; 100 Kč students. **Map 3 J4**
Intelligent programming, good sound, brilliant location, dreadful space. The best in new jazz talents are showcased in what looks disconcertingly and distressingly like a Holiday Inn conference room. The small lobby bar makes for the only relief.

Jazz Club Železná
Železná 16, Prague 1 (2423 9697). Metro Můstek. **Open** 3pm-midnight daily. **Admission** 70 Kč. **Map 3 J3**
The music at Železná is finally catching up with its prime location (just off Old Town Square). All in all, this is a fun, dungeon-like cellar space, with low prices and excellent CD shop. 'Ethno' nights on Sunday fill the space with conga beats and reggae while Latino nights spice up the more traditional midweek jazz programme.

Metropolitan Jazz Club
Jungmannova 14, Prague 1 (2421 6925). Metro Můstek or Národní třída/3, 9, 14, 24, 52, 53, 55, 56 tram. **Open** 11am-1am Mon-Fri; 7pm-1am Sat, Sun; concerts start at 9pm. **Admission** 80 Kč. **Map 3 J5**
All Dixie all the time. Fun cellar space if you're not a Coltrane snob, and can enjoy the romantic little corners, basic dinner menu and easygoing atmosphere, which may step out on a limb with swing or ragtime. Potentially painful otherwise.

Reduta

Národní třída 20, Prague 1 (2491 2246/294 340). Metro Národní třída/6, 9, 18, 22, 51, 54, 57, 58 tram. **Open** 9pm-midnight daily; *box office* 3-9pm Mon-Fri; 5-9pm Sat; 7-9pm Sun. **Admission** around 120 Kč. **Map 3 H5**

That Bill Clinton once played sax here to entertain Václav Havel hardly makes up for the steep cover, bland repertoire and boring interior. Even so, some of the best musicians in town often sit in with the evening's band.

U Malého Glena

Karmelitská 23, Prague 1 (535 8115). Metro Malostranská/12, 22, 57 tram. **Open** 10am-2am daily. **Admission** 70 Kč. **Credit** AmEx, EC, MC, V. **Map 2 D4**

Intimate jazz trios somehow sound wonderful in the closet-sized basement beneath the rowdy main floor café (*see p151*). This despite an appalling sound system, about six tables, rock-hard seats and noise from above. Rising Czech players like David Dorůžka or veteran Roman Pokorný meld grooves impressively and without pretence. Popular midweek theme nights can land anywhere on the cool end of the club music spectrum and Sunday night open jams are a treat.

U staré paní

Michalská 9, Prague 1 (264 920/267 267). Metro Můstek. **Open** 6.30pm-4am daily; concerts start at 9pm. **Admission** 90 Kč; 60 Kč students, OAPs. **Credit** AmEx, EC, MC, V. **Map 3 H4**

Doubling as a good restaurant, this central establishment is a late-night favourite with top local musicians. Once finished performing for the tourist trade, they come here for informal jams. Though the 150 Kč cover charge alienates most locals, this is one of the best places in town for serious jazz.

Folk/country & western

Folk and C&W seem to connect with the Czech rural heritage and locals are fascinated by the American cowboy lifestyle. They may live in block housing, intimidated by bureaucracy five days a week, but come Friday they're free-livin', guitar-packin' Willie Nelsons. Some of the biggest of the many annual folk/C&W festivals include July's **Zahrada** in Moravia, and **Prázdniny v Telči** in southern Bohemia in August.

První Prag Country Saloon Amerika

Korunní 101, Prague 3 (2425 6131). Metro Náměstí Míru/16 tram. **Open** 7.30-11.30pm Mon-Sat. **Admission** 80 Kč. **Map 8 B3**

The place for an all-Czech cowboy fiddle jam. Strange pelts on the walls and six-shooters on the waiting staff add up to one gol-danged hootenanny of an evening. *See also p152.*

Festivals

The summer **ET JAM** (*0800 155 555* or 10:15 Promotion at *2481 0161*) is a massive outdoor concert weekend in late spring. Past line-ups have included everyone from Björk to INXS, usually trading off with local DJs. **D Smack U Promotion** (*www.techno.cz/D_Smack_U*), with a much more underground electronic bent, is chief organiser of **summer raves** in such unlikely places as the Prague Castle Stag Moat. The city centre is usually plastered with posters for the above at such times.

The summer and autumn **AghaRTA Jazz Festival** (*2221 1275*) brings world-class talents like Ray Brown and Maceo Parker to the **Lucerna** music bar, while the curiously named **Jazz Meets World** (*697 6411*) festival is an all-year series that brings everything from world beat to klezmer to the **Akropolis**.

Join in the ho-down fun at the succinctly named **První Prag Country Saloon Amerika**.

Nightlife

Dance clubs may be in short supply – but sex and gambling dens are on a roll.

Big cities look better by night. While this may generally be accepted, in Prague the transformation somehow transcends physics. Both time and space become fluid to the nocturnal rambler in the Old Town, where you float from Gothic to Romantic to cyberspace and back in the length of a block. Even the beery haze that blurs the borders is a form of communion with the ages – Praguers have been christening the evening with a quaff of sublime brew or a wine tap since they laid the first cobblestone here a millennium ago. These days, sublime – and dirt-cheap – beer is still available all night long, but is accompanied more and more by slick mixed-drinks bars that tend to focus on sheer variety of libation rather than expert mixology.

So throw on some utilitarian black, and start with a bite, then a classic drink rendezvous. As 9pm arrives and restaurants and music halls start making closing noises, head out into the all-night refuges listed in this chapter. Basic club goings-on are covered in the local press, but to really get in on the scene *du jour*, head over to whatever was listed on that bizarre poster you spotted at Náměsti Republiky or on the flyer you picked up at **Terminal Bar** (*see page 144*). 'Global psychedelic ethno trance from St Petersburg', 'Bratislava ska' or a one-off skate party at some vacant warehouse dubbed the 'Fucktory' are typical offerings, though scouting out Malá Strana or Žižkov hotspots is just as likely to work.

Having a great night out in Prague always involves luck, mainly because of its size – just over a million souls with less than a decade of real clubbing experience don't make for likely trendsetters. Add to this the recent closure of more than half of the city's most popular clubs (developer takeovers and harassment campaigns from early-rising neighbours have taken their toll), and it adds up to a club scene that could be called anaemic. But even if Prague isn't defined by dance scenes, avant-garde culture or cutting-edge lifestyles, at least the coming and going of trends and clubs keeps things fresh.

But it would be highly premature to despair the collapse of Bohemian nights. There are still world-class suds, all-night eats and every vice you can imagine, from artistic to strictly corporeal. Remember, the hedonists and oddballs have loved Prague since the days of Rudolf II, so history is on

your side. Or maybe gambling is your thang, in which case you can choose from a range of *herna* bars and casinos.

Remember, though, before you set out: recent legislation means that Czech police now have the discretion to arrest anyone with what they deem 'more than a little' of a controlled substance. You have been warned.

Note that any tram with a number in the 50s is a night tram. *See page 256.*

Clubs

Bílý koníček
(The White Horse) Staroměstské náměsti 20, Prague 1 (2422 0947). Metro Můstek, Náměsti Republiky or Staroměstská. **Open** 5pm-4am daily; *disco* 9pm-5am daily. **Admission** 50 Kč cover charge on some nights. **Map 3 J3**
Billed as 'Prague's oldest disco', this twelfth-century cellar right on Old Town Square is usually full of young German tourists dancing to piss-poor pop techno, with the occasional go-go dancer getting her kit off. It can be fun – when you're in the mood.

Cibulka
corner of Plzeňská & Nad Hliníkem, Prague 5 (no phone). Tram 4, 7, 9, 58. **Open** 9pm-3am Fri, Sat. **Admission** 50-100 Kč.
Good weather-only club with Prague's best line-up of techno raves and multi-band marathons of local fringe rockers. Amenities are basic, to say the least: a bonfire, a rope swing, a sofa or two for seating and construction-site toilets. But it only proves the credentials of this anti-commercial scene and provides an unforgettably anarchic dance night that's rare in big cities. If you go by tram, get off at the Poštovky stop.

Delta
Vlastina 887, Prague 6 (301 9222). Tram 20, 26, 51. **Open** 7pm-1am Thur-Sat. **Admission** 60-120 Kč.
This fringe rock refuge in the midst of suburban apartments on the city's western border attracts a local crowd that's young, bored and aching to break out. This translates into a steady supply of uncommercial live bands from the expat-heavy Deep Sweden to local underground, such as drum-crazed Pluto. Worth the trip for the chance to see just what the old regime was trying to stamp out.

Dream Mansion
Husitská 54, Prague 3 (no phone). Tram 5, 9, 26, 55, 58. **Open** 7pm-3am daily. **Admission** 50 Kč. **Map 8 B1**
Irony is the only possible explanation for the name of this tiny bar, which stands amid hundreds in the pub heaven of Žižkov. Electronic music addicts are used to making sacrifices in Prague, though, and have been known to party in mausoleums for the chance of adequate space. If you think of it as a techno bar, rather than a club, this place actually works quite well.

RADOST FX

BELEHRADSKA 120 / PRAGUE 2 / METRO I.P. PAVLOVA

MUSIC NIGHT CLUB
NEW INTERIOR
THE BEST DOMESTIC AND INTERNATIONAL D.J'S

10:00 P.M. / 5:00A.M.

FX CAFE FX
VEGETARIAN RESTAURANT
AMERICAN
STYLE BRUNCH
EVERY WEEKEND
11:00 A.M / 3:00 P.M.

FX LOUNGE FX
MULTI-MEDIA CENTER WITH LIVE MUSIC, GALLERY AND D.J'S

WWW.CZECHTECHNO/RADOSTFX
E-MAIL:RADOSTFX@TERMINAL.CZ
PHOTO: JEFREE RENET @ THINK MAGAZINE / TYPOGRAPHY: TIMOTHY OTIS

Fromin

Václavské náměstí 21, Prague 1 (2423 5793). Metro Můstek/3, 9, 14, 24, 52, 55, 56, 58 tram. **Open** 9pm-3am daily. **Admission** 100 Kč. **Map 3 J5**
If hair mousse and B-52s are part of your ultimate night out, then Fromin is your destiny. Buffed bodies and microdresses undulate before three levels of glass walls, all of them offering breathtaking views of Wenceslas Square rooftops. Entry, drinks and cruising soon add up; the music is neither live nor anywhere near cutting-edge; and the bar staff are too busy primping to worry about competent mixing. Still, the cappuccino is hot and so is the action. So hot, in fact, you might need to chill on the penthouse terrace. *See also p123.*

La Habana

Míšenská 12, Prague 1 (5731 5104). Metro Malostranská/12, 22, 57 tram. **Open** 5pm-5am daily. **Admission** free. **Map 2 E3**
Looks like a comfortable Malá Strana rum bar at street level, but don't miss the back stairs in the hall – they lead to an all-night fever of mambo and salsa tracks in an arched stone cellar. Cerdo asado, Spanish tortillas, Daquiris and watery sangria fuel the fire in the blissful Cuban ghetto of Prague. Dance lessons can be arranged with Jorge 'Cuba Step' Concepcion.

Jo's Garáž

Malostranské náměstí 7, Prague 1 (530 9421). Metro Malostranská/12, 22, 57 tram. **Open** 9pm-5am daily (sometimes earlier). **Admission** free. **Map 2 E3**
The Gothic cellar adjunct to the backpacker's first-stop, Jo's Bar (*see p150*). This rock and funk cave plays predictable DJ rock tracks, which are eagerly lapped up by budget partiers from all over Europe and the States. That said, it's a cheap, infectious and packed environment of booty-shaking and shouted monosyllabic conversation. When that fails, suggestive gestures are generally understood, particularly by the frequent bar-top dancers.

Lucerna music bar

Vodičkova 36, Prague 1 (2421 7108). Metro Můstek/3, 9, 14, 24, 52, 53, 55, 56, 58 tram. **Open** 6pm-2am daily. **Admission** 60-300 Kč. **Map 4 K5**
In between top-notch jazz concerts (*see p198*), this vast basement bar and dancefloor doubles as a rising rock scene, with crowds of hip young Czechs and internationals turning out for '80s kitsch and getting down to Bowie and Iggy Pop tracks. As the only surviving dance space in the centre of town with boogie room to spare and a regular run of live rock and jazz, it's a must on the nocturnal party circuit. It maintains its funky integrity with barely painted-over 1920s décor, rambling balcony vogue space and dark wood trim.

Malostranská beseda

Malostranské náměstí, Prague 1 (539 024). Metro Malostranská/12, 22, 57 tram. **Open** 2pm-1am daily. **Admission** 40-80 Kč cover charge after 7pm. **Map 2 E3**
Surprisingly classy rock and roots bands grace this faded glory, including Prague ska kings Sto Zvířat or the occasional retro jazz act, such as the impressive Original Prague Syncopated Orchestra. Bottled beer is the only drawback to this welcoming, well worn-in bar and next-door dance room of clunky wood surfaces and windows overlooking Malá Strana's main square. A local favourite, it also offers a well-stocked jazz and alterna-rock CD shop.

Mánes

Masarykovo nábřeží 250, Prague 1 (299 438). Tram 17, 18, 51, 54. **Open** 9pm-4am Fri, Sat. **Admission** 50-100 Kč. **Map 5 G7**
This classy 1930s functionalist gallery space is more than living art history. It's also an increasingly popular riverside dance venue, with – remarkably for Prague – an international flavour. The current rage, 'Tropicana' nights on Friday and Saturday, brings out some of the city's hottest Cuban mambo kings. Stick to the edge of the dancefloor unless you know your stuff. The attached terrace café is nice for cooling off, though it closes around 11pm.

Music Park

Francouzská 4, Prague 2 (691 1491). Metro Náměstí Miru/4, 22, 34, 57 tram. **Open** 9pm-5am Tue-Thur; 9pm-6am Fri, Sat. **Admission** 50 Kč. **Map 8 A3**
The undisputed centre of Euro-trash disco culture, Music Park is a great place to show off your new leather jacket that says something stupid in big letters on the back, have cheery conversations with the po-faced bouncers and pick up a girl in a denim mini-skirt.

Night Club Fenix/Disco Astra

Václavské náměstí 4, Prague 1 (no phone). Metro Můstek/3, 9, 14, 24, 52, 53, 55, 56, 58 tram. **Open** 9pm-4am Wed-Sat. **Admission** 30-100 Kč. **Map 3 J5**
The last surviving remnant of the once-great Wenceslas Square cheesy disco epoch, and, as such, arguably worth a look. Lost-looking young Germans and 'working girls' flop around to Top 40 tunes upstairs, while adroit Gypsy electric guitar players and strippers trade off down below in Fenix. Hang out near the bar and it's inevitable that a heavily made-up woman will slip her arm into yours.

Propast

Lipanská 3, Prague 3 (9000 3371). Tram 5, 9, 26, 55, 58. **Open** 6pm-midnight Mon-Thur; 6pm-3am Fri, Sat. **Admission** free. **Map 8 C1**
Punk's not dead – it's just moved to Propast. The walls alternately pay homage to the Ramones and Plasmatics, and scream anarchy and Anti-Nazi League slogans. The club no longer has a live music licence, but that doesn't stop people from coming here to bang heads. Friendly, very grotty atmosphere and dirt-cheap Kozel beer.

Punto Azul

Kroftova 1, Prague 5 (551 029). Tram 6, 9, 12, 58. **Open** 8pm-2am daily. **Admission** 40 Kč.
Nothing Spanish about it but the name, this little Smíchov hole in the wall is on every wirehead's map. The techno dance space is just about the size of a circuit board and half of this place is routine student drinking dive, but a consistent groove is achieved with a line-up of Prague's most popular spacey house DJs.

Radost/FX

Bělehradská 120, Prague 2 (2425 4776/www.techno.cz/radostfx). Metro I.P. Pavlova/4, 6, 11, 16, 22, 34, 51, 56, 57 tram. **Open** 11.30am-6am daily. **Admission** 80-150 Kč. **Map 6 L8**
A rare survivor of the recent plague of club closures, probably because it continues to offer the best all-night mix of enticements in the city. A creative, credible veggie café, a spaced-out backroom lounge and art gallery, a small but slick downstairs club featuring absurdly glam theme parties (such as *Elle* night), a steady supply of the local stars of house and techno mixing, and, to revive you after all this, one of the best Sunday brunches around. *See also p129 & p152.*

Rock Café

Národní třída 20, Prague 1 (2441 4416/www.radio.cz/rock-cafe). Metro Národní třída/6, 9, 18, 22, 51, 54, 57, 58 tram. **Open** 10pm-3am Mon-Fri; 8pm-3am Sat, Sun. **Admission** 50-100 Kč. **Map 3 H5**
This was once a fairly respected rock 'n' roll joint. These days it's been bequeathed to tourists and out-of-touch Czechs, but the interior is still worth a look. It tends to attract the countless Czech 'revival' bands who cover everyone from ABBA to the Velvet Underground. For some reason, there are endless screenings of rock documentaries by day.

*There's nothing poxy about the foxy **Roxy**.*

Roxy

Dlouhá 33, Prague 1 (2481 0951). Metro Náměstí Republiky or Staroměstská/5, 14, 26, 53 tram. **Open** *tearoom* noon-midnight Mon-Sat; 5pm-midnight Sun; *club* 8pm-late daily. **Admission** 50-250 Kč. **Map 3 J2**
Still bucking the disco pack after all these years, the Roxy remains a proud, semi-legal, local shrine to the best in techno, house, drum 'n' bass, jungle and trance music. With DJs imported from Berlin and London, bizarre cabaret menageries, a hidden tearoom (*see p149* **Dobrá čajovna**) and vastly improved sound and light systems, this former movie house also enchants with its cratered dancefloor and balcony bar. The summer Alternativa festival, also held here, is an excellent showcase of local fringe rock.

Újezd

Újezd 18, Prague 1 (538 362). Metro Malostranská/9, 12, 22, 58 tram. **Open** 6pm-4am daily. **Admission** free. **Map 2 E5**
In its earlier days as Borát, this three-storey madhouse was an important dissident/alternative music club. Today it's home to some loud, badly amplified Czech rock tracks, battered wooden chairs in the café upstairs and shouted conversation in the bar below.

U zlatého stromu

Karlova 6, Prague 1 (2422 1385). Metro Staroměstská/ 17, 18, 51, 54 tram. **Open** 24 hours daily. **Admission** 50 Kč. **Map 3 G4**
One of the strangest combinations in the Old Town area: a non-stop disco, striptease, bar, restaurant and hotel a few metres from Charles Bridge. Descend into the stone cellar labyrinth of bad pop and softcore strippers, and you'll end up in a peaceful outdoor garden or a cosy nook for con-

versing. The upstairs café has a full menu plus coffee and drinks. Make no mistake, though: it's 100 per cent tourist and the staff are uncompromisingly neanderthal.

Late bars

See also chapter **Cafés, Pubs & Bars**.

Akropolis

Kubelíkova 27, Prague 3 (697 5491/akropol@jk.anet.cz/ www.spinet.cz/akropolis). Metro Jiřího z Poděbrad/5, 9, 11, 26, 55, 58 tram. **Open** 10am-1am Mon-Fri; 4pm-1am Sat, Sun. **Admission** 100-250 Kč (concerts only). **Map 8 B2**
Dependably iconoclastic world music concerts are only half the appeal here – the rest is in the variety and number of ways to perch and imbibe. At the last count, three bars and the new Kaaba Café were operating on the premises, but by now they may have tunnelled out a few more. All are hip, smoky, well mixed with locals and expats, and done up in suitably bizarre décor ranging from sham country and western to tropical cyberpunk. *See also p152 & p198*.

Banana Bar/Tapas

Štupartská 9, Prague 1 (232 4801). Metro Náměstí Republiky/5, 14, 26, 53 tram. **Open** 8pm-1am daily. **Map 3 J3**
Don't be too encouraged by the name: visions of authentic Spanish bar food aren't really justified, unless you normally go to Barcelona for pesto popcorn. It's a tanned, rippling business crowd in these twin bars that isn't too discriminating about its entertainment, judging by Banana's bartop go-go dancers. Distinctly unlike the mellow **La Provence** restaurant (*see p127*) below the floorboards.

Bar-Herna non-stop

Kralodvorská 9, Prague 1 (231 6239). Metro Náměstí
Republiky/5, 14, 26, 53 tram. **Open** 24 hours daily.
Map 4 K3
Catering to *herna* machine players (*see below*) and obliterated exiles from the nearby Taz bar, this non-stop bar provides a sobering glimpse of typical Prague nocturnal low-life. Drink here only if you're researching social aberration.

Battalion Rock Club

28 října 3, Prague 1 (2010 8148). Metro Můstek/
3, 6, 9, 14, 18, 22, 51, 52, 54, 55, 56, 57, 58 tram.
Open 24 hours daily. **Map 3 J5**
Grubby, throbbing with generic hip-hop tracks, packed with teenage skate punks and offering an intriguing décor of tree limbs and battered vinyl sofas, this is just the place to relive your yoof.

Belle Epoque

Křižovnická 8, Prague 1 (232 1926). Metro
Staroměstská/17, 18, 51, 54 tram. **Open** noon-2am
daily. **Map 3 G3**
Belle Epoque has picked up on the formula that made **Kozička** (*see below*) a hit. Jackets and little black dresses fit the bill best – just try to avoid getting paraffin all over them from the church candles set into the brick walls. Then again, you might need to get them dry-cleaned anyway if you sit too close to the sizzling rump steaks. As for the mixed drinks… well, you'd better stick to shots. *See also p139.*

Billiard club Trojická

Trojická 10, Prague 2 (299 551). Tram 3, 7, 17, 54.
Open 1pm-4am daily. **Map 5 H10**
A two-storey billiard hall in an old theatre building next to the Vltava. The tables are in excellent shape and go for 60 Kč an hour. It's quite surprising, then, that the place is often practically empty.

Chapeau Rouge

Jakubská 2, Prague 1 (no phone). Metro Náměstí
Republiky/5, 14, 26, 53 tram. **Open** *winter* 4pm-4am,
summer 4pm-5am, daily. **Map 4 K3**
Prague's main hangout for young Americans has much in common with hell. It's unbearably hot, crowded, loud, red and full of suckers who deserve to burn for eternity. It's also the most popular bar in town, which is a solid argument against democracy. So why do people love it so much? One patron summed it up: 'It's open late and it's a good place to meet little backpacker girls with noserings who are heading to Greece in a couple of days.' Charming. *See also p140.*

Corona Bar

Novotného lávka 9, Prague 1 (2108 2208). Metro
Staroměstská/17, 18, 51, 54 tram. **Open** 6pm-1am Mon-Wed; 6pm-3am Thur-Sat; 6pm-midnight Sun. **Map 3 G4**
Part of the Prague restaurant empire that includes Bellevue, U Patrona, Avalon and V Zátiší (*see chapter* **Restaurants**), this has been made over into an upscale Mexican village mock-up. Complete with four separate but equally glossy bars, Corona naturally features the namesake Mexican bottled beer – at several times the price of good old Gambrinus – along with swinging guitar players and singers from Brazil and Russia. *See also p140.*

Kozička

Kozí 4, Prague 1 (2481 8308). Metro Staroměstská/5,
14, 26, 53 tram. **Open** noon-4am Mon-Fri; 4pm-4am Sat,
Sun. **Map 3 J2**
A popular, unpretentious local scene in the heart of the Old Town – hard to beat if only for that reason – with homely nooks throughout, mighty steaks until 11pm and Krušovice on tap. *See also p141.*

Marquis de Sade

Templová 8, Prague 1 (no phone). Metro Náměstí
Republiky/5, 14, 22, 53 tram. **Open** 11am-2am
(food until 11pm) daily. **Map 4 K3**
Despite its name, there's nothing sadistic about this member of the Chapeau Rouge/La Provence expat hangout ghetto. Boring live music every night is saved by an inexpensive snack menu and top-notch bar. The atmosphere is undeniably pleasant, though they could've done much more with the space. Not bad for conversation, at least. *See also p141.*

Ostroff

Střelecký ostrov (Shooter's Island) 336, Prague 1
(2491 9235). Tram 6, 9, 17, 18, 22, 57, 58.
Open 11am-3am daily; *terrace* 11am-midnight daily.
Map 2 F5
Phenomenally well-stocked, professionally poured and with Vltava river views no one can touch. Ostroff's Italian barmen run an affable, sophisticated show in a setting of blond wood, designer seating and late-night limoncello just for close friends – like you (*see also p120*). If you go by tram, get off before the bridge, then walk over Legionnaires' Bridge (most Legii).

Sféra

(Sphere) Michalská 19, Prague 1 (2423 0841).
Metro Můstek/6, 9, 18, 22, 51, 54, 57, 58 tram.
Open 10am-4am daily. **Map 3 H4**
Bridging the gap between the backpacker mecca of **Chapeau Rouge** (*see above*) and the strictly expense-account **Bugsy's** (*see p139*), Sféra aims to launch Central Europe's first trash culture lounge in September 1998, complete with the latest in ultra-cool San Francisco-style retro amenities. Vinyl booths, 'sleaze/porno' music tracks, fresh fruit vodka shots, Belgian fruit 'n' nut beers, food wraps (those focaccia/burrito hybrids that are all the rage in SoMa), a sound stage for live combos and late, late hours. Run by the same management as **Jo's Bar** (*see p150*), it looks as though an experienced hand has finally come up with a direly needed touch of style for Prague's nascent bar scene.

Studio A Rubín

Malostranské náměstí 9, Prague 1 (535 015). Metro
Malostranská/12, 22, 57 tram. **Open** 5pm-4am daily.
Map 2 E3
Popular with young Czechs, this cellar pub has maintains a consistently great vibe, which sometimes becomes so irresistible that even the bar staff are infected and end up abandoning the bar in favour of the dancefloor. Local, affordable and not bad fun.

U Kotvy

(The Anchor) Spálená 11, Prague 1 (no phone).
Metro Národní třída/6, 9, 18, 22, 51, 54, 57, 58 tram.
Open 24 hours daily. **Map 5 H6**
Late-night, would-be tram passengers, stranded at the infamous Lazarská crossroads, end up here every night. A final dash of Becherovka? One last beer? A light snack? A wafer-thin mint? Okay, so the last one's a lie, but the rest is cheap and it's cheap.

ZanziBar

Lázeňská 6, Prague 1 (no phone). Metro Malostranská/
12, 22, 57 tram. **Open** noon-3am Mon-Sat; 5pm-3am
Sun. **Map 2 E3**
If you've just spent half your salary on Italian boots and a Joe Camel expedition jacket, you won't find a better place to show it off – nor more competition. Crowds of revellers orbit around the drink specials lists, grooving to James Brown tracks, and nobody seems to mind the steepest prices in town for clumsily mixed drinks. Or maybe everyone's too cool to care. *See also p151.*

Nice 'n' sleazy

Call it a credit to Czech entrepreneurial spirit. Call it a national disgrace, but wherever you come down on the sleaze question, one thing's clear: business is booming in Prague.

The Social Democratic party, needful of revenue to pay for badly neglected social programmes, has estimated the potential of a tax on prostitution at anywhere between one and 25 billion Kč. If the 'Gold Rush' days of post-Velvet Revolution foreign capital are over, nobody has told the city's sex barons.

But sleaze has always abounded in Eastern Europe, where once-forbidden porn popped up within days of the old regime's demise and still features on late-night TV Nova. Though prostitution is not legal under Czech law, it's clear from any newsstand that nobody's making any arrests: maps of 'Erotic Prague' are on sale everywhere, alongside the 'Prague Sex Guide,' a promotional full-colour bordello guide, complete with coupons giving free entry, so to speak.

'Disko striptýz', a slightly more innocent entertainment particular to the former Eastern Bloc, still features at clubs such as **Arena**. More usual, and, quite professional strip shows, run all night at **Alhambra, Go-Go Bar Cascade** and the new **Cabaret Atlas** in the city centre and at **Black & White** in Smíchov.

At the latter two, as at many places further afield, stripping is only a preview of further offerings. A vast range of extra services are on hand (as it were), at rates from 2,500-6,000 Kč per hour; entry fees and drinks can push it up by a further 500-1000 Kč. Go for centrally located, populist places like **Klub Marthy** and **Hanka Servis**, laps of luxury at **Lotos** and **Escade**, or S&M doctors and nurses at **Satanela**. Those without a date for the night need look no further than Perlova, Prague's unofficial Sunset Strip, which has survived all official attempts to ban it, or for that matter, the lobby bar of many of the city's more upscale hotels if you're a guest.

Alhambra
Václavské náměstí 5, Prague 1 (2419 3856). Metro Můstek/3, 9, 14, 24, 52, 53, 55, 56, 58 tram Open 9pm-4am daily. **Admission** 450 Kč. **Map 3 J5**
Viva Prague's Vegas. The original king of skin, with drinks on a James Bond theme and a theatrical setting.

Arena
Melantrichova 5, Prague 1 (2421 2573). Metro Můstek. **Open** 9pm-5am daily. **Admission** 50 Kč. **Map 3 H4**
Essentially a glossy, utterly square disco, though amusing if you're in the right frame of mind (and during the twice-nightly peeling).

Black & White
Štefánikova 7, Prague 5 (542 348). Metro Anděl/6, 9, 12, 58 tram. **Open** 9pm-5am daily. **Admission** 1,100 Kč.

Late-night eating

See also page 135 **Fast food**.

FX Café
Bělehradská 120, Prague 2 (2425 4776). Metro I.P. Pavlova/4, 6, 11, 16, 22, 34, 51, 56, 57 tram. **Open** 11.30am-6am daily. **Map 6 L8**
After a long night of dancing and drinking, you'll swear you're eating the best fettucine alfredo in the world, served by the most beautiful waitress you've ever seen. At least there's some chance that at least the latter might be true. Part of the unavoidable, multi-functional **Radost** complex (*see above*).

Masarykovo nádraží
Havlíčkova 2, Prague 1 (no phone). Metro Náměstí Republiky/5, 14, 24, 26, 52, 53, 56 tram. **Open** 9am-11pm daily. **Map 4 L3**
Desperate hunger has been known to drive men to cannibalism, or worse – to this incomparable train station buffet where the fried cheese has the subtle flavour of dirty socks. Yum.

Rebecca
Olšanské náměstí 8, Prague 3 (627 6920). Metro Flora/5, 9, 26, 55, 58 tram. **Open** 9am-8am daily. **Map 8 D2**
This (almost) non-stop in Žižkov packs out with clubbers, who trek from miles around to sit in the narrow, hideously purple setting and eat reasonably stale food.

Snack Bar Agnes
Hybernská 1, Prague 1 (no phone). Metro Náměstí Republiky/3, 5, 14, 24, 26, 53, 56 tram. **Open** 11am-3am Mon-Fri; 2pm-3am Sun. **Map 4 L3**
Emergency food best described as edible, and sometimes criminally overcharged, but available when little else is. Just check the price on the menu before ordering.

U Havrana
Hálkova 6, Prague 2 (9620 0020). Metro I.P. Pavlova/4, 6, 16, 22, 34, 51, 56, 57 tram. **Open** 24 hours Mon-Fri; 6pm-6am Sat, Sun. **Map 6 K7**
Near **Radost** (*see above*), **Music Park** (*see above*) and **AghaRTA** (*see p199*), this all-night pub is clean, serves good food and beer, and has attentive service (if you manage to get the right waitress).

A bit out of centre, but who else combines impressive striptease with late-night sushi bar?

Cabaret Atlas

Ve Smečkách 31, Prague 1 (9622 4260). Metro Muzeum/4, 6, 16, 22, 34, 51, 56, 57 tram. **Open** 24 hours. **Admission** 200 Kč.
Map 6 K6
Striptease and whirlpools… and that's just for starters.

Escade

Křesomyslova 5, Prague 4 (436 916). Tram 7, 18, 24, 53, 55. **Open** 24 hours. **Admission** 300 Kč.
The latest and most splashy show and bar in the market. Provides own taxi service but be prepared to shell out.

Go-Go Bar Cascade

Rybná 8, Prague 1 (231 0537). Tram 5, 14, 26, 53. **Open** 9pm-4am daily. **Admission** 300 Kč.
Map 4 K3
A dozen dancers, as dizzying as the drink prices.

Hanka Servis

Bulharská 10, Prague 10 (734 011/734 794). Bus 135, 139, 213. **Open** 24 hours. **Admission** 200 Kč.
No, that's not 'hankie'. Sin of choice for the average Prague Tomáš cat.

Klub Marthy

Seifertova 35, Prague 3 (627 8013). Tram 5, 9, 26, 55, 58. **Open** 2pm-2am Mon-Sat, Sun.
Admission free. **Map 8 B1**
Could be any Žižkov bar, but cleaner and remarkably more accommodating.

Lotos

Kupeckého 832, Prague 4 (791 6825). Metro Háje. **Open** 24 hours. **Admission** 500 Kč.
Prime practitioners, known here and abroad – not for the bargain-hunter.

Satanela

Vílová 9, Prague 10 (781 6618). Metro Strašnická/ 7, 19, 26, 51, 55 tram. **Open** 10pm-4am Mon-Sat; 10pm-2am Sun. **Admission** free.
Whips and chains, lab coats and fetish.

Gambling

Gambling is big business in Prague – and one that seems to be getting bigger every year. First came the *hernas* ('gambling halls' – essentially, bars full of one-arm bandits). Then came the bigger casinos that now line Wenceslas Square. Most casinos in Prague are legit, geared towards tourists, encourage small-time betting and have fairly relaxed atmospheres. The *hernas* cater mostly to locals, pay a maximum of 300 Kč for a 2 Kč wager, and operate on a legally fixed ratio of 60 to 80 odds.

Casino Admiral Praha

5 května 65, Prague 4 (6117 3297/643 3715). Metro Vyšehrad. **Open** 5pm-5am. **Credit** EC, MC, V.
Map *see p85.*
The largest casino in the Czech Republic sits atop the Palace of Culture – a triumph of communist architecture in Vyšehrad. It's the most professionally operated gambling hall in town, offering roulette, card games, slot machines and an upscale bar. Bets from 20-5,000 Kč.

Casino Jalta Happy Days

Václavské náměstí 35, Prague 1 (643 3958). Metro Můstek/3, 9, 14, 24, 52, 53, 55, 58 tram. **Open** 24 hours daily. **Credit** EC, MC, V. **Map 4 K5**
With all the lights and the motorbike in the window, this ridiculously named place is hard to miss. The front room is an upscale *herna*, while the back offers a dim and glittery casino. Roulette, blackjack and poker. Bets from 20-10,000 Kč.

Palais Savarin

Na příkopě 10, Prague 1 (2422 1648). Metro Můstek/5, 14, 26, 53 tram. **Open** 1pm-4am daily. **Credit** DC, EC, MC, V. **Map 4 K4**
The elegant interior, with sterling candelabra and baroque frescoes, is worth a look even if you don't gamble. American roulette and stud poker are offered along with all the traditional games of chance. Bets from 20-5,000 Kč. Hurry, though – rumour has it that a McDonald's buyout is pending.

VIP Club Casino

Václavske náměsti 7, Prague 1 (2419 3837). Metro Můstek/3, 9, 14, 24, 52, 53, 55, 56, 58 tram. **Open** 24 hours daily. **Credit** EC, MC, V. **Map 3 J5**
Located in the Hotel Ambassador (it's not called VIP for nothing). Roulette, blackjack, poker, punto banco, craps, slots. Wagers from 25-5,000 Kč.
Branches: Hotel Panorama, Milevská 7, Prague 4 (6116 1111); Hotel Forum, Kongresová 1, Prague 4 (6119 1111).

Herna bars

Herna Můstek

inside Můstek metro station (no phone). Metro Můstek/3, 9, 14, 24, 52, 53, 55, 56, 58 tram. **Open** 9am-11pm daily. **Map 4 K5**
Most *herna* bars are pretty seedy places, but this one, inside Prague's main metro station, is relatively unthreatening.

Poker club

Václavské náměsti 7, Prague 1 (no phone). Metro Můstek/3, 9, 14, 24, 52, 53, 55, 56, 58 tram. **Open** 24 hours daily. **Map 3 J5**
A particularly dark non-stop *herna* on the main avenue.

Reno

Vodičkova 39, Prague 1 (260 553). Metro Můstek/3, 9, 14, 24, 52, 53, 55, 56, 58 tram. **Open** 11am-4am daily. **Map 5 J6**
Patronised by nervous-looking types. Light food served.

Late-night shops

Agip

Olbrachtova 1, Prague 4 (692 1465). Metro Budějovická/ 504, 505 bus. **Open** 24 hours daily.
A 24-hour petrol station with a weird assortment of gourmet and snack foods, including caviar and imported beers.

Potraviny-Lahůdky

Národní třida 37, Prague 1 (2421 2393). Metro Narodni třida/6, 9, 18, 22, 51, 54, 57, 58 tram. **Open** 6am-midnight Mon-Fri; 8am-midnight Sat, Sun. **Map 3 H5**
Last-chance groceries for the ride home on the nearby night tram terminus on Lazarská.

Samoobsluha

Uhelný trh 2, Prague 1 (2421 0548). Metro Můstek or Narodní třida/6, 9, 18, 22, 51, 54, 57, 58 tram. **Open** 6.30am-11pm Mon-Fri; 8am-11pm Sat; 9am-11pm Sun. **Map 3 H5**
Potraviny near Old Town Square with a large food selection.

Sport & Fitness

Now that even the Czechs are getting fit, you've no excuse for not working off all that beer. So either shape up or ship out.

Believe it or not, the Czech Republic is actually shaping up. More and more people are saying yes to life, crowding the city's fitness centres and pools during lunch breaks and after work. Okay, so they might guzzle down three beers afterwards, but, let's face it – health-consciousness isn't built in a day. The downside to this is the onslaught of protein drinks, steroids and weight-watch programmes aimed at guilting people into shedding pounds. And though this negative aspect gives cause for concern, the general focus on fitness is good news for Czechs, and has arrived not a moment too soon: after all, this is a country whose daily diet consists largely of beer and cigarettes, coupled with meals that raise your cholesterol count if you so much as look at them. As demand increases, so too do the quality and range of services: gone are the days of medieval torture chambers that passed for fitness equipment.

Participation sports

Bungee jumping

What to say? They string you up. You jump. You don't hit the ground. In theory, at least. Beats Nova TV re-runs on a Friday night.

KI Bungee Jump
Hvězdova 2, Prague 4 (424 271/0602 250 125). Metro Pankrác/134, 188, 193 bus. **Open** *office 9am-3pm Mon-Fri; jumps May-June, Sept, Oct 11am-5pm Sat, Sun; July, Aug 11am-6pm Wed-Sun.* **Cost** 650 Kč.
Jumps are made from Zvikovské podhradi, the bridge over the Vltava.

Cycling & mountain biking

Beware of biking in Prague – if the fumes don't kill you, the cars will do their best. But if you make it outside the city limits, you'll find a network of reasonably maintained bike trails. Bike maps are available at nearly every bookstore, and if you're afraid to brave it alone, try the following places, which organise cycling tours and stock equipment.

Bike Ranch
Palackého náměsti 2, Prague 2 (294 933). Metro Karlovo náměsti/3, 4, 7, 16, 17, 34 tram. **Open** 10am-noon, 1-6pm, Mon; 10am-noon, 1-7.30pm, Tue; 10am-noon, 1-6pm, Wed-Fri. **Map 5 G9**

Landa
Šumavská 33, Prague 2 (2425 6121). Metro Náměsti Miru/11, 16 tram. **Open** 9am-6pm Mon-Fri. **Map 8 B3**

Sport S-cyclo
Korunni 19, Prague 2 (25 86 21). Metro Náměsti Miru/11, 16 tram. **Open** 10am-6pm Mon-Fri; 9am-noon Sat. **Map 8 B3**
Branches: Jaromírova 8, Prague 2 (0602 309 296); Plzeňská 61, Prague 5 (547 753).

U Tyrše
Eliasova 12, Prague 6 (2431 5594). Metro Hradčanská/ 131 bus. **Open** 9am-7pm Mon-Fri; 9am-noon Sat.
Branch: Bělohradská 57 (296 888).

Fishing

The Czech Fishing Association unapologetically makes it tough for foreigners to procure even temporary licences, but if you're really serious, it will fork over the necessary paperwork and give advice. Different fish are in season at different times of the year; river fishing is allowed from mid-June to mid-August.

Czech Fishing Association
(Český rybářský svaz) Nad Olšinami 31, Prague 10 (7811 7513/fax 7811 1754). Tram 22, 26. **Open** 7am-3pm Mon, Tue, Thur; 7am-4pm Wed; 7am-2pm Fri. **Licence** *with trout* 1,050 Kč a year; *without trout* 950 Kč a year.

Fitness centres

As the city is growing more and more body-conscious, fitness centres are cropping up everywhere you turn – but there's still no one central, modern, fully equipped gym. The places listed below have knowledgeable, helpful staff.

Body Island
Uruguayská 6, Prague 2 (250 592). Metro Náměsti Miru/4, 22, 34 tram. **Open** 10am-10pm Mon-Thur; 10am-9pm Fri; 9am-7pm Sat; 3pm-9am Sun.
Admission *sauna* 150 Kč per hour; 250 Kč per two hours; *classes* 60 Kč; 50Kč students. **Membership** *3-month (12 visits)* 700 Kč; 580 Kč students; *10-month (48 visits)* 2,400 Kč; 1,920 Kč students. **Map 6 M9/8 A3**
The nautilus machines are nothing to write home about, but this body-care complex – including a wide range of aerobics and dance classes, a sauna, and a masseur and hairstylist when you're all worked out – offers something for (nearly) every conceivable bodily need.

Erpet Golf Centrum
Strakonická 510, Prague 5 (548 086). Metro Smíchovské nádraži/12 tram. **Open** 8am-11pm daily.
Admission *massage* 300 Kč; *squash* 300 Kč per hour; *solarium* 5 Kč per minute. **Membership** 15,000 Kč per year. **Credit** AmEx, DC, EC, MC, V.
With quality fitness equipment and good assistance at a low price, you can see why this workout centre is so popular with the expat community. Facilities include a

whirlpool, sauna, full workout systems, as well as fitness consultation and an excellent juice bar. Non-members can only come for a massage, a game of squash or a fry in the solarium. *See also* **Golf** *below*.

Fitness Centre Hilton

Pobřežní 1, Prague 8 (2484 2013). Metro Florenc/3, 24 tram. **Open** 6.30am-10pm daily. *Tennis* 7am-10pm daily. **Admission** *gym* 170 Kč; *classes/swimming* 220 Kč. **Membership** 35,000 Kč per year; *tennis* 10-17,000 Kč plus 400 Kč per game. **Credit** AmEx, EC, MC, V.
The Hilton's small luxury fitness centre offers rowing machines, Airsteppers and Soloflex, plus a warm, if small, pool. Good English-speaking assistance and a tropical poolside juice bar are bonuses.

Fitness Club Intercontinental

Náměstí Curieových 43, Prague 1 (2488 1525). Metro Staroměstská/17 tram. **Open** 6am-11pm Mon-Fri; 9am-10pm Sat, Sun. **Admission** 150 Kč per hour. **Credit** AmEx, DC, EC, MC, V. **Map 3 H1**
Popular among the rich and moderately famous. Come flex with the movers and shakers (and treadmillers and Stairmaster-ers) of Prague's burgeoning business community. Good cardio machines and an eager staff of trainers. They even have TVs in front of the treadmills, so you won't be (too) bored.

Fitness Forum International

Kongresová 1, Prague 4 (6119 1326). Metro Vyšehrad. **Open** 7am-10pm Mon-Fri; 9am-9pm Sat, Sun. **Admission** 150 Kč per hour; *swimming & sauna* 250 Kč for two hours. **Membership** 30,000 Kč. **Credit** DC, EC, MC, V.
This 25th-floor fitness centre is as relaxing as it is invigorating. There are squash courts, aerobics and a good, though fairly small, assortment of training equipment. Treat yourself to a sauna, cold dip or tanning session, or just slob out in a white robe by the small pool with a panoramic view.

Fit studio Pohořelec

Diskařská 1, Prague 6 (353 488). Tram 8, 22. **Open** 9am-10pm Mon-Fri; 9am-6pm Sat. **Admission** *fitness studio* 50 Kč per hour. **Membership** 4,500 Kč per year; 2,000 Kč students.
Located just beyond Strahov Monastery, Fit Studio has an excellent gym – used by the Czech gymnastic squad for training – and also provides proper instruction. There's a range of aerobic classes (high, low and step) in the evenings, some of which are taken by an American instructress (but don't let that put you off). Club membership allows you a ten per cent discount on classes, which start at 35 Kč.

Holiday Inn Prague

Koulova 15, Prague 6 (2439 3838). Tram 20, 25. **Open** 7am-10pm daily **Admission** 80 Kč.
The machines at this well-equipped fitness centre still maintain their just-from-the-factory sparkle, probably because the remote location means they don't get too much use. More for you, then.

Golf

Though not exactly world-renowned for its golfing facilities, the Czech Republic does have 13 courses. Okay, so only four are 18-hole, but two of these are in dramatic settings: **Karlštejn** (*0311 684 716-7; see also page 229*) and **Karlovy Vary** (*017 333 1101; see also page 234*). Prague, in particular, is poorly served. Most are open from April to October, though some operate year-round.

Erpet Golf Centrum

See above. **Green fee** 100 Kč per hour.
Prague's only 18-hole course is only available for members. Full-swing golf simulators offer a choice of ten courses from around the world, and there's also an indoor putting green and pitching course. Club rentals and instruction are available. The pro shop has English-language brochures on golf courses in the Czech Republic.

Golf club Praha

Plzeňská, Prague 5 (tel/fax 544 586/651 2464). Metro Anděl, then 4, 7, 9 tram. **Green fee** 7-800 Kč per round.
A nine-hole course and driving range on a hilltop. The course can get very dry in the summer months, but at least you can blame your bad form on the ground.

Horse riding

For better or for worse, most horse-riding outfits will be more than willing to seat you on the steed of your choice and let you loose in the open plain. Which means that, for your own sake, don't exaggerate your experience.

TJ Žižkov Praha

Císařský ostrov 76, Žižkov, Prague 7 (878 476/878 181). **Open** call between 9am-5pm daily. **Rates** 300 Kč per hour.
Good facilities, plus a dressage ring and a showjumping arena. Probably not the best place for complete beginners as there are no structured classes, but all riders are accompanied. For a 200 Kč supplement you can ride on trails in Stromovka park (*see below*), a far more enjoyable setting. Reserve in advance.

Ice skating

Though you can no longer skate on the Vltava, the reservoirs at Hostivař and Divoká Šárka (*see above* and *below*) still come alive in December with bundled skaters and grog vendors. Most indoor facilities operate from October to April, and are quite inexpensive.

Krasobruslařský Stadion

Sámova 1, Prague 10 (no phone). Tram 6, 7, 24. **Open** *Sept-June* 10am-noon Mon-Fri. **Admission** 15 Kč.

Sportovní hala (HC Sparta)

Za elektrárnou 419, Prague 7 (372 204). Tram 5, 12, 17. **Open** *Sept-Mar* 3.15-5.15pm Sat, Sun. **Admission** 20 Kč. **Map 7 D1**

Vokovice

Za lány 1, Prague 6 (362 759). Metro Dejvická, then 26 tram. **Open** *Sept-Mar* 3.30-5.45pm Sun. **Admission** 20 Kč.

Jogging

Jogging, even in the parks of central Prague, is the aerobic equivalent of smoking a pack a day – no joke. But if you must get your running shoes out of the closet, try one of the following, which are far enough from the pollution to make the endeavour just less than harmful. No park, however, is safe from the menace of dogs, which will snap at your heels as their owners stand by laughing.

Heading for a fall: skateboarding in the shadow of the metronome in Letná Park.

Divoká Šárka

Prague 7. Tram 20, 26/119, 216, 218 bus.
'Wild' Šárka lives up to its name, with bulbous rock formations and forests so thick you'll think you've left all
civilisation far behind. There are challenging, hilly trails
for joggers. Šárka is most easily accessible from Evropská,
heading towards the airport. Take any of the trams or buses
above from Dejvická metro. *See also p83 & p227.*

Michelský les

Prague 4. Metro Roztyly.
Avert your eyes from the hideous *panelák* (tower block) eye-
sore at the base of the hill and head straight for the green
hills behind. Within minutes, you'll forget you're anywhere
near a city.

Obora Hvězda

Prague 6. Tram 8, 22/179, 191 bus.
All trails are designed to wind you back to the park's centrepiece, the stunny, star-shaped, Renaissance summer
palace. *See also p83.*

Stromovka

*Prague 7. Metro Nádraží Holešovice, then 5, 12 or 17
tram.* **Map 7 B1**
The most centrally located of Prague's large parks. After
the initial sprint to avoid the Výstaviště fairground crowds,
you can have the woods to yourself – the park was developed by Rudolf II, who was keen on communing with
nature. *See also p82.*

Skateboarding

To get a glimpse of local talent, check out the concrete pavilion next to the National Theatre ticket
office or the area around the giant metronome in
Letná Park. The following places sell skate gear.

Mystic Sk8

*Štěpánská 31, Prague 1 (264 675). Metro Muzeum/3, 9,
14, 24 tram.* **Open** 10am-7pm Mon-Fri; 10am-2pm Sat.
Credit EC, MC, V. **Map 6 K6**
Undoubtedly the best skate shop in Prague, and a good place
to hook up with the underground graffiti scene.

Total Board Shop

*Čertouská 23, Prague 9 (861 190). Tram 3, 8 or Metro
Českomoravská, then 277 bus.* **Open** 10am-5pm Mon-Fri.
Big pants and big boards – you're halfway there.
Branch: Balbinova 5, Prague 2 (2423 3517).

Skiing & snowboarding

Serious ski buffs head for the Tatra mountain
range in Slovakia. Somewhat surprisingly, the ominous peaks of the High Tatras, though more visu-
ally impressive, don't provide the most challenging
skiing opportunities. The area's highest point – and
only black-diamond slope – can be found in the

eastern High Tatra town of Tatranská Lomnica, though it tends to be a run of solid ice. Beginners, meanwhile, will find the hilly region near Zdiar, near the High Tatras' Polish border, ideal for gaining their snow legs. Hardcore skiiers head for the Low Tatras, where the slopes are varied and complicated enough to challenge even the most seasoned. The area around Jasná and Chopok is especially thrilling. If you don't want to cross the border, the Krkonoše mountains offer your best bet for downhill skiing. Stock up in Prague, at one of the places listed below, and head for the mountains – Špindlerův Mlýn has regular competitions.

Kastner Öhler

Václavské náměstí 66, Prague 1 (2422 5432). Metro Muzeum/3, 9, 14, 24 tram. **Open** 9.30am-7pm Mon-Sat. **Credit** EC, MC, V. **Map 6 K6**
The lower level of this general sports store is packed with ski equipment from Solomon, Rosignol and Head.

Snowboardel

Husitská 29, Prague 3 (627 9900). Metro Florenc, then bus 133, 207. **Open** 10am-6pm Mon-Fri. **Map 8 B1**
A huge selection of new and used snowboards, sold by goatee-wearing hardcore aficionados of the pastime. Also a good selection of stylish snowboardwear.

Sport Slivka

Újezd 40, Prague 1 (5700 7231). Tram 12, 22. **Open** 10am-8pm Mon-Fri; noon-6pm Sat, Sun.
Good, reasonable rentals for skiers – a wise idea as resorts often have little to offer.

Squash

Squash is becoming increasingly popular in the Czech Republic, especially in the winter months, when it's not unheard of to reserve more than a month in advance. The courts listed below rent out playing space and equipment by the hour. *See also* **Fitness Forum International** and **Erpet Golf Centrum** *above.*

Squash Centrum Strahov

Strahov 1230, Prague 6 (2051 3609). Metro Dejvická, then 132, 143, 149, 219 bus. **Open** 7am-11pm Mon-Fri; 8am-11pm Sat, Sun. **Rates** 160-330 Kč per hour.
One of the city's oldest squash centres. Often mobbed with students from the adjacent dorm.

Squashové centrum

Václavské náměstí 15, Prague 1 (2400 9232). Metro Můstek/3, 9, 14, 24 tram. **Open** 7am-11pm Mon-Fri; 9am-11pm Sat, Sun. **Rates** 260-420 Kč.
Three courts and an unbeatable location.

Swimming

As the winter is long and the summer fickle, your most reliable bet is indoor pools. But choose with care; many of Prague's pools are thick with chlorine, hysterical children or amorous teenagers who steadfastedly ignore the designated areas for lap-swimmers. Also, don't be too squeamish about stray hairs. If you prefer to do your swimming in the open air, the dams on *page 225* are even dirtier, but wildly popular. *See also above* **Fitness centres** for hotels with pools.

Areál Strahov Stadion

Olympijská, Prague 6 (355 226/353 095). Tram 22/132, 143, 149, 217 bus/cable car from Újezd, then walk along Olympijská. **Open** 6am-8pm Mon, Thur, Fri; 6am-5pm Tue; 6am-5pm, 7-8pm, Wed; 8am-2pm Sat. **Closed** July, Aug. **Admission** 25 Kč. **Map 1 A5**
A large, well-kept indoor pool that serves as a training site for competitive Czech swimmers. There are also sauna facilities, making it one of the best swimming centres.

Divoká Šárka

Prague 6 (368 022). Tram 26, then short walk through a rocky valley. **Open** May-mid-Sept 9am-7pm daily. **Admission** 20 Kč; 10 Kč children.
Follow the other swimmers on the red- and white-striped trail up the valley to find this outdoor pool. The setting is idyllic and the lawned sunbathing area gets more crowded than the pool.

Džbán Reservoir

(vodní nádrž Džbán) Vokovice, Prague 6 (366 068). Tram 26. **Open** May-Sept 9am-7pm daily. **Admission** 20 Kč; 10 Kč children.
A large, popular reservoir and naturist beach, close to the tram stop. You can also play volleyball and table tennis.

Hostivař Reservoir

(vodní nádrž Hostivař) Prague 10. Metro Skalka, then bus 147, 154/tram 22, 26, or Metro Háje, then bus 165, 170, 212, 213/tram 22, 26, then short walk through forest. **Open** May-Sept 10am-7pm daily. **Admission** 10 Kč.
Larger and deeper than Džbán, and with more activities, including rowing, wind-surfing, tennis, volleyball and a water slide. There's also a naturist beach if you're feeling daring.

Hotel Axa

Na Poříčí 40, Prague 1 (232 3967). Metro Florenc or Náměstí Republiky/3, 5, 14, 24, 26 tram. **Open** 7am-10pm Mon-Fri; 9am-9pm Sat, Sun. **Admission** 60 Kč per hour. **Map 4 M2**
The pool in this hotel is a good length and, if you go in the morning, mercifully free of shrieking children.

Podolí

Podolská 74, Prague 4 (6121 4343). Tram 16, 17, 32. **Open** 6am-9.45pm Mon-Fri; 8am-7.45pm Sat, Sun. **Admission** *indoor* 60 Kč for 3 hours; 20-30 Kč children; *outdoor* 80 Kč per day; 20-40 Kč children.
Watch the Darwinian struggle between overexcited kids and heroic proportions of chlorine. It's quite a pick-up joint for tanned young singles, as well as a notorious centre of male prostitution.

SK Slávia

Stadion SK Slávia Praha, Vladivostocká 2, Prague 10 (735 552). Tram 4, 7, 22, 24. **Open** *indoor* Sept-Apr 6am-8pm Mon-Fri; 9am-7pm Sat, Sun; *outdoor* May-Sept 6am-8pm daily. **Admission** *indoor* 25 Kč per hour; 20 Kč children; *outdoor* 50 Kč per day; 20 Kč children. **Sauna** *(733 191).* **Open** 10am-10pm Mon-Fri; 10am-6pm Sat, Sun. **Admission** 90 Kč for 2 hours.
The Slávia complex has indoor and outdoor pools, both of a respectable size. On hot days, however, the outdoor pool gets so packed that you can virtually abandon all hope of swimming.

YMCA

Na Poříčí 12, Prague 1 (2487 2220). Metro Náměstí Republiky/5, 14, 26 tram. **Open** 6.30am-noon, 4-10pm, Mon-Fri; 10am-10pm Sat, Sun. **Admission** 1 Kč per minute. **Map 4 L3**
Though the tiny nautilus rooms get rather claustrophobic if more than a handful of people are using them, the pool is more spacious, and is established ground for reasonably serious swimmers.

Tennis

The Czech Republic has long been renowned for its tennis stars – most notably Ivan Lendl and Martina Navrátilová. Although both of them defected to the West, they're still national heroes. Czech success at the 1996 Olympics and the international rise of Jana Novotná – sealed when she took the 1998 Women's Championship title at Wimbledon – have also helped boost the game in the Republic.

1. ČLTK

Ostrov Štvanice 38, Prague 7 (232 4601/2481 0272). Metro Florenc or Vltavská. **Open** 6am-11pm daily. **Rates** *before 1pm* 300 Kč per hour; *after 1pm* 600 Kč per hour. **Map 7 E3**
In the first week of August, the annual Škoda Czech Open (ATP tour) is held at these six outdoor floodlit courts, located on an island in the Vltava. The locals love it, so booking is essential.

Fit studio Pohořelec

Diskařská 1, Prague 1 (353 488). Tram 22. **Open** 8am-9pm Mon-Sun. **Rates** 150 Kč per hour.
Three outdoor courts that can be booked in advance.

TCVŠ Praha

Nad Hliníkem, Prague 5 (tel/fax 5721 0647). Tram 4, 7, 9. **Open** *summer* 7am-9pm daily; *winter (indoor)* 7am-11pm daily. **Rates** *summer* 120 Kč per hour; *winter* 350 Kč per hour.
These courts, on a wooded hillside in front of the Hotel Golf, are hired out to the public at off-peak times. Booking is essential during the summer.

Tenis Club

Střelecký ostrov, Prague 1 (2492 0136). Tram 6, 9, 22. **Open** 9am-9pm daily. **Rates** 200 Kč per hour. **Map 2 F5**
These courts are on an island in the middle of the Vltava and, as such, not for the shy.

Tenisový klub Slávia Praha

Letenské sady 32, Prague 7 (3337 4033). Tram 1, 8, 25. **Open** *Apr-Oct* 7am-8pm daily; *Nov-Mar (indoor)* 7am-10pm. **Rates** *outdoor* 200 Kč per hour; *indoor* 500 Kč per hour. **Map 7 B3**
Just opposite the National Technical Museum on Letná Hill are eight floodlit outdoor clay courts. The courts are in good condition and the shaded outdoor café is convivial, but otherwise the facilities are pretty shoddy. Booking is essential during the summer.

TJ Vyšehrad

V Pevnosti 6, Prague 2 (427 578). Metro Vyšehrad.
Open 9am-7pm daily (in good weather). **Rates** 200 Kč
per hour.

An excellent outdoor complex of clay courts, nestled in
sunken red-brick castle walls. The public is allowed in only
when not in use by members. Phone for information.

Spectator sports

Football

Internationally, Czech teams have suffered a bit of
a beating in the last few years, as most of their top
players have skipped town in favour of higher
salaries and greater prestige. Domestically, the
age-old rivalry between Sparta and Slávia, the two
top football teams, remains fierce. Though Sparta
is generally acknowledged to be the superior of the
two, the competition between them is the lifeblood
of spectator sport in this country. Prague's other
first division team is FK Victoria Žižkov.

Up in arms

Czech firearms are respected worldwide – in
fact, the word 'pistol' is one of the few Czech
words to weasel its way into the English language. And plenty of people use the word in
its mother tongue: over 40,000 people in
Prague alone own a firearm. It's all perfectly
legal, involving a barrage of tests and strict
regulations concerning the exposure of guns
in public places. And as the city still has a
miniscule amount of violent crime, you'll
most likely see very few of those 40,000-odd
firearms in the light of day. But if you've got
an itchy trigger finger and don't want to go
through the bureaucratic hassle getting
licensed to kill, never fear: any number of
shooting galleries in Prague will be more than
happy to slap a class-A weapon in your
hands and let you loose. Take your pick:
indoor ranges afford a creaky-basement
ambience straight out of a grade-B horror
flick, and a colourful cast of two-dimension-
al characters to serve as your target practice.
Outdoor ranges, most of which are located
in the peripheries of Prague, offer a wider
range of guns and greater distance between
you and your target, and a whole troop of
humourless supervisors to make sure you
don't get carried away.

Rambo Shooting Range

*Za pořičskou branou 7, Prague 8 (231 3712).
Metro Florenc.* **Open** 9am-noon, 1-6pm, daily.
Admission 60 Kč for 30 minutes; 500 Kč for
10 visits.

FC Sparta Praha

*Stadion Sparta, M Horákové 98, Prague 7 (2057 0323).
Metro Hradčanská/8, 25, 26 tram.* **Admission** *league
games* 60-200 Kč; *European games* 120-600 Kč.
Map 7 B2

FK Viktoria Žižkov

*Stadion TJ Viktoria Žižkov, Seifertova 130, Prague 3
(272 775). Tram 5, 9, 26.* **Admission** *league games*
20-50 Kč; *European games* 130 Kč. **Map 8 B2**

SK Slávia Praha

*Stadion SK Slávia Praha, Vršovice, Prague 10 (6731
2705). Tram 4, 7, 22, 24.* **Admission** *league games* 50-
100 Kč; *European games* 100-160 Kč.

Horse racing

It's no Kentucky Derby, but the Chuchle race track
on the outskirts of Prague offers regular chances
to spend a day at the races. If you really enjoy
watching quadrupeds sweat, hold out for the
Pardubice steeplechase, the longest in the world,
held in late October – but leave your animal-rights
activist friends at home: the jumps are among
the most dangerous in Europe. Betting works in a
similar way to the British system, with two agents
accepting minimum bets, of 20 Kč and 50 Kč
respectively. You can bet to win (*vítěz*) or place
(*místo*) as well as on the order (*poradní*). Handi-
capper's information is contained on the programme. There's both outdoor seating and indoor
monitors, and a selection of appealingly dilapidated bars and restaurants for inter-race libations.

Chuchle

*Radotínská 69, Prague 5 (543 091/fax 536 610). Metro
Smíchovské nádraží, then 129, 172, 241, 244 bus.*
Admission 30 Kč adults; 10 Kč children.
On race days, you can get a train from Smíchovské nádraží
to Chuchle. Races start at 2pm on Sundays.

Dostihový spolek

*Pražská 607, Pardubice, 110km (68 miles) east of Prague
(040 633 5300). Metro Florenc, then ČSAD bus to
Pardubice.* **Race meets** Saturdays in May-October.
Admission 40 Kč.
Velká Pardubická is on the second Sunday in October,
admission 200-2,000 Kč.

Ice hockey

Sport, of course, can never fully compensate for
history, but the Czech national ice-hockey team's
victory in the 1998 Winter Olympics in Tokyo
came pretty damned close. What followed was the
biggest city-wide party since the wall came tumbling down.

HC Sparta Praha

*Za Sportovní hala Sparta Praha, Za elektárnou 419,
Prague 7 (2423 2251). Trams 5, 12, 17.* **Admission** 70-
90 Kč; *European games* 150 Kč. **Map 7 B2**
Sparta's home ground in Holešovice resembles the one at
Wembley, both architecturally and acoustically.

Slávia Praha

*Stadion SK Slávia Praha, Vršovice, Prague 10 (6731
1415). Tram 4, 7, 22, 24.* **Admission** 50-100 Kč.

Theatre & Dance

After a post-revolution barren period, the Prague theatre and dance scene is on the up again. And you don't even have to understand Czech to enjoy the pickings.

The theatrical arts have long enjoyed considerable popularity and influence in the Czech lands – how many other countries could conceive of electing a playwright as president? Through much of the communist era, strict censorship helped shape Czech theatre into a deliciously clever, richly double-entendred form of subversion. Since the 1989 revolution many of Prague's theatrical artists have been busily modernising their techniques and repertoires. Judging by a recent upswing in theatre attendance, audiences seem to approve.

Theatre has played a consistently vital role in Czech culture and identity ever since the National Revival of the late nineteenth century. Completed in 1881, the magnificent **National Theatre** (*see below* and *page 55*) symbolised both Czech independence and national pride, presenting opera and drama in the Czech language. During the First Czechoslovak Republic, **Jan Werich** and **Jiří Voskovec**'s popular Liberated Theatre (Osvobozené divadlo) fused Brechtian satire with Czech cabaret and folk traditions. In 1921, **Karel Čapek**'s expressionist sci-fi masterpiece *R.U.R.* gave the world a new word: robot.

During the Nazi occupation, theatre was savagely suppressed along with all other forms of native cultural expression. From 1948 to the early 1960s communist leaders took over where the Germans left off by demanding rigid adherence to socialist realism. When his first full-length play, *The Garden Party*, premièred at the Theatre on the Balustrade in 1963, **Václav Havel** helped usher in a new and hopeful renaissance of Czech culture, tolerated by authorities under the policy of 'destalinisation'. After the communist crackdown of 1968, however, the outspoken actors, directors and playwrights who had created this mid-sixties 'Golden Age' of Czech theatre either emigrated or found themselves constantly harassed by the freshly oppressive regime. In 1977, Havel and a number of other theatrical artists signed the Charter 77 declaration; some signatories, including Havel, were subsequently banned from Czech theatres.

This close relationship between theatre and political subversion led to a minor identity crisis after the 1989 revolution when Prague's theatrical artists, suddenly able to say anything, seemed devoid of anything significant to say. This, combined with the flood of incoming Western films and television programmes, helped cause a decline in theatre attendance. Since 1995, however, audiences have been swelling again. With ticket prices ranging from a mere 20 to 500 Kč, enjoying one of Prague's many and varied live performances can cost less than catching the latest Hollywood action flick. Accordingly, Czech theatre still occupies a populist role long relegated to the cinema in most countries, and contemporary productions are more likely to concentrate on entertainment than subversion.

Today, some pessimistic critics claim that Czech playwrights have floundered for subject matter ever since communism collapsed. Others maintain that Czech theatre has been slowly developing a less reactionary and more contemporary voice, in line with current international trends that integrate theatre with dance, music, video or computer graphics. Despite the Czech theatre's rich political history, there has been little movement since the revolution toward theatre as a method of social critique or political subversion. Given the almost daily political scandals rocking the Czech Republic, however, the further development of theatre as a critical voice seems inevitable.

Tickets & information

Not all box-office staff will speak English; consequently you might be better off buying tickets through one of the agencies listed below (though they are likely to charge commission). Another advantage is that the agencies accept credit cards, unlike the majority of the venues listed below (unless otherwise stated).

Bohemia Ticket International

Malé náměstí 13, Prague 1 (2422 7832/2161 2123/ fax 2161 2126/www.csad.cz/bti). Metro Staroměstská. **Open** 9am-6pm Mon-Fri; 9am-2pm Sat. **Credit** MC, V. **Map 3 H4**
Book your theatre tickets via Bohemia Ticket International's website, or visit one of its numerous concessions throughout the city, including the following hotels: **Renaissance** (2182 2201), **Diplomat** (2439 4117) and **Holiday Inn** (2439 3892) – for addresses, *see chapter* **Accommodation**. **Branches:** Na příkopě 16, Prague 1 (2421 5031); **Best Tours**, Václavské náměstí 27, Prague 1 (9003 2776).

Mozart woz 'ere: the classy neo-classical **Estates Theatre**. *See page 217.*

Ticketpro
*Salvátorská 10, Prague 1 (2481 4020/vstupenky@
ticketpro.cz/www.ticketpro.cz). Metro Staroměstská/17, 18
tram.* **Open** 8am-8pm Mon-Fri; 9am-8pm Sat; noon-8am
Sun. **Credit** AmEx, EC, MC, V. **Map 3 J3**
Major ticket outlet for theatre and concerts. See *Zlaté stránky*
(Yellow Pages) for other branches too numerous to list here.

Selected Czech theatres

On any given night, Prague's theatrical options are
likely to include works by contemporary local
playwrights, Czech-language versions of recent
international plays, standard presentations of
classics, innovative interpretations of traditional
material, and even translated stage versions of
Western films such as *Harold and Maude* or the
works of Woody Allen. Musical theatre is also
immensely popular, both in neighbourhood theatres and in large, splashy productions such as
Dracula, the long-running Czech version of *Jesus
Christ Superstar* and *Evita*, which opened in
summer 1998.

Adria Theatre/Palác Adria
*Jungmannova 31, Prague 1 (2449 4601). Metro Národní
třída or Můstek/3, 6, 9, 14, 18, 22, 24 tram.*
Tickets *from* **Ticketpro** (*see above*). **Map 5 J6**

During the regular Czech season (September to June), this
newly renovated theatre presents classic plays by writers
like Chekhov and Molière, as well as newer international
works, performed by the members of **Divadlo Bez
zábradlí** (Theatre Without a Balustrade). Well-known film
director Jiří Menzel (*Closely Observed Trains*) directs and
occasionally acts for the troupe. In the summer months, other
groups rent out the theatre, usually presenting tourist-
friendly fare such as the 1998 multimedia extravaganza
Faust. The Adria complex also houses a jazz club, a restaurant, an elegant bar, a café and an exhibition space.

Alfred ve dvoře Theatre
*(Divadlo Alfred ve dvoře) Františka Křižka 36, Prague 7
(2057 1584). Metro Vltavská/1, 5, 8, 12, 17, 25, 26
tram.* **Open** *box office* 4-8pm Mon-Fri. **Map 7 D3**
Headed by mime, experimental theatre artist, director and
teacher Ctibor Turba, this funky new theatre presents
mostly innovative dance and theatre projects and is a special venue for Turba's students in the alternative theatre
department at HAMU, Prague's music academy.

Archa Theatre
*(Divadlo Archa) Na Poříčí 26, Prague 1 (232 7570/fax
232 2089/reservations 232 8800/theatre@archa.aret.cz).
Metro Náměstí Republiky or Florenc/3, 24 tram.*
Open *box office* 9am-9pm daily (*summer* 10am-6pm
Mon-Fri). **Map 4 M2**
Prague's hippest and possibly finest theatre brings interna-
tionally renowned avant-garde dance, theatre, musical per-
formances and multimedia productions to its versatile and
well-equipped space, which also houses a café. As well as

laterna magika

laterna magika
Národní 4, Praha 1
Ticket Office Tel.: 2491 4129

Sales Department
Tel.: 2421 2691, Fax: 2422 7567

E-mail: latmag@bsdi.infima.cz
Internet: http://www.laterna.cz

Metro stop: Národní třída (B)

Tickets available at all Ticketpro outlets

providing a venue for alternative Czech performances, Archa sponsors frequent collaborations between local and international artists. If there's anything by Robert Wilson, David Byrne, Min Tanaka or Diamanda Galas happening in Prague, this is where you'll see it.

Celetná Theatre

(Divadlo v Celetné) Celetná 17, Prague 1 (2480 9168/ 232 6483). Metro Náměstí Republiky/5, 14, 26 tram.
Open tickets available at the theatre's Gaspar Kašpar Coffee Bar 9am-midnight Mon-Fri; 1pm-midnight Sat, Sun. **Map 3 J3**
This charming, small theatre space, with a pleasant adjoining café, is run by Jakub Spalek, mastermind of Kašpar, a talented group of actors. Celetná serves as a frequent venue for the English-language group **Misery Loves Company**

(*see below*), and for performances by students at (and recent graduates of) DAMU, Prague's leading drama school. It also showcases Kašpar's own high-energy productions.

Estates Theatre

(Stavovské divadlo) Ovocný trh 1, Prague 1 (2421 5001). Metro Můstek. **Open** *box office* 10am-6pm Mon-Fri; 10am-12.30pm, 3-6pm Sat, Sun; and half an hour before performances. Tickets are also available across the street at the Kolowrat Palace box office. **Map 3 J4**
Famous for premièring Mozart's *Don Giovanni* and known during the communist period as one of the 'Stone Theatres' that presented politically risk-free works, the Estates still favours a classical repertoire, including Mozart operas, and mainstream dramatic works by the likes of Shakespeare, Eugene O'Neill and Arthur Miller.

In the mood for dancing?

Classical ballet still prevails in Prague, with performances by the **National Ballet** at the **National Theatre**, the **Estates Theatre** and the **State Opera** (*see page 194*). The **Prague Chamber Ballet** performs amalgamations of traditional and modern dance.

In a different traditional vein, Bohemian folk-dancing is still vital in Prague. Folklore shows combine live music, high-energy dance, and colourful, elaborate costumes, featuring enthusiastic, athletic young ensembles of male and female dancers.

Currently, experiments in modern dance theatre are on the increase. Many international dance troupes visit Prague, feeding a growing desire among young Czech dancers to break away from traditional forms. Since few of the city's venues are devoted exclusively to dance, local and international dance companies perform at assorted Prague theatres, including **Archa Theatre, Alfred ve dvoře Theatre** and the **Roxy** (*see page 204*).

Dance venues

Duncan Center

Branická 41, Prague 4 (4446 1810/4446 1342/4446 2354). Tram 3, 16, 17.
This contemporary dance school doubles as the home performance space for **Deja Donne Productions**, the company run by Lenka Flory and Simone Sandrone. The Duncan Center sometimes presents exciting student productions and also hosts interesting touring foreign artists.

Ponec

Husitská 24A, Prague 3 (2481 7886/2481 3899). Metro Florenc, then 133 bus. **Map 8 B1**
Slated to open in 1999, this converted cinema was recently acquired by **Tanec Praha** (*see below*), a non-profit organisation. Devoted exclusively to contemporary dance, Ponec will present both Czech and international productions, as well as housing rehearsal studios and spaces for ongoing dance training.

Dance festivals

Progressive European Dance Theatre Festival

information from Duncan Center (see above).
Tickets 100-200 Kč. **Date** October.
This yearly autumn festival brings performers from all over the world to Prague for wildly diverse recitals in dance and dance theatre. Intended to educate as well as entertain, the performances are followed by seminars where anyone interested can learn more from the artists.

Tanec Praha

information: Jirsíkova 4, Prague 8 (2481 7886/2481 3899/fax 2319 576). Metro Florenc/8, 24 tram.
Tickets phone for details. **Date** June/July.
Every summer, usually in June or July, **Dance Prague** (Tanec Praha) stages an international dance and movement theatre festival. Attracting acclaimed Czech and international choreographers and companies, the festival aims to establish contact with foreign artists, stimulate public interest in contemporary dance, and encourage innovation among Czech choreographers and dancers.

Folklore shows & performances

Restaurace U Marčanů

Veleslavínská 14, Prague 6 (367 910). Tram 20, 26.
Open 6pm-midnight Mon-Sat. **Credit** EC, MC, V.
Prague's version of dinner theatre includes a folklore show of live music, song and dance, along with a traditional Czech three-course meal, aperitifs, wine, and coffee – all at a very reasonable flat price.

Theatre at the Fire Brigade

(Divadlo u hasičů) Řimská 45, Prague 2 (255 141 ext 266 or 286). Metro Náměstí Míru/4, 11, 16, 22, 34 tram. **Open** 10am-noon; 4-8pm daily.
Map 6 M7
Offers decent seasonal folklore shows (*see above*) from June to September.

Theatre on Klárova

(Divadlo na Klárově) Nábřeží Edvarda Beneše 3, Prague 1 (539 837/fax 539 845). Metro Malostranská/12, 18, 22 tram. **Open** 7.30-9pm Mon-Sat. **Map 3 G1**
Performs folklore shows from April to October.

Ta Fantastika *takes you black to the '60s. See page 219.*

National Theatre

(Národní divadlo) Národní třída 2, Prague 1 (2491 3437/2490 1520). Metro Národní třída/6, 9, 18, 17, 22 tram. **Open** *box office* 10am-6pm Mon-Fri; 10am-12.30pm, 3-6pm, Sat, Sun. **Map 5 G6**

Completed in 1881 during the Czech National Revival (and then rebuilt almost immediately when it burned down), this stunning neo-Renaissance building by the Vltava is an important symbol of Czech patriotism and cultural autonomy. The traditional repertoire includes opera, ballet, concerts and classical drama. Children get in for half price, and there are also discounts on unsold tickets that normally cost more than 30 Kč: arrive half an hour before the start of the performance.

Theatre on the Balustrade

(Divadlo Na zábradlí) Anenské náměstí 5, Prague 1 (2422 1933/2422 0920/232 6333). Metro Staroměstská/17, 18 tram. **Open** *box office* 2-7pm Mon-Fri; two hours before start of performance Sat, Sun. **Map 3 G4**

Before 1989 this theatre was a gathering place for disgruntled intellectuals, and is best known for premièring the works of Václav Havel and other former dissident playwrights. Its repertoire still includes Havel, but mostly features Czech translations of foreign plays. Thanks to imaginative artistic director Petr Lébl, it is still one of Prague's best theatres. The bar, despite suffering from idiosyncratic opening hours, can be a lively spot for a cheap beer *(see p139)*.

English-language companies

Black Box International Theatre

(information 9614 4139/777 493). **Tickets** *from* **Ticketpro** *(see above) and the* **Globe Bookstore & Coffeehouse***, Janovského 14, Prague 7 (357 9161; see p151).*

Prague's oldest and most prolific English-language theatre group performs at various venues. During the main season it mounts contemporary classics by Czech and international playwrights, frequently bringing in quality guest directors and collaborators. Black Box is especially acclaimed for its summer theatre festivals, which present important Czech plays in English translation. Recent productions have included Brian Friel's *Translations* and Doug Wright's *Quills*.

Misery Loves Company

Celetná 17, Prague 1 (2480 9168). Metro Náměstí Republiky/5, 14, 26 tram. **Open** tickets available at the theatre's Gaspar Kašpar Coffee Bar 9am-midnight Mon-Fri; 1pm-midnight Sat, Sun. **Map 3 J3**

Founded in 1994, Misery Loves Company has staged high-energy plays by respected international and Czech authors as well as budding Prague-based English-language playwrights. The company's English translation of Josef Topol's *A Nightingale for Dinner*, for example, featured actors from the National Theatre and played at the Edinburgh Fringe Festival. Branches of the company extend to San Francisco and New York City.

'Black Light' and 'Magic Lantern' theatre

At the World Expo '58 in Brussels, Czech innovators Alfred Radok and Josef Svoboda wowed the world with a fresh, contemporary blend of theatre, film, large-screen projection, pantomime and dance, known as **'Magic Lantern'** (Laterna Magika). At the same time, Josef Lamka was busy developing **'Black Theatre'** (Černé divadlo), in which black-clad actors, blending in with a black velvet backdrop, were able to 'invisibly' manipulate objects illuminated by special, luminescent violet light.

Since the 1989 revolution, several fledgling groups have imitated and merged the Magic Lantern and Black Theatre styles, exploiting these non-verbal genres to attract tourists craving a uniquely Czech form of theatre. Unfortunately, the styles have developed little beyond their 1960s heyday, resulting in extravagant but sometimes comically dated theatre pieces. The theatres listed below present comparatively high-quality productions interesting at least for their novelty value; many other similarly touted productions are so shoddy that viewers might be tempted to laugh – if the ticket prices weren't so high.

Laterna Magika

Národní třída 4, Prague 1 (2491 4129/box office 2421 2691). Metro Národní třída/6, 9, 18, 22 tram. **Open** *box office* 10am-8pm Mon-Fri; 3-8pm Sat, Sun. **Map 6 G5**
Famous for pioneering the Magic Lantern style, this company's glossy, high-tech multimedia productions are professional though no longer at the cutting edge. Performances are held at **Nová Scéna**, the controversial glass 'new stage' addition to the National Theatre designed by Karel Prager in 1983.

Ta Fantastika

Karlova 8, Prague 1 (2422 9078/2423 8287/2423 2711). Metro Staroměstská/17, 18 tram. **Open** *box office* 11am-9pm daily. **Closed** Nov-Mar. **Map 3 G4**
The best of Prague's black light theatres sometimes succeeds in milking real wonder and magic out of the hackneyed 'Black Theatre' techniques. The well-choreographed movement, quality music, fine stage sets and sense of humour of Ta Fantastika's productions make for an enjoyable evening's entertainment.

Puppet theatre

The Bohemian lands boast a strong puppet tradition – here puppetry is not just for children, and formed an intrinsic part of the Czech National Revival in the 1800s. Even so, much of the puppet theatre in Prague today is aimed unashamedly at tourists: slick, professional and entertaining, perhaps, but rarely innovative or challenging. However, quality Czech puppeteers and productions do appear frequently in Prague. Some to look out for are: the **Dragon Theatre** (Divadlo Drak), **Buns and Puppets** (Buchty a Loutky),

Petr Nykl, and František and Věra Vitek's amazing show *Puppetry, Subtitled Josef!* (Piskanderdula podtitul Josefe!). In addition, the following theatre spaces regularly present puppet performances.

National Marionette Theatre

(Národní divadlo marionet) Žatecká 1, Prague 1 (232 3429/232 2536). Metro Staroměstská/17, 18 tram. **Open** *box office* 10am-6pm (8pm on performance days). **Credit** EC, MC. **Map 3 H3**
Performing the long-running *Don Giovanni* and *Yellow Submarine* puppet shows, this touristy company presents overlong and artistically inferior productions set to recorded music. The puppets and scene design, however, can be quite interesting.
    Magic Theatre of the Baroque World and the **International Institute of Marionette Art** present tourist-oriented versions of the Orpheus myth, similar in quality and production values to the National Marionette Theatre shows.

Spejbl and Hurvínek Theatre

(Divadlo Spejbla a Hurvínka) Dejvická 38, Prague 6 (312 1241/1243). Metro Hradčanská/2, 20, 25, 26 tram. **Open** *box office* 3-6pm Wed-Fri; 1-5pm Sat, Sun.
Spejbl and Hurvinek, a father and son duo, are perhaps Bohemia's most famous puppet characters. Created by Josef Skupa in the inter-war period, these characters also appear on Czech television. Their subject matter is mostly aimed at children.

Theatre Minor

(Divadlo Minor) Senovážné náměstí 28, Prague 1 (2421 4304 ext 31 or 38). Metro Náměstí Republiky/3, 5, 9, 14, 24 tram. **Open** *box office* 2-5pm Mon-Fri, and one hour before start of performance. **Map 4 L4**
Before 1989, the Minor was the National Puppet Theatre. Since the revolution it has produced shows combining puppetry and live drama; many of them, such as *Peter Rabbit* and *The Hobbit*, are directed at children. Though productions aren't particularly innovative, some of the puppeteers are excellent.

Festivals

Bohnice Festival

Ústavní 91, Prague 8 (8574 524/765 2725). Metro Nádraží Holešovice, then 152 or 200 bus. **Tickets** phone for details. **Date** May.
This yearly two-day theatre, music and art festival, held on the grassy grounds of a mental institution on the outskirts of Prague, usually takes place in May, and features performances by top Czech theatre companies along with occasional productions by Bohnice's patients.

Next Wave Theatre Festival

information from Theatre on the Balustrade (2422 1933) or on 232 2356/232 4589. **Tickets** 100 Kč. **Date** October.
Taking place in autumn at a variety of Prague venues, this alternative festival includes performances of theatre, puppets and dance.

Four Days in Motion Festival

Box office: Ekomuzeum, Papírenská 6, Prague 6 (2480 9116). Metro Hradčanská, then 131 bus. **Tickets** 130 Kč. **Date** November.
This excellent festival of dance and visual theatre, usually held every two years, brings prominent international movement theatre to various venues around Prague for four exciting days.

PIZZERIA RUGANTINO

Praha 1, Dušní 4
tel.: 231 8172

The Original Italian
Pizzeria in Prague

Delicious Pizza, Salad and Pasta
- Forno a legna -

Trips Out of Town

Trips Out of Town

Castles and forests, picture-postcard towns and creepy caves – the perfect antidote to the bustle of the capital.

If you're in Prague for just a weekend, then it would be silly to suggest you flee the city for the country (though this is precisely what many Praguers do at the end of the working week). Should you be staying for longer than a couple of days, however, then you really ought to see some of the rest of the country. The glories of Prague are, of course, the number one draw for visitors to the Czech Republic – but it is about as typical of the country as a whole as, say, London is of the UK or New York is of the USA, which is to say, not at all. You'll learn far more about modern Czech life by joining the natives and hiking through the countryside or pottering around a small town for an afternoon than you'll ever glean from Old Town tours, Mozart concerts and kitschy beer halls.

The chapter is divided into two basic sections: **Easy day trips** – perfectly feasible even if you had one too many beers the night before and don't rise before mid-morning; and **Overnighters** – possible in a day but more rewarding if you allow longer. The former includes a run-down of the best (and worst) Central Bohemian **Castles**. Within the latter category, destinations are divided into **Towns** and **Country**. Most have been included with ease of access by public transport in mind – but, if you can stretch to a hire car (*see page 257*), then you'll find your travelling made enormously easier, particularly for the most distant places and getting about the countryside.

If you want to make minimal effort, then there are organised trips galore to the big places (Terezín, Karlštejn, Karlovy Vary, etc), available from the office of **Matana** (*see page 49*) and **Čedok** (*see page 246*), travel agents and countless booths scattered across the centre of Prague. But unless you enjoy feeling like a sheep, there's no substitute for travelling independently.

If you plan to stay overnight, all tourist offices listed should be able to book accommodation for you. Private houses all over the country offer rooms, and this can be the best way to learn more of the way Czechs live.

A TOUR OF THE COUNTRY

Divided into the provinces of Bohemia in the north-west and Moravia in the south-east, the terrain within the Czech Republic is surprisingly diverse. Riddled with vineyards and undulating hills, **Moravia** is prettiest in autumn, where a leisurely week could easily be spent vineyard-hopping, combing through the region's caves, and getting your urban fix in **Brno**, the Czech Republic's second city.

Eastern Bohemia is notable largely for **Olomouc**, a pretty town populated largely with university students, and the bizarre and beautiful **Český ráj** (Czech paradise), a playground for hikers and clean-air addicts throughout the country. Conversely, you may find it difficult to draw a good, deep breath in even the more pastoral parts of **northern Bohemia** – particularly in the north-east – as the bulk of the country's industry is concentrated here, including the Škoda plant and the Thonet chair factory. Take solace further west, where the banks of the **Labe** (Elbe) river feature striking sandstone cliffs.

Southern Bohemia is heavily trafficked in the summer, both by tourists revelling in the medieval charm of Český Krumlov and by cottagers taking weekends and summer holidays in their summer houses — nearly every Czech, no matter what their income bracket, has at least one of these little houses. What with scores of carp ponds and the dense woods of the Šumava, this is ye olde Bohemia at its best. In **western Bohemia**, the closer you venture to the German border, the more you'll see tacky hotels and roadside stands choked with garden gnomes. The landscape surrounding the famed spa towns, however, is dramatically verdant (once you get past the open-cast mines), with rolling hills and spruce forests.

Getting out of town

By bus

Many intercity bus services depart from Florenc bus station in Prague 8 (by the metro stop of the same name). Bus services are more frequent in the morning and it's worth checking the return times before you leave, as often the last bus back leaves disappointingly early (commonly before 6pm). The bus information line (in Czech) is on *1034* and operates between 6am and 6pm, Monday to Friday. A few buses leave from Nádraží Holešovice across the river in Prague 7. Most destinations are covered by the state bus company ČSAD, although a number of private services have been set up offering competitive prices and times. One of the largest of these is **Čebus** *Ke štvanici, Prague 8 (2481 1676)*.

By train

Trains often follow more scenic routes than buses, but they cover less ground and usually take longer. There are four main railway stations in Prague but no fixed pattern as to which destinations or even part of the country they serve. **Hlavní nádraží** (Metro Hlavní nádraží) is the most central station and one of two principal departure points for international services, although some domestic services also leave from there. Timetables can be obtained at the state railways (ČSD) information office at that station *(2422 4200/2461 4030)*. **Nádraží Holešovice** (Metro Nádraží Holešovice) is also principally used for international services. **Masarykovo nádraží** (Metro Náměstí Republiky) serves most destinations in northern and eastern Bohemia. Domestic routes to the south and west leave from **Smíchovské nádraží** (Metro Smíchovské nádraží). Travel is priced by the kilometre and, despite recent enormous price hikes, still cheap by West European or American standards.

For more on train services, *see page 253*.

By road

There are very few motorways in the Czech Republic, although more are planned for the future, and you'll mostly be confined to A roads.

Petrol stations (some marked by a big sign saying *benzina*) are thin on the ground, so if you see one it's a good idea to fill up. Petrol comes in two grades, super and special; the latter is recommended for most West European cars. Unleaded is called *natural* and diesel is *diesel* or *nafta*. The maximum speed limit is 60kph in built-up areas and 90kph elsewhere. On the motorways you can cruise at up to 110kph. If you have an accident call the **Emergency Road Service** on *154*. (*See page 257* for more on driving.)

For car hire, *see page 258*.

HITCH-HIKING

The basic rules of courtesy and common sense apply to hitch-hiking within the Czech Republic. It's a time-honoured method of transport, particularly among students and soldiers. As in any city, station yourself just outside the city limits; brandish a sign bearing your destination of choice; offer to help with petrol money, though your money will most likely be waved away; and be wary of accepting rides from German-speakers

with Playboy air-fresheners hanging from their rearview mirrors.

Easy day trips

Kutná Hora

Kutná Hora's short-lived wealth but lasting fame began with the discovery of silver ore here in the late thirteenth century. A boom town was born, the silver rush financing the construction of a sparkling new Gothic town, even after the Bohemian kings had siphoned off a lion's share of the profits. For 250 years Kutná Hora was second in importance only to Prague.

Don't panic when you get off the train at the main station in **Sedlec**, a couple of kilometres north-east of the centre. Kutná Hora's beauty, and the reason for its UNESCO World Heritage Site listing, lies beyond the horizon of communist-era apartment blocks. But while in Sedlec, don't miss the extraordinary bone chapel, the last resting place of an estimated 40,000 skeletons that have been used as ornate and macabre decoration. The **Cistercian Abbey** was founded in Sedlec in 1142. Today, the remaining church – an eighteenth-century structure rebuilt by Giovanni Santini-Aichel after the fourteenth-century version was gutted by fire – is in a permanent state of restoration, and the role of the adjoining monastic buildings could hardly be more secular (they're occupied by the largest tobacco factory in Central Europe).

But while the monks were still in control, they built the **ossuary** (kostnice; *see below*), a few hundred metres north of the church on Zámecká. From the outside, as a result of some nineteenth-century remodelling, this chapel looks like a stray chunk that has fallen off St Barbara's Cathedral (*see below*). In the late thirteenth century Abbot Jindřich returned from a trip to Jerusalem with a pot of soil he had swiped from the holy grave. As a result, the abbey quickly gained a name throughout central and northern Europe and corpses from Poland, Bavaria and even Belgium came flooding in. The plague of 1318 contributed some 30,000 bodies and the crypt was close to bursting point when the Schwarzenberg family acquired it in 1784.

A rudimentary arrangement of bones had already been carried out by a half-blind monk in the sixteenth century, but the Schwarzenbergs had altogether grander designs and hired a local wood-carver in 1870 to fashion the creative display seen today. The result is truly remarkable. Every single bone in the human body has been utilised – skulls, femurs, tibias and pelvises are combined in ornate and grotesque combinations. From the ceiling hangs a skeletal chandelier, the centrepiece shaped from human skulls. There are urns made

Průhonice

If you lack the time or momentum to plan a thorough, rough-and-tumble day or weekend trip from Prague, console yourself by spending an afternoon just beyond the city limits in the lush gardens of Průhonice. Although the town's thirteenth-century château is off limits to the public, you'll be way too distracted by the lavish landscaping to care. Enclosed within the walls of château's vast gardens, the three man-made ponds, arched bridges, winding paths and colossal beech trees allow for hours of easy strolling and fresh air – if, that is, you don't mind the hordes of locals who can be found pacing the paths at the first glimpse of sunlight.

If you tire of the park itself, you can admire from without the château, which was reconstructed in a combination of neo-Gothic and neo-Renaissance styles in the late 1800s – and if you make it on time for the 5pm Sunday mass, you'll get to see the adjacent chapel, which still retains its original trappings. A ticket to the park costs 10 Kč.

Getting there

ČSAD buses leave from the Opatov metro station, on the C line, every half an hour or so – the service steps up on the weekends. The ride costs 10 Kč, and lasts about 15 minutes.

of thigh bones, several monstrances, an anchor and even the coat of arms of the Schwarzenberg family, all made out of bones.

It's a long walk or a short bus ride through Sedlec's industrial ugliness before you reach the charmingly delapidated town centre. The town's highlight is undoubtedly the **Cathedral of St Barbara** (sv. Barbora; *see below*). Designed in Peter Parler's workshop, it is a magnificent building, with an exterior outclassing that of Parler's St Vitus's Cathedral in Prague. Work was started on St Barbara's in 1388 but was interrupted by the Hussite wars. Benedict Ried (architect of the Vladislav Hall in Prague's Old Royal Palace) took over in 1512 and undertook the construction of the nave, giving it his distinctive flower-patterned vaulting. Remarkably, the money for the entire construction came not out of the royal coffers, but from the miners' pockets, and the church is a monument to their hazardous profession. Their spiritual welfare was protected by St Barbara, their patron saint, and the ceiling is decorated with the emblems of the guilds, guardians of their worldly interests. Numerous other interior details dignify their labours, most

notably the Miners' Chapel, where recent renovation has uncovered late Gothic frescoes depicting miners with wheelbarrows and pickaxes. The silver minters also sponsored a chapel and it is similarly homely, the paintings showing the craftsmen perched on three-legged stools hammering out coins.

If you want to get some idea of life in a medieval mine, head downhill from the cathedral to the **Hrádek** on Barborská. Here, the **Czech Silver Museum** (*see below*), housed in a late Gothic fort, prepares you for a trip, clad in protective white suits and hard hats, into the tunnels themselves.

Continuing towards the centre of the town you'll come to the site of the former royal mint. Tiny cell-like workshops line the walls of the **Vlašský dvůr** (Italian Court; *see below*), so named because Italian artisans were drafted in to hammer out the silver Prague groschens (*pražské groše*) in the fifteenth century – the days when Bohemia could boast a hard currency that was used throughout Europe. Today the architecture is a mix of Gothic and neo-Gothic and the inside houses a collection of rare coins.

Above the Court looms the 83-m (272-ft) high tower of the Gothic **Church of St James** (sv. Jakub; *see below*), dating from 1300-25. It was closed to visitors at the time of going to press, but it is worth checking to see if it's reopened – its tower offers the best view in town, taking in a broad sweep of the verdant Vrchlice valley and the dizzying towers of St Barbara.

The rest of the town is pleasant to wander around. There are plenty of quiet side streets lined with some interesting Renaissance houses, and although the main square (Palackého náměstí) is not overly exciting, it's where most of the bars and restaurants are to be found. It's also worth making your way to the Plague column on Šultyskovo náměsti. These monuments are typical features of many Bohemian towns: this one dates from 1713, when the survivors of the plague had good reason to count their blessings, although it's unclear if the bulbous forms on which the cherubs are perched are stylistic representations of clouds or graphic representations of bubonic swellings.

Getting there

By bus: Buses leave five times a day from outside Želivského metro, and once daily from Florenc bus station. The journey takes around one hour 15 minutes.

By car: The fastest route is to head out through Žižkov and follow signs to Kolín to get on to Route 12; then change to road 38 to Kutná Hora. The scenic way is on Route 333 via Říčany, further south.

By train: Trains run from Hlavní nádraži or Masarykovo nádraži, and take 50 minutes. The main Kutná Hora station is actually located in Sedlec. Local trains meet express trains coming from Prague upon arrival and take visitors into Kutná Hora proper.

Tourist information

Palackého náměstí 377 (0327 515 556). **Open** *summer* 9am-6.30pm Mon-Fri; 9am-5pm Sat, Sun. *Winter* 9am-5pm Mon-Fri.
Staff can book accommodation in private houses.
Branch: Barborská (0327 515 797).

Sights

Cathedral of St Barbara

(Kostel sv. Barbory). **Open** *Apr, Oct* 9-11.30am, 1-3.30pm; *May-Sept* 9am-5.30pm, *Oct-Mar* 9-11.30am, 2-3.30pm, Tue-Sun. **Admission** 30 Kč; 15 Kč children.

Czech Silver Museum & Medieval Mine

(Muzeum a středověké důlní dílo) Barborská 28 (0327 512 159). **Open** *Apr, Oct* 9am-5pm, *May-Sept* 9am-6pm, Tue-Sun. **Admission** 100 Kč; 50 Kč children.
If you want to see the mine, a guided tour is compulsory. Booking is advisable.

The Ossuary (kostnice)

Zámecká. **Open** *Apr, Oct* 9am-5pm, *May-Sept* 8am-6pm, *Nov-Mar* 9am-noon, 1-4pm, daily; otherwise the key may be collected from the vegetable shop at Zámecká 127. **Admission** 30 Kč; 15 Kč children.

Vlašský dvůr (Italian Court)

Havlíčkovo náměstí 552 (0327 512 873). **Open** *Apr-Oct* 9am-5pm, *May-Sept* 9am-6pm, *Nov-Mar* 10am-4pm, daily. **Admission** 50 Kč; 25 Kč children.

Where to eat

Harmonia

Husova 105 (0327 512 275). **Open** 11am-11pm daily. **Average** 180 Kč.
If the weather is fine there's a beautiful terrace overlooking a picturesque lane, and the menu's relatively extensive.

U groše

Kollárova 313 (0327 515 330). **Open** 10am-10pm daily. **Average** 120 Kč.
Named after the silver coins once mined here, this comfortable, affordable pub-restaurant serves typical Czech cuisine upstairs, while the brew flows below.

U Morového sloupu

Šultysova 173 (0327 513 810). **Open** 10am-midnight daily. **Average** 200 Kč.
The main decorative feature of the interior is a wall covered in visiting cards – not as good as the Renaissance frescoes and sculptures of reclining dames that adorn the façade, but the traditional Czech food is decent and cheapish.

Mělník

In the heart of fertile grape-growing country, Mělník is a sleepy little town just 33km (20 miles) north of Prague with a fine castle, a bizarre ossuary and spectacular views over the surrounding countryside. It's also the home of **Ludmila wine**, the beverage its producers claim gave Mozart the creative energy he needed to write *Don Giovanni*.

The main sights are concentrated near the lovely **castle** (*see below*), now more château than stronghold. It was rebuilt during the sixteenth and seventeenth centuries and occupies a prime position on a steep escarpment overlooking the confluence of the Vltava and Labe (Elbe) rivers. Although a settlement has existed here since the tenth century, it was Charles IV who introduced vines to the region from his lands in Burgundy in the fourteenth century, and he established a palace for the Bohemian queens. Up until the end of the fifteenth century, this was where the royal ladies of the court would come when they needed a break from Prague. Under recent restitution laws, the castle has been returned to the Lobkowicz family, who were one of the most powerful aristocratic clans in Bohemia before they were driven into exile by the

Dam fine swimming

If you've seen your fill of castles and need a break from the city streets, do what the Czechs do and head for one of these two popular plunging places, both within relatively easy reach of Prague.

Slapy dam

The long, narrow, snaking lake created by the enormous Slapy dam is a prime weekend spot with Praguers. Surrounded by the verdant hills of the Vltava valley, this is as picturesque a place as you could wish for to have a swim and watch the motor boats that cruise up and down the waters.

Getting there

By bus: Buses leave from Na Knížecí bus terminal (Anděl metro) and the journey takes about an hour. From the village of Slapy you can walk to the water or catch a local bus.

By car: 30km (19 miles) south of Prague. Head out of the city through Smíchov and join Route 4, then turn off to Slapy at Zbraslav.

Malá Ameriká

Malá Ameriká (Little America) is so called because of its resemblance to the Grand Canyon, although it's not quite in the same league. It's really a flooded stone quarry, but the absurdly turquoise waters make it the most scenic place to go for a dip in the vicinity of Prague. The one disadvantage is that it is only accessible by car.

Getting there

By car: About 25km (15.5 miles) south of Prague. Follow signs to Plzeň to join the E50, leave the motorway at exit 10 and follow signs to Karlštejn. The path leading down to the gorge is about seven kilometres (four miles) before Karlštejn – the only clue as to the exact spot is the number of cars parked along an unremarkable stretch of country road.

communists. You can take a tour around the castle's interior, and even better, one round the splendidly gloomy wine cellars, where a lesson in viticulture is followed by a chance to sample the end product and walk over a bizarre arrangement of tens of thousands of upturned bottles.

Opposite the castle is the church of **Sts Peter and Paul** (sv. Petr a Pavel), a late Gothic structure with a 60-m (197-ft) high tower that was topped with an onion-shaped cupola in the sixteenth century. For a resoundingly weird experience, visit the **ossuary** (*see below*) in the church's crypt. Pass through red velvet curtains and descend to the basement, where skulls and bones are piled to the ceiling. Two speakers precariously balanced on top of a stack of femurs broadcast a breathless English commentary delivered in Hammer horror style, accompanied by liberal doses of Bach organ music.

The site was established as a burial place for plague victims in the sixteenth century and sealed off for the next few hundred years. However, in 1914, a social anthropology professor from Charles University cracked open the vault and shipped in his students to lend their artistic talents to arranging the 15,000 skeletons he found piled up there. The end result includes the Latin for 'Look death!' spelled out in skulls, and a cage displaying the remains of people with spectacular physical deformities.

The main square below the castle, Náměstí Míru, is lined with typically Bohemian baroque and Renaissance buildings. The fountain dates from considerably later.

Getting there
By bus: There are roughly ten departures a day from stand 18 at Prague's Florenc station. The trip takes around 50 minutes.
By car: Head north out of Prague on route 608 and follow signs to Zdiby, then Mělnik on Route 9.

Tourist information
Náměstí Míru 30 (0206 627 503). **Open** *May-Sept* 9am-5pm daily; *Oct-Apr* 9am-5pm Mon-Fri.

Sights
The Castle
Svatováclavská 19 (0206 622 121/622 127). **Open** *Mar-Dec* 10am-5pm daily. **Closed** Jan, Feb. **Admission** *castle tour* 60 Kč; 40 Kč children; *short wine-tasting tour* 70 Kč; *long wine-tasting tour* 110 Kč.
The Ossuary (kostnice)
Church of Sts Peter & Paul (0206 621 2337). **Open** *English-language tours* 10.30am, 1pm, 3pm, 5pm, daily. **Admission** 30 Kč; 15 Kč children.

Where to eat
The Castle restaurants
Svatováclavská 19 (0206 622 121/622 127). **Open** 11am-6pm Wed-Sun. **Average** 250 Kč.
There are currently two restaurants inside the castle with two more due to open. The **vinárna** is the swankiest: the crockery is embossed with the Lobkowicz insignia, the vaulted walls are painted peach and it's one of the best places to splash out on an expensive meal in Bohemia.

Restaurace Stará škola
Na vyhlídce 159 (0603 482 748). **Open** 11am-11pm daily. **Average** 190 Kč.
This basic restaurant, close to the Church of Sts Peter and Paul, knocks up a mean steak and chips. The terrace has a stunning view over the surrounding countryside and the Vltava/Labe confluence.

Tábor

If you're a bit nonplussed by the sleepy streets of Tábor, bear in mind that things haven't really been hopping in the town since the fifteenth century, when a band of religious radicals founded the place (in 1420) as their stronghold following Jan Hus's execution (*see page 14*). Led by Jan Žižka, the one-eyed general whose statue sits astride a hill overlooking Prague 3 (as well as the more modest affair in Tábor's main square), some 15,000 Taborites (as this sect of Hussites called themselves) battled the Catholic forces for nearly 15 years. Their policies of equal rights for men and women and common ownership of property were never likely to endear them to the rul-

ing classes and eventually the Taborites were crushed by the moderate Hussite forces under George of Poděbrady.

Bone up on more details of Hussite history at the town's **Hussite Museum** (*see below*), which features one of Žižka's military innovations, a crude sort of tank consisting of cannons balanced on a wagon. The museum also runs tours of a section of the underground passages, used as stores and refuges, that snake under much of the centre. Most of the town's other bona fide points of interest are also located on the main square, Žižkovo náměstí, from which the city's many labyrinthine streets and alleys radiate. Their confusing layout is not the result of ad hoc medieval building, but a deliberate ploy to confuse the town's enemies. The square is also adorned with a Hussite immortalised in stone in a fountain, and two stone tablets believed to have been used for religious services.

Getting there

By bus: connections from Prague are plentiful, with buses leaving from several of Prague's stations –

including Florenc, Roztyly and Dejvická. The trip usually takes around two hours.

By car: 82km (51 miles) south of Prague. Take the D1 south-east towards Jihlava and Brno, exiting at junction 21 on to highway 3 south.

By train: trains to Vienna from Prague make a stop in Tábor; the journey lasts just under two and a half hours.

Tourist information

Infocentrum, Žižkovo náměstí 2 (0361 252 385).
Open *Apr-Sept* 8.30am-7pm Mon-Fri; 8am-1pm Sat; 1-5pm Sun; *Oct-Mar* 9am-4pm Tue-Fri.

Sights

Hussite Museum
Žižkovo náměstí 1 (0361 254 286). **Open** 9am-5pm daily. **Admission** 40 Kč; *tunnel tours* 40 Kč.

Where to eat & stay

Beseda
Žižkovo náměstí (no phone). **Open** 10am-10pm daily. Popular beer hall in the town hall on the main square.

Černýleknín
Příběnická 695 (0361 256 405). **Rates** (including breakfast) *single* 1,290 Kč; *double* 1,550 Kč.
This neo-Gothic villa is Tábor's best accommodation option.

Call of the wild

Prague's car-free Old Town makes it one of the greatest walking cities in the world, but if you hanker after fresh air, trees and grass, you'd best look further afield.

Wholly apart from the precious charms of Malá Strana gardens (*see page 80*), three suburban nature preserves offer solid strolling and gentle hiking possibilities: **Divoká Šárka**, **Prokopské údolí** and **Kunratický les**. Each of these rolling, wooded areas, while technically within Prague city limits, are large enough to shut out the urban surrounds.

Divoká Šárka is named after 'Wild Šárka', leader of a mythic matriarchal society that briefly held sway in Prague's pagan days, and her tribute in Prague 6 is appropriately rough, rocky, wooded and rambling. A noisy, popular swimming lake with a few food stands around it forms the southern flank (accessed from Evropská) but the real appeal is to the west and north: the 363-m (1,190-ft) Džbán peak attracts climbers while further west is a network of trails covering a kilometre and a half of woods and scrub, after which it's possible to circle back or veer north to the suburb of Nebušice (from which buses 164 and 251 run back to the Dejvická metro).

Prokopské údolí, tucked away above the Barrandov district of Prague 5 to the south, is a narrower preserve (best traversed from west to

east), but includes some dramatic rocky overlooks. Like Šárka and Kunratický les, it's a protected refuge where you may come across deer, rabbits, hedgehogs, owls, woodpeckers, cuckoos, and even falcons. (If you do, don't tangle with them – considering Prague's population density, air and water quality, it's clear that these fauna are some pretty tough customers.) The park is best accessed by following Do Klukovic street west and north from the terminus of the 120 bus line, then crossing the under the railroad and over Prokopský potok stream, and heading up the hill into the wooded ridge. Wander back eastward along the ridge for a kilometre and a half, then you're in Hlubočepy, a good spot for the pubs along Slivenecká street, where you can again pick up bus 120 back to the centre.

Kunratický les, and the adjoining Michelský les back right up to the Roztyly metro station in Prague 4, but offer peace and tranquillity almost unthinkable in Prague. A system of trails lead south away from the remarkably ugly hospital complex on the northern end of the preserve and weave about for two kilometres, eventually taking you to a small castle ruin in the park's south-west corner, its only real landmark. Just beyond it, across the Kunratický potok stream, buses 114, 272 and 275 run along Videřská back to the Kačerov metro.

Terezín

Terezín, originally known as Theresienstadt, was purpose-built as a fortress town in 1780 on the orders of Emperor Joseph II, to protect his empire from Prussian invaders. However its notoriety dates from this century: in 1941 the whole town became a holding camp for Jews before they were sent on to the death camps further east.

Today, the atmosphere of the town is still distinctly eerie, accentuated by soulless streets laid out to a grid pattern. The Nazis expelled the native population and, unsurprisingly, few of them chose to return after the war.

The **Ghetto Museum** (*see below*) is the best place to start a tour of the area. Documentary films are shown in several languages and you can request the ones you'd like to see. Without a doubt the creepiest is the one that contains clips from the Nazi propaganda film *The Führer Gives a Town to the Jews*. The film was part of the sophisticated Nazi strategy to hoodwink the world. Red Cross officials visited the camp twice, and saw specially rehearsed gymnastic performances, a children's playground and new street signs with names instead of numbers. The impression was successfully conveyed of a self-governing Jewish community with a flourishing cultural life. To complete the illusion, the Nazis established the Terezín Family Camp in Auschwitz, where the inmates were kept in special conditions for long enough to write a postcard home before being sent to the gas chambers.

The ground-floor exhibition of harrowing artwork produced by the prisoners, many of them children, has been temporarily removed to Prague's Pinkas Synagogue (*see page 95*). Upstairs is a well laid-out exhibition documenting the Nazi occupation of Bohemia and Moravia. Decrees of discriminating measures taken against Jews are detailed – including the certificate that a customer in a pet shop intending to buy a canary had to sign, promising that the pet would not be exposed to any Jewish people – as well as more gruesome facts. Out of 140,000 men, women and children who passed through Terezín, 87,000 left on transport to the death camps in the east (mainly Auschwitz) and only 3,000 returned alive; 34,000 people died within the ghetto of Terezín itself.

A 15-minute walk back down the road from Prague brings you to the **Small Fortress** (Malá pevnost; *see below*), which was built at the same time as the larger town fortress. The high, red-brick walls that surround it made it an opportune site for the Gestapo to establish a prison here in 1940. Until it was liberated in 1945, 32,000 political prisoners passed through it, and about 2,500 of them died within its walls.

The first thing you see on approaching the Small Fortress is the National Cemetery where some 10,000 Nazi victims are buried. Most of their graves are marked by numbers rather than names and are interspersed with hundreds of red roses. In the middle stands a giant wooden cross – an insensitive memorial considering the tiny percentage of non-Jews who lost their lives here.

The whole fortress is now a museum and a free map (available from the ticket office) enables you to explore the network of courtyards, cells and exhibitions. To the left of the main entrance is an arch that still displays the infamous Nazi slogan 'Arbeit Macht Frei'. Walking through the arch brings you to the main prison courtyards, lined with mass cells that housed more than 250 inmates at any one time, and 20 tiny windowless solitary confinement cells. On the wall of Number One is a plaque commemorating an earlier inmate, Gavrilo Princip, who was sent here in 1918 after taking a pot-shot at Archduke Francis Ferdinand. The plaque, a present from the Yugoslav Ambassador, commemorates him as a national hero.

Continuing past the hospital, a long dank tunnel takes you out to the Gestapo's execution ground where prisoners were variously shot or hanged. The former SS Commander's house is now a museum with displays detailing the appalling physical condition of the inmates, as well as a chronological overview of the Nazi occupation. There's also one of the few references you'll find in the Czech Republic to the fact that in 1945 Terezin became a holding camp for three million Sudeten Germans, before their mass expulsion later that year.

If Terezín gets too much for you, head for the little town of **Litoměřice**, three kilometres (two miles) to the north. Its typically lovely sgraffitoed-town-hall-and-a-plague-column formula might do the trick of persuading you there is still good in this world. The most interesting feature in the town's main square, Mírové náměsti, is the Mrázovský dům, which has had an incongruous wooden chalice, a symbol of the Hussite movement, on its roof since 1537 when it was erected by the devoutly Hussite owner. As most of the other buildings were made redundant by fire or the Thirty Years' War, many of the ones you'll see today date from the eighteenth century.

Getting there
By bus: buses leave Florenc station about once every two hours and the journey takes between an hour and 75 minutes.
By car: join Route 8 or the E55 at Holešovice, via Veltrusy.

Tourist information
Náměsti čs armády 85, Terezin (0416 782 369).
Open *Apr-Sept* 9am-4pm Sun-Fri.

Sights
Ghetto Museum

A chilling but necessary excursion: the former Nazi holding camp at **Terezín**.

Komenského 411, Terezín (0416 782 577). **Open** *Oct-Mar* 9am-4.30pm; *April* 9am-5.30pm daily; *May-Sept* 9am-6.30pm, daily. **Admission** 90 Kč; 70 Kč children, students, OAPs. Joint ticket for museum and fortress (*see below*) 160 Kč; 120 Kč children, students, OAPs.

Small Fortress
(Malá pevnost). **Open** *Oct-Mar* 8am-4.30pm; *April* 8am-5.30pm; *May-30 Sept* 8am-6.30pm, daily. **Admission** 90 Kč; 70 Kč children, students, OAPs; *guided tour* 230 Kč.

Where to eat & stay
Light meals and snacks can be had in the former guards' canteen just inside the entrance to the Small Fortress.

Hotel Salva Guarda
Mírové náměstí 12, Litoměřice (0416 732 506). **Rates** *single* 800 Kč; *double* 1,200 Kč. **Credit** AmEx, EC, MC, V. The best hotel in town – with the best restaurant, too.

Restaurace u Hojtašů
Komenského 152, Terezín (0416 782 203). **Open** 10am-11pm daily. **Average** 150 Kč.
The best bet for a bite within Terezin town.

Easy day trips: Castles

Karlštejn

Without a doubt the Czech Republic's most traf-ficked castle, it must be said that Karlštejn is not wholly undeserving of the attention. Situated in a lush bend of the Berounka river, the fourteenth-century stronghold (heavily remodelled in the nineteenth century) once housed the royal jewels, and is certainly impressive from afar – and afar is exactly where you should stay. If the walk up to the castle – clogged with overpriced snack bars and postcard, crystal and lace vendors – doesn't kill you, the castle tour itself definitely will. Only a very few of the rooms – excluding the castle's masterpiece, the **Holy Rood Chapel**, whose walls are encrusted with over 2,000 semiprecious stones – are open to the public; those that are are crammed with mediocre portraits and tour groups in nearly every conceivable language. With no dearth of lovely castles that boast better ambience than your average international airport terminal, you most likely won't regret skipping Karlštejn.

The Castle
(0311 684 617). **Open** *Mar, April, Oct-Dec* 9am-noon, 1-4pm, Tue-Sun; *May-Sept* 9am-noon, 1-6pm, Tue-Sun. **Admission** 150 Kč; 90 Kč children, students, OAPs. Last tour one hour before closing; tours available in English.

Getting there
By car: 30km (19 miles) south-west of Prague. Take the E50-D5 or Route 5 towards Plzeň, then leave the motorway at exit 10 and follow the signs to Karlštejn.
By train: Trains leave Prague's Smíchovské nádraží or Hlavní nádraží for Karlštejn about every hour. The trip takes roughly 40 minutes, runs through the beautiful Berounka valley, as well as through Řevnice, Martina Navrátilová's home town. It's a 10-minute walk from the station up to the village, and a further 15 minutes up to the castle.

Konopiště Castle: *a monument to taxidermy.*

Where to eat

There are plenty of unpromising eating possibilities lining the road to the castle. The best are the cosy **U Janů** (*0311 684 210*), with antlers hanging from the ceiling and a nice terrace garden, and the **Koruna** (*0311 684 465*), where good food and a solid quota of old men sitting around drinking beer prove it's not just for the tourists.

Konopiště

Other castles may showcase their tapestried bedrooms, tranquil gardens or rows of stuffy portraits, but at Konopiště, taxidermy is the main attraction. This castle, which dates back to the 1300s, was refurbished by the Habsburgs to act as a hunting lodge to satisfy the passions of its most famous occupant, Archduke Franz Ferdinand, whose convenient assassination in Sarajevo triggered World War I. Brace yourself for the accusing, glassy stares of several long halls' worth of disembodied heads of your fuzzy forest friends. The halls are crammed with the heads and torsos of nearly every kind of fauna imaginable, birds of prey with outstretched wings, hundreds and hundreds of sawn-off antlers – and only one per cent of the actual collection is on display.

The Archduke is purported to have felled an average of 20 animals a day, every day for 40 years. Habsburg royalty took their recreation seriously; several fearsome-looking hunting weapons are also on display here. The tour lets you down gently with some more sedate rooms featuring collections of wooden Italian cabinets and Meissen porcelain.

A second tour of the castle, which requires a further ticket, takes you through the Archduke's private chambers, the chapel and a Habsburg-era version of a gentlemen's club, where only the old boys were allowed to do their partying.

The castle's large grounds won't exactly let you detox from the animal overdose, but at least the peacocks and pheasants aren't affixed to the wall, and the bears in the castle's moat pace incessantly, oblivious of their unluckier counterparts within.

Konopiště's popularity with visitors is second only to that of Karlštejn, so brace yourself for the revenge of the coach party.

The Castle

(0301 21366) **Open** *Apr, Oct* 9am-noon, 1-3pm, daily; *May-Aug* 9am-noon, 1-5pm, daily; *Sept* 9am-noon, 1-4pm Tue-Sun. **Admission** 110 Kč; 60 Kč children.

Getting there

By bus: buses leave from Florenc bus station nearly every 45 minutes; the trip lasts a little over an hour.
By car: go south on the D1 and exit near Benešov, following the signs for Konopiště.
By train: hourly trains to Benešov from Hlavní nádraží take around one hour. The castle is a two-kilometre walk from the station, or you can catch one of the infrequent buses.

Křivoklát

From the outside, the Gothic fortress of Křivoklát is perhaps something of a disappointment when compared with its flashy upstream neighbour,

Karlštejn. But the interior is among the finest in the whole country, less by virtue of any one attraction than the meticulous care that's been devoted to restoring the rooms. The approach to Křivoklát is just as satisfying; the road winds along the banks of the Berounka river, passing cornfields and meadows, and up a densely forested hill before the castle (perched on a high promontory) appears before you.

It's actually a hotchpotch of different structures and styles. Křivoklát was originally one of the Přemyslid princes' hunting lodges. It was converted into a defensible castle at the beginning of the twelfth century by King Vladislav I, but the biggest building projects took place under the auspices of the Polish King Vladislav II Jagiellon (1471-1516), whose trademark 'W' insignia can be seen all over the castle.

The barley-sugar pillars and vaulted ceiling of the **Castle Chapel** are the work of the second Vladislav's architect and woodcarver, Hans Spiess. The nineteenth-century pews are decorated with carved dragons, armadillos and other reptilian horrors, while the fine Gothic altarpiece includes an elaborate polychrome statue of Christ surrounded by sweet-looking angels holding medieval instruments of torture in their hands. A much more varied selection of instruments of torture is to be found in the **dungeon**, which the official guide saves until last and relishes demonstrating. The unrestored chamber contains some impressively unpleasant pain-inflicting devices, including a fully operational rack, two cages, a thumb screw, the so-called Rosary of Shame (an attractive necklace made out of lead weights) and the Iron Maiden, a body box lined with pointed prongs.

The castle's most impressive feature is the enormous **Round Tower**, which dwarfs the other buildings. It dates from 1280 and was a prison up until the sixteenth century, when the Habsburgs came to power, lost interest in the place and eventually sold it to the Wallenstein family in 1685. Before they did, however, the English would-be alchemist Edward Kelley was locked away here after Rudolf II tired of his excuses. Prisoners were lowered in through the small hole in the ceiling and left there to rot. A door on the lower level, cut through the three-metre (10-ft) thick walls, allows rather easier access today.

The Castle

(info 0313 558 120). **Open** *June-Aug* 9am-noon, 1-5pm, *May, Sept* 9am-noon, 1-4pm, *Mar, Apr, Oct-Dec* 9am-noon, 1-3pm, Tue-Sun. **Admission** *long tour* 110 Kč; 55 Kč children; *short tour* 60 Kč; 30 Kč children.
The castle can only be visited by one of two guided tours held every half hour (last tour one hour before closing). They are only conducted in English if a group of five or more English-speakers can be assembled (or if you're willing to pay up for five tickets). The 70-minute tour includes all the interiors, while a 20-minute version is just

the tower and exterior walk. But you can take a translated script and muddle through, wondering what the jokes were.

Getting there

By car: This is much the best way to get to Křivoklát and means the excursion can, say, be combined with a trip to Karlovy Vary. To travel on the most picturesque route, take the E50-D5 out of Prague in the direction of Beroun, turn off at junction 14 and follow the Berounka valley west, as if you were going to Rakovník. Křivoklát is 21km (13 miles) north-west of Beroun.

By train: Trains leave for Beroun from Smíchovské nádraží or Hlavní nádraží about every half hour and take around 45 minutes. There are occasional direct trains, but most require a change at Beroun. Trains depart from Beroun to Křivoklát around ten times a day and take about 40 minutes.

Where to eat & stay

Hotel u Dvořáků *Rostoky 225, Křivoklát (0313 558 355).* **Rates** *single* 250 Kč; *double* 500 Kč.

Orlík & Zvíkov

Popular with Czechs but rarely visited by foreign tourists, and situated on a lake as pretty as the castle itself, **Orlík** is bound to please the castle-hopper. The castle itself, astride the Orlík dam, used to be perched at the top of a hill, until massive flooding in the 1960s, caused by the construction of the dam, brought the water up to its current level, just below the castle's walls. The terrain isn't the only thing that's changed over the years; the castle itself suffered a series of destructive fires since its construction in the thirteenth century, undergoing extensive reconstruction each time. In 1992 it was returned to the Schwarzenberg family, the castle's owners from 1719 until 1945.

Once you're done with the castle tour (which probably won't change your life), you can easily spend the rest of the afternoon, or even a weekend, sunning yourself or camping on the shores of the dam, or swimming and sailing. If you're planning on making a weekend of it, though, you'd be advised to stock up on groceries back in Prague, since the local grocery store closes at noon on Saturday and the town's one pub only dispenses *klobása* (the ubiquitous grilled sausage) and beer.

Those who prefer their castles wild and unprettified might find **Zvíkov**, a further 14km (nine miles) south along the Vltava, more to their taste. The thirteenth-century structure commands a better position than Orlík and has retained its original medieval austerity. The few visitors who come here can wander amid the buildings, taking in the fine frescoes in the chapel and the beautiful arcaded courtyard.

Another possibility is taking the one-hour boat trip from Orlík to Zvíkov (operating Tuesday-Sunday in July and August; weekends only in late

June and early September) or the marked trail by the river.

Orlík Castle
(0362 841 101). **Open** *Apr, Oct* 9am-3pm, *May, Sept* 9am-4pm, *June-Aug* 9am-5pm, Tue-Sun. **Admission** 120 Kč; 50 Kč children.

Zvíkov Castle
(0362 899 676). **Open** *Apr, Oct* 9am-noon, 1-3.30pm Sat, Sun; *May, Sept* 9am-noon, 1-4pm, Tue-Sun; *June* 9am-noon, 1-5pm, Tue-Sun; *July, Aug* 9am-5pm Tue-Sun. **Admission** 50 Kč; 30 Kč children.

Getting there
By bus: Buses leave every two hours or so from Prague's Florenc station to Orlík; the trip takes around an hour and 20 minutes.

By car: 82km (51 miles) south-west of Prague. Take highway 4 heading to Příbram, changing to the 19 towards Orlík.

By train: A circuitous route that lasts over two hours involves a change in Pisek; you're better off with the bus.

Where to eat & stay
U Nováků
Kožli u Orlika, Orlík (0602 467 886). **Rates** *single* 150 Kč; *double* 300 Kč. **Average** 80-150 Kč.

Hotel Zvíkov
Zvíkovské podhradí (1km from castle), Zvíkov (0362 899 659). **Rates** (including breakfast) *single* 1,200 Kč; *double* 1,850 Kč. **Credit** AmEx, EC, MC, V.

Overnighters: Towns

České Budějovice

České Budějovice is the regional capital of south Bohemia and, although it's surrounded by some smoky suburbs, the old centre retains its original medieval town plan. It was founded in 1265 by Otakar II and its main square, which bears his name (Náměsti Přemysla Otakara II) is enormous.

There are some attractive crumbling streets in the town, but if you're combining the trip with Český Krumlov (a mere 22 kilometres – 14 miles – away; *see below*) you'll have already been spoilt in such matters. Beer is the town's reason for existence today, and it's also the best excuse for a visit. Since 1894, when bottle-fermented beer really took off, the **Budvar brewery** has been producing the legendary lager. The brewery has only recently opened to the public, in response to the tours operated by its biggest rival, Pilsner Urquell in Plzeň. It's worth taking the longer tour, as the extra half hour is devoted to a comprehensive sampling of the product. If you're staying overnight, the New York nightclub in the Družba shopping centre on Pražská offers decent dance music and is open until 5am every morning.

České Budějovice is at the centre of the south Bohemian lakeland, and it's a good starting point to explore the UNESCO-protected region. It has some 270 ponds, created in the sixteenth century and used ever since for breeding carp, the national Christmas dish. These days most of the fish are exported to Germany, where they can be sold for three times the Czech market price. The best stopping-off place along the way is **Třeboň**, a tiny Renaissance town. It boasts a miniature, but nonetheless stunning, square and an interesting château where there's a series of tranquil courtyards, decorated with sgraffitoed façades and connected by ornate archways. Also worth noting is **Hluboká nad Vltavou**, with its gorgeous, glitzy, thirteenth-century castle – it's like no other in the country. When the Schwarzenbergs took over the castle in the mid-nineteenth century, they gave it a full-on facelift to emulate Windsor Castle. Although the tour only takes you through a third of the castle's 141 rooms, the rooms that are on display give an ample taste of decadence at its most manic.

Getting there
By bus: five buses leave from Florenc bus station during the morning and take about four hours. In the afternoons buses depart from Roztyly.

By car: leave Prague on the D1-E60 towards Brno and then at Mirošovice take the E55 to České Budějovice, passing through Tábor.

By train: nine trains daily leave from Hlavní nádraži. Fast trains take around two and a half hours.

Tourist information
Náměsti Přemysla Otakara II (038 635 2589). **Open** *Apr-Sept* 8.30am-6pm daily; *Oct-Mar* 9am-5.30pm Mon-Fri; 9am-noon Sat.

Sights
Budvar Pivovar
K Světlé 4 (038 770 5341/770 5340). **Open** 9am-3pm Mon-Fri. **Admission** 70 Kč; 16 Kč a beer.
Take bus 2 or 4 to the brewery, a few kilometres north of the centre. There are two different tours; the first lasts one hour and costs 85 Kč, the second lasts an hour and a half, involves sampling the product and costs 155 Kč.

Where to eat & stay
The Tourist Information Office can book a pension for around 250 Kč a night, although a better selection is available in nearby Český Krumlov.

Hotel Malý Pivovar
ulice Karla IV 100 (038 731 3285/731 3286).
Rates (including breakfast) *single* 1,840 Kč; *double* 2,290 Kč. **Credit** AmEx, DC, EC, MC, V.
A cavernous beer hall with clean white walls and an unprecedented no-smoking area. It serves Samson beer, a lesser-known local brew that (judging from the packed tables) has many fans among the locals.

Restaurace Masné krámy
Krajinská 29 (038 37957). **Open** 10am-11pm daily. **Credit** V.
The long, thin room looks rather like a train carriage and has cosy alcoves leading off it. It's the most popular place in town to down the mighty Budvar.

Český Krumlov

In 1992 Český Krumlov's outstanding beauty led UNESCO to declare the tiny south Bohemian town second only in importance to Venice on the World Heritage list. The castle and fantastical pink Renaissance tower rise high above the town, which is idyllically positioned on a double loop of the Vltava river. It's almost impossible not to be impressed and charmed. The streets are a labyrinth of tiny cobbled alleyways and almost every building is an architectural gem, the crumbling Renaissance façades and overhanging balconies made even more attractive by flower-filled window boxes and lines of washing strung across the passageways.

The Castle (*see below*), and in particular the tower, dominates the town. It's one of the most extensive complexes in Central Europe, consisting of 40 buildings spread through five courtyards, gradually added over the course of six centuries.

Taking the waters

If you've seen the dreamy, dazzling film *Last Year at Marienbad*, which depicts an elliptical encounter between two high-society élites, your preconception of spa towns may well supersede the humble realities of the present. The Czech Republic's spa towns – particularly the oft-cited trio of **Karlovy Vary**, **Mariánské Lázně** and **Františkovy Lázně** (known to many by their German names of Carlsbad, Marienbad and Franzenbad, respectively; *see page 234*) – had more than their fair share of cinema-worthy intrigue, with Europe's rich and soon-to-be-famous sipping the waters, strolling the grounds, and orchestrating liaisons behind the carved, mirrored doors. Among the spas' biggest patrons were habitués of haute culture such as Franz Kafka, Ludwig van Beethoven, Karl Marx and JS Bach.

But contemporary spa culture ain't quite what it used to be. A summer-time visit to some of these towns in high season might even send you fleeing back to the city for respite. Packed with bad restaurants and quasi-upscale, loud boutiques, the narrow streets can become overwhelmed with braying foreigners. The public taps – each of which dispense thermal water of varying temperature – are often crowded with backpackers sticking plastic water bottles underneath the spigots or German tourists with kitschy Becher (those wacky ceramic cups with straws attached).

And the treatments themselves? Under socialism, a sympathetic doctor could easily scrawl off an official prescription for a stint at a spa town as a cure for nearly any imaginable ailment: digestive problems, nervous disorders, run-of-the-mill stress. Today, the full gamut of spa treatments comes at a cost: some travel agencies can arrange spa weekends, and many of the high-class hotels in the town offer their own five-star spa treatments.

For lay folk who don't want to splurge on underwater massage and electrotherapy treatments (the *fin-de-siècle* spa-goers would have been appalled at such things, anyway), the pathways through a myriad of parks surrounding every spa town's centre, or public baths (at around 60 Kč for a half-hour, a far better deal than anything the hotels offer), or simply slurping up the cloudy water dispensed from public taps can compete with the best of placebos. Much of the murky, mineral-rich spa water tastes suspiciously of rotten eggs, but remember – it's good for you. If you want to go all out, cut the taste of the water by munching on *oplatky*, the frisbee-sized, sugary wafers that have long been a tradition of these towns.

If none of this sounds especially appealing, please do remember that the Czech Republic's spa towns are at their core pillars of grandiose, decadent beauty – when enjoyed in the off-season, they command an almost mystical air, their walls infused with the trysts of decades. Though there's little in the way of nightlife in these towns – remember, they're usually frequented by retirees who came here to rest – you might best be served roaming the colonnades at night, when the daytrippers have returned to Prague and the spa-goers have retreated to their hotels. Then, the colonnades and dark springs cutting through the promenade can easily transport you back to more genteel days.

Though the troika of spas near the German border are the best known, Bohemia is littered with spa towns – but for the bulk of them, there's not much more evidence of the spas than a public spigot in the street. Still, if you're a serious fan of spa treatments, **Teplice** and **Poděbrady**, near Prague, are worth a visit for a quiet session of detoxing.

Particularly in the towns listed below, beware two-tiered pricing, especially at hotels used to floods of Germans who won't notice the difference. If you think you're being overcharged, make a stink about it and you might guilt them into giving you the Czech price.

West Bohemian spa towns

Karlovy Vary

Though far and away the most touristed of the bunch, Karlovy Vary holds its own as the oldest, largest and most grandiose of the Czech Republic's spa towns. The town began its ascent to fame in 1358 when one of Charles IV's hunting hounds leapt off a steep crag in hot pursuit of a more nimble stag. The unfortunate dog fell to the ground and injured its paw, but then made a miraculous recovery as it limped through a pool of hot, bubbling water. Experts were summoned to test the waters and declared them beneficial for all kinds of ills. From that moment, Karlovy Vary's future was ensured.

The river Teplá runs through the centre of town and disappears beneath the hulking Hotel Thermal, a perversely fascinating symbol of the communist notion of absolute luxury, especially when contrasted with the gracious elegance of the **Grand Hotel Pupp** (*see below*). The garish boutiques and inescapable wafer shops may not be your idea of relaxation – but you can always retreat to the parks, adorned with the busts of some of the spa's more famous guests, or down a few Becherovkas – the herbal liqueur that works magic with its base of the city's pungent spa water. If you fancy a cheap splash about, try the state baths, Vojenský lážeňský ústav, at Mlýnské nábřeží 7 (0117 22206).

Getting there

By bus: Starting at 5.30am, buses run at least every hour from Prague's Florenc station. The journey takes around two and a half hours.
By car: 130km (81 miles) west of Prague on E48.
By train: Trains leave Prague's Hlavní nádraží three times a day, but the route takes about four hours.

Tourist information

Kur-Info, Vřídelní kolonáda (017 322 9312/322 4097). **Open** 7am-5pm Mon-Fri; 8am-3pm Sat, Sun.
In the big glass complex built around the main spring. Staff are helpful. Karlovy Vary hosts a number of arts festivals, including the annual international film festival held in July (*see p9 & p184*) and a number of classical music festivals. Or try the **Čedok** office at dr. Davida Bechera 21 (017 322 2994; *open* 9am-5pm daily).

Where to eat & stay

Grand Hotel Pupp
Mírové náměstí 2 (017 310 9111). **Rates** *single* US$135; *double* US$165 Kč. **Credit** AmEx, DC, EC, MC, V.
If you splurge on this lavish hotel – purportedly the finest in the country – be careful to ask for a room that has not yet been refurbished; several of the rooms have been unsympathetically 'modernised'. The hotel's elegant restaurant is also worth a visit if you're feeling flush.

Pension Holiday
Ondříčkova 26 (017 322 0649). **Rates** (including breakfast) *double* 1,000 Kč.
Friendly, family-run pension with an excellent local reputation, located a ten-minute walk from the town centre. More modern than charming but very clean.

Promenáda
Tržiště 31 (017 322 5648). **Average** 300 Kč.
Karlovy Vary is notorious for its lack of acceptable restaurants. If you can't stretch to the Pupp's dining room, try this place – a cut above the usual goulash-and-dumplings places, with reasonably quick service, freshwater trout and steaks.

Františkovy Lázně

Though often mentioned in the same breath as the aforementioned spas, few visitors bother to make the jog over to near the German border – which means that these days Františkovy Lázně, founded in 1793 and named after the Habsburg emperor Franz II, will be all but deserted. And not without reason – the architecture and relatively uninteresting environs don't compare to the grandeur of its sibling spa towns to the east. But if you're here for the cure – the spa is most touted for its ability to cure infertility among women – you have absolutely no one to blame but yourself if you can't manage to relax, since most of the town's distractions – the highlight of which are the springs at the end of Národní – can be dispensed with in a matter of hours. The most amusing of these is the curio-crammed **Spa Museum** (Lázně muzeum) at dr. Pohoreckého 8 (0166 549 344; *open* 10am-noon, 1-5pm, Tue-Fri; 10am-4pm Sat, Sun).

Getting there

By bus: The easiest route is to take a bus to Karlovy Vary and change to a bus to Františkovy Lázně; buses leave from Karlovy Vary five times a day, and the trip takes just over 30 minutes.
By car: Take the E48 on past Karlovy Vary, exiting to the North on E49 – all told, a three-hour drive from Prague.
By train: The train from Prague to Karlovy Vary continues on to Františkovy Lázně; the trip takes around four and a half hours.

Tourist information

Četour, Národní třída 5 (0166 542 210).
Open 9am-4.30pm Mon-Fri; 9-11.30am Sat.

Where to eat & stay

Hotel Slovan
Národní 5 (0166 542 841). **Rates** *single* 865 Kč; *double* 1,660 Kč. **Credit** AmEx, EC, MC, V.
Comfortable and central, if a bit sterile, with a reasonable Czech-food restaurant on site.

Hotel Tři lillie
Jiráskova 17 (0166 542 415). **Rates** *single* 100 DM;
double 160 DM. **Credit** AmEx, EC, MC, V.
This old-fashioned hotel has been sensitively restored
and is conveniently central on a colonnade with attached
garden, restaurant and art gallery, which hosts exhibitions of local work.

Mariánské Lázně

Regarded by many as the plainer sister of
Karlovy Vary, Mariánské Lázně was founded in
the early nineteenth century by an abbot from
the Teplá monastery, Karl Reitenberger, and a
local physician, Josef Nehr. Although the spa
town consists in large part of one main drag,
Hlavní třída, this avenue of pastel Empire wedding-cake buildings and the elegant cast-iron
colonnades across the way is compact and
coherent enough to preserve the hushed air of
an exclusive spa town – unlike ever-eager
Karlovy Vary, which spreads itself a bit too
thin. Compound that with half the number of
tourists, 39 springs of varying temperatures
and remedial powers, a web of attractive paths
to stroll and densely forested environs, and
you may well find Mariánské Lázně far more
agreeable a slice of old-world spa life than
Karlovy Vary.

Visitors can have a soak and a massage at the
Nové lázně (New Baths; 0165 3001; *open* 7am-
3pm Mon-Fri). If you're itching for bona fide
attractions, check out the **Chopin Museum** –
the composer stayed here in 1836 – at Hlavní 47
(no phone; *open* 2-5pm Tue, Sun) or the red and
yellow **Orthodox Church of St Vladimír** at
Ruská 347-9.

Getting there
By bus: Buses from Florenc bus station take
between three and three and a half hours, and leave
four times daily.
By train: Around ten express trains a day from
Hlavní nádraží make the trek in around three hours.
By car: Go west on E50 to Plzeň, turning off to the
north at highway 21.

Tourist information
Infocentrum, Hlavní třída 47 (0165 622 474).
Open 9am-6pm Mon-Fri; 9am-5pm Sat, Sun.

Where to eat & stay
Classic Café Restaurant
Hlavní třída 131 (0165 622 807). **Average** 120 Kč.
A good selection of light meals and desserts in a glar-
ingly white but cheery setting.
Hotel Bohemia
Hlavní třída 100 (0165 623 251). **Rates** *single* 1,800
Kč; *double* 2,300 Kč. **Credit** AmEx, DC, EC, MC, V.
One of the classier places in town.
U Zlaté koule
Nerova 26 (0165 622 691). **Average** 210 Kč.
Beautifully elevated Czech cuisine, in a rosy, gracious
dining room that feels more like an old-world parlour.

Booking spa treatments in Prague

If you want to visit these spa towns the way they
were meant to be experienced, try one of the
agencies below.
Balnex
Křižovnická 3, Prague 1 (2481 0415).
Bohemia lázně
Kozlovská 14a, Prague 6 (2431 4742).

Founded before 1250, the castle's heyday began when the Rožmberk family adopted it as their seat in 1302, and as their riches and influence increased with each successive generation, it was gradually transformed into the Renaissance palace that still exists today. Craftsmen and artists flocked to the town to work on the extensive building schemes, creating a cosmopolitan community; the Rožmberks, enlightened humanists and generous patrons, endowed the town with a vigour and vitality unmatched in the region. The castle was sold in 1602 and, after various owners, was inherited by the Schwarzenberg family in 1715 with whom it remained until 1947.

As you cross the dry moat to enter the complex, note the bored-looking live bears that roam around below. The tower, the castle's most obvious feature, dates from the thirteenth century and was transformed into a whimsical Renaissance affair in 1591. It's painted pink and yellow, covered with murals, and topped with marble busts and gold trimmings. Walk up to the arcaded gallery and there's a bird's-eye view of the steeply pitched red tiled roofs below.

You can wander through the five interconnecting courtyards, all of which are covered with ornate Renaissance murals, the last of which is reached via **Plášťový Bridge** (Plášťový most). This is a spectacular five-tiered affair, which rises at an angle between two steep escarpments, although you can only get a true sense of its unique structure from the ground. For the best view descend to the **Stag Gardens** (Jelení zahrada) and look upwards.

If you want to see the inside, you have to go with a guide through the warren-like enclosure; highlights of the tour include the Eggenberg coach, a gilded carriage built in 1638 to convey presents to the Pope. The Mirror and Masquerade Halls are triumphs of the art of stucco and *trompe l'oeil* painting, while the baroque theatre is a uniquely preserved monument complete with original auditorium, stage scenery, lighting and costumes. It has been closed for seemingly endless refurbishment since 1966, but it's worth checking to see whether it has finally reopened.

Note that the castle and gardens are closed between October and April.

The best way to see the town itself is to indulge in some aimless wandering. The streets aren't merely tourist showpieces – this is still a working town whose residents are employed in mining, beer-making or at the nearby paper mills. Before World War II, Český Krumlov was predominantly German-speaking, but, as a part of the Sudetenland, it was annexed by Hitler in 1938. In 1945 the majority of the region's three million German-speaking inhabitants were expelled and the town's centuries-old bi-cultural life came to an abrupt end. Český Krumlov originally developed as two separate settlements on either side of the river, one (called Latrán) around the castle, the other on a gentle slope between the two bends of the Vltava. Although the two were united in 1555, the main street on the castle side is still called Latrán and winds its way from the delightful, painted Budějovická Gate and over to the wooden Lazebnický Bridge on the other side.

Take the street called Na novém městě ('to the New Town'; the name refers to alterations carried out seven centuries ago) and you'll end up at the **Eggenberg Brewery**, which moved here from its original Renaissance house on the main square in 1945. Although tours of the brewery are not officially encouraged, they have been known to happen. If you're unlucky, console yourself in the rollicking *pivnice* next door. Follow the river path back and you'll see the entrances to the medieval graphite mines that run underneath the town and are still worked today.

Crossing Lazebnický Bridge will bring you up to **Náměstí Svornosti**, the main square. It's a small, intimate space by Bohemian standards, dominated by the Old Town Hall built in the Renaissance style in the sixteenth century and stamped with emblems of various noble families and, since 1992, the UNESCO insignia. Close by on Horní is the **Church of St Vitus**, the long slender tower of which is visible from all parts of the town. It was finished in 1439 and the baroque ornamentation that was added inside at a later date is somewhat at odds with the clean, vertical lines of the nave.

The **Egon Schiele Cultural Centre** (*see below*), just west of the main square on Široká, is worth a visit but may be disappointing to diehard fans. Český Krumlov was the home town of the painter's mother and he spent some time here before 1918. In 1993 his former studios were adapted into an exhibition space, showing 80 of his works that the founders have somehow managed to procure on permanent loan from private American collectors. Occasionally, these make way for mediocre modern art.

West of Český Krumlov lies the unspoilt, heavily forested **Šumava** region (*see below*).

Getting there

By bus: two buses a day leave from Roztyly bus station in the afternoon. The trip takes about four hours.

By car: the fastest and easiest way to get to the town. There are two possible routes: either leave Prague on the Brno motorway (D1-E50) and then take the E55 at Mirošovice past Tábor and České Budějovice, and then take the 159 road to Český Krumlov; or go via Písek leaving Prague on Route 4, in the direction of Strakonice.

By train: the trip from Hlavní nádraží takes five hours and includes a change at České Budějovice.

Tourist information

Náměstí Svornosti 1 (0337 711 183). **Open** 9am-7.30pm daily.
Staff can book canoe and boat tours down the fast-flowing Vltava. Trips range from a one-hour jaunt to an eight-hour expedition.

Sights

The Castle

(0337 711 687/711 465). **Open** *Apr, Oct* 9am-noon, 1-3pm, *May, Sept* 9am-noon, 1-4pm, *June-Aug* 9am-noon, 1-5pm, Tue-Sun. **Admission** 110 Kč; 55 Kč children.
The last ticket is sold one hour before closing time. The only way to see the castle is to take an hour-long tour. The tower is open at the same times as the castle.

Egon Schiele Cultural Centre

Široká 70-72 (0337 711 224). **Open** 10am-6pm daily. **Admission** 120 Kč; 80 Kč children.

Where to eat & stay

Finding a room in Český Krumlov is not a problem. Dozens of tiny cottages offer *Zimmer frei* (rooms for rent). Some of the best are located on Parkán, a tranquil terrace with abundant flowers that looks on to the river.

Hospoda Na louži

Kajovská 66 (0337 711 280). **Open** 10am-11pm daily. **Average** 200 Kč.
A good place to experience 'Southern Bohemian Cuisine' in a central pub with traditional food and atmosphere.

Penzion Katka

Linecká 51 (0337 711 902). **Rates** *single* 600 Kč; *double* 1,000 Kč.
Just a minute's stroll from the town square, this restored but still charming old spot has a pleasantly rustic atmosphere.

Pension ve věži

Pivovarská 28 (0337 711 742). **Rates** (including breakfast) *double* 1,000 Kč.
Call well in advance to reserve one of the four rooms inside this former fortress tower with metre-thick walls.

U Šatlavy

Šatlavská (no phone). **Open** 10am-10pm daily. **Average** 150 Kč.
Medieval dining simulated in small, candlelit Gothic cellar where waiting staff in period costume serve up mead and spit-roasted meat dishes.

Slavonice

Few places with a mere 2,000 inhabitants can boast such wonderful Renaissance architecture as Slavonice. Located in the south-western tip of Moravia just three kilometres (two miles) from the Austrian border, the town was off bounds to visitors during the communist years and still retains the atmosphere of a village lost in a time-warp. The peeling sgraffitoed façades of the houses are testimony to its heyday in the sixteenth century when it thrived as an important trading post for merchants on the Vienna-Prague stage-coach route.

However, its prosperity was shortlived; decline set in early with extensive destruction during the Thirty Years' War and the eventual relocation of the trade route. Until World War II the inhabitants were mainly Austrian, but they were forced to leave in 1945 under the mass expulsion of the German-speaking population, and the town has been gradually repopulated by Czechs.

Slavonice consists of little more than two adjoining squares. The lower one, and larger of the two, contains the **Municipal Museum** (which documents the history of Slavonice's architecture; *see below*), the sixteenth century parish **Church of the Virgin Mary** and Slavonice's most original architectural feature: diamond vaulting. Step into the local police station or the *cukrárna* (sweetshop) to gawp at this geometric wonder that preempts cubism by some 400 years.

The most famous building on the upper square is the **Besídka snack bar and gallery**, owned and run by members of the former dissident Prague-based theatre group Sklep. They bought the building in 1989, and decided to put the long-neglected Slavonice back on the map by opening an arty café that would function as a base for summer workshops.

A little further up from the Besídka, the friendly Italian owner of no.85 will show you the sixteenth-century prayer room on the first floor of his house. A complete cycle of biblical frescoes is preserved in what was once a secret Protestant chapel. Look out for the crocodile wearing a papal tiara, one of the more unusual expressions of anti-papal sentiment, and, in the final fresco, the pathetic 'beast' that looks like a depressed cartoon character with a sagging bosom and bulbous eyes.

All the streets branching off the main square lead almost immediately into the countryside. There are lots of good picnic spots around the dilapidated village of Mariz, which lay in no man's land until 1989.

Summer workshops

Multilingual classes on sculpture, drawing, painting, theatre, music and photography are held annually in July. For more information contact Jan Boháč at the Besídka, Slavonice *(0332 493 292)* or in Prague *(643 4233).*

Getting there

By bus: Catch a bus to Dačice (famous for giving the sugar cube to the world); from there you can get a local bus or train to Slavonice. Between April and November a private line runs buses out of Palmovka (697 8850 *ext* 254).
By car: From Telč follow signs to Dačice, and then to Slavonice. The journey takes about half an hour.
By train: Local trains leave every hour from Telč.

Sights

Municipal Museum

Náměstí Míru 478 (0332 493 502). **Open** *June-Sept* 8am-noon, 1-5pm, daily. **Admission** 10 Kč; 7 Kč students; 5 Kč children.

Where to eat & stay

Besídka

Horní náměstí 522 (0332 493 293). **Rates** *dorm beds* 160 Kč.
Dormitory-style accommodation above the café of the same name. By far the most interesting place to eat and drink in Slavonice, it serves cheap and tasty Czech food and excellent coffee.

Hotel Alfa
Náměsti Miru 482 (0332 493 161). **Rates** *single* 150 Kč;
double 300 Kč.
Comfortable if unthrilling rooms.

Telč

The tiny town of Telč, with its immaculately
preserved Renaissance buildings, still partly
enclosed by medieval fortifications and surrounded by lakes, undoubtedly deserves its place on
UNESCO's World and Natural Heritage list. The
large rhomboid **central square** dates back to the
fourteenth century, but its present appearance – a
delicate colonnade runs down three of its sides,
which are lined with absurdly photogenic gabled
houses – was determined in the sixteenth century
during Zacharia of Hradec's period of administration. A trip to Genoa and a fortuitous marriage to
Katerina of Wallenstein gave this Renaissance
man the inspiration and means to reconstruct the
town following a devastating fire in 1530. Each of
the pastel-hued buildings has a different façade

Marked trails cover the Czech Republic.

adorned with frescoes, sgraffito or later baroque
and rococo sculptures.

The narrower end of the square is dominated by
the onion-domed bell-towers of the seventeenth
century Jesuit **church** on one side and the
Renaissance **castle** opposite. In 1552 Zachariá
decided to turn this fourteenth-century family seat
into his principal residence; at his invitation the
Italian architect Baldassare Maggi arrived in town
with a troupe of master masons and stuccodores
and set to work transforming the Gothic fort into
the Italianate palace you can see today. The cof-
fered ceilings of the Golden Hall and of the Blue
Hall, and the monochrome *trompe l'oeil* decorations that cover every inch of plaster in the
Treasury, count among the finest Renaissance
interior decorations in Central Europe. In the
Marble Hall is some fantastic armour for both
knight and steed, while the African Hall contains
a motley collection of hunting trophies including
a stuffed rhino and a very large elephant's ear.

The castle also houses a permanent exhibition
of works by the Moravian surrealist Jan Zrzavý
(1890-1977), and a small municipal museum that
contains an unusual nineteenth century mechanical nativity crib, which the custodian will willing-
ly activate for you. After you've exhausted the
interior possibilities, relax in the peaceful gardens
that stretch down to the lake.

Getting there
By bus: buses leave five times daily from Florenc bus
station and once per afternoon from Roztyly. The journey
takes just under four hours.
By car: 150km (93 miles) from Prague. Head out of Prague
in the direction of Brno on the E50/D1 motorway. At Pávov
follow signs to Jihlava; at Třešť follow signs to Telč.

Tourist information
Náměsti Zachariáše z Hradce 10 (066 962 233).
Open 8am-6pm Mon-Fri; 10am-6pm Sat, Sun.
Staff can book accommodation, plus fishing, horse riding
and hunting expeditions.

Sights
The Castle
Náměsti Zachariáše z Hradce (066 962 943).
Open *Apr, Sept, Oct* 9am-noon, 1-4pm, *May-Aug* 9am-
noon, 1-5pm, Tue-Sun. **Admission** *castle & gallery* 90 Kč;
45 Kč children.
Tours of the castle are conducted in Czech but you can pick
up a detailed English text at the ticket counter.

Where to eat & stay
Hotel pod kaštany
Štepnická 409 (066 721 30 42). **Rates** *single* 300 Kč;
double 660 Kč. **Credit** EC, MC.
Past its prime, perhaps, but a friendly place.
Pension Privát Nika
Náměsti Zachariáše z Hradce 45 (066 962 104).
Rates *single* 500 Kč; *double* 800 Kč.
Comfortable and good value.
Šenk pod věži
Palackého 116 (066 962 889). **Open** 10am-10pm daily.
Average 150 Kč.
There are various choices, but this is the most charming. It
serves good Czech fare, has friendly staff and a terrace.

*The magnificent and deeply improbable **Trosky Castle** in **Český ráj**.*

Overnighters: Country

Český ráj

Český ráj literally means 'Czech Paradise' and this protected **national park** is a peaceful haven of densely forested hills, giant rock formations and ruined castles in the otherwise industrial and polluted north-east of Bohemia. For many Czechs, donning walking boots and venturing into the great outdoors comes close to paradise. Praguers flock here at weekends for activities ranging from gentle hiking to scaling the huge sandstone rocks. Though the area is accessible by road, the best way to explore it is on foot; even reluctant amateurs can cross the region in two days. The neighbouring towns of **Jičín** and **Turnov** provide a good base from which to begin your exploration, and, as signposted trails can be followed almost from the centres of the towns, a great way to see the region is to get the train to one of them and hike over to the other for the return train journey.

The greatest concentration of protruding rocks is to be found around **Hrubá skála**: follow any of the marked footpaths from the village and you'll soon find yourself surrounded by these pockmarked giants covered in human spiders. The two hotels here (*see below*) probably make the best base for exploring the region.

Supreme among the ruined castles in the area is **Trosky** (the name means 'ruins'). Its two towers, built on absurdly inaccessible basalt outcrops, form the most prominent silhouette in the region. The taller, thinner rock goes by the name of Panna (Maiden), while the smaller one is Bába (Grandmother). In the fourteenth century,

Čeněk of Vartemberk undertook a monumental feat of medieval architecture by building a tower on each promontory, with a series of interconnecting ramparts joining the two peaks together. The towers still remained virtually impenetrable, though, as they could only be reached by an ingenious wooden structure that could be dismantled in times of siege, leaving invaders with the choice of scaling the impossibly steep rocks or, more likely, beating a hasty retreat. In the nineteenth century Trosky Castle became a favourite haunt of Romantic poets, painters and patriots. Now you can climb to the base of the tower on Panna for outstanding views of the surrounding countryside.

Trosky Castle

Open *April, Oct* 9am-4pm Sat, Sun, public holidays; *May-Aug* 8am-5pm Tue-Sun; *Sept* 9am-5pm Tue-Sun.

Getting there

By bus: four buses a day go to Malá skála from Holešovice bus station in Prague. A private bus line leaves each morning from Palmovka metro for Jičín. Call *6631 1040* for information. It's roughly a two-hour ride.

By train: a local train goes from Jičín to Turnov; eight trains a day leave from Prague's Hlavní nádraží to Turnov. There are local connections from Turnov to Hrubá skála and Malá skála.

By car: about 90km (56 miles) from Prague; follow signs to Mladá Boleslav and join the E65 or Route 10, which continues all the way to Turnov. Jičín lies 23km (14 miles) south-west of Turnov. Hrubá skála and Trosky are both just off route 35 – the Turnov-Jičín road.

Getting around on foot: the best map is the *Český ráj Poděbradsko*, which can be bought at any decent bookshop in Prague.

Where to eat & stay

There are no sizeable towns within the national reserve area, but close to each of the main tourist sights there are places offering filling, if uninspiring, Czech fare.

Hotel Štekl

Hrubá skála (0436 916 284). **Rates** *single* 490 Kč; *double* 650 Kč. **Credit** EC, MC, V.

Resembles an alpine resthouse, and has views over the sur-

The most romantic spot to stay in **Český ráj** *– Hotel Zámek in Hrubá skála.*

*View of stunning **Český ráj** scenery from the battlements of the Hotel Zámek.*

rounding valleys; rooms are old-fashioned. The decent dining room tends to close alarmingly early.

Hotel Zámek
Hrubá skála castle (0436 916 281). **Rates** *single* 865 Kč; double 1,100 Kč.
Fabulous location, keen prices and fantastic views from the ivy-covered turret rooms. Not to be missed.

Camping is the other option; there are several campsites but most people just pitch their tent unofficially on an appealing plot of land.

Climbing

From 1 April until 31 October climbers can scale the sandstone pinnacles in the region.

České Švýcarsko

North Bohemia typically gets – and deserves – a bad rap for its rampant ecological neglect, in the form of brown coal mines and the factories that love them. But whether you're into hiking or simply gawping, the Labe (Elbe) valley boasts some of the most dramatic scenery to be found in the Czech Republic. Known as the 'Czech Switzerland' (České Švýcarsko) – purportedly after two Swiss painters who settled in the region in the eighteenth century – the sweeping sandstone cliffs will even produce oohs and ahhs from passengers on the train that runs beside the river all the way up into Germany. The hills beyond, laced with trails, are a hiker's paradise, with steep cliffs and spectacular gorges carved out of the sandstone by streams and rivers, and thick spruce and pine forests.

Though not especially compelling in its own right, **Děčín** – originally two towns on opposite sides of the river, Děčín and Podmolky, that were grafted together in 1948 – is your best base for exploring the pleasures of the rocks beyond. You can while away a day in the town proper, with a visit to the **Town Museum** on Mládeže, which – in addition to the requisite hum-drum old photos and mediocre portraits – features a well-planned exhibit on the 450,000 Czechs who were shipped to Germany during World War II as forced labour. But even in the town, the best attractions are on high – take the lift to the 150-metre (492-ft) tall **Pastýřská stěna** (Shepherd's Rock) on the Podmolky side to the sixteenth-century château and its accompanying baroque rose garden on the Děčín side.

Once you've oriented yourself in Děčín, head for the hills and wear good shoes, since the area is best explored by foot. Get hold of a map of the area (widely available from bookshops) and tramp the well-travelled, clearly marked trails. Tackle the trails via the pretty village of **Hřensko**, 12km (7.5 miles) north of Děčín on the German border, from which one of the region's most spectacular attractions can be reached – the **Pravčická brána**. At 30-m (98-ft) long, 21-m (69-ft) high, it's the highest natural bridge in Europe and the third highest in the world (the other two are in Utah). Or head 20km (12.5 miles) west from Děčín to the rock village of **Tiské Stěny**, an otherworldly collection of rock towers that resemble dripping sandcastles. Whatever route you chose, keep a Zen-like attitude: the journey along the way is just as worthwhile as the destination.

Getting there

By bus: three buses leave Prague's Florenc station daily; the trip takes around two and a half hours.

By car: 108km (67.5 miles) north of Prague. Take the E55-D8 north out of Prague towards Veltrusy and pick up highway 30 at Lovosice and then, following the Labe, the 253 or 261 from Ústí nad Labem.

By train: Express and local trains leave Prague's Hlavní Nádraží for Děčín up to six times a day; depending on the train, the trip can take less than two hours.

Where to stay

There are cheap rooms galore available in villages all over the region.

Hotel Bowling Club
Klicperova 174, Děčín (0412 548 508).
Rates (breakfast included) *single* 550 Kč; *double* 1,100 Kč.
Credit EC, MC, V.
Suffers from that unmistakable late-'70s injection of 'modernism', but the rooms are clean and the basement bowling alley is delightfully tacky.

Moravian caves

The whole country is riddled with caves (jeskyně), the most notable of which are located north of Brno. But caving in this country is not for spelunkers alone: it's common to see busloads of children and, less frequently, pensioners unloading at the mouths of many of these caves. The rarefied air is touted as remedial to pesky ailments, particularly allergies and asthma. Whether or not you're looking for a cure, guided tours through the limestone caves are a particularly welcome respite in the summer months. But bring a sweater and, if possible, try to avoid going at the weekend – on hot summer days, the lines can be torturously long.

By far the most concentrated and easily accessible network of caves – all told, around 400 – the **Moravský kras** are best visited as a day trip from Brno. All of these are limestone caves, formed as a cumulative process of slightly acidic rain water and underground streams that have been gradually carving out caves for the last 350 million years. The **Kateřinská**, **Sloupsko-šošůvské** and **Balcarka** caves are all within easy reach of the Moravian capital. But if you're looking to do all your caving in one go, your best bet is the **Punkevní jeskyně**, the largest in the country – although only around three kilometres (two miles) of the caves' 12-km (7.5-mile) length is open to the public. This is one of the more dramatic cave tours you'll find, with some run-of-the-mill stalactite sightings giving way to the colossal **Macocha Abyss**: 140-m (459-ft) deep, it was formed in part by the collapse of the ceiling of a cave farther below. The tour then sends you down the narrow tunnels of the cave via a skinny little boat – take heed that any latent claustrophobia you might have will probably come shining through, since the passages are barely wide enough to handle the boat, and you'd most likely be impaled by a stalactite if you stood erect. Be sure to arrive early in peak season as tours can sell out by mid-morning. And when you emerge from

underground, walk off the claustrophobia with a wonderful surrounding countryside.

Brno itself is a diverting city (providing you ignore the industrial suburbs), and there are many other attractions within easy reach. The most popular is the spectacular Gothic castle of **Pernštejn**; others include the Napoleonic battlefield of **Austerlitz** (Slavkov) and the **Alfons Mucha Museum** at the Renaissance château of **Moravský Krumlov**.

Getting there

By bus: buses run roughly every hour between Brno and Prague. The journey time is two hours.

By car: 202km (126 miles) south-east of Prague. The D1 motorway runs all the way from the Czech to the Moravian capital.

By train: hourly trains to Brno from Prague take between three and four hours.

From Brno to the caves: the caves are 22km (14 miles) north-east of Brno, with a battery of a dozen trains leaving Brno for the nearby town of Blansko daily. Local buses then run to the caves. A tourist train travels between the Punkevní and the centre of Skalní Mlýn, from which the other three caves are accessible. It's all a lot easier if you have a car.

Tourist information

Old Town Hall, Radnická 8 (0542 211 090).
Open 8am-6pm Mon-Fri; 9am-5pm Sat, Sun.

Where to eat & stay

Hotel Skalní Mlýn
Skalní Mlýn (0506 418 113). **Rates** *single* 690 Kč; *double* 890 Kč. **Credit** AmEx, DC, EC, MC, V.
Heavily touristed but the best base for the caves – and with a decent restaurant, too.

The Šumava

The dark, earthy terrain of the Šumava in southern Bohemia has something of a sombre, even ghostly air to it – and with good reason, as this region was once the heavily patrolled border between the Czech Republic and Germany, in which lurked not woodland spirits but attack dogs and watchmen. Today its wilds remain largely untrafficked, partly because camping outside sites is still forbidden and partly due to the difficulty of exploring the area without a car and a good amount of legwork. More reminiscent of the Black Forest than of Český ráj's rocky outcrops (*see page above*), the dense forests, ruined castles, matchbook-sized towns and smatterings of dark-wood Alpine-style housing make for rewarding wandering. Don't be put off by the amount of walking necessary: the trails are generally gentle.

Few venture farther into the region than **Český Krumlov** (*see page above*) on its north-eastern border. But the secrets of the Šumava are divulged even close to that overly touristed town; visit the extensive fourteenth-century castle ruins of **Dívčí Kámen**, 12km (7.5 miles) to the north, accessible only by foot along a path that winds three kilometres (one mile) from the station at Třísov. Follow the train line further north, and another two-kilometre (one-mile) walk from Holubov station will take you to the 1,083-m- (3,553-ft-) high peak of **Klet**, accessible by chairlift if your legs are tired.

Further west into the Šumava, the castle near **Kašperské hory** – a charming town in its own right, with an elaborate Renaissance-style town hall – is, surprise surprise, accessible only by trail. Though the castle has been closed due to reconstruction for several years, the massive walls are even more impressive when viewed up-close. Ditto for **Rabí**, where General Jan Žižka (*see page 15*) parted with one of his eyes in a Hussite siege of the now-ruined castle.

Dominated by its evil-twin towers – one bone-white, the other jet black – **Klatovy**, at the Šumava's western border, can be a fearsome sight when approached by night. The town's main sights are located on its steep main square: the looming towers (the only way to shake the feeling that they're watching you is to climb them yourself, affording a fantastic view of the Šumava mountains) and an adjacent museum of the town's history; the **House at the White Unicorn** (Dům u bílého jednorožce), a quirky pharmaceutical museum; and a collection of accidental mummies from the 1600s that were unearthed in the early part of this century. Due to a ventilation system that happened to perfectly preserve its contents, a whole colony of mummies was discovered at the beginning of this century. A few fell victim a second time to bad storage condition or plagues of insects, but around 20 stunted, shrivelled bodies remain on display.

Located on a main highway connecting Munich to Prague, Klatovy is a useful base more in terms of accessibility than its real proximity to Šumava destinations. Since much of the Šumava does not have a well-developed tourist network, information, meals and reservations might be better had in Klatovy, which has no dearth of *Zimmer frei* options and reliable pub grub.

The beautiful medieval town of **Prachatice**, known in hackneyed tourist parlance as 'the gateway to the Šumava', is perhaps a preferable and more central base for exploring the region. Fourteenth-century fortifications surround the miniscule, circular old town, centred on Velké náměstí with its wonderfully sgraffitoed houses.

Husinec, five kilometres (three miles) north of Prachatice, is the birthplace of ubiquitous Czech hero **Jan Hus** (*see page 14*). A small museum (*see below*) in the house where Hus is alleged to have been born commemorates the life of the proto-Protestant martyr.

Getting to Klatovy & Prachatice

By train: some of the trains that pass through Plzeň continue on to Klatovy; these leave Prague's main

station three times daily. The trip lasts around two and a half hours. Prachatice is on a minor line – it's far easier to come by bus.

By car: Klatovy is 136km (85 miles) south-west of Prague. Take the E50-D5 south-west of Prague to Plzeň, then highway 27 south. Prachatice is 140 km (88 miles) south of Prague. Take highway 4 south out of Prague along the Vltava as far as Volyně, then the 144, 145 and 141 to Prachatice.

By bus: buses from Prague to Klatovy and Prachatice leave three or four times daily (twice on weekends); both journeys last around three hours.

Getting around the Šumava

Bus connections are few and trains only run the spine of the region, which makes a car a virtual necessity – especially since, after what might amount to a half-day's worth of riding and waiting for any number of buses or trains, you're usually finished with most of the castles or ruins within five minutes. If you can't secure a car, the train ride south from Klatovy to Železná Ruda, then north again to Sušice, is a picturesque, hassle-free way to window shop the prettiest parts of the Šumava.

Tourist information

Pergolia Informservis, Náměstí Míru 63, Klatovy (0186 23515). **Open** 9am-5pm Mon-Fri; 9am-noon Sat, Sun.

Infocentrum, Velké náměstí, Prachatice (0338 22563). **Open** *June-Aug* 8am-5pm Mon-Fri; 9am-noon Sat; *Sept* 8am-4.30pm Mon-Fri; *Oct-May* 7.30am-4pm Mon-Fri.

Sights

House at the White Unicorn
(Dům u bílého jednorožce) Náměstí Míru, Klatovy (0186 22049/24361). **Open** 9am-noon, 1-5pm, daily. **Admission** 20 Kč; 10 Kč children, students.

Jan Hus Museum
Husinec (0338 331 284). **Open** 9am-noon, 1-4pm, Tue-Sun. **Admission** 10 Kč; 5 Kč children.

Tower & Town Museum
Neumannova 13, Prachatice (0338 311 419/314 202). **Open** *July, Aug* 9am-5pm Tue-Fri; 10am-5pm Sat, Sun; *Sept-June* 9am-4pm Tue-Fri; 10am-4pm Sat, Sun. **Admission** 20 Kč; 10 Kč children.

Where to eat & stay

Private rooms abound in Klatovy, and are a good alternative to the pricier hotels.

Hotel Parkán
Věžní 51, Prachatice (0338 311 868). **Rates** (including breakfast) *single* 890 Kč; *double* 1,290 Kč. **Credit** EC, MC, V.

Pension U bílé věžé
Křižová 165, Klatovy (0186 23385/0601 263 007). **Rates** *single* 250 Kč; *double* 450 Kč. Just five cheerful rooms in an old town-centre building.

Restaurant Královská
Husova 106, Prachatice (0338 21950). **Open** 11am-10pm Mon-Fri; 11am-11pm Sat, Sun. **Average** 120 Kč. Good regional dishes.

Vinárna u Radů
Pražska 22, Klatovy (0186 24594). **Open** 10am-11pm Mon-Thu; 10am-midnight Fri, Sat; 10am-9pm Sun. **Average** 170 Kč. Moravian wines on tap and an adequate selection of meals – the chicken dishes are especially good.

Directory

Resources A-Z **244** Getting to Prague **253** Getting around Prague **254**
Business **260** Media **263** Studying in Prague **266**

Resources A-Z

Customs

There are no restrictions on the import and export of Czech currency, but if you're carrying more than 200,000 Kč out of the country, you must declare it at customs. The allowances for importing goods are:

- 200 cigarettes or 100 cigars at 3g each or 250g of tobacco;
- 1 litre of liquor or spirits and 2 litres of wine;
- Medicine in any amount for your own needs.

If you want to export an antique, you must have a certificate stating that it is not important to Czech cultural heritage. Every once in a while and usually without warning or much reason, EC countries limit the import of some Czech foodstuffs – even for personal consumption.

Customs Office

(Oblastní celní úřad Praha)
Washingtonova 11, Prague 1 (6133 1111). Metro Muzeum. **Open** 8am-4pm Mon-Fri. **Map 6 L6**
Branch: *Ruzyně airport (2011 4380).*

Disabled access

According to law, all buildings constructed after 1994 must be barrier-free. Reconstructed buildings, however, need not provide wheelchair access, but many do voluntarily. Even so, it is no picnic to be in Prague in a wheelchair. There are few ramps. Most hotels provide no wheelchair access and only five railway stations in the entire country are wheelchair-friendly. The guidebook *Accessible Prague (Přístupná Praha)*, available from the Prague Wheelchair Association, maps hotels, toilets, restaurants, galleries and theatres that are wheelchair-friendly. For travel information for the disabled, *see page 256*.

Prague Wheelchair Association

(Pražská organizace vozíčkářů) Centre for Independent Living (Centrum samostatného života), Benediktská 6, Prague 1 (232 5831/232 5803/fax 2481 6231). Metro Náměstí Republiky. **Open** 10am-5pm Mon-Thur; 10am-3pm Fri. **Map 4 K2**
This organisation is run by the disabled for the disabled. In addition to its *Accessible Prague* guidebook, it provides helpers and operates a taxi service and an airport pick-up service for the disabled. Service is limited and should be ordered as far as possible in advance.

Embassies

All embassies and consulates are closed on Czech holidays as well as their own national holi-

International dialling codes

Australia	*00 61*
Canada	*00 1*
Ireland	*00 353*
New Zealand	*00 64*
UK	*00 44*
US	*00 1*

AT&T International Operator

Australia	*00 420 06101*
Canada	*00 420 04401*
Ireland	*00 420 35301*
UK	*00 420 00151*
USA	*00 420 00101*

MCI International Operator

Call Australia	*00 420 06110*

Call UK	*00 420 04450*
Call USA	*00 420 00112*

For other countries and for rates see the front section of the *Zlaté stránky* (Yellow Pages).

Operator Services

Note: very few of the numbers listed have English-speaking operators.

Directory enquiries (local)	*120*
National directory enquiries	*121*
International directory enquiries	*0149*
Speaking clock	*112*
Repairs	*129*
Telegram	*0127*
Alarm call	*125*
Weather	*116*

days. For other embassies, you will need to consult the *Zlaté stránky* (Yellow Pages) under 'Zastupitelské úřady'.

American Embassy
Tržiště 15, Prague 1 (5732 0663/fax 5732 0920). Metro Malostranská/12, 22 tram. **Open** 8am-4pm Mon-Fri. **Map 2 D3**

Australian Trade Commission and Honorary Consulate
Na Ořechovce 38, Prague 6 (2431 0743/2431 0071). Metro Dejvická/ 132, 216 bus. **Open** 8.30am-5pm Mon-Thur; 8.30am-2pm Fri.

British Embassy
Thunovská 14, Prague 1 (5732 0355/fax 5732 1023). Metro Malostranská/12, 22 tram. **Open** 9am-noon Mon-Fri. **Map 2 D3**

Canadian Embassy
Mickiewiczova 6, Prague 6 (2431 1108/fax 2431 0294). Metro Hradčanská/18, 22 tram. **Open** 8.30am-11pm Mon-Fri. **Map 7 A3**

Electricity

Electricity is 220 volts with two-pin plugs almost everywhere. Bring continental adaptors or converters with you, as they are expensive here when available at all.

Health

Prague isn't a very healthy place to live. The Czech diet is fatty, pork-laden and low on fresh vegetables. The Czechs top world beer consumption charts and are unrepentant smokers. The city also has serious smog problems and nitrate-infested water. (*See also page 29* **Prague Today**.)

Prague is a great place for hypochondriacs. The damp climate is a haven for various moulds that can be hell for anyone with allergies. Summer is the time for salmonella-infected ice-cream, and for a nice trip to the countryside, which could be preceded by a visit to the doctor for inoculations against tick-borne encephalitis (*see also page 179*)

Emergencies

The following emergency numbers are toll-free.
First Aid	155	**Prague City Police**	156
Czech Police	158	**Fire**	150
		Road Accidents	154, 0123, 0124

and other horrible things lurking in trees.

But if you really do get ill, the semi-privatised ex-socialist health-care system means you'll be smothered with attention whenever you go to the doctor. If you have health insurance, the doctors will try to rack up points for the care they give, which they redeem for money from the health insurance companies. If you pay cash you'll get even better treatment than the locals.

General health-care

Medical facilities are usually open 7.15am-6pm weekdays. It's usually best to find a GP (*rodinný* or *praktický lékař*), dentist (*zubní lékař*) and paediatrician (*dětský lékař*) close to your home or workplace. Many Czech doctors speak English or German, especially at larger facilities like a hospital (*nemocnice*) or medical centre (*poliklinika*) and in the larger cities.

Health insurance

For longer stays, you should take out health insurance. As long as you are a legal resident, this is no problem. Czech law requires your employer to provide you with health insurance. If you are self-employed, you have to get your own policy. Be careful, though: individual policies don't necessarily cover all medical procedures (like childbirth) the way group policies do.

There have been a number of scandals in the banking and

insurance industries since regulations in both sectors were eased. It's much safer to go with the formerly state-run Central Health Insurance Office or with a trusted international firm than to use a smaller company, no matter how stable they may seem.

Central Health Insurance Office
(Všeobecná zdravotní pojišťovna) Tyršova 7, Prague 2 (2197 2111). Metro I.P. Pavlova/4, 16, 22 tram. **Open** 8am-6pm Mon-Thur; 8am-4pm Fri. **Map 6 L9**

Gay health
See page 187.

Helplines

Helplines generally run around the clock, but you have a better chance of catching an English-speaker if you call during regular office hours.

Alcoholics Anonymous
Na Poříčí 16, Prague 1 (2481 8247). Metro Florenc or Náměstí Republiky. **Open** (for English speakers) 7.30pm Tue, Wed; noon Fri; 5.30pm Sun. **Map 4 M2**
Twelve-step programmes. Anyone with alcohol problems is welcome.

Crisis Centre Prague
(Krizové centrum Praha) Ke Karlovu 11, Prague 2 (297 900). Metro I.P. Pavlova. **Open** 24 hours daily. **Map 6 K8**
This is a general helpline.

Crisis Intervention Centre
(Centrum krizové intervence – Psychiatrická léčebna Bohnice) Ústavní 91, Prague 8 (8385 0666). Metro Nádraží Holešovice, then 102, 177, 200 bus. **Open** 24 hours daily. Bohnice is the biggest and best-equipped mental health facility in Prague, with lots of outreach programmes.

Drop In
Karoliny Světlé 18, Prague 1 (tel/fax 265 730). Metro Národní třída.
Open 9am-5.30pm Mon-Thur; 9am-4pm Fri. **Map 3 G5**
Focusing on problems related to drug addiction, including HIV testing and counselling, Drop In is an informal clinic. You can call or just drop in 24 hours a day.

Emergency Health Care
toll-free call *155*.

Pharmacies

Many central pharmacies (*lékárna* or *apothéka*) have been doing business in exactly the same place for centuries, and have gorgeous period interiors that are worth a visit even if you don't need any aspirin. Over-the-counter medicines are only available at pharmacies, which are usually open 7.30am-6pm, though some operate extended hours. All pharmacies are supposed to post directions to the nearest 24-hour pharmacy in their window, though this information will be in Czech. Ring the bell for after-hours service, for which there is usually a surcharge of about 30 Kč.

24-hour pharmacies
(Lékárna s nepřetržitou službou):
Anny Drabíkové 534, Prague 4 (791 2743). Metro Háje.
Belgická 37, Prague 2 (258 189/2423 7207). Metro Náměstí Míru. **Map 6 M9**
Štefánikova 6, Prague 5 (5732 0918/537 039). Metro Anděl/6, 7, 12, 14 tram.

Women's health

Dr Kateřina Bittmanová
Mánesova 64, Prague 2 (office 627 1951/home 793 6895). Metro Jiřího z Poděbrad/11 tram. **Map 8 B3**
Dr Bittmanová speaks fluent English. She runs a friendly private practice and is on call 24 hours a day. Her fee for a general examination is 900 Kč; a smear costs an additional 450 Kč.

Bulovka Hospital
Budínova 2, Prague 8 (6608 3239/6608 3240). Tram 12, 14.
Housed within a huge state hospital complex, the privately run MEDA Clinic is favoured by British and American women living in Prague. Prices are reasonable, the

gynaecologists speak English, and facilities are clean and professional. Contraception and HIV testing available. Multilingual staff.

Podolí Hospital
Podolské nábřeží 157, Prague 4 (6121 4518 ext 485). Tram 3, 16, 17.
The Podolí Hospital has obstetricians/gynaecologists who speak English. With modern facilities and neo-natal care, Podolí handles most births for expats.

RMA Centrum
Dukelských hrdinů 17, Prague 7 (373 791/379 900). Tram 4, 12, 14, 17, 26. **Map 7 D2**
An alternative medicine centre that offers homeopathy, acupuncture and acupressure, traditional Chinese medicine and massage as well as gynaecology and mammography. There's even a sauna and beauty salon.

Information sources

The English-language weekly *Prague Post* carries entertainment sections as well as survival hints. Monthly entertainment listings magazines are the pocket-sized *Exit* (in Czech), *Kulturní přehled* (in Czech), *Kultura v Praze* and its shorter English equivalent *Culture in Prague*. (*See also page 264*.) The Prague Information Service (PIS) also publishes a free monthly entertainment listings programme in English.

The use of the international blue and white 'i' information sign is not regulated, so the places carrying it are not necessarily official.

The best map for public transport or driving is the *Kartografie Praha Plán města* (a book with a yellow cover), costing about 100 Kč, though for central areas the co-ordinates are sometimes far too vague. Check you've got the latest edition. For central areas the free map from **PIS** (*see above*) is very useful.

Čedok
Na příkopě 18, Prague 1 (2419 7642/2419 7615/262 904/fax 2422 2300). Metro Můstek or Náměstí Republiky. **Open** 8.30am-6pm Mon-Fri; 8.30am-1pm Sat. **Map 4 K4**
The former state travel agency is still

the biggest in the Czech Republic. A handy place to obtain train, bus and air tickets and information.

Prague Information Service (PIS)
(Pražská informační služba) Na příkopě 20, Prague 1 (264 022/ general info 187/544 444). Metro Můstek or Náměstí Republiky.
Open 9am-7pm Mon-Fri; 9am-5pm Sat, Sun (longer in summer).
Map 4 K4
After decades of truly awful service, the PIS woke up and started to do what it was always supposed to do – provide free information, maps and help with a smile.
Branches: Hlavní nádraží (main station), Wilsonova, Prague 1 (2423 9258); Old Town Hall, Staroměstské náměstí, Prague 1 (2448 2202); Charles Bridge – Malá Strana-side Tower (summer only) (536 010).

Prague Public Transit Company (DP) Information Offices
(Informační střediska dopravního podniku hl. m. Prahy) Metro Můstek, B line lobby beneath Jungmannovo náměstí (Lines A and B; 2264 6350).
Open 7am-9pm daily. **Map 3 J5**
Employees usually have at least a smattering of English and German, and are unusually helpful. They provide free information booklets, sell tickets, maps, night transport booklets, individual tram and bus schedules.
Branches: Metro Muzeum, Main Lobby (lines A and C) (2264 0103). Metro Karlovo náměstí (Line B) (294 682). Metro Nádraží Holešovice, Plynární street exit (Line C) (806 790).

Insurance

Insuring personal belongings is always wise and should be arranged before leaving home.

While there is no Czech law governing the provision of emergency care to those who need it, most Czech doctors feel it is their duty to provide such care. The Czech Republic has reciprocal agreements (for free emergency care only) with the United Kingdom, Greece and most of the Republic's former allies in the ex-Warsaw Pact countries. Other nationals are expected to pay for emergency care, the costs of which can vary wildly as they are not regulated. If you are on a

Finding a flat to rent

Apartment space is tight in Prague. Before you begin your search, you should be aware of a few of the realities of life for the local population. Under the old regime, there was a 20-year waiting list for flats in the town centre, and at least a ten-year wait in the outlying districts. Divorced couples often had to continue living together; newlyweds had to live with one set of parents; and families fought over who would get granny's flat decades before her death.

It's perhaps not surprising, then, that the average Czech simply cannot understand foreigners' demands for luxuries like a fully equipped kitchen, a washing machine, telephone and parking. You should be happy just to have a roof over your head. This gap in expectations can cause problems when looking at flats. Whatever your requirements, the landlord or estate agent will show you somewhere completely unsuitable, far away from the centre, devoid of public transport connections and furnished with the ugliest stuff you've ever seen in your life – and tell you that it's the only place available in your price range. This is unlikely to be true. There are good flats on the market, but you have to be patient, lucky and persistent to find one.

Legal rights

Landlord-tenant rights have not been legally defined in the new free market economy. Even after restitution, which restored property to those who owned it before the communist nationalisation, many residential apartments in Prague are still state-owned. This means that people often find themselves renting a black market apartment. To meet the increasing demand, families rent out their flats to foreigners, at ten times the average rent of 1,000 Kč a month, while not declaring your presence to the state authorities. Consequently, any lease you sign won't be legally binding, leaving you with no legal rights if you have any problems. You're best off finding a privately owned flat and signing a legally binding lease that can protect you from being evicted at the whim of your landlord, though how much protection this really affords you is open to conjecture.

Flat hunting

There is no consistency in rent prices for foreigners. The price you pay (generally in dollars or marks) depends on who you are negotiating with, the security of the lease, and how rich the landlord thinks you are. An executive on a generous allowance may pay US$2,500 per month for an apartment in the Old Town Square, while an English-language teacher may live in the same flat in the same building for US$400 per month. There are four basic ways to find a flat in Prague:

1. Word of mouth
Both the most effective and the most elusive way of finding somewhere to live. Hang out at the expat bars and restaurants – such as **Jo's Bar** (*see p150*), **Radost** (*see p152*) and **The Globe** (*see p151*) – and tell people you're looking for a flat. Keep an eye on the notice boards in these places, too.

2. Advertising
Look through the rental section in *Annonce*, the classified ads paper that comes out three times a week on Monday, Wednesday and Friday. Also look through the classifieds section of the *Prague Post*, which occasionally lists flats available.

3. Bulletin boards
There are bulletin boards at **Radost**, **Laundry Kings** (*see p161*) and **The Globe** which frequently have notices up about flats available for rent. You can also try putting up a notice yourself.

4. Estate agents
If you are not on a tight budget, getting an agent can be the most painless way to find a flat (*see p261*). Like the property market itself, agents are inconsistent. They usually charge a success fee of between one and two months' rent for finding you somewhere to live.

Agentura Kirke
Moskevská 58, Prague 10 (7172 0399/fax 7172 3726). Metro Náměstí Míru/4, 22 tram. **Open** 8.30am-4pm Mon-Fri.
Run by British expat Nicholas Kirke, this estate agency has been helping people find flats since 1990.

Directory

short-term stay, it is advisable to take out travel insurance (and make sure that it covers Central and Eastern European countries).

For more on health insurance, *see page 245*.

Left luggage

There are left luggage offices/ lockers at Main Station (Hlavní nádraží), Holešovice Station (Nádraží Holešovice) and Florenc bus station (*see page 254*).

Lost property

Most railway stations have a Lost Property Office (Ztráty a nálezy). If you lose your passport, contact your embassy (*see above*).

FRIDAY'S
★ ★ ★ ★ ★
AMERICAN BAR

Malé Nám. 2, Prague 1

Central Lost Property Office

Karoliny Světlé 5, Prague 1 (2423 5085). Metro Narodní třída/6, 9, 17, 18, 22 tram. **Open** 8am-noon, 12.30-5.30pm, Mon, Wed; 8am-noon, 12.30-4pm, Tue, Thur; 8am-noon, 12.30-2pm, Fri. **Map 3 G5**

Money

The currency of the Czech Republic is the Česká koruna or Czech crown (abbreviated as Kč). One crown equals 100 hellers (haléřů). Hellers come as small, light 10, 20 and 50 coins. There are also 1, 2, 5, 10, 20 and 50 Kč coins in circulation. Banknotes come in denominations of 20, 50, 100, 200, 500, 1,000 and 5,000 Kč.

At the time of going to press, the exchange rate was approximately 52 Kč to the pound, or around 32 Kč to the US dollar.

The crown was the first fully convertible currency in the former Eastern Bloc. A bizarre indicator of its viability is the number of convincing counterfeit Czech banknotes in circulation. If someone stops you in the street, asking if you want to change money, it's a fair bet that he'll be trying to offload dodgy notes.

The Czech Republic has long been a cash economy, and conveniences like cash machines (ATMs), credit cards and cheques are not nearly as ubiquitous here as they are in EC countries or the US, though they're becoming more common. It's easier to cash cheques at a bank than to pay with them in a shop. However, the situation is changing and, particularly in Prague, it's not difficult to find ATMs that will pay out cash on the major credit cards. Many of the classier restaurants and shops also accept credit cards.

Banks & currency exchange

Exchange rates are usually the same all over, but banks offer a better commission rate (usually one to two per cent). Unfortunately, they are only open during regular business hours (usually 8am-5pm Mon-Fri).

Bureaux de change usually charge higher rates of commission, although some outlets (such as those at the Charles Bridge end of Karlova) may only take one per cent, but bear in mind that this means little if you're getting a poor exchange rate.

The number of bank failures of late appears to have improved service at the survivors. At some, like Komerční banka, there is no minimum requirement to open an account and foreign currency accounts are also available without the outlandish fees once charged.

Money transfer

To get money fast, try the American Express office or, in the case of a serious emergency, your embassy. The Na příkopě branch of ČSOB processes transfers faster than other Czech banks.

American Express

Václavské náměstí 56, Prague 1 (2421 9992/fax 2422 7708). Metro Můstek or Muzeum/3, 9, 14, 24 tram. **Open** 9am-7pm daily. **Map 4 K5** Card-holders can send and receive mail and faxes here.

Československá obchodní banka (ČSOB)

Na příkopě 14, Prague 1 (2411 1111). Metro Můstek or Náměstí Republiky/3, 5, 9, 14, 24 tram. **Open** 8am-5pm Mon-Fri. **Map 4 K4** Specialises in international currency transactions.

Komerční banka

Na příkopě 33, Prague 1 (2243 2111). Metro Můstek or Náměstí Republiky/3, 5, 9, 14, 24 tram. **Open** 8am-5pm Mon-Fri. **Map 4 K4** The country's largest full-service bank. Large branch network throughout the country. The ATM network accepts international credit cards. Represents MasterCard and Eurocard. Its card emergency number is 2424 8110.

Živnostenská banka

Na příkopě 20, Prague 1 (2412 1111). Metro Můstek or Náměstí Republiky/3, 5, 9, 14, 24 tram. **Open** 8.30am-5pm Mon-Fri. **Map 4 K4** This old trading bank, housed in one of the most beautiful buildings in Prague, has long experience in working with foreign clients and English is generally spoken by tellers. Represents Visa. For lost or stolen Visa cards phone 2423 2423, 00 44 71 9378 1111 (for the UK) or 00 1 410 581 3836 (for the US).

Opening hours

Standard opening hours for most shops and banks are from 8am or 9am to 5pm or 6pm Monday to Friday. Many shops are open a bit longer and from 9am to noon or 1pm on Saturday. Shops with extended hours are called *večerka* (open until 10pm or midnight) and 'non-stop' (open 24 hours). Outside the centre, most shops are closed on Sundays and holidays. Shops frequently close for a day or two for no apparent reason, some shops close for an hour or two at lunch, and many shops and theatres close for a month's holiday in August. Most places have shorter opening hours in winter (starting September or October) and extended hours in summer (starting April or May). Castles and some other attractions are only open in summer.

Police & security

Police in the Czech Republic are not regarded as serious crimefighters, or protectors of the public, and are just barely considered keepers of law and order. Their past as pawns for the regime, combined with a present reputation for corruption, racism and incompetence, has prevented them from gaining much respect. If you are the victim of crime while in Prague, don't expect much help – or even concern – from the local constabulary.

Legalities

You are expected to carry your passport or residence card at all times. If you have to deal with police, they are supposed to provide an interpreter for you. Buying or selling street drugs is illegal, and a controversial new law has outlawed the possession of even small quantities. The legal drinking age is 18, but nobody pays any attention.

Street crime

Prague's pickpockets concentrate in tourist areas like Wenceslas Square, Old Town Square, Charles Bridge and the Castle. Keep an eye on your handbag or wallet, especially in crowds and on public tranport. Seedier parts of Prague include parts of Žižkov, parts of Smíchov, the park in front of the Main Station (Hlavní nádraaži), and the lower end of Wenceslas Square and upper end of Národní třída.

Postal services

Stamps are available from the post office, newsagents, tobacconists and most places where postcards are sold. Postcards cost 6 Kč within Europe and 7 Kč outside Europe; regular letters cost 8 Kč within Europe and 10-11 Kč airmail elsewhere. Packages should be wrapped in plain white or brown paper.

Post offices are scattered all over Prague. Though they are being thoroughly modernised, many have different opening hours, offering varying degrees of services and all are confusing. Indeed, the system designating what's on offer at which window is perplexing, even for some Czechs.

The Main Post Office on Jindřišská in Prague 1 offers the most services but is no longer open 24 hours a day pending complete remodelling. At the time of going to press, the Masarykovo nádraži

(Masaryk Station) post office offers the closest thing to 24-hour service (*see below*). Fax, telegram and international phone lines are now located in the annex around the corner at Politických vězňů 4. Some services, like Poste Restante and EMS (Express Mail Service), are theoretically available at all post offices, but are much easier to use at this branch.

You can buy special edition stamps and send mail overnight within the Czech Republic and within a few days to Europe and the rest of the world via EMS – a cheaper but less reliable service than Federal Express and other international courier services For details, *see page 261*.

To send or collect restricted packages or items subject to tax or duty, you must go to the **Customs Post Office** (*see below*). Bring your passport, residence permit and other ID. For incoming packages, you will also need money to pay duties and tax. Outgoing packages weighing more than 2kg, valued upwards of 30,000 Kč or containing 'unusual contents' like medicine or clothing, must officially be cleared through customs, but in practice it is not usually necessary. The export of antiques is strictly restricted. The biggest queues at customs form between 11am and 1.30pm.

Main Post Office

(Hlavní pošta) Jindřišská 14, Prague 1 (postal info 2113 1445/telecom info 232 0837). Metro Můstek/ 3, 9, 14, 24 tram. **Open** all services are available 7am-8pm daily. **Map 4 K5**

Non-Stop Post Office

Masarykovo nádraži, Hybernská 15, Prague 1 (2421 9715/2122 5847). Metro Náměstí republiky. **Open** 12.15am-11.15pm daily. **Map 4 L3**

Customs Post Office

Plzeňská 139, Prague 5 (5701 9105). Metro Anděl, then 4, 7, 9 tram. **Open** 7am-3pm Mon, Tue, Thur, Fri; 7am-6pm Wed.

Useful postal vocabulary

letters   *příjem – výdej listovin*
packages   *příjem – výdej balíčků or balíků*
money transactions   *platby*
stamps   *známky* – usually at window marked *Kolky a ceniny*
special issue stamps   *filatelistický servis*
registered mail   *doporučeně*

Public holidays

See page 5.

Religious services in English

Anglican Church of Prague

Kostel U Klimenta, Klimentská, Prague 1 (231 0094). Metro Náměstí Republiky. **Service** 11am Sun. **Map 4 L4**

Beth Simcha

Uruguayská 7, Prague 2 (2481 2325). Metro Náměstí Míru. **Service** 6pm Fri. **Map 8 A3**

Church of St Joseph

(Sv. Josef) Josefská 4, Prague 1 (5731 5242). Metro Náměstí Republiky. **Service** 10.30am, 6pm Sat, Sun. **Map 4 K3** Catholic services.

International Baptist Church of Prague

Vinohradská 68, Prague 3 (2425 4646). Metro Jiřího z Poděbrad. **Service** 11am Sun. **Map 8 B3**

International Church of Prague

Vrázova 4, Prague 5 (543 072). Metro Anděl. **Service** 11.15am Sun.

Prague Christian Fellowship

Ječná 19 (entry at back of house), Prague 2 (290 623). Metro Karlovo Náměstí. **Service** 3pm Sun. **Map 5 J8**

Telecommunications

Telephones

Virtually all of the public telephones that still take 2 Kč coins are broken; the rest run on telephone cards, which come in denominations from 50-150 units and can be bought at newsstands, post offices and anywhere you see the blue and yellow Telecom sticker in the window. Calls cost 3 Kč for one unit (lasting three minutes from 7am-7pm weekdays, and six minutes from 7pm-7am weekdays, all day weekends and Sundays) for a local call. International calls, which are horrendously expensive, can be made from any telephone box or at the Main Post Office (*see above*).

The international dialling code to the Czech Republic **is 420 and the city code for Prague is 2** (02 within the Czech Republic). To call abroad, dial the prefix 00, the country and the area codes (for UK area codes omit the 0) and then the number. *See page 244.* Eight digits indicate that the number is on a digital switchboard while a four-, five-, six- or seven-digit number indicates an analogue switchboard. Czech Telecom is rapidly digitalising the entire system.

The phone system can never be described as any better than bad, and it's worse when it's raining and the underground lines get wet. It often takes several attempts to get through, and you may get a disconnected tone even when a number is in service.

SPT Czech Telecom

Olšanská 6, Prague 3 (6714 1111). Metro Želivského/5, 9, 16, 19 tram. **Open** 9am-3pm Mon, Wed; 9am-6pm Tue, Thur. **Map 8 D2**

A woman's lot

In the early twentieth century, Czechoslovakia had a vital and progressive feminist tradition. First the Nazis, then the communists, however, executed the era's major feminist leaders, effectively eradicating all traces of the tradition. After the 1948 communist takeover, the party introduced its own brand of so-called feminism. With slogans such as 'Socialism liberates women', this movement's primary aim was to push women into the workforce; meanwhile, tradition demanded that women continue to perform nearly all domestic tasks. Unable to pay full attention to either their families or their careers, many females grew understandably suspicious of anyone promising 'Women's Liberation'.

A decade after the 1989 revolution, it's still common to find a Czech woman who wakes up at five o'clock to cook her family's breakfast, cleans up afterwards, heads off to her full-time job before seven, grocery shops during her lunch hour, hurries home after work to prepare dinner, washes up, then helps the children with their homework or tidies the flat until it's finally time to sleep. While Western women now expect their partners to at least pay lip-service to the idea of domestic equality, many Czech men will cheerfully admit that they have no idea how to boil an egg or wash their own clothes.

On the career front, at least, there are some encouraging signs. With women comprising just over half of the Czech workforce, wage discrepancies have narrowed. Women's wages now average 74 per cent of men's – no triumph, to be sure, but similar to ratios in the West. Unfortunately, though the percentage of women in management positions has more than doubled since the revolution, only two per cent of Czech CEOs are female, and women in positions of power and authority often complain of not being respected or taken as seriously as their male counterparts.

Personal and domestic oppression also linger. The stunning 'supermodel' looks of many Czech women is not as natural as Western visitors may think: experts claim that anorexia affects 60 to 80 per cent of Czech women between 18 and 23. Neither is Czech women's usual deference to their husband's decisions always chosen: wife-battering is estimated to take place in 11.5 per cent of Czech families.

One huge advantage that Czech women have over their Western counterparts is greater governmental and familial support in child-rearing. Czech women taking maternity leave receive 90 per cent of their normal salary for the first six months and can choose to stay home for a further three and a half years without fear of losing their jobs. Since career ramifications can be severe, though, few Czech women stay home the full four years allowed by law. The emotional, and geographical, closeness of most extended families means that Czech grandparents (grandmothers, especially) assume many day-care duties, helping ease the double work-family burden most women face.

With feminism still considered a dirty word here, progress-minded Czech women are little organised to alter the imbalances in their society. Post-communist women's foundations have rarely banded together for strength; instead, scattered small foundations independently promote a number of causes. In spring 1998, however, four of these groups – the **Center for Gender Studies, ProMluv, ProFem** and **La Strada** – teamed up under one roof to open Prague 5's Ženské centrum ('Women's Centre') at Náměstí 14. října 16.

Directory

Faxes & telegrams

You can send faxes and telegrams from the Main Post Office (see page 150) and major hotels. A fax costs the same per minute as for a phone call, a telegram is usually 26 Kč plus 1.70 Kč per word (up to ten letters). Faxes to your name can be received at any time of the day or night at 00 420 2 2423 0303/2421 5146, for a cost of 30 Kč for the first page and 9 Kč per page thereafter.

Mobile phones, pagers & voicemail

The recent introduction of competition has led to improved services and lower rates in the past year. The two main companies are listed below – they offer different payment schemes and coverage areas, so it's best to get details of both before deciding.

EuroTel
Sokolovská 855/225, Prague 9 (6701 6711/6701 1111/0601 601 601/infotel 670 1666/fax 6701 1266/www.eurotel.cz). Metro Českomoravská/8 tram. **Open** 8am-6pm Mon-Fri.
The leading provider of cellphone services and a subsidiary of telephone monopoly SPT Telecom.

Paegas
Londýnská 57-59, Prague 2 (0603 603 603/fax 0603 603 606). Metro I.P. Pavlova. **Open** 9am-5pm Mon-Fri. **Map 6 M8**
The new kid on the block. Prices are generally lower than at Eurotel, but the coverage (especially outside of Prague) may not be as extensive.

Radiokontakt Operator
Skokanská 1, Prague 6 (323 434/328 451-3/fax 328 754). Bus 191. **Open** 8am-5pm Mon-Fri.
The pager service subsidiary of SPT Czech Telecom.

Radiomobil
Londýnská 57, Prague 2 (0603 603 603/fax 691 9330/2162 0225). Metro I.P. Pavlova. **Open** 9am-5pm Mon-Fri. **Map 6 M8**
The welcome arrival of this new mobile phone company should precipitate a price war that will bring down the prohibitive cost of cell services.

Venus International
Sokolská 42, Prague 2 (9618 1818/fax 9618 7780). Metro I.P. Pavlova. **Open** 9am-5pm Mon-Fri. **Map 6 K8**
Offers voicemail services starting at around 300 Kč a month. The company can also provide a callback service.

Internet

The number of companies offering Internet access is growing and services are improving. The standard rate for individual accounts, including browsing time and e-mail, starts at about 500 Kč a month. Corporate and leased lines are also available and rates rise according to the connection speed and number of accounts.

The main Internet providers in Prague are listed below. Alternatively, a good list of Czech providers is kept at *sgi.felk.cvut.cz/~prikryl/providers.html*. You can check out this and other sites at one of Prague's growing number of Internet cafés (see page 139).

Spinet
Pod Smetankou 12, Prague 9 (2462 4461/fax 825 493/info@spinet.cz). Metro Palmovka, then 168, 261 bus. **Open** 8am-4.30pm Mon-Fri.
Spinet offers dial-up service at competitive rates. Also does design work to order.

Terminal Bar
Soukenická 6, Prague 1 (2187 1111/fax 2187 1910/online@terminal.cz/www.terminal.cz). Metro Náměstí Republiky. **Open** 9am-2am Mon-Fri; 10am-2am Sat; 10am-1am Sun. **Map 4 L2**
The market leader, offering dial-up services for PC and Macintosh users. Standard rates, generally friendly and reliable (but occasionally rather flaky) service. Specialises in web page design. Not bad coffee, too.

Video On Line
Rybná 14, Prague 1 (2184 4333/fax 2184 4335/info@i.vol.cz). Metro Náměstí Republiky. **Open** 9am-5.30pm Mon-Fri. **Map 4 K2**
Oriented mainly towards corporate accounts, and also provides consulting and intranet services.

The Czech Republic is on Central European Time (CET), one hour ahead of the UK, and uses the 24-hour clock. The Czechs are prompt, and you should never be more than 15 minutes late for a meeting.

That Prague is such a beautiful city helps to make up a little for its lousy weather.

Spring
The best season in Prague – that is, when it bothers to show at all. The city comes out of hibernation from a long, cold, cloudy winter. While it is not unheard of for there to be snow lingering on as late as 1 May, temperatures are often perfect for strolling. *Averages*: **March** 0 to 7°C (5 hours sun/65mm rain); **April** 3 to 12°C (6 hours sun/78mm rain); **May** 8 to 17°C (8 hours sun/63mm rain).

Summer
Prague citizens usually abandon the city to the tourist hordes by heading for their summer cottages (*chatas*) or to the seaside. Summers are pleasant, warm (rarely hot) and prone to thundery showers. The days are long, and it stays light until 10pm. *Averages*: **June** 12 to 21°C (9 hours sun/50mm rain); **July** 13 to 23°C (9 hours sun/25mm rain); **August** 14 to 22°C (8 hours sun/50mm rain).

Autumn
This can be the prettiest time of year, with crisp cool air and sharp blue skies, but can also be the wettest. September is a good month to visit the city. The streets are once again jammed with cars, the parks full of children, and the restaurants full of local business people plotting their next move. The days grow shorter alarmingly quickly. By the end of October, the sun sets at around 5.30pm. *Averages*: **September** 10 to 17°C (6 hours sun/55mm rain; **October** 5 to 14°C (4 hours sun/100mm rain); **November** 1 to 5°C (2 hours sun/110mm rain).

Winter
Street-side carp sellers and Christmas markets help break the monotony of the long, cold, grey winter. When it snows, Prague is so beautiful and white that you forget for a few minutes the winter-long gloom that blankets the city. Sadly, bright, white snows are rarely accompanied by clear blue skies. Many residents still burn coal for heating, and by midwinter the smog is so bad, you can't see across the river.

Averages: **December** -2 to 0°C (1 hour sun/76mm rain); **January** -5° to 0°C (22 hours sun/62mm rain); **February** -4 to 1°C (3 hours sun/73mm rain).

Tipping

Czechs tend to round up restaurant bills, often only by a few crowns, but foreigners are more usually expected to leave a ten per cent tip. If service is bad, however, don't feel obliged to leave anything. Service is often added on automatically for large groups. Taxi drivers expect you to round the fare up, but, if you've just been ripped off, don't give a heller.

Toilets

Usually called a 'WC' (pronounced 'veh-tseh'), the word for toilet is *záchod* and the usual charge for using one is 2 or 3 Kč. Calls of nature can be answered in all metro stations 8am-8pm or longer, many fast-food joints and department stores. 'Ladies' in Czech is *Dámy* or *Ženy*, and 'Gents' is *Páni* or *Muži*.

Visas

Citizens of the US, EC and most other European countries don't need a visa to enter the Czech Republic for stays of up to 30 days – just a valid passport with at least six months to run by the end of your visit. Citizens of most other countries can usually get a visa at Prague airport or at these border crossing points: Znojmo-Hatě, Dolni Dvořiště and Rozvadov. For visa information call *00 420 2 6144 1119*. Australians should obtain a single-entry six-month visa from a Czech embassy abroad or they face a 1,500 Kč charge for a visa at the border, good for only five days. Canadians need no visa and are, like Americans, allowed 30 days as tourists.

For stays of up to three months, you are technically required to register at the local police station within 30 days of arriving (if you are staying at a hotel this will be done for you). After three months, all foreigners must obtain

extended visas or a residence permit (*občanský průkaz*), which isn't easy to get (*see page 265*).

The Czech police conduct periodic crackdowns on illegal aliens. They're usually aimed at Romanians, Ukrainians, Vietnamese and other nationals considered undesirable, though a few Brits and Americans usually get caught. Even so, most expats reside here illegally. Many solve the problem by leaving the country once every three months. If you choose this option, be sure to get the required stamp in your passport as you leave by saying 'razítko prosím'.

Weights & measures

The Czechs use the metric system, and even sell eggs in batches of five or ten. Things are usually measured out in decagrams or *deka* (10 grams) or *deciliters* or *deci* (10 centilitres). So a regular glass of wine is usually two *deci* (abbreviated *dcl*), and ham enough for a few sandwiches is 20 *deka* (abbreviated *dkg*).

Getting to Prague

By air

Prague's only airport, **Ruzyně**, has been recently expanded and is about 20km (12.5 miles) north-west of the centre, and is not directly accessible by metro or tram. Some hotels provide a pick-up service from the airport if you book ahead and there is a regular public bus service.

For information in English on arrivals and departures call *2011 3314*, for other airport information call *2011 3321*.

Taxi

Airport taxis are regulated but often charge illegally high prices. The ride, which should take about 20-25 minutes, should cost around 300 Kč to the centre. Check the airport

information kiosk for the going rate to your destination. For a more honest taxi try taking your luggage to the customs depot (where people accept air-freighted shipments from abroad), and phone one of the local taxi services to fetch you (*see p256*). They will not pick you up at the regular arrivals /departures area, though.

Express airport bus

Two express buses run every half hour from the airport into town, first stopping in Prague 6 at Dejvická metro – the end station on the green Line A – and then at Revoluční třída in Prague 1. The Welcome Touristic bus runs 8.30am-7pm, and the Čeda bus runs 4.30am-11.30pm. The express bus service is quick and cheap at 15 Kč for the 20-minute ride to Dejvická and 30 Kč for the 35-minute ride to Revoluční třída in Prague 1. Night bus 510 goes from the airport to Divoká Šárka, where you can catch night tram 51 to the centre.

Local bus

Three local buses run from the airport to metro stations about every 20 minutes from 5am to midnight. Bus 119 runs from the airport to Dejvická metro (green Line A), bus 108 goes to Hradčanská metro (green Line A) and bus 179 goes to Nové Butovice metro (yellow Line B). This is the cheapest, slowest and most crowded alternative. If you have a lot of luggage, you will need to buy extra tickets for your bags. The buses depart from the stands in front of the arrivals hall. There you'll find orange public transport ticket machines (you'll need change to buy tickets). There are also ticket machines and an information office in the airport lobby. For ticket details, *see below*.

By train

International trains arrive at the Main Station (Hlavní nádraži, sometimes called

Directory

Wilson Station or Wilsonovo nádraži) and Holešovice Station (Nádraži Holešovice) – both on the red Line C of the metro. It's easy to get off at Holešovice thinking that it is the main station. If your train stops at both, wait for the last stop.

The centrally located Main Station is a beautiful art nouveau building with communist-period lower halls. It's got food stalls and a PIS information office in the main hall and showers and a 24-hour left luggage area below in the lower hall.

It's not a good idea to hang around in the small park outside the station – locals have nicknamed it Sherwood Forest because so much illegal redistribution of wealth goes on here.

24-hour rail infoline

(2422 4200/2461 4030).
National and international timetable information. English spoken. For ticket prices, call *2461 5249* (8am-7pm daily).

Holešovice Station

(Nádraži Holešovice) Vrbenského, Prague 7 (2461 5865). Metro Nádraži Holešovice/12, 25 tram. **Map 7 E1**

Main Station

(Hlavní nádraži) Wilsonova, Prague 2 (2422 4200/2461 4030). Metro Hlavní Nádraži/12, 25 tram. **Map 4 M5**

Masaryk Station

(Masarykovo nádraži) Hybernská, Prague 1 (2461 4030/2422 4200). Metro Náměstí Republiky/3, 5, 14, 24, 26 tram. **Map 4 L3**

Smíchov Station

(Smíchovské nádraži) Nádražní, Prague 5 (542 797). Metro Smíchovské nádraži/12 tram.

By coach

Florenc coach station may be the least pleasant place in Prague. Perhaps its best feature is that it is on two metro lines (yellow Line B and red Line C) so you can make a quick getaway. Late-night arrivals can take the night tram or a taxi or stay overnight in one of the hotels on Na Poříčí, the main street in front of the station.

The easiest place to buy coach tickets is **Čedok** (*see page 246*).

Kingscourt Express

Havelská 8, Prague 1 (2423 4583/ 2423 3334). Metro Můstek.
Open 8am-6pm Mon-Fri; 9am-1pm Sat.
Kingscourt Express is the biggest company running coach services to and from the UK.

Getting around Prague

Walking is the best way to see central Prague. Every twist of the city's ancient streets reveals some new curiosity. The centre is full of intriguing alleys, sudden broad squares, covered arcades and pedestrian-only precincts. Walking is also often faster than taking a taxi or public transport.

Greater Prague is a different story, spreading out into a sprawl of distant tower blocks. But the city has an excellent, inexpensive and pretty much 24-hour integrated public transport system that will get you almost anywhere you want to go.

Driving in Prague takes some getting used to, and it really isn't worth the bother on a short visit. Taxis are ubiquitous but unreliable – pretty cheap if you find an honest driver; ruinous if you let one rip you off.

Because the communists dammed the Vltava so thoroughly, there isn't any real freight or passenger traffic on the river – just pleasure cruises.

An assortment of eccentric conveyances – horse-drawn carriages, bike-taxis and an electric train thing that takes tourists up to the Castle and back – can all be found in Old Town Square.

Public transport

The places in Prague you can't get to using a combination of metro, tram, bus and occasionally train are places you wouldn't want to go anyway.

There are bus and/or tram connections and usually taxi stands at every metro station, and all of Prague's railway stations except Masaryk are connected to the metro network.

Public transport runs round the clock. Regular day service is from about 5am to noon. Peak times are 5am-8pm Monday to Friday. From about midnight to 5am, night buses and night trams take over.

Metro, tram and bus lines are shown on most city maps, but roadworks often cause unpredictable stoppages or

detours, especially during summer.

Timetables can be found at each tram and bus stop. Posted times apply to the stop where you are – which is highlighted on the schedule. If your destination is listed below the highlighted stop, you are in the right place.

Tickets (jízdenky)

Tickets are good for any mode of transport (metro, bus, tram, even the funicular). In 1996, the city introduced transit zones – two inside and four outside Prague city limits. Most locals have passes (which is why you don't see them punching tickets). Buying a pass is probably the easiest option for you, too – if only to avoid the rigmarole at ticket machines.

The machines have control panels covered with buttons, but only two ticket types need concern you. An 8 Kč ticket entitles you to one 15-minute ride on one piece of transport above ground, or one ride of up to four stops on the metro. It is not valid for night transport, the historical tram or the funicular. A 12 Kč ticket lasts for 60 minutes at peak times and 90 minutes at slow times, allowing unlimited travel throughout Prague, including transfers between metros, buses and trams.

Babies in carriages, children under six, handicapped people, small bags and skis ride free. Children aged six to 15, large items of luggage and other sizeable items need a half-price ticket. Enormous luggage and 'items that stink or look disgusting' aren't allowed on Prague public transport at all. Check with the nearest DP (Prague's Public Transport authority) information office or read the posted information for exhaustive details.

The orange ticket machines are marvels of Czechnology. They have buttons marked with prices. Press once for the ticket you want, twice if you want two tickets (and so on), and then press the 'enter' button. Insert the total amount in coins (the machines do give change) and wait an agonisingly long time for the machine's screeching mechanism to print out each ticket individually. It's worth stocking up on tickets in advance. They can be bought at most tobacconists, DP Information and PIS offices (*see page 264*), or anywhere you see the red-and-yellow DP sticker in the window.

Buy your ticket before entering the transport and stamp it (face up in the direction of the arrow) in a machine as soon as you board a bus or tram or as you enter the 'paid area' of the metro. There are no guards or gates, but plain-clothes inspectors (*revizoři*) carry out random ticket checks. They'll flash a shiny red-and-yellow badge at you and spot fine you 200 Kč if you're travelling without a

valid ticket. The guard should also, on your request, show you his or her photo ID badge and make out a receipt for the fine. Playing the dumb foreigner usually doesn't work.

Travel passes

At most of the places listed above, you can also buy transit passes, which allow unlimited travel on the metro, trams and buses. During working hours, metros with a DP window also sell individual tickets, short-term passes for tourists and long-term passes for residents. Only the 24-hour pass is available at automatic ticket machines.

You must first fill in your full name and date of birth on the reverse side, and then stamp short-term passes as you would an ordinary ticket. The pass is then valid from the time it was stamped. It is invalid if the information on the reverse side is not filled in – even if it is stamped.

24-hour pass	**70 Kč**
3-day pass	**180 Kč**
7-day pass	**250 Kč**
15-day pass	**280 Kč**

Residents usually have long-term passes. All you need to get one is a recent photo and some ID. They are available at the DP windows in some metro stations or at the transit company main offices at Na bojišti 5, Prague 2 (2498 2770). Passes must be filled in with your full name and 'rodné číslo' or other ID number. Coupons inserted in the pass are valid for one day before and three days after the month or other time period shown on the face of the coupon and are not stamped.

One-month pass	**380 Kč**
Three-month pass	**1,000 Kč**
One-year pass	**3,400 Kč**

The metro

The Prague metro network, with a total length of 43.6km (27 miles) running between 46

stations along three lines, is a little copy of the grandiose Moscow metro. The stations are well lit and clearly signposted; trains are clean and frequent. A digital clock on each platform informs you of the time elapsed since the last train came along.

The Prague metro consists of three lines: the **green Line A** (Skalka-Dejvická); the **yellow Line B** (Českomoravská-Zličín); the **red Line C** (Nádraží Holešovice-Háje). A fourth line is due to open sometime early in the twenty-first century.

Transfers (*přestup*) are possible at three stations: Muzeum (between the green Line A and the red Line C), Můstek (between the green Line A and the yellow Line B) and Florenc (between the yellow Line B and the red Line C).

The metro runs from 5am to midnight. At peak times, expect trains every two minutes; at other times every five or ten minutes.

Trams (*tramvaje*)

An electric tram service began in Prague in 1891 and trams have been the preferred method of transport for most Praguers ever since, as they are the most picturesque and convenient of the city's transport services.

Twenty-three daytime tram lines stop at 606 stations along 494km (309 miles) of tram track between 4.30am to midnight – after which eight night trams take over (*see below*). Trams come every six to eight minutes at peak times and ten to 15 minutes at other times. With the newer, boxier trams, you may need to open the automatic doors by pressing the green button.

The best tram lines for seeing the city are the 22, which runs from the Castle to Národní třída and beyond, and the Historical Tram (number 91), which runs from the

Directory

Výstaviště in Prague 7 through Malá Strana, Wenceslas Square, Náměstí Republiky and back to Prague 7. It runs on Saturdays, Sundays and holidays from Easter to the end of October and leaves Výstaviště every hour on the hour from 1pm to 7pm. The complete ride takes 40 minutes, and tickets cost 15 Kč for adults and 7 Kč for children.

Buses (*autobusy*)

Since 1925, buses in Prague have provided transport to places where no other means of public transport dare to go. There are 196 daytime bus lines stopping at 2,060 stations along a 697.5km network. Buses run from about 5am to midnight, after which ten night bus lines take over (*see below*). Buses run every five to 18 minutes at peak times and 15-30 minutes at other times.

Bus infoline
(1034, only in Czech). **Open** 6am-8pm Mon-Fri; 8am-4pm Sat, Sun.

Night trams & buses (*noční tramvaje, noční autobusy*)

Night buses and trams run about every 40 minutes from midnight to 4.30am. Every night tram (with numbers in the 50s) stops at Lazarská crossroads on Spálená. Night buses (501-512) don't have one similar central stop, but many stop at the top of Wenceslas Square (near Muzeum metro) and around the corner from I.P. Pavlova metro. You can buy a guide to night transport – showing all lines, times and stations – at the DP information offices for about 10 Kč.

Disabled access

There are lifts at the following metro stations: Dejvická, Skalka on the green Line A; Zličín, Stodůlky, Luka, Lužiny, Hůrka on the yellow Line B; Nádraží Holešovice, Hlavní

nádraží, Florenc, I.P. Pavlova, Pankrác, Roztyly, Chodov, Opatov and Háje on the red Line C. At some, you must be accompanied by another person to operate the lift. There are two bus lines – 498 and 499 – that consist only of kneeling buses. All of the newer, boxier trams kneel also, but there's no counting on when one is going to come along. You can find out which tram lines are using the newer cars at DP information offices (*see page 246*).

Funicular railway (*lanovka*)

The funicular runs for half a kilometre from the bottom of Petřín hill at Újezd (around the corner from the tram stop of the same name), stopping midway at Nebozízek (at the pricey restaurant of the same name) and continuing to the top of Petřín hill. It runs every ten or 15 minutes between 9.15am and 8.45pm and costs 10 Kč for adults and 5 Kč for children.

Taxis

The appalling reputation of Prague's taxi drivers has caused Prague City Hall to introduce strict guidelines. Even so, you will still get ripped off. The drivers waiting at ranks in obvious tourist locations are all crooks, so avoid them. Hail a moving cab or call one of the services listed below. Make sure you are getting into an authorised taxi (it should be clearly marked as a taxi, with registration numbers and fares printed clearly on the doors and a black-and-white checked stripe along the side). If the driver doesn't turn on the meter, insist that he do so. If he doesn't, either get out of the car immediately, or agree a fee to your destination. Do neither, and the driver will almost certainly demand a ruinous fare at the end of your journey – and maybe resort to violence in collecting it.

Ideally, your taxi experience should go something like this: the driver does not turn on the meter (*taximetr*) until you enter the cab. When he does, 10 Kč appears as the initial amount. While you are driving inside Prague, the rate is set at '1' and should never be more than 12 Kč per kilometre.

When your ride is over, the driver provides you with a receipt (*účet* or *paragon*) that must include the name and address of the taxi company, the taxi registration number, the date of your journey, the times and places of departure and arrival, the rate per kilometre and total mileage, the price of the trip, the driver's name and signature. If the driver does not provide this receipt or if the information on it is incorrect, you are theoretically not required to pay the fare.

In reality, few drivers will provide a receipt unless you request one. Honest cabbies will print one out on the agonisingly slow machine attached to the meter. Rip-off merchants will write you one out on a pad.

At the time of writing, the maximum rates for taxi service – 10 Kč for entering the cab (no matter how many people), 1 Kč a minute for waiting (because of a passenger request or heavy traffic), and no more than 12 Kč per kilometre for normal rides – were scheduled for a slight increase.

AAA
(1080/312 2112).

Acro Taxi
(1088/8388 0153)

ProfiTaxi
(1035/2213 5551).

Taxi complaints
Prague City Hall
Department of Local Revenues (Magistrát hl. m. Prahy), Mariánské náměstí 2, Prague 1 (2448 1111).
Map 3 H3
You could also try the **Taxi Guild** *(2491 6666).*

On foot

It is generally safe to walk anywhere in Prague anytime – using common sense and appropriate caution in the wee hours, of course. Prague does not (yet) have any 'bad' areas that you should avoid (*see page 250* **Street crime**). Beware of bad drivers, though – they'll often try to run you down even if you are on a zebra crossing (crosswalk).

By bicycle

Cycling in Prague is hellish. There are no bike lanes, drivers are oblivious to your presence, and pedestrians yell at you if you ride on the pavement. Mountain bikes are best, as the wide wheels shouldn't get stuck in the tram tracks. Prague does, however, have acres of parkland inside and outside of the centre. On public transport, bicycles are allowed in the last car of metro trains only, and your bike is expected to purchase and stamp its own 6 Kč ticket.

By boat

The Prague Steamship Company (Pražská paroplavební služba) had a monopoly on river traffic way back in 1865 – and still provides the most boat services on the river today. You'll find these, other boat companies plying sightseeing and booze cruises, and rowing boats for hire (*see page 176*) along the right bank of the Vltava.

Prague Steamship Company

(Pražská paroplavební služba) Rašínovo nábřeží, Prague 2 (298 309/293 803). Metro Karlovo náměstí/3, 16, 17 tram. **Map 5 G9**

Driving

One of the first things the Nazis did after occupying the country in 1939 was to switch traffic flow from the left to the right

side of the street. Czechs have been driving on the right side ever since.

The worst driving days are Friday and Sunday, when people who don't know the difference between the clutch and the brake pack their families into old Škodas for a weekend trip to their summer cottage, or *chata*. Czech drivers tend to stop in the middle of intersections on a red light and, since they don't usually bother to stop for pedestrians on a zebra crossing, pedestrians don't usually bother to use them.

Traffic regulations in the Czech Republic are similar to those in most European countries. There is zero tolerance for drinking and driving, though – drivers are not allowed to drink any alcohol at all before driving. Ditto for drugs. Use of safety belts is required in the front and – if the car is equipped with them – in the back seat as well. Children under the age of 12 or anybody shorter than 150cm (5ft 1in) may not ride in the seat next to the driver. Small children must be in approved child safety seats. Trams, which follow different traffic lights than cars, always have the right of way. You must stop behind trams when passengers are getting on and off at a stop where there is no island, and you should avoid driving on tram tracks unless the road offers no alternative.

The maximum speed limit for cars and buses is 90kph (56mph) on roads, 110kph (69mph) on highways, and 60kph (37mph) in villages and towns.

Motorcyclists and their passengers are required to wear helmets, and the maximum speed limit for motorcycles is 90kmph (56mph) on roads and highways and 60kmph (37mph) in villages and towns.

You are required to notify the police of any accident

involving casualties or serious damage to a car. Letters of credit issued by the AIT, FIA or your local national motoring club are usually accepted in the Czech Republic.

If you are driving your own car, you will need international proof of insurance (known as a Green Card – *see below*) and you must pay an annual toll for using the Czech roads. If you rent a car, insurance and toll should be taken care of for you. The toll sticker – which should be displayed on the windshield – costs 400 Kč and can be bought at post offices, most border crossing points and petrol stations. For caravans and other vehicles weighing 3.5-21 metric tons, the cost is 1,000 Kč.

Car hire

Renting a car can be expensive in Prague, with many Western firms charging more than they would back home. It is definitely worth shopping around, as many small local firms charge far less than the big boys. When renting a car be sure to bring your driving licence, passport and credit card with you. The agency should provide you with a green insurance card that permits you to drive across the border. It is also wise to arrange your rental a few days in advance to be sure you get the car you want. In addition to the places listed below, both **American Express** (*see page 249*) and **Čedok** (*see page 246*) can arrange car rental.

A Rent Car

Washingtonova 9, Prague 1 (2421 1587). Metro Muzeum. **Open** 7am-7pm daily. **Rates** *from* 1,990 Kč per day. **Credit** AmEx, DC, MC, V. **Map 4 L5**
Branch: Ruzyně Airport, Prague 6 (2011 4370/367 807).

Autopůjčovna Car-Lend

Hovorčovice (suburb east of Prague). (687 0519/0602 229 155). **Open** 8am-6pm Mon-Fri. **Rates** *from* 550 Kč per day. **No credit cards**.

Expats: the Left Bank left behind

Expatriate Prague isn't what it used to be. As the city slowly solidifies into a normal European capital, not only bohemian slacker-types but also expatriate businesspeople are leaving the city in increasing numbers.

The *Prague Post*'s editor-in-chief Alan Levy is largely responsible – or guilty, depending on your viewpoint – for sparking the media rush that publicised Prague as the new bohemia. After Levy dubbed the city 'the Left Bank of the '90s' back in 1991, wads of newspaper and magazine articles, TV news features, documentary films and even master's theses hurried to cash in on the clever catchphrase, drawing convenient (if stunningly oversimplified and often patently untrue) parallels between the American expatriate communities in Paris in the 1920s and Prague in the 1990s.

Unfortunately, the journalists involved often ignored the actual goings-on and misquoted the participants – most of whom had no desire to categorise their adopted city as anything but the Prague of the 1990s – in their eagerness to portray Bohemia's foreign residents as beret-wearing, Gauloise-puffing, hard-drinking, Hemingway-emulating literary wannabes. Nonetheless, the cliché sold well, and the media attention encouraged still more arrivals. Between 1992 and 1995, liberal doses of Aussies, Brits, Scandinavians and Germans mingled with loads of Americans, creating a vital and transient expatriate 'scene' that swirled around Sunday-night poetry readings, buskers on Charles Bridge and an ever-changing smattering of nightclubs and bars.

Meanwhile, a less transient bunch of foreigners existed quietly alongside the bohemians. English teachers, office workers, lawyers, environmentalists, businesspeople (often with their families in tow) and entrepreneurs were all taking advantage of the city's ample job opportunities and as-yet-unfilled market niches.

These days, the numbers of Western expatriates are dwindling in all categories. The salary-to-cost-of-living ratio has worsened in the past few years, the excitement of participating in a historical political transition has dulled as Prague grows more and more Western, and the lure of untapped business opportunities has faded as the underlying shakiness of the Czech economy becomes evident. The number of expatriates working in managerial, professional and administrative positions in the Czech Republic has declined steadily over the past several years, as most companies now prefer Czech employees, who are cheaper to hire and tend to stay longer.

Record levels of Czech unemployment (five per cent in early 1998) have induced government promises to toughen the procedures by which non-natives obtain residence permits. But analysts complain that these procedures are already unusually difficult, and that Prague's five per cent foreign population is far lower than the 10-15 per cent seen in most major European capitals, and that anyhow most work permits are for blue collar jobs, which foreigners are content to take for less pay than Czechs. In fact, contrary to all the Western media hype, Slovaks, Ukrainians and Russians comprise the largest number of foreign residents in Prague, with Chinese and Vietnamese next in line and Americans and other Western nationals trailing far behind. Despite the threats, however, the government's instability since autumn 1997 has prevented the proposed laws from being passed and, while 54,000 foreigners held legal work permits in Prague in early 1998, experts estimate hundreds of thousands more work illegally.

As for the remains of Prague's expatriate bohemian community, some still party heavily. Nowadays, though, they mingle extensively with hip young Czechs, who often constitute half the clientele at foreign-operated bars and cafés such as **Terminal Bar** (*see page 144*), **Chapeau Rouge** (*see page 139*) and **The Globe** (*see page 151*). Most of the artsy types have moved away, gone into journalism, or turned into serious writers who spend more time at the keyboard than tippling in bars. Some can be sighted at the long-running Beefstew readings at **Radost** (*see page 152*), but the open mike now provides a forum for at least as many stand-up comics, storytellers and musicians as writers.

Free delivery of a Škoda Favorit (550 Kč per day) to your door, or the more upmarket Felicia (600 Kč per day). Long-term leases also available. Call in advance to reserve your vehicle with the help of a Czech speaker.

Avis

Klimentská 46, Prague 1 (2185 1225). Metro Florenc/3, 8 tram. **Open** 7am-6pm Mon-Fri; 8am-2pm Sat; 8am-1pm Sun. **Rates** *from* 2,852 Kč for 1 day; 3,500 Kč for 2 days. **Credit** AmEx, DC, EC, MC, V. **Map 4 M1**

Branch: Ruzyně Airport, Prague 6 (316 6739/2011 4270).

Budget

Čistovická 100, Prague 6 (302 5713). Tram 8, 22. **Open** 8am-4.30pm Mon-Fri. **Rates** *from* 2,690

Kč per day. **Credit** AmEx, DC, EC, MC, V. **Map 3 H1**
Branch: Ruzyně Airport, Prague 6 (316 5214; 7am-10pm daily).

European Inter Rent/ National Car Rental

Pařížská 28, Prague 1 (2481 0515/ 2481 1920). Metro Staroměstská/17, 18 tram. **Open** 8am-8pm daily.
Rates *from* 3,200 Kč per day.
Credit AmEx, MC, V. **Map 3 H2**
Branches in most of the major cities in the Czech Republic.

Hertz

Karlovo náměsti 28, Prague 2 (291 851/290 122/292 147). Metro Karlovo náměsti/3, 4, 6, 14, 16, 18, 22, 24, 34 tram. **Open** 8am-8pm daily. **Rates** *from* 999 Kč per day.
Credit AmEx, DC, EC, MC, V.
Map 5 H7

Car insurance

You need a Green Card as international proof of insurance. This should be issued by your usual insurer at home before you go. Should the Green Card expire, you can buy short-term insurance from the Czech insurance agency Česká pojišťovna for 3,000 Kč a month. For long-term insurance, you'll need to register your car with the Czech authorities (paying something like half the cost of the car in duties and tax), get a *technický průkaz* and sign up for *Povinné ručeni* – the minimum insurance necessary by law.

Česká pojišťovna

Spálená 14, Prague 1 (2409 2904/2409 2111). Metro Národni třída/6, 9, 18, 22 tram. **Open** 8am-6pm Mon-Fri; 9am-4pm Sat; 9am-noon Sun. **Map 5 H6**

Czech motoring clubs

ÚAMK/Central Office of the Central Motoring Club Prague

(Ústředni automotoklub) Na strži 9, Prague 4 (6110 4111). Metro Budějovická, then 118, 121, 124, 205 bus. **Open** 8.30am-4.30pm Mon-Fri.
Call *123/6122 0220* for 'Yellow Angel' 24-hour emergency road service.

Czech Automobile Club

(Autoklub České republiky) Opletalova 29, Prague 1 (2422 1820/2423 0506). Metro Hlavni nádraži.
Open 8am-6pm Mon-Fri.
Call *124* for 'ABA' 24-hour emergency road service.

Parking

Parking can be hellish in Prague and in larger cities in the Czech Republic. Look out for special zones (usually providing one to five parking spaces) reserved for area residents and businesses. If you park illegally, your car can be towed away (call *158*) or clamped – both of which are a major pain. It could cost around 1,000 Kč to retrieve your vehicle, more if it is towed away and left for a while. Don't be surprised if you are ripped off. If you're new in town, the easiest and safest option is to leave your vehicle in a car park. Choose a guarded one if possible.

Parking meters dispense tickets that should be placed face up on the dashboard and

Road emergencies

ABA Autoklub
Bohemia Assistance
124, 0124, 261 491
ADOS Assistance
6731 0713
Central Automobile Club (ústředni automotoklub)
123, 0123, 154, 777 521, 773 455
Service *24*
(for lorries) *472 6243*

be visible through the windscreen. There are three parking zones – orange, green and blue. The orange zone is for stops up to two hours and costs a minimum of 10 Kč for 15 minutes, and 40 Kč for one hour. The green zone is for stays of up to six hours. It costs 15 Kč for 30 minutes, 30 Kč for an hour and 120 Kč for six hours. Parking is free in green zones from 6pm to 8am and on Sundays (on Saturdays, too, in some areas). The blue zone only permits long-term parking for local residents and businesses. Ignore the restrictions at your peril.

Park & ride car parks with direct metro access

Green A line Hradčanská – Milady Horákové; Dejvická – Vítězné náměsti (Prague 6); Strašnická – V olšinách; Skalka – V Rybničkách (both Prague 10).

Yellow B line Nové Butovice – Bucharova; Radlická – Radlická (both Prague 5).

Red C line Opatov – Hrnčiřská (Prague 4).

Directory

Remember, remember the fifth of Leaves Falling

The Slav months are designated by descriptive nouns. So here you have New Year's Day on the 1st of Icy; beware the Ides of Pregnancy; lament that Oak is the cruellest month; go gathering nuts in Blossom; celebrate Summer Solstice on the 21st of Redder; head off on your summer holiday in Sickle; hum along to Kurt Weill's Blazing Song; commemorate Lenin's Rutting Revolution; remember, remember the fifth of Leaves Falling; and celebrate Christmas on the 25th of Please.

Petrol & service

An increasing number of petrol filling stations are open 24 hours a day. Leaded fuel (octane 90) is called Special, leaded fuel (octane 96) is known as Super, and unleaded fuel (95D) is called Natural. Super Plus 98 and diesel fuel are also available. A booklet listing all the petrol and service stations (and also including information on selected car parks) in Prague is available from the Prague Information Service offices (*see page 246*).

Business

National agencies

The following can provide their fellow countrymen with market research, useful contacts, potential Czech partners, publications and trade directories, and low-cost consulting services. Advice is also available on reciprocal trade agreement, tax treaties and other issues.

British Embassy Commercial Section

Na příkopě 21, Prague 1 (2224 0021/fax 2224 3625). Metro Můstek. **Open** 8.30am-5pm Mon-Fri. **Map 4 K4**

Irish Trade Board

Tržiště 13, Prague 1 (530 914/5/fax 5731 1494). Metro Malostranská/12, 22 tram. **Open** 9am-1pm, 2-5pm, Mon-Fri. **Map 2 D3**

US Embassy Foreign Commercial Service

Tržiště 15, Prague 1 (5732 0663/fax 5732 0920). Metro Malostranská/12, 22 tram. **Open** 9am-1pm, 2-5pm, Mon-Fri. **Map 2 D3**

Government agencies

Czechinvest

Politických vězňů 20, Prague 1 (2422 1540/fax 2422 1804). Metro Muzeum/3, 9, 14, 24 tram. **Open** 9am-4.30pm Mon-Fri. **Map 4 L5**
This Czech government agency encourages large-scale direct foreign investment and assists in joint ventures. Staff can research Czech contacts in fields of interest.

Economic Chamber of the Czech Republic

(Hospodářská komora ČR) Argentinská 38, Prague 7 (6679 4883/fax 6671 0805/ hkcrinf@traveller.cz). Metro Nádraží Holešovice. **Open** 8am-4pm Mon-Thur. **Map 7 E2**

Provides background information on Czech industrial sectors, companies and economic trends. The chamber also establishes trade contacts and provides business information for foreign and local companies.

Banking

Anyone can open a bank account in the Czech Republic, although some banks will require a minimum deposit. Corporate bank accounts require special paperwork. Banks generally charge high fees and current accounts do not bear interest. Most banks have some English-speaking staff. Service is improving, but still expect long queues, short opening hours and lots of burdensome paperwork – even on relatively simple transactions. Czech banks usually cater to individual account holders, while foreign banks are largely geared to corporate accounts. The four main Czech banks are listed below. All provide a similar range of services.

Česká spořitelna

Rytířská 29, Prague 1 (2410 1111). Metro Můstek. **Open** 8am-5pm Mon-Thur; 8am-4pm Fri. **Map 3 J4**
Geared toward domestic savings accounts. Operates a large ATM network throughout the city.

Československá obchodní banka (ČSOB)

See p249.

Komerční banka

See p249.

Živnostenská banka

See p249.

About 30 international and foreign banks are represented in the Czech Republic. Many offer at least some traditional banking services, although most cater exclusively to wealthier private clients or corporate accounts, or offer only consulting or other secondary services.

Bank Austria

Revoluční 15, Prague 1 (2489 2111). Metro Náměstí Republiky. **Open** 8.30am-noon, 1-4pm, Mon-Thur; 8.30am-2pm Fri. **Map 4 K2**

Citibank

Evropská 178, Prague 6 (2430 4111). Tram 20, 26. **Open** 9am-4.30pm Mon-Fri.

Hypobank

Štěpánská 27, Prague 1 (2110 6111). Metro Můstek. **Open** 9am-noon, 1-4pm, Mon-Thur; 9am-12.30pm Fri. **Map 6 K6**
Offers a full range of banking services. Growing number of branches around the country.

Publications

See also page 163 **Media**.

Business Central Europe

(Editorial offices) Schwarzenbergplatz 8/4, 1030 Vienna, Austria (431 713 3363/fax 431 714 0113).
Monthly economic and business magazine published by *The Economist*. Covers the whole of Central Europe and the former Soviet Union and regularly includes stories on the Czech Republic.

Central European Business Weekly

Sudoměřská 32, Prague 3 (627 4479/fax 627 4479). Metro Flora.
Prague-based business weekly with full coverage of Central and Eastern Europe.

Central European Economic Review

(Editorial offices) Boulevard Brand Whitlock 87, 1200 Brussels, Belgium.
A monthly regional overview published by the *Wall Street Journal*. Tends to focus on finance, banking and capital markets.

The Fleet Sheet
PO Box 67, Prague 3 (2210 5515/
fax 2422 1580/fleet@traveller.cz).
A daily one-page digest of the Czech
press with good coverage of major
political and financial events. Sent
out as a fax each morning.

Newsline/Radio Free Europe
Vinohradská 1, Prague 2 (2112
1111/webmaster@rferl.org/
www.rferl.org).
Dry but highly informative daily
overview of events in Eastern Europe
and the former Soviet Union.
Produced in co-operation with
Prague-based Radio Free
Europe/Radio Liberty. Information is
available as an e-mail service or from
RFE's comprehensive website.

Prague Business Journal
Sokolská 22, Prague 2 (2426 1360/
fax 2426 1361/subscribe@pbj.cz/
www.ceebiz.com).
Weekly business newspaper focusing
on Prague and the Czech Republic.
Highly informative.

The Prague Post
Na Poříčí 20, Prague 1 (2487 5000/
fax 2487 5050/www.praguepost.cz).
Weekly newspaper with good
coverage of business, banking and
capital markets. Highlights and major
stories available free on its website.

The Prague Tribune
Nádražní 32, Prague 5 (548 072/
fax 542 289).
Glossy, bilingual Czech-English
monthly mag with an emphasis on
business, social issues and features.

Radio Prague E-News
Vinohradská 12, Prague 2
(2409 4608/www.radio.cz).
Czech state radio offers free e-mail
copy of daily news bulletins in
English, Czech and other languages.
Informative website with links to
other Internet-based info sources.

Resources
Ječná 39, Prague 2 (2494 1800/fax
2494 3884/resource@mbox.vol.cz/
www.resources.cz).
Offers a comprehensive and practical
directory of business contacts in
Prague and Bratislava.

Stock exchange

The Prague Stock Exchange
trades about 50 companies in its
top-tier listing. Several dozen
brokerages, including most of
the major banks, can place buy
and sell orders. Liquidity is
good, although insider trading
has been a problem.

Prague Stock Exchange (PX)
Rybná 14, POB 49, Prague 1 (2183
1111/fax 2183 3040/program@
pse.vol.cz). Metro Náměstí Republiky.
Open 8am-4.30pm Mon-Fri.
Map 4 K3

Business services

Accounting firms

The 'Big Six' international
accounting firms are well established on the market and can
offer a full range of services.
There are also hundreds of
local companies and
partnerships that provide basic
book-keeping and payroll
services. All operate standard
business hours (9am-5pm
Mon-Fri).

Coopers & Lybrand
Karlovo náměstí 17, Prague 2 (2491
7074/fax 290 095). Metro Karlovo
náměstí. **Map 5 H7**

Deloitte & Touche
Týn 4/641, Prague 1 (2489 5500/
fax 2489 5555). Metro Náměstí
Republiky. **Map 3 J3**

KPMG
Jana Masaryka 12, Prague 2 (691
0194/fax 691 0480). Metro Náměstí
Míru. **Map 6 M10**
Smaller and more personal than the
other agencies, KPMG is known for
its financial planning and technical
expertise.

Price Waterhouse
Římská 15, Prague 2 (2440 8333/
fax 2440 8444). Metro Náměstí
Míru. **Map 8 A3**
Accounting specialists whose
auditors have a good reputation.

Computer rental & leasing
See also page 159.

APS
Opletalova 55, Prague 1 (2421 5147/
apscorp@mbox.vol.cz). Metro Hlavní
nádraží. **Open** 9am-5pm Mon-Fri.
No credit cards. Map 4 L4
Flexible PC leasing options.

MacSource
Krkonošská 2, Prague 2 (627
2224/fax 627 2228). Metro Jiřího z
Poděbrad. **Open** 9am-6pm Mon-Fri.
Credit AmEx, MC, V.
Map 8 B2
Specialises in Macintosh equipment.
Can lease or rent, short or long term.

Courier/messenger services

Express Parcel System (EPS)
Patočkova 3, Prague 6 (2031 6111).
Open 8am-6.30pm Mon-Fri.
Citywide cycle service. Also delivers
to destinations within the Czech
Republic. Offers 'urgent' collection
service within 30 minutes.

Messenger Service
Patočkova 3, Prague 6 (2031 6111).
Open 7.30am-11pm daily.
Guarantees one-hour collection and
two-hour delivery.

Estate agents

Finding reasonably priced and
adequate office space can be
challenging. Estate agents tend
to push more expensive proper-
ties in order to maximise their
commissions. Make sure that
any space has adequate (ie
modern) phone lines and isn't
due in the near future for noisy
or disruptive repairs. If
parking is important, choose
a space outside of the
congested centre.

Apollo
Záhřebská 33, Prague 2 (258 359/
fax 2425 4361). Metro Náměstí
Míru. **Open** 9am-5.30pm Mon-Fri.
Map 6 M9
Lease and sale of commercial and
private real estate. Provides financial
and development consulting.

Nexus
Belgická 36, Prague 2 (2423 1730/
fax 2423 1731). Metro Náměstí
Míru. **Open** 9am-6pm Mon-Fri.
Map 6 M9
Serves small and medium-sized
businesses.

Express mail services

DHL
Aviatická 1048/12, Prague 6 (2030
0111/fax 2151 2424). Metro
Dejvická, then bus 191 or Metro
Nové Butovice, then bus 179 to
Letiště Ruzyně stop. **Open** 24 hours
for phone deliveries.
Offers a daily pick-up service until
6pm weekdays and 3pm on
Saturdays.
Branches: Na Poříčí 4, Prague 1
(2422 9887); Klimentská 46, Prague 1
(2185 1093); Lipová 10, Prague 2 (296
585); Jankovcova 2, Prague 7 (6678
2195); IBC Building, Pobřežní 3,
Prague 8 (232 3712); Počernická 96,
Prague 10 (6702 1235).

Directory

Vocab

For food and drink vocabulary, *see page 133.*

Pronunciation

a	as in g*a*p	á	as in f*a*ther
e	as in l*e*t	é	as in *ai*r
i, y	as in l*i*t	í, ý	as in s*ee*d
o	as in l*o*t	ó	as in l*o*re
u	as in b*oo*k	ú, ů	as in l*oo*m
c	as in i*ts*	č	as in *ch*in
ch	as in lo*ch*		
ď	as in *d*uty		
ň	as in o*ni*on		
ř	as a standard r, but flatten the tip of the tongue making a short forceful buzz like **ž**		
š	as in *sh*in		
ť	as in s*t*ew		
ž	as in plea*s*ure		
dž	as in *G*eorge		

Handy words & phrases

Czech words are always stressed on the first syllable.

hello/good day	*dobrý den*
good evening	*dobrý večer*
good night	*dobrou noc*
goodbye	*na shledanou*
yes	*ano* (often abbreviated to *no*)
no	*ne*
please	*prosím*
thank you	*děkuji*
excuse me	*promiňte*
sorry	*pardon*
help!	*pomoc!*
attention!	*pozor!*
I don't speak Czech	*Nemluvím česky*
I don't understand	*Nerozumím*
do you speak English?	*mluvíte anglicky?*
sir	*pán*
madam	*paní*
open	*otevřeno*
closed	*zavřeno*
I would like…	*chtěl bych…*
how much is it?	*kolik to stojí?*
may I have a receipt, please?	*účet, prosím?*
can we pay, please?	*prosím, zaplatíme?*
where is…?	*kde je…?*
go left	*doleva*
go right	*doprava*
straight	*rovně*
far	*daleko*
near	*blízko*
good	*dobrý*
bad	*špatný*
big	*velký*
small	*malý*
no problem	*to je v pořádku*
who are you rooting for?	*máš rád(a)?*
cool shades!	*máš dobře vychytaný brejle!*
It's a rip-off	*to je zloděejina*
I'm absolutely knackered	*jsem úplně na dně*
the lift is stuck	*výtah zůstal viset*
could I speak to Václav?	*mohl bych mluvit s Václavem?*

Street names, etc

avenue	*třída*
bridge	*most*
church	*kostel*
embankment	*nábřeží* or *nábř.*
gardens	*sady* or *zahrada*
island	*ostrov*
lane	*ulička*
monastery, convent	*klášter*
park	*park*
square	*náměstí* or *nám.*
station	*nádraží* or *nádr.*
steps	*schody*
street	*ulice* or *ul.*
tunnel	*tunel*

In conversation, as in this Guide, most Prague addresses are referred to by their name only, leaving off *ulice, třída* and so on.

Numbers

0 *nula* 1 *jeden* 2 *dva* 3 *tři* 4 *čtyři* 5 *pět* 6 *šest* 7 *sedm* 8 *osm* 9 *devět* 10 *deset* 11 *jedenáct* 12 *dvanáct* 13 *třináct* 14 *čtrnáct* 15 *patnáct* 16 *šestnáct* 17 *sedmnáct* 18 *osmnáct* 19 *devatenáct* 20 *dvacet* 30 *třicet* 40 *čtyřicet* 50 *padesát* 60 *šedesát* 70 *sedmdesát* 80 *osmdesát* 90 *devadesát* 100 *sto* 1,000 *tisíc*

Days of the week

Monday *pondělí* **Tuesday** *úterý* **Wednesday** *středa* **Thursday** *čtvrtek* **Friday** *pátek* **Saturday** *sobota* **Sunday** *neděle*

Months & seasons

January *leden* **February** *únor* **March** *březen* **April** *duben* **May** *květen* **June** *červen* **July** *červenec* **August** *srpen* **September** *září* **October** *říjen* **November** *listopad* **December** *prosinec*

Spring *jaro* **Summer** *léto* **Autumn** *podzim* **Winter** *zima*

Pick-up lines

What kind of music do you listen to?
Jakou posloucháš hudbu?
I lost my keys to my flat. Is there any room for me at your place?
Ztratily se mi klíče od bytu. Nemáš místečko pro mě u sebe?
Do you want to take a look at my butterfly collection? *Chceš se podívat na moji sbírku motýlů?*
I love you *Mám tě rád(a)*

Put-down lines

Don't make me laugh!	*Ty mě chceš rozesmát!*
Kiss my arse!	*Polib mi prdl*
Shit your eye out!	*Vyser si oko!*
That pisses me off!	*To mě sere!*
You jerk!	*Ty vole!*
You bitch!	*Tý děvko!*
Jump into a dirty toilet!	*Běž do hajzlíku!*

Directory

UPS

*Výtvarná 4, Prague 6 (3300 3111).
Metro Hradčanská, then bus 108 to
Pod hřbitovem stop.* **Open** 7am-6pm
Mon-Fri.
For domestic and international
packages weighing up to 31.5 kg
(70lbs).

Internet providers

See page 252.

Interpreting &
translating agencies

Prague has dozens of
translation companies, with
most offering services in all the
major European languages and
many languages further afield.
Rates are usually determined
by the page (30 lines per page
at 60 characters per line).

Abram

*Dlouhá 16, Prague 1 (232 2068/
fax 232 2068). Metro Staroměstská.*
Map 3 J2
Claims to translate all languages.
Operates a freelance pool of about
1,500 translators.

Interlingua

*Spálená 17, Prague 1 (2490 9250/
fax 290 721). Metro Národní třída.*
Map 5 H6
Specialises in legal and financial
documents.

Law firms

There are dozens of local and
international law firms that
can help establish a company
and provide standard legal
services. Local firms tend to

have a better grasp of arcane
bits of Czech law, while
international firms offer better
linguistic skills and more
polish (at a much higher price).
For a local lawyer, contact
the Czech Chamber of
Commercial Lawyers.

Czech Chamber of
Commercial Lawyers

*Senovážné náměstí 23, Prague 1
(2414 2457). Metro Náměstí
Republiky.* **Open** 8am-6pm Mon-
Thur; 8am-3pm Fri.
Map 4 L4

Altheimer & Gray

*Platnéřská 4, Prague 1 (2481
2782/fax 2481 0125). Metro
Staroměstská.* **Map 3 H3**
Offers advice on privatisation,
acquisitions and foreign investment.

Cameron McKenna

*Husova 5, Prague 1 (2424 8518/fax
2424 8524). Metro Staroměstská.*
Map 3 H4
Claims to have the largest network of
law offices in Central Europe.

Čermák, Hořejš & Vrba

*Národní třída 32, Prague 1 (9616
7401/fax 2494 6724). Metro
Národní třída.* **Map 3 H5**
Local firm specialising in patent and
other types of corporate law.

Mobile phones, pagers
& voicemail

See page 252.

Office hire

Chronos

*Václavské náměstí 66, Prague 1
(2422 6612/fax 2221 1327). Metro*

Muzeum. **Open** 8am-6pm Mon-Fri.
Map 6 K6
Offers temporary office space, tele-
phone services and secretarial help.

Regus

*Klimentská 46, Prague 1 (2185
1055/fax 2185 2099). Metro
Náměstí Republiky.* **Open** 8.30am-
6pm Mon-Fri. **Map 4 L1**
Can provide short-term offices
and conference rooms, as well as
temporary access to the Internet
and e-mail.

Photocopying

See page 171.

Recruitment agencies

Finding good employees in
Prague can be challenging
given the city's booming
economy and the general
shortage of English speakers.

AYS

*Žitná 8, Prague 2 (2499 3137).
Metro Karlovo náměstí.*
Open 8.30am-5pm Mon-Fri.
Map 6 J7
Specialises in secretarial and adminis-
trative support.

Helmut Neumann
International

*Národní třída 10, Prague 1 (2495
1530). Metro Národní třída.* **Open**
9am-6pm Mon-Fri. **Map 3 H5**
One of several international head-
hunting agencies. Fills positions in all
sectors of the economy.

Work Plus – Inter Staff

*Vodičkova 33, Prague 1 (2423
5787). Metro Můstek.* **Open** 9am-
6pm Mon-Fri. **Map 5 J6**
Provides a range of temporary office
support staff.

Directory

Media

The New Presence

This is the English-language version
of *Nová přítomnost*, a journal dating
back to inter-war Bohemia that offers
a liberal and stimulating selection of
opinion writings, some translated
from their original Czech, by both
local and international writers. Not
easy to find, but worth seeking out
for an in-depth look at the Czech
Republic. Try **The Globe**, **U
Knihomola** and **Big Ben**
bookstores *(see p158).*

Prague Business Journal/
Central European
Business Weekly/
Prague Tribune

The *Prague Business Journal*, the
best of this business-oriented bunch,
is part of a chain that also puts out
the *Budapest BJ* and the *Warsaw BJ*.
The *PBJ* often scoops the fat-cat
Czech press, but is still of little
interest to the general public. And
even loyal readers acknowledge its
role as a supplement to papers with a
more general business scope. The
CEBW seems to be dying a slow
death, and the *Tribune* clings to life,
if not relevance, from issue to issue.

Prague Post

Among younger Prague types, the
Prague Post often gets a bad rap for
being dull and lifeless. Its local news
is steady (if, perhaps, overly heavy
on the party politics) but rarely
seems to do more than scratch the
surface of Czech life. Still, as
competitors fall by the wayside, the
Post – with its useful cultural
listings, business focus and
entertainment features – is still
around after all these years. Editor-
in-Chief Alan Levy's self-promoting
'Prague Profile' column is loved by
many and hated by many. Check
out the *Post*'s website at
www.praguepost.cz.

Think

A free 'zine with the look of a ransom note but an authoritative list of club events and parties in the back, plus occasionally useful website tips, hidden among conspiracy theory rants and silly stabs at counter-culture. Find it at **Radost** (*see p152*) or **U Melého Glena** (*see p151*).

Czech press

Newspapers

Blesk

One of the country's most popular newspapers, *Blesk* ('Lightning') is a daily tabloid full of sensationalised news, celebrity scandals, UFO sightings and busty page-three girls.

Hospodářské noviny

The Czech equivalent of the *Financial Times*, this respected daily brings news of capital markets, exchange rates and business transactions. Required reading for Czech movers and shakers.

Lidové noviny

An underground dissident paper in the communist days, *Lidové noviny*'s finest hour came in the early 1990s. Today, the paper is still respected in some right-wing and intellectual circles, but commercialism has taken its toll.

Mladá fronta Dnes

A former communist newspaper, *Dnes* has been the country's leading serious newspaper for several years. It now offers fairly balanced domestic and international news, and a reasonable level of independence. The reporting and editing, however, are often inexcusably poor.

Právo

The former communist party newspaper (the name means 'Justice'; it used to be *Rudé Právo* – 'Red Justice') is now a respectable, left-leaning daily with an equally respectable circulation.

Respekt

A weekly newspaper, *Respekt* takes a close look at the good, the bad and the ugly effects of the Czech Republic's transformation to a market economy. Not only does it ask the questions other newspapers don't but it also has some cutting-edge cartoons.

Sport

Daily sports paper, and you don't need Czech to figure out the results from home and abroad. Predictably heavy on European football, ice hockey and tennis coverage. *Sport* also lists results from the NBA and NFL.

Periodicals

Cosmopolitan/Elle

Cosmopolitan fails to stand up against its Western counterparts, but Czech *Elle* appeals to both teens and middle-aged women with flashy fashion spreads, décor and interviews.

Reflex

Reflex is a popular, low-rent style weekly with glossy format, some interesting editorial and some very boring design.

Živel

A cool cyberpunk mag with an interesting design and a sub-cultural editorial slant – like a cross between *The Face* and *Wired*. Hip, small circulation and more likely to be found in bookshops than at newsagents. Was quarterly but now publishes irregularly.

Listings

Annonce

A classified ad sheet into which bargain-hunting Czechs delve to find good deals on second-hand washing machines, TVs, cars, etc. Also a good apartment-hunting tool. Place your ad for free, then wait by the phone – it's a proven success formula.

Culture in Prague

A privately run monthly alternative to *Kulturní přehled* (*see below*) covering all major cultural events; available in English at bookstores around Wenceslas Square.

Do města

'Downtown' is a tall-format entertainment freesheet in Czech with English translations. Good for weekly listings of galleries, cinemas, theatres and clubs. New edition every Thursday. You'll find it lying around in bars, cafés and clubs.

Kulturní přehled

A reliable monthly listing of cultural events in Prague. In Czech only but not hard to understand and it gives schedules for the main cultural venues, including theatres, operas, museums, clubs and exhibitions.

Týdeník

A weekly guide to what's on TV. If you're looking for the occasional English-language movie with Czech subtitles, better to check the listings in the *Prague Post* (*see above*).

Literary magazines

Though many have folded over the past few years, a whole pile of literary

magazines is still published in Prague, in both Czech and English. You should be able to track down most of them at **The Globe**, **U Knihomola** and **Big Ben** bookstores (*see page 158*). The Czech-language *Revolver Review*, supposedly published quarterly (but distinctly irregularly), is a hefty periodical with *samizdat* roots. The *RR* presents new works by well-known authors plus lesser-known pieces by pet favourites such as Kafka. *Labyrint Revue*, a monthly magazine, and *Literární noviny*, a weekly, are the other two main Czech publications offering original writing and reviews of new work. *Labyrint* also has music and art reviews.

English publications tend to come and go. The best and most widely known is *Trafika*, a 'quarterly' showcase for international writers that tends to lapse into an 'occasionally'. Although it has recently been out of action, *Trafika*'s editors now look to be reviving this early pioneer.

The *Prague Review*, formerly the *Jáma Review*, is a slim quarterly of plays, prose and poetry from Czechs and Czech-based expats. Its editors – who have included such Czech literary heavyweights as Bohumil Hrabal, Ivan Klima and Miroslav Holub – generously subtitle the volume 'Bohemia's journal of international literature'.

Optimism is a more-or-less monthly literary mag that somehow has not missed a single issue since it was founded in 1995, which makes it impressive for that reason, if no other. A forum for Prague's English-speaking expatriate community, its content ranges from the intriguing to hopelessly trite but is genuinely open to young, unproven writers.

Job hunting in Prague

Native English speakers with conversational Czech are highly sought after, but if you can't speak any Czech don't expect a special welcome. If you are a recent graduate, the easiest way in is by teaching English. Possession of a TEFL (Teaching English as a Foreign Language) certificate should merit you a choice of jobs. A TEFL certificate can be earned in Prague from **ITC** (*see below*), which guarantees job placement for its graduates. If you don't have a TEFL certificate, try a large language school which provides training in its own teaching methods (*see page 267*).

Teaching private English lessons is always more lucrative than teaching at a language school, especially as most private teachers work tax-free; however, private teaching income is notoriously unreliable and provides none of the benefits of a legal job. Most teachers begin at a school and then pick up private students on the side. Students can also be found through word of mouth and by checking bulletin boards at expat-friendly businesses such as **The Globe** (*see page 151*), **Radost** (*see page 152*) and **Terminal Bar** (*see page 144*).

Bookstores, restaurants, bars and cafés which cater to foreigners often hire native English speakers; people in such positions, however, will rapidly need to learn enough Czech to deal with native colleagues and customers. Pay tends to be low, but you'll meet a lot of people quickly.

Any legal position in the Czech Republic includes employer/state-paid health insurance, paid vacation, 47 per cent income tax, and a lot of responsibility for little money. After word of mouth, the best way of finding a job is by consulting the *Prague Post*, the *Resources* directory, the weekly advertising paper *Annonce*, or by doing the rounds of the recruitment agencies.

ITC (International TEFL Certificate)
(301 9784/voice mail 9614 1014/www.itc-training.com).
Four-week evening and weekend courses, including several hours weekly teaching practice with Czech students, resulting in a TEFL certificate and guaranteed job placement. The course costs US$1,200.

Legalities

The number of foreigners living illegally in Prague may surprise visitors, as may the number of foreign residents who regularly travel to the country's border to have their passports stamped (allowing another month of legal 'tourism'). But anyone who actually tries to get a residence permit will immediately understand

the phenomenon. Horror stories abound of endless queues, eternal employee lunch breaks and frequent hostility encountered in the dreaded Foreigners' Police (*see below*) office. Once it's done, though, getting an annual renewal is easy.

When visiting Czech bureaucracies, arrive early and have nothing else planned for the day. There are four official reasons for going legit: 'family reasons' (marrying a Czech), study, work or setting up a small business. In all cases, you need a letter from your landlord or a copy of your rental agreement confirming your address. But because many apartments are rented on the black market, your landlord may be reluctant to declare your presence for tax reasons. An alternative is to falsely register temporary residence with a friend.

Residence permits

Residence permits (*Průkaz o povolení pobytu cizince*) are granted for up to five years (*trvalý*) for family reasons, or for one year (*dlouhodobý*) for other reasons. For both types of permit you'll need a 1,000 Kč revenue stamp (*kolková známka*) and three passport pictures. Get the revenue stamp from the Foreigners' Police station where you file for your permit. Take your passport, proof of address, clean criminal record certificate (*Výpis z trestního rejstříku – see below*) and proof that you have a valid reason for requesting residency – for instance, a work permit, Czech student card or trading licence.

Foreigners' Police
(Cizinecká policie) Olšanská 2, Prague 3 (recorded info in Czech 6144 1119/6144 1352/6144 1356/live Czech-speaker 6614 1540). Tram 5, 9. **Open** 7.30am-2.30pm Mon, Tue, Thur; 7.30am-5pm Wed; 7.30am-noon Fri. **Map 8 D2**

Work permits

The Czech Republic is not yet a member of the EU, so EU citizens also need work permits. If at all possible, have your employer apply on your behalf by providing the authorities with your passport and a translation of your educational qualifications (university diploma, teaching certificate, etc). Otherwise, you can do it yourself by taking the same documents to the employment office (*Úřad práce*) in the district where you work, and then go to the main office (*see below*).

Úřad práce
Zborovská 11, Prague 5 (2192 1111). Metro Anděl/4, 7, 12, 14, 34 tram.

Foreign press

Foreign newspapers are available at various stalls on and around Wenceslas Square and at major hotels. The *International Guardian, International Herald-Tribune* and the international edition of *USA Today* are available on the day of publication. Most other newspapers arrive 24 hours later.

Broadcast media

Television

ČT1/ČT2

The two national public channels. ČT1 tries to compete with TV Nova, but is out of its depth financially. ČT2 serves up serious music (including frequent spotlights on the jazz greats), theatre and documentaries to the small percentage of the population that tunes in. ČT2 sometimes broadcasts English-language movies with Czech subtitles; Woody Allen flicks are popular as are Monty Python classics. It also airs *Euronews*, an English-language pan-European

programme, on weekdays at 8am and on weekends at 7am.

Prima TV

A Prague-based regional broadcaster that lamely follows the lead of TV Nova (*see below*) but is slowly being revamped by new foreign partners from the West.

TV Nova

One of the first national private television stations in Eastern Europe. Initially funded by Ronald Lauder, son of Estée, Nova TV looks like American television with lots of old Hollywood movies and recycled sitcoms dubbed into Czech. Appallingly successful.

Radio

BBC World Service (101.1 FM)

English-language news on the hour plus regular BBC programming, with occasional Czech and Slovak news broadcasts. For 30 minutes a day around teatime it transmits local Czech news in English, courtesy of Radio Prague.

Limonádový Joe (90.3 FM)

Lemonade Joe pumps out nothing but corny, old Czech hits from the 1960s

and '70s, plus an Elvis song here and there. Named after a classic Czech parody of American westerns, Joe is worth tuning in to for a giggle.

Radio Free Europe

Now the world HQ for RFE, it still beams the same old faintly propagandist stuff to Romania, Ukraine and other former Soviet republics. It is now based in Prague at the former Czechoslovak Federal Assembly building, next to the National Museum.

Radio Kiss (98.0 FM)/ Radio Bonton (99.7 FM)/ Evropa 2 (88.2 FM)

Pop music, pop music and more pop music.

Radio 1 (91.9)

Excellent alternative music station that plays everything from Jimi Hendrix to techno. Evening calendar listings have everything the hip partygoer needs to know.

Radio Prague (92.6 FM & 102.7 FM)

Daily news in English, interviews, weather and traffic. Nothing too inspired, but an established and connected source with some history behind it.

Students

Charles University courses

Founded in 1348 by King Charles IV, Prague's Charles University (*Universita Karlova*) is the oldest university in Central Europe, and the undisputed hub of Prague's student activity. Its heart is the **Carolinum**, a Gothic building on Ovocný trh near the Estates Theatre, which houses the central administration offices, though university buildings are scattered all over the city.

Several cash-hungry faculties now run special courses for foreigners. Contact the relevant dean or the International Relations Office during the university year (October to May) for information on courses and admissions procedures.

Below is a selection of the more popular offerings. For

courses outside Prague, contact the British Council.

International Relations Office

Universita Karlova Rektorát, Ovocný trh 3-5, Prague 1 (2449 1310/fax 2422 9487). Metro Staroměstská or Můstek. **Open** 8am-4pm Mon-Fri. **Map 3 J4**

FAMU

Smetanovo nábřeží 2, Prague 1 (2422 0955/fax 2423 0285). Metro Staroměstská or Národní třída. **Open** 9am-3pm Mon-Fri. **Map 3 G4** Famous for turning out such Oscar-winning directors as Miloš Forman, Prague's foremost school of film, TV and photography runs several English courses under its Film For Foreigners (3F) programme, including summer workshops, six-month and one-year courses in aspects of film and TV production, and a BA in photography.

Institute of Language & Professional Training

(Ústav jazykové a odborné přípravy) Universita Karlova, Jindřišská 29 (entrance at Senovážné náměstí 25), Prague 1 (2423 0027/fax 2422

9497). Metro Můstek. **Open** 9-11am, 1-3pm, Mon, Wed; 9-11am Tue, Fri; 1-3pm Thur. **Fees** six-week session $410; intensive semester $1,210; individual lesson 500 Kč per hour. **Map 4 L4** Aimed at preparing foreign nationals who want to embark on degree courses at Czech universities, this branch of Charles University offers six-week summer courses, semester-long intensive courses and pricey individual lessons.

School of Czech Studies

Filosofická fakulta, Universita Karlova, náměstí Jana Palacha 2, Prague 1 (2161 9111). Metro Staroměstská. **Open** Oct-May 10.30am-6pm Mon-Fri. **Fees** $2,010 per two-semester year. **Map 3 G3** Runs year-long courses during the school year, offering a mix of language instruction and lectures in Czech history and culture. Classes are available for beginners, intermediate and advanced speakers of Czech.

Summer School of Slavonic Studies

Filosofická fakulta, Universita Karlova, náměstí Jana Palacha 2, Prague 1 (tel/fax 231 9645).

Metro Staroměstská. **Fees** $440 (course fee only) or $960 (includes dorm accommodation & meals).
Map 3 G3
This one-month summer course, held yearly in August, is designed for professors and advanced students in Slavonic studies. It's best to correspond by mail. A registration deadline of 1 May is recommended, but not enforced.

Other courses

Anglo-American College
Sokolská 21, Prague 1 (291 346-8/fax 291 349). Metro I.P. Pavlova. **Open** 9am-5pm Mon-Fri. **Fees** 47,000 Kč per five-course semester. **Map 6 K8**
A private college offering Western-style degree courses in business, economics, the humanities and law. While the entire syllabus and all classes are in English, the student body is a mix of Czechs, Slovaks and foreign nationals. Limited course offerings during the summer session.

Language courses

Many schools offer Czech-language instruction. If you prefer a more informal approach, place a notice on one of the boards at the Charles University Faculty, **The Globe** bookstore (*see page 158*), **Radost** (*see page 152*) or any other place where young Czechs and foreigners meet. Many students and other young people are happy to offer Czech conversation in exchange for English conversation. But, since Czech grammar is difficult, most serious learners require systematic, professional instruction to master the language's basics.

Accent
Bitovská 3, Prague 4 (420 595/fax 422 848). Metro Budějovická. **Fees** individual session 550 Kč per 45-minute session; intensive 5,200 Kč; standard 7,800 Kč.
A co-operative run and owned by the senior teachers, both Czech and foreign, this school has a good reputation for standards and quality. Choose a one-month intensive course (two hours daily instruction) or a more relaxed 'standard' five-month course (four hours weekly). All classes have a maximum size of six. A bit out of the way, but worth the travel.

Angličtina Expres Office
Korunni 2, Prague 2 (261 526). Metro Náměstí Míru. **Fees** 30-hour course 4,300 Kč. **Open** 8am-8pm Mon-Fri. **Map 8 A3**
Well-established, Czech-run school, originally set up to teach the locals English but now with years of experience in teaching rudimentary Czech to expats. Instructors use materials developed in-house. The 30-hour course runs every weekday for four weeks, and includes no more than eight students.

Berlitz
Ječná 12, Prague 2 (299 959/fax 299 958). Metro I.P. Pavlova. **Open** 8am-8pm Mon-Fri. **Fees** 40-minute lesson 600 Kč. **Map 5 J8**
The staggering cost of lessons is testament, supposedly, to the efficiency of the Berlitz method, which emphasises speaking drills and discourages systematic grammar teaching and note-taking. With an internationally standardised method of teaching and branches all over the world (several in Prague alone), Berlitz is the McDonald's of language schools, and it gets results.

State Language School
(Státní jazyková škola) Školská 15, Prague 1 (Slavonic languages & Czech for foreigners 2223 2238/ summer courses 297 114). Metro Můstek or Národní třída. **Open** 12.30-3.30pm Tue; 12.30-6.30pm Wed; 12.30-3.30pm Thur, Fri. **Fees** intensive 13,420 Kč; standard 3,730 Kč; summer 6,000 Kč. **Map 5 J6**
The largest and cheapest language school in Prague is state-run and teaches just about every language under the sun. The Czech for Foreigners department offers both intensive courses (16 hours weekly for five months) and standard courses (three hours weekly for five months) during the normal school year, as well as shorter intensive summer courses (20 hours weekly for one month). Classes tend to start very large, but many students drop out over the course of the semester, leaving a smaller, more dedicated, but still dead cheap, class.

Libraries

For a full list of Prague's libraries, ask at the National Library or look in the *Zlaté stránky* (Yellow Pages) under 'knihovny'. Admission rules vary; generally, you don't need to register to use reading rooms, but you do to borrow books, and for this you'll need your passport and sometimes a

document stating that you are a student, teacher, researcher or Prague resident. Most libraries have restricted opening hours or close in July and August.

American Center for Culture and Commerce
Hybernská 7, Prague 1 (switchboard/resource center 2423 1085/library 2423 9947). Metro Náměstí Republiky. **Open** 8am-4.30pm Mon-Fri. **Map 4 L3**
Formerly housing Prague's best, and most up-to-date, English-language library and reading room, this arm of the US Embassy has recently gone computer-age. The result: an 'Information Resource Center', equipped with Internet facilities, intended for experts and serious researchers and only open by appointment 8am-4.30pm Monday to Friday. A separate Foreign Commercial Service and Commercial Library provides English info, statistics and directories of Czech business and business law, which can only be read in-house. At press time, the Foreign Commercial Service and Commercial Library was planning to move to the American Embassy (Tržiště 15, 5732 0663).

British Council
Národní třída 10, Prague 1 (2491 2179/fax 2491 3839). Metro Národní třída. **Open** *reading room Sept-June* 9am-7pm Mon-Thu; 9am-4pm Fri; *July, Aug* 10am-6pm Mon-Thur, 10am-4pm Fri. *Library* 10am-1pm, 3-8pm, Mon, Tue, Thur; 11am-1pm, 3-8pm, Wed; 11am-1pm, 4-8pm, Fri (closed in summer). **Map 3 H5**
The light and airy reading room has a cheap, excellent café and free Internet terminals. The downstairs library is packed with materials and aids for TEFL and TESL teachers, but virtually no literature. The video selection is eclectic, and the free screenings can be excellent. The library is open to everyone. Membership entails providing solid proof of your status as either a teacher or a student.

City Library
(Městská knihovna v Praze) Mariánské náměstí 1 (2211 3338/232 8208). Metro Staroměstská. **Open** *July, Aug* 1-6.30pm Mon; 10am-6.30pm Tue-Fri; *Sept-June* 1-8pm Mon; 10am-8pm Tue-Fri; 10am-5pm Sat. **Map 3 H3**
The freshly renovated main branch of the City Library is now spacious, calm and state-of-the-art. You'll find an excellent English-language reference section, a handful of English-language magazines, fine music and audio collections and plenty of comfortable spaces for studying, scribbling and flipping through tomes.

National Library

Národní knihovna v Praze (Klementinum). Křižovnické náměsti 4, Prague 1 (2166 3331/fax 2166 3261/www.nkp.cz). Metro Staroměstská. **Open** 9am-7pm Mon-Sat. **Map 3 G4**

A comprehensive collection of just about everything published in Czech and a reasonably good international selection, housed in a confusing warren of occasionally gorgeous halls. Hours vary somewhat depending on which reading room you want to use. It is possible to take books out but you'll need your passport and a residence permit.

CKM

Jindřišská 28, Prague 1 (268 532/2423 0218/fax 268 623). Metro Můstek. **Open** *July-Sept* 9.30am-6pm Mon-Thur; 9.30am-4pm Fri; 9.30am-1pm Sat; *Oct-June* 9.30am-5pm Mon-Thur; 9.30am-4pm Fri. **Map 4 K5**

Specialises in cheap travel in and outside the Czech Republic for young people, students and teachers. ISIC cards are very liberally issued; just show a letter from your university vouching that you are studying in Prague, pay 180 Kč, hand over a passport photo and –

bingo! – you're a bona fide student. (No factchecking has ever been witnessed.)

GTS

Ve Smečkách 27, Prague 1 (9622 4301-3/fax 2221 0478). Metro Museum or Můstek. **Open** 9am-6pm Mon-Fri; 10am-2pm Sat. **Map 6 K6**

The best place for ISIC card-holders to find cheapo student fares. Especially good international flight bargains, as well as occasional deals on bus and train travel. Also offers travel insurance and issues ISIC cards. **Branch**: Lodecká 3, Prague 1 (2481 2770).

Prague on the Net

Akropolis

www.spinet.cz/akropolis
The month's line-up at Prague's coolest (and only) world music venue and pub labyrinth.

Archa Theatre

voskovec.radio.cz/archa/index1.html
The most progressive performance space in the Republic posts its monthly calendar here in Czech and English with links to performers' homepages worldwide.

Central Europe Online

www.centraleurope.com
A flashy and popular website offering news, business and special reports on the Czech Republic and other Central European countries. Crisply designed pages but somewhat dry content.

Charles University

www.cuni.cz
The official site of Charles University, much of it in English, with links to a university-run news service (available via e-mail), the university library, departments and courses for foreigners.

Czech National Theatre

www.anet.cz/nd
The official page of the Czech National Theatre with complete listings of opera, theatre and ballet at the city's top three performance venues, with descriptions in English.

Czech Techno

www.techno.cz/news.htm
All the party and club news in the Czech Republic with links to techno-favouring clubs and promoters and the bands that rock them.

FAN

www.capitol.cz
A free weekly events calendar covering film listings and just about everything else in Prague. In Czech but generally decipherable.

The Globe Bookstore & Coffeehouse

www.ini.cz/globe
The month's programme of readings, the menu and an impressive range of Czech links (though they may need updating).

Ministry of Foreign Affairs

www.czech.cz
A somewhat clunky, though thorough, overview of Czech history and culture.

Nazdar

www.nazdar.cz/nazdar.html
Nazdar ('greetings') is a slick, complete and lightning-quick source on culture, finance, the government and technology in the Czech Republic and internationally, all in English and created by the fast-growing European Internet Network.

Prague Post Tourist Information Page

www.praguepost.cz/tourist/tour2.html
A must stop for net surfers who plan to visit the city. This page offers a goldmine of tips on the Golden City, from medical/safety issues to accommodation to pub and restaurant reviews.

Prague Summer Writers' Workshop

www.gnofn.org/~writer/PSWW.html
The best scam ever conceived for getting university credits while writing in Prague (under the tutelage of some impressive international authors).

Praha Interactive Street Index

cech.cesnet.cz/cgi-bin/st
Find where your hotel is located by looking it up on this complete online map of Prague.

Radio Free Europe/Radio Liberty

www.rferl.org/bd/cz/index.html
News, maps, facts and figures and lots of info about Czech life.

Seznam

www.seznam.cz
A fast Czech-language search engine with data on all things Czech.

Time Out Prague Guide

www.timeout.co.uk:81/TO/Prague/Prague.html
Shameless self-promotion it may be, but here's where you'll find the online version of the best guide available.

The Weather Channel

www.weather.com/weather/int/cities/CZ_Prague.html

Further Reading

Look out for editions from the small Prague-based Twisted Spoon Press. Founded in 1992, this unique independent publisher is devoted to new writing and English translations of Central European writers largely unavailable elsewhere. *See also p188* **Literary Prague.**

Literature & Fiction

Brierley, David *On Leaving A Prague Window*
Readable but dated thriller set in post-communist Prague.

Buchler, Alexander (ed) *This Side of Reality*
Absorbing anthology of modern Czech writing.

Chatwin, Bruce *Utz*
Luminous tale of a Josefov porcelain collector.

Hašek, Jaroslav *The Good Soldier Švejk*
Rambling, picaresque comic masterpiece set in World War I, by Bohemia's most bohemian writer.

Havel, Václav *The Memorandum/Three Vaněk Plays/Temptation*
The President's work as playwright. *The Memorandum* is his ground-breaking absurdist work.

Hrabl, Bohumil *I Served The King Of England*
The living legend's most Prague-ish novel tracks its anti-hero through a decade of fascism, war and communism.

Klima, Ivan *Love And Garbage*
Reflections on the lives of intellectuals as street-sweepers.

Kundera, Milan *The Joke/The Book Of Laughter And Forgetting/The Unbearable Lightness Of Being*
Smug, disliked in Prague and by discerning Westerners.

Leppin, Paul *Others' Paradise/Severin's Journey Into The Dark*
Recently translated work from pre-War Prague German writer, both in beautiful editions from Twisted Spoon Press.

Meyrink, Gustav *The Golem*
The classic version of the tale of Rabbi Loew's monster, set in Prague's Jewish Quarter.

Neruda, Jan *Prague Tales*
Wry and bitter-sweet stories of life in nineteenth-century Malá Strana, from Prague's answer to Dickens.

Šimečká, Martin M. *The Year Of The Frog*
Award-winning debut about dissidence in Bratislava.

Škvorecký, Josef *The Bass Saxophone*
Black humour and underground jazz.

Topol, Jáchym *A Trip To The Train Station*
A wide-eyed, cynical wander through a corrupt contemporary Prague, from one of the city's leading young writers.

Wilson, Paul (ed.) *Prague: A Traveller's Literary Companion*
Fruitily introduced but excellent collection, from Meyrink to Škvorecký, organised to evoke Prague's sense of place.

Kafka

Kafka, Franz *The Castle; The Transformation & Other Stories; The Trial*
Worth re-reading, if only to note how postmodern Prague has completely lost all sense of Kafkaesque menace.

Kafka, Franz *Contemplation*

Observations, vignettes and reflections in a beautiful illustrated edition from Twisted Spoon Press.

Anderson, Mark M *Kafka's Clothes*
Erudite, subtle and unconventional book encompassing Kafka, dandyism and the Habsburg culture of ornament.

Brod, Max *Franz Kafka: A Biography*
The only biography by anyone who actually knew the man.

Hayman, Ronald *K: A Biography of Kafka*
Widely available, dependable, but a bit boring.

Hockaday, Mary *Kafka, Love And Courage: The Life Of Milena Jesenská*
Best biography of Kafka's lover, and excellent on Prague.

Karl, Frederick *Franz Kafka: Representative Man*
Hefty for a holiday read, but a thorough and thoughtful account of the man, his work, and the Prague he inhabited.

History, memoir & travel

Brook, Stephen *The Double Eagle: Vienna, Budapest & Prague*
Fussy but entertainingly detailed travelogue of the Habsburg capitals in the early 1980s.

Fermor, Patrick Leigh *A Time Of Gifts*
Evocative 1930s travelogue, culminating in inter-war Prague.

Garton Ash, Timothy *The Magic Lantern: The Revolution of 1989 Witnessed in Warsaw, Budapest, Berlin And Prague*
Instant history by on-the-spot Oxford academic.

Pynsent, Robert B. *Questions of Identity: Czech and Slovak Ideas of Nationality and Personality*
Witty, erudite and incisive look at Czech self-perception.

Rimmer, Dave *Once Upon A Time In The East*
Communism seen stoned and from ground level.

Ripellino, Angelo Maria *Magic Prague*
Mad masterpiece of literary and cultural history, mixing fact and fiction as it celebrates the city's sorcerous soul.

Shawcross, William *Dubček*
Biography of the Prague Spring figurehead, updated to assess his role in the 1989 Velvet Revolution.

Essays & argument

Čapek, Karel *Towards The Radical Centre*
Selected essays from the man who coined the word 'robot'.

Klima, Ivan *The Spirit Of Prague*
Selected essays, of which the title piece is highlight.

Havel, Václav *Living In Truth/Letters To Olga/Disturbing The Peace*
His most important political writing, his prison letters to his wife, and his autobiographical reflections.

Miscellaneous

Iggers, Wilma A. *Women Of Prague*
Fascinating – the lives of 12 women, across 200 years.

Sís, Peter *Three Golden Keys*
Children's tale set in Prague, with wonderful drawings.

Putz, Harry *Do You Want To Speak Czech?*
If the answer is yes, this is the book (and the cassette).

Various eds. *Prague: Eleven Centuries of Architecture*
Solid, substantial, not too stodgy and widely available.

Index

Notes:
Numbers in bold indicate the section giving key information on the topic; italics indicate illustrations.

In line with standard Czech practice, words beginning or containing Č, É, Ř, Š and Ž are listed after those starting or including C, E, R, S and Z respectively.

absinthe 150
accommodation **104-117**
  agencies 116-7
  camping 117
  gay and lesbian 187
  hostels 115-6
  renting 247
accountants *see under* business
A-club 186
Adam Pharmacy 53
Adonis 137
Adria Theatre/Palác Adria 215
Aeronautical & Cosmonautical
  Exhibition 91-2
AghaRTA 199
AIDS/HIV *see under* health, gay and
  lesbian
air travel *see under* travel and
  transport
Akropolis 129, 152, 198, *198*, 204
Alcoholics Anonymous 245
Alfred ve dvoře Theatre 215
All Souls' Day 8
Ambiente 126
ambulance *see under* health,
  helplines/emergencies
American Center for Culture and
  Commerce 54
American Express *see under* money
Andy's Café 138
Anniversary of the Creation of
  Czechoslovakia 8
apartments *see under*
  accommodation and flat hunting
ApriLes 187
Aqua club 2000/Connections 187
arcades 53, **57**
Archa Theatre 215
Archbishop's Palace 71
architecture **34-40**
  art nouveau 38;
  baroque 36-7;
  communist 40;
  cubist 38-9, 85;
  Gothic 35-6;
  modernist 39-40;
  Renaissance 36;
  revivalist 37;
  Romanesque 34-5;
  rondo-cubist 39
Army Museum 92
art galleries **96-102**
  commercial galleries 101-2

municipal galleries 96-102
  religious 73
  see also individual museums and
    galleries
Astra 2 40
Astronomical Clock 43, *43*, **52**
Astronomical Tower 51
Autocamp Trojská 117
Avalon 124
AVE 116-7

Baba Villas 40, **83**
babies *see under* children
Ball Game Court 36, 69
ball season 7
  dress hire 163
Balšánek, Antonín 38
Bambino di Praga 78, 80
Banana Bar/Café 139, 204
Bank of the Czechoslovak Legions
  39-40
banks and banking
  business 260
  currency exchange 249, 260
  opening hours 249
Baráčnická rychta 148
Bar Bar 129
Bar-Herna non-stop 205
Barock Bar & Café 123
Barracuda 126
Barrandov **83-4**, 180
bars **138-152**
  gay and lesbian 186
  in Holešovice/Karlín 81, 151
  in Malá Strana/Hradčany 74-5, 78,
    148-151
  in Nové Město 142-8
  in Staré Město 42-3, **138-142**
  in Vinohrady/Žižkov 85, **152**
  late-night 204-5
  see also clubs; pubs
Battalion Rock Club 205
Battle of Hradec Kralové 9
Battle of Lipany 15
Battle of White Mountain (Bila Hora)
  10, 17, 83
Baťa 53, 163
Bazaar Mediterranée 126
beer 146-7
  Budvar 146, 232
  Karlovy Vary Beer Olympiad 9
Bella Napoli 126
Belle Epoque 139
Bellevue 119
Belvedere, the 36, **69**, 99
Bendelmayer, Bendřich 54
Beneš, Edvard 20
Berlioz, Hector 57
Bertramka 83, 192; *see also* Mozart
  Museum
Best Western City Hotel Moráň 105
Bethlehem Chapel 47, **51**
Betlém Club 111

Bilá Hora 83; *see also* Battle of White
  Mountain
Bilá labuť 55, **154**
Bilek Villa 97-8
Billiard Club Trojická 205
Bilý koníček 201
Le Bistrot de Marlène 123
Black Box International Theatre 218
Black Tower 63
Blatnička 139
Blatouch 139
Blecha, Matěj 53
Blue Light 148
boat trips *see under* travel and
  transport
Bohemia Bagel 148
Bohemian Chancellery 61, **73**
Bohemia Ticket International 195,
  214
Bontonland 168
Botanical Gardens 58
Brahe, Tycho 51, 71
Brasserie Le Molière 123
La Brise 123
broadcast media 266
Brod, Max 55
Bromová, Veronika 100
Březnov Monastery 83
Buchlov Festival of Folk Music 9
Buffalo Bill's 126
Bugsy's 139
Bull Staircase 65
bungee jumping 208
Buquoy Palace 77
Burčák 8
bureaux de change *see under* banks
  and banking, currency exchange
buses *see under* travel and transport
business **260-63**
  accountants 261
  banking 260
  estate agents 261
  express mail 261-3
  government agencies 260
  interpreters/translators 263
  law firms 263
  office hire 263
  publications 260-61
  recruitment agencies 263
  resources and organisation 260
  stock exchange 261

Café Archa 142
Café bar Na zábradlí 139
Le Café Colonial 125
Café Louvre 139
Café Milena 43, 139
Café Rincon 139
cafés, pubs & bars **138-52**
  see also bars and pubs
La Cambusa 126
campsites 117
Cantina 126
Carolinum 46, 99

cars and driving
  hire 257-9
  insurance 259
  parking 259
  petrol/service 260
Casablanca 123
La Casa Blů 139
casinos 207; *see also* gambling
castles 225, 229-33, 239; *see also*
  Prague Castle
caves 242
Celetná Theatre 217
Ceremonial House/Former
  Ceremonial Hall 48, 50, **94**
Chapeau Rouge 139-40, 205
Charles IV 52, 53, 57-8, 61
Charles Bridge 13, 35, **44-5**, *45*, *75*,
  176
  sculptures 45
Charles University 30, 266;
  accommodation 115
Charter 77 25
Chez Marcel 140
children **176-9**
  activities for 176-9
  baby requirements 179
  child-minding 179
  health 179
  transport 179
Chochol, Josef 39, 84
Chrasten Castle *see* Vyšehrad
Christmas 9
churches and cathedrals
  Basilica of St George 35, **60**
  Basilica of St Margaret 83
  Cathedral of Sts Cyril & Methodius
    8, *20*, 22, 58, **59**
  Chapel of the Holy Rood 47, 61
  Chapel of St Wenceslas 61
  Hussite 85
  Loreto, the 37, *37*, **71-3**
  Minorite Church of St Francis 35
  Na Karlově 58
  Nativity, the 73
  Our Lady 73
  Our Lady before Týn 36, 42, **51**
  Our Lady Beneath the Chain 77
  Our Lady of the Snows 55, **58-9**,
    59
  Our Lady Victorious 78, **80**
  Sacred Heart 39-40, 85
  services in English 25
  St Barbara 224
  St Clement 51
  St Francis 44
  St George's Basilica 61
  St Giles 47
  St Havel (Gall) 46
  St Ignatius 58
  St James 42, **51**, 192224
  St John on the Rock 58
  St Joseph 76
  St Ludmila 85
  St Nicholas (Malá Strana) 36-7, 74,
    80, 193
  St Nicholas (Staré Město) **43**, 193
  St Saviour 36, 44, 51
  St Thomas 76, **80**
  St Simon & St Jude 193
  St Vitus's Cathedral 13, 35, 45, 51,
    61-2, *64*
  St Wenceslas 85
  Sts Peter and Paul 84, 226
Cibulka 201

Cicala 126
cinemas 183
Circle Line 119
City of Prague Information Service
  117, 246
City Transport Museum 93
Civic Forum 25
Clam-Gallas Palace 44
Clementinum 37, 44, **51**
  Astronomical Tower 51
  Chapel of Mirrors 51, 193
Clinton, Bill 55
Cloister Inn 111
Clown & Bard 116, 152
Club Habitat (hostel) 116
clubs 201-4
  gay and lesbian 186
  jazz 7, 57, 74
La Colline Oubliée 126
communism 22-5
computers 159
  rental and leasing 261
  sales and repairs 159
  see also Internet
concert halls and venues 192-4
Corinthia Hotel Forum 104
Corona Bar 140, 205
Country Life 137, 165
courses 266-7
crime; organised 30-31
crystal 157
cubist lamp post 39
cubism *see* architecture, cubism
customs 244
Cybeteria 143
cycling 208
Czech Museum of Fine Arts 99
Czech National Symphony Orchestra
  191
Czech Silver Museum 224
Czech Union of Fine Arts 102

č

Čedok 195, 246
Černého vola, U 138, **150**
Černín Palace 71, 73
Černý pivovar 129
Čertovka 76
České Budějovice 232
České Švýcarsko 241
Český Krumlov 232-3
Český ráj 238-40
Čínské Zátiší 129

d

Dalibor Tower 63
dance 217
Dance Prague 8
David 120
defenestration 58, 61, 65, 71, **73**
Dejvice 29, 82-3
della Stella, Paolo 36, 69
Delta 201
Devil Pillars 84
Diamant House 39, *39*, 58
diamond monstrance 73
Dientzenhofer, Christoph 36
Dientzenhofer Kilian Ignaz 36
Diplomat Hotel Praha 105
directory **244-68**
disabled access 244, 256; public
  transport 256

Divoká Šárka 83, 177, 210, 212, **225**
Dobrá čajovna 149, 165
Don Giovanni (hotel) 107
Don Giovanni (restaurant) 125
Drake's 186
Dream Mansion 201
drugs 31
Drýak, Alois 54
Dubček, Alexander 23, *26*, 53, 55
Duncan Center 217
Dunkin' Donuts 143
Dům U kamenného zvonu 35-7, 44;
  see also House at the Stone Bell
Dům U Velke Boty 113
Dvořák, Antonin 190-91
Dvořák Museum 58, **92**

e

Easter 5
Eben, Petr 191
electricity 245
Eluard, Paul 62
embassies 244-5
emergencies 245
Emmaus Monastery 57
English-language publications
  263
Èrra Café 140
Estates Theatre 37, 46, 194, *215*, 217
Estia 125
Evropa Café 143
exhibitions 99-101
expatriate Prague 258

f

Fakhreldine 123
Faros 126
Faust House 58
feminism 251
Ferdinand I 15-16
Ferdinand II 17
Ferdinand V 19
festivals and events
  dance 217
  film 9, 184
  music 9, 194-5
  Prague Film Festival 184
  puppetry 8
  theatre 8, 219
film **180-84**
  classic Czech films 182
  festivals 9, 184
  information 182
first aid 246
First Republic 20-21
fishing 208
fitness centres 208-9
flat hunting 247
food 33; *see also* restaurants; cafés
football 213
Former Ceremonial Hall/Ceremonial
  House 50, **94**
Fotogalerie U Řečických 102
Franciscan Gardens 55
Francouská Restaurace 123
Františkovy Lázně 233-5
Franz Josef, Emperor 19
'Fred and Ginger' building
  40, *56*, 57
French Institute Café 143
Fromin *120-21*, 123, 203
FX Café *see* Radost

Gabčik, Josef 22, 59
Gagarin, Yuri, monument to 33
Galerie Baraka Café 150
Galerie Behémót 101
Galerie Café Chiméra 150
Galerie Hollar 100
Galerie Jaroslav Fragnera 47
Galerie Jednorožec s harfou 101
Galerie Jiří Švestka 101, *101*
Galerie Módy 143
Galerie MXM 102
Galerie Na Jánském Vršku 102
Galerie Peithner-Lichtenfels 102
Galerie Rudolfinum 100
Galerie Václava Špály 102
Galerie Vltavín 102
galleries 47; *see also* National Gallery
Gallery of Modern & Contemporary
    Art 81, 96-7, *98-9*
gambling 207; *see also* casinos and
    herna bars
Gambra 71, **102**
game 135
Gandy Galerie 102
gay and lesbian Prague **185-7**
Gay Man Pageant 187
Gay Penzion David 187
Gehry, Frank 40, 57
Globe, the 151, 158, 258, 265
Gočár, Jan 39
Golden Lane 62
Golden Portal 61
Golem 16
golf 209
La Golosina 127
Golz-Kinský Palace 44
Good 'King' Wenceslas 12; *see also* St
    Wenceslas
Gottwald, Klement **23**, 86
Le Gourmand 137
Grand Hotel Bohemia 105
Grand Hotel Evropa 38, 54, **113**
Great Tower 61
Grill Bono/Občerstvení 137
Gulu Gulu 140
gyms *see* fitness centres
gypsies *see* Romanies
Gyros Falafel Arik 137

La Habana 150, 203
Habsburgs 15-18
Haffenecker, Antonin 37
hairdressers 167-8
Háje 86
Havel, Václav 25, *26*, 53, 189, 214
Havelská Market 137, *153*, 155
health 245
    gay and lesbian 187
    helplines/emergencies 245-6
    insurance 245
    women's 246
helplines 245-6
    gay and lesbian 187
Henlein, Konrad 21
Herna bars 207
Heydrich, Reinhard 8, 21, 59, 62
High Synagogue 49
hiking 227
Historical museum (Lobkowicz
    Palace) 63, **91**

history **10-27**
hitchhiking 223
Hitler, Adolf 46
Hogo Fogo 130
Holešovice 81-2
Holiday Inn Prague (Hotel
    International) 40, 82, **107**, *111*, 209
holidays 5-7
horse-racing 213
horse riding 209
Hospodka U Kašpárka 133
hostels 115-6
Hostel Sokol 116
Hostivař reservoir 86
Hotel 16 U sv. Kateřiny 111
Hotel Anna 113-4
Hotel Axa 111
Hotel Central 38
Hotel Hoffmeister 107
Hotel International *see* Holiday Inn
    Praha
Hotel Legie 115
Hotel Palace Praha 105, *107*
Hotel Pařiž Praha 105, *109*
Hotel Pod Věži 109
Hotel Praha 109
hotels 104-115
    budget 113-5
    gay and lesbian 187
    luxury/expensive 104-111
    mid-range 111-113
Hotel Savoy 105
Hotel Sax 111
Hotel U páva 109
House at the Black Madonna 39, 42,
    98
House at the Stone Bell 100, 193; *see*
    also Dům U kammeného zvonu
House of the Gold Ring 98
House of the Lords of Kunštát and
    Poděbrady 35, 47, **52**
Hrabal, Bohumil 189
Hradčany 60, *69*, **71**
Hunger Wall 78
Hus, Jan **14**, 19, 47, 51, 243
    Jan Hus Monument 44
Husák, Gustav **25**, 55
Hvězda Hunting Lodge 36, 83
Hybernů, U 54

ice hockey 213
ice skating 209
Imperial Stables 100
Indická restaurace 130
information sources 246
insurance 246
Interkoncerts 195, 198
Internet 252
    cafés 139
    Prague on the Net 268
Internet Café 140
interpreters *see under* business

Jalta Hotel 54
Jáma 143
James Joyce 140
Janáček, Leos 190-93
Janák, Pavel 55
Jazz & Blues Café 199
Jazz Café č. 14 143

Jazz Club Železná 199
Jewel of India 120
jewels, crown 61
Jewish Cemetery (New) 8, **86**
Jewish Cemetery (Old) 49, **95**
Jewish Museum 48, **94-5**
Jewish Prague 48
Jewish quarter *see* Josefov
Jewish Town Hall 47
Jirásek & Aleš Museum 83, **94**
Jižní Město 86
job hunting 265
jogging 209-10
John Bull Pub 143
Jo's Bar 150
Jo's Garáž 203
Josefov 47-50, *50*
Joseph II 18, 48
Julián (hotel) 111

Kafirna U českého pána 186
Kafka, Franz 48, 55, 188
    anniversary pilgrimage 8
Kampa Island 76
Kampa Park 76
Kampa Park (restaurant) 123
Kampa Stará Zbrojnice (hotel) 113
Karlin 37
Karlovo náměsti 58
Karlovy Vary 233-4
    Beer Olympiad 9
    International Film Festival 9, 184
    Rainbow Festival 187
Karlštejn 229
Kaunitz Palace 74
Kavárna Obecni dům 144
Kavárna Rudolfinum 140
Keltská Restaurace 133
key cutting & locksmiths 168
Klaus, Václav 27, 33
Klausen Synagogue 49, 50, **94**
Klima, Ivan 188
Klub Architektů 130
Kmotra Pizzeria 130
Knast/Arco bar 186
Kogo Pizzeria & Caffeteria 130
Komenský Pedagogical Museum 91
Konirna 141
Konopiště 230
Koruna (hotel) 115
Koruna Palace 54, 154
Kotěra, Jan 38-9, 53
Kotva 154
Kozička 141, 205
Králíček, Emil 53, 55, 58
Krone/Julius Meinl 154
Křivoklát 230-31
Kubiš, Jan 22
Kubišta, Bohumil 39
Kundera, Milan 188
Kutna Hora 223-5
Kvicala, Petr 100
Kysela, Ludvik 53

Labour Day 7, *7*
Lapidárium 82, **98**
Laterna Magika 219
L club 186
Ledebur Gardens 65, **79**
left luggage 247

Lennon Wall, John 76, 77
Letná Park 7, 81-2, *210-11*
Ležáky 22
Libra-Q (hostel) 116
libraries 267-8
Libuše **11**, 84
Lichtenstein Palace 193
Lidice 22
Literární kavárna GPlusG 152
literary Prague **188-9**, 269
Lobkowicz Palace 63, 78, 91, 193
Loos, Adolf 39
Loreto, the 37, *37*, **71-3**
lost property 247-9
Lotos 127
Löw, Rabbi **16**, 47, 51
Lucerna 53, **57**
Lucerna music bar 198, *199*, 203
Lunapark 82, 178

Mácha, Karel Hynek 7, 80
Mailsi 127
Mainer, Martin 100
Main Station (Hlavní nádraží) 38, 40, 55, 254
Maisel, Rabbi 47
Maisel Synagogue 49, **95**
Malá Strana 10, 30, 33, 45, **74-80**
Malostranská beseda 198, 203
Malostranská Kavárna 150
Malý Buddha 149
Mánes 39, 40, 57-8, 102, 203
Mariánské Lázně 233, 235, *235*
Maria Theresa, Empress 18
markets 46, 137, 155
Marquis de Sade 141, 205
Martinů, Bohuslav 190-91
Mary's Accommodation Service 117
Masaryk, Jan 22-3, 71
Masaryk Station 37, 55, 254
Masaryk, Tomaš Garrigue 19, *19*
Massada 125
Master's Bar 23 144
Matthew of Arras 61
Matthias Gate 61
May rituals *6*, 7
May Day 7
Mečiar, Vladimír 27
media 263-6
Medúza 152
Melantrich Building 53
Memorial to the 'victims of communism' *24*, 54
Mendelssohn, Felix 50
Metamorphosis 141
metro *see* public transport
Metropolitan Jazz Club 199
Mělník 225-6
Michna Palace 78
Mihulka *see* Powder Tower
Military Museum 71, **92**
Minute House 43
Mirror Maze 78, **80**, 178, *178*
Misery Loves Company 218
Miss Czech Republic 9
Místodržitelský letohrádek 82
Modrá Zahrada 130
Molly Malone's 141
money 249
Moravia 222, 242
Morzin Palace 75
Mozart, Wolfgang Amadeus 10, 46

Mozart Museum 83, **92**
Mucha, Alfons 59
Mucha Museum 55, **90**, *90*
Municipal House (Obecní dům) 38, 40, 52, 54, **59**, 144, 192
   Exhibition Hall 100
Municipal Library 100-101
Museum of the City of Prague 55, **91**
Museum of Decorative Arts 50, **90**
museums **90-95**; *see also* individual museums
mushrooms 9
music: classical **190-95**
   festivals 194-5;
   opera 194
   recommended CDs 192-3
   shops 44, 171
   ticket agencies 195
   see also individual composers
Music Park 203
music: rock, folk and jazz **197-200**
   festivals 200
   folk & country 9, 200
   jazz 199-200
   shops 44, **168-71**
   ticket agencies 198
   tickets & information 197-8
   venues 198-9
Music Shop Trio 44, 171
Myslbek Center 154
Myslbek, Václav 40, 53, 85

Najada 151
Na Kampě 15 135
Náprstek Museum 47, **91**
Na rybárně 127
National Ballet 217
National Gallery 51, 62, 71, **96-7**
National Marionette Theatre 219
National Memorial 85, **86**
National Monument of Heydrich Terror *see* Churches and Cathedrals, Cathedral of Sts Cyril & Methodius
National Museum 37, 53, **91**, *92*
National Technical Museum 81, **93**, 176
National Theatre 37, *54*, **55**, 194, 214, 218
Na zvonařce 152
Němcova, Božena 57
Neruda, Jan 75, 85
newspapers & magazines 264
   gay and lesbian 187
New Town Hall 58, 73
New Town *see* Nové Město
New Year Celebrations 9
Night Club Fenix/Disco Astra 203
nightlife **201-7**; *see also* clubs
Nostic Palace 193
Nová síň 102
Nové Město 13, **53-9**
Novoměstský Pivovar 135
Nový Svět 71
Nusle Bridge 40

Obecní dům *see* Municipal House
O'Ché's 141
Ohmann, Friedrich 38
Old Council Hall 52

Old Jewish Cemetery 49, **95**
Old-New Synagogue 35, *46*, 47, 48, **52**
Old Royal Palace 60, **62**
Old Town *see* Staré Město
Old Town Bridge Tower 45
Old Town Hall 43, **52**
Old Town Square (Staroměstské náměsti) *42*, 43
Olšany Cemetery 85-6
Opera Grill 120
Opera Mozart 195
opticians 171
Orlík Castle 231
Ostroff 120, 205
Otakar I 12
Otakar II 13

Pacassi, Niccolo 36, 60
Palace of Culture 40, 84, 198
Palach, Jan 9, *24*, **25**, 50, 54, 86
Palacký, František 57
Palffy Gardens 65
Palffy Palác 127
La Palma 127
Paradise Gardens 63-4, **79**
Parler, Peter 35, 45, 61
Parnas 121
Parník 187
Pavilon 154
Pension City 115
Pension Dientzenhofer 115
Pension Unitas 115
Pension Větrník 115
Pension Vyšehrad 115
La Perle de Prague 121
permits
   residence 266
   work 266
Peterka House 53
Petřín Hill **78**, 178
Petřín Tower *77*, 78, **80**, 178
pharmacies 246
Philosophical Hall 73
photocopying 171-2
photography galleries 102
Piano bar 186
picnics 137
Pinkas Synagogue 49, 50, **95**
Pivnice U Pivrnice 135
Pizza Roma Due 130
Pizzeria Grosseto 127
Pizzeria Rugantino 130
Pl@neta 152
Plečnik, Josip 39, 61, 65, 85
Poděbrady 233
police 31, 245, **249-50**
Police Museum 58, *93*, **94-5**
Polivka, Osvald 38
Ponec 217
Posezeni Na řece 144
Postage Stamp Museum 55, **95**
postal services 250, 261-3
Powder Bridge 65
Powder Gate 42, **52**, 54
Powder Tower 60, **62**
Pragokoncert 195, 198
Prague Autumn 8
Prague by Season **5-9**
Prague Castle & Hradčany 34, 39, **60-69**
Prague Castle Picture Gallery 61, **98**

Prague Castle Riding School 101
Prague Chamber Ballet 217
Prague Chamber Philharmonic
  Orchestra 191
Prague Film Festival 184
Prague Hilton Atrium 105
Prague Information Service 117, 246
Prague Insurance Building 38
Prague International Book Fair and
  Writer's Festival 7
Prague Jazz Festival 7
Prague Spring 23-5
Prague Spring Festival 7, 190, *190*
Prague Symphony Orchestra 190
Prague Today **29-33**
Prague Wax Museum **93-4**, 176
Praha-Roma 144
Praha Tamura/Japanese Bufet Dai
  124
Pravěk 130
Propast 152, 203
prostitution 53
La Provence 127
Průhonice 224
Prvni Prag Country Saloon Amerika
  152, 200, *200*
Přemysl and the Přemyslid dynasty
  10-11
Příhoda, Jiři 100
Pták Loskuták 152
public holidays 5
public transport 254-60
  buses 256
  disabled access 256
  metro 255
  night 256
  railway 256
  taxis 256
  tickets and passes 254-5
  trams 176, **255**
pubs **138-152**
  food 131-5, 140
  gay and lesbian 142, 186
  Irish 44, 51, 141
  jazz 74
  see also cafés; bars; clubs
Punto Azul 203

Radegast Pub 141
Radio Free Europe 53
Radio Prague Symphony Orchestra
  191
Radost/FX Café 129, 152, *185*, 203,
  206
railways *see* public transport
Rainbow Festival in Karlovy Vary
  187
Rasputin 124
Reduta 200
Renaissance Prague Hotel 105
Reno 141
Restaurace Jáma 130
Restaurace Pivovarský dům 135
Restaurant Delfy 127
Restaurant Fondue 127
restaurants **118-137**
  American 124, 126, 127, 130
  bills/menus 118-9
  budget 129-137
  Chinese/Eastern 128-9
  etiquette 119
  expensive 119-124

fast food 137
food delivery 166
French 123, 125-8
gay and lesbian 187
Greek 125-7, 131
Indian 120, 127, 128, 129
inexpensive 126-131
Italian 125-7, 130
Japanese 123-4
kosher 125
late-night 137, 206
Mexican 126-7, 137
Middle Eastern 123, 129, 137
moderate 124-6
North African 126
pizzerias 127, 130
pub dining 131-5
Russian 124
seafood/fish 120, 125-7
traditional 124, 125-6, 129, 131
vegetarian 118, 120, 127, 129, 130,
  131, 137
vocabulary 133
see also cafés
Reykjavik 125
RHIA Tours 117
Rhythmeen 152
Rider's Steps 61
Ried, Benedict 35
Il Ritrovo 127
Rock Café 198, 203
Rokoko passage 57
Romanies 31
Romantik Hotel U raka 109
Rott House 44
Rotunda of the Holy Cross 35
Rotunda of St Longinus 35
Rotunda of St Martin *34*, 35, 84
Roxy, the 51, 198, 204, *204*, 217
Royal Garden 65
Royal Route 42
Rudolf II 16, 50
Rudolfinum 37, **50**, 192
Rudolphine Renaissance summer
  festival 96
Rybi trh 125

Safir Grill 137
St Agnes's Convent 35, 51, **97**, 194
St Felix of Valois 45
St George's Convent 60, 62, **97**
St Ivan 45
Le Saint-Jacques 128
St John of Matha 45
St John of Nepomuk 45, 62
St Luitgard 45
St Michael's Mystery 46, 52
St Nicholas Café 150
St Nicholas's Eve 9
St Sylvester's Day *see* New Year
  Celebrations
St Vitus's Cathedral 13, 35, **45**, 51,
  61-2, *64*
St Vitus's Celebration 8
St Wenceslas 12, 53, 61; *see also*
  Good 'King' Wenceslas
Sakura 124
Saloun, Ladislav 59
Sam's club 186
Santa Casa 57
saunas, gay and lesbian 187
Scarlett O'Hara's 150

Schönborn Palace 78
Schulz, Josef 37, 53
Schwarzenberg Palace 36, *36*, 71
Segafredo 125
Sféra 205
Shalimar 128
shooting ranges 213
shopping & services **153-73**
  antiques 155-7
  books/periodicals 157-9
  cameras 172-3
  children's/toys 162, 173
  computers 159, 261
  cosmetics/perfumes 160
  department stores 154
  dry cleaners/launderettes 160-1
  fashion 161-3
  florists 163
  food and drink 165-6
  gifts/sweets 167
  hair and beauty 167-8
  household 168
  jewellery 162
  keycutting & locksmiths 168
  late-night 207
  lingerie 162
  malls 154
  markets 155
  music 168-9
  opening hours 249
  opticians 171
  shoes/leather 162-3
  stationery/art materials 173
  supermarkets 166
shots 143
Sigismund bell 61
Singing Fountain 69
Skála, František 100
skateboarding 210
skiing and snowboarding 210-11
Slanský, Rudolf 23
Slavia 57, 141, *141*, **142**
Slavonice 237
sleaze 206
Slovanský Island 57, *177*
Smetana, Bedřich 7, 190-91
Smetana Hall 59, **191**
Smetana Museum 93
Smichov 83-4
Soldiers' Gardens 76, **79**
Soviet House of Science and Culture
  46
Spanish Hall 61
Spanish Synagogue 50
spas 233-5
Spejbl and Hurvinek Theatre 219
Spillar, Karel 59
sport and fitness **208-13**
Sports Café Cornucopia 137, 166
squash 211
Stag Moat 65
Stalin, Josef, former monument to 81
Staré Město 30, 33, **42-52**
State Opera 55, 194, 217
stations (rail/bus) 253-4
Stella 186
Sternberg Palace 71, **97**
Stone Ram, the 36
Stop City 117
Strahov Gallery 73, **99**
Strahov Monastery 71, **73**
Strahov Stadium 198
Stratil, Václav 100
striptease 206-7

Stromovka 82, 178
students 266-8
Studio A Rubin 150, 205
Sucharda, Stanislav 57
Sudek Gallery, Josef 102
Suk, Josef 191, 193
Summer House 69
Summer Palace *see* Belvedere, the
Supich Building 53
swimming 212, 225
  hotels with pools 104-9
synagogues
  Old-New 35, *46*, 47, 48, **52**
  High 49
  Klausen 49, 50, **94**
  Maisel 49, **95**
  Pinkas 49, 50, **95**
  Spanish 50

š

Šimutová, Adriena 100
Štefánik Observatory 78, **80**, 178
Šumava 242-3

t

Tábor 226-7
Ta Fantastika *218*, 219
Taj Mahal 128
Taverna 131
teahouses 138, **149**
Telč 237-8
telecommunications 250-51
  faxes 252
  international dialling codes 251
  mobiles/pagers/voicemail 252
  telephones 250
tennis 212-3
Teplice 233
Tequila Sunrise 142
Terezin 227-9
Terminal Bar 144, 201, 258, 265
Tesco 154, *155*
Thajský Restaurant 128
Thanh Long 128
theatre and dance **214-9**
  Black Light and Magic Lantern 219
  dance festivals 217
  dance venues 217
  English-language 218
  folklore shows and performances 217
  puppet 8, 219
  theatre festivals 219
  tickets 215-6
Theatre Minor 219
Theatre on the Balustrade 218
Theological Hall 73
Thirty Years' War 10, **17-18**, 71
Thun-Hohenstein Palace 75
Ticketpro 195, 198, 214
time and seasons **252**, 259
tipping 253
toilets 253
Tom's bar 186
Tom's Travel 117
Topič Building 38
tourist offices 246
Toy Museum 60, **95**, 176
Trade Fair Palace *see* Gallery of Modern & Contemporary Art
trams *see* public transport
travel and transport 222-3, **253-60**

air 253
bicycle 257
boat 176-7, 257
bus 222, 253
car 257
children and 179
road 223, **253-4**
student 258
train 223, **253-4**
walking 257
see also public transport
Travellers' Hostels 116
Trips Out of Town **222-43**
Troja 81-2
Troja Château 37, **82**
Tunel sex club 186
Tyrš Sport and Physical Training Museum 78

u

U Bakaláře 137
U Cedru 129, 166
U Černého Vola 151
U červeného páva 142
U Čížků 129
U dubu 186
U Fleků 58, **145**
U Govindy Vegetarian Club
U kapra 187
U Knihomola 152, 158
U Kotvy 145, *148*, 205
U krále Jiřího 113, 142
U krále Karla (hotel) 109-10
U Kristiána 129
U Malého Glena 151, 200
U malířů 121
U Maltézských rytířů *124*, 125
U Matouše 124
U medvídků 115, 142, *142*
U modré kachničky 125
U pastýřky 129
U Patrona 125
U Petra Voka 186
U Radnice 131
Urbánek Publishing House 38-9
U Rozvařilů 137, 145
U starého songu 187
U staré pani 200
U střelce
U Sudu 145
U Supa 129
U Svatého Vojtěcha 148
U Ševce Matouše 129
U Tři pštrosů (hotel) 111
U Vystřelenýho oka 152
U Závěsného kafe 151
U zeleného čaje 149
U Zlatého kohouta 149
U zlatého stromu 204
U Zlatého tygra 142
U Zlaté studny (hotel) 113, *113*
Újezd 204

v

VE Day 7
Veletržní palác 39-40, 81
  see also Gallery of Modern and Contemporary Art
Velryba 148
Velvet Revolution 8, **25-7**, 29, 51, 53
video rental 173
Villa Andy 187

Vinohrady 29, **84-6**
visas 253
Vladislav Hall 35, *35*, 62
Vltava (pub) 148
vocabulary 263
Vyšehrad 34, **84-5**
Vyšehrad cubist houses 39
Vyšehrad Museum 91
Výstaviště **82**, 178, 198
Výstavní siň Mánes 102; *see also* Mánes building
V Zátiší 124
Vzpomínky na Afriku 142, 166

w

Wagner, Richard 50
Wallenstein, General 18, 76
Wallenstein Palace and Garden 37, 76, 79, *79*
Wallenstein Riding School 101
Wax Museum Prague **94**, 176
weather 5-9
weights and measures 253
Wenceslas *see* St Wenceslas and Good 'King' Wenceslas
Wenceslas IV 14
Wenceslas Square 30, 35, **53-4**
Wiehl, Antonín 53
Wiehl House 37, *38*, 53
wine 144-5
  Burčák season 8
  shops 144, 166
  Ludmila 225
wine bars 139
Witches' Night 5-7
Wohlmut, Bonifác 36
women 251
World War I 20
World War II 21

y

YMCA 212
Young Czechs 19
youth hostels 115-6

z

Zajíc, Jan *24*, 54
ZanziBar 151, 205
Zitek, Josef 37
Zlatá ulička 131
zoo 176
Zvíkov Castle 231-2

ž

Žíznivý pes 142
Žižka, Jan 15, 85, 226
Žižkov 84-6
Žižkov TV Tower 40, 85, **86**, *87*
Žofín 58

Advertisers' Index

Please refer to the relevant sections for addresses/telephone numbers

Budweiser Budvar Beer	**IFC**
American Medical Center	**2**
Laundryland Praha	**2**

By Season

Kingscourt Express	**4**
Cityrama Praha	**4**
AT&T	**6**

Prague Today

Casinos Czechoslovakia	**32**
Everyday Prague	**48**

Sightseeing

The St. Michael Mystery	**64**
Amor Granát	**64**
Bohemia Ticket International	**66**
Staropramen Beer-Pražské Pivovary	**68**
Air Ostrava	**70**
Pražské Panoptikum	**72**

Museums

Galerie Alexander Onishenko	**88**
Galerie Peithner- Lichtenfels & Čubrda	**88**

Accommodation

AVE Travel Agency	**106**
Hotel Savoy	**108**
Hotel Palace Praha	**108**
Hotel Diplomat	**108**
Hotel Don Giovanni	**110**
Hotel Mövenpick	**110**
Zlatá Praha	**110**
Radisson SAS Hotel Praha	**112**
Hotel Inter·Continental	**114**

Restaurants

Café Konvikt	**122**
Klub Architektů	**122**
Gourmet Club Restaurant-Hotel Palace	**132**
Restaurant Hradčany-Hotel Savoy	**132**
Buffalo Bill's	**134**
Zlatá Ulička	**134**
Il Giardino Restaurant	**134**
Buenos Aires Restaurant	**136**

Shopping & Services

Boutique Bim, Bam, Bum	**156**
Big Ben Bookshop	**156**
KV Crystal	**156**
Celetná Crystal	**164**
Nový Svět	**170**

Arts & Entertainment

Top Theatre Tickets	**174**
Stone Bell Series	**196**
Bohemia Ticket International	**196**
Radost	**202**
Laterna Magika	**216**

Trips

Pizzeria Rugantino	**220**

Directory

Friday's American Bar	**248**

Prague Metro

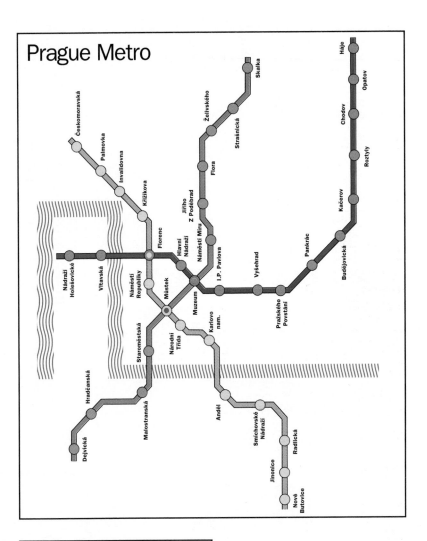

Place of Interest and/or Entertainment	
Railway Stations	
Metro Stations	Ⓜ
Parks	
Pedestrian Zones	
Churches	✚
Steps	
Area Name	JOSEFOV
Tram Routes	

Maps

Pedestrians

Possibilities

TimeOut London's Living Guide.

http://www.timeout.com

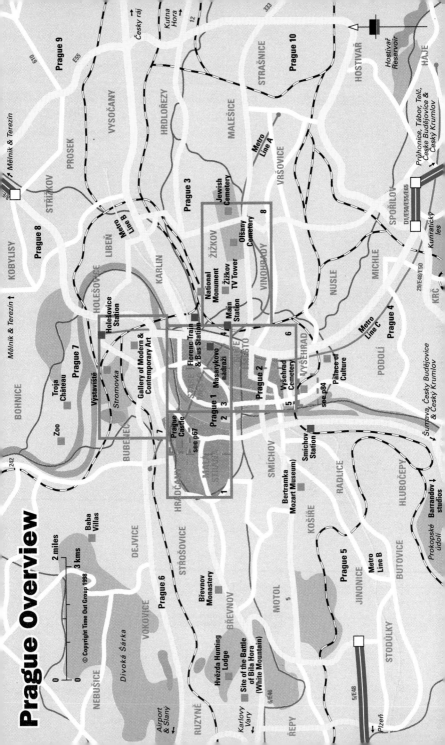

Prague Overview

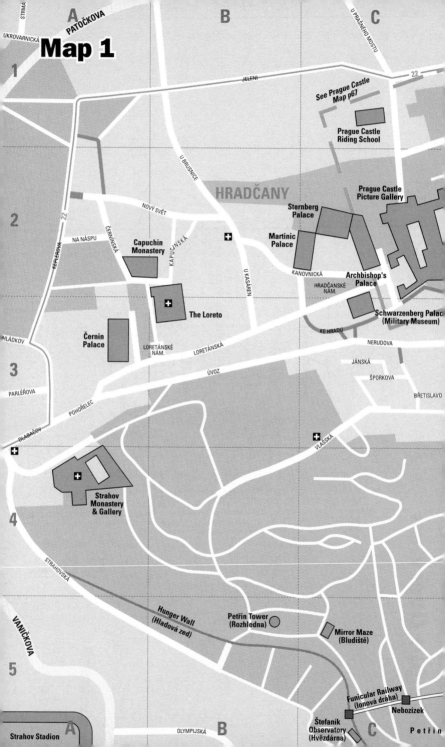

Map 1

A   **B**   **C**

STRMA

PATOČKOVA

UKROVARNICKÁ

1

JELENÍ

U PRAŠNÉHO MOSTU

22

See Prague Castle
Map p67

Prague Castle
Riding School

U BRUSNICE

HRADČANY

Prague Castle
Picture Gallery

NOVÝ SVĚT

KEPLEROVA

22

2

NA NÁSPU

ČERNÍNSKÁ

Capuchin
Monastery

KAPUCÍNSKÁ

Sternberg
Palace

Martinic
Palace

KANOVNICKÁ

Archbishop's
Palace

U KASÁREN

HRADČANSKÉ
NÁM.

The Loreto

Schwarzenberg Palac
(Military Museum)

Černin
Palace

LORETÁNSKÉ
NÁM.

LORETÁNSKÁ

KE HRADU

NERUDOVA

HLÁDKOV

JÁNSKÁ

ŠPORKOVA

3

ÚVOZ

PARLÉŘOVA

BŘETISLAVO

POHOŘELEC

DLABAČOV

VLAŠSKÁ

Strahov
Monastery
& Gallery

4

STRAHOVSKÁ

VANIČKOVA

Hunger Wall
(Hladová zeď)

Petřín Tower
(Rozhledna)

Mirror Maze
(Bludiště)

5

Funicular Railway
(lanová dráha)

Nebozízek

Štefánik
Observatory
(Hvězdárna)

A   **B**   **C**

Strahov Stadion

OLYMPIJSKÁ

Petřín

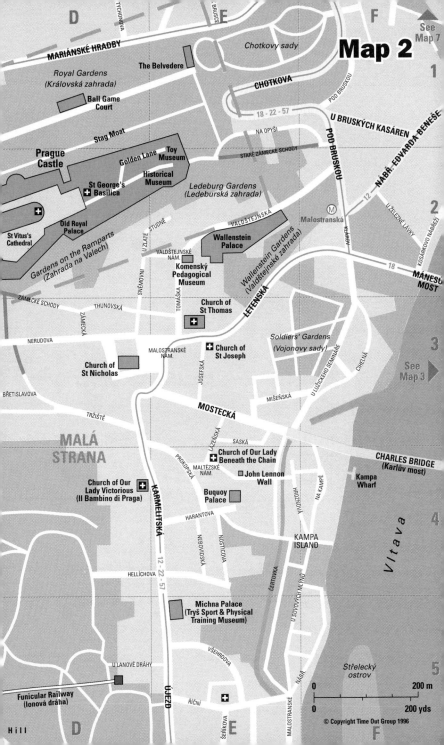

Map 2

See Map 7

D   E   F

Chotkovy sady

1

MARIÁNSKÉ HRADBY

*Royal Gardens
(Královská zahrada)*

The Belvedere

CHOTKOVA

POD BRUSKOU

U BRUSKÝCH KASÁREN

Ball Game
Court

18 · 22 · 57

NÁBŘ. EDVARDA BENEŠE

Stag Moat

NA OPYŠI

POD BRUSKOU

**Prague
Castle**

Golden Lane

Toy
Museum

STARÉ ZÁMECKÉ SCHODY

12

U ŽELEZNÉ LÁVKY

KOŠÁROVO NÁBŘEŽÍ

Historical
Museum

St George's
Basilica

*Ledeburg Gardens
(Ledeburská zahrada)*

M
Malostranská

2

KLÁROV

Old Royal
Palace

VALDŠTEJNSKÁ

St Vitus's
Cathedral

U ZLATÉ STUDNĚ

Wallenstein
Palace

18

MÁNESŮV
MOST

*Gardens on the Ramparts
(Zahrada na Valech)*

VALDŠTEJNSKÉ
NÁM.

Komenský
Pedagogical
Museum

*Wallenstein Gardens
(Valdštejnské zahrada)*

ZÁMECKÉ SCHODY

THUNOVSKÁ

SNĚMOVNÍ

TOMÁŠSKÁ

LETENSKÁ

*Soldiers' Gardens
(Vojanovy sady)*

3

ZÁMECKÁ

Church of
St Thomas

CHELNÁ

See
Map 3

NERUDOVA

Church of
St Joseph

MALOSTRANSKÉ
NÁM.

JOSEFSKÁ

U LUŽICKÉHO SEMINÁŘE

Church of
St Nicholas

MIŠEŇSKÁ

BŘETISLAVOVA

TRŽIŠTĚ

MOSTECKÁ

**MALÁ
STRANA**

LÁZEŇSKÁ

SASKÁ

CHARLES BRIDGE
(Karlův most)

Church of Our Lady
Beneath the Chain

Kampa
Wharf

PROKOPSKÁ

MALTÉZSKÉ
NÁM.

John Lennon
Wall

Church of Our
Lady Victorious
(Il Bambino di Praga)

KARMELITSKÁ

Buquoy
Palace

HROZNOVÁ

V l t a v a

HARANTOVA

NA KAMPĚ

4

NEBOVIDSKÁ

NOSTICOVA

KAMPA
ISLAND

ČERTOVKA

HELLICHOVA

12 · 22 · 57

Michna Palace
(Tryš Sport & Physical
Training Museum)

U SOVOVÝCH MLÝNŮ

VŠEHRDOVA

*Střelecký
ostrov*

5

U LANOVÉ DRÁHY

0   200 m

Funicular Railway
(lanová dráha)

ÚJEZD

ŘÍČNÍ

ŠEŘÍKOVA

NÁBŘ.

MALOSTRANSKÉ

0   200 yds

© Copyright Time Out Group 1996

Hill

D   E   F

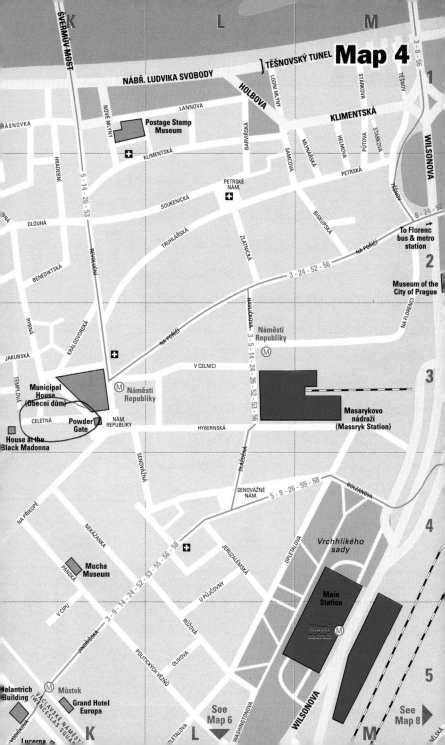

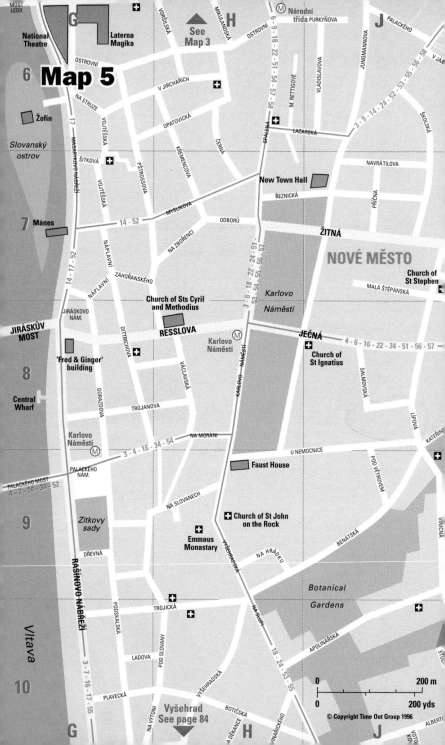

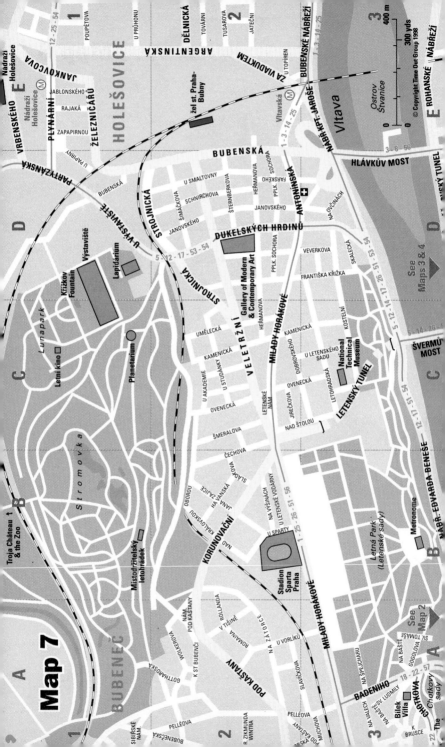

Map 7

A **B** **C** **D** **E**

BUBENEČ

HOLEŠOVICE

ARGENTINSKÁ

DĚLNICKÁ

JANKOVCOVA

VRBENSKÉHO

PLYNÁRNÍ

PARTYZÁNSKÁ

POUPETOVA

U PRŮHONU

TOVÁRNÍ

TUSAROVA

JATEČNÍ

BUBENSKÉ NÁBŘEŽÍ

ZA VIADUKTEM

Nádraží Holešovice Ⓜ

Nádraží Holešovice

JABLONSKÉHO

RAJAKÁ

ZAPAPIRNOU

ŽELEZNIČÁŘŮ

U PAPÍRNY

BUBENSKÁ

žel st. Praha-Bubny

U UTOPÍREN

12 - 25 - 54

1 - 3 - 14 - 25

Vltavská Ⓜ

1 - 3 - 14 - 25

ROHANSKÉ NÁBŘEŽÍ

ROHANSKÉ NÁBŘEŽÍ

BUBENSKÁ

U SMALTOVNY

ŠTERNBERKOVA

HEŘMANOVA

FARSKÉHO

STROJNICKÁ

ŠIMÁČKOVA

SCHNIRCHOVA

JANOVSKÉHO

PPLK. SOCHORA

JANOVSKÉHO

NA OVČÍNÁCH

ANTONÍNSKÁ

HLÁVKŮV MOST

3 - 8 - 56

Vltava

DUKELSKÝCH HRDINŮ

Gallery of Modern & Contemporary Art

VEVERKOVA

SKALECKÁ

FRANTIŠKA KŘIŽKA

5 - 12 - 17 - 53 - 54

Výstaviště

Lapidárium

U VÝSTAVIŠTĚ

STROJNICKÁ

VELETRŽNÍ

UMĚLECKÁ

KAMENICKÁ

U AKADEMIE

U STUDÁNKY

HEŘMANOVA

KAMENICKÁ

MILADY HORÁKOVÉ

DOBROVSKÉHO

U LETENSKÉHO SADU

KOSTELNÍ

National Technical Museum

5 - 12 - 14 - 17 - 26 - 51 - 53 - 54

See Maps 3 & 4

ŠVERMŮ MOST

5 - 10 - 26

Křižíkov Fountain

Lunapark

Letní kino

Planetarium

OVENECKÁ

LETOHRADSKÁ

LETENSKÝ TUNEL

12 - 17 - 51 - 54

ŠMERALOVA

LETENSKÉ NÁM.

NAD ŠTOLOU

JIREČKOVA

OVENECKÁ

Stromovka

ČECHOVA

SLÁDKOVA

JANA ZAJÍCE

OBORU

U VÝŠINÁCH

U LETENSKÉ VODÁRNY

U SPARTY

Místodržitelský letohrádek

KORUNOVAČNÍ

NAD KRÁLOVSKOU

JANA HA ZAJÍCE

1 - 25 - 26 - 51 - 56

Metronome

Letná Park (Letenské sady)

NÁBŘ. EDVARDA-BENEŠE

MILADY HORÁKOVÉ

Troja Château & the Zoo

SIBIŘSKÉ NÁM.

BUBENEČSKÁ

GOTTHARDSKÁ

K ST BUBENČÍ

WOLKEROVA

NÁM. POD KAŠTANY

V ROLLANDA

V TIŠINĚ

ROMAINA

NA ZÁTORCE

SLAVÍČKOVA

U VORLÍKŮ

MILADY HORÁKOVÉ

Stadion Sparta Praha

POD KAŠTANY

PELLÉOVA

MUCHOVA

NA VALECH

K BRUSCE

BADENIHO

R. ZIKMUNDA WINTRA

NA BAŠTĚ SV. LUDMILY

NA BAŠTĚ

NA ŠPEJCHARU

GOGOLOVA

SV. TOMÁŠE

See Map 2

CHOTKOVA

Bílek Villa

The Chotkovy sady

18 - 22 - 57

22

BUBENEČ

POD KAŠTANY

0   300 yds
0   400 m

© Copyright Time Out Group 1998

Ostrov Štvanice

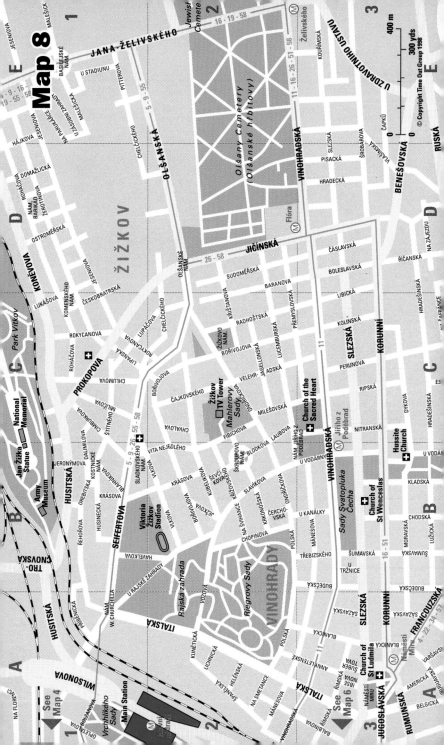

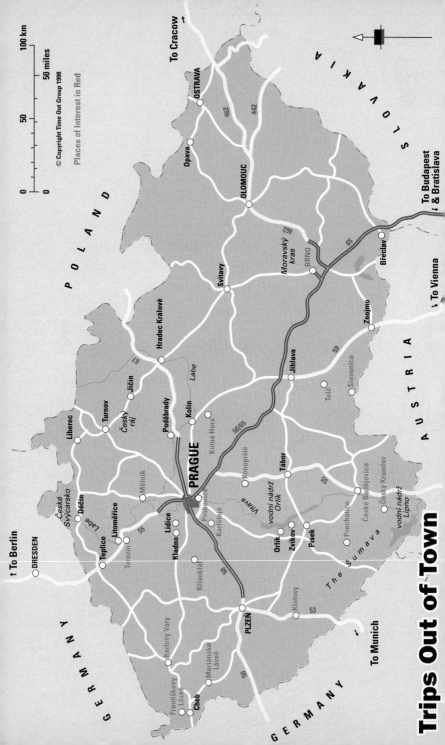

Trips Out of Town

Street Index

In accordance with standard Czech practice, all streets beginning with 'Č', 'Ř' and 'Š' are listed before those starting 'C', 'R' and 'Š' respectively.

17. LISTOPADU - Map 3G2/H2
28. ŘÍJNA - Map 3 J5

ALBERTOV - Map 5 J10
ALŠOVO NÁBŘ. - Map 3 G3
AMERICKÁ - Map 6 M8/9
AMERICKÁ - Map 8 A3
ANENSKÁ - Map 3 G4
ANENSKÉ NÁM. - Map 3 G4
ANGLICKÁ - Map 6 L7
ANNY LETENSKÉ - Map 6 M7
ANNY LETENSKÉ - Map 8 A2/3
ANTONÍNSKÁ - Map 7 D2
APOLINÁŘSKÁ - Map 5 J10
APOLINÁŘSKÁ - Map 6 K9
ARGENTINSKÁ - Map 7 E1/2

BADENIHO - Map 7 A3
BALBÍNOVA - Map 6M7
BALBÍNOVA - Map 8 A2/3
BARANOVA - Map 8 D2
BARTOLOMĚJSKÁ - Map 3 G5/H5
BARVÍŘSKÁ - Map 4 L1
BASILEJSKÉ NÁM. - Map 8 E1
BĚLEHRADSKÁ - Map 6 L7/8/M9/10
BELGICKÁ - Map 6 M8/9
BELGICKÁ - Map 8 A3
BENÁTSKÁ - Map 5 H9/J9
BENEDIKTSKÁ - Map 4 K2
BENEŠOVSKÁ - Map 8 D3/E3
BETLÉMSKÁ - Map 3 G5
BETLÉMSKÉ NÁM. - Map 3 G4/5
BILKOVA - Map 3 J2
BISKUPSKÁ - Map 4 M2
BLAHNÍKOVA - Map 8 B1
BLANICKÁ - Map 8 A2/3
BLODKOVA - Map 8 B2
BOLESLAVSKÁ - Map 8 D3
BOLZANOVA - Map 4 M4
BOLZANOVA - Map 8 A1
BORŠOV - Map 3 G5
BOTIČSKÁ - Map 5 H10
BOŘIVOJOVA - Map 8 B2/C2
BRUSELSKÁ - Map 6 M9
BUBENEČSKÁ - Map 7 A1/2
BUBENSKÁ - Map 7 D1/2
BUBENSKÉ NÁBŘEŽÍ - Map 7 E3
BUDEČSKÁ - Map 8 B3
BŘEHOVÁ - Map 3G2/H2
BŘETISLAVOVA - MAP 1 C3/D3
BŘETISLAVOVA - MAP 2 D3

CELETNÁ - Map 3 J3
CELETNÁ - Map 4 K3
CHARLES BRIDGE (KARLŮV MOST) - MAP 2 F4
CHARLES BRIDGE (Karlův most) - Map 3 G4
CHARVÁTOVA - Map 3 J5
CHELČICKÉHO - Map 8 C2/D1/E1
CHLUMOVA - Map 8 C1
CHODSKÁ - Map 8 B3
CHOPINOVA - Map 8 B2
CHOTKOVA - MAP 2 E1/F1
CHOTKOVA - Map 7 A3
CHVALOVA - Map 8 C2
CIHELNÁ - MAP 2 F3
CIMBURKOVA - Map 8 C1
CUKROVARNICKÁ - MAP 1 A1

ČAJKOVSKÉHO - Map 8 C2

ČAPKŮ - Map 8 E3
ČÁSLAVSKÁ - Map 8 D3
ČECHOVA - Map 7 B2/C2
ČECHŮV MOST - Map 3 H1
ČERCHOVSKÁ - Map 8 B2
ČERNÁ - Map 5 H6/7
ČERNÍNSKÁ - MAP 1 A2
ČESKOBRATRSKÁ - Map 8 C1/D1

DALIMILOVA - Map 8 B1/C1
DĚLNICKÁ - Map 7 E2
DITTRICHOVA - Map 5 G8
DIVADELNI - Map 3 G5
DLABAČOV - MAP 1 A3
DLÁŽDĚNÁ - Map 4 L3/4
DLOUHÁ - Map 3 J2/3
DLOUHÁ - Map 4 K2
DOBROVSKÉHO - Map 7 C2/3
DOMAŽLICKÁ - Map 8 D1
DR. ZIKMUNDA WINTRA - Map 7 A2
DUKELSKÝCH HRDINŮ - Map 7 D2/3
DUŠNI - Map 3 H1/2
DUŠNÍ - Map 3 J3
DVOŘÁKOVO NÁBŘ. - Map 3G2/H1
DYKOVA - Map 8 C3
DŘEVNÁ - Map 5 G9

EL. KRÁSNOHORSKÉ - Map 3 H2

FIBICHOVA - Map 8 C2
FRANCOUZSKÁ - Map 8A3
FRANTIŠKA KŘIŽKA - Map 7 D3
FÜGNEROVO NÁM. - Map 6 L9

GOGOLOVA - Map 7 A3
GORAZDOVA - Map 5 G8
GOTTHARDSKÁ - Map 7 A1/2

HA VANSKÁ - Map 7 B2
HÁJKOVA - Map 8 E1
HÁLKOVA - Map 6 K7/8
HARANTOVA - MAP 2 E4
HAVELKOVA - Map 8 B1/2
HAVELSKÁ - Map 3 H4/J4
HAVÍŘSKÁ - Map 3 J4
HAVLÍČKOVA - Map 4 L2/3
HAŠTALSKÁ - Map 3 J2
HAŠTALSKÉ NÁM. - Map 3 J2
HELÉNSKÁ - Map 6 M6
HELÉNSKÁ - Map 8 A2
HELLÍCHOVA - MAP 2 D4
HELMOVA - Map 4 M1/2
HEŘMANOVA - Map 7 C2/D2
HLÁDKOV - MAP 1 A3
HLÁVKŮV MOST - Map 7 D3
HOLBOVA - Map 4 L1
HORSKÁ - Map 6 K10
HRADEBNÍ - Map 4 K1/2
HRADECKÁ - Map 8 D3
HRADEŠÍNSKÁ - Map 8 C3/D3
HRADČANSKÉ NÁM. - Map 1 C2
HROZNOVÁ - MAP 2 E4/F4
HUSINECKÁ - Map 8 B1
HUSITSKÁ - Map 8 A1/B1
HUSOVA - Map 3 H4
HYBERNSKÁ - Map 4 L3

IBSE NOVA - Map 6 M7
IBSNOVA - Map 8 A3
ITALSKÁ - Map 6 M7
ITALSKÁ - Map 8 A1/2/3

JABLONSKÉHO - Map 7 E1
JÁCHYMOVA - Map 3 H3
JAGELLONSKÁ - Map 8 C2
JAKUBSKÁ - Map 4 K3

JALOVCOVÁ - Map 3 H4
JANA MASARYKA - Map 6 M9/10
JANA ZAJICE - Map 7 B2
JANA-ŽELIVSKÉHO - Map 8 E1/2
JANKOVCOVA - Map 7 E1
JANOVSKÉHO - Map 7 D2
JÁNSKÁ - MAP 1 C3
JATEČNI - Map 7 E2
JELENI - MAP 1 A1/B1/C1
JERONÝMOVA - Map 8 B1
JERUZALÉMSKÁ - Map 4 L4
JESENIOVA - Map 8 C1/D1/E1
JEČNÁ - Map 5 H8/J8
JEČNÁ - Map 6 K8
JEŽKOVA - Map 8 B2
JILSKÁ - Map 3 H4
JINDŘIŠSKÁ - Map 4 K4/5
JIRÁSKOVO NÁM. - Map 5 G8
JIRÁSKŮV MOST - Map 5 G8
JIREČKOVA - Map 7 C2
JIČÍNSKÁ - Map 8 D2
JOSEFSKÁ - MAP 2 E3
JUGOSLÁVSKÁ - Map 6 L8/M8
JUGOSLÁVSKÁ - Map 8 A3
JUNGMANNOVA - Map 3 J5
JUNGMANNOVA - Map 5 J6
JUNGMANNOVO NÁM. - Map 3 J5

K BRUSCE - MAP 2 E1
K BRUSCE - Map 7 A3
K ST BUBENČI - Map 7 A2
KAMENICKÁ - Map 7 C2/3
KANOVNICKÁ - MAP 1 B2/C2
KAPROVA - Map 3 G3/4/H4
KAPUCINSKÁ - MAP 1 B2
KARLOVO NÁMĚSTÍ - Map 5 H7-9
KARMELITSKÁ - MAP 2 E4
KAROLINY - Map 3 G5
KATEŘINSKÁ - Map 5 J8
KATEŘINSKÁ - Map 6 K8
KE HRADU - MAP 1 C3
KE KARLOVU - Map 6 K8/9/10
KEPLEROVA - MAP 1 A1/2/3
KLADSKÁ - Map 8 B3
KLÁROV - MAP 2 F2
KLÁŠTERSKÁ - Map 3 J1
KLIMENTSKÁ - Map 4 K2/L1/M1
KOLINSKÁ - Map 8 C3
KOMENSKÉHO NÁM. - Map 8 C1
KONĚVOVA - Map 8 C1/D1
KONVIKTSKÁ - Map 3 G5/H5
KORUNNÍ - Map 8 A3/B3/C3/D3
KORUNOVAČNÍ - Map 7 B2
KOSÁRKOVO NÁBŘEŽÍ - MAP 2 F2
KOSÁRKOVO NÁBŘEŽÍ - Map 3 G1/2
KOSTELNÍ - Map 7 C3/D3
KOSTEČNA - Map 3 H3
KOSTNICKÉ NÁM. - Map 8 B1
KOUBKOVA - Map 6 L9
KOUŘÍMSKÁ - Map 8 E3
KOZÍ - Map 3 J1/2
KOŽNÁ - Map 3 J4
KRAKOVSKÁ - Map 6 K6/7
KRÁLODVORSKÁ - Map 4 K3
KRÁSOVA - Map 8 B1/2
KRKONOŠSKÁ - Map 8 B2
KROCÍNOVA - Map 3 G5
KUBELIKOVA - Map 8 B2
KUNĚTICKÁ - Map 8 A2
KŘEMENCOVA - Map 5 H6/7
KŘIŠTANOVA - Map 8 C2/D2
KŘIŽOVNICKÁ - Map 3 G3
KŘIŽOVNICKÉ NÁM. - Map 3 G4
KŘÍŽOVSKÉHO - Map 8 B2

LADOVA - Map 5 G10
LANNOVA - Map 4 L1
LAUBOVA - Map 8 C2

LAZARSKÁ - Map 5 H6/J6
LÁZEŇSKÁ - MAP 2 E3/4
LEGEROVA - Map 6 L6-10/M6
LETENSKÁ - MAP 2 E2/3/F2
LETENSKÉ NÁM - Map 7 C2
LETENSKÝ TUNEL - Map 7 C3
LETOHRADSKÁ - Map 7 C3
LIBICKÁ - Map 8 C3/D3
LICHNICKÁ - Map 8 A2
LILIOVÁ - Map 3 G4
LINHARTSKÁ - Map 3 H3
LIPANSKÁ - Map 8 C1
LÍPOVÁ - Map 5 J8
LODNI MLÝNY - Map 4 L1
LONDÝNSKÁ - Map 6 M8/9
LONDÝNSKÁ - Map 6 L7/8
LORETÁNSKÁ - MAP 1 A3/B3
LORETÁNSKÉ NÁM. - MAP 1 B3
LUBLAŇSKÁ - Map 6 L8-10
LUCEMBURSKÁ - Map 8 C2
LUKÁŠOVA - Map 8 C1/2/D1
LUŽICKÁ - Map 8 B3

M. RETTIGOVÉ - Map 5 H6
MAISELOVA - Map 3 H3
MALÁ STUPARSKÁ - Map 3 J3
MALÁ ŠTĚPÁNSKÁ - Map 5 J7
MALÉ NÁM. - Map 3 H4
MALEŠICKA - Map 8 E1
MALOSTRANSKÉ NÁBŘ. - MAP 2 E5/F5
MALOSTRANSKÉ NÁM. - MAP 2 E2
MALTÉZSKÉ NÁM. - MAP 2 E4
MÁNESOVA - Map 6 M6/7
MÁNESOVA - Map 8 A2/3/B3
MÁNESŮV MOST - Map 2 F2
MÁNESŮV MOST - Map 3 G2/3
MARIANSKÉ NÁM. - Map 3 H3
MARIÁNSKÉ HRADBY - MAP 2 D1/E1
MARTINSKÁ - Map 3 H5
MASARYKOVO NÁBŘEŽÍ - Map 5 G6/7
MASNÁ - Map 3 J3
MELANTRICHOVA - Map 3 H4
MEZIBRANSKÁ - Map 6 L6/7
MICHALSKÁ - Map 3 H4
MIKOVCOVA - Map 6 L7
MIKULANDSKÁ - Map 3 H5
MIKULANDSKÁ - Map 5 H6
MILADY HORÁKOVÉ - Map 7 A3/B2/3/C2/D2
MILEŠOVSKÁ - Map 8 C2
MILIČOVA - Map 8 C1
MIŠENSKÁ - MAP 2 E3
MLYNÁŘSKÁ - Map 4 M1/2
MORAVSKÁ - Map 8 B3
MORSTADTOVA - MAP 1 A3
MOST LEGII - Map 5 G6
MOSTECKÁ - MAP 2 E3
MUCHOVA - Map 7 A2/3
MYSLIKOVA - Map 5 G7/H7

NA BAŠTĚ SV. LUDMILY - Map 7 A3
NA BAŠTĚ SV. TOMÁŠE - Map 7 A3
NA BOJIŠTI - Map 6 K8/9
NA DĚKANCE - Map 5 H10
NA FLORENCI - Map 4 M2/3
NA FLORENCI - Map 8 A1
NA FRANTIŠKU - Map 3 H1/J1
NA HRÁDKU - Map 5 H9
NA HROBCI - Map 5 G10/H10
NA KAMPĚ - MAP 2 F4
NA MORÁNI - Map 5G9/H8
NA MŮSTKU - Map 3 J4
NA NÁSPU - MAP 1 A2
NA OPYŠI - MAP 2 E1

NA OVČINÁCH - Map 7 D3
NA PARUKÁŘCE - Map 8 E1
NA PERŠTÝNĚ - Map 3 H5
NA POŘÍČÍ - Map 4 K3/L2/3M2
NA PŘIKOPĚ - Map 4 K4
NA RYBNÍČKU - Map 6 K7
NA SLOVANECH - Map 5 H9
NA SLUPI - Map 5 H10
NA SMETANCE - Map 6 M6
NA SMETANCE - Map 8 A2
NA STRUZE - Map 5 G6
NA VALECH - Map 7 A3
NA VÝTONI - Map 5 G10/H10
NA VÝŠINÁCH - Map 7 B2
NA ZÁBRADLÍ - Map 3 G4
NA ZÁJEZDU - Map 8 D3
NA ZÁTORCE - Map 7 A2
NA ZBOŘENCI - Map 5 H7
NA ŠAFRÁNCE - Map 8 C3
NA ŠPEJCHARU - Map 7 A3
NA ŠVIHANCE - Map 8 B2
NÁBŘ KPT. JAROŠE - Map 7 E3
NÁBŘ. EDVARDA BENEŠE - MAP 2 F1/2
NÁBŘ. EDVARDA BENEŠE - Map 3 G1/H1
NÁBŘ. EDVARDA BENEŠE - Map 7 B3/C3
NÁBŘ. LUDVIKA SVOBODY - Map 4 K1/L1
NAD KRÁLOVSKOU OBOROU - Map 7 B2
NAD ŠTOLOU - Map 7 C2/3
NÁM. BARIKÁD - Map 8 D1
NÁM. CURIEOVÝCH - Map 3 H1/2
NÁM. J. PALACHA - Map 3 J3
NÁM. JIŘÍHO Z PODĚBRAD - Map 8 B2/C2
NÁM. POD KAŠTANY - Map 7 A2
NÁM. REPUBLIKY - Map 4 K3
NÁM. W. CHURCHILLA - Map 8 A1
NÁMĚSTÍ MÍRU - Map 8 A1
NÁPLAVNÍ - Map 5 G7
NÁPRSTKOVA - Map 3 G4
NÁRODNÍ TŘÍDA - Map 3 G5/H5/J5
NAVRÁTILOVA - Map 5 J7
NEBOVIDSKÁ - MAP 2 E4
NEKÁZANKA - Map 4 K4
NERUDOVA - MAP 1 C3
NERUDOVA - Map 2 D3
NITRANSKÁ - Map 8 C3
NOSTICOVA - MAP 2 E4
NOVÉ MLYNY - Map 4 K1
NOVOTNÉHO LÁVKA - Map 3 G4
NOVÝ SVĚT - MAP 1 A2/B2

ODBORŮ - Map 5 H7
OLIVOVA - Map 4 L5
OLYMPIJSKÁ - MAP 1 A5/B5
OLŠANSKÁ - Map 8 D2/E1
OLŠANSKÉ NÁM. - Map 8 D2
ONDŘÍČKOVA - Map 8 B2/C2
OPLETALOVA - Map 4 L4/5/M4
OPLETALOVA - Map 6 K6/L/6
OPLETALOVA - Map 8 A2
OREBITSKÁ - Map 8 B1
OSTROMĚŘSKÁ - Map 8 D1
OSTROVNÍ - Map 5 G6/H6
OVENECKÁ - Map 7 C2/3
OVOCNÝ TRH - Map 3 J4

PALACKÉHO - Map 5 J6
PALACKÉHO MOST - Map 5 G9
PALACKÉHO NÁM. - Map 5 G9
PANSKÁ - Map 4 K4
PARLÉŘOVA - MAP 1 A3
PARTYZÁNSKÁ - Map 7 D1
PATOČKOVA - MAP 1 A1
PAŘÍŽSKÁ - MAP 3 H2
PAŘÍŽSTÁ - Map 3 H3
PELLÉOVA - Map 7 A2/3
PERLOVÁ - Map 3 J5
PERUNOVA - Map 8 C3
PETRSKÁ - Map 4 L2
PETRSKÉ NÁM. - Map 4 L2

PISACKÁ - Map 8 D3
PITTEROVA - Map 8 E1
PLATNÉRSKÁ - Map 3 G3/H3
PLATNÉRSKÁ - Map 3 H3
PLAVECKÁ - Map 5 G10
PLYNÁRNÍ - Map 7 E1
POD BRUSKOU - MAP 2 F1/2
POD KAŠTANY - Map 7 A2/3
POD SLOVANY - Map 5 H10
POD VĚTROVEM - Map 5 J9
POD ZVONAŘKOU - Map 6 M10
PODSKALSKÁ - Map 5 G9/10
POHOŘELEC - MAP 1 A3
POLITICKÝCH VĚZŇŮ - Map 4 K5/L5
POLSKÁ - Map 8 A2/B2
POUPĚTOVA - Map 7 E1
PPLK. SOCHORA - Map 7 D2
PROKOPOVA - Map 8 C1
PROKOPSKÁ - MAP 2 E4
PROVAZNICKÁ - Map 3 J4
PURKYŇOVA - Map 5 J6
PŮTOVA - Map 4 M1/2
PŘEMYSLOVSKÁ - Map 8 C2/D2
PŘÍBĚNICKÁ - Map 8 A1
PŘÍČNA - Map 5 J7
PŠTROSSOVA - Map 5 G6/7

RADHOŠTSKÁ - Map 8 C2
RAJAKÁ - Map 7 E1
RAŠÍNOVO NÁBŘEŽÍ - Map 5 G9/10
RESSLOVA - Map 5 G8/H8
REVOLUČNÍ - Map 4 K2
RIPSKÁ - Map 8 C3
ROHANSKÉ NÁBŘEŽÍ - Map 7 E3
ROHÁČOVA - Map 8 C1/D1
ROKYCANOVA - Map 8 C1
ROLLANDA - Map 7 A2
ROMAINA - Map 7 A2
RUBEŠOVA - Map 6 L7
RUMUNSKÁ - Map 6 L8/M8
RUMUNSKÁ - Map 8 A3
RUSKÁ - Map 8 D3/E3
RYBNÁ - Map 4 K2/3
RYTÍŘSKÁ - Map 3 J4
RŮŽOVÁ - Map 4 L4/5

ŘÁSNOVKA - Map 3 J1/2
ŘÁSNOVKA - Map 4 K1
ŘEHOŘOVA - Map 8 B1
ŘETĚZOVÁ - Map 3 H4
ŘEZNICKÁ - Map 5 H7/J7
ŘÍMSKÁ - Map 6 L7/M7
ŘÍMSKÁ - Map 8 A3
ŘÍČNÍ - MAP 2 E5
ŘÍČANSKÁ - Map 8 D3

SA FAŘÍKOVA - Map 6 M10
SALMOVSKÁ - Map 5 J8
SALVÁTORSKÁ - Map 3 H3/J3
SAMCOVA - Map 4 L1/2
SASKÁ - MAP 2 E3
SÁZAVSKÁ - Map 8 A3
SCHNIRCHOVA - Map 7 D2
SEIFERTOVA - Map 8 B1
SEMINÁŘSKÁ - Map 3 H4
SENOVÁŽNÁ - Map 4 K3/4
SENOVÁŽNÉ NÁM. - Map 4 L4
SIBIŘSKÁ NÁM. - Map 7 A1
SKALECKÁ - Map 7 D3
SKOŘEPKA - Map 3 H5
SLÁDKOVA - Map 7 B2
SLADKOVSKÉHO NÁM. - Map 8 B1
SLAVÍKOVA - Map 8 B2
SLAVÍČKOVA - Map 7 A2/3
SLEZSKÁ - Map 8 A3/B3/C3/D3/E3
SMETANOVO NÁBŘ - Map 3 G4/5
SNĚMOVNI - MAP 2 D2
SOKOLSKÁ - Map 6 K7/8/L8-10
SOUKENICKÁ - Map 4 K2/L2
SPÁLENÁ - Map 5 H6/7
SRBSKÁ - Map 7 A2/3
STARÉ ZÁMECKÉ SCHODY - MAP 2 E2
STARKOVA - Map 4 M1/2

STAROMĚSTSKÉ NÁM. - Map 3 H3/J3
STRAHOVSKÁ - MAP 1 A4/5
STRMÁ - MAP 1 A1
STROJNICKÁ - Map 7 D1/2
STUDNIČKOVA - Map 5 J10
STUDNIČKOVA - Map 6 K10
SUDOMĚŘSKÁ - Map 8 D2
SVĚTLÉ - Map 3 G5

ŠEVČÍKOVA - Map 8 B2
ŠEŘÍKOVA - MAP 2 E5
ŠIMÁČKOVA - Map 7 D2
ŠIROKÁ - Map 3 H2/3
ŠITKOVÁ - Map 5 G7
ŠKOLSKÁ - Map 5 J6/7
ŠKRÉTOVA - Map 6 L7
ŠKROUPOVO NÁM. - Map 8 B2
ŠMERALOVA - Map 7 C2
ŠPANĚLSKÁ - Map 6 M6
ŠPANĚLSKÁ - Map 8 A2
ŠPORKOVA - MAP 1 C3
ŠROBÁROVA - Map 8 D3/E3
ŠTĚPÁNSKÁ - Map 6 K6/7
ŠTERNBERKOVA - Map 7 D2
ŠTÍTNÉHO - Map 8 C1
ŠTUPARTSKÁ - Map 3 J3
ŠUBERTOVA - Map 6 M7
ŠUBERTOVA - Map 8 A3
ŠUMAVSKÁ - Map 8 B3
ŠVERMŮV MOST - Map 4 K1
ŠVERMŮV MOST - Map 7 C3

TEMPLOVÁ - Map 4 K3
TĚSNOV - Map 4 M1/2
TĚŠNOVSKÝ TUNEL - Map 4 L1/M1
TĚŠNOVSKÝ TUNEL - Map 7 D2
THUNOVSKÁ - MAP 2 D1D3
TOMÁŠSKA - MAP 2 E2/3
TOVÁRNI - Map 7 E2
TROCNOVSKÁ - Map 8 B1
TROJANOVA - Map 5 G8/H8
TROJICKÁ - Map 5 G10/H10
TRUHLÁŘSKÁ - Map 4 K2/L2
TRŽIŠTĚ - MAP 2 D3
TUSAROVA - Map 7 E2
TYCHONOVA - MAP 2 D1
TYLOVO NÁM. - Map 6 L8
TYRŠOVA - Map 6 L9
TŘEBIZSKÉHO - Map 8 B3
TÝNSKÁ - Map 3 J3

U AKADEMIE - Map 7 C2
U BRUSKÝCH KASÁREN - MAP 2 F1
U BRUSNICE - MAP 1 B1/2
U KASÁREN - MAP 1 B2/3
U LANOVÉ DRÁHY - MAP 2 E3
U LETENSKÉ VODÁRNY - Map 7B2
U LETENSKÉHO SADU - Map 7 C3
U LUŽICKEHO SEMINÁŘE - MAP 2 F3
U MILOSRDNÝCH - Map 3 J2
U NEMOCNICE - Map 5 H9/J8
U OBECNÍHO DVORA - Map 3 J2
U PAPIRNY - Map 7 D1
U PRAŠNÉHO MOSTU - MAP 1 C1
U PRŮHONU - Map 7 E1
U PŮJČOVNY - Map 4 L4/5
U RADNICE - Map 3 H3
U RAJSKÉ ZAHRADY - Map 8 B1/2
U SMALTOVNY - Map 7 D2
U SOVOVÝCH MLÝNŮ - MAP 2 E5/F4
U SPARTY - Map 7 B2
U STADIUNU - Map 8 E1
U STUDÁNKY - Map 7 C2
U TOPÍREN - Map 7 E2
U TRŽNICE - Map 8 B3
U VODÁMY - Map 8 B3
U VODÁRNY - Map 8 B3
U VORLÍKŮ - Map 7 A2/3
U VÝSTAVIŠTĚ - Map 7 D1
U ZÁSOBNI ZAHRADY - Map 8 E1
U ZLATÉ STUDNĚ - MAP 2 D2/E2

U ZVONAŘKY - Map 6 M10
U ŽELEZNÉ LÁVKY - MAP 2 F2
UHELNÝ TRH - Map 3 H5
ÚJEZD - MAP 2 E5
UMĚLECKÁ - Map 7 C2
URUGUAYSKÁ - Map 6 M8/9
URUGUAYSKÁ - Map 8A3
ÚVOZ - MAP 1 A3/B3

V CELNICI - Map 4 L3
V CÍPU - Map 4 K4/5
V JÁMĚ - Map 5 J6
V JÁMĚ - Map 6 K6
V JIRCHÁŘÍCH - Map 5 G6/H6
V KOLKOVNĚ - Map 3 J2
V KOTCÍCH - Map 3 J4
V TIŠINĚ - Map 7 A2
V TŮNÍCH - Map 6 K7/8
VÁCLAVSKÁ - Map 5 H8
VÁCLAVSKÉ NÁMĚSTÍ - Map 3 J5
VÁCLAVSKÉ NÁMĚSTÍ - Map 4 K5
VÁCLAVSKÉ NÁMĚSTÍ - Map 6 K6/L6
VALDŠTEJNSKÁ - MAP 2 E2
VALDŠTEJNSKÉ NÁM. - MAP 2 E2
VALENTINSKÁ - Map 3 H3
VANÍČKOVA - MAP 1 A5
VARŠAVSKÁ - Map 8 A3
VE SMEČKÁCH - Map 6 K6/7
VEJVODOVA - Map 3 H4
VELEHRADSKÁ - Map 8 C2
VELESLAVÍNOVÁ - Map 3 G3
VELETRŽNÍ - Map 7 C2
VEVERKOVA - Map 7 D3
VĚZEŇSKÁ - Map 3 J2
VINAŘICKÉHO - Map 5 H10
VINIČNÁ - Map 5 J9
VINOHRADSKÁ - Map 6 M6/7
VINOHRADSKÁ - Map 8 A2/3
VINOHRADSKÁ - Map 8 B3/C3/D3/E2
VINOHRADSKÁ - Map 8 D3/E2
VITA NEJEDLÉHO - Map 8 B2
VITĚZNÁ - MAP 2 E5
VLADISLAVOVA - Map 5 J6
VLAŠSKÁ - MAP 1 B4/C3
VLAŠÍMSKÁ - Map 8 D3/E3
VLKOVA - Map 8 B2
VOCELOVA - Map 6 L8
VODIČKOVA - Map 4 K5
VOJTĚŠSKÁ - Map 5 G6
VOJTĚŠSKÁ - Map 5 G7
VORŠILSKÁ - Map 5 H6
VOTOČKOVA - Map 5 J10
VOZOVÁ - Map 8 A2/B2
VRBENSKÉHO - Map 7 E1
VYŠEHRADSKÁ - Map 5 H9/10
VŠEHRDOVA - MAP 2 E5

WASHINGTONOVA - Map 4 L5
WASHINGTONOVA - Map 6 L6
WENZIGOVA - Map 6 K10/L10
WILSONOVA - Map 4 L5/M1/2/4/5
WILSONOVA - Map 6 L6
WILSONOVA - Map 8 A1
WOLKEROVA - Map 7 A2

ZA VIADUKTEM - Map 7 E2
ZÁHOŘANSKÉHO - Map 5 G7
ZÁHŘEBSKÁ - Map 6 M9
ZÁMECKÁ - MAP 2 D3
ZÁMECKÉ SCHODY - MAP 2 D2/3
ZAPAPIRNOU - Map 7 E1
ZLATNICKÁ - Map 4 L2

ŽATECKÁ - Map 3 H3
ŽELEZNÁ - Map 3 J4
ŽELEZNIČÁŘŮ - Map 7 E1
ŽEROTINOVA - Map 8 D1
ŽITNÁ - Map 5 H7/J7
ŽITNÁ - Map 6 K7
ŽIŽKOVO NÁM. - Map 8 C2

TimeOut **Prague Guide** Please let us know what you think.

(THIRD EDITION)

About this guide...

1. How useful did you find the following sections?

	Very	Fairly	Not very
In Context	☐	☐	☐
Sightseeing	☐	☐	☐
Accommodation	☐	☐	☐
Eating & Drinking	☐	☐	☐
Shopping & Services	☐	☐	☐
Arts & Entertainment	☐	☐	☐
Trips Out of Town	☐	☐	☐
Directory	☐	☐	☐

2. Did you travel to Prague:

Alone? ☐   With partner? ☐
As part of a group? ☐   With children? ☐

3. How long was your trip to Prague?

Less than three days ☐
Three days to one week ☐
One to two weeks ☐
Over two weeks ☐

4. Did you visit any other destinations?
If so, which?

_____
_____
_____
_____

5. Is there anything you'd like us to cover in greater depth?

_____
_____
_____
_____
_____
_____
_____

Lisbon Guide ☐
London Guide ☐
Los Angeles Guide ☐
Madrid Guide ☐
Miami Guide ☐
Moscow Guide ☐
New Orleans Guide ☐
New York Guide ☐
Paris Guide ☐
Rome Guide ☐
San Francisco Guide ☐
Sydney Guide ☐

Film Guide ☐
Kids Out magazine ☐
London Eating & Drinking Guide ☐
London Pubs & Bars Guide ☐
London Visitors' Guide ☐
ici Londres ☐
Paris Eating & Drinking Guide ☐
Paris Free Guide ☐
London Shopping Guide ☐
Student Guide ☐
Book of Country Walks ☐
Book of Interviews ☐
Book of London Walks ☐
Book of New York Short Stories ☐
Time Out New York magazine ☐
Time Out Roma ☐
Time Out Diary ☐
www.timeout.com ☐

About other Time Out publications...

6. Have you bought/used other Time Out publications? If so, which ones?

Time Out magazine ☐

City Guides:
Amsterdam Guide ☐
Barcelona Guide ☐
Berlin Guide ☐
Brussels Guide ☐
Budapest Guide ☐
Dublin Guide ☐
Edinburgh Guide ☐

Florence & Tuscany Guide ☐
Las Vegas Guide ☐

About you...

(BLOCK CAPITALS PLEASE)

7. Title (Mrs, Miss etc):

First name:
_____

Surname:
_____

Address:
_____
_____

Postcode:
_____

8. Year of birth:
_____

9. Sex: Male ☐   Female ☐

10. Are you:

employed full-time ☐   employed part-time ☐
self-employed ☐   unemployed ☐
student ☐   home-maker ☐

11. At the moment do you earn:

under £10,000 ☐
over £10,000 and up to £14,999 ☐
over £15,000 and up to £19,999 ☐
over £20,000 and up to £24,999 ☐
over £25,000 and up to £39,999 ☐
over £40,000 and up to £49,999 ☐
over £50,000 ☐

☐ Please tick here if you do not want to receive information on other Time Out products.
If you prefer to return this in an envelope, please use the FREEPOST address overleaf.

Time Out Guides

FREEPOST 20 (WC3187)
LONDON
W1E 0DQ

City Guides are available from all good bookshops or through Penguin Direct.

Simply call 0181 899 4036 (9am–5pm) or fill out the form below, affix a stamp and return.

Payment: Please note your order may be delayed if payment details are incorrect.
Postage and Packing £1.50. Please tick which book(s) you'd like to order.

ISBN	title	retail price	quantity	total
0140273115	Time Out Guide to **Amsterdam**	£9.99		
0140273123	Time Out Guide to **Barcelona**	£9.99		
0140257187	Time Out Guide to **Berlin**	£9.99		
0140273166	Time Out Guide to **Brussels**	£9.99		
014026745X	Time Out Guide to **Budapest**	£9.99		
0140266879	Time Out Guide to **Dublin**	£9.99		
0140266844	Time Out Guide to **Edinburgh**	£9.99		
0140266860	Time Out Guide to **Florence & Tuscany**	£9.99		
0140270620	Time Out Guide to **Las Vegas**	£9.99		
0140273158	Time Out Guide to **Lisbon** (published 1/99)	£9.99		
0140259767	Time Out Guide to **London**	£9.99		
0140259740	Time Out Guide to **Los Angeles**	£9.99		
0140257179	Time Out Guide to **Madrid**	£9.99		
0140266852	Time Out Guide to **Miami**	£9.99		
014027314X	Time Out Guide to **Moscow** (published 1/99)	£9.99		
0140274480	Time Out Guide to **New Orleans**	£9.99		
0140273107	Time Out Guide to **New York**	£9.99		
0140270647	Time Out Guide to **Paris**	£9.99		
0140257160	Time Out Guide to **Prague**	£9.99		
0140266887	Time Out Guide to **Rome**	£9.99		
0140267468	Time Out Guide to **San Francisco**	£9.99		
0140259732	Time Out Guide to **Sydney**	£9.99		
		+ postage & packing		£1.50
		Total Payment		

(Please Use Block Capitals)

Cardholder's Name

Address

Town _____ Postcode

Daytime Telephone Number

Method of Payment (UK Credit cards only)

Barclaycard/Visa

Access Card/Mastercard

Signature (if paying by credit card) _____

Expiry date

Cheque

I enclose a cheque £ _____ made payable to Penguin Direct

Delivery will normally be within 14 working days. The availability and published prices quoted are correct at time of going to press but are subject to alteration without prior notice. Order form valid until May 2000. Please note that this service is only available in the UK.

Penguin Direct
Penguin Books Ltd
Bath Road
Harmondsworth
West Drayton
Middlesex
UB7 0DA